M000302913

The Official (ISC)²® Guide
to the SSCP® CBK®

Fourth Edition

The Official (ISC)² Guide
to the SSCP® CBK®

Fourth Edition

ADAM GORDON
CISSP-ISSAP, CISSP-ISSMP, SCCP, CCSP, CISA, CRISC

STEVEN HERNANDEZ
MBA, HCISPP, CISSP, CSSLP, SSCP, CAP, CISA

(ISC)²®

SYBEX®
A Wiley Brand

The Official (ISC)²® Guide to the SSCP® CBK®, Fourth Edition

Published by
John Wiley & Sons, Inc.
10475 Crosspoint Boulevard
Indianapolis, IN 46256
www.wiley.com

Copyright © 2016 by (ISC)2®

Published by John Wiley & Sons, Inc., Indianapolis, Indiana
Published simultaneously in Canada

ISBN: 978-1-119-27863-4
ISBN: 978-1-119-27864-1 (ebk)
ISBN: 978-1-119-27865-8 (ebk)

Manufactured in the United States of America

10 9 8 7 6 5 4 3 2 1

For general information on our other products and services please contact our Customer Care Department within the United States at (877) 762-2974, outside the United States at (317) 572-3993 or fax (317) 572-4002.

Wiley publishes in a variety of print and electronic formats and by print-on-demand. Some material included with standard print versions of this book may not be included in e-books or in print-on-demand. If this book refers to media such as a CD or DVD that is not included in the version you purchased, you may download this material at http://booksupport.wiley.com. For more information about Wiley products, visit www.wiley.com.

Library of Congress Control Number: 2016937576

About the Editors

 **Adam Gordon** With over 25 years of experience as both an educator and IT professional, Adam holds numerous professional IT certifications including CISSP-ISSAP, CISSP-ISSMP, SCCP, CCSP, CISA, CRISC. He is the author of several books and has achieved many awards, including EC-Council Instructor of Excellence for 2006–07 and Top Technical Instructor Worldwide, 2002–2003. Adam earned his bachelor's degree in International Relations and his master's degree in International Political Affairs from Florida International University.

Adam has held a number of positions during his professional career including CISO, CTO, consultant, and solutions architect. He has worked on many large implementations involving multiple customer program teams for delivery.

Adam has been invited to lead projects for companies such as Microsoft, Citrix, Lloyds Bank TSB, Campus Management, US Southern Command (SOUTHCOM), Amadeus, World Fuel Services, and Seaboard Marine.

 **Steven Hernandez** Steven Hernandez, MBA, HCISPP, CISSP, CSSLP, SSCP, CAP, CISA, is a chief information security officer practicing in the U.S. Federal Government in Washington DC. Hernandez has over 17 years of information assurance experience in a variety of fields including international healthcare, international heavy manufacturing, large finance organizations, educational institutions, and government agencies. Steven is an honorary professor at California State University – San Bernardino and affiliate faculty at the National Information Assurance Training and Education Center located at Idaho State University. Through his academic outreach, he has lectured over the past decade on numerous information assurance topics including risk management, information security investment, and the implications of privacy decisions to graduate and postgraduate audiences. In addition to his credentials from (ISC)², Hernandez also holds six U.S. Committee for National Security Systems certifications ranging from systems security to organizational risk management. Steven also volunteers service to (ISC)²'s Government Advisory Board and Executive Writers Bureau. Steven enjoys relaxing and traveling with his wife, whose patience and support have been indispensable in his numerous information assurance pursuits.

Credits

Project Editor
Kelly Talbot

Technical Editors
Adam Gordon
Steven Hernandez

Production Manager
Kathleen Wisor

Copy Editor
Andrew Schneiter

**Manager of Content Development &
Assembly**
Mary Beth Wakefield

Marketing Manager
Carrie Sherrill

**Professional Technology &
Strategy Director**
Barry Pruett

Business Manager
Amy Knies

Executive Editor
Jim Minatel

Project Coordinator, Cover
Brent Savage

Proofreader
Kim Wimpsett

Indexer
Johnna VanHoose Dinse

Cover Designer
Mike Trent

Cover Image
Mike Trent

Contents

Foreword

CONGRATULATIONS! YOU HAVE MADE the decision to take control of your career with *The Official (ISC)² Guide to the SSCP CBK*. The fact that you've taken this step shows your commitment to the field and the high importance you place on continuing your professional education. It should be no surprise to you that IT professionals, who are doing hands-on work, need to be doing that work in accordance with the best practices, policies, and procedures found in the *SSCP CBK*.

This fourth edition of the *SSCP CBK* will help facilitate the practical knowledge you need to assure strong information security for your organization's daily operations. Practitioners who have proven hands-on technical ability would do well to include the *SSCP CBK* in their arsenal of tools to competently handle day-to-day responsibilities and secure their organization's data.

Reflecting the most pertinent issues that security practitioners currently face, along with the best practices for mitigating those issues, the *SSCP CBK* offers step-by-step guidance through seven domains:

- Access Controls
- Security Operations and Administration
- Risk Identification, Monitoring, and Analysis
- Incident Response and Recovery
- Cryptography
- Networks and Communications Security
- Systems and Application Security

Drawing from a comprehensive, up-to-date global body of knowledge, this book prepares you to join the thousands of practitioners worldwide who have obtained the (ISC)² Systems Security Certified Practitioner (SSCP) credential. For those with proven technical skills and practical security knowledge, the SSCP certification is the ideal credential. The SSCP confirms the breadth and depth of practical security knowledge expected of those in hands-on operational IT roles. The certification provides industry-leading confirmation of a practitioner's ability to implement, monitor, and administer information security policies and procedures that ensure data confidentiality, integrity, and availability (CIA).

In order to meet continuing professional education requirements, SSCPs must also stay current on security issues related to changing technologies and emerging threats. As a result, SSCP practitioners can be confident that they have the know-how to competently handle day-to-day responsibilities in support of information security and business requirements.

As the recognized global leader in the field of information security education and certification, (ISC)²'s mission is to promote the development of information security professionals throughout the world. Working in coordination with members, (ISC)² also strives to raise the profile of the profession through security awareness programs for schoolchildren and an information security career program for colleges and their students. Earning an (ISC)² credential puts you in great company with a global network of professionals who echo (ISC)²'s focus to inspire a safe a secure cyber world.

As you make plans for your career, you will find that *The Official (ISC)² Guide to the SSCP CBK* most accurately reflects the technical and practical security knowledge required for the daily job functions of today's frontline information security practitioner.

I wish you good luck and success as you work toward achieving your goals.

Regards,

David P. Shearer, CISSP, PMP
Chief Executive Officer (CEO)
(ISC)²

Introduction

THERE ARE TWO MAIN requirements that must be met in order to achieve the status of SSCP: one must take and pass the certification exam, and one must be able to demonstrate a minimum of one year of direct full-time security work experience in one or more of the seven domains of the (ISC)² SSCP CBK. A firm understanding of what the seven domains of the SSCP CBK are, and how they relate to the landscape of business, is a vital element in successfully being able to meet both requirements and claim the SSCP credential. The mapping of the seven domains of the SSCP CBK to the job responsibilities of the information security practitioner in today's world can take many paths, based on a variety of factors such as industry vertical, regulatory oversight and compliance, geography, as well as public versus private versus military as the overarching framework for employment in the first place. In addition, considerations such as cultural practices and differences in language and meaning can also play a substantive role in the interpretation of what aspects of the CBK will mean and how they will be implemented in any given workplace.

It is not the purpose of this book to attempt to address all of these issues or provide a definitive prescription as to what is "the" path forward in all areas. Rather, it is to provide the official guide to the SSCP CBK and, in so doing, to lay out the information necessary to understand what the CBK is, how it is used to build the foundation for the SSCP, and its role in business today. Being able to map the SSCP CBK to your knowledge, experience, and understanding is the way that you will be able to translate the CBK into actionable and tangible elements for both the business and its users that you represent.

1. Although **Access Control** is a single domain within the SSCP Common Body of Knowledge (CBK), it is the most pervasive and omnipresent aspect of information security. Access controls encompass all operational levels of an organization:

   - **Facilities**—Access controls protect entry to, and movement around, an organization's physical locations to protect personnel, equipment, information, and other assets inside that facility.

- **Support Systems**—Access to support systems (such as power, heating, ventilation and air conditioning [HVAC] systems; water; and fire suppression controls) must be regulated so that a malicious entity is not able to compromise these systems and cause harm to the organization's personnel or the ability to support critical systems.

- **Information Systems**—Multiple layers of access controls are present in most modern information systems and networks to protect those systems, and the information they contain, from harm or misuse.

- **Personnel**—Management, end users, customers, business partners, and nearly everyone else associated with an organization should be subject to some form of access control to ensure that the right people have the ability to interface with each other and not interfere with the people with whom they do not have any legitimate business.

The goals of information security are to ensure the continued confidentiality-integrity-availability of an organization's assets. This includes both physical assets (such as buildings, equipment, and, of course, people) and information assets (such as company data and information systems). Access controls play a key role in ensuring the confidentiality of systems and information. Managing access to physical and information assets is fundamental to preventing exposure of data by controlling who can see, use, modify, or destroy those assets. In addition, managing an entity's admittance and rights to specific enterprise resources ensures that valuable data and services are not abused, misappropriated, or stolen. It is also a key factor for many organizations that are required to protect personal information in order to be compliant with appropriate legislation and industry compliance requirements.

2. The **Security Operations and Administration** domain is used to identify critical information and the execution of selected measures that eliminate or reduce adversary exploitation of critical information. It includes the definition of the controls over hardware, media, and the operators with access privileges to any of these resources. Auditing and monitoring are the mechanisms, tools, and facilities that permit the identification of security events and subsequent actions to identify the key elements and report the pertinent information to the appropriate individual, group, or process. The information security practitioner should always act to maintain operational resilience, protect valuable assets, control system accounts, and manage security services effectively. In the day-to-day operations of the business, maintaining expected levels of availability and integrity for data and

services is where the information security practitioner impacts operational resilience. The day-to-day securing, monitoring, and maintenance of the resources of the business, both human and material, illustrate how the information security practitioner is able to protect valuable assets. The use of change and configuration management by the Information Security practitioner, as well as reporting and service improvement programs (SIP), ensures that the actions necessary to manage security services effectively are being carried out.

3. The **Risk Identification, Monitoring, and Analysis** domain focuses on determining system implementation and access in accordance with defined IT criteria. The use of risk management processes plays a central part in the activities of the security practitioner within this domain. Knowledge, awareness, and understanding of risk within the context of the business is an element critical to the successful implementation of an information security management system (ISMS) today, and one that this domain helps the Security Practitioner to understand and focus on. In addition, this domain also discusses collecting information for identification of, and response to, security breaches or events.

4. The **Incident Response and Recovery** domain focuses on the review, analysis, and implementation of processes essential to the identification, measurement, and control of loss associated with adverse events. The security practitioner will be expected to understand the incident handling process and how to support forensics investigations within the enterprise. In addition, knowledge of both business continuity and disaster recovery planning and processes will be important.

5. The **Cryptography** domain is a fascinating domain in the SSCP CBK. Few information security topics have the history, challenge, and technological advancements that cryptography enjoys. Throughout history, cryptography has been a crucial factor in military victories or failures, treason, espionage, and business advantage. Cryptography is both an art and a science—the use of deception and mathematics, to hide data as in steganography, to render data unintelligible through the transformation of data into an unreadable state, and to ensure that a message has not been altered in transit. Another feature of some cryptographic systems is the ability to provide assurance of who sent the message, authentication of source, and proof of delivery. Information security practitioner expectations according to the (ISC)² Candidate Information Bulletin are that an SSCP candidate will be expected to know basic concepts within cryptography; public and private key algorithms in terms of their applications and uses; algorithm construction, key distribution and management, and methods of attack; the

applications, construction, and use of digital signatures to provide authenticity of electronic transactions; and nonrepudiation of the parties involved.

6. The **Networks and Communication Security** domain encompasses the structures, transmission methods, transport formats, and security measures used to provide confidentiality, integrity, and availability for transmissions over private and public communications networks and media. Network security is often described as the cornerstone of IT security. The network is a central asset, if not the most central, in most IT environments. Loss of network assurance (the combined properties of confidentiality, integrity, availability, authentication, and non-repudiation) on any level can have devastating consequences, while control of the network provides an easy and consistent venue of attack. Conversely, a well-architected and well-protected network will stop many attacks in their tracks.

7. **Systems and Application Security** covers countermeasures and prevention techniques for dealing with viruses, worms, logic bombs, Trojan horses, and other related forms of intentionally damaging code. In addition, the implementation and operation of end-point device security are discussed, along with the security of big data systems. The operation and configuration of cloud computing security is a focus for the security practitioner within this domain, as is the operation and security of virtualized computing environments.

CONVENTIONS

To help you get the most from the text, we've used a number of conventions throughout the book.

> ▶▶ **REAL WORLD EXAMPLE**
>
> Real-world examples take the concepts that are being discussed and describe scenarios about how these concepts are actually handled in the real world.

WARNING   Warnings draw attention to important information that is directly relevant to the surrounding text.

NOTE   Notes discuss helpful information related to the current discussion.

As for styles in the text:

- We show URLs and code within the text like so: `persistence.properties`.
- We present code like this:

```
We use a monofont type for code examples, just as you see it in the real
world.
```

Access Controls

ACCESS CONTROL IS CONCERNED with determining the allowed activities of legitimate users, mediating every attempt by a user to access a resource in the system. Access controls permit the security practitioner to specify what users can do, which resources they can access, and what operations they can perform on a system. Access controls provide the security practitioner with the ability to limit and monitor who has access to a system and to restrain or influence behavior on that system. In some systems, complete access is granted after successful authentication of the user, but most systems require more sophisticated and complex control. In addition to the authentication mechanism such as a password, access control is concerned with how authorizations are structured. Access control systems define what level of access an individual has to the information contained within a system based on predefined conditions such as authority level or group membership. Access control systems are based on varying technologies, including passwords, hardware tokens, biometrics, and certificates, to name a few. Each access control system offers different levels of confidentiality, integrity, and availability to the user, the system, and stored information.

TOPICS

The following topics are addressed in this chapter:

- ❑ Implement authentication mechanisms
  - ■ Single/multifactor authentication
  - ■ Single sign-on
  - ■ Offline authentication
  - ■ Device authentication
- ❑ Operate internetwork trust architectures (e.g., extranet, third-party connections, federated access)
  - ■ One-way trust
  - ■ Two-way trust
  - ■ Transitive trust
- ❑ Administer identity management lifecycle
  - ■ Authorization
  - ■ Proofing
  - ■ Provisioning
  - ■ Maintenance
  - ■ Entitlement
- ❑ Implement access controls (e.g., subject-based, object-based)
  - ■ Mandatory
  - ■ Non-discretionary
  - ■ Discretionary
  - ■ Role-based
  - ■ Attribute-based

OBJECTIVES

A Systems Security Certified Practitioner (SSCP) is expected to demonstrate knowledge in how different access control systems operate and are implemented to protect the system and its stored data. In addition, the security practitioner must demonstrate knowledge in the following:

- Account management
- Access control concepts
- Attack methods that are used to defeat access control systems

ACCESS CONTROL CONCEPTS

Security practitioners planning to implement an access control system should consider three constructs: access control policies, models, and mechanisms. Access control policies are high-level requirements that specify how access is managed and who may access information under what circumstances. For instance, policies may pertain to resource usage within or across organizational units or may be based on need-to-know, competence, authority, obligation, or conflict-of-interest factors. At a high level, access control policies are enforced through a mechanism that translates a user's access request, often in terms of a structure that a system provides. An access control list is an example of an access control mechanism. Access control models bridge the gap between policy and mechanism. Rather than attempting to evaluate and analyze access control systems exclusively at the mechanism level, the security practitioner should use security models, which are usually written to describe the security properties of an access control system. Security models are formal presentations of the security policy enforced by the system and are useful for proving the theoretical limitations of a system. Discretionary access control (DAC), which allows the creator of a file to delegate access to others, is one of the simplest examples of a model.

Access controls provide for the ability to control "who" can do "what" with respect to data, applications, systems, networks, and physical spaces. In the simplest of terms, an access control system grants system users only those rights necessary for them to perform their respective jobs. The following definitions of key terms will be helpful for the security practitioner:

- A *subject* is an active entity that requests access to an object or the data within an object. The subject is the actor.
- An *object* is a passive entity being accessed, or the item being acted upon.

- *Access* is the ability of a subject to do something, such as read, create, delete, or modify. Access is also considered the flow of information between a subject and object.

- *Access control* is focused on the security features that control how subjects and objects communicate and interact with each other and the flow of information.

Applying Logical Access Control in Terms of Subjects

An access control subject is an active entity and can be any user, program, or process that requests permission to cause data to flow from an access control object to the access control subject or between access control objects.

Access control subjects include

- Authorized users
- Unauthorized users
- Applications
- Processes
- Systems
- Networks

The authorization provided to the access control subject by an access control system can include but is not limited to the considerations shown in Table 1.1.

TABLE 1.1 **Access Control Subject/Object Comparison**

ACCESS CONTROL SUBJECT	ACCESS CONTROL OBJECT
Temporal—time of day, day of request.	Data content of the object.
Locale from where the access control subject was authenticated.	The access control subject may be restricted from accessing all or part of the data within the access control object because of the type of data that may be contained within the object.
Inside or outside of the network.	Transaction restrictions may also apply.
Password or token utilized.	
An individual access control subject may have different rights assigned to specific passwords that are used during the authentication process.	

The attributes of a subject are referred to as privilege attributes or sensitivities. When these attributes are matched against the control attributes of an object, privilege is either granted or denied.

In a typical access control system, there are additional subject-specific requirements:

- A secure default policy should be applied to any newly created subject.

- The attributes of the subject should not be expressed in terms that can easily be forged, such as an IP address.

- The system should provide for a default deny on all permissions for the subject, thereby requiring that access to any object be explicitly created by an administrator.

- In the absence of policy for a given subject, the default policy should be interpreted as default deny.

- A user ID should remain permanently assigned to a subject.

The configuration of privileges in access control for an individual subject affords maximum granularity to the security practitioner. In systems with perhaps hundreds or thousands of users, this granularity can quickly become a management burden. By incorporating multiple subjects with similar permissions within a group, the granularity is thereby coarsened and the administration of the access control system is simplified. For example, look at Figure 1.1. Notice that the access control entry for Student\NHM_E4 has five permissions associated with it. Managing these permissions for a single user is not very difficult, nor does it present the security practitioner with a situation that would be too challenging to document and manage over the lifecycle of the SSCP Access Control Example document. However, even with just a single user and the permissions associated with their access to the document, there are a minimum of 10 different possible outcomes that the security practitioner will have to keep in mind as potential access levels for the user with regards to the document if the *standard* permissions are considered only. When the *special* permissions are added as well, the number jumps to a minimum of 26 potential outcomes if all permissions were employed.

The total number of permissions available for use in a Windows operating system such as Windows 7 or Windows 8 that uses the NTFS file system would be 14 if all possible standard and special permission options were included for potential use. This would include the five standard permissions, the additional eight special permissions available, as well as the 14th permission, which would be **no access** (full control = DENY). The security practitioner always needs to keep in mind what permissions have been assigned to a resource, either explicitly or implicitly, and, by extension, which permission(s) have not been assigned. A complete listing of the NTFS special permissions is as follows:

- Full control
- Traverse folder/execute file
- List folder/read data
- Read attributes
- Read extended attributes
- Create files/write data
- Create folders/append data
- Write attributes
- Write extended attributes
- Delete
- Read permissions
- Change permissions
- Take ownership

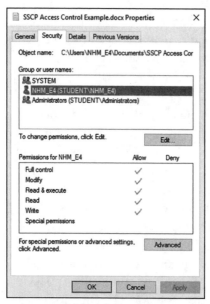

FIGURE 1.1 **Subject Group Access Control—User**

The security practitioner needs to keep in mind that permissions can be assigned to the user, or set, as either ALLOW or DENY, as shown in Figure 1.2.

When Figure 1.3 is examined, one will notice that there are access control entries for multiple users. Each user has the potential to have different permissions assigned to them by the owner of the SSCP Access Control Example document. As a result, the security practitioner now has a situation that will require them to manage and document permissions assigned to multiple users. Managing these permissions for multiple users is more challenging, as there are a minimum of 10 different possible outcomes multiplied by the four users that the security practitioner will have to keep in mind as potential access levels for the user concerning the document if the standard permissions are considered only. This means that the security practitioner will now have to keep track of a potential minimum of 40 different user/permission combinations. When the special permissions are added as well, the number jumps to a minimum of 26 potential outcomes multiplied by the four users, which is a minimum of 104 outcomes, if all permissions were employed.

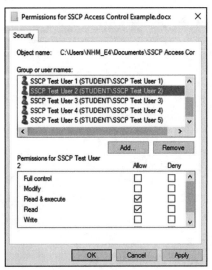

FIGURE 1.2 **Subject Group Access Control—User permissions Allow and Deny**

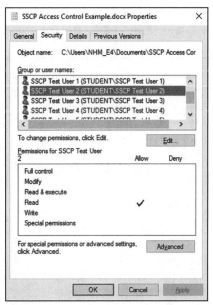

FIGURE 1.3 **Subject Group Access Control—Multiple Users**

In Figure 1.4, the access control entry for the Student\Administrators group has five permissions associated with it. On the surface, this group presents the same scenario to the security practitioner that the Student\NHM_E4 user from Figure 1.1 does, and the same minimum number of outcomes for both the standard and special permissions. The key difference for the security practitioner is the ability to leverage the power of membership in the group in order to simplify the management overhead involved with assigning, documenting, and tracking permission combinations. By placing users with similar access needs into a single group, the security practitioner will be able to use the power of the group to *assign once and manage many,* resulting in two key advantages. The first advantage is that the security practitioner will be able to streamline the permission provisioning process for the users requiring access to the SSCP Access Control Example document, resulting in less management overhead as more users require access over the lifetime of the document. The second advantage is that the likelihood of an incorrect permission assignment being made for one or more users, leading to either too little or too much access to the SSCP Access Control Example document, is greatly reduced if the security practitioner is focused on ensuring that the group permissions are assigned based on job role or access need, and as a result, that membership in the groups are managed the same way. The security practitioner should always strive to use group membership as the basis for assigning access to resources when planning access control solutions, as it offers more flexibility and forces the data owner to carefully consider the requirements for data access *prior* to assignment.

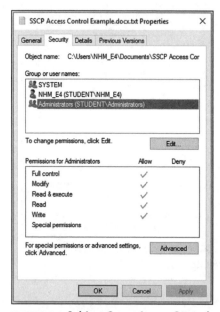

FIGURE 1.4 **Subject Group Access Control—Group**

Applying Logical Access Control in Terms of Objects or Object Groups

An access control object is a passive entity that typically receives or contains some form of data. The data can be in the form of a file, can be in the form of a program, or may be resident within system memory.

Access control objects include:

- Data
- Applications
- Systems
- Networks
- Physical space, for example, the data center

Typical access control object considerations can include but are not limited to the following:

- Restrict access to operating system configuration files and their respective directories to authorized administrators.
- Disable write/modify permissions for all executable files.
- Ensure that newly created files inherit the permissions of the directory in which they were created.
- Ensure that subdirectories cannot override the permissions of parent directories unless specifically required by policy.
- Log files should be configured to only permit appending data to mitigate the risk of a log file's contents being purposely deleted or overwritten by a malicious user or process.
- Encryption of data at rest can afford additional security and should be a consideration in the determination of the policies for access control objects.

The configuration of privileges to access an individual object affords maximum granularity. It is common today for the number of objects within an access control system to number in the tens or even hundreds of thousands. While configuring individual objects affords maximum control, this granularity can quickly become an administrative burden. It is a common practice to assign the appropriate permissions to a directory, and each object within the directory inherits the respective parent directory permissions. By incorporating multiple objects with similar permissions or restrictions within a group or directory, the granularity is thereby coarsened and the administration of the access control system is simplified. Figure 1.5 shows the permission entries for the SSCP_1 folder, a child object of the parent SSCP folder object. As a child object, the SSCP_1 folder automatically upon creation is set to accept inheritable permissions from the object's parent as indicated by the button with the text "Disable inheritance." This setting ensures that *all* objects created within the SSCP_1 folder will inherit the existing access control settings already in place at the parent object, the SSCP folder, in addition to whatever new settings are assigned once the object is created by the object owner.

The "Replace all child object permission entries with inheritable permissions from this object" setting is never set by default and must be manually selected to be used. This setting indicates that the object owner has decided to break the original hierarchical inheritance chain between the parent and child objects and, as a result, all additional hierarchical generations that are created below the child as well. Further, the breaking of the hierarchical inheritance chain at this point will result in all new objects that are created being blocked from inheritance of the parental object's existing access control settings, thus ensuring that these newly created child objects are not bound by *any* of the access control settings in place at the parent object.

Figure 1.6 illustrates this exact outcome, as the language "This will replace explicitly defined permissions on all descendants of this object with inheritable permissions from" indicates. This action will also effectively promote the current child to the status of a parent for any/all newly created objects at this level, as well as all sublevels, ensuring that these objects inherit their access control settings from their newly created parent object, not the original parent object that they are now disassociated from due to the breaking of the inheritance chain.

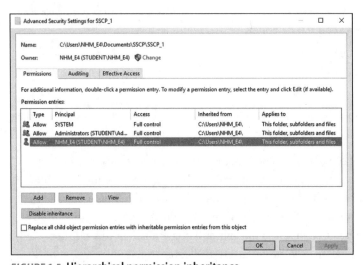

FIGURE 1.5 **Hierarchical permission inheritance**

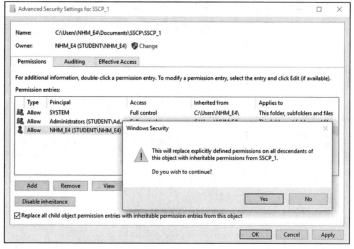

FIGURE 1.6 **Replacement of all child object permissions**

IMPLEMENTING ACCESS CONTROLS

Access controls are used in a system to ensure that authorization and authentication are properly implemented. Authorization is the process where requests to access a particular resource should be granted or denied. Authentication is providing and validating identity. The SSCP should be familiar with the different types of access control methods available, as well as how they work.

Discretionary Access Control

A *Discretionary Access Control* (DAC) policy is a means of assigning access rights based on rules specified by users. This class of policies includes the file permissions model implemented by nearly all operating systems. In Unix, for example, a directory listing might yield "... rwxr-xr-x ... SSCP File 1.txt," meaning that the owner of SSCP File 1.txt may read, write, or execute it, and that other users may read or execute the file but not write it. The set of access rights in this example is {read, write, execute}, and the operating system mediates all requests to perform any of these actions. Users may change the permissions on files they own, making this a discretionary policy. A mechanism implementing a DAC policy must be able to answer the question: "Does subject Sayge have right Read for object SSCP File 1?" More practically, the same information could also be represented as an access control matrix. Each row of the matrix corresponds to a subject and each column to an object. Each cell of the matrix contains a set of rights. Table 1.2 shows an example of an access control matrix.

TABLE 1.2 **An Access Control Matrix**

	SSCP FILE 1	SSCP FILE 2
Aidan	Read | Write | eXecute	Read | eXecute
Sayge	Read	Read | Write

Systems typically store the information from this matrix either by columns or by rows. An implementation that stores by columns is commonly known as an access control list (ACL). File systems in Windows and Unix typically use such an implementation: Each file is accompanied by a list containing subjects and their rights to that file. An implementation that stores by rows is commonly known as a capability list. For example, it is easy in an ACL implementation to find the set of all subjects who may read a file, but it is difficult to find the set of all files that a subject may read.

The underlying philosophy in DAC is that subjects can determine who has access to their objects. In Discretionary Access Control (DAC), the owner of the access control object would determine the privileges (i.e., read, write, execute) of the access control subjects. In the DoD 5200.28-STD, Department of Defense Standard Department of Defense Trusted Computer System Evaluation Criteria, Discretionary Access Control is defined as "a means of restricting access to objects based on the identity of subjects and/ or groups to which they belong. The controls are discretionary in the sense that a subject with certain access permission is capable of passing that permission (perhaps indirectly) on to any other subject (unless restrained by mandatory access control)."[1]

This methodology relies on the discretion of the owner of the access control object to determine the access control subject's specific rights. Hence, security of the object is literally up to the discretion of the object owner. DACs are not very scalable; they rely on the decisions made by each individual access control object owner, and it can be difficult to find the source of access control issues when problems occur.

Rule Set–Based Access Controls

Rule Set–Based Access Controls (RSBAC) are discretionary controls giving data owners the discretion to determine the rules necessary to facilitate access. RSBAC is an open source access control framework for current Linux kernels, which has been in use since January 2000 (version 1.0.9a). RSBAC allows full fine-grained control over objects (files, processes, users, devices, etc.), memory execution prevention (PaX, NX), real-time integrated virus detection, and much more. The RSBAC framework logic is based on the work done for the Generalized Framework for Access Control (GFAC) by Abrams and LaPadula.[2]

All security relevant system calls are extended by security enforcement code. This code calls the central decision component, which in turn calls all active decision modules (the different modules implementing different security models) and generates a combined final decision. This decision is then enforced by the system call extensions. Decisions are based on the type of access (request type), the access target, and the values of attributes attached to the subject calling and to the target to be accessed. Additional independent attributes can be used by individual modules. All attributes are stored in fully protected directories, one on each mounted device. Thus, changes to attributes require special system calls to be provided.

RSBAC works at the kernel level and affords flexible access control based on several modules:

- Mandatory Access Control (MAC) module
- Privacy module (PM)
- Function Control module (FC)
- File Flag module (FF)
- Malware Scan module (MS)
- Role Compatibility module (RC)
- Function Control module (FC)
- Security Information Modification module (SIM)
- Authentication module (Auth)
- Access Control List module (ACL)

Figure 1.7 illustrates the RSBAC access request process.

✔ **Try It for Yourself—With a Live CD**

Test RSBAC with a Debian-based live CD, or use it on a USB key/drive. This will allow full testing of RSBAC functionality without having to install it. Just insert the CD or USB key, reboot, and try it!

Download here:

```
https://www.rsbac.org/download
```

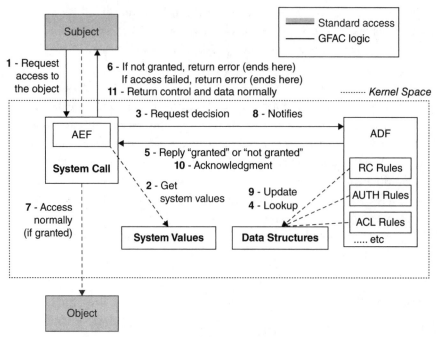

FIGURE 1.7 **The Rule Set Based Access Control (RSBAC) Generalized Framework for Access Control (GFAC) logic for data access request**

Role-Based Access Controls

With role-based access control, access decisions are based on the roles that individual users have as part of an organization. Users take on assigned roles (such as Backup Operator, Performance Log Users, and Administrators). The process of defining roles should be based on a thorough analysis of how an organization operates and should include input from a wide spectrum of users in an organization.

Access rights are grouped by role name, and the use of resources is restricted to individuals authorized to assume the associated role. For example, within a network the role of Performance Log User can include operations to open, read, save, and delete log files; and the role of Backup Operators can be limited to activities related strictly to the backing up of specified data, but not be designed to include the activities associated with restoring the data if required.

Under the RBAC framework, users are granted membership into roles based on their competencies and responsibilities in the organization. The operations that a user is permitted to perform are based on the user's role. User membership in roles can be revoked easily and new memberships established as job assignments dictate. Role associations can be established when new operations are instituted, and old operations can be deleted as organizational functions change and evolve. This simplifies the administration and management of privileges; roles can be updated without updating the privileges for every user on an individual basis.

Under RBAC, when a user is associated with a role, the user should be given no more privileges than are necessary to perform their role. This concept of least privilege requires identifying the user's job functions, determining the minimum set of privileges required to perform that function, and restricting the user to a role with those privileges and nothing more. In less precisely controlled systems, this is often difficult to achieve. Someone assigned to a job category may be allowed more privileges than needed because it is difficult to tailor access based on various attributes or constraints. Since many of the responsibilities overlap between job categories, maximum privilege for each job category could cause undesired or unlawful access.

Under RBAC, roles can have overlapping responsibilities and privileges; that is, users belonging to different roles may need to perform common operations. Role hierarchies can be established to provide for the natural structure of an enterprise. A role hierarchy defines roles that have unique attributes and that may contain other roles; that is, one role may implicitly include the operations that are associated with another role.

✔ Try It for Yourself—RBAC in a Box

Now you will interact with RBAC first hand.

What's Needed?

A Windows-based computer and a user account with administrative rights.

How to Do It

Use the following step-by-step guidance:

1. Open the Control Panel from the Windows desktop, or simply type **control panel** in the Run line and hit Enter. (Alternately, you can type `compmgmt.msc` directly in the Run line to bypass the Control Panel and go directly to the Computer Management Console.)

2. From the Control Panel open Computer Management.

3. From within the Computer Management Console go to the Local Users and Groups item and then select the Groups folder in the left window. You will see the various groups that are already present on the system displayed in the right portion of the window. (See Figure 1.8.)

CONTINUES

CONTINUED

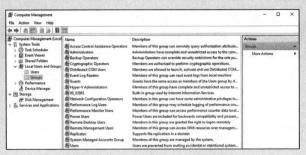

FIGURE 1.8 **Local Users and Groups in a Windows 7 computer**

4. Select a group to examine the permissions for, such as the Backup Operators group or the Power Users group.

5. Open the Windows Explorer window to examine the files and folders on the system.

6. Pick a file or folder from within the Windows Explorer window in order to examine the RBAC permissions for the group you chose in step 4. Any file or folder in the computer may be used, but it would be best if one were created specifically to test with, so existing file permissions are not mistakenly changed.

7. Once the file or folder has been selected, right-click on it from within the Windows Explorer window and choose Properties from the shortcut menu that pops up. When the Properties window for the file or folder has opened, click on the Security tab (second in line, moving left to right). Something similar to Figure 1.9 should be displayed.

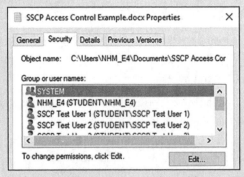

FIGURE 1.9 **File permissions** *before* **adding an RBAC example in Windows 7/Windows 8 computer**

8. Click the Edit button and then click the Add button on the Security tab that will appear once the Edit button has been clicked.

9. Use the group that was selected in step 4. Type the name of the group into the dialog within the Select Users or Groups screen that has appeared, as shown in Figure 1.10.

    Please note the following: Type the group name into the window in the format shown in Figure 1.10, which is **Machine Name\Group Name**. You can find the machine name listed under the "From this location" area, right above where the machine name\group name information will be typed.

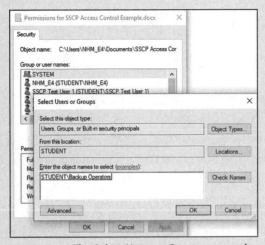

FIGURE 1.10 The Select Users or Groups screen that appears after the Edit button has been clicked

10. Once done entering the group information, click the OK button. Something similar to Figure 1.11 should be displayed.

CONTINUES

CONTINUED

11. Figure 1.11 shows the Backup Operators group and the Role Based Access Control permissions associated with the group. RBAC has been successfully demonstrated!

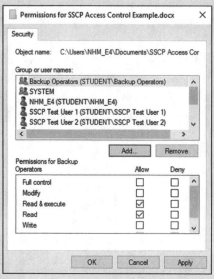

FIGURE 1.11 Folder permissions *after* adding an RBAC example in Windows 7/ Windows 8; resultant set of permissions for Backup Operators group

Constrained User Interface

Constrained User Interface (CUI) is a methodology that restricts the user's actions to specific functions by not allowing them to request functions that are outside of their respective level of privilege or role. One of the most common examples of a Constrained User Interface can be found in online banking applications and ATMs where the limited menus are not readily apparent until after the user has properly authenticated, thereby establishing their respective role/level of privilege.

Three major types of restricted interfaces exist: menus and shells, database views, and physically constrained interfaces.

- **Menu and Shells**—When menu and shell restrictions are used, the options users are given are the commands they can execute. For example, if an administrator wants users to be able to execute only one program, that program would be the only choice available on the menu. This limits the users' functionality. A shell is a type of virtual environment within a system. It is the user's interface to the operating system and works as a command interpreter. If restricted shells were used, the shell would contain only the commands the administrator wants the users to be able to execute.

- **Database Views**—Database views are mechanisms used to restrict user access to data contained in databases.

- **Physically Constraining a User Interface** — Physically constraining a user interface can be implemented by providing only certain keys on a keypad or certain touch buttons on a screen. You see this when you get money from an ATM. This device has a type of operating system that can accept all kinds of commands and configuration changes, but it is physically constrained from being able to carry out these functions.

Another type of CUI is often referred to as View-Based Access Control (VBAC); it is most commonly found in database applications to control access to specific parts of a database. The CUI in VBAC restricts or limits an access control subject's ability to view or perhaps act on "components" of an access control object based on the access control subject's assigned level of authority. Views are dynamically created by the system for each user-authorized access.

Simply put, VBAC separates a given access control object into subcomponents and then permits or denies access for the access control subject to view or interact with specific subcomponents of the underlying access control object.[3]

Content-Dependent Access Control

Content-Dependent Access Control (CDAC) is used to protect databases containing sensitive information. CDAC works by permitting or denying the access control subjects access to access control objects based on the explicit content within the access control object. An example would be the use of CDAC in a medical records database application where a health-care worker may have been granted access to blood test records. If that record contains information about an HIV test, the health-care worker may be denied access to the existence of the HIV test and the results of the HIV test. Only specific hospital staff would have the necessary CDAC access control rights to view blood test records that contain any information about HIV tests.

While high levels of privacy protection are attainable using CDAC, they come at the cost of a great deal of labor in defining the respective permissions. It should be further noted that CDAC comes with a great deal of overhead in processing power as it must scan the complete record to determine if access can be granted to a given access control subject. This scan is done by an arbiter program to determine if access will be allowed.

Context-Based Access Control

Context-Based Access Control (CBAC) is used in firewall applications to extend the firewall's decision-making process beyond basic ACL decisions to decisions based on state as well as application-layer protocol session information. A static packet-filtering firewall is a good example of a firewall that does not use CBAC. It looks at each packet and compares the packet to an ACL rule base to determine if the packet is to be allowed or denied. A stateful inspection firewall is a good example of a firewall that uses CBAC. The firewall also considers the "state of the connection"; i.e., if a packet arrives that is part of a continuing session that had previously been permitted to pass through the firewall, then subsequent packets that are part of that session are allowed to pass without the overhead associated with comparing the packet to the ACL rules. CBAC affords a significant performance enhancement to a firewall.[4]

CBAC is often confused with CDAC, but they are two completely different methodologies. While CDAC makes decisions based on the content within an access control object, CBAC is not concerned with the content; it is concerned only with the context or the sequence of events leading to the access control object being allowed through the firewall.

In the example of blood test records for CDAC in the previous section, the access control subject would be denied access to the access control object because it contained information about an HIV test. CBAC could be used to limit the total number of requests for access to any blood test records over a given period of time. Hence, a health-care worker may be limited to accessing the blood test database more than 100 times in a 24-hour period.

While CBAC does not require that permissions be configured for individual access control objects, it requires that rules be created in relation to the sequence of events that precede an access attempt.

Temporal Isolation (Time-Based) Access Control

Temporal Isolation (Time-Based) Access Control is used to enhance or extend the capabilities of RBAC implementations. This combined methodology is often referred to as Temporal Role-Based Access Control (TRBAC).[5] TRBAC supports periodic role enabling and disabling and temporal dependencies among such actions. Such dependencies expressed by means of role triggers (active rules that are automatically executed when the specified actions occur) can also be used to constrain the set of roles that a particular user can activate at a given time instant. The firing of a trigger may cause a role to be enabled/ disabled either immediately or after an explicitly specified amount of time. Enabling/ disabling actions may be given a priority that may help in solving conflicts, such as the simultaneous enabling and disabling of a role. As expected, the action with the highest priority is executed. TRBAC effectively applies a time limitation to when a given role can be activated for a given access control subject.

- A high-level *top secret* role would be assigned to a given access control subject during the normal 8 a.m. to 5 p.m. working hours.
- A lower-level *confidential* role would be assigned to the same access control subject during the 5 p.m. to 8 a.m. nonworking hours.

To decrease the effort associated with assigning TRBAC rules to many individual access control subjects, most implementations of TRBAC assign the temporal-based classification levels to the access control objects rather than to the access control subject. Hence, a given access control object would have a temporal-based classification level that is effective against all access control subjects.

Temporal extensions are also used to enhance other access control methodologies. It is common today to find access control devices that support time-based access control rules. The temporal enhancement of the access control rule only allows the rule to be effective during the specified time period.

Nondiscretionary Access Control

According to the United States National Institute of Standards and Technology (NIST), in general, all access control policies other than DAC are grouped in the category of non-discretionary access control (NDAC). As the name implies, policies in this category have rules that are not established at the discretion of the user. Non-discretionary policies establish controls that cannot be changed by users, but only through administrative action.[6]

Mandatory Access Control

Mandatory Access Control (MAC) is typically used in environments requiring high levels of security such as government or military systems. In MAC, the inherent problems of trying to rely on each system owner to properly control access to each access control object is eliminated by having the system participate in applying a mandatory access policy; the system owner applies the "need to know" element. This policy affords typically three object classification levels: *top-secret*, *secret*, and *confidential*. Each access control system subject (users and programs) is assigned clearance labels, and access control system objects are assigned sensitivity labels. The system then automatically provides the correct access rights based on comparing the object and subject labels. MAC allows multiple security levels of both objects and subjects to be combined in one system securely.

Mandatory access control (MAC) policy means that access control policy decisions are made by a central authority, not by the individual owner of an object, and the owner cannot change access rights. An example of MAC occurs in military security, where an individual data owner does not decide who has a top secret clearance, nor can the owner change the classification of an object from top secret to secret. The need for a MAC mechanism arises when the security policy of a system dictates that

1. Protection decisions must not be decided by the object owner.
2. The system must enforce the protection decisions (i.e., the system enforces the security policy over the wishes or intentions of the object owner). Usually a labeling mechanism and a set of interfaces are used to determine access based on the

MAC policy; for example, a user who is running a process at the secret classification should not be allowed to read a file with a label of top secret. This is known as the *simple security rule*, or *no read up*. Conversely, a user who is running a process with a label of Secret should not be allowed to write to a file with a label of Confidential. This rule is called the **-property* (pronounced "star property") or *no write down*. The *-property is required to maintain system security in an automated environment. A variation on this rule called the *strict *-property* requires that information can be written at, but not above, the subject's clearance level. Multilevel security models such as the Bell–LaPadula Confidentiality and Biba Integrity models are used to formally specify this kind of MAC policy.

Attribute-Based Access Control

The following is a high-level definition of ABAC, according to NIST Special Publication 800-162, *Guide to Attribute Based Access Control (ABAC) Definition and Considerations:*[7]

> *Attribute Based Access Control (ABAC) is an access control method where subject requests to perform operations on objects are granted or denied based on assigned attributes of the subject, assigned attributes of the object, environment conditions, and a set of policies that are specified in terms of those attributes and conditions.*

Here are some vocabulary terms that will help the security practitioner understand and apply the definition:

- *Attributes* are characteristics of the subject, object, or environment conditions. Attributes contain information given by a name-value pair.

- A *subject* is a human user or NPE, such as a device that issues access requests to perform operations on objects. Subjects are assigned one or more attributes. For the purpose of this document, assume that subject and user are synonymous.

- An *object* is a system resource for which access is managed by the ABAC system, such as devices, files, records, tables, processes, programs, networks, or domains containing or receiving information. It can be the resource or requested entity, as well as anything upon which an operation may be performed by a subject including data, applications, services, devices, and networks.

- An *operation* is the execution of a function at the request of a subject upon an object. Operations include read, write, edit, delete, copy, execute, and modify.

- *Policy* is the representation of rules or relationships that makes it possible to determine if a requested access should be allowed, given the values of the attributes of the subject, object, and possibly environment conditions.

- *Environment conditions* represent the operational or situational context in which access requests occur. Environment conditions are detectable environmental characteristics. Environment characteristics are independent of subject or object and may include the current time, day of the week, location of a user, or current threat level.

Separation of Duties

This aspect of access control establishes guidelines that require that no single person should perform a task from beginning to end and that the task should be accomplished by two or more people to mitigate the potential for fraud in one person performing the task alone. Separation of duties is a key element in the Clark–Wilson formal model.

SECURITY ARCHITECTURE AND MODELS

Security architects often use established security models as points of reference in design work. Established, tested models identify the major components in a security solution and how they interact. Chief among these models are the Bell–LaPadula confidentiality model, and the Biba and Clark–Wilson integrity models.

Bell–LaPadula Confidentiality Model[8]

The Bell–LaPadula model was designed as an architectural reference for controlling access to sensitive data in government and military applications. The components of the model are subjects, objects, and an access control matrix. *Objects* (access targets) are classified into a hierarchy of security levels based on sensitivity, from low to high. If information has been previously classified (top secret, secret, etc.), then classification levels corresponding to the organization's policy are used. *Subjects* (actors) — which may be human actors, application programs, or system processes — are assigned security levels called *clearance levels.* The relation between the sensitivity level of objects and the clearance level of subjects is defined in the *access control matrix.* The access control matrix defines permissions (read-only, read/write, append, execute) for each clearance level and object classification. Each access operation is defined within the matrix by a subject, object, and access permission triple. The matrix provides assurance that the confidentiality of the system will remain stable despite transitions in state; that is, a system that is in a secure state before an operation will be in the same secure state at the conclusion of the operation.

The basic tenet of Bell–LaPadula is that a given subject can read objects at the same or lower sensitivity level, but not those at a higher sensitivity level; this is called the *simple security property* and can be remembered as "no read up." The simple property is usually sufficient for implementing systems that control access to classified documents and files when the files have corresponding read-only attributes. However, it does not take into consideration the possibility that a subject may add, append, or transmit sensitive information to an area of lower sensitivity and thus create a channel that defeats the access control mechanism. Bell–LaPadula adds another property to counteract this called the star (*) property. The * property blocks the channel between areas of different sensitivities such that when a subject has accessed an object for a read operation, then objects at a lower sensitivity level cannot be accessed for create and modify operations ("no write down"). Covert channels, such as backup and monitoring channels and image capture utilities, still present a risk for systems designed using Bell–LaPadula confidentiality models as these processes may be used for legitimate as well as illegitimate purposes.

Bell–LaPadula is not without its limitations. It is concerned only with confidentiality and makes no mention of other properties (such as integrity and availability) or more sophisticated modes of access. These have to be addressed through other models. More importantly, it does not address important confidentiality goals such as need-to-know, or the ability to restrict access to individual objects based on a subject's need to access them. Since Bell–LaPadula does not provide a mechanism for a one-to-one mapping of individual subjects and objects, this also needs to be addressed by other models.

Biba[9] and Clark–Wilson Integrity Models[10]

Like Bell–LaPadula, Biba is also a lattice-based model with multiple levels. It uses the same modes of access (read, write, and read/write) and describes interactions between subjects and objects. Where Biba differs most obviously is that it is an integrity model: It focuses on ensuring that the integrity of information is being maintained by preventing corruption. At the core of the model is a multilevel approach to integrity designed to prevent unauthorized subjects from modifying objects. Access is controlled to ensure that objects maintain their current state of integrity as subjects interact with them. Instead of the confidentiality levels used by Bell–LaPadula, Biba assigns integrity levels to subjects and objects depending on how trustworthy they are considered to be. Like Bell–LaPadula, Biba considers the same modes of access but with different results. Table 1.3 compares the BLP and Biba models.

For example, consider a subject that wishes to add two numbers together. The subject needs information that is reasonably accurate to two decimal places and has different values to choose from. Some of these values are accurate to more than two decimal places. Some are less accurate. To prevent corruption, the subject must only use information that is at least as accurate as two decimal places; information that is accurate only to one decimal place must not be used or corruption may occur.

TABLE 1.3 BLP and Biba Model Properties

PROPERTY	BLP MODEL	BIBA MODEL
ss-property	A subject cannot read/ access an object of a higher classification (no read up).	A subject cannot observe an object of a lower integrity level (no read down).
*-property	A subject can save an object only at the same or higher classification (no write down).	A subject cannot modify an object of a higher integrity level (no write up).
Invocation property	Not used.	A subject cannot send logical service requests to an object of a higher integrity.

Source: Hare, C., "Policy Development," *Information Security Management Handbook*, 6th ed., Tipton, H.F. and Krause, M., Eds., Auerbach Publications. New York, 2007.

In the * integrity property, a given subject has the ability to write information to different types of objects with differing levels of integrity or accuracy. In this case, the subject must be prevented from corrupting objects that are more accurate than it is. The subject should then be allowed to write to objects that are less accurate, but not to objects that are more accurate. To allow otherwise may result in corruption. Biba also addresses the problem of one subject getting a more privileged subject to work on their behalf. In the invocation property, Biba considers a situation where corruption may occur because a less trustworthy subject was allowed to take advantage of the capabilities of a more trustworthy subject by invoking their powers. According to Biba, this must be prevented or corruption could occur.

David D. Clark and David R. Wilson developed their Clark–Wilson integrity model to address what they viewed as shortcomings in the Bell–LaPadula and Biba models.[11] While these models were useful for protecting classified information from unauthorized access or leakage to unclassified systems, they did not provide any framework to prevent corruption of data (either maliciously or unintentionally) during processing of the data. Clark–Wilson's model addresses this risk using the idea of a well-formed transaction operating on the data. The components of this model also form a triple: authenticated principals (users), programs acting on data (transaction processes), and the data items themselves. Each triple or relation between user, transaction, and data item must be maintained in the system.

Systems designed to enforce the Clark–Wilson integrity policy consist of well-formed transactions, that is, transactions that maintain a consistent level of integrity between the initial and end state. Integrity verification processes ensure the integrity of data items before, during, and after a transaction. Clark–Wilson also protects against malicious users by requiring separation of duties between people who can create relations used in a process and those who can execute the process.

Additional Models

Bell–LaPadula, Biba, and Clark–Wilson are all useful frameworks for designing so-called multilevel security (MLS) systems, in which information with various sensitivities or integrity requirements can be processed concurrently in a single system by users or actors with multiple levels of clearance or need to know. Some additional models that the security practitioner will want to familiarize themselves with are mentioned in the following sections.

Brewer–Nash (the Chinese Wall) Model

This model focuses on preventing conflict of interest when a given subject has access to objects with sensitive information associated with two competing parties. The principle is that users should not access the confidential information of both a client organization and one or more of its competitors. At the beginning, subjects may access either set of objects. Once, however, a subject accesses an object associated with one competitor, they are instantly prevented from accessing any objects on the opposite side. This is intended to prevent the subject from sharing information inappropriately between the two competitors even unintentionally. It is called the Chinese Wall Model because, like the Great Wall of China, once on one side of the wall, a person cannot get to the other side. It is an unusual model in comparison with many of the others because the access control rules change based on subject behavior.

Graham–Denning Model

Graham–Denning is primarily concerned with how subjects and objects are created, how subjects are assigned rights or privileges, and how ownership of objects is managed. In other words, it is primarily concerned with how a model system controls subjects and objects at a very basic level where other models simply assumed such control.

The Graham–Denning access control model has three parts: a set of objects, a set of subjects, and a set of rights. The subjects are composed of two things: a process and a domain. The domain is the set of constraints controlling how subjects may access objects. Subjects may also be objects at specific times. The set of rights govern how subjects may manipulate the passive objects. This model describes eight primitive protection rights called commands that subjects can execute to have an effect on other subjects or objects. The model defines eight primitive protection rights:

1. **Create Object**—The ability to create a new object
2. **Create Subject**—The ability to create a new subject

3. **Delete Object**—The ability to delete an existing object

4. **Delete Subject**—The ability to delete an existing subject

5. **Read Access Right**—The ability to view current access privileges

6. **Grant Access Right**—The ability to grant access privileges

7. **Delete Access Right**—The ability to remove access privileges

8. **Transfer Access Right**—The ability to transfer access privileges from one subject or object to another subject or object

Harrison–Ruzzo–Ullman Model

This model is very similar to the Graham–Denning model, and it is composed of a set of generic rights and a finite set of commands. It is also concerned with situations in which a subject should be restricted from gaining particular privileges. To do so, subjects are prevented from accessing programs or subroutines that can execute a particular command (to grant read access for example) where necessary.

IMPLEMENTING AUTHENTICATION MECHANISMS— IDENTIFICATION, AUTHENTICATION, AUTHORIZATION, AND ACCOUNTABILITY

The process flow involved in the implementation of authentication mechanisms is to identify, authenticate, and authorize. Identification is the process used to allow the access control subject to provide information as to their identity, which can be used to validate them. Authentication is the act of providing and validating identity within the access control system. Authorization is the process where requests to access a particular resource should be granted or denied, based on the outcome of the authentication process. One example of a technology used to provide authentication services within an access control system is Biometrics. The SSCP should be familiar with the identification, authentication, and authorization processes and how they work together to create accountability within access control systems.

Identification (Who Is the Subject?)

Identification asserts a unique user or process identity and provides for accountability. Identification of an access control subject is typically in the form of an assigned user name. This user name could be public information whether intentional or not. A good example is that in most networks, the user name that identifies the user for network access is also the identification used as the e-mail account identifier. Hence, all one would have to do to determine the account holder's user name would be to know the account holder's e-mail address. An access control that relied on the user name alone to provide access would be an ineffective access control. To prove that the individual who presented the user name to the access control is the individual who the user name was assigned to, a secret is shared between the access control system and the respective user. This secret is the user's password and is used to authenticate that the user who is trying to gain access is in fact the user who owns the rights associated with the respective identification.

Methods (User ID, PIN, Account Number)

The three most common methods used to provide user identity in an access control system are

- User ID — User name and password combination assigned to the user
- PIN — Typically a four-digit numerical combination created by the user during a sign-up/on-boarding process
- Account number — Typically an eight- to sixteen-digit unique numerical sequence assigned to an individual by the owner of the system

Regardless of the method used (user ID, PIN, or account number), each one must be unique to be valid for any user. Further care must be taken so that users are not readily identifiable from that of another user's user ID. An example of this problem would be to simply use the user's first initial and last name as his user ID. Anyone knowing the user's first and last names would then easily know the user's user ID.

Registration of New Users

Manual user registration provides for the greatest granularity but is also regarded as having too high of an administrative burden to be effective. Today it is often replaced with an automated provisioning solution. Automated provisioning solutions (identity management) provide a framework for managing access control policies by role, interconnection with IT systems, workflows to guide sign-off, delegated administration, password management, and auditing.

Periodic Review of Access Levels

The periodic review of user access levels is no longer simply a best practice and has been incorporated into current regulations including Sarbanes–Oxley. The mandatory periodic review of user access levels is necessary to ensure that each user's privilege continues to be appropriate and reflects any changes in their access requirements as their role and or responsibilities within the enterprise change.

Clearance

The proper application of clearance is critical in systems where access controls are based on security labels such as implementations of access control using the Bell–LaPadula model. Access control systems using clearances typically do so using a trusted user directory. Access to the directory is available only after successful authentication, and the directory must be trusted. Clearance levels, like other general access levels, must routinely be verified against each user's actual requirements, designated access, and status.

Certificates play an important role today in improving trust within a user directory. Instead of simply looking up a user in a directory to determine the level of clearance, a certificate with additional attributes, such as clearance lifecycle, can be used to verify by its digital signature that the clearance is valid.

Authentication (Proof of Identity)

Authentication is the process of verification that the identity presented to the access control system belongs to the party that has presented it. The three common factors in authentication are something you know, something you have, and something you are. In network authentication, the identification of the user is authenticated using a secret password that only the user should know. This would be referred to as simple authentication. There are more complex authentication methodologies such as *dual factor authentication* that not only require the secret that the user knows but also require another layer of authentication in the form of something the user "has" in their possession (such as a security token) or something the user "is" (as in the case of biometric authentication, a fingerprint or retina scan). We will discuss complex authentication methodologies such as dual factor later in this chapter. Again, the objective of authentication is to prove the identity of the user who is asking for some type of access from the access control system.

Knowledge (Static Passwords)

Knowledge is something someone knows, such as a password. Static passwords can be a password, a PIN, a passphrase, a graphic, etc. Regardless of length and character construction, static passwords that are not frequently changed are inherently insecure.

Secure storage is a necessity as legacy encryption of passwords in storage is typically easy to crack and makes unauthorized use of accounts a trivial matter for a determined malicious hacker. Tools such as Cain & Able along with Rainbow Tables can defeat the most commonly used password encryption methodologies in seconds. There are also Linux distributions such as KALI Linux that have a much broader toolset and function than just password cracking and are specifically engineered to provide an arsenal of tools to the security professional, password crackers among them, for detailed penetration testing. (Find it here: https://www.kali.org/.)[12] Password resets when the user forgets their password consume a large volume of time in most IT support departments and also provide an effective entry vector for social engineering attacks. All too often password lockout mechanisms are disabled to reduce the number of required password resets, further increasing the risk of potential compromise. Automated password reset mechanisms range from the user being required to answer a series of personal questions that they previously provided responses for to newer technology-based reset mechanisms that use voice recognition to further automate the process.

Mass lockouts of user accounts are an effective denial-of-service attack. If a malicious hacker learns that you are using a standard "not unique" user name format, making the user names for authentication easy to guess, and that your access control system will lock out a user account after a given number of failed login attempts, it is a simple matter to quickly script an attack that walks through a failed login attempt, creating a locked-out account for every user. An example of this behavior can be found in the eBay Account Lockout Attack. At one time, eBay displayed the user ID of the highest bidder for a given auction. In the final minutes of the auction, an attacker who wanted to outbid the current highest bidder could attempt to authenticate three times using the targeted account. After three deliberately incorrect authentication attempts, eBay password throttling would lock out the highest bidder's account for a certain amount of time. An attacker could then make their own bid and the legitimate user would not have a chance to place a counter-bid because they would be locked out of their account.

Ownership

Ownership is something the user has in his possession such as a smart card or a token.

Smart Cards

Typically, smart cards are credit card size, contain a tamper-resistant security system, are managed by a central administration system, and require a card reader device, such as the typical card reader on an ATM or fuel pump at a gasoline station. There are contact and contactless smart cards and readers.

A contact card reader requires physical contact with the card reader. There are two primary methodologies for contact card readers. A landing contact requires physical contact with the contacts (landing zone) on the card when it is placed within the reader. Typical standards for landing contact readers include ISO 7816.[13] Landing contact readers are popular in physical access applications. A friction contact requires that the card landing contacts are wiped against the contact reader. Typical friction card readers are those used in credit card transactions at merchants.

Contactless card readers are quickly gaining in popularity and typically rely on radio-frequency identification (RFID) technology to facilitate reading. The additional security mechanisms found in contactless card applications can include challenge/response-based encryption safeguards to reduce the risk of *card skimming*, whereby the account information is stolen in an otherwise legitimate transaction. Smart cards are discussed in more depth later.

Dynamic Passwords

A dynamic password methodology, also known as a *one-time password*, is typically implemented by utilizing hardware or software token technology. The password is changed after each authentication session. This effectively mitigates the risk of shoulder surfing or password sniffing, as the password is valid for only one session and cannot be reused.

Tokens

While tokens are available in many different form factors, there are two basic types of tokens in use today: *synchronous* and *asynchronous*.

With a synchronous token, time is synchronized between the token device and the authentication server. The current time value is enciphered along with a secret key on the token device and is presented to the access control subject for authentication. A popular synchronous token from RSA called "SecureID" provides for a new six- to eight-digit code every 60 seconds; it can operate for up to 4 years and can be programmed to cease operation on a predetermined date. The synchronous token requires fewer steps by the access control subject to successfully authenticate:

- The access control subject reads the value from his or her token device.

- The value from the token device is entered into the login window along with the access control subject's PIN.

- The authentication server calculates its own comparative value based on the synchronized time value and the respective access control subject's PIN. If the compared values match, access is granted.

An asynchronous token, such as the event-driven asynchronous token from Secure Computing called the SafeWord eToken PASS, provides a new one-time password with each use of the token. While it can be configured to expire on a specific date, its lifetime depends on its frequency of use. The token can last from 5 to 10 years and effectively extends the time period typically used in calculating the total cost of ownership in a multifactor authentication deployment. In the use of an asynchronous one-time password token, the access control subject typically executes a five-step process to authenticate identity and have access granted:

1. The authentication server presents a challenge request to the access control subject.

2. The access control subject enters the challenge into his/her token device.

3. The token device mathematically calculates a correct response to the authentication server challenge.

4. The access control subject enters the response to the challenge along with a password or PIN.

5. The response and password or PIN is verified by the authentication server and, if correct, access is granted.

The use of a PIN together with the value provided from the token helps to mitigate the risk of a stolen or lost token being used by an unauthorized person to gain access through the access control system. Tokens are discussed in more depth later in the "Tokens" section.

Radio Frequency Identification (RFID)

RFID is the wireless non-contact use of radio-frequency electromagnetic fields to transfer data, for the purposes of automatically identifying and tracking tags attached to objects. The tags contain electronically stored information. Some tags are powered and read at short ranges, typically a few meters, via magnetic fields. Others use a local power source such as a battery, or else have no battery but collect energy from the interrogating EM field, and then act as a passive transponder to emit microwaves or UHF radio waves. Battery-powered tags may operate at hundreds of meters. Unlike a bar code, the tag does not necessarily need to be within line of sight of the reader and may be embedded in the tracked object.

According to Technovelgy.com, some common problems with RFID are reader collision and tag collision:

> "Reader collision occurs when the signals from two or more readers overlap. The tag is unable to respond to simultaneous queries. Systems must be carefully set up to avoid this problem; many systems use an *anti-collision protocol* (also called a *singulation protocol*). Anti-collision protocols enable the tags to take turns in transmitting to a reader. Tag collision occurs when many tags are present in a small area; but since the read time is very fast, it is easier for vendors to develop systems that ensure that tags respond one at a time."[14]

Characteristics

A characteristic is defined as a physical trait of the user, also referred to as "what a person does" or "what a person is," that allows for the confirmation of an individual's identity based on either a physiological condition such as a fingerprint or retina scan or a behavioral characteristic such as keystrokes, speech recognition, or signature dynamics.

Characteristics are generally identified by using biometrics. Biometrics is discussed at length in the "Biometrics" section.

Biometrics

Biometrics is the science and technology of measuring and analyzing biological data. In information technology, biometrics refers to technologies that measure and analyze human body characteristics, such as DNA, fingerprints, voice patterns, facial patterns, and hand measurements, for authentication purposes. Biometric data cannot be considered to be secret in the way that private keys or passwords can. In contrast with private keys, biometric data is given to possibly hostile hosts to which a user wishes to authenticate. As opposed to passwords, biometric data cannot be changed, and a user cannot conveniently choose different biometric data to present to different hosts in the way that one might use a different password for a webmail account or a bank account. Moreover, in contrast with keys and passwords, biometric data such as user's facial characteristics and fingerprints are in the public domain and can be captured without the user's consent or knowledge. For this reason, protocols for biometric authentication should rely on proof of freshness of biometric data and cannot rely on its secrecy.

The processes involved within a biometric authentication solution could be classified as two steps: enrollment and verification. During the enrollment process, the user's registered biometric code is stored either in a system or on a smart card that is kept by the user. During the verification process, the user presents their biometric data to the system so that the biometric data can be compared with the stored biometric code. User verification can be carried out either within the smart card, a process called on-card matching, or in the system outside the card, known as off-card matching. The on-card matching algorithm protects the user's stored biometric code. The biometric code is not necessarily transferred to the outside environment if using this type of matching. Even though the biometric data is not considered to be secret, the protocol should not reveal it without the user's agreement. When the biometric data is used for biometric authentication, it should not only be protected from disclosure to an attacker, but also its origin should be guaranteed; this prevents an attacker from presenting the previously captured biometric data to the system in order to authenticate himself as the authorized user.

Biometrics can be broken down into two main classifications: behavioral and physiological.

Behavioral Biometrics

Behavioral biometrics includes signature analysis, voice pattern recognition, and keystroke dynamics.

Signature Analysis

The handwritten signature is unique to each individual. Most access control signature analysis access devices use a 3D analysis of the signature, which includes both the pressure and form of the signature. Signature analysis dynamically measures the series of movements, which contain biometric characteristics such as acceleration, rhythm, pressure, and flow. Signature analysis access control devices have become popular with credit card merchants for authorization of credit card transactions (see Figure 1.12).

FIGURE 1.12 Electronic signature pad. PHOTO OF ELECTRONIC SIGNATURE PAD (MODEL TM-LBK755) COURTESY OF TOPAZ SYSTEMS

> ### ✔ Experience It!
>
> To discover more about signature analysis, and the systems used to implement a solution, here is a list of vendors that provide systems:
>
> - http://www.topazsystems.com/Software/index.htm
> - http://www.kofax.com/products/kofax-signature-solutions

Voice Pattern Recognition

Voice pattern recognition works by creating a database of unique characteristics of the access control subject's voice. The access control subject then simply speaks at or near a microphone, and the access control device compares the current voice pattern characteristics to the stored characteristics to determine if access is to be granted. Biology, not technology, is the issue with voice recognition. As the subject ages, the characteristics of the voice naturally change. Voice characteristics can change under stress, and during an emergency situation the access control subject could be denied access simply because of the stress he/she was under at that moment. Further, it is possible to create an error through the altering of the inflection of a given phrase. Voice recognition is an inexpensive methodology to implement, but because of the high probability of error it is best used to complement another more accurate technology, such as iris scanning, and not to be relied on as a primary access control device.

✔ **Experience It!**

To discover more about voice pattern recognition, and the systems used to implement a solution, here is a list of vendors that provide systems:

- http://www.authentify.com/
- http://www.biovalidation.com/index.aspx

Keystroke Dynamics

Keystroke dynamics rely on characteristics that are unique to an individual. Specifically, these are the characteristics of the access control subject's keystrokes as the user name and password are typed on the keyboard. The normal characteristics of the individual are learned over time and typically can be enrolled with six or eight samples. The individual characteristics used by the typical keystroke analysis device include but are not limited to

- The length of time each key is held down
- The length of time between keystrokes
- The typing speed
- The tendencies to switch between a numeric keypad and keyboard numbers
- The keystroke tendencies involved in capitalization

Figure 1.13 shows some standard aspects of keystroke dynamics that are measured.

The accuracy of keystroke dynamics can be affected by hand injuries, fatigue, arthritis, and perhaps temperature. In addition, the security of the keystrokes committed by the subject is open to compromise.[15] Hence, while keystroke dynamics is regarded as the lowest-cost authentication mechanism, it cannot yet be used reliably in a single-factor or perhaps two-factor (using passphrase) authentication methodology and is better suited to complement another technology such as iris scanning in a two-factor authentication scheme. It is important to note, however, that it does provide continuous authentication, if that is desirable.

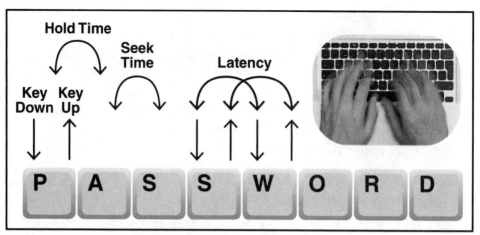

FIGURE 1.13 Sample keystroke dynamics measurements

Physiological Biometrics

There are several biometric devices that make use of the user's personal physiological data in access control applications. These apply fingerprint, hand, vascular, eye, or facial recognition technology.

Fingerprint Verification Technology

Fingerprint verification typically requires seven characteristics or matching points either to enroll a new access control subject or to verify an existing access control subject. The task is not as difficult as it may seem as the human finger contains 30–40 characteristics or matching points. The fingerprint reader does not store an image of the fingerprint. Rather, it creates a geometric relationship between the characteristics or matching points and stores and then compares that information. See Figure 1.14.

FIGURE 1.14 A fingerprint reader scans the loops, whorls, and other characteristics of a fingerprint and compares it with stored templates. When a match is found, access is granted.
PHOTO OF BIOMETRIC ID SIGNATURE PAD WITH OPTICAL FINGERPRINT SENSOR (MODEL TF-LBK464) COURTESY OF TOPAZ SYSTEMS.

One of the biggest challenges facing biometric technology in general, and fingerprint verification in particular today, is the ability to carry out performance evaluations unambiguously and reliably. One way this challenge is being addressed is through an innovative program called FVC-onGoing. FVC-onGoing is a web-based automated evaluation system for fingerprint recognition algorithms. Tests are carried out on a set of sequestered datasets, and results are reported online by using well-known performance indicators and metrics. While previous FVC initiatives were organized as "competitions," with specific calls and fixed time frames, FVC-onGoing is

- An "ongoing competition" always open to new participants
- An evolving online repository of evaluation metrics and results

Furthermore, FVC-onGoing performance evaluation is not only limited to fingerprint verification algorithms: ad hoc metrics and datasets for testing specific modules of fingerprint verification systems are available. This allows to better understand the limits and the challenges not only of the whole recognition problem but also of its modules (e.g., feature extractor, matcher), with clear benefits for researchers and algorithms' developers. The aim is to track the advances in fingerprint recognition technologies, through continuously updated independent testing and reporting of performances on given benchmarks. The algorithms are evaluated using strongly supervised approaches to maximize trustworthiness.

FVC-onGoing is the evolution of FVC: the international Fingerprint Verification Competitions organized in 2000, 2002, 2004, and 2006. Find out more about FVC-onGoing at `https://biolab.csr.unibo.it/FVCOnGoing/UI/Form/Home.aspx`.

✔ Experience It!

To discover more about fingerprint verification, and the systems used to implement a solution, here is a list of vendors that provide systems:

- `www.supremainc.com`
- `http://usa.morpho.com`
- `http://www.zvetcobiometrics.com/`

Hand Geometry Technology

Hand geometry and geometry recognition technology is in broad use for access control as well as time and attendance applications (see Figure 1.15). An individual places their hand on a reader, and their identity is verified based upon the location of a number of key points on their hand (e.g., length of fingers, position of knuckles, etc.). Hand geometry technology measures the dimensions of hands and fingers, being mostly used in physical security applications. Applications include frequent traveler verification, identification of season pass holders for Walt Disney, and building security for hospitals. The advantage of hand geometry is that it provides a proven reliable verification even within difficult environments while being simple to operate. However, compared to other identification and verification methods, the method is less accurate and requires large and expensive equipment. Hand geometry verification is typically accomplished by building a five-element array of finger lengths determined from scanned matching points at the base and end of each finger. The stored five-element array is compared to a new hand scan, and a mathematical calculation is performed to determine the geometric distance between the respective arrays.

FIGURE 1.15 **Hand geometry reader**

✔ **Experience It!**

Discover more about hand geometry, and the systems used to implement a solution; here is a list of vendors that provide systems:

- ` http://us.allegion.com/Products/biometrics/handkey2/Pages/default.aspx `

- ` http://www.morphotrust.com/ `

Vascular Patterns

This is the ultimate palm reader (see Figure 1.16). Vascular patterns are best described as a picture of the veins in a person's hand or finger. The thickness and location of these veins are believed to be unique enough to an individual to be used to verify a person's identity. The NTSC Subcommittee on Biometrics reports that researchers have determined that the vascular pattern of the human body is unique to the specific individual and does not change as people age. Claims for the technology include

- **Difficult to forge**—Vascular patterns are difficult to re-create because they are inside the hand, and for some approaches, blood needs to flow to register an image.

- **Contactless**—Users do not touch the sensing surface, which addresses hygiene concerns and improves user acceptance.

- **Many and varied uses**—It is deployed at ATMs, hospitals, and universities in Japan. Applications include ID verification, high security physical access control, high security network data access, and POS access control.

- **Capable of 1:1 and 1:many matches**—Users' vascular patterns are matched against personalized ID cards/smart cards or against a database of many scanned vascular patterns.

FIGURE 1.16 **Vascular pattern reader.** PHOTO OF PALMSECURE® ID MATCH COURTESY OF FUJITSU FRONTECH NORTH AMERICA

Eye Features/Retina Scan

The retina scan is one of the oldest and most accurate biometric authentication methodologies. Traditionally, the retina scan has been reserved only for the most secure application of physical access systems control. The retina scan simply maps the blood vessels in the back of the eye and only requires 10 or so seconds to complete a scan. There is no known technology that can forge a retina scan signature, and as the blood vessels quickly decay upon death, a retina scan on a dead individual will not create the same signature as that of the live individual.

How it works:

- The eye is read by a small green infrared light.

- Low-intensity infrared light is used because blood vessels on the retina absorb the infrared light faster than the surrounding eye tissues and the light is reflected back to a video camera.

- Initial scanning takes 10–15 seconds total, but verification scanning takes 2 seconds.

- Patterns of blood vessels are converted into mathematical patterns.

See Figure 1.17 for an overview of how retinal scanning works.

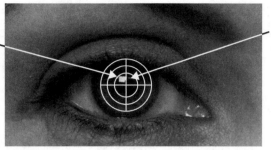

1. The EOFTI retinal scanner reads from the outer iris in to the pupil edge

2. The scanner then plots distinct patterns of blood vessels using infrared light

3. The information is then sent to a central server and the results are compressed

4. To gain access, a retinal scan will be compared with the stored, compressed image

FIGURE 1.17 How retinal scanners record identity source

Eye Features/Iris Scan

Iris scanning is based on scanning the granularity of the richly detailed color bands around the pupil. The color bands are well defined at birth and change little over the subject's lifetime. The typical iris scanner maps nearly 247 variables in the iris and can do so at a distance of 19–20 inches. This makes the iris scanner potentially more accurate than a fingerprint, with only 40–80 characteristics, and is less obtrusive then a retina scanner as it does not require the same close proximity to the reading device or a light shining into the eye.

How it works:

- A person stands 1–3 feet away, and a wide-angle camera calculates the position of the eye.

- A second camera zooms in on the eye and takes a black-and-white image.

- The camera lays a circular grid on the image of the iris so the iris system can recognize patterns within the iris to generate points.

- The captured image or "eyeprint" is checked against previously stored reference template in the database.

- Software localizes the inner/outer boundaries of the iris and eyelid contours.

- Demodulation, or mathematical software, encodes the iris pattern.

- Then it captures the unique features of the iris, like a template (the IrisCode).

The template is immediately encrypted to eliminate the possibility of identity theft and maximize security.

Figure 1.18 shows a simplified overview of how iris scanning works.

1. Scanner reads from the outer edge of the iris inwards toward the pupil edge

2. The scanner then plots distinct markings on the iris and maps a unique shape

3. After plotting many marks within the iris the data is saved to a database

4. Other scanners will compare this data to verify identity

FIGURE 1.18 **How iris scanners record identity**

Here are some interesting facts about iris scan technology:

- No two irises are alike, not even with identical twins.

- The left eye and right eye are not the same on one person.

- The iris has six times more distinct identifiable features than fingerprints.

- The probability of having two irises that are alike is one in 10 to the 78th power (the population of the earth is approximately 10 to the 10th power).

- There is no known way to copy a retina, unlike an iris.

- A retina from a dead person would deteriorate too fast to be useful, so no extra precautions have been taken with retinal scanning to make sure the person is alive.

Security concerns have recently come up with regards to iris scans, which are considered to be one of the most secure biometric solutions currently in use. Announced during the annual Black Hat security conference in 2012, a team at the Universidad Autonoma de Madrid was able to re-create the image of an iris from digital codes of real irises stored in security databases. The researchers were able to print out synthetic images of irises, and as they tested their fake irises against one of the leading commercial recognition systems, they achieved an 80% false accept rate.[16] Another problem that has recently come to light is the effect that alcohol can have on iris scans. Research has shown that alcohol consumption causes recognition degradation as the pupil dilates/constricts, which causes deformation in the iris pattern. Experiments performed show that in matching pre- and post-alcohol consumption images, the overlap between genuine and impostor match scores increased by approximately 20%. This means that one in five subjects under alcohol influence potentially could be able to evade identification by iris recognition systems.[17]

The ISO/IEC standard 19794-6:2011, "Information technology—Biometric data interchange formats—Part 6: Iris image data," specifies two alternative image interchange formats for biometric authentication systems that utilize iris recognition. The first is based on a rectilinear image storage format that may be a raw, uncompressed array of intensity values or a compressed format such as that specified by ISO/IEC 15444-1:2004/Amendments 1–5. The second format is based on a polar image specification that requires certain pre-processing and image segmentation steps but produces a much more compact data structure that contains only iris information. Data that complies with either one of the iris image formats specified in ISO/IEC 19794-6:2011 are intended to be embedded in a CBEFF-compliant structure in the CBEFF Biometric Data Block (BDB) as specified in ISO/IEC 19785-1:2006 and ISO/IEC 19785-1:2006 / AMD1:2010.

✔ Try It for Yourself— Open Source Iris Scan Project in a Box

Now you will work directly with an iris scan project.

What's Needed?

A Linux-based computer and a user account with administrative (root) privileges.

How to Do It

Use the following step-by-step guidance:

1. Download the source tarball from here (tarball name is **iris-0.1.tar.gz**):

   ```
   http://projectiris.co.uk/
   ```

2. To install for any Linux distribution:

   ```
   tar zxf iris-version.tar.gz
   cd iris-version/
   qmake
   make ./iris
   ```

Facial Recognition

Like the fingerprint reader and hand geometry devices, facial recognition uses a mathematical geometric model of certain landmarks of the face such as the cheekbone, tip of the nose, and eye socket orientation, and measures the distance between them. There are approximately 80 separate measurable characteristics in the human face, but most facial recognition systems rely on only 14–22 characteristics to perform their recognition.

Figure 1.19 shows how geometric properties are used for facial recognition.

Here are some interesting facts about facial recognition technology:

- Google's Picasa digital image organizer has a built-in face recognition system starting from version 3.5 onwards. It can associate faces with people so that queries can be run on pictures to return all pictures with a specific group of people together.
- Windows Live Photo Gallery includes face recognition.
- Sony's Picture Motion Browser (PMB) analyzes photos, associates photos with identical faces so that they can be tagged accordingly, and differentiates between photos with one person, many people, and nobody.
- OpenBR is an open source face recognition system and research platform for biometric algorithm development.

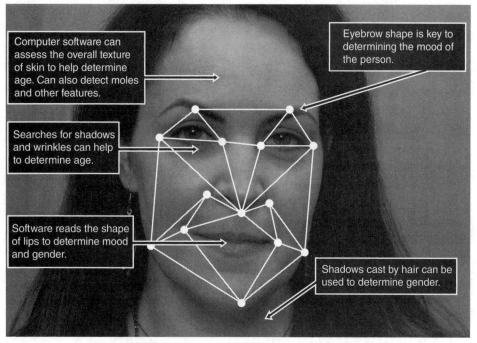

Computer software can assess the overall texture of skin to help determine age. Can also detect moles and other features.

Eyebrow shape is key to determining the mood of the person.

Searches for shadows and wrinkles can help to determine age.

Software reads the shape of lips to determine mood and gender.

Shadows cast by hair can be used to determine gender.

FIGURE 1.19 Geometric properties of a subject's face used in facial imaging

Biometric Implementation Issues

User acceptance is one of the most critical factors in the success of any biometric-based implementation. To minimize the risk of improper use, which can cause failed access, the device should not cause discomfort or concern and must be easy to use.

Biometric accuracy is measured by two distinct rates: the False Rejection Rate (FRR), referred to as a type 1 error, and the False Acceptance Rate (FAR), referred to as a type 2 error.

- **False Rejection**—Failure to recognize a legitimate user. While it could be argued that this has the effect of keeping the protected area extra secure, it is an intolerable frustration to legitimate users who are refused access because the scanner does not recognize them.

- **False Acceptance**—Erroneous recognition, either by confusing one user with another or by accepting an imposter as a legitimate user.

Failure rates can be adjusted by changing the threshold ("how close is close enough") for declaring a match, but decreasing one failure rate will increase the other.

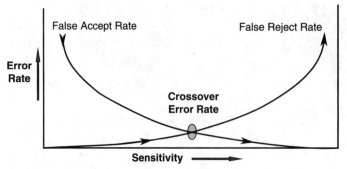

FIGURE 1.20 **Crossover error rate is one of three categories of biometric accuracy measurements.**

The actual methodologies of the measurement of accuracy may differ in each type of biometric device, but simply put, you can obtain a good comparative accuracy factor by looking at the intersection point at which the type 1 error rate equals the type 2 error rate as shown in Figure 1.20. This value is commonly referred to as the Crossover Error Rate, (CER). The biometric device accuracy increases as the crossover value becomes smaller, as shown in Table 1.4.

TABLE 1.4 **Biometric Crossover Accuracy**

BIOMETRIC CROSSOVER ACCURACY	
Retinal scan	1:100,00,000
Iris scan	1:131,000
Fingerprint	1:500
Hand geometry	1:500
Signature dynamics	1:50
Voice dynamics	1:50

A further comparison of biometric technologies is provided in Table 1.5.

In reusable password authentication, the access control subject had to remember a perhaps difficult password. In token-based authentication, the access control subject had to retain possession of the token device. In biometric, characteristic-based authentication, the actual access control subject *is* the authentication device.

TABLE 1.5 Comparison of Biometric Technologies

CHARACTERISTIC	FINGERPRINTS	HAND GEOMETRY	RETINA	IRIS	FACE	SIGNATURE	VOICE
Ease of Use	High	High	Low	Medium	Medium	High	High
Error Incidence	Dryness, dirt, age	Hand injury, age	Glasses	Poor lighting	Lighting, age, glasses, hair	Changing signatures	Noise, colds, weather
Accuracy	High	High	Very high	Very high	High	High	High
User Acceptance	Medium	Medium	Medium	Medium	Medium	Medium	High
Required Security Level	High	Medium	High	Very high	Medium	Medium	Medium
Long-Term Stability	High	Medium	High	High	Medium	Medium	Medium

Source: Liu, S., and Silverman, M., "A practical guide to biometric security technology," *IT Professional*, 3, 27–32, 2005. With permission.

Physical Use as Identification

Biometrics takes advantage of the unique physical traits of each user and arguably is the most effective methodology of identifying a user. It is important to note that in physical security, biometrics is often used as an identification mechanism, while in logical security biometrics is often used as an authentication mechanism. As biometric technologies evolve, accuracy rates are increasing, error rates are declining, and improved ease-of-use is increasing user acceptance.

Biometric Standards Development

Numerous activities regarding the interoperability of biometrics are ongoing at both the national and international levels. On the national level, ANSI INCITS 395-2005 specifies a data interchange format for representation of digitized sign or signature data, for the purposes of biometric enrollment, verification, or identification through the use of Raw Signature/Sign Sample Data or Common Feature Data. The data interchange format is generic, in that it may be applied and used in a wide range of application areas where electronic signs or signatures are involved. No application-specific requirements or features are addressed in this standard. At the international level, there are two corresponding documents currently published: The first is ISO/IEC 19794-7:2014: Information technology—Biometric data interchange formats—Part 7: Signature/sign time series data, and the second is ISO/IEC 19794-11:2013/Amd.1:2014: Information technology—Biometric data interchange formats—Part 11: Signature/Sign Processed Dynamic Data.

The ISO JTC 1/SC 37 Biometrics working group homepage can be found here:

```
http://www.iso.org/iso/home/standards_development/list_of_iso_technical_
committees/jtc1_home/jtc1_sc37_home.htm
```

Tokens

Security tokens are used to prove one's identity electronically. There are four different ways in which this information can be used, according to Wikipedia:[18]

> **Static Password Token**—The device contains a password that is physically hidden (not visible to the possessor) but that is transmitted for each authentication. This type is vulnerable to replay attacks.
>
> **Synchronous Dynamic Password Token**—A timer is used to rotate through various combinations produced by a cryptographic algorithm. The token and the authentication server must have synchronized clocks.
>
> **Asynchronous Password Token**—A one-time password is generated without the use of a clock, from either a one-time pad or a cryptographic algorithm.
>
> **Challenge Response Token**—Using public key cryptography, it is possible to prove possession of a private key without revealing that key. The authentication server encrypts a challenge (typically a random number, or at least data with some random parts) with a public key; the device proves it possesses a copy of the matching private key by providing the decrypted challenge.

Smart Cards

A smart card, typically a type of chip card, is a plastic card that contains an embedded computer chip—either a memory or microprocessor type—that stores and transacts data. This data is usually associated with either value, information, or both and is stored and processed within the card's chip. The card connects to a reader with direct physical contact or with a remote contactless radio frequency interface. With an embedded microcontroller, smart cards have the unique ability to store large amounts of data, carry out their own on-card functions (e.g., encryption and mutual authentication), and interact intelligently with a smart card reader. Smart card technology conforms to international standards (ISO/IEC 7816 and ISO/IEC 14443) and is available in a variety of form factors, including plastic cards, fobs, subscriber identity modules (SIMs) used in GSM mobile phones, and USB-based tokens.

There are two general categories of smart cards: contact and contactless. According to the Smart Card Alliance,[19]

> A contact smart card must be inserted into a smart card reader with a direct connection to a conductive contact plate on the surface of the card (typically gold plated). Transmission of commands, data, and card status takes place over these physical contact points.

> A contactless card requires only close proximity to a reader. Both the reader and the card have antennae, and the two communicate using radio frequencies (RF) over this contactless link. Most contactless cards also derive power for the internal chip from this electromagnetic signal. The range is typically one-half to three inches for non-battery-powered cards, ideal for applications such as building entry and payment that require a very fast card interface.

> Two additional categories of cards are dual-interface cards and hybrid cards. A hybrid card has two chips, one with a contact interface and one with a contactless interface. The two chips are not interconnected. A dual-interface card has a single chip with both contact and contactless interfaces. With dual-interface cards, it is possible to access the same chip using either a contact or contactless interface with a very high level of security.

Improvements to Authentication Strategies

For many years knowledge-based authentication in terms of passwords was the most common methodology in use in access control systems. Weaknesses in the implementation of encryption (hashing) for passwords has effectively rendered these knowledge-based methodologies obsolete.

Multifactor Authentication

In October 2005, the Federal Financial Institutions Examination Council provided a recommendation to U.S. banks that included, in part, a requirement to replace passwords and single-factor authentication with multifactor authentication.[20] The recommendation clearly pointed out that passwords alone were simply no longer a secure methodology for authenticating users in the current Internet environment.

The best practice in access control is to implement at least two of the three common techniques for authentication in your access control system:

- Knowledge-based
- Token-based
- Characteristic-based

Two-Factor vs. Three-Factor Authentication

In two-factor authentication, typically the mechanism used provides for something the user has in the form of a physical token that generates a one-time password and something the user knows in the form of a PIN that is appended to the one-time password that is generated by the token. This methodology is regarded as more secure than historical single-factor methodologies such as traditional passwords; however, it does little to definitively identify the user. This can be significantly improved upon by incorporating a third factor in the form of a biometric that in fact identifies the user. An example of a three-factor authentication solution is the RSA AuthenTec Fingerprint device from Privaris. It incorporates a fingerprint reader to identify the user, as well as being something the user "has," and also incorporates the traditional one-time password and PIN combination found in common two-factor authentication tokens.

Dual Control

Dual control, also referred to as "split-knowledge," is built on the principle that no one person should have access to information that would allow the person to determine the encryption key used to encrypt protected information more quickly than a brute-force attack of the entire key-space. Effectively, the determination of any part of the encryption key would require collusion between at least two different trusted individuals. Encryption—splitkeys—is just one example of dual control. It has been said that because of its inherent complexity, dual control is not difficult to accomplish but is easy to get wrong.

Continuous Authentication

While traditional one-time authentication, otherwise known as transactional authentication, takes place only once before granting access, continuous authentication takes place both before granting access and then continuously through the entire duration of the user's connection to maintain the granted access.

Periodic Authentication

The most common use of periodic authentication first provides for traditional challenge/response authentication requiring user interaction and then begins periodically to issue challenge/response authentication queries with the user's token to determine if the user has physically left the area where he had authenticated. This methodology aids in reducing the risk that a user would walk away from a device or system he has authenticated access to before properly logging out.

Time Outs

If the user leaves the proximity of the device authenticated after a specific time period, the user is automatically logged off and the authentication process would start over, requiring user intervention to accomplish initial authentication before continuous authentication could again resume. Naturally, the shorter the timeout period, the higher the security that can be provided; however, as always, it comes at the cost of being intrusive to the user.

Reverse Authentication

With the advent of phishing it is no longer enough to simply authenticate the user in web-based transactions. Today, it is necessary to also authenticate the website/page to the user as part of the authentication process. Bank of America was a pioneer in reverse authentication with its roll-out of PassMark, a reverse authentication system that relies on a series of pictures that the user could identify and use to accomplish the authentication of the Bank of America website. Some had believed that the picture approach of PassMark was too simplistic and raised doubts about the technology. However, PassMark quickly grew in acceptance and was adopted by more than 50% of the online banking market.

Certificate-Based Authentication

Certificate-based authentication relies on the machine that the user authenticates from having a digital certificate installed that is used in part along with the encrypted user's password to authenticate both the user and the device the user is authenticating from. Effectively, the use of a certificate in the authentication process adds an additional element in security by validating that the user is authorized to authenticate from the device they are using because of the presence of the digital certification within the device. Great care must be taken in the management of the digital certificates by the certificate authority to ensure that the use of certificates is properly controlled and certificate renewal and revocations are accomplished in a timely and effective manner.

Authorization

What a user can do once authenticated is most often controlled by a reference monitor. A reference monitor is typically defined as the service or program where access control information is stored and where access control decisions are made. A reference monitor will typically decide if access is to be granted based on an ACL within the reference monitor. Once access is granted, what the subject can then do is controlled by the authorization matrix or table (see Table 1.6).

TABLE 1.6 Authorization Table—Matrix of Access Control Objects, Access Control Subjects, and Their Respective Rights

ACCESS CONTROL SUBJECTS	ACCESS CONTROL OBJECTS					
	Procedure A	Procedure B	File A	File B	File C	File D
Bob	Execute		Read	Read/Write		Read
Tom		Execute			Read	
Mary		Execute			Read	
Process A			Read/Write			Write
Process B			Write			Read/Write

Access to Systems vs. Data, Networks

Defining ACLs that only address access to systems can facilitate unintended user access to data that perhaps the user should not have had access to. Including access controls to specific data within a given system increases overall security. Consideration must also be given to ensuring that users only have access to intended networks, systems, and data.

Access Control Lists/Matrix

An authorization table is a matrix of access control objects, access control subjects, and their respective rights, as shown in Table 1.6. The authorization table is used in some DAC systems to provide for a simple and intuitive user interface for the definition of access control rules. While an authorization table provides for an increase in ease of use, it does not solve the inherent issue of DAC in that the system is still relying on the access control object owner to properly define the access control rules. Further, the use of an authorization table does not decrease the instance of errors or violations that may occur when changes are made within the authorization table.

An access control matrix is used in a DAC system to provide for a simple user interface to implement an ACL. The access control matrix determines the access rights for access control objects to access control subjects, as shown in Table 1.7. Like the authorization table mentioned earlier, the access control matrix does not decrease the instance of errors or violations that may occur when changes are made within the access control matrix.

TABLE 1.7 **Access Control Matrix Determines the Access Rights for Access Control Objects to Access Control Subjects**

ACCESS CONTROL SUBJECTS	ACCESS CONTROL OBJECTS															
	1	2	3	4	5	6	7	8	9	10	11	12	13	14	15	16
1	X		X		X	X		X					X	X		
2	X		X	X						X	X					
3	X	X				X	X	X						X		X
4				X	X	X										
5		X			X		X	X	X					X	X	
6												X				
7						X	X	X	X	X	X					
8		X	X										X	X		

Directories

Lightweight Directory Access Protocol (LDAP) is an application protocol used for querying and modifying directory services over TCP/IP. An LDAP directory is a logically and hierarchically organized group of objects and their respective attributes using an LDAP directory tree. An LDAP directory tree typically starts with domain names at the top of the hierarchy followed by organizational boundaries, then groups followed by users and data, such as groups of documents.

X.500 relies also on the use of a single Directory Information Tree (DIT) with a hierarchical organization of entries that are distributed across one or more servers. Every directory entry has what is referred to as a Distinguished Name (DN), which is formed by combining its Relative Distinguished Name (RDN), one or more attributes of the entry itself, and the RDN of the superior entries reaching all the way up to the root of the DIT.

The Microsoft Active Directory Domain Services (ADDS, originally called NT Directory Services) stores data and information within a central database, is highly scalable, and provides a wide variety of other network services including LDAP-like directory services, authentication, and Domain Name System–based naming. While ADDS is primarily used for assignment of policies because of its many attributes, it is commonly used by separate services to facilitate software distribution within a network.

Think of directory structures like LDAP, X.500, and ADDS as telephone directories where all entries are based on an alphabetical order and have attached addresses and telephone numbers.

Single Sign-On

Single sign-on (SSO) can best be defined as an authentication mechanism that allows a single identity to be shared across multiple applications. Effectively, it allows the user to authenticate once and gain access to multiple resources.

The primary purpose of SSO is the convenience of the user. With that in perspective, SSO can also help in mitigating some of the inherent risks of access control subjects using a different password or authentication mechanism for each of the many systems they access in a large network. Simply put, the chances of a security breach naturally increase as the number of passwords and or authentication mechanisms increase. This must, of course, be balanced against the additional risk of using SSO in that once it's implemented, a malicious hacker now only has to obtain a single set of authentication credentials and then has access to all of the systems that the respective access control subject was permitted to access. The advantages as well as disadvantages of SSO must also be considered (Table 1.8).

TABLE 1.8 **Advantages and Disadvantages of SSO**

ADVANTAGES OF SSO	DISADVANTAGES OF SSO
More efficient log-on process.	Difficult to implement across the enterprise.
Easier administration.	Many systems use proprietary authentication systems that will not work well with standard SSO systems.
When a new employee is hired, all of the accounts on all of the systems the new employee needs to access can be quickly added from a single administration point.	Time-consuming to implement properly.
When an existing employee is terminated, all access can be quickly and simultaneously restricted at a single administration point.	Many underestimate the amount of time necessary to properly implement SSO across all systems in the enterprise.
If an existing user loses their token or forgets their password, the administrator can quickly update the user's authentication credentials from a single administration point.	Expensive to implement.
Can mitigate some security risks.	Because of the difficulty and time involved to properly implement SSO, it is expensive. A redundant authentication server is required to avoid a single point of failure.
Reduces the inherent risk of a user having to remember passwords for multiple systems, within the enterprise.	
Because only a single password is used, the user is more apt to use a much stronger password.	

ADVANTAGES OF SSO	DISADVANTAGES OF SSO
Timeout and attempt thresholds are enforced consistently across the entire enterprise. SSO generally offers a good return on investment for the enterprise. The reduced administrative costs can often pay for the cost of implementing SSO in a short period of time. However, it should be noted that if scripting is used to facilitate the implementation of SSO, the typical reduced administration costs associated with SSO could in fact be negated because of the effort required to maintain numerous scripts.	Proprietary authentication systems may need expensive custom programming to be used in an SSO implementation, and more often than not this cost is not considered in the original estimates and results in SSO implementation cost overruns. In some cases the original authentication system for a difficult to implement system has to be weakened in an effort to get it to work reliably in an SSO system.

There are a couple of significant risks inherent with SSO:

- **Single point of failure**—With all of the users' credentials stored on a single authentication server, the failure of that server can prevent access for those users to all applications that it had provided authentication services for.

- **Single point of access**—Because SSO affords a single point of access, it is more prone to mass denial-of-service attacks whereby entire groups of users can be denied access to systems by attacking the single point of access.

Authentication Using Kerberos

Kerberos, described in RFC 1510, was originally developed by the Massachusetts Institute of Technology (MIT) and has become a popular network authentication protocol for indirect (third-party) authentication services.[21] It is designed to provide strong authentication using secret-key cryptography. It is an operational implementation of key distribution technology and affords a key distribution center, authentication service, and ticket granting service. Hosts, applications, and servers all have to be "Kerberized" to be able to communicate with the user and the ticket granting service.

Like the previously discussed indirect authentication technologies, Kerberos is based on a centralized architecture, thereby reducing administrative effort in managing all authentications from a single server. Furthermore, the use of Kerberos provides support for

1. **Authentication**—A user is who they claim to be.
2. **Authorization**—What can a user do once properly authenticated?
3. **Confidentiality**—Keep data secret.
4. **Integrity**—Data received is the same as the data that was sent.
5. **Nonrepudiation**—Determines exactly who sent or received a message.

The process in the use of Kerberos is substantially different from those indirect authentication technologies previously reviewed and is considerably more complex. The following is a simplified explanation of the Kerberos process that was adapted for use here from *Applied Cryptography: Protocols, Algorithms, and Source Code in C* by Bruce Schneier (New York, NY: Wiley, 1993).

1. Before an access control subject can request a service from an access control object, it must first obtain a ticket to the particular target object; hence, the access control subject first must request from the Kerberos Authentication Server (AS) a ticket to the Kerberos Ticket Granting Service (TGS). This request takes the form of a message containing the user's name and the name of the respective TGS.

2. The AS looks up the access control subject in its database and then generates a session key to be used between the access control subject and the TGS. Kerberos encrypts this session key using the access control subject's secret key. Then, it creates a Ticket Granting Ticket (TGT) for the access control subject to present to the TGS and encrypts the TGT using the TGS's secret key. The AS sends both of these encrypted messages back to the access control subject.

3. The access control subject decrypts the first message and recovers the session key. Next, the access control subject creates an authenticator consisting of the access control subject's name, address, and a time stamp, all encrypted with the session key that was generated by the AS.

4. The access control subject then sends a request to the TGS for a ticket to a particular target server. This request contains the name of the server, the TGT received from Kerberos (which is already encrypted with the TGS's secret key), and the encrypted authenticator.

5. The TGS decrypts the TGT with its secret key and then uses the session key included in the TGT to decrypt the authenticator. It compares the information in the authenticator with the information in the ticket, the access control subject's network address with the address the request was sent from, and the time stamp with the current time. If everything matches, it allows the request to proceed.

6. The TGS creates a new session key for the user and target server and incorporates this key into a valid ticket for the access control subject to present to the access control object server. This ticket also contains the access control subject's name, network address, a time stamp, and an expiration time for the ticket—all encrypted with the target server's secret key—and the name of the server. The TGS also encrypts the new access control subject target session key using the session key shared by the access control subject and the TGS. It sends both messages to the access control subject.

7. The access control subject decrypts the message and extracts the session key for use with the target access control object server. The access control subject is now ready to authenticate himself or herself to the access control object server. He or she creates a new authenticator encrypted with the access control subject target session key that the TGS generated. To request access to the target access control object server, the access control subject sends along the ticket received from Kerberos (which is already encrypted with the target access control object server's secret key) and the encrypted authenticator. Because this authenticator contains plaintext encrypted with the session key, it proves that the sender knows the key. Just as important, encrypting the time of day prevents an eavesdropper who records both the ticket and the authenticator from replaying them later.

8. The target access control object server decrypts and checks the ticket and the authenticator, also confirming the access control subject's address and the time stamp. If everything checks out, the access control object server now knows the access control subject is who he or she claims to be, and the two share an encryption key that they can use for secure communication. (Since only the access control subject and the access control object server share this key, they can assume that a recent message encrypted in that key originated with the other party.)

9. For those applications that require mutual authentication, the server sends the access control subject a message consisting of the time stamp plus 1, encrypted with the session key. This serves as proof to the user that the access control object server actually knew its secret key and was able to decrypt the ticket and the authenticator.

To provide for the successful implementation and operation of Kerberos, the following should be considered:

1. Overall security depends on a careful implementation.

2. Requires trusted and synchronized clocks across the enterprise network.

3. Enforcing limited lifetimes for authentication based on time stamps reduces the threat of a malicious hacker gaining unauthorized access using fraudulent credentials.

4. The key distribution server must be physically secured.

5. The key distribution server must be isolated on the network and should not participate in any non-Kerberos network activity.

6. The AS can be a critical single point of failure.

Kerberos is available in many commercial products, and a free implementation of Kerberos is available from MIT.[22] Table 1.9 shows the ports used by Kerberos during the authentication process.

TABLE 1.9 Network Ports Used During Kerberos Authentication

SERVICE NAME	UDP	TCP
DNS	53	53
Kerberos	88	88

User/Device Authentication Policies

Security and authentication policies are often unique to a given organization; effective security is never a one-size-fits-all proposition. A basic security policy—defining what information is sensitive, who can have access to this information and under what circumstances, and what to do in the event of a breach—is a must. Simple and obvious elements, like requiring PIN codes on mobile devices and regular password changes, are essential. Policy can go further to explain what a given user/device combination can do based on credentials and context. Only after policies are set and tested in an isolated or pilot setting should specific user/device authentication technologies be considered.

Authentication can take many forms. The security practitioner should familiarize themselves with the methods listed here:

Computer Recognition Software   Using the computer as a second authentication factor is accomplished by installing a small authentication software plug-in that places a cryptographic device marker onto the user's computer, which can then be verified as a second factor during the authentication process. The authentication process would then include two factors: a password (something you know) and the device marker on the user's computer (something you have). Because the device marker is always present on the user's computer, the user only has to enter their username and password to log in.

Biometrics   Using biometrics as a second factor is accomplished by verifying physical characteristics such as a fingerprint or eye using a dedicated hardware device. We discussed biometrics at length earlier in this chapter.

E-mail or SMS One-Time Password (OTP)   Using e-mail or SMS OTP as a second factor is accomplished by sending a second one-time use password to a registered e-mail address or cell phone. The user must then input that second one-time password in addition to their normal password to authenticate. This method is generally considered too cumbersome for everyday logins because there is a time lag before users get the OTP they need to login but is often used for the initial enrollment before providing another form of authentication.

One Time Password (OTP) Token Using an OTP token as a second factor is accomplished by providing users with a hardware device that generates a constantly changing second password that must be entered in addition to the normal password. OTP tokens require the user to carry the token with them to login.

Out of Band Using an out-of-band verification for authentication involves the target system calling a registered phone number and requesting that the user enter their password over the phone prior to allowing the user to log in. Similar to e-mail or SMS OTPs, this requirement introduces a time lag and requires that the user be at the location of the registered phone number during the login sequence.

Peripheral Device Recognition Using peripheral device recognition as a second factor is accomplished by placing a cryptographic device marker on a user's existing device such as a USB flash drive, an iPod, or smart phone memory card and then requiring that device to be plugged into the computer when the user logs in. This can be a good alternative to the OTP token because it provides a hardware-based second factor but does not require the user to carry an additional device. In addition, device markers from multiple systems can reside on a single hardware device.

COMPARING INTERNETWORK TRUST ARCHITECTURES

Computers are connected together using networks, and different types of networks provide different levels of trust. Primarily, there are four types of trust architectures: the Internet, an intranet, an extranet, and a demilitarized zone (DMZ, or perimeter network). The security practitioner is expected to understand all of them.

Internet

The Internet is a global system of interconnected computer networks that use the standard Internet protocol suite (TCP/IP) to link several billion devices worldwide. It is an international network of networks that consists of millions of private, public, academic, business, and government packet-switched networks, linked by a broad array of electronic, wireless, and optical networking technologies. The terms Internet and World

Wide Web are often used interchangeably in everyday speech; it is common to speak of "going on the Internet" when invoking a web browser to view web pages. However, the World Wide Web or the Web is just one of a very large number of services running on the Internet. The Web is a collection of interconnected documents (web pages) and other web resources, linked by hyperlinks and URLs. In addition to the Web, a multitude of other services are implemented over the Internet, including e-mail, file transfer, remote computer control, newsgroups, and online games. All of these services can be implemented on any intranet, accessible to network users.

Intranet

An intranet is a network based on TCP/IP protocols (an internet) belonging to an organization, usually a corporation, accessible only by the organization's members, employees, or others with authorization. Intranets utilize standard network hardware and software technologies like Ethernet, Wi-Fi, TCP/IP, web browsers, and web servers. An organization's intranet typically includes Internet access but is firewalled so that its computers cannot be reached directly from the outside.

Extranet

An extranet is a computer network that allows controlled access from the outside for specific business or educational purposes. Extranets are extensions to, or segments of, private intranet networks that have been built in many corporations for information sharing and ecommerce. In a business-to-business context, an extranet can be viewed as an extension of an organization's intranet that is extended to users outside the organization, usually partners, vendors, and suppliers, in isolation from all other Internet users. An extranet is similar to a DMZ in that it provides access to needed services for channel partners, without granting access to an organization's entire network.

Demilitarized Zone (DMZ)

A DMZ is a computer host or small network inserted as a "neutral zone" between a company's private network and the outside public network (see Figure 1.21). It prevents outside users from getting direct access to a server that has company data.

In addition to the four types of trust architectures, the security practitioner should be familiar with the trust types, which are discussed in the following section.

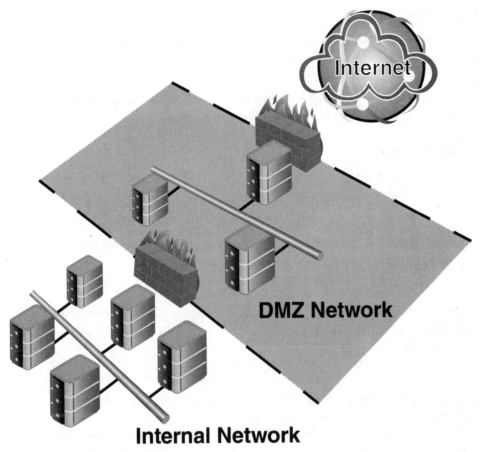

FIGURE 1.21 A typical DMZ design

TRUST DIRECTION

The trust type and its assigned direction affect the trust path that is used for authentication. A trust path is a series of trust relationships that authentication requests must follow between domains. Before a user can access a resource in another domain, the security system on domain controllers must determine whether the trusting domain (the domain that contains the resource that the user is trying to access) has a trust relationship with the trusted domain (the user's logon domain). To determine this, the security system computes the trust path between a domain controller in the trusting domain and a domain controller in the trusted domain.

One-Way Trust

A one-way trust is a unidirectional authentication path that is created between two domains. This means that in a one-way trust between Domain A and Domain B, users in Domain A can access resources in Domain B. However, users in Domain B cannot access resources in Domain A. Some one-way trusts can be either a non-transitive trust or a transitive trust, depending on the type of trust that is created.

Two-Way Trust

In a two-way trust, Domain A trusts Domain B, and Domain B trusts Domain A. This means that authentication requests can be passed between the two domains in both directions. Some two-way relationships can be either non-transitive or transitive, depending on the type of trust that is created.

Trust Transitivity

Transitivity determines whether a trust can be extended outside the two domains between which the trust was formed. You can use a transitive trust to extend trust relationships with other domains. You can use a non-transitive trust to deny trust relationships with other domains.

ADMINISTERING THE IDENTITY MANAGEMENT LIFECYCLE

There are five areas that make up the identity management lifecycle:

- Authorization
- Proofing
- Provisioning
- Maintenance
- Entitlement

Authorization

Authorization determines whether a user is permitted to access a particular resource. Authorization is performed by checking the resource access request against authorization policies that are stored in an Identity Access Management (IAM) policy store. Moreover, authorization could provide complex access controls based on data or information or policies including user attributes, user roles/groups, actions taken, access channels, time, resources requested, external data, and business rules.

Proofing

According to Gartner's IT Glossary, identity-proofing services, which verify people's identities before the enterprise issues them accounts and credentials, are based on "life history" or transaction information aggregated from public and proprietary data sources. These services are also used as an additional interactive user authentication method, especially for risky transactions, such as accessing sensitive confidential information or transferring funds to external accounts. Identity-proofing services are typically used when accounts are provisioned over the Web or in a call center. However, they can also be used in face-to-face interactions.[23]

Provisioning

According to the Encyclopedia of Cryptography and Security, provisioning is the automation of all procedures and tools to manage the lifecycle of an identity: creation of the identifier for the identity, linkage to the authentication providers, setting and changing attributes and privileges, and decommissioning of the identity.

Maintenance

This area is comprised of user management, password management, and role/group management. User management defines the set of administrative functions such as identity creation, propagation, and maintenance of user identity and privileges.

Entitlement

According to the Open Group, entitlement is a set of rules, defined by the resource owner, for managing access to a resource (asset, service, or entity), and for what purpose. The level of access not only is conditioned by your identity but is also likely to be constrained by a number of further security considerations such as your company policy, your location (i.e., are you inside your secure corporate environment, connected via a hotspot, or working from an Internet café, etc.), or time of day.[24]

SUMMARY

Controlling physical access to IT assets is an important element in protecting the availability and integrity of services provided by the assets. Many considerations factor into the selection and implementation of physical access controls. Using multiple layered controls such as deterrence and detection safeguards and response and recovery plans provide the greatest span of asset protection. Different types of assets may require specific access control systems to be able to effectively limit access to authorized personnel. Since information systems are comprised of various components, the availability of the information system as a whole is one of the main goals of an effective access control. The availability of the entire information system is only as strong as the weakest control afforded each component. The security practitioner should always be focused on the systems that are deployed to achieve access control within the environment, as well as how they are being monitored and maintained.

SAMPLE QUESTIONS

1. What type of controls are used in a Rule Set–Based Access Control system?
   a. Discretionary
   b. Mandatory
   c. Role Based
   d. Compensating

2. What framework is the Rule Set–Based Access Controls logic based upon?
   a. Logical Framework for Access Control
   b. Specialized Framework for Access Control
   c. Technical Framework for Access Control
   d. Generalized Framework for Access Control

3. View-Based Access Controls are an example of a(n):
   a. Audit control
   b. Constrained User Interface
   c. Temporal constraint
   d. Side Channel

4. Which of the following are supported authentication methods for iSCSI? (Choose two.)
   a. Kerberos
   b. Transport Layer Security (TLS)
   c. Secure Remote Password (SRP)
   d. Layer 2 Tunneling Protocol (L2TP)

5. According to the following scenario, what would be the most appropriate access control model to deploy?

Scenario: A medical records database application is used by a health-care worker to access blood test records. If a record contains information about an HIV test, the health-care worker may be denied access to the existence of the HIV test and the results of the HIV test. Only specific hospital staff would have the necessary access control rights to view blood test records that contain any information about HIV tests.

   a. Discretionary Access Control

   b. Context-Based Access Control

   c. Content-Dependent Access Control

   d. Role-Based Access Control

6. Which of the following is *not* one of the three primary rules in a Biba formal model?

   a. An access control subject cannot request services from an access control object that has a higher integrity level.

   b. An access control subject cannot modify an access control object that has a higher integrity level.

   c. An access control subject cannot access an access control object that has a lower integrity level.

   d. An access control subject cannot access an access control object that has a higher integrity level.

7. Which of the following is an example of a firewall that does not use Context-Based Access Control?

   a. Static packet filter

   b. Circuit gateway

   c. Stateful inspection

   d. Application proxy

8. Where would you find a singulation protocol being used?

   a. Where there is a Radio Frequency ID system deployed and tag collisions are a problem

   b. Where there is router that has gone offline in a multi-path storage network

   c. Where there is a Radio Frequency ID system deployed and reader collisions are a problem

   d. Where there is switch that has gone offline in a multi-path storage network

9. Which of the following are not principal components of access control systems? (Choose two.)

   a. Objects

   b. Biometrics

   c. Subjects

   d. Auditing

10. Which of the following are behavioral traits in a biometric device?

    a. Voice pattern and keystroke dynamics

    b. Signature dynamics and iris scan

    c. Retina scan and hand geometry

    d. Fingerprint and facial recognition

11. In the measurement of biometric accuracy, which of the following is commonly referred to as a "type 2 error"?

    a. Cross-over error rate (CER)

    b. Rate of false rejection—False Rejection Rate (FRR)

    c. Input/output per second (IOPS)

    d. Rate of false acceptance—False Acceptance Rate (FAR)

12. What is the difference between a synchronous and asynchronous password token?

    a. Asynchronous tokens contain a password that is physically hidden and then transmitted for each authentication, while synchronous tokens do not.

    b. Synchronous tokens are generated with the use of a timer, while asynchronous tokens do not use a clock for generation.

    c. Synchronous tokens contain a password that is physically hidden and then transmitted for each authentication, while asynchronous tokens do not.

    d. Asynchronous tokens are generated with the use of a timer, while synchronous tokens do not use a clock for generation.

13. What is an authorization table?

    a. A matrix of access control objects, access control subjects, and their respective rights

    b. A service or program where access control information is stored and where access control decisions are made

    c. A listing of access control objects and their respective rights

    d. A listing of access control subjects and their respective rights

14. What ports are used during Kerberos Authentication?

    a. 53 and 25

    b. 169 and 88

    c. 53 and 88

    d. 443 and 21

15. What are the five areas that make up the identity management lifecycle?

    a. Authorization, proofing, provisioning, maintenance, and establishment

    b. Accounting, proofing, provisioning, maintenance, and entitlement

    c. Authorization, proofing, provisioning, monitoring, and entitlement

    d. Authorization, proofing, provisioning, maintenance, and entitlement

NOTES

[1] See the following for the full DoD 5200.28 TCSEC Standard: http://csrc.nist.gov/publications/history/dod85.pdf

[2] See the following for the original paper by Leonard J. LaPadula, "Rule-Set Modeling of a Trusted Computer System": http://www.acsac.org/secshelf/book001/09.pdf

[3] See the following for RFC 3415—View-based Access Control Model (VACM) for the Simple Network Management Protocol (SNMP): http://tools.ietf.org/html/rfc3415. This document describes the View-based Access Control Model (VACM) for use in the Simple Network Management Protocol (SNMP) architecture. It defines the Elements of Procedure for controlling access to management information. This document also includes a Management Information Base (MIB) for remotely managing the configuration parameters for the View-based Access Control Model.

[4] Firewalls make context-based access decisions when they collect state information on a packet before allowing it to transit the network. A stateful firewall understands the necessary steps of communication for specific protocols. For example, in a TCP connection, the sender sends a SYN packet, the receiver sends a SYN/ACK, and then the sender acknowledges that packet with an ACK packet. A stateful firewall understands these different steps and will not allow packets to go through that do not follow this sequence. Therefore, if a stateful firewall receives a SYN/ACK and there was not a previous SYN packet that correlates with this connection, the firewall "understands" that the context for this packet is not right and disregards the packet.

[5] See the following for the original research paper that defined TRBAC as a model. "TRBAC: A Temporal Role-Based Access Control Model" by Elisa Bertino, Piero Andrea Bonatti, and Elena Ferrari. ACM Transactions on Information and Systems Security, Vol. 4, No.3, August 2001, 191-223.

[6] See the following for the NIST Interagency Report 7316: "Assessment of Access Control Systems." http://csrc.nist.gov/publications/nistir/7316/NISTIR-7316.pdf

[7] http://nvlpubs.nist.gov/nistpubs/specialpublications/NIST.sp.800-162.pdf

[8] Read more about Bell–La Padula here: http://www.acsac.org/2005/papers/Bell.pdf

[9] Read more about the Biba Integrity Model here: http://www.dtic.mil/cgi-bin/GetTR-Doc?AD=ADA166920 (Page 27).

[10] Read more about the Clark–Wilson model here: http://www.cs.clemson.edu/course/cpsc420/material/Policies/Integrity%20Policies.pdf

[11] As it turns out, Biba addresses only one of three key integrity goals. The Clark–Wilson model improves on Biba by focusing on integrity at the transaction level and addressing three major goals of integrity in a commercial environment. In addition to preventing changes by unauthorized subjects, Clark and Wilson realized that high-integrity systems would also have to prevent undesirable changes by authorized subjects and to ensure that the system continued to behave consistently. It also recognized that it would need to ensure that there is constant mediation between every subject and every object if such integrity was going to be maintained.

[12] See the following for an overview of the major Linux Security Distros: http://www.itproportal.com/2016/02/02/the-top-10-linux-security-distros/

[13] For an overview of the entire ISO 7816 Standards set, see the following: http://www.smartcardsupply.com/Content/Cards/7816standard.htm

[14] See the following: http://www.technovelgy.com/ct/Technology-Article.asp?ArtNum=20

[15] Although it requires a higher level of skill, keystrokes can be hacked. At DEFCON 17, Andrea Barisani and Daniele Bianco demonstrated how to sniff keystrokes using unconventional side channel attacks. Wires in PS/2 keyboards leak information from the data wire into the ground wire, which acts like an antenna. The leaked information about the keyboard strokes can be detected on the power outlet, as well as other wires on the same electrical system. By slicing open one of these lines, cutting the ground wire, and attaching a probe, the line can be monitored and the signal isolated by filtering out the noise using software such as Scilab. The waves from the oscilloscope and the data can be streamed to the hacker's computer where additional software is used to extract the victim's keystroke information. In addition, a research team from the Ecole Polytechnique Federale de Lausanne was able to pick up electromagnetic radiation that is generated every time a computer keyboard is tapped by using an oscilloscope and an inexpensive wireless antenna; the team was able to pick up keystrokes from virtually any keyboard, including laptops, with 95 percent accuracy. See the following for more information on each of these instances:

1. DEFCON 17: Sniff Keystrokes With Lasers/Voltmeters—YouTube video: http://www.youtube.com/watch?v=xKSq9efXmh8

2. Robert McMillan. "A Way to Sniff Keystrokes From Thin Air," *PCWorld*. http://www.pcworld.com/article/161166/article.html

[16] See the following for the BBC News article describing the events at Black Hat 2012:
`http://www.bbc.co.uk/news/technology-18997580#`

[17] See the following for the complete report on the research findings: Arora, S.S.; Vatsa, M. ; Singh, R. ; Jain, A. "Iris recognition under alcohol influence" (Conference Publications). 978-1-4673-0397-2. Biometrics (ICB), 2012 5th IAPR International Conference, pp. 336–341.

[18] See the following: `http://en.wikipedia.org/wiki/Security_token`

[19] See the following: `http://www.smartcardalliance.org/smart-cards-intro-primer/`

[20] See the following for the Authentication in an Internet Banking Environment recommendation: `http://www.ffiec.gov/pdf/authentication_guidance.pdf`

[21] See the following for RFC 1510, The Kerberos Network Authentication Service (V5):
`http://www.ietf.org/rfc/rfc1510.txt`

[22] See the following for the MIT Kerberos home page: `http://web.mit.edu/kerberos/`

[23] See the following: `http://www.gartner.com/it-glossary/identity-proofing-services`

[24] See the following: `http://blog.opengroup.org/2012/08/07/`
`entities-and-entitlement-the-bigger-picture-of-identity-management/`

ACCESS CONTROLS

1

Security Operations

SECURITY OPERATIONS AND ADMINISTRATION entails the identification of an organization's information assets and the documentation required for the implementations of policies, standards, procedures, and guidelines that ensure confidentiality, integrity, and availability. Working with management information owners, custodians, and users, the appropriate data classification scheme is defined for proper handling of both hardcopy and electronic information.

TOPICS

The following topics are addressed in this chapter:

☐ **Understand and comply with Codes of Ethics**

  ◾ (ISC)² code of ethics

  ◾ Organizational code of ethics

☐ **Understand security concepts**

  ◾ Confidentiality

  ◾ Integrity

  ◾ Availability

  ◾ Non-repudiation

  ◾ Privacy

  ◾ Least privilege

  ◾ Separation of duties

  ◾ Defense-in-depth

  ◾ Risk-based controls

  ◾ Authorization and accountability

☐ **Document and operate security controls**

  ◾ Deterrent controls

  ◾ Preventative

  ◾ Detective

  ◾ Corrective

☐ **Participate in asset management**

  ◾ Lifecycle

  ◾ Hardware

  ◾ Software

  ◾ Data

❏ **Implement and assess compliance with controls**

■ **Technical controls**

■ **Operational controls**

■ **Managerial controls (e.g., security policies, baselines, standards, and procedures)**

❏ **Participate in change management duties**

■ **Implementation and configuration management plan**

■ **Security impact assessment**

■ **System architecture/interoperability of systems**

■ **Testing patches, fixes, and updates**

❏ **Participate in security awareness and training**

❏ **Participate in physical security operations**

OBJECTIVES

A Systems Security Certified Practitioner (SSCP) is expected to demonstrate knowledge in:

■ Privacy issues

■ Data classification

■ Data integrity

■ Audit

■ Organizational roles and responsibilities

■ Policies

■ Standards

■ Guidelines

■ Procedures

■ Security awareness

■ Configuration control

■ Application of accepted industry practices

The terms *security administration* and *security operations* are often used interchangeably by organizations to refer to the set of activities performed by the security practitioner to implement, maintain, and monitor effective safeguards to meet the objectives of an organization's information security program. In many organizations, security administrators are responsible for configuring, managing, and participating in the design of technical and administrative security controls for one or more operating system platforms or business applications, while security operations personnel primarily focus on configuring and maintaining security-specific systems such as firewalls, intrusion detection and prevention systems, and antivirus software. Placing knowledgeable practitioners in operations and administration roles is critical to security program effectiveness. This chapter focuses on the knowledge and skills needed to become an effective security administrator.

CODE OF ETHICS

All (ISC)²-certified security practitioners must comply with the Code of Ethics, which sets forth standards of conduct and professionalism that characterize dealings with employers, business associates, customers, and the community at large. There are four mandatory tenets of the Code of Ethics:

1. Protect society, the commonwealth, and the infrastructure.
2. Act honorably, honestly, justly, responsibly, and legally.
3. Provide diligent and competent service to principals.
4. Advance and protect the profession.

Additional guidelines for performing your role in a professional manner are also provided in the Code of Conduct.

Violations of the (ISC)² Code of Conduct are a serious matter and may be subject to disciplinary action pursuant to a fair hearing by the Ethics Committee established by the (ISC)² Board of Directors. The complete Code of Conduct is available at the (ISC)² website.[1]

The following section is an excerpt from the (ISC)² Code of Ethics preamble and canons, by which all (ISC)² members must abide. Compliance with the preamble and canons is mandatory to maintain membership and credentials. Professionals resolve conflicts between the canons in the order of the canons. The canons are not equal and conflicts between them are not intended to create ethical binds.

Code of Ethics Preamble

Safety of the commonwealth, duty to our principals, and to each other requires that we adhere, and be seen to adhere, to the highest ethical standards of behavior. Therefore, strict adherence to this Code is a condition of certification.

Code of Ethics Canons

- Protect society, the commonwealth, and the infrastructure.

- Promote and preserve public trust and confidence in information and systems.

- Promote the understanding and acceptance of prudent information security measures.

- Preserve and strengthen the integrity of the public infrastructure.

- Discourage unsafe practice.

- Act honorably, honestly, justly, responsibly, and legally.

- Tell the truth; make all stakeholders aware of your actions on a timely basis.

- Observe all contracts and agreements, express or implied.

- Treat all constituents fairly. In resolving conflicts, consider public safety and duties to principals, individuals, and the profession in that order.

- Give prudent advice; avoid raising unnecessary alarm or giving unwarranted comfort. Take care to be truthful, objective, cautious, and within your competence.

- When resolving differing laws in different jurisdictions, give preference to the laws of the jurisdiction in which you render your service.

- Provide diligent and competent service to principals.

- Preserve the value of their systems, applications, and information.

- Respect their trust and the privileges that they grant you.

- Avoid conflicts of interest or the appearance thereof.

- Render only those services for which you are fully competent and qualified.

- Advance and protect the profession.

- Sponsor for professional advancement those best qualified. All other things equal, prefer those who are certified and who adhere to these canons. Avoid professional association with those whose practices or reputation might diminish the profession.

- Take care not to injure the reputation of other professionals through malice or indifference.

- Maintain your competence; keep your skills and knowledge current. Give generously of your time and knowledge in training others.

Applying a Code of Ethics to Security Practitioners

In 1998, Michael Davis, a professor of philosophy at the Illinois Institute of Technology, described a professional code of ethics as being a "contract between professionals." In this sense, professionals cooperate in serving a unified ideal better than they could if they did not cooperate. Information security professionals serve the ideal of ensuring the integrity, confidentiality, availability, and security of information. A code of ethics for information security professionals should specify how professionals pursue their common ideals so that each may best ensure information's security, confidentiality, integrity, and availability.

The code of ethics sets expectations for every single information security professional. Other information security professionals and even members of other professions are likely to judge your actions and behavior in relationship to this code of ethics. Beyond that, every individual is more than just a member of a profession and has responsibilites that extend beyond their code of ethics. Each person ultimately is answerable not only their own conscience but also the perceptions, criticism, and legal ramifications of other professionals and society. As information security professionals perform their duties in a variety of unique environments and circumstances, it is important that they balance the code of ethics with legal and regulatory responsibilities.

Donn B. Parker, an information security researcher and a 2001 Fellow of the Association for Computing Machinery, identified five ethical principles that apply to processing information. These principles and how they might be applied are described in the following list:

1. **Informed consent.** When contemplating any action, be sure to communicate it clearly and honestly to the people who will be affected by it. For example, if an employee wants a member of another team to collaborate with them on a project, the managers of both teams should be consulted to be sure that there aren't any conflicts with overall workload, divisions of departmental responsibilities, or breaches of department-based security clearance.

2. **Higher ethic in the worst case.** When considering your available courses of action, choose the actions that will cause no harm or as little harm as possible even in the worst circumstances. For instance, if a manager suspects that an employee might be involved in illegal or inappropriate activity in the workplace, the manager the manager might choose to check with the legal department to determine whether it is legally possible to monitor the employee's e-mail, which could be a potential violation of his privacy and rights.

3. **Change of scale test.** Consider whether your action performed on an individual scale or only one time would be more harmful if you repeated it or if many others engage in the same activity. Examples include checking personal e-mail on company time, surfing the Internet, and using company software for personal use. One instance seems innocent, but when you multiply these actions

repeatedly by a person or by many people, it can result in a loss of productivity (and profitability), violation of license agreements, and violation of employment contracts.

4. **Owners' conservation of ownership.** When you own or are otherwise responsible for information, take reasonable steps to secure it and be sure to clearly communicate ownership and rights to users. For example, a company that has a public web site and a corporate network should take adequate measures to protect its customers' and employees' passwords, Social Security numbers, and other personal information.

5. **Users' conservation of ownership.** When you use information, you should always assume that someone owns it and protect their interests. For instance, an employee shouldn't take software that is licensed to their employer and distribute illegal copies to their friends and family.[2]

SECURITY PROGRAM OBJECTIVES: THE C-I-A TRIAD AND BEYOND

The essential mission of any information security program is to protect the confidentiality, integrity, and availability of an organization's information systems assets. Effective security controls, whether they are physical, technical (logical), or administrative, are designed and operated to meet one or more of these three requirements.

Confidentiality

Confidentiality refers to the property of information in which it is only made available to those who have a legitimate need to know. Those with a need to know may be employees, contractors and business partners, customers, or the public. Information may be grouped into a logical series of hierarchical "classes" based on the attributes of the information itself; the parties authorized to access, reproduce, or disclose the information; and the potential consequences of unauthorized access or disclosure. The level of confidentiality may also be dictated by an organization's conduct and operating principles, its need for secrecy, its unique operating requirements, and its contractual obligations. Each level of confidentiality is associated with a particular protection class; that is, differing levels of confidentiality require different levels of protection from unauthorized or unintended disclosure. In some cases, the required level of protection—and thus the protection class or confidentiality level—is specified by laws and regulations governing the organization's conduct.

It is important to distinguish between confidentiality and privacy. Many states have privacy laws that dictate how and for what purpose personal, nonpublic information may be accessed. However, privacy also refers to an individual's ownership of his or her information and includes not only the need to maintain confidentiality on a strict "need-to-know" basis, but also the individual's right to exercise discretionary control over how his or her information is collected, the accuracy of the information, and how, by whom, and for what purpose the information is used.

Authorization, identity and access management, and encryption and disclosure controls are some methods for maintaining an appropriate level of confidentiality. Detective controls such as Data Leakage Prevention (DLP) tools may be used to monitor when, how, and by whom information is accessed, copied, or transmitted.

The consequences of a breach in confidentiality may include legal and regulatory fines and sanctions, loss of customer and investor confidence, loss of competitive advantage, and civil litigation. These consequences can have a damaging effect on the reputation and economic stability of an organization. When certain types of an individual consumer's information such as personally identifying data, health records, or financial information are disclosed to unauthorized parties, consequence such as identity and monetary theft, fraud, extortion, and personal injury may result. Information central to the protection of government interests may have serious public safety and national security consequences if disclosed.

Confidentiality supports the principle of *least privilege* by providing that only authorized individuals, processes, or systems should have access to information on a need-to-know basis. The level of access that an authorized individual should have is at the level necessary for them to do their job. In recent years, much press has been dedicated to the privacy of information and the need to protect it from individuals, who may be able to commit crimes by viewing the information. Identity theft is the act of assuming one's identity through knowledge of confidential information obtained from various sources.

An important measure to ensure confidentiality of information is data classification. This helps to determine who should have access to the information (public, internal use only, or confidential). Identification, authentication, and authorization through access controls are practices that support maintaining the confidentiality of information. A sample control for protecting confidentiality is to encrypt information. Encryption of information limits the usability of the information in the event it is accessible to an unauthorized person.

Integrity

Integrity is the property of information whereby it is recorded, used, and maintained in a way that ensures its completeness, accuracy, internal consistency, and usefulness for a stated purpose. Systems integrity, on the other hand, refers to the maintenance of a known good configuration and expected operational function. In both cases, the key to ensuring integrity is knowledge of state. Specifically, the ability to document and understand the state of data or a system at a certain point, creating a *baseline*. Going forward from that baseline, the integrity of the data or the system can always be ascertained by comparing the baseline to the current state; if the two match, then the integrity of the data or the system is intact; if the two do not match, then the integrity of the data or the system has been compromised. Integrity is a key factor in the reliability of information and systems.

Integrity controls include system edits and data validation routines invoked during data entry and update; system, file, and data access permissions; change and commitment control procedures; and secure hashing algorithms. Detective controls include system and application audit trails, balancing reports and procedures, antivirus software, and file integrity checkers.

The need to safeguard information and system integrity may be dictated by laws and regulations, such as the Sarbanes–Oxley Act of 2002, which mandates certain controls over the integrity of financial reporting. More often, it is dictated by the needs of the organization to access and use reliable, accurate information. Integrity controls such as digital signatures used to guarantee the authenticity of messages, documents, and transactions play an important role in non-repudiation (in which a sending or signing party cannot deny their action) and verifying receipt of messages. Finally, the integrity of system logs and audit trails and other types of forensic data is essential to the legal interests of an organization.

Consequences of integrity failure include an inability to read or access critical files, errors and failures in information processing, calculation errors, and uninformed decision making by business leaders. Integrity failures may also result in inaccuracies in reporting, resulting in the levying of fines and sanctions, and in inadmissibility of evidence when making certain legal claims or prosecuting crime.

Availability

Availability refers to the ability to access and use information systems when and as needed to support an organization's operations. Systems availability requirements are often defined in service level agreements (SLAs), which specify percentage of uptime as well as support procedures and communication for planned outages. In disaster recovery planning, system recovery time objectives (RTOs) specify the acceptable duration of an unplanned outage due to catastrophic system non-availability. When designing safeguards, security practitioners must balance security requirements with the need for availability of infrastructure services and business applications.

Availability controls include hardware and software RAID (redundant array of independent disks) controllers, UPS (uninterruptable power supply), backup and recovery software and procedures, mirroring and journaling, load balancing and failover, and business continuity plans.

Consequences of availability failures include interruption in services and revenue streams, fines and sanctions for failure to provide timely information to regulatory bodies or those to whom an organization is obliged under contract, and errors in transaction processing and decision making.

Non-repudiation

Non-repudiation is a service that ensures the sender cannot deny a message was sent and the integrity of the message is intact. NIST's SP 800-57 defines non-repudiation as:

> A service that is used to provide assurance of the integrity and origin of data in such a way that the integrity and origin can be verified by a third party as having originated from a specific entity in possession of the private key of the claimed signatory. In a general information security context, assurance that the sender of information is provided with proof of delivery and the recipient is provided with proof of the sender's identity, so neither can later deny having processed the information.[3]

Non-repudiation can be accomplished with digital signatures and PKI. The message is signed using the sender's private key. When the recipient receives the message, they may use the sender's public key to validate the signature. While this proves the integrity of the message, it does not explicitly define the ownership of the private key. A certificate authority must have an association between the private key and the sender (meaning only the sender has the private key) for the non-repudiation to be valid.

Privacy

Privacy can be defined as "the rights and obligations of individuals and organizations with respect to the collection, use, retention, and disclosure of personal information."[4] Personal information is a rather generic concept and encompasses any information that is about or on an identifiable individual. Although international privacy laws are somewhat different in respect to their specific requirements, they all tend to be based on core principles or guidelines. The Organization for Economic Cooperation and Development (OECD) has broadly classified these principles into the collection limitation, data quality, purpose specification, use limitation, security safeguards, openness, individual participation, and accountability. The guidelines cover the following:

- The collection of personal data should be limited, obtained by lawful and fair means, and done with the knowledge of the data subject.

- The collection of personal data should be done relevant to the specific purposes for which it is to be used and should be accurate, complete, and up to date.

- The purposes of personal data collection should be specified no later than the time of data collection. Subsequent use of the personal data should be limited to the fulfillment of the stated purposes or for compatible purposes that are specified on each occasion of change of the purpose.

- Personal data should not be used, disclosed, or made available for purposes other than those specified above except by the authority of law or with the consent of the data subject.

- Reasonable security safeguards should be in place against risks such as unauthorized access, loss, destruction, misuse, modification, or disclosure of data.[5]

A general policy of openness about developments, practices, and policies concerning personal data should be in place. There should also be a means for establishing the existence and nature of personal data, the main purposes of its use, and the identity and location of the data controller. A person should have the following rights:

- To obtain confirmation of whether the data controller or similar party has data relating to him.

- To have communicated to him the data that relates to him in a reasonable time, at a reasonable charge, in a reasonable manner, and in an intelligible form.

- To be given valid reasons if his request for his data is denied.

- To be able to challenge a denial of his request for his data.

- To be able to challenge data relating to him and, if the challenge is successful to have the data deleted, corrected, completed, or amended.

- To challenge data relating to him and, if the challenge is successful, to have the data erased, rectified, completed, or amended. A data controller should be accountable for complying with measures that give effect to the principles stated above.

A data controller should be accountable for complying with measures that establish and enforce these principles.[6]

In most industries internationally there is a consensus that these principles should form the minimum set of requirements for the development of reasonable legislation, regulations, and policy, and that nothing prevents organizations from adding additional principles. However, the actual application of these principles has proved more difficult and costly in almost all circumstances; there has been a vast underestimation of the impact of the various privacy laws and policies both domestically and with cross-border commerce. This is not an excuse to abandon, block, or fail to comply with applicable laws, regulations, or policies. However, information security practitioners need to appreciate that business practices have changed due to the need to be in compliance (often with international regulations) and that budgets must be appropriately increased to meet the demand. Like it or not, the privacy genie is out of the bottle and there is no putting it back.

Security Best Practices

When designing and implementing a security program, the security practitioner seeks to combine the needs of the organization with industry best practices. Best practices are defined as processes and methods that have been proven by thorough testing and real-world experience to consistently lead to desired results. A best practice may set the standard for performing a particular process such as managing system access or configuring a specific type of security device, or it may be broader in scope, covering one or more aspects of a security program such as risk management or personnel security. Security practitioners should refer to best practices where available to make use of the industry knowledge and experience that has gone into their creation and avoid reinventing the wheel. Be mindful, however, that citing best practices is rarely, in itself, a sufficient argument for adopting a particular strategy for the organization. The technologies and practices that the security practitioner implements should first and foremost address the specific risks, objectives, and culture of the organization. Many best practices documents are designed with sufficient flexibility to allow a security practitioner to readily adapt their principles into the specific set of practices that best meet the unique needs of the organization.

Designing a Security Architecture

Security architecture is the practice of designing a framework for the structure and function of information security systems and practices in the organization. When developing security architecture—whether at the enterprise, business unit, or system level—security best practices should be referenced for guidance when setting design objectives. Essential best practice considerations include

- Defense-in-depth
- Risk-based controls
- Least privilege
- Authorization and accountability
- Separation of duties

Defense-in-Depth

There is no such thing as perfect security. Preventive measures designed to safeguard an organization's assets can and do fail due to the presence of unknown vulnerabilities, hardware or software failures, human error, weaknesses in dependent processes, and the efforts of external attackers and malicious insiders. Reliance on a single safeguard to protect any critical asset is an invitation to a security breach. Security practitioners understand this and avoid single points of failure by designing safeguards using a layered approach.

Designing for defense-in-depth requires an understanding of the specific threats to the target asset and the anatomy of potential attacks or *attack vectors*, that is, the specific means by which a particular attack can occur. Defenses may be designed to prevent or deter attack using an outside-in or inside-out approach. By placing safeguards at two or more points along the access path to the asset, failure of one safeguard can be counteracted by the function of another safeguard further along the access path. For example, a firewall protecting an organization's web server may be designed to only allow web browsing (HTTP or HTTPS) to the server from the external network. An attacker may either circumvent the firewall policy by following an indirect path, for example, accessing a web server via a compromised host or user account with access to the server; by exploiting vulnerabilities in the firewall itself; or by using the allowed ports and protocols for purposes other than that for which they were intended. A defense-in-depth strategy might go beyond perimeter defenses, adding safeguards to the web server and hosted web applications, for example by disabling unnecessary services such as FTP (File Transfer Protocol), Telnet (terminal emulation), and remote procedure calls, requiring use of a unique identifier and strong authentication method to gain access to services, implementing protections against brute force of passwords, etc. If the actual target lies downstream from the interface, further protection along the access path is advisable. For example, if the web server uses a database to store data, it can be protected by using stored procedures, using strong input validation, requiring additional authentication for people and applications, or installing a host-based intrusion prevention system on the database server. It is important to note that a true defense-in-depth strategy requires that safeguards not share a common mechanism or be dependent on one another for proper operation. This is because failure of a common mechanism causes failure of all safeguards that rely on that mechanism.

Network segmentation is also an effective way to achieve defense-in-depth for distributed or multi-tiered applications. The use of a demilitarized zone (DMZ), for example, is a common practice in security architecture. Host systems that are accessible through the firewall are physically separated from the internal network by means of secured switches or by using an additional firewall (or multi-homed firewall) to control traffic between the web server and the internal network. Application DMZs are more frequently used today to limit access to application servers to those networks or systems that have a legitimate need to connect. The security practitioner should examine Figure 2.1 to see a logical design for network segmentation and the use of a DMZ.

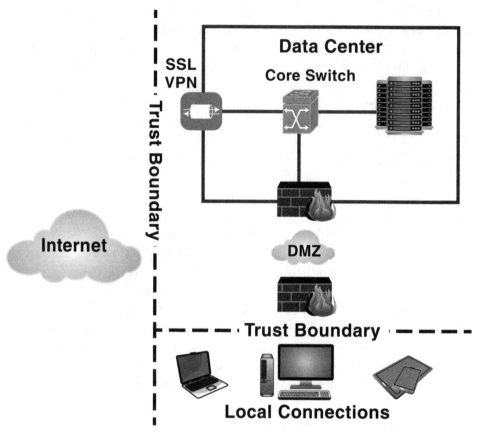

FIGURE 2.1 **Defense-in-depth through network segmentation**

Although preventive controls are usually the first and primary design elements in a security architecture, no preventive mechanism is 100% foolproof. Furthermore, not all attacks can be prevented even by layering preventive safeguards along the access path to an asset without interfering with legitimate activity. For that reason, defense-in-depth design also includes detective and corrective controls along the attack path. Detective controls are designed to inform security practitioners when a preventive control fails or is bypassed. Activity logs, audit trails, accounting and balancing procedures, and intrusion detection systems (IDSs) are typical detective controls. Intrusion detection systems, which operate in real-time or near real-time, are the best choice for critical assets. Signature-based intrusion detection systems are designed to flag activity that the security practitioner has identified as suspicious or malicious. Such systems are useful for known attack scenarios. However, the so-called zero-day attacks for which no signature is yet available can evade these systems. Anomaly-based IDS have the advantage of identifying new attacks, but they must be constantly tuned as new applications or functions are introduced to avoid alarming on legitimate activity.

Finally, corrective controls seek to minimize extent or impact of damage from an attack and return compromised systems and data to a known good state. Furthermore, they seek to prevent similar attacks in the future. Corrective controls are usually manual in nature, but recent advances in intrusion detection and prevention system (IDPS) technology have allowed security practitioners to place these systems in-line along the access path where they can automatically close ports, correct vulnerabilities, restore previous configurations, and redirect traffic because of a detected intrusion. Caution must be taken when implementing these systems to avoid interfering with legitimate activity, particularly when detective controls are set to automatically trigger corrective action.

Risk-Based Controls

Security has traditionally been considered "overhead" in many organizations, but this attitude is changing as more security practitioners enter the field armed with an understanding of business practices and the concept of risk-based security controls. All organizations face some degree of risk. Information security risk can be thought of as the likelihood of loss due to threats exploiting vulnerabilities; that is:

$$RISK = THREAT + VULNERABILITY + IMPACT$$

The degree of risk tells the organization what losses can be expected if security controls are absent or ineffective. The consequences or impact to assets may be tangible, as when computer equipment is lost or stolen, operations are interrupted, or fraudulent activity occurs. They may also be intangible, such as damage to an organization's reputation, decreased motivation of staff, or loss of customer and investor confidence. A "reasonable" expectation of loss may or may not be a result of a known probability or frequency of occurrence; for critical assets, large losses could result from a single security incident and, therefore, the risk may be high even if the probability of an incident occurring is low. Conversely, highly probable events that incur minimal losses may be considered acceptable as a cost of doing business, depending on the organization's risk tolerance, or risk appetite.

The concept of risk-based controls states that the total costs to implement and maintain a security measure should be commensurate with the degree to which risks to the confidentiality, integrity, and availability of the assets protected by the security measure must be reduced to acceptable levels. Safeguards that address multiple risks can and should be implemented to provide economies of scale wherever possible, as long as they are a part of an overall defense-in-depth strategy. The cost of safeguards includes not only capital expenses for software and equipment but also the use of resources to implement and maintain the safeguard and the impact, if any, on current business processes and productivity levels. An objective presentation of risk, including the likelihood and anticipated impact of adverse events, will help the security practitioner gain needed support from financial decision makers and line staff. Risk treatment decisions—that is, whether and to what extent to transfer, mitigate, or accept a certain level of risk—are management decisions that should be founded in an objective view of the facts. Similarly, the prioritization and selection of safeguards is guided by the extent and nature of the risks uncovered in the risk assessment.

Using a standard process for assessing and documenting risk provides consistent and repeatable results that can be readily compared, trended, and understood by decision makers. Methodologies such as the Carnegie Mellon Software Engineering Institute's OCTAVE (Operationally Critical Threat, Asset, and Vulnerability Assessment) and COBRA (Consultative, Objective and Bi-Functional Risk Analysis), and guidance from industry best practices such as National Institute of Standards and Technology (NIST) Special Publication 800-30 R1: "Risk Management Guide for Information Technology Systems," enhance the credibility of results and promote more efficient and effective use of time and resources.[7]

A risk assessment may be qualitative or quantitative in nature; whenever possible, use quantitative data to document incident probability and impact. Data for the risk assessment may be based on internal events and historical data, surveys, interviews and questionnaires, and industry experience available through various publications and industry forums. The use of metrics and cost/benefit analyses are key success factors in gaining the organization's buy-in for security measures. Transparency of process, open communication, and a willingness to include nontechnical management and line staff as participants in the risk assessment process make the risk assessment a collaborative effort and promote effective adoption of risk treatment recommendations.

Least Privilege

The least privilege concept is the analog of "need to know." Under least privilege, access rights are permissions granted based on the need of a user or process to access and use information and resources. Only those rights and privileges needed to perform a specific function are granted. Eliminating unnecessary privileges reduces the potential for errors committed by users who may not have the knowledge or skills necessary to perform certain functions and protects against random errors such as unintentional deletion of files. Limiting the number of privileged users on critical systems and auditing the activities of those who have a high privilege level also reduces the likelihood of authorized users performing unauthorized functions. On the desktop, least privilege or least user access

(LUA) is often implemented to prevent casual users from installing software, modifying system settings, or falling prey to malicious code operating in the context of the logged-in user. Some organizations assign administrators two logins, one with administrative privileges and one with ordinary user privileges, to reduce the impact of mistakes when performing routine activities that do not require administrative authority. As an alternative, some systems provide temporary augmentation of privileges under "run as" or privilege adoption schemes in which additional privileges are granted for a specific task or session and then removed when the task is complete.

Least privilege can be implemented at the operating system, application, process, file, data element, or physical security layers. Unfortunately, many COTS (commercial, off-the-shelf) applications are developed in environments that have not adopted least privilege principles and, as a result, these products often require elevated privilege to run. For desktop applications, the use of Microsoft's Process Monitor and similar tools can identify system files, registry keys, and other protected resources accessed by the application so that policy configuration can be modified to provide specific permissions as needed. (See Figure 2.2.)

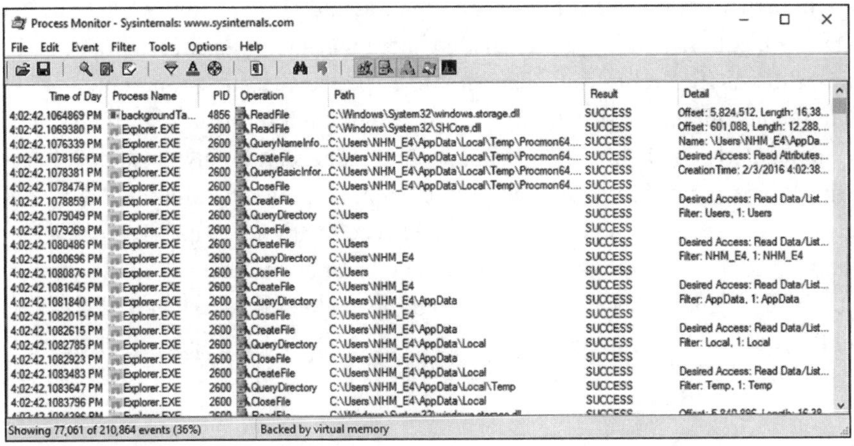

FIGURE 2.2 **Microsoft/Sys-internals Monitor Process**

However, this is time consuming and only useful in certain operating environments. When a full implementation of least privilege is not feasible or possible, adopting a defense-in-depth strategy using such things as audit logs, event monitoring, and periodic audits can be used as a compensating control strategy.

In practice, privileges are typically set by associating specific roles or groups with an access control entry. Maintaining role- or group-based privileges is much more efficient than granting these rights at an individual level, which requires frequent modifications across multiple access entries to accommodate changes in each individual's status and job function. The groups Everyone, Public, Authenticated Users, and the like, which contain all authorized users of a system, should be associated with access control entries that grant only the minimum privileges needed to authenticate to the system.

Authorization and Accountability

Access control systems are designed with the assumption that there is an appropriate process in place to authorize individuals to specific access privileges. The decision of which privileges to grant to which individuals or groups should not be made by the security practitioner, but rather by the owners of the data or system to be accessed. A system or data owner is the individual who has the most vested interest in maintaining the confidentiality, integrity, or availability of a particular system or data set and is typically a business line manager or above. A record of authorizations should be kept to support access control system validation testing, in which actual access is compared to authorized access to determine whether the process of assigning access entitlements is working as intended and is aligned with the stated policy. Testing also helps to catch errors in assigning access privileges before a breach can occur. Documented authorizations are also used in forensic work when determining whether an incident occurred at the hands of a legitimate or illegitimate user.

Accountability is a principle that ties authorized users to their actions. Accountability is enforced through assigning individual access accounts and by generating audit trails and activity logs that link identifying information about the actor (person, system, or application) with specific events. Audit data should be protected against unintentional or malicious modification or destruction, as it is an important forensic tool. It should be backed up regularly and retained for a sufficient period to support investigations and reporting. Some regulations require a specific retention period for audit trail data. Individuals should be cautioned never to share their access with others and to protect their credentials from unauthorized use. They should be informed that any information recorded under their unique access accounts will be attributed to them; that is, they will be held accountable for any activity that occurs through use of the access privileges assigned to them.

Separation of Duties

Separation of duties is an operational security mechanism for preventing fraud and unauthorized use that requires two or more individuals to complete a task or perform a specific function. (Note: Separation of duties does not necessarily require two people to perform a task but requires that the person performing is not the person checking on the task.) Separation of duties is a key concept of internal control and is commonly seen in financial applications that assign separate individuals to the functions of approving, performing, and auditing or balancing a transaction. This ensures that no single person operating alone can perform a fraudulent act without detection. Most COTS financial software packages have built-in mechanisms for enforcing appropriate separation of duties, using transaction segmentation and role-based access control. In nonfinancial systems, separation of duties may be implemented in any system subject to abuse or critical error to reduce the impact of a single person's actions. For example, most program change control processes separate development, testing, quality assurance (QA), and production release functions.

Dual control is similar to a separation of duties in that it requires two or more people operating at the same time to perform a single function. Examples of dual control include use of signature plates for printing, supervisor overrides for certain transactions and adjustments, and some encryption key recovery applications.

Separation of duties does not prevent collusion, that is, cases where two or more persons cooperate to perpetuate a fraudulent act. Careful transaction balancing and review of suspicious activity and output captured in logs, transaction registers, and reports are the best methods of detecting collusion. In some organizations, additional operational security practices such as mandatory vacation periods or job rotations are enforced to provide management with an opportunity to prevent and detect collusion.

Documenting and Operating Security Controls

In addition to the best practices discussed thus far for designing a security architecture, there are several more considerations regarding controls and documentation that should be addressed.

Controls

Controls are safeguards and counter measures that are implemented to mitigate, lessen, or avoid a risk. Controls are generally grouped into different categories. U.S. NIST uses three classes in their descriptions of controls based on definitions from U.S. FIPS 200[8] that are based on a control's function:

- **Management**—Controls based on the management of risk and the management of information systems security. These are generally policies and procedures.

- **Technical**—Controls that are primarily implemented and executed through mechanisms contained in the hardware, software, and firmware of the components of the system.

- **Operational**—Controls that are primarily implemented and executed by people (as opposed to systems).

In addition to these classes, U.S. NIST has defined 18 control families based on the minimum security requirements defined in U.S. FIPS 200. Table 2.1 illustrates their relationship to the classes.[9]

TABLE 2.1 Security Control Classes, Families, and Identifiers

IDENTIFIER	FAMILY	CLASS
AC	Access Control	Technical
AT	Awareness and Training	Operational
AU	Audit and Accountability	Technical
CA	Security Assessment and Authorization	Management
CM	Configuration Management	Operational
CP	Contingency Planning	Operational
IA	Identification and Authentication	Technical
IR	Incident Response	Operational
MA	Maintenance	Operational
MP	Media Protection	Operational
PE	Physical and Environmental Protection	Operational
PL	Planning	Management
PM	Project Management	Management
PS	Personnel Security	Operational
RA	Risk Assessment	Management
SA	System and Services Acquisition	Management
SC	System and Communications Protection	Technical
SI	System and Information Integrity	Operational

Other organizations within the industry may have different terms or a different number of categories depending on their definitions and how they choose to delineate their categories. For example, some relate control categories to the time line of a security incident as illustrated in Figure 2.3.

- **Directive**—Controls designed to specify acceptable rules of behavior within an organization

- **Deterrent**—Controls designed to discourage people from violating security directives

- **Preventive**—Controls implemented to prevent a security incident or information breach

- **Compensating**—Controls implemented to substitute for the loss of primary controls and mitigate risk down to an acceptable level
- **Detective**—Controls designed to signal a warning when a security control has been breached
- **Corrective**—Controls implemented to remedy circumstance, mitigate damage, or restore controls
- **Recovery**—Controls implemented to restore conditions to normal after a security incident

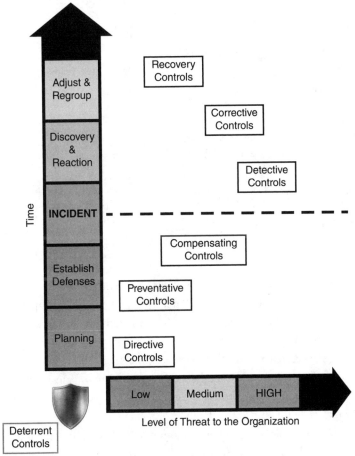

FIGURE 2.3 Continuum of controls relative to the time line of a security incident

In either example, controls are still identified for the purpose of safeguards and countermeasures to address risk, and different labels can be used in conjunction with each other. An example is illustrated in Table 2.2.

TABLE 2.2 **Control Example for Types and Categories**

	ADMINISTRATIVE	TECHNICAL	PHYSICAL
Directive	Policy	Configuration standards	Authorized Personnel Only signs Traffic lights
Deterrent	Policy	Warning banner	Beware of Dog sign
Preventative	User Registration Procedure	Password-based login	Fence
Detective	Review Violation reports	Logs	Sentry CCTV
Corrective	Termination	Unplug, isolate, and terminate connection	Fire extinguisher
Recovery	DR Plan	Backups	Rebuild
Compensating	Supervision Job rotation Logging	CCTV Keystroke logging	Layered defense

Compensating controls were mentioned in one of the examples and should be discussed further because of their importance with the risk management process. Compensating controls are introduced when the existing capabilities of a system do not support the requirements of a policy. Compensating controls can be technical, procedural, or managerial. Although an existing system may not support the required controls, there may exist other technology or processes that can supplement the existing environment, closing the gap in controls, meeting policy requirements, and reducing overall risk. For example, the access control policy may state that the authentication process must be encrypted when performed over the Internet. Adjusting an application to natively support encryption for authentication purposes may be too costly. Secure Sockets Layer (SSL), an encryption protocol, can be employed and layered on top of the authentication process to support the policy statement. In addition, management processes, such as authorization, supervision, and administration, can be used to compensate for gaps in the control environment. The critical points to consider when addressing compensating controls are

■ Do not compromise stated policy requirements.

- Ensure that the compensating controls do not adversely affect risk or increase exposure to threats.

- Manage all compensating controls in accordance with established practices and policies.

- Compensating controls designated as temporary should be removed after they have served their purpose and another, more permanent control should be established.

System Security Plans

A system security plan is a comprehensive document that details the security requirements for a specific system, the controls established to meet those requirements, and the responsibilities and expected behaviors of those administering and accessing the system. It is developed with input from system and information owners, individuals with responsibility for the operation of the system, and the system security officer. The system security plan and its supporting documents are living documents that are periodically reviewed and updated to reflect changes in security requirements and in the design, function, and operation of the system. Security plans are developed and reviewed before system certification and accreditation; during these later stages of preproduction review, system security plans are analyzed, updated, and finally accepted.

Roles and responsibilities in the system security planning process include

- **System Owner**—Responsible for decisions regarding system procurement or development, implementation and integration, and operation and ongoing maintenance. The system owner has overall responsibility for system security plan development in collaboration with the information owner, system security officer, and users of the system, and for maintaining current plans. In addition, he/she is responsible for ensuring that the controls specified in the plan are operating as intended.

- **Information Owner**—Has overall authority for the information stored, processed, or transmitted by the system. The information owner is responsible for specifying policies for appropriate use of information and security requirements for protecting information in the system. He/she determines who can access the system and the privileges that will be granted to system users.

- **Security Officer**—Responsible for coordinating development, review, and acceptance of security plans and for identification, implementation, administration, and assessment of security controls.

- **Authorizing Official or Approver**—A senior executive or manager with the authority to assume full responsibility for the system covered in the system security plan. This is the person empowered to authorize operation of the system and accept any residual risk that remains after security controls have been implemented.

The system security plan scope is determined by performing a boundary analysis to identify the information, hardware, system and application software, facilities, and personnel included in the overall system's function. Typically, the resources constituting a system are under the same management control and work together to perform a discrete function or set of functions. If scoping is difficult, it may be helpful to start with the specific type or set of information assets in question and define the hardware, software, and personnel involved in its storage, processing, and use. Larger systems may be subdivided into subsystems that perform one or more specific functions. The controls documented in the system security plan should consist of administrative, technical, and physical mechanisms to achieve the desired level of confidentiality, integrity, and availability of system assets.

The system security plan should include the following information:

- **System Name and a Unique ID**—An ID is assigned to the system to aid in inventory, measurement, and configuration management.

- **System Categorization**—The system should be categorized low, medium, or high (or some other relative ranking) for each element of the C-I-A triad.

- **System Owner**—Identify the name, title, and organization of the system owner.

- **Authorizing Official**—The name, title, and organization of the authorizing official.

- **Technical and Administrative Contacts**—Contact information for personnel who have knowledge of the configuration and operation of the system.

- **Security Requirements**—Security requirements for confidentiality, integrity, and availability of system resources.

- **Security Controls**—Administrative, physical, and technical controls applied to meet security requirements.

- **Review and Maintenance Procedures**—Roles, responsibilities, and procedures for reviewing and maintaining the system security plan.

Additional Documentation

In addition to the documentation described previously, the security practitioner maintains associated documentation such as security recommendations, technical specifications, design documents, and implementation checklists to support administration and troubleshooting. General information documents may be created to provide an overview of specific security systems for new employees or for those performing backup functions.

Security recommendations are developed to address specific issues that are identified as a result of a risk, vulnerability, or threat assessment. Recommendations may be presented as a section in a formal risk assessment report; may be presented to management as follow up to an incident report; or may be published as guidelines for developers, administrators, or users of a system. Recommendations are not mandatory actions but instead are suggested steps that, if taken, can achieve a specific security outcome.

Disaster recovery documentation is created and maintained for any critical system that must be restored onsite or offsite in the event of system interruption. System restoration does not always follow the same steps as building a new system; for example, policy and other configuration files and application data may need to be backed up and restored to bring systems back to the state they were in when the interruption occurred. A copy of disaster recovery documentation should be maintained at a sufficient distance from the organization's offices to support restoration activities in the event of local or regionalized disaster.

Another type of documentation maintained by the security practitioner is the collection of audit and event logs, incident data, and other information captured during the course of operating the organization's security systems. These data are necessary for system tuning, troubleshooting and problem resolution, forensics investigations, reporting, and validation of security controls. It may also be used to validate compliance with applicable policies, procedures, and regulations. Audit and event data should be protected from unauthorized access and modification and retained for a predetermined period. Most security systems are self-documenting, although you may be required to document procedures for collecting, reviewing, and securing the data.

Secure Development and Acquisition Lifecycles

Software applications have become targets of an increasing number of malicious attacks in recent years. Web-based applications that are exposed over public networks are a natural choice for criminal hackers seeking entry points to an organization's data and internal network infrastructure. Internal applications are also at risk due to internal fraud and abuse, logical processing errors, and simple human mistakes. While firewalls and other network security devices offer a great degree of protection, they are often bypassed by legitimate users, attackers using stolen login credentials or hijacked user sessions, and unauthorized activity conducted over allowed ports and protocols. Indirect access through a remote access gateway or compromised internal host can also bypass perimeter protections. Safeguards built into applications early in systems design are needed to counteract these threats, thwart application-level attacks, and maintain data and system integrity in the face of human error.

The security practitioner will be better able to build security into his or her organization's application systems by actively participating through all phases of the development and acquisition process. Rather than becoming an impediment to productivity, secure design and development practices introduce efficiencies and enhance quality if they are applied consistently throughout the development life cycle. This process of building security in requires an understanding of commonly used application software development methods, common threats and vulnerabilities, and application-level safeguards.

Most organizations adhere to a standard methodology to specify, design, develop, and implement software applications. Various models exist for developing software applications. Some of the more prevalent are described in the following sections.

The Waterfall Model

The waterfall model[10] consists of a linear sequence of six steps. Steps are taken in order, and as each step in the process is completed, the development team moves on to the next step. Steps in the waterfall model are

1. **Requirement Gathering and Analysis**—Various stakeholders are consulted to identify the system requirements, and the results are compiled in a requirement specification document.

2. **System Design**—The requirement specifications document is consulted to determine the architecture, software requirements, hardware requirements, and other aspects of system design.

3. **Implementation**—The system is now developed in small programs that are often referred to as units. Each unit is developed and tested and modified until it works well.

4. **Integration**—All the units are integrated into a system. The entire system is tested for any faults and failures.

5. **Deployment**—The product and its related instructions are officially released into the corporate, government, or consumer market.

6. **Maintenance**—The existing product is maintained, patches for technical problems are released, functionality is updated, minor upgrades are released, and so on.

In addition to these phases, testing takes place as necessary in the process, often occuring during implementation, after integration, after deployment, and sometimes as part of maintenance.

Let's delve a little deeper into each phase.

Requirements Gathering and Analysis

A feasibility analysis usually precedes approval of any development project. In this stage, the business problem and a recommended approach are documented in the project charter. The project charter also includes a preliminary plan, resource estimates and budget, and constraints. The person designated as the project sponsor typically signs off on the charter, giving the go-ahead to proceed. Additional stakeholders may be named to participate in review and approval at key milestone points. The security practitioner who is fully hooked in to the development process will ideally be asked to participate in charter development and review.

Functional and nonfunctional requirements are documented in this phase. Functional requirements specify user interactions and system processing steps and are often documented in the form of sequences of action called use cases, documented using Unified Modeling Language (UML). Nonfunctional requirements, such as those for performance and quality or those imposed by design or environmental constraints, are documented using narratives and diagrams. Security requirements may be incorporated within the nonfunctional requirements specification. Examples of this type of security requirement include user and process authentication, maintaining access logs and audit trails, secure session management, and encryption of passwords and sensitive data. Functional security requirements, such as how an application responds to incorrect passwords, malformed input, or unauthorized access attempts, can be documented in the form of "abuse" or "misuse" case diagrams. Security requirements are typically derived through a risk or threat assessment conducted during this stage of development.

The project sponsor and stakeholders sign off on the completed requirements before the team begins solution development.

System Design

Software design activities are typically performed by architects or programmer analysts who are well versed in both the business process to be developed and the environment in which the application will operate. Specifications elicited during the requirements phase are documented into application events using a set of flow charts and narratives. Design may first be laid out in a *general design document*, which is then refined to produce specifications for the *detailed design*. Design walkthroughs are often held to review the design before construction to ensure that all of the requirements have been accounted for in the application design. A security architect or administrator should participate in the design phase to ensure that security design requirements are integrated with the overall application design.

Implementation

Software programming is completed in this phase. Functional design specifications, typically created by analysts, are translated into executable processes using one or more programming languages. The usual scenario has multiple programmers working concurrently on discrete functional units or modules that comprise the whole application. Each capability is separately tested by the developer before being rolled up, or integrated, with other functions.

Integration

Integration occurs when multiple functional units of code or modules that form the application are compiled and run together. This ensures, for example, that outputs produced by one process are received as expected by a downstream process.

Deployment of System

When the application has been system tested, it is installed into a controlled environment for quality assurance and user acceptance testing. At this stage, the application is considered to be in its final form, installation and operational documentation has been developed, and changes are tightly controlled. Typically, a separate QA team performs quality testing before releasing the application to end users for the final acceptance testing phase. User acceptance testing requires formal signoff from the project sponsor to indicate that the application has met all requirements. Certification and accreditation may also be required before an application project can be closed. Release management, discussed in a later section, is a set of controlled processes used to implement the final, approved application into the production environment.

Maintenance

Applications rarely remain in the form in which they were originally released to production. Changes in business needs and practices, newly discovered bugs and vulnerabilities, and changes in the technical environment all necessitate changes to production applications.

The waterfall model described is the oldest and most widely used formal development model; it is common practice in defense applications and in large, established organizations. Key differentiators of the waterfall model are its adherence to a highly structured linear sequence of steps or phases, an emphasis on completeness of up-front requirements and design, and the use of documentation and formal approvals between phases as primary control mechanisms. Major benefits of using the waterfall method are its ease of use and management (even with large teams) and the broad scope and detailed specificity of systems documentation that is available to certification, accreditation, and application maintenance and enhancement teams. A major drawback of the waterfall model is that it assumes a static set of requirements captured before design and coding phases begin. Thus, errors may not be noticed until later testing phases, where they are more costly to address. Even in the absence of errors, new requirements may surface during development due to regulatory and operational changes and emergence of new threats that impact the automated process. To correct for this, project managers must establish rigorous change management processes to reduce the disruption, delays, and cost overruns that can occur as a result of having to retrofit new requirements into the application. The later in development requirements surface, the more potentially disruptive they are, and the more likely they are to be shelved for future development. For this reason, security practitioners are urged to actively contribute to requirements gathering and documentation and maintain awareness of the change management process to address any functional changes that may introduce new security requirements.

Testing

Testing is not a separate phase of waterfall development projects; instead, different types of testing and debugging occur from construction to installation and beyond. Programmers perform unit testing to validate proper functioning of code at the lowest level of functionality, which can be a process, function, program, or method in the case of object-oriented programming. Automated tools built into the developer's programming environment are often used for unit testing.

Integration testing is the next phase, in which individually tested units are assembled in functional groups and retested as a whole, following a test script or plan. Use and abuse cases generated during requirements gathering may form the basis of functional testing at this stage. The purpose of integration testing is to ensure that major application functions specified in the design are working together. All interactions, such as program calls, messages, etc., are tested in this phase.

System testing is performed on a complete, integrated system to ensure that all requirements and approved changes have been incorporated into the application. Some organizations create separate environments, such as servers, databases, files, and utilities, for the purpose of system testing. Objects in the system test environment should be secured in the same manner as in production to avoid "breaking" the application once it is released.

Additional Application Development Methods

There are several popular application development models other than the waterfall model. These include the spiral model, rapid application development, agile development, and component development and reuse.

Spiral Model

The spiral model is based on the waterfall development life cycle but adds a repeated PDCA (Plan–Do–Check–Act) sequence at each stage of the waterfall progression. A first pass through the steps of the waterfall model is taken using a subset or high-level view of overall requirements, which are used as a basis for an initial *prototype* (working model) of the application. The spiral model assumes that requirements are naturally flushed out in a hierarchical way, with high-level or basic requirements giving rise to more detailed functional requirements.

Extreme Programming and Rapid Application Development

Rapid Application Development (RAD) was designed to fully leverage modern development environments that make it possible to quickly build user interface components as requirements are gathered. Application users are intimately involved in RAD projects, working with the screen flows as they are being built and providing feedback to the developers. The advantages of RAD include high error detection rates early in development, bypassing the need for extensive retrofitting and regression testing. RAD projects thus require less project change management overhead. This very fact can be a downside, however; RAD projects may suffer fatal "scope creep," as new requirements are continually added and teams lose sight of the end goal while cycling through an unending series of prototypes.

Agile Development

Agile is built on the example of iterative development models. Agile development methods rely on feedback from application users and development teams as their primary control mechanism. Software development is seen as a continuous evolution, where results from continuous release testing are evaluated and used to enhance subsequent releases of the developing code. Enhanced team productivity, increased development speed, and a reduction in production defects are all stated benefits of agile development. IT personnel who are well versed in traditional development methods take some time to get used to agile development, and performance gains in the first year are expected to double—or better—in the second year after adopting agile methods.

Component Development and Reuse

The idea of component-based development is based on the reuse of proven design solutions to address new problems. This is not really a new concept; traditional utility programs such as date conversion routines are an example of components that have been in existence for decades. Components may be retained as design patterns, common modules, or architectural models in a component library that is searchable by developers looking to incorporate them in their applications. Component reuse reduces development and testing time and cost, increases quality and reliability, and promotes consistency and ease of maintenance among applications.

User and application authentication sequences, authorization checks, and encryption and decryption methods are examples of security functions that can be developed for reuse across applications. Some development platforms, such as J2EE (Java 2 Enterprise Edition), incorporate security methods in their programming libraries. Using prepackaged components is encouraged whenever possible to avoid vulnerabilities that can easily be introduced into homegrown security logic.

System Vulnerabilities, Secure Development, and Acquisition Practices

Exposing applications, infrastructure, and information to external users via the Internet creates an opportunity for compromise by individuals and groups wishing to steal customer data and proprietary information, interfere with operations and system availability, or damage an organization's reputation. Vulnerabilities within web-facing applications provide opportunities for malicious attack by unauthorized users, authorized but malicious users, and malicious code executing locally or on a compromised machine connected to the application. Internal development projects should combine secure coding practices, appropriate program and infrastructure change control, and proactive vulnerability management to reduce vulnerabilities.

The Open Web Application Security Project (OWASP) provides a freely available listing of the top vulnerabilities found in web applications; in reality, the list contains a mix of vulnerabilities and exploits that frequently occur as a result of compromised web browsers and, in some cases, web servers.[11] Most of these attacks are platform independent, although specific platforms have been targeted by variants. At a minimum, coding standards and guidelines should be developed to protect applications against the OWASP Top Ten, which are in Table 2.3.[12]

TABLE 2.3 OWASP Top Ten—2013: "The Ten Most Critical Web Application Security Risks"

#	APPLICATION SECURITY RISKS	DESCRIPTION
1	Injection	Injection flaws, such as SQL, OS, and LDAP injection, occur when untrusted data is sent to an interpreter as part of a command or query. The attacker's hostile data can trick the interpreter into executing unintended commands or accessing data without proper authorization.
2	Broken Authentication and Session Management	Application functions related to authentication and session management are often not implemented correctly, allowing attackers to compromise passwords, keys, or session tokens, or to exploit other implementation flaws to assume other users' identities.
3	Cross Site Scripting (XSS)	XSS flaws occur whenever an application takes untrusted data and sends it to a web browser without proper validation and escaping. XSS allows attackers to execute script in the victim's browser, which can hijack user sessions, deface websites, or redirect the user to malicious sites.
4	Insecure Direct Object References	A direct object reference occurs when a developer exposes a reference to an internal implementation object, such as a file, directory, or database key. Without an access control check or other protection, attackers can manipulate these references to access unauthorized data.
5	Security Misconfiguration	Good security requires having a secure configuration defined and deployed for the application, frameworks, application server, web server, database server, and platform. Secure settings should be defined, implemented, and maintained, as defaults are often insecure. Additionally, software should be kept up to date.
6	Sensitive Data Exposure	Many web applications do not properly protect sensitive data, such as credit cards, tax IDs, and authentication credentials. Attackers may steal or modify such weakly protected data to conduct credit card fraud, identity theft, or other crimes. Sensitive data deserves extra protection such as encryption at rest or in transit, as well as special precautions when exchanged with the browser.
7	Missing Function Level Access Control	Most web applications verify function-level access rights before making that functionality visible in the UI. However, applications need to perform the same access control checks on the server when each function is accessed. If requests are not verified, attackers will be able to forge requests in order to access functionality without proper authorization.

#	APPLICATION SECURITY RISKS	DESCRIPTION
8	Cross Site Request Forgery (CSRF)	A CSRF attack forces a logged-on victim's browser to send a forged HTTP request, including the victim's session cookie and any other authentication information, to a vulnerable web application. This allows the attacker to force the victim's browser to generate requests the vulnerable application thinks are legitimate requests from the victim.
9	Using Components with Known Vulnerabilities	Components, such as libraries, frameworks, and other software modules, almost always run with full privileges. If a vulnerable component is exploited, such an attack can facilitate serious data loss or server takeover. Applications using components with known vulnerabilities may undermine application defenses and enable a range of possible attacks and impacts.
10	Un-validated Redirects and Forwards	Web applications frequently redirect and forward users to other pages and websites, and use untrusted data to determine the destination pages. Without proper validation, attackers can redirect victims to phishing or malware sites or use forwards to access unauthorized pages.

As the vulnerabilities described in this chapter have illustrated, guidelines for developers should include the following areas:

- **Authentication**—Use standard, secure authentication mechanisms for users and applications, including mechanisms for forgotten passwords and password changes (require the old password be entered first), secure encrypted storage of authentication credentials, and enforcement of strong passwords not susceptible to dictionary attacks.

- **Authorization**—Perform authorization checks to requested objects such as files, URLs, and database entries. Secure objects from unauthorized access.

- **Session Management**—Most web application platforms include session management functions that link individual requests to an authenticated user account so that the user does not need to manually re-authenticate to each web page. Custom cookies should be avoided for authentication (user and session) where possible. Proper session management includes timing out inactive sessions, deleting session information after timeout, not passing credentials in URL strings, and using salted hashes to protect session IDs.

- **Encryption of Sensitive Data**—Encryption of data at rest may not be feasible for your organization, with the exception of authentication credentials, which should always be encrypted. Encryption of sensitive data in transit is simple and inexpensive to configure and should be required of all applications. Avoid home-grown encryption methods wherever possible.

- **Input Validation**—Applications should never assume that data sent to them in the form of HTTP requests, form field input, or parameters are benign and in the proper format. User input should be validated using an *accepted known good* approach wherever possible (matching input to a set or range of acceptable values). String length or field size limits, data types, syntax, and business rules should be enforced on all input fields.

- **Disallow Dynamic Queries**—Dynamic queries and direct database access should not be allowed within web applications. Stored procedures (routines precompiled in the database or callable as program code) should be used wherever possible. Use strongly typed, parameterized APIs for queries and stored procedure calls.

- **Out-of-Band Confirmations**—Consider sending confirmations out of band when there has been a password change or significant business transaction performed via the website.

- **Avoid Exposing System Information**—Avoid exposing references to private application objects in URL strings, cookies, or user messages.

- **Error Handling**—Avoid exposing information about the system or process, such as path information, stack trace and debugging information, and standard platform error messages in response to errors and consider setting a low debug level for general use. Also consider, consider using a standard default error handling routine for all application components, including those in the application environment (server operating system, application system, etc.). Ensure that error messages do not expose any information that could be exploited by hackers; for example, a return "incorrect password" indicates that the supplied UserID is valid, while "login failed" does not expose any such information. Timing attacks can be avoided by enforcing a consistent wait time on certain transactions.

Hardware/Software

IT asset management (ITAM) entails collecting inventory, financial, and contractual data to manage the IT asset throughout its life cycle. ITAM depends on robust processes, with tools to automate manual processes. Capturing and integrating auto discovery/inventory, financial, and contractual data in a central repository for all IT assets enables the functions to effectively manage vendors and a software and hardware asset portfolio from requisition through retirement, thus monitoring the asset's performance throughout its life cycle.

A vulnerable condition is required for a successful attack on unmanaged hardware/software. Unmanaged hardware/software assets are more likely to be vulnerable to attacks;

successful attacks on these assets often go undetected because no one is attending to them. The Hardware Asset Management (HWAM) capability is one of four capabilities that focus on device management. The other device management capabilities are

- Software Inventory Management (SWAM)
- Configuration Setting Management (CSM)
- Vulnerability (Patch) Management (VUL)

According to the "Continuous Diagnostics and Mitigation (CDM) Hardware Asset Management (HWAM) Capability" report published by the U.S. Department of Homeland Security:

> "The Hardware Asset Management capability addresses whether someone is assigned to manage the machine and whether the machine is authorized. It does not address how well the machine is managed. Quality of management is covered by Software Asset Management (SWAM), Configuration Setting Management (CSM), and Vulnerability Management (VUL). One reason unmanaged devices are more vulnerable is that no one is actively managing software installation, configuration settings, and vulnerabilities. This leaves the software on those devices with a higher risk of successful attack. If we do not know who is managing the device, we cannot send the responsible individual(s) data to identify problems with software installed (SWAM), configuration settings (CSM), and patching (VUL). In addition, we cannot hold anyone responsible for poor management of the device."[13]

For the purposes of Hardware Asset Management, a device is

- Any hardware asset that is addressable (i.e., has an IP address) and is connected to your organization's network(s). These devices and their peripherals are remotely attackable.
- Any USB device connected to a hardware asset that has an IP address. These devices are a vector to spread malware among devices.

This definition is used by FISMA and is documented on page 23 of the annual FISMA reporting instructions. Thus, not every "device" in a property inventory is included in the Hardware Asset Management definition of devices. For example, a monitor (not addressable, thus not included) can be attacked only through an addressable computer.[14]

According to the U.S. Department of Homeland Security report, the minimal Hardware Asset Management data recorded for desired state devices should include the following, as reproduced from the report in Table 2.4.[15]

TABLE 2.4 Minimal Hardware Asset Management Data to Be Recorded for Desired State

DATA ITEM	JUSTIFICATION
Expected CPE (vendor, product, version, release level) or equivalent	For reporting device types
	For supply chain management
	To know what CVEs may apply to these devices
Person or organization who is responsible for managing the hardware asset (Note: Such assignments should ensure that the designee is not assigned too many assets to effectively manage them)	To know who should fix specific risk conditions
	To assess the responsible individuals' risk management performance
Data necessary to link desired state inventory to actual state inventory	To be able to identify unauthorized and unmanaged devices
Data necessary to physically locate hardware assets	So managers can find the device to fix it
	To identify mobile devices so that extra controls can be assigned
The period of time the asset is authorized	To allow previously authorized devices to remain in the inventory, while knowing they are no longer authorized
Expected status of the device (active, inactive, stolen, missing, transferred, etc.)	To know which authorized devices are not likely to be found in actual inventory
Data necessary to physically identify the asset (such as property number or serial number)	To be able to validate that the remotely found device is actually this device, and not an imposter

Data

The definition of data management provided by the Data Management Association (DAMA) is: "Data management is the development, execution and supervision of plans, policies, programs, and practices that control, protect, deliver, and enhance the value of data and information assets."[16] The SSCP needs to be able to engage in data management activities in order to ensure the confidentiality, integrity, and availability of data.

Secure Information Storage

Laptops and other mobile devices are at significant risk of being lost or stolen. Sensitive mobile data may be encrypted at the file or folder level, or the entire disk may be encrypted. File/folder encryption is simpler and faster to implement but presents exposures if the operating system or user of the machine writes data to an unencrypted location. Full disk encryption protects the entire contents of a laptop's hard drive, including the boot sector, operating system, swap files, and user data. Since it does not rely on user discretion to determine what information to encrypt, it is typically the preferred method of protecting sensitive mobile data from unintended disclosure. There are some drawbacks; full disk encryption comes at the cost of a more complicated setup process that includes changes to the drive's boot sequence, and it may take hours during initial implementation to encrypt the hard drive (subsequently, new data are encrypted on the fly).

Typically, disk encryption products use software-generated symmetric keys to encrypt and decrypt the contents of the drive. Keys are stored locally and protected by a password or passphrase or other authentication mechanism that is invoked at boot time to provide access to the decryption key. Devices containing a TPM (Trusted Platform Module) chip contain a unique, secret RSA key burned into the chip during manufacture to securely generate derivative keys. Using hardware encryption in conjunction with software-based encryption products is a more secure approach to protecting highly sensitive mobile data. In addition, TPM chips provide additional security features such as platform authentication and remote attestation, a form of integrity protection that makes use of a hashed copy of hardware and software configuration to verify that configurations have not been altered.

Authentication may be integrated with a network directory service such as LDAP or Active Directory, or other external authentication service or two-factor authentication method such as smart cards, hardware tokens, and biometric devices.

Encrypted data can be irrevocably lost when a disk crashes or a user forgets his or her password, unless there is a mechanism in place to recover from such events. Some software allows for a master key or passphrase that can access the data without knowledge of the user password. Recovery disks containing backed-up data and boot information can be created during the initial installation; however, for ease of administration, it is best to combine disk encryption with a network-based backup solution.

Before implementing an encryption solution, care must be taken to thoroughly test all laptop software for compatibility, particularly software that interacts directly with operating system processes. Applications used for asset tracking, desktop intrusion prevention, patch management, and desktop administration may not be able to access encrypted information. If the organization uses other mobile devices such as PDAs, encryption software should support these devices as well for ease of integration, support, and maintenance.

Encryption is a relatively straightforward and cost-effective means of protecting mobile data, but it is not a silver bullet. Encryption keys are vulnerable to discovery during encryption/decryption operations while the key data are stored in system memory, and users may inadvertently or knowingly reveal the password to unlock the decryption key. Personal firewalls, antivirus software, and appropriate physical and personnel security are essential elements of an overall mobile data protection program.

Backup tapes lost or diverted during transport and offsite storage have been another source of security breaches. Backup tapes can be encrypted during the backup operation using software built into or integrated with your backup management solution. In many implementations, the server containing the backup software acts as a client to the key management server whose function is to create, store, manage, and distribute encryption keys. Special encrypting tape drives or libraries must be used to encrypt and decrypt the tapes. When implementing a backup tape encryption solution, you may need to update internal hardware as well as hardware specified in disaster recovery equipment schedules. Thorough planning and testing should be performed to ensure that data on encrypted backup tapes will be accessible when needed.

Data residing on a storage area network (SAN) can be encrypted at various levels. Both internal and external disk array controllers offer encryption capabilities. Alternatively, data may be encrypted on the host system or at the individual disk level, offering the possibility of encrypting individual files and directories. SAN encryption implementations typically make use of a key management server, a corresponding client, and an encryption processing device integrated into the SAN infrastructure.

In an enterprise environment, sensitive data is often stored in centralized databases for access by a variety of applications. Database encryption is used to protect these data from unauthorized access by human and software agents. Database encryption has the distinct advantage of protecting sensitive data from the eyes of even the most privileged system and database administrators (except, of course, those with access to the key management system). Encryption mechanisms may be built into the database management system itself, or those provided by third-party software compatible with the database and operating system platform may be employed. Database encryption may occur at the file, database, or column/field level. It is not necessary and, in fact, is detrimental to encrypt an entire database when only one data element is confidential. Database encryption solutions are available for most common database management systems. Implementing these solutions presents a number of challenges. When selecting a solution, the SSCP needs to understand how each addresses the following:

- **Database Size**—Encryption may increase the size of data elements in your database by padding smaller chunks of data to produce fixed block sizes. If the database is not sized to accommodate these changes, it may need to be altered.

- **Performance**—Performance degradation, particularly when encrypting indexed or frequently accessed fields, may be noticeable. If application performance is a concern, databases may need to be reorganized and re-indexed to accommodate the additional overhead of decrypting fields.

- **Application Compatibility**—While some newer, integrated encryption solutions provide transparent decryption services to applications, most communicate through APIs, which must be compiled into business applications that access encrypted data. A thorough inventory of such applications is needed to prevent unanticipated failures, and resources will be required to modify impacted applications.

Data Scrubbing

Wholesale replication of data from production to test is a common practice. Wholesale replication of security controls from production to test is not. There is a practical reason for this; if developers do not have access to accurate representations of data to work with, test results cannot be a reliable indicator of application performance in the production environment. Organizations that outsource development or testing are especially at risk of unauthorized access to sensitive production data because of difficulties in supervising and monitoring third-party account activity. One method of addressing this issue is to sanitize the data, that is, to mask, scramble, or overwrite sensitive data values with meaningless data, which nonetheless conforms to data format and size restrictions. Data sanitization is also known as scrubbing or de-identification. It is not to be confused with encryption, which implies that data can be decrypted and viewed in its original form. The goal of data sanitization is to obfuscate sensitive data in such a way that the actual data values cannot be deduced or derived from the sanitized data itself, or through inference by comparing the sanitized data values with values of other data elements (the so-called inferential disclosure). For example, if a sanitization routine transposes characters on a one-for-one basis, substituting Q for A and W for S, and so on, original values for each character of a data element may be easily guessed.

Merely replacing data with null values is not an effective way to sanitize data, as most developers require a fairly accurate representation of the actual data element to interpret test results. Masking replaces characters in specified fields with a mask character, such as an X; for example, the masked credit card number 0828 2295 2828 5447 may be represented as 0828 XXXX XXXX 5447. Since the values of particular fields (such as those containing card issuer details) may need to remain intact for adequate testing, masking data in this manner requires coordination with the development teams. Another sanitization technique is substitution, wherein certain field values are replaced with randomly generated values that have no relationship to the original value. An example is substituting salary information in a payroll database with values randomly selected from a table of salaries. This technique produces data that is true to the original format, but it may be difficult to generate and maintain tables containing the large variety and amount of random data needed to meet data sanitization requirements for large systems. Shuffling and other techniques that merely rearrange existing data—for example, reorganizing the salary column so that salaries are associated with different employees—are fast and efficient, but are effective only on large databases and do not address all the needs of de-identification, particularly if the operation is not entirely random.

One concern with applying data sanitization is the maintenance of referential integrity within the database or file system. That is, relationships between files and tables cannot be altered or broken when data are sanitized; for example, if an account number used as a primary key in one table is used as a foreign key in another table, the relationship will be broken if the account number is converted to different values in each table. Data sanitization solutions should thus allow the administrator to define all critical relationships during configuration so that consistent values are produced across database tables. Sanitization is typically a batch operation that is run when production data are copied or refreshed into the test environment. It should be performed by an administrator who is not part of the development group that maintains the test environment.

Data Deduplication

Modern storage area networks (SANs) offer the ability to deduplicate data. Deduplication is a process that scans the entire collection of information looking for similar chunks of data that can be consolidated. The security practitioner must understand the implications of deduplication on integrity and encryption. Since data deduplication involves the deletion of similar information in favor of a reference or pointer, the integrity of a file in storage may be modified. This means it may not be possible or very difficult to prove the file on the drive is the same file that was created prior to saving to the deduplicated drive. Most modern SANs offer a way to hash files for comparison before and after deduplication. However, this hashing often comes at a performance trade-off.

Because deduplication works on finding common areas of files, it should come as no surprise encryption works against deduplication. The same file encrypted with different keys by different users will not be deduplicated by the system and will take up possibly twice as much space as if the files were deduplicated. The security practitioner must work with system administrators and SAN experts to ensure the performance necessary for the system can be achieved with the security configuration required.

Managing Encryption Keys

Because encryption keys control access to sensitive data, the effectiveness of any encryption strategy hinges on an organization's ability to securely manage these keys. Key management refers to the set of systems and procedures used to securely generate, store, distribute, use, archive, revoke, and delete keys. Defining a key management policy that identifies roles, responsibilities, and security requirements is a critical yet often overlooked component of any successful encryption strategy. The key management policy and associated documentation should be part of the organization's overall systems security plan. Considerations for key management policy and for selecting and deploying an effective key management system include the following:

- **Roles and Responsibilities**—Responsibilities for generation, approval, and maintenance of the key management system and its associated processes should be clearly articulated in the policy document. The key management system access control mechanism must operate at sufficient level of granularity to support the policy, including any provisions for separation of duties or dual control required by the organization's security plan.

- **Key Generation and Storage**—Random number generators are used to generate keys. The key generation process should produce keys of the desired length and be sufficiently random and contain sufficient entropy so that keys cannot be easily guessed. Some systems generate entropy to seed keys by collecting timing data from random system events. The server used to generate and store keys may be a software application running on a standard server operating system or may be a purpose-built, hardened platform dedicated to key management. One advantage of using a purpose-built system is that common operating system vulnerabilities that might be exploited to compromise encryption keys can be avoided. Another is that key management roles can be separated from database and server administration roles, reducing the risk of data compromised by privileged administrator accounts. The keys themselves, key control material (such as the unique key identifier or GUID created during key generation that uniquely identifies the key within a particular name space), and key server event logs must be protected from unauthorized access.

- **Distribution**—The key distribution center or facility should be capable of authenticating and checking authorization for key requests. The authentication mechanism should be sufficiently robust and protected from compromise. The client should have an integrity mechanism to validate the authenticity of the issuer and proper format of the keying material before accepting a key and to verify receipt once the key has been accepted.

- **Expiration**—Encryption keys are assigned a cryptoperiod, or time span in which they are authorized for use. In general, shorter cryptoperiods are more secure but create logistical issues for rekeying and updating keys, especially for enterprise applications in which the cost of rekeying and re-encrypting large amounts of data can be prohibitively high. Typically, keys generated to secure stored data have longer cryptoperiods than those used to secure communications. Strong keys combined with other forms of access control can compensate for longer cryptoperiods.

- **Revocation and Destruction**—The key management system should support timely revocation of expired and compromised keys and secure destruction of key material that is no longer valid.

- **Audit and Tracking**—All key management operations should be fully audited, and event logs or audit records should be protected from unauthorized access and modification. Facilities must be available to track keying material throughout its life cycle and should include mechanisms to detect and report on key compromise. Key labeling may be used to identify attributes of keys such as its identity, cryptoperiod, key type, and the like; labels should be stored with the key for identification purposes.

- **Emergency Management**—The key management policy should specify the requirements for emergency replacement and revocation of encryption keys. Availability should be protected by storing backup or archive copies of keys in a separate location. The appropriate disaster recovery procedures must be created to address both key recovery and recovery of the key management system itself.

Information Rights Management (IRM)

IRM functions to assign specific properties to an object such as how long the object may exist, what users or systems may access it, and if any notifications need to occur when the file is opened, modified, or printed. IRM works extremely well in organizations where IRM is deployed wildly and users understand how to configure the restrictions of IRM when sharing information. When information is sent outside of the organization, IRM can start to fall apart. For example, if a document is marked in the IRM system so only Bob can print it, within the organization and the systems supporting the IRM, only Bob can print the file. However, if Bob sends the file to Julie who doesn't have the IRM software on her computer, the file may either not open or open and not enforce the IRM restrictions.

Secure Output

Many print processing functions send output to printers in the form of print spooler files, which contain human-readable copies of data to be printed. Securing spooled files is necessary to preserving confidentiality. One way to accomplish this would be to direct certain sensitive output to a secure document or print server for processing. If this is not possible, you should limit the number of individuals who have print operator authority or who are otherwise able to view, redirect, or manage output files and control functions. Printers receiving sensitive output should be located in secured areas or, in some cases, in individual offices. Users should be instructed to monitor their print jobs and pick up their output as soon as it is produced. Some printers support authentication for jobs.

Some printers support encrypted file transfer and storage, which should be considered for highly sensitive documents.

Data Retention and Disposal

A record retention policy and schedule (list of records, owners, retention periods, and destruction methods) is an important component of an organization's information handling procedures. Information owners are responsible for designating retention periods and assigning custodial duties, typically in IT, to ensure that record integrity is preserved for the specified retention period. Audits may be performed to ensure policy compliance. Many organizations use a commercial document management system to organize and automate aspects of their record retention policy.

Handling procedures for confidential information must include provisions for secure destruction of records containing sensitive information. For private industry in the United States, such procedures may be required by U.S. privacy regulations such as the Fair and Accurate Credit Transactions Act of 2003 (FACTA), HIPAA, and GLBA. Additional mandates apply to government entities and contractors working with national interest information. Records destruction should be authorized, appropriate to the level of sensitivity of the record, secure, timely, and documented. The goal of secure destruction is to assure the appropriate sanitization of sensitive information so that it is no longer legible and so that insufficient data remains to be pieced together to derive protected data elements. Secure destruction methods are designed to combat the problem of data remanence, which is generally used to refer to the information left in a record or file after the original data has been deleted, or moved to another location. Secure destruction methods include burning, shredding, disk cleaning or reformatting, and tape degaussing.

Due to environmental concerns, it is often not considered appropriate to burn paper records or disks. Instead, paper documents and CD/DVD media should be shredded using special equipment designed for this purpose. Paper shredders typically cut documents into thin strips or small fragments. They come in a variety of capacities, from personal shredders to industrial-strength models. Several types of shredders are available, such as the following:[17]

- **Strip-cut shredders**—Cut paper in long, thin strips.
- **Cross-cut shredders**—Preferable to strip-cut, these cut paper into small rectangular fragments.
- **Particle-cut shredders**—Similar to cross-cut; create tiny square or circular fragments.
- **Hammermills**—Pound paper through a screen.
- **Granulators (or Disintegrators)**—Repeatedly cut paper into fine, mesh-size particles.

Shredding services can be contracted to process large volumes of information, either onsite using mobile equipment or at a specially designed facility. Depending on the application, such companies may require a security clearance and may be suitable only for some classification levels. For typical applications, such clearance may not be necessary, but it is wise to request a certificate of destruction, which most companies will supply on request.

Magnetic media, including diskettes, CD/DVDs, disk drives, and tapes, may be destroyed using a number of methods. Often, however, these methods are not environmentally friendly, require excessive manual effort, and are not suitable for high-volume enterprise application. CD/DVD shredders are available at nominal cost and are practical for small business units. Fixed disk shredders are also available, but they are mainly geared to the consumer market and may not produce consistent results with data in disparate formats. When disk shredders are used, they should produce fragments that contain less than one (512Kb) block of data. Many organizations may wish to preserve the media for reuse or redeployment to another location. For example, many organizations donate used PCs to schools or charitable organizations. Even when media is redeployed within an organization, care should be taken to remove sensitive information before the media is reused.

Cleaning/Sanitizing

Methods of destroying data contained on magnetic media include various techniques for clearing or sanitizing data. Clearing refers to any operation that removes or obscures stored data such that it cannot be reconstructed using operating system or third-party utilities. Sanitizing or purging removes data in such a way that it cannot be reconstructed at all. While disk clearing may be acceptable protection against accidental or random disclosure, it is not adequate to prevent someone with intent and commonly available tools from restoring data.

Cloud service providers should support eradication of data when deleted. Ensure when selecting a cloud provider that the provider can support overwriting and scrubbing information from the shared infrastructure when a deletion occurs.

Erasure or Reformatting

Conventional magnetic recording heads do not operate at sufficient density to totally erase the contents of disk and tape; therefore, merely erasing or reformatting magnetic media using conventional drives will not eliminate all the stored information. Furthermore, most operating system file management utilities do not delete the data itself but instead remove the entry in the system directory or address table so that it cannot be immediately accessed. The data itself will typically remain on disk until the sector it occupies is overwritten with new data. Metadata, or schema information, usually remains intact as well. Even when metadata is erased or overwritten, forensic software that performs direct reads on the disk sectors is available to retrieve the information.

Formatting, repartitioning, or reimaging a disk drive is only slightly more secure than erasing the data. Modern disk drives cannot be reformatted by older, low-level methods that skew sector or track numbers or interleave sectors, as certain data are necessary for the servo mechanism in the drive to locate a desired track. Instead, many reformatting utilities (such as the UNIX dd utility) write a zero byte to each sector on the disk (also known as zero filling) in a single pass. High-level reformatting methods operate by creating a file system on disk and installing a boot sector. Although space is marked as available on disk and data appears to be erased, data is not actually deleted or overwritten in the reformatting process.

Disk Wiping/Overwriting

Disk wiping or overwriting is a method of writing over existing data—typically with a stream of zeroes, ones, or a random pattern of both. Special procedures may be required, such as using certain combinations of patterns or making a certain number of passes over the disk, each time writing a different pattern. Overwriting is acceptable for clearing media for reuse but is not a sufficient method of sanitizing disk or tape. Overwriting before reformatting is a much more effective technique than reformatting alone and can be a suitable means of clearing less sensitive content from disk.

Degaussing

Degaussing is a technique of erasing data on disk or tape (including video tapes) that, when performed properly, ensures that there is insufficient magnetic remanence to reconstruct data. This is performed with a machine called a degausser, which applies a magnetic field to the media and then removes it, eliminating the residual magnetic signals on the media. Media can be classified in terms of coercivity, or the intensity of the magnetic energy a disk or tape can store, measured in a unit called Oersteds. To perform properly, the degausser must be capable of creating a magnetic field with two to three times the intensity of the capacity of the media. Magnetic tape may be classified by coercivity as type I, II, or III, and must be degaussed with a machine rated for the type of tape employed.

Degaussers may be operated manually or be automatic using a conveyor belt assembly. Because of the strength of the magnetic field generated, not all media can be successfully degaussed without destroying the information needed by the servo mechanism used to read the disk or tape, which would render the media unusable. This is particularly true of some disk and tape cartridges used in midrange and mainframe systems. Therefore, the manufacturer's specifications should be consulted before planning a degaussing strategy.

The U.S. NIST SP 800-88 provides a matrix (reproduced in Table 2.5) for determining requirements for clearing and sanitizing media at various levels.[18]

TABLE 2.5 NIST SP 800-88 Matrix for Determining Requirements for Clearing and Sanitizing Media at Various Levels

CATEGORY	SUBCATEGORY	CRR REFERENCE	RMM REFERENCE	INFORMATIVE REFERENCES
Asset Management (AM): The data, personnel, devices, systems, and facilities that enable the organization to achieve business purposes are identified and managed consistent with their relative importance to business objectives and the organization's risk strategy.	**ID.AM-1:** Physical devices and systems within the organization are inventoried.	AM:G2.Q1 (Technology)	ADM:SG1.SP1	• CCS CSC 1 • COBIT 5 BAI03.04, BAI09.01, BAI09.02, BAI09.05 • ISA 62443-2-1:2009 4.2.3.4 • ISA 62443-3-3:2013 SR 7.8 • ISO/IEC 27001:2013 A.8.1.1, A.8.1.2 • NIST SP 800-53 Rev. 4 CM-8
	ID.AM-2: Software platforms and applications within the organization are inventoried.	AM:G2.Q1 (Technology)	ADM:SG1.SP1	• CCS CSC 2 • COBIT 5 BAI03.04, BAI09.01, BAI09.02, BAI09.05 • ISA 62443-2-1:2009 4.2.3.4 • ISA 62443-3-3:2013 SR 7.8 • ISO/IEC 27001:2013 A.8.1.1, A.8.1.2 • NIST SP 800-53 Rev. 4 CM-8
	ID.AM-3: Organizational communication and data flows are mapped.	AM:G2.Q2	ADM:SG1.SP2	• CCS CSC 1 • COBIT 5 DSS05.02 • ISA 62443-2-1:2009 4.2.3.4 • ISO/IEC 27001:2013 A.13.2.1 • NIST SP 800-53 Rev. 4 AC-4, CA-3, CA-9

CATEGORY	SUBCATEGORY	CRR REFERENCE	RMM REFERENCE	INFORMATIVE REFERENCES
	ID.AM-4: External information systems are catalogued.	AM:G2.Q1 (Technology)	ADM:SG1.SP1	• COBIT 5 APO02.02• ISO/IEC 27001:2013 A.11.2.6• NIST SP 500-291 3, 4• NIST SP 800-53 Rev. 4 AC-20, SA-9
	ID.AM-5: Resources (e.g., hardware, devices, data, and software) are prioritized based on their classification, criticality, and business value.	AM:G1.Q4	ADM:SG2.SP1	• COBIT 5 APO03.03, APO03.04, BAI09.02• ISA 62443-2-1:2009 4.2.3.6• ISO/IEC 27001:2013 A.8.2.1• NIST SP 800-34 Rev. 1IDENTIFY(ID)• NIST SP 800-53 Rev. 4 CP-2, RA-2, SA-14
	ID.AM-6: Cybersecurity roles and responsibilities for the entire workforce and third-party stakeholders (e.g., suppliers, customers, partners) are established.	AM:MIL2.Q3	ADM:GG2.GP7	• COBIT 5 APO01.02, DSS06.03• ISA 62443-2-1:2009 4.3.2.3.3• ISO/IEC 27001:2013 A.6.1.1• NIST SP 800-53 Rev. 4 CP-2, PM-11

DISCLOSURE CONTROLS:
DATA LEAKAGE PREVENTION

Various implementations of DLP systems exist; the two most common are those that protect transfer of sensitive data to mobile storage devices such as USB keys and smartphones and those that prevent data leakage via web and e-mail at an organization's Internet gateway. Less prevalent are those solutions that tackle confidentiality of data at rest in files, databases, and mass storage facilities. An effective data leakage prevention strategy includes use of both host- and network-based components that perform the following functions:

- **Data Discovery**—The process of "crawling" distributed files and databases to locate sensitive data is the first step in implementing data leakage prevention tools. The discovery process has intrinsic value, even without implementing loss prevention tools, in that organizations can use it to pinpoint exactly where their sensitive data are stored and design additional safeguards, such as policies and access control mechanisms, to protect the data. One may uncover, for example, cases where users run queries over sensitive data that are stored in a secured database and then save the results to their desktops or to an unsecured public file, where access control safeguards may be weaker. Note—This violates the "*" property of the Bell–LaPadula model!

- **Labeling**—Data may be labeled or "tagged" with an identifier that can be used to subsequently monitor movement of that data across the network. This is particularly useful in identifying documents and files containing sensitive information. Labels used may correspond to the sensitivity levels defined in the organization's information classification policy or may identify specific types of data such as PHI (Private Health Information).

- **Policy Creation**—Content monitoring and usage policies specify which data is sensitive and define rules for copying or transmitting that data, typically using a combination of predefined labels, keywords, and regular expressions (e.g., nnn-nn-nnnn to identify a social security number) to identify unique data elements.

- **Content Detection/Monitoring**—Data communications over local and wide area networks, data traversing perimeter gateway devices, and data leaving host computers via USB or serial connections are monitored by inspecting the contents of the communication at the file, document, and packet levels. At the network layer, packet-level monitoring can be used to identify and intercept transmission of sensitive data through FTP, SSL, and posting to blogs and chat rooms among other things. Documents transferred as attachments to e-mail and instant messages can also be monitored and blocked at gateways if they contain sensitive content. To identify data transferred to removable storage, software agents are typically employed on target machines to monitor traffic over USB, wireless, and FireWire ports.

- **Prevention or Blocking**—When policy violations are detected, user actions may be prevented or network traffic may be dropped, depending on the location of the violation. Alternatively, encryption may be enforced before a write operation to CD, USB, or other removable media.

- **Reporting**—Violations of data disclosure policies are reported, typically showing the policy that was violated, the source IP address, and the login account under which the violation occurred.

Regardless of the method used to detect and prevent data leakage, it should be supplemented with traditional safeguards such as physical and logical access controls, encryption, and auditing. It must also be kept current to accommodate changes in applications, business processes and relationships, and infrastructure.

Technical Controls

Technical controls are security controls that the computer system executes. The controls can provide automated protection from unauthorized access or misuse, facilitate detection of security violations, and support security requirements for applications and data. The implementation of technical controls, however, always requires significant operational considerations and should be consistent with the management of security within the organization.

Some of the technical controls that the SSCP may encounter in the organization can be identified by category. The following sections explore these categories.[19]

Identification and Authentication

Regardless of who accesses the system, the SSCP should discuss the identification and authentication security controls that are used to protect the system. These include the following:

- The system's user authentication control mechanisms along with the processes used to control changes to those mechanisms should be detailed.

- If passwords are to be used as a control element in a system, the minimum and maximum values for password length should be provided.

- If passwords are to be used as a control element in a system, the character sets to be used for password creation should be provided.

- If passwords are to be used as a control element in a system, the procedures for password changes of a voluntary nature should be provided.

- If passwords are to be used as a control element in a system, the procedures for password resets due to compromise should be provided.

- The mechanisms used to create accountability, audit trails, and the protection of the authentication process should be described.

- All policies that allow for the bypassing of the authentication system along with the controls used should be detailed.

- The number of invalid access attempts to be allowed and the actions taken when that limit is exceeded should be described.

- The procedures for key generation, distribution, storage, entry, use, archiving, and disposal should be detailed.

- How biometric and token controls are to be used and implemented should be described.

Logical Access Controls

Logical access controls authorize or restrict the activities of users. This discussion includes hardware and software features that permit only authorized access to the system, restrict users to authorized functions and actions, and detect unauthorized activities. These include the following:

- How access rights and privileges are granted

- Temporal restrictions used to prevent system access outside of allowable work periods

- Mechanisms used to detect unauthorized transaction attempts by authorized and/ or unauthorized users

- Inactivity timeout periods for system lockout

- Whether or not encryption is used to prevent access to sensitive files

- How separation of duties is enforced

- How often ACLs are reviewed

- Controls that regulate how users may delegate access permissions or make copies of files or information accessible to other users

Public Access Controls

If the general public accesses the system, the following should be described or detailed:

- Information classification schemes.

- What form(s) of identification and authentication will be acceptable?

- Controls to be used to limit what the user can read, write, modify, or delete.
- Will copies of information for public access be made available on a separate system?
- How will audit trails and user confidentiality be managed?
- What are the requirements for system and data availability?

Audit Trails

Regardless of who is able to access the system, the SSCP should be able to describe the additional security controls used to protect the system's integrity:

- What is the process to review audit trails? How often are they reviewed? By whom? Under what conditions?
- Does the audit trail support accountability by providing a trace of user actions?
- Are there mechanisms in place to safeguard individual user privacy and confidentiality of user information (PII) captured as part of the audit trail?
- Are audit trails designed and implemented to record appropriate information that can assist in intrusion detection and remediation?
- Is separation of duties between those who administer the access control function and those who administer the audit trail used and enforced?

Operational Controls

Operational control policies address process-based security controls that are implemented and executed by people. Examples of operational controls may include the following:

- Change management processes
- Configuration management processes
- Authorization processes

Managerial Controls

Management controls address security topics that can be characterized as managerial. They are techniques and concerns that are normally addressed by management in the organization's computer security program. In general, they focus on the management of the computer security program and the management of risk within the organization.

Security policies are formal, written documents that set the expectations for how security will be implemented and managed in an organization. Security policies may be specific, setting forth the rules or expectations for administering or managing one aspect of the security program or a particular type of technology, or they may be more general, defining the types of practices the organization will adopt to safeguard information systems assets. Policies are relatively static and typically do not reference specific technology platforms or protocols. Because of this, policies remain current in the face of technical changes. Examples of general security policies are security program policies, which set forth the operating principles of the security program, and acceptable usage policies, which prescribe the authorized uses of information systems assets. General policies, especially those governing acceptable usage of e-mail, Internet, and other assets, may require employee signatures indicating that they have read, understood the policy, and agree to comply with it.

Subject-specific security policies typically address a limited area of risk related to a particular class of assets, type of technology, or business function. Examples of specific security policies include

- E-Mail and Internet Usage Policies
- Antivirus Policy
- Remote Access Policy
- Information Classification Policy
- Encryption Policies

Policy Document Format

The security practitioner should understand the basic elements of an information security policy that defines and enforces the organization's security practices. Typical policy elements include

- **Objective**—This statement provides the policy's context. It gives background information and states the purpose for writing the policy, including the risk or threat the policy addresses and the benefits to be achieved by policy adherence.
- **Policy Statement**—A succinct statement of management's expectations for what must be done to meet policy objectives.
- **Applicability**—This lists the people to whom the policy applies, the situations in which it applies, and any specific conditions under which the policy is to be in effect.
- **Enforcement**—How compliance with the policy will be enforced using technical and administrative means. This includes consequences for noncompliance.

- **Roles and Responsibilities**—States who is responsible for reviewing and approving, monitoring compliance, enforcing, and adhering to the policy.

- **Review**—Specifies a frequency of review, or the next review date on which the policy will be assessed for currency and updated if needed.

To be effective, security policies must be endorsed by senior management, communicated to all affected parties, and enforced throughout the organization. When policy violations occur, disciplinary action commensurate with the nature of the offense must be taken quickly and consistently.

Policy Life Cycle

Security policies are living documents that communicate management expectations for behavior. Policy development begins with determining the need. The need for a policy may arise due to a regulatory obligation, in response to an operational risk, or a desire to enforce a particular set of behaviors that facilitate a safe, productive work environment. Impacted parties, such as human resources, legal, audit, and business line management, should be identified so that they can participate throughout the development process. Once the need is determined and the team assembled, the security practitioner should address the following areas:

- **State the Objective**—A clear statement of policy objectives answers the question, "Why are we developing this policy?" The statement of objective will guide development of the specific points in the policy statement and will help keep team discussions in scope and focused.

- **Draft the Policy Specifics**—The policy statement should be drafted in simple, clear language that will be easily understood by those who must comply with the policy. Avoid vague statements that could be open to multiple interpretations, and be sure to define all technical terms used in the policy document.

- **Identify Methods for Measurement and Enforcement**—Policy enforcement mechanisms may include technical controls such as access management systems, content blocking, and other preventive measures as well as administrative controls such as management oversight and supervision. Compliance with policy expectations can be measured through audit trails, automated monitoring systems, random or routine audits, or management supervision. The means of monitoring or measuring compliance should be clearly understood, as well as the logistics of enforcement. The logistics of taking and documenting disciplinary action should be established at this time to ensure that the organization is willing and able to enforce policy and prepared to apply corrective action quickly and consistently.

- **Communication**—The timing, frequency, and mechanism by which the policy will be communicated to employees and others should be established before final policy approval. Expectations must be clearly communicated and regularly enforced so that everyone remains apprised of what the appropriate conduct is considered to be. Whenever disciplinary action may be taken in response to policy violations, it is especially important that management make every effort to ensure that employees are made aware of the policy and what they must do to comply. Some organizations require employees to sign a form acknowledging their receipt and understanding of key policies and agreeing to comply with expectations.

- **Periodic Review**—Policies should be reviewed at least annually to ensure that they continue to reflect management's expectations, current legal and regulatory obligations, and any changes to the organization's operations. Policy violations that have occurred since the last review should be analyzed to determine whether adjustments to policy or associated procedures or enhancements to communication and enforcement mechanisms may be needed.

Standards and Guidelines

A standard is a formal, documented requirement that sets uniform criteria for a specific technology, configuration, nomenclature, or method. Standards that are followed as common practice but are not formally documented or enforced are so-called de facto standards; such standards often become formalized as an organization matures. Some examples of security standards include account naming conventions, desktop and server antivirus settings, encryption key lengths, and router ACL (access control list) configurations. Standards provide a basis for measuring technical and operational safeguards for accuracy and consistency. A *baseline* is a detailed configuration standard that includes specific security settings. Baselines can be used as a checklist for configuring security parameters and for measurement and comparison of current systems to a standard configuration set.

Guidelines, on the other hand, are recommended practices to be followed to achieve a desired result. They are not mandatory and provide room for flexibility in how they are interpreted and implemented; therefore, they are rarely enforced except through an organization's culture and norms. Guidelines are often instructional in nature. They are useful for cases where an organization wishes to provide enough structure to achieve an acceptable level of performance while allowing room for innovation and individual discretion. Some examples of security guidelines include methods for selecting a strong password, criteria for evaluating new security technology, and suggested training curricula for security staff.

Standards, baselines, procedures, and, to a lesser extent, guidelines help organizations maintain consistency in the way security risks are addressed and thus provide assurance that a desirable level of security will be maintained. For example, a desktop antivirus standard might specify that all desktops be maintained at the current version of software, configured to receive automatic updates, and set to scan all executable files and templates whenever a file is opened or modified. By consistently applying the same criteria across the board, all desktops are equally protected from virus threats, and this can be assured through periodic scanning or auditing. In addition, unlike guidelines, standards specify repeatable configurations. This enhances productivity by allowing practitioners to develop reusable templates that can be applied quickly and easily either manually or through automated configuration management tools. Similarly, programmers can create standard security logic for functions such as login sequences, input validation, and authority checks, and store this logic in a central repository as reusable components that can be compiled into new business applications. This saves time and effort, reduces errors, and ensures enforcement of application security rules during the development life cycle.

Standards differ from policies in that they are typically more technical in nature, are more limited in scope and impact, do not require approval from executive management, and are more likely than policies to change over time. Standards are often developed to implement the details of a particular policy. Because of their more detailed technical nature, security practitioners responsible for administering security systems, applications, and network components typically play a more active role in the development of standards than in policy development, which largely occurs at management levels in an organization. Many organizations have formal standards and procedures review committees composed of IT practitioners, whose role is to assist in the development of standards documents; review documents for clarity, accuracy, and completeness; identify impacts; and often implement approved standards.

A baseline is a special type of standard that specifies the minimum set of security controls that must be applied to a particular system or practice area in order to achieve an acceptable level of assurance. Baselines may be derived from best practices frameworks and further developed according to your organization's unique needs. They are often documented in the form of checklists that can be used by teams to specify the minimum security requirements for new and enhanced systems.

Standards should be reviewed at specified intervals, at a minimum annually, to ensure they remain current. Standards must often be modified in response to:

- Introduction of new technology
- Addition of configurable features to a system
- Change in business operations
- Need for additional controls in response to new threats or vulnerabilities

External to the organization, the term *standards* is used in two special contexts: *industry standards* and *open standards*. Industry standards are generally accepted formats, protocols, or practices developed within the framework of a specific industrial segment, such as engineering, computer programming, or telecommunications. Industry standards may be developed by leading manufacturers, such as IBM's ISA (Industry Standard Architecture) PC bus standard, for use in its equipment and compatible equipment developed by other vendors. They may also be developed by special-interest groups such as the Institute of Electrical and Electronic Engineers (IEEE), American National Standards Institute (ANSI), or International Telecommunications Union (ITU). Industry standards are not always formally developed and accepted but may be so widely adopted by organizations across industries that they become necessary for the industry to incorporate them in products and services in order to serve their customers' needs. Examples of these de facto industry standards include the PCL print control language developed by Hewlett-Packard and the Postscript laser printer page description language developed by Adobe.

In contrast to industry standards, open standards are specifications that are developed by standards bodies or consortia and made available for public use without restrictions. They are designed to promote free competition, portability, and interoperability among different implementations. The standards themselves are platform independent and are published as source code or as a set of detailed specification documents that can be used to develop new products and services that can be integrated into existing, standards-based products.

Development of open standards follows due process and is a collaborative venture. Typically, an expert committee or working group develops a draft and publishes it for peer review and open comment before formalizing the results in a standards document. Some bodies such as the Internet Engineering Task Force (IETF) produce documents called RFCs (Requests for Comment) for this purpose. Formal approval completes the process of codifying a standard for final publication. The Internet and many of its protocols and services are based on open standards. For example, TCP/IP (Transmission Control Protocol/Internet Protocol) is an open standard that is implemented in every operating system and network device. Just imagine what would happen if vendors decided to implement their own version of TCP/IP—the Internet would simply cease to function.

Organizations choosing to adopt open standards find that they are not as locked in to specific vendor solutions and proprietary interoperability requirements and may be able to streamline their approach to securing and managing distributed systems. Open standards allow such organizations to adopt a "best-of-breed" strategy when selecting security and other technologies—that is, where individual solutions are selected for depth of functionality and ability to meet most requirements—rather than a uniform, single-vendor strategy that may be comprehensive yet not provide all the functionality desired in individual components. When all components of a security system are implemented according to open standards, they can work together without cumbersome manual intervention to provide a comprehensive security solution.

Note that the term "open standards" should never be confused with open source. Open source is software that is freely distributed and available for modification and use at little or no cost. To be considered open source, software must be distributed in source code and compiled form; must allow for derivative works; must not discriminate against any person, group, or use; and must not be tied to any specific product or restrict distribution of any associated software with the license. Licensing is covered by public agreement, which typically includes "copyleft" provisions requiring that any derived works be redistributed to the community as open source. A popular example of open source licensing is the GPL (Gnu Public License).

While many organizations have begun to adopt open source, others are more cautious. Some drawbacks to using open source are lack of vendor support, incompatibility with proprietary platforms, and inability to protect the organization's intellectual property rights to systems built on open source. Because of these limitations, many organizations prefer to limit their use of open source to noncritical systems.

Procedures

Procedures are step-by-step instructions for performing a specific task or set of tasks. Like standards, procedures are often implemented to enforce policies or meet quality goals. Despite the fact that writing documentation can be one of a technical person's least favorite activities, the importance of documenting security procedures cannot be overemphasized. When followed as written, procedures ensure consistent and repeatable results, provide instruction to those who are unfamiliar with how to perform a specific process, and provide assurance for management and auditors that policies are being enforced in practice. In addition, clear procedures often allow organizations to delegate routine functions to entry-level staff, or develop programs to automate these functions, freeing up more experienced practitioners to perform higher-level work. For example, account provisioning software has been implemented in many organizations to automate procedures that contain multiple steps such as establishing login credentials, home directories, assigning users to groups and roles, and the like. This software can be used by junior staff who lack the depth of knowledge and understanding of the systems configuration behind these procedures. Organizations justify the cost based on savings in salaries, an ability to free up senior staff to perform more complex activities, improvements in consistency and quality by reducing human error, and eliminating the manual effort needed to create an audit trail of account management activity.

When developing procedures, the security practitioner should not take the reader's level of knowledge or skill for granted; instead, each step in the process should be explained in sufficient detail for someone who is unfamiliar with the process to be able to perform it independently. All technical terms should be defined, and acronyms should be spelled out. A procedure, like a good novel, has a beginning, middle, and an end. Typical components of a procedure are

- **Purpose**—The reason for performing the procedure, usually the desired outcome.
- **Applicability**—Who is responsible for following the procedure, and in what circumstances the procedure is followed.
- **Steps**—The detailed steps taken to perform the procedure.
- **Figures**—Illustrations, diagrams, or tables used to depict a workflow, values to enter in specific fields, or display screen shots to show formats and to enhance ease of use.
- **Decision Points**—Yes/no questions whose answers result in branching to different steps in the procedure. These may be written as steps in the procedure or included in a workflow diagram or decision tree.

✔ Try It for Yourself: Security Operations Exercise

This exercise will have you create a policy, standard, and procedure for passwords.

Setup

The organization has no consistent password methodology, approach, or standard configuration. The security practitioner researches best practices and discovers the best password strategy for her organization is a complex passphrase of 16 to 32 characters with at least two numbers, one special character, and one uppercase letter.

As the security practitioner, you must create the following:

- A policy explaining the organization's position on passwords
- A standard explaining the minimum specifications for creating a password and password lifecycle considerations
- A procedure explaining common password-related processes

Solutions

Policy

Organizational Password Policy

February 2, 2015

TO: All organizational information system users

FROM: Chief Information Officer

SUBJECT: Organizational Password Policy No 11032014

Information security is a shared responsibility. A single risk assumed by one is a risk assumed by all; therefore it is important we practice strong information assurance practices in creating and using passwords. Effective immediately, the organizational chief information security officer is authorized to establish the minimum standards and procedures for the creation and maintenance of secure passwords throughout the organization. All organizational users will adhere to the standards and procedures put forth by the CISO and furthermore may be subject to disciplinary action should violations of this policy or associated standards or procedures occur.

Sincerely,

Organizational CIO

Standard

Organizational Password Standard

Effective immediately, all organizational passwords shall conform to the following minimal standards:

> **Length:** 16–32 characters.
>
> **Complexity:** Two numeric digits, one upper-case digit, no dictionary words, no names, and no repeating numbers.
>
> **Reuse:** Passwords may not be reused within the past 10 passwords.
>
> **Expiration:** Passwords shall expire no longer than 30 days after initial creation.
>
> **Storage:** Passwords may only be stored in approved electronic vaults. Writing down passwords is not permissible.

CONTINUES

Procedures

Setting a Password

Users will be issued an initial password by the help desk after validation of the user's ID has taken place. Upon receipt of the temporary password, the user will need to

1. Log in to an authorized organizational system.
2. Acknowledge the prompt to create a new password.
3. Enter a new password consistent with the organizational password policy.
4. Re-enter the new password to confirm.
5. Click OK to accept the new password.
6. Enter the new password in an approved electronic vault if desired.

The development of policies, standards, and processes is a daily occurrence for the security practitioner. Policies should be created with high-level organizational support and be written to last year's if possible. Policies should direct users to standards and procedures. Standards and procedures should be written as specifically as possible and reference their parent policy when necessary. The role involved in keeping the standards and procedures updated must ensure the updates remain consistent with the policy and the technology environment of the organization.

Implementation and Release Management

Release management is a software engineering discipline that controls the release of applications, updates, and patches to the production environment. The goal of release management is to provide assurance that only tested and approved application code is promoted to production or distributed for use. Release management also seeks to meet timeliness goals, minimize disruption to users during releases, and ensure that all associated communication and documentation is issued with new releases of software. The most important role is that of the release manager. The release manager is responsible for planning, coordination, implementation, and communication of all application releases. This function may be situated within a unit of a quality assurance or operational group or may be part of a separate organization responsible for overall change and configuration management. The decision of where to locate release management functions should be based on the need to achieve separation of duties and rigorous process oversight during application installation or distribution and ongoing maintenance. This is essential to mitigate risks and impacts of unplanned and malicious changes, which could introduce new vulnerabilities into the production environment or user community.

Release management policy specifies the conditions that must be met for an application or component to be released to production, roles and responsibilities for packaging, approving, moving, and testing code releases, and approval and documentation requirements.

The release management process actually begins with the QA testing environment. It is important to ensure that any defects found and corrected in QA are incorporated back into the system test environment, or previously corrected bugs may resurface. An organization may have separate user acceptance and preproduction or staging environments that are subject to release management before code is released to production. Typically the configuration and movement of objects into these environments are controlled by the release management team. Once user acceptance testing is complete, the application is packaged for deployment to the production or preproduction environment, and the final package is verified. Automated build tools are typically used to ensure that the right versions of source code are retrieved from the repository and compiled into the application. In organizations that use automated deployment tools, builds are packaged together with automated installers (such as Windows MSI service for desktop operating systems) and other necessary components such as XML configuration and application policy files.

To ensure integrity of the source code or application package and to protect production libraries from the release of unauthorized code, applications may be hashed and signed with a digital signature created with a public key algorithm. *Code signing*, which is typically used for web applications such as those based on Java and ActiveX to assist users in validating that the application was issued by a trusted source, also has an application in release management. For example, Sun provides a jarsigner tool for Java JAR (Java Archive) and EAR (Enterprise Archive) files that allows an authorized holder of a private key to sign individual JAR files, record signed entries into a file called a manifest, and convert the manifest into a signature file containing the digest of the entire manifest. This prevents any modifications to the archive file once it has been approved and signed. The public key used to verify the signature is packaged along with the archive file so that the person responsible for deploying the file can verify the integrity of the release, also using the jarsigner tool.

Release management tools aid in automating application deployments and enforcing an organization's release policy. Such features include role-based access control to enforce separation of duties; approval checking and rejection of unapproved packages; component verification tools to ensure that all required application components, documentation, etc., are included in the release; rollback and demotion facilities to protect against incomplete deployments; and auditing and reporting tools to track all aspects of the release process. Automated tools may also be capable of verifying integrity by interrogating a digital signature.

Applications deployed into preproduction or production environments may be smoke tested as part of the release process. Smoke testing is high-level, scripted testing of the major application components and interfaces to validate the integrity of the application before making it publicly available.

The release manager ensures that all documentation and communication regarding the release are prepared and distributed before going "live" with a new or modified application. Any planned outages or other impacts should be communicated in advance, and contacts for assistance with the application should be made available. Following the release, a "burn in" period may be instituted in which special problem resolution and support procedures are in effect.

Release management policy is typically enforced through access control mechanisms that prevent developers from modifying production programs and data. Sensitive system utilities should reside in their own libraries and should be executed only by authorized personnel and processes. Utility programs such as compilers and assemblers should never be executed in production environments.

Systems Assurance and Controls Validation

Systems assurance is the process of validating that existing security controls are configured and functioning as expected, both during initial implementation and on an ongoing basis. Security controls should never be assumed to be functioning as intended. Human error, design issues, component failures, and unknown dependencies and vulnerabilities can impact the initial configuration of security controls. Even once properly implemented, controls can lose effectiveness over time. Changes in the control environment itself, in the infrastructure that supports the control, in the systems that the control was designed to protect, or in the nature of threats that seek to bypass controls all contribute to reduced control effectiveness. Even in the absence of known changes, a "set it and forget it" mentality can expose an organization to risk. Therefore, controls should be tested on a periodic basis against a set of security requirements.

Change Control and Management

Change control refers to the formal procedures adopted by an organization to ensure that all changes to system and application software are subject to the appropriate level of management control. Change control seeks to eliminate unauthorized changes and reduce defects and problems related to poor planning and communication of changes. Change control is often enforced through use of a Change Control Board, which reviews changes for impact, ensures that the appropriate implementation and backout plans have been prepared, and follows changes through approval and post-implementation review.

The change control policy document covers the following aspects of the change process under management control:

1. **Request Submission**—A request for change is submitted to the Change Control Board for review, prioritization, and approval. Included in the request should be a description of the change and rationale or objectives for the request, a change implementation plan, an impact assessment, and a backout plan to be exercised in the event of a change failure or unanticipated outcome.

2. **Recording**—Details of the request are recorded for review, communication, and tracking purposes.

3. **Analysis/Impact Assessment**—Changes are typically subject to peer review for accuracy and completeness and to identify any impacts on other systems or processes that may arise as a result of the change.

4. **Decision Making and Prioritization**—The team reviews the request, implementation and backout plans, and impacts and determines whether the change should be approved, denied, or put on hold. Changes are scheduled and prioritized, and any communication plans are put in place.

5. **Approval**—Formal approval for the change is granted and recorded.

6. **Status Tracking**—The change is tracked through completion. A post-implementation review may be performed.

Systems experience frequent changes. Software packages are added, removed, or modified. New hardware is introduced, while legacy devices are replaced. Updates due to flaws in software are regular business activities for system managers. The rapid advancement of technology, coupled with regular discovery of vulnerabilities, requires proper change control management to maintain the necessary integrity of the system. Change control management is embodied in policies, procedures, and operational practices.

Maintaining system integrity is accomplished through the process of change control management. A well-defined process implements structured and controlled changes necessary to support system integrity and accountability for changes. Decisions to implement changes should be made by a committee of representatives from various groups within the organization such as ordinary users, security, system operations, and upper-level management. Each group provides a unique perspective regarding the need to implement a proposed change. Users have a general idea of how the system is used in the field. Security can provide input regarding the possible risks associated with a proposed change. System operations can identify the challenges associated with the deployment and maintenance of the change. Management provides final approval or rejection of the change based on budget and strategic directions of the organization. Actions of the committee should be documented for historical and accountability purposes.

The change management structure should be codified as an organization policy. Procedures for the operational aspects of the change management process should also be created. Change management procedures are forms of directive controls. The following subsections outline a recommended structure for a change management process.

- **Requests**—Proposed changes should be formally presented to the committee in writing. The request should include a detailed justification in the form of a business case argument for the change, focusing on the benefits of implementation and costs of not implementing.

- **Impact Assessment**—Members of the committee should determine the impacts to operations regarding the decision to implement or reject the change.

- **Approval/Disapproval**—Requests should be answered officially regarding their acceptance or rejection.

- **Build and Test**—Subsequent approvals are provided to operations support for test and integration development. The necessary software and hardware should be tested in a nonproduction environment. All configuration changes associated with a deployment must be fully tested and documented. The security team should be invited to perform a final review of the proposed change within the test environment to ensure that no vulnerabilities are introduced into the production system. Change requests involving the removal of a software or a system component require a similar approach. The item should be removed from the test environment and have a determination made regarding any negative impacts.

- **Security Impact Assessment**—A security impact assessment is performed to determine the impact of the proposed change to confidentiality, integrity, or availability. Should the change introduce risk, the security impact assessment should qualify and quantify the risk as much as possible and provide mitigation strategies.

- **Notification**—System users are notified of the proposed change and the schedule of deployment.

- **Implementation**—The change is deployed incrementally, when possible, and monitored for issues during the process.

- **Validation**—The change is validated by the operations staff to ensure that the intended machines received the deployment package. The security staff performs a security scan or review of the affected machines to ensure that new vulnerabilities are not introduced. Changes should be included in the problem tracking system until operations has ensured that no problems have been introduced.

- **Documentation**—The outcome of the system change, to include system modifications and lessons learned, should be recorded in the appropriate records. This is the way that change management typically interfaces with configuration management.

Change management can involve several different roles, each with their own responsibilites. The division of these roles can vary from organization to organization, but here are some of the common major roles:

- **Change Manager**—Individual in charge of CM policies and procedures, including mechanisms for requesting, approving, controlling, and testing changes.

- **Change Control Board**—Responsible for approving system changes.

- **Project Manager**—Manages budgets, timelines, resources, tasks, and risk for systems development, implementation, and maintenance.

- **Architects**—Develop and maintain the functional and security context and technical systems design.

- **Engineers and Analysts**—Develop, build, and test system changes, and document the rationale for and details of the change.

- **Customer**—Requests changes and approves functional changes in the design and execution of a system.

- **System Security Officer**—Ensures planned changes do not have adverse security impacts by performing security impact assessments for each change. The system security officer is also responsible for assisting the system's owner with updating relevant security documentation.

Configuration Management

Throughout the system life cycle, changes made to the system, its individual components, or its operating environment can introduce new vulnerabilities and thus impact this security baseline. Configuration management (CM) is a discipline that seeks to manage configuration changes so that they are appropriately approved and documented, so that the integrity of the security state is maintained, and so that disruptions to performance and availability are minimized. Unlike change control, which refers to the formal processes used to ensure that all software changes are managed, configuration management refers to the technical and administrative processes that maintain integrity of hardware and system software components across versions or releases.

Typical steps in the configuration management process are: change request, approval, documentation, testing, implementation, and reporting. A configuration management system consisting of a set of automated tools, documentation, and procedures is typically used to implement CM in an organization. The system should identify and maintain:

- Baseline hardware, software, and firmware configurations

- Design, installation, and operational documentation

- Changes to the system since the last baseline

- Software test plans and results

The configuration management system implements the four operational aspects of CM: identification, control, accounting, and auditing.

Organizational hardware and software require proper tracking, implementation testing, approvals, and distribution methods. Configuration management is a process of identifying and documenting hardware components, software, and the associated settings. A well-documented environment provides a foundation for sound operations management by ensuring that IT resources are properly deployed and managed. The security professional plays an important role in configuration management through the identification and remediation of control gaps in current configurations.

Detailed hardware inventories are necessary for recovery and integrity purposes. Having an inventory of each workstation, server, and networking device is necessary for replacement purposes in the event of facility destruction. All devices and systems connected to the network should be in the hardware list. At a minimum, configuration documentation should include in the hardware list the following information about each device and system:

- Make
- Model
- MAC addresses
- Serial number
- Operating system or firmware version
- Location
- BIOS and other hardware-related passwords
- Assigned IP address if applicable
- Organizational property management label or bar code

Software is a similar concern and a software inventory should minimally include

- Software name
- Software vendor (and reseller if appropriate)
- Keys or activation codes (note if there are hardware keys)
- Type of license and for what version
- Number of licenses
- License expiration
- License portability
- Organizational software librarian or asset manager
- Organizational contact for installed software
- Upgrade, full, or limited license

The inventory is also helpful for integrity purposes when attempting to validate systems, software, and devices on the network. Knowing the hardware versions of network components is valuable from two perspectives. First, the security professional will be able to quickly find and mitigate vulnerabilities related to the hardware type and version. Most hardware vulnerabilities are associated with a particular brand and model of hardware. Knowing the type of hardware and its location within the network can substantially reduce the effort necessary to identify the affected devices. Additionally, the list is invaluable when performing a network scan to discover unauthorized devices connected to the network. A new device appearing on a previously documented network segment may indicate an unauthorized connection to the network.

A configuration list for each device should also be maintained. Devices such as firewalls, routers, and switches can have hundreds or thousands of configuration possibilities. It is necessary to properly record and track the changes to these configurations to provide assurance for network integrity and availability. These configurations should also be periodically checked to make sure that unauthorized changes have not occurred.

Operating systems and applications also require configuration management. Organizations should have configuration guides and standards for each operating system and application implementation. System and application configuration should be standardized to the greatest extent possible to reduce the number of issues that may be encountered during integration testing. Software configurations and their changes should be documented and tracked with the assistance of the security practitioner. It is possible that server and workstation configuration guides will change frequently due to changes in the software baseline.

Identification

Identification captures and maintains information about the structure of the system, usually in a configuration management database (CMDB). Each component of the system configuration should be separately identified and maintained as a configuration item (CI) within the CMDB using a unique identifier (name), number (such as a software or hardware serial number), and version identifier. The CMDB may be a series of spreadsheets or documents or may be maintained within a structured database management system (DBMS). Use of structured databases is preferred to enforce consistency and maintain the integrity of information (such as preventing duplicate entries and preserving associations between CIs) and to safeguard against unauthorized modifications and deletions.

Within the CMDB, changes are tracked by comparing the differences between a CI before and after the change in a change set or delta. The CMDB thus is capable of storing the baseline configuration plus a sequence of deltas showing a history of changes. In addition, the system must maintain a consistent mapping among components so that changes are appropriately propagated through the system. Dependencies between components are identified so that the impacts of logical changes to any one component are known.

Automated Configuration Management Tools

Many in-house software development teams use automated tools for software version change control and other aspects of configuration management. Most development platforms include features such as source code comparators, comment generators, and version checkers. When linked to a central repository, these tools use check in/check out functions to copy code from the repository into a development library or desktop environment, make and test modifications, and place the modified code back into the repository. Branching and merging tools help resolve concurrency conflicts when two or more individuals modify the same component. Standalone or add-on tools are available commercially or as open source and typically contain more robust functionality suited to teams of developers. Tool vendors do not always distinguish between features that manage the CM process and those that manage actual configurations. Datacenter CM tools, for example, range from standalone CMDBs to full suites that include workflow engines, access control, policy enforcement, and reporting capabilities.

Control

All configuration changes and releases must be controlled through the life cycle. Control mechanisms are implemented to govern change requests, approvals, change propagation, impact analysis, bug tracking, and propagation of changes. Control begins early in systems design and continues throughout the system life cycle. Before changes are implemented, they should be carefully planned and subjected to peer review. Implementation and rollback plans (in case of change failure) should accompany the change request. Technical controls to enforce this aspect of CM include access control for development, test, and production environments, as well as to the CMDB itself.

Accounting

Accounting captures, tracks, and reports on the status of CIs, change requests, configurations, and change history.

Auditing

Auditing is a process of logging, reviewing, and validating the state of CIs in the CMDB, ensuring that all changes are appropriately documented and that a clear history of changes is retained in such a way that they can be traced back to the person making the change and provide detail on the delta (difference) between the baseline and the current state of the system. Auditing also compares the information in the CMDB to the actual system configuration to ensure that the representation of the system is complete and accurate, and association between components is maintained.

Security Impact Assessment

Security impact assessment is the analysis conducted by qualified staff within an organization to determine the extent to which changes to the information system affect the security posture of the system. Because information systems are typically in a constant state of change, it is important to understand the impact of changes on the functionality of existing security controls and in the context of organizational risk tolerance. Security impact analysis is incorporated into the documented configuration change control process.

The analysis of the security impact of a change occurs when changes are analyzed and evaluated for adverse impact on security, preferably before they are approved and implemented but also in the case of emergency/unscheduled changes. Once the changes are implemented and tested, a security impact analysis (and/or assessment) is performed to ensure that the changes have been implemented as approved and to determine if there are any unanticipated effects of the change on existing security controls.

Security impact analysis supports the implementation of NIST SP 800-53r4 control CM-4 Security Impact Analysis.

System Architecture/Interoperability of Systems

Interoperability describes the extent to which systems and devices can exchange data and interpret that shared data. For two systems to be interoperable, they must be able to exchange data and subsequently present that data such that it can be understood by a user. If two or more systems are capable of communicating and exchanging data, they are exhibiting syntactic interoperability. Specified data formats, communication protocols, and the like are fundamental. XML or SQL standards are among the tools of syntactic interoperability. Syntactical interoperability is a necessary condition for further interoperability. Beyond the ability of two or more computer systems to exchange information, semantic interoperability is the ability to automatically interpret the information exchanged meaningfully and accurately in order to produce useful results as defined by the end users of both systems. To achieve semantic interoperability, both sides must refer to a common information exchange reference model. The content of the information exchange requests are unambiguously defined: what is sent is the same as what is understood.

With respect to software, the term interoperability is used to describe the capability of different programs to exchange data via a common set of exchange formats, to read and write the same file formats, and to use the same protocols. (The ability to execute the same binary code on different processor platforms is *not* contemplated by the definition of interoperability.) The lack of interoperability can be a consequence of a lack of attention to standardization during the design of a program. Indeed, interoperability is not taken for granted in the non-standards-based portion of the computing world.

According to ISO/IEC 2382-01, "Information Technology Vocabulary, Fundamental Terms," interoperability is defined as follows: "The capability to communicate, execute programs, or transfer data among various functional units in a manner that requires the user to have little or no knowledge of the unique characteristics of those units."[20]

Patch Management

The application of software and firmware patches to correct vulnerabilities is a critical component of vulnerability and configuration management practices. Most security breaches that have occurred over the past decade are not the result of the so-called zero-day attacks but rather were perpetrated by attackers exploiting known vulnerabilities. The SQL Slammer worm, which exploited a buffer overflow vulnerability in Microsoft's SQL server and desktop engines, cost between $950 million and $1.2 billion in lost productivity and denial of service during its first five days in the wild. Yet not seven months later, Blaster arrived on the scene to wreck similar havoc. These attacks could have been prevented by timely and effective application of patches that were already available to administrators—so why did not the affected organizations keep up to date on patches? The answer is that patching, and patching distributed desktop and laptop systems in particular, is not a straightforward process. Vulnerabilities can target a number of systems, including desktop and server operating systems; database management systems; client software such as browsers and office productivity software; and network devices such as routers, switches, and firewalls. The sheer volume of vendor patches to be deployed across these disparate systems necessitates an automated solution that accommodates an organization's core platforms. The patches themselves must be acquired, tested, distributed, and verified in a coordinated and controlled manner, which means processes must be designed and followed religiously to ensure effectiveness. Application of patches can be disruptive to operations, slowing down systems or making them unavailable during the installation window and often requiring reboot or restart after installation, and some can be "bad," meaning that they introduce new vulnerabilities, create downstream impacts, or do not deploy correctly on all target systems. Not all patches are of equal criticality to an organization, meaning that someone must make a decision regarding when and why to deploy patches as they are made available. This is typically done through the organization's change control system.

Despite these obstacles, an organization must adopt some form of patch management discipline to mitigate vulnerabilities. Decisions regarding when, what, and how to patch should not be left up to individual administrators but should be backed by a formal patch management policy or process and carried out by a specifically designated team or committee. The policy should identify roles and responsibilities, criteria for determining whether and how to deploy patches, and service-level objectives for fully deploying patches at each criticality level. The patch management process includes the following steps:

- **Acquisition**—Patches are most often supplied via download from the vendor's website. Some patch distribution and management systems may automatically scan these sites for available patches and initiate downloads to a centralized, internal site.

- **Testing**—Patches must be tested to ensure that they can be correctly distributed and installed and that they do not interfere with normal system or application functioning. Despite a vendor's best efforts, patches are often created under pressure to fix critical vulnerabilities and may not be thoroughly regression tested. Furthermore, each organization's operating environment is unique, and it is impossible to test these myriad variations, so impacts on dependent services and applications and compatibility with all possible configurations are not always identified during vendor testing. Patches should initially be tested in a laboratory environment that contains replicas of standard target machine configurations. A limited pilot deployment may then be used for further testing in the production environment.

- **Approval**—Not all patches will be immediately approved for deployment. Non-critical patches and patches that are not applicable to the platforms and services used in the organization may be deferred to a later date, or to a time when they are included in a more comprehensive vendor update. Patches that cannot be deployed via standard means or those that cause issues on test machines may require further planning and testing before they are approved. The approval process should include provisions for emergency deployments of critical security patches.

- **Packaging**—Patches must be packaged or configured for distribution and installation on target systems. Depending on how patches are deployed, packaging can take several forms. Some platforms such as Windows provide installation software or scripts that are bundled with the patch and automatically invoked when distributed. Custom scripts can also be written to execute a series of installation actions. Patch management software typically includes facilities to package as well as deploy patches.

- **Deployment**—Having an accurate inventory of machines and their current patch levels is critical to successful deployment of patches. Automated patch management and software deployment tools may maintain an independent inventory or CMDB or may integrate with third-party configuration and asset management software. Deployment features include scheduling, user notification of patch and reboot (with or without a "snooze" option), and ordering options for multiple-patch deployments.

- **Verification**—Automated patch management tools should be able to verify correct application of patches and report all successful and unsuccessful deployments back to a centralized console or reporting engine.

To minimize user disruption during the workday, organizations can purchase Wake-on-LAN (WOL) compliant network cards, now standard on most end-user computers and servers. These cards respond to wake-up transmissions (called *magic packets*) from a centralized configuration management server that are sent before distributing the patch. The server will send the transmission only to those systems that require the scheduled patch updates.

Monitoring System Integrity

A comprehensive configuration and change management program should include a mechanism to monitor or periodically validate changes to system configuration. Sophisticated integrity monitors such as Tripwire integrate with the organization's CMDB to produce a detailed history of system changes. Integrity checkers work by taking a "snapshot" of the approved system configuration, including UNIX object properties and Windows registry keys, access control lists, and contents of system configuration files. This snapshot is then hashed and cryptographically signed to protect against modification. Periodically, the snapshot is compared to a hash of the current configuration, and any changes are reported back to the administrator or noted directly in the CMDB, if an automated interface exists.

Integrity checkers such as Tripwire do not necessarily record who made the change or prevent unauthorized changes from occurring. Use of additional protections such as host-based IPS and log collection and correlation is recommended to supplement integrity checking functions.

Security Awareness and Training

Common sense tells us that the security posture of any organization is only as strong as its weakest link. Increased focus on technical and administrative safeguards in the wake of data security breaches, international terrorism, and large-scale fraud and abuse have improved the situation, but many organizations still fail to consider the human element. Basel III defines operational risk, of which information security risk is a component, as "the risk of direct or indirect loss resulting from inadequate or failed internal processes, people, and systems or from external events."[21]

Security Awareness

Security awareness seeks to reduce the risk related to human error, misjudgment, and ignorance by educating people about the risks and threats to confidentiality, integrity, and availability, and how they can help the organization be more resistant to threats in the performance of their daily job functions. Many national and international regulatory and standards bodies recognize the importance of security awareness and awareness training by making them security program requirements. Critical success factors for any security awareness program are:

- **Senior Management Support**—Security success stories happen when individuals begin to treat security as part of their job function. Too many security programs fail because senior management does not buy in to the security team's mission and message. To get this buy-in, start your awareness program at the top. Involve senior management in the design and oversight of the program, and tie awareness program goals to business goals.

- **Cultural Awareness**—There is no such thing as a "one size fits all" awareness program. Is your organization a large, established, hierarchical institution or an agile, high-tech, entrepreneurial firm? Are workers unionized or independent professionals? Does your organization value customer service, operational efficiency, or personal achievement? These and other questions help define your target audience and deliver a message whose content, style, and format are designed to have impact on your specific audience.

- **Communication Goals**—Set communication goals and build a strategy to meet these goals. Perform a needs assessment to identify gaps in security awareness and develop objectives to close these gaps. Be as specific as you can when stating your goals. Do you intend to alert users to social engineering threats? Communicate policy? Teach people how to spot and report incidents? Your objectives will dictate how your awareness program is delivered.

- **Taking a Change Management Approach**—The end goal of awareness programs is to produce changes in behavior in your target audience. Understanding barriers to change and methods that successfully stimulate people to change will help you reach this goal. People change because they are motivated to change. Motivators include small prizes and awards, financial incentives, time off, peer recognition, feelings of personal pride and accomplishment, feelings of job competency, and just plain fun. Organizations that tie security awareness to their formal system of salary and performance management are the most likely to foster interest in security issues and compliance with expectations. Promoting awareness that "hits home" by spotlighting issues such as identity theft, spyware and malicious code, online shopping safety, and protection of children on the Internet and tying these to workplace issues is an effective way to capture employee interest.

- **Measurement**—Measuring success against stated objectives not only helps justify the awareness program to senior management, but will allow you to identify gaps and continuously improve on your delivery.

General security awareness differs from awareness training, in that awareness is designed to get people's attention while training instructs people on practices they can adopt to identify, respond to, and protect against security threats. Some specific vehicles for delivering general security awareness include:

- Threat alerts distributed by e-mail
- Security-specific newsletters or articles in your company's newsletter
- Security awareness intranet sites
- Screen savers and computer wallpaper
- Posters and notices in prominent locations
- Brochures or pamphlets

Awareness efforts should also focus on user responsibilities for promoting ethical practices and a productive work environment. RFC 1087, "Ethics and the Internet," promotes personal responsibility and provides sound general principles for behavior when using computing resources. These include prohibitions against unauthorized access, wasteful use of resources, and violations of confidentiality, integrity, and availability of information and systems.

Awareness training is typically more formal in nature and produces more directly measurable results. It is a good idea to make security awareness training a mandatory annual or semiannual event by partnering with Human Resources or training areas. Some organizations require specific training on security policies and procedures and appropriate use of information systems, and may maintain a record of attendance and formal, signed acknowledgment that training has been received. Training can be general or it can focus on specific areas such as:

- Labeling and handling of sensitive information
- Appropriate use policies for e-mail, Internet, and other services
- Customer privacy laws, policies, and procedures
- Detecting and reporting security incidents
- Protecting intellectual property and copyright

Training typically addresses issues that are specific to the work environment and provides explicit instruction on policies, standards, and procedures. Training should be required for employees, contractors, and third parties that use or manage the organization's information systems assets. Instructors providing security awareness training should be well versed in the security domain as well as related policies and procedures.

To measure the effectiveness of security awareness training, consider using surveys or quizzes that test knowledge of key issues before and after training. Other tests for improved awareness include password analyzers or crackers that test the strength of user-selected passwords, number of incidents reported by personnel using established procedures, number of security policy violations, or number of help desk calls or system-related issues due to malicious code, social engineering attacks, etc. You should determine what metrics you will use when designing your awareness program. Results should be reported to senior management to ensure their continued support.

Security Staff Training

Personnel with specific security job responsibilities must have specialized knowledge and skills in traditional security domains as well as the specific tools, technologies, and practices used on the job. Training should begin by identifying roles and responsibilities and determining the specific knowledge and skills needed to perform security functions. Training should cover the basics of the seven SSCP domains and offer continuing advancement in each of these specialized areas:

- Access controls
- Analysis and monitoring
- Cryptography
- Malicious code
- Networks and telecommunications
- Risk, response, and recovery
- Security operations and administration

In addition, training in the specific industry regulations, laws, and standards applicable to the security practitioner's role in the organization should be included in the curriculum.

Most organizations do not have the capacity to provide specialized professional training in these areas, and must look outside the organization for assistance. When selecting a security training provider, take care to ensure that the company employs only highly qualified, experienced trainers who will be prepared to explore topics in depth and provide answers to technical questions. A number of organizations provide security training and training programs and general and advanced security certifications. Some of them (this is by no means an all-inclusive list) are

- **(ISC)² SSCP, CISSP, and CAP**—Review seminars conducted by (ISC)² and Authorized Education Affiliates (see `http://www.isc2.org` for more details).

- **CPP–ASIS–International**—Offers the Certified Protection Professional (CPP), Professional Certified Investigator (PCI), and Physical Security Professional (PSP) credentials. Information on certification review courses and domain-specific classroom and e-learning courses are available at `https://www.asisonline.org/Certification/Board-Certifications/Pages/default.aspx`.

- **CISA, CISM**—Certified Information Systems Auditor and Certified Information Security Manager certifications are offered by ISACA (Information Systems Audit and Control Association), as well as security courses and conference programs. More information can be found at `https://www.isaca.org/Pages/default.aspx`.

Interior Intrusion Detection Systems

Within the facility, it is still necessary to maintain levels of security. The layered approach provides for additional security measures while inside the perimeter of the facility. Specifically, not all employees need access to the sensitive areas, such as the phone closets, or need access into the data center. It is not practical or economical to have guards stationed at every security point within the facility; however, an access control system can provide the necessary security controls throughout the building.

A card reader can control access into a specific room. This can be controlled through the access control software, which will be maintained within the security control center. If the individual has access to the room, the employee will place his badge up to the reader and it will release the electric lock and allow entry.

Other elements necessary for this control of interior access are described in the following sections.

Balanced Magnetic Switch (BMS)

This device uses a magnetic field or mechanical contact to determine if an alarm signal is initiated. One magnet will be attached to the door and the other to the frame; when the door is opened, the field is broken. A BMS differs from standard magnetic status switches in that a BMS incorporates two aligned magnets with an associated reed switch. If an external magnet is applied to the switch area, it upsets the balanced magnetic field such that an alarm signal is received. Standard magnetic switches can be defeated by holding a magnet near the switch. Mechanical contacts can be defeated by holding the contacts in the closed position with a piece of metal or taping them closed. Balanced magnetic switches are not susceptible to external magnetic fields and will generate an alarm if tampering occurs. These switches are used on doors and windows (Figure 2.4).

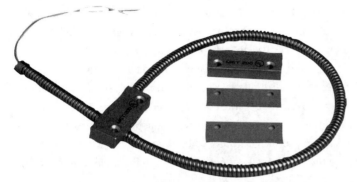

FIGURE 2.4 Balanced Magnetic Switch (BMS), used on doors and windows, uses a magnetic field or mechanical contact to determine if an alarm signal is initiated. PHOTO OF BOSCH ISN_CMET_200AR COMMERCIAL METAL CONTACT COURTESY OF BOSCH SECURITY SYSTEMS, INC.

Motion-Activated Cameras

A fixed camera with a video motion feature can be used as an interior intrusion point sensor. In this application, the camera can be directed at an entry door and will send an alarm signal when an intruder enters the field of view. This device has the added advantage of providing a video image of the event, which can alert the security officer monitoring the camera and he can make a determination of the need to dispatch a security force. Typically, one camera can be associated with several doors along a hallway. If a door is forced open, the alarm will trigger the camera to begin recording and can give the monitoring officer a video view starting one minute before the alarm was tripped, so as to allow the operator all the possible information before dispatching a security response. This system uses technology to supplement the guard force. It can activate upon motion and can give a control center operator a detailed video of actual events during alarm activation.

Acoustic Sensors

This device uses passive listening devices to monitor building spaces. An application is an administrative building that is normally occupied only in daylight working hours. Typically, the acoustic sensing system is tied into a password-protected building entry control system, which is monitored by a central security monitoring station. When someone has logged into the building with a proper password, the acoustic sensors are disabled. When the building is secured and unoccupied, the acoustic sensors are activated. After hours intruders make noise, which is picked up by the acoustic array and an alarm signal is generated. The downside is the false alarm rate from picking up noises such as air conditioning and telephone ringers. This product must be deployed in an area that will not have any noise. Acoustic sensors act as a detection means for stay-behind covert intruders. One way to use the system is as a monitoring device: when it goes into alarm, the system will open up an intercom and the monitoring officer can listen to the area. If no intruder is heard, then the alarm is cancelled.

Infrared Linear Beam Sensors

Many think of this device from spy movies, where the enduring image of secret agents and bank robbers donning their special goggles to avoid triggering an active infrared beam is recalled. This is the device found in many homes on garage doors. A focused infrared (IR) light beam is projected from an emitter and bounced off of a reflector that is placed at the other side of the detection area (Figure 2.5). A retroreflective photoelectric beam sensor built into the emitter detects when the infrared beam is broken by the passing of a person or the presence of an object in the path of the infrared beam. If the beam is broken, the door will stop or the light will come on. This device can also be used to notify security of individuals in hallways late at night, when security is typically at its reduced coverage.

Passive Infrared (PIR) Sensors

A PIR sensor (Figure 2.6) is one of the most common interior volumetric intrusion detection sensors. It is called passive because there is no beam. A PIR picks up heat signatures (infrared emissions) from intruders by comparing infrared receptions to typical background infrared levels. Infrared radiation exists in the electromagnetic spectrum at a wavelength that is longer than visible light. It cannot be seen, but it can be detected. Objects that generate heat also generate infrared radiation, and those objects include animals and the human body. The PIR is set to determine a change in temperature, whether warmer or colder, and distinguish an object that is different from the environment that it is set in. Typically, activation differentials are three degrees Fahrenheit. These devices work best in a stable, environmentally controlled space.

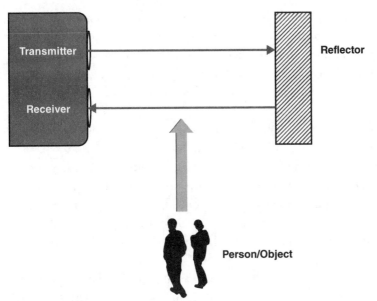

FIGURE 2.5 **Infrared linear beam sensors**

FIGURE 2.6 **A passive infrared (PIR) sensor is one of the most common interior volumetric intrusion detection sensors. Because there is no beam, it is called passive.** PHOTO OF BOSCH COMMERCIAL SERIES TRITECH MOTION DETECTOR COURTESY OF BOSCH SECURITY SYSTEMS, INC.

A PIR is a motion detector and will not activate for a person who is standing still because the electronics package attached to the sensor is looking for a fairly rapid change in the amount of infrared energy it is seeing. When a person walks by, the amount of infrared energy in the field of view changes rapidly and is easily detected. The sensor should not detect slower changes, like the sidewalk cooling off at night.

PIRs come in devices that project out at a 45° angle and can pick up objects 8 to 15 meters away. There are also 360° PIRs, which can be used in a secured room, so when there is entry, the PIR will activate. These motion detection devices can also be programmed into an alarm key pad located within the protected space. When motion is detected, it can be programmed to wait for a prescribed time while the individuals swipe their badge or enter their pass code information into the keypad. If identification is successful, the PIR does not send an intruder notification to the central station.

While not only a security application, PIRs are often used as an automatic request to exit (REX) device for magnetically locked doors. In this application, the REX (Figure 2.7) acts as the automatic sensor for detecting an approaching person in the exit direction for magnetically locked doors and deactivates the alarm.

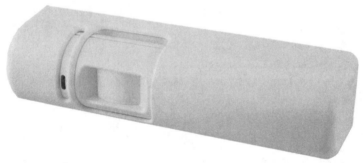

FIGURE 2.7 **An automatic request to exit (REX) device.** PHOTO OF MD-31REQUEST-TO-EXIT (REX) MOTION DETECTOR DEVICE COURTESY OF SECURITY DOOR CONTROLS

Dual-Technology Sensors

These provide a commonsense approach for the reduction of false alarm rates. For example, this technology uses a combination of microwave and PIR sensor circuitry within one housing. An alarm condition is generated only if both the microwave and the PIR sensor detect an intruder. Since two independent means of detection are involved, false alarm rates are reduced when configured into this setting. Integrated, redundant devices must react at the same time to cause an alarm. More and more devices are coming with dual-technology that will reduce the need for multiple devices and will significantly reduce the false alarm rates.

Escort and Visitor Control

All visitors entering the facility should sign in and sign out on a visitor's log to maintain accountability of who is in the facility, the timeframe of the visit, who they visited, and in the case of an emergency, have accountability of everyone for safety purposes.

All visitors should be greeted by a knowledgeable receptionist who in turn will promptly contact the employee that they are there to visit or meet with. There should be some type of controlled waiting area within the lobby so the receptionist can keep track of the visitor and can direct the employee to them, in the event they have never met previously.

Visitors are given temporary badges, but this badge does not double as an access card. The temporary badge will be issued at an entry control point only after the visitor identifies the purpose of the visit and receives approval by the employee being visited. In some organizations, only certain employees may approve visitor access along with the day and time of the visit. In many operations, the visitor is escorted at all times while inside the facility. When the visitor arrives, he will present a form of photo identification, such as a driver's license, to the receptionist for verification. Some visitor badges are constructed of paper and may have a feature that causes a void line to appear after a preset time period. Typically, the pass is dated and issued for a set period, usually one day. In most cases, a visitor will wear a conspicuous badge that identifies him or her as a visitor and clearly indicates whether an escort is required (often done with color-coded badges). If an escort is required, the assigned person should be identified by name and held responsible for the visitor at all times while on the premises. A visitor management system can be a pen and paper system that records basic information about visitors to the facility. Typical information found in an entry includes the visitor's name, reason for the visit, date of visit, and the check-in and checkout times.

Other types of visitor management systems use a computer-based system or specific visitor software product. They can be manually inserted into the system by the receptionist or, on a higher-end visitor management system, the visitor provides the receptionist with identification, such as a driver's license or a government or military ID. The receptionist then swipes the person's identification through a reader. The system automatically populates the database with ID information and recognizes whether the ID is properly formatted or false. The receptionist who is registering the guest identifies the group to which the person belongs—guest, client, vendor, or contractor. Then the badge is printed.

It is best for the employee to come to the lobby area and greet the visitor personally. This is more than a common courtesy because it provides the necessary security in proper identification, escorting, and controlling the movement of the visitor. Some companies initiate a sound security practice by properly identifying the visitor and signing him or her into a visitor management system, but then they allow the visitor to wander the halls of the company trying to find his or her contact. This completely defeats the prior work of identifying and badging the visitor.

Building and Inside Security

Securing the perimeter and interior of a building is always a high priority. There is a wide array of door-securing technologies available. Beyond that, safes, vaults, and containers are important. All of these security measures are almost meaningless without a good key control system in place. These aspects of building security are all discussed in the following sections.

Doors, Locks, and Keys

Door assemblies include the door, its frame, and anchorage to the building. As part of a balanced design approach, exterior doors should be designed to fit snugly in the doorframe, preventing crevices and gaps, which also helps prevent many simple methods of gaining illegal entry. The doorframe and locks must be as secure as the door in order to provide good protection.

Perimeter doors should consist of hollow steel doors or steel-clad doors with steel frames. Ensure the strength of the latch and frame anchor equals that of the door and frame. Permit normal egress through a limited number of doors, if possible, while accommodating emergency egress. Ensure that exterior doors into inhabited areas open outward. Locate hinges on the interior of restricted areas. Use exterior security hinges on doors opening outward to reduce their vulnerability.

If perimeter doors are made of glass, make sure that the material is constructed of a laminate material or stronger. Ensure that glass doors only allow access into a public or lobby area of the facility. High security doors will then need to be established within the lobby area where access will be controlled. All doors that are installed for sensitive areas such as telephone closets, network rooms, or any area that has access control will require the door to have an automatic door closing device.

Electric Locks

The electric lock is a secure method to control a door. An electric lock actuates the door bolt. For secure applications, dual locks can be used. In some cases, power is applied to engage the handle, so the user can retract the bolt instead of the electric lock door operator actually retracting the bolt. Most electric locks can have built-in position switches and request-to-exit hardware. Although offering a high security level, electric locks are expensive. A special door hinge that can accommodate a wiring harness and internal hardware to the door is required. For retrofit applications, electric locks usually require the purchase of a new door.

Electric Strikes

The difference between an electric strike and an electric lock is in the mechanism that is activated at the door. In an electric-lock door, the bolt is moved. In an electric-strike door, the bolt remains stationary and the strike is retracted. As in electric locks, electric strikes can be configured for fail-safe or fail-secure operation. The logic is the same. In fail-safe configuration, the strike retracts when de-energized on loss of power. This allows the door to be opened from the public side. In fail-secure configuration, the strike remains in place, causing the door to be locked from the public side requiring manual key entry to unlock the door from the public side. Again, as with electric locks, unimpeded access is allowed for in the direction of exit by manual activation of the door handle or lever when exiting from the secure side. For retrofit situations, electric strikes rarely require door replacement and can often be done without replacing the doorframe.

Magnetic Locks

The magnetic lock is popular because it can be easily retrofitted to existing doors (Figure 2.8). The magnetic lock is surface-mounted to the door and doorframe. Power is applied to magnets continuously to hold the door closed. Magnetic locks are normally fail-safe but do have a security disadvantage. In requirements for the U.S. Life Safety Codes, doors equipped with magnetic locks are required to have one manual device (emergency manual override button) and an automatic sensor (typically a passive infrared sensor [PIR] or request to exit [REX] device) to override the door lock signal when someone approaches the door in the exit direction.[22] All locks are controlled by a card reader that, when activated, will release the secured side portion of the door and allow entry into the facility. While enhancing overall building safety, the addition of these extra devices allows possible compromise of the door lock. In the scenario, where a REX is used with magnetic locks, it not only turns off the alarm when the individual exits but also deactivates the locking device. This can be a problem if an adversary can get something through or under the door to cause the REX to release the magnetic lock.

FIGURE 2.8 Magnetic Lock. PHOTO OF 1511 EMLOCK MAGNETIC DOOR LOCK COURTESY OF SECURITY DOOR CONTROLS

Anti-passback

In high security areas, a card reader is utilized on both entry and exit sides of the door. This keeps a record of who went in and out. *Anti-passback* is a strategy where a person must present a credential to enter an area or facility and then again use the credential to "badge out." This makes it possible to know how long a person is in an area and to know who is in the area at any given time. This requirement also has the advantage of instant personnel accountability during an emergency or hazardous event. Anti-passback programming prevents users from giving their cards or PIN number to someone else to gain access to the restricted area. In a rigid anti-passback configuration, a credential or badge is used to enter an area and that same credential must be used to exit. If a credential holder fails to properly badge-out, entrance into the secured area can be denied.

Turnstiles and Mantraps

A common and frustrating loophole in an otherwise secure ACS can be the ability of an unauthorized person to follow through a checkpoint behind an authorized person, called "piggybacking" or "tailgating."

The traditional solution is an airlock-style arrangement called a "mantrap," in which a person opens one door and waits for it to close before the next door will open (Figure 2.9). A footstep-detecting floor can be added to confirm there is only one person passing through. A correctly constructed mantrap or portal will provide for tailgate detection while it allows roller luggage, briefcases, and other large packages to pass without causing nuisance alarms. People attempting to enter side-by-side are detected by an optional overhead sensing array. The mantrap controller prevents entry into secured areas if unauthorized access is attempted.

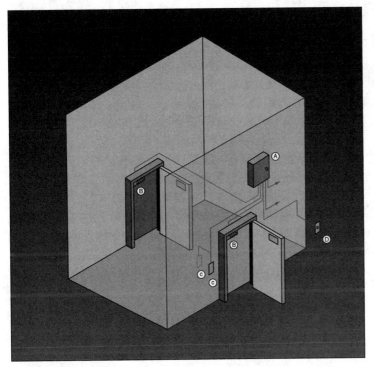

FIGURE 2.9   **A mantrap**

Another system that is available is a turnstile, which can be used as a supplemental control to assist a guard or receptionist while controlling access into a protected area. Anyone who has gone to a sporting event has gone through a turnstile. In this approach, the individual's badge is used to control the turnstile arm and allow access into the facility (Figure 2.10).

FIGURE 2.10 **A turnstile can be used as a supplemental control to assist a guard or receptionist while controlling access into a protected area.** PHOTO OF FASTLANE® PLUS 400 TURNSTILE COURTESY OF SMARTER SECURITY, INC.

A higher-end turnstile is an optical turnstile, which is designed to provide a secure access control in the lobby of a busy building. This system is designed as a set of parallel pedestals that form lanes, which allow entry or exit. Each barrier is equipped with photoelectric beams, guard arms, and a logic board (Figure 2.11).

To gain access to the interior of the building, an authorized person uses his access card at the optical turnstile. When the access card is verified, the guard arm is dropped, the photoelectric beam is temporarily shut off, and the cardholder passes without creating an alarm. The concept behind these options is to create a secure perimeter just inside the building to ensure only authorized people proceed further into the building, thereby creating the secure working environment.

FIGURE 2.11 A higher-end turnstile is an optical turnstyle, which is designed to provide a secure access control in the lobby of a busy building. PHOTO OF FASTLANE GLASSGATE® 200 TURNSTILE COURTESY OF SMARTER SECURITY, INC.

Types of Locks

Key locks are one of the basic safeguards in protecting buildings, personnel, and property and are generally used to secure doors and windows. According to UL Standard 437, door locks and locking cylinders must resist attack through the following testing procedures: the picking test, impression test (a lock is surreptitiously opened by making an impression of the key with a key blank of some malleable material—wax or plastic—which is inserted into the keyway and then filed to fit the lock), forcing test, and salt spray corrosion test for products intended for outdoor use. The door locks and locking cylinders are required by UL standards to resist picking and impression for ten minutes.[23]

Rim Lock   A rim lock, shown in Figure 2.12, is a lock or latch typically mounted on the surface of a door. It is typically associated with a dead bolt type of lock.

Mortise Lock   A mortise lock, shown in Figure 2.13, is a lock or latch that is recessed into the edge of a door rather than being mounted to its surface. This configuration has a handle and locking device all in one package.

FIGURE 2.12 **A rim lock is a lock or latch typically mounted on the surface of a door.**
PHOTO OF BEST 1E RIM CYLINDER COURTESY OF STANLEY SECURITY

FIGURE 2.13 **A mortise lock is a lock or latch that is recessed into the edge of a door rather than being mounted to its surface.** PHOTO OF BEST 45H MORTISE LOCK COURTESY OF STANLEY SECURITY

Locking Cylinders   The pin tumbler cylinder is a locking cylinder that is composed of circular pin tumblers that fit into matching circular holes on two internal parts of the lock (Figure 2.14). The pin tumbler functions on the principle that the pin tumblers need to be placed into a position that is entirely contained with the plug. Each pin is of a different height, thus accounting for the varying ridge sizes of the key. When the pins are properly aligned, the plug can be turned to unlock the bolt.

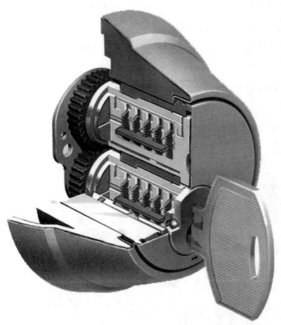

FIGURE 2.14 A pin tumbler cylinder is a locking cylinder that is composed of circular pin tumblers that fit into matching circular holes on two internal parts of the lock.
PHOTO OF STANLEY COMMERCIAL HARDWARE QDB100 REKEY COURTESY OF STANLEY SECURITY

Cipher Lock   A cipher lock, shown in Figure 2.15, is controlled by a mechanical key pad, typically 5 to 10 digits. When it is pushed in the right combination, the lock will release and allow entry. The drawback is someone looking over a shoulder can see the combination. However, an electric version of the cipher lock is in production in which a display screen will automatically move the numbers around, so if someone is trying to watch the movement on the screen, they will not be able to identify the number indicated unless they are standing directly behind the victim.

Remember locking devices are only as good as the wall or door that they are mounted in, and if the frame of the door or the door itself can be easily destroyed, then the lock will not be effective. A lock will eventually be defeated, and its primary purpose is to delay the attacker.

FIGURE 2.15 A cipher lock is controlled by a mechanical key pad with digits that when pushed in the right combination will release the lock and allow entry. PHOTO OF BEST KEYPAD EZ LOCK COURTESY OF STANLEY SECURITY

Hi-Tech Keys

Not all lock and key systems are standard metal composite. There have been developments in key technology that offer convenient, reliable access control.

"Intelligent keys" are keys with a built-in microprocessor, which is unique to the individual key holder and identifies the key holder specifically (Figure 2.16). The lock also contains a minicomputer and the key exchange data, allowing the lock to make valid access decisions based on the parameters established for the key holder. For example, the key will know if the employee is allowed access into the facility after normal business hours; if not, the key will not work. Also, it will keep track of whose key is being used to access specific locked doors and when the attempts are taking place. When an employee resigns from the organization, the relevant key is disabled.

"Instant keys" provide a quick way to disable a key by permitting one turn of the master key to change a lock. This method of changing a lock can save both time and money in the event a master key is lost. According to a manufacturer, a 50-story bank building can be rekeyed in six hours by two security guards. The system can go through 10 to 15 changes before having to be re-pinned.

Safes

Safes are often the last bastion of defense between an attacker and an asset. Several types of safes not only protect against theft but also fire and flood. A safe (Figure 2.17) is defined as a fireproof and burglarproof iron or steel chest used for the storage of currency, negotiable securities, and similar valuables.

FIGURE 2.16 "Intelligent keys" have a built-in microprocessor that is unique to the individual key holder and identifies the key holder specifically. PHOTO OF CLIQ® INTELLIGENT KEY COURTESY OF MUL-T-LOCK USA, INC.

FIGURE 2.17 A safe is a fireproof and burglarproof iron or steel chest used for the storage of currency, negotiable securities, and similar valuables. PHOTO OF MICROVAULT COURTESY OF INTERNATIONAL VAULT, INC.

The categories for safes depend on the amount of security needed. Underwriters Laboratories lists several classifications of safe. The following is one such classification, provided here solely as an example:

Tool-Resistant Safe Class TL-15. This type of combination lock safe is designed to be resistant to entry (by opening the door or making a six-inch hand hole through the door) for a networking time of 15 minutes using any combination of the following tools:

- Mechanical or portable electric hand drills not exceeding a half-inch
- Grinding points, carbide drills (excluding the magnetic drill press and other pressure-applying mechanisms, abrasive wheels, and rotating saws)
- Common hand tools such as chisels, drifts, wrenches, screwdrivers, pliers, and hammers and sledges not to exceed the 8-pound size, pry bars and ripping tools not to exceed 5 feet in length
- Picking tools that are not specially designed for use against a special make of safe

A TL-15 safe must

- Weigh at least 750 pounds or be equipped with anchors and instructions for anchoring in larger safes, in concrete blocks, or to the floor of the bank premises.
- Have metal in the body that is solid cast or fabricated open-hearth steel at least 1 inch thick with a tensile strength of 50,000 pounds per square inch (psi) and that is fastened to the floor in a manner equal to a continuous 1/4-inch penetration weld of open-hearth steel having an ultimate tensile strength of 50,000 psi.
- Have the hole to permit insertion of electrical conductors for alarm devices not exceeding a 1/4-inch diameter and be provided in the top, side, bottom, or back of the safe body, but it must not permit a direct view of the door or locking mechanism.
- Be equipped with a combination lock meeting UL Standard No. 768 requirements for Group 2, 1, or 1R locks.
- Be equipped with a relocking device that will effectively lock the door if the combination lock is punched.

The UL classifications mean that a Tool-Resistant Safe Class TL-30 will take 30 minutes to break into using tools. A TRTL-30 safe means it will take 30 minutes for a combination of tools and torches to break into the safe. The categories go up to a safe that can resist tools, torches, and explosives.

Vaults

A vault (Figure 2.18) is defined as a room or compartment designed for the storage and safekeeping of valuables and has a size and shape that permits entrance and movement within by one or more persons. Vaults generally are constructed to withstand the best efforts of man and nature to penetrate them.

The UL has developed standards for vault doors and vault modular panels for use in the construction of vault floors, walls, and ceilings. The standards are intended to establish the burglary-resistant rating of vault doors and modular vault panels according to the length of time they withstand attack by common mechanical tools, electric tools, cutting torches, or any combination thereof. The ratings, based on the networking time to affect entry, are as follows:

- **Class M**—One quarter hour
- **Class 1**—One half-hour
- **Class 2**—One hour
- **Class 3**—Two hours

FIGURE 2.18 A vault is a room or compartment designed for the storage and safe-keeping of valuables and has a size and shape that permits entrance and movement within by one or more persons. PHOTO OF VAULT COURTESY OF INTERNATIONAL VAULT, INC.

Containers

A container is a reinforced filling cabinet that can be used to store proprietary and sensitive information. The standards for classified containers are typically from a government. For example, the U.S. government lists a class 6 container (Figure 2.19) as approved for the storage of secret, top secret, and confidential information. The container must meet the protection requirements for 30 man-minutes against covert entry and 20 hours against surreptitious entry with no forced entry.

FIGURE 2.19 **A class 6 container is approved for the storage of secret, top secret, and confidential information.**

Key Control

Key control, or more accurately the lack of key control, is one of the biggest risks that businesses and property owners face. Strong locks and stronger key control are the two essentials in a high-security locking system. In most cases, master and sub-master keys are required for most building systems so that janitorial and other maintenance personnel may have access. Thus, the control of all keys becomes a critical element of the key lock system: All keys need to be tightly controlled from the day of purchase by designated personnel responsible for the lock system.

Without a key control system, an organization cannot be sure who has keys or how many keys may have been produced for a given property. Not having a patent-controlled key system leads to unauthorized key duplication, which can lead to unauthorized access or employee theft. Most key control systems utilize patented keys and cylinders. These lock cylinders employ very precise locking systems that can be operated only by the unique keys to that system. Because the cylinders and the keys are patented, the duplication of keys can be done only by factory-authorized professional locksmiths.

The key blanks and lock cylinders are made available only to those same factory authorized professional locksmiths. Procedures may be in place to allow the organization to contract another security professional should the need arise.

All high-security key control systems require specific permission to have keys originated or duplicated. These procedures assure the property owner or manager that they will always know who has keys and how many they possess. If an employee leaves and returns the keys, the organization can be reasonably assured that no copies of the keys were made. Most systems have cylinders that will retrofit existing hardware, keeping the cost of acquisition lower. Some systems employ different levels of security within the system, still giving patented control, but not requiring ultra-high security where it is not needed. These measures are again aimed at cost control.

Most systems can be master keyed; some will coordinate with existing master key systems. There are systems available that allow interchangeable core cylinders for retrofitting of existing systems.

Locks, keys, doors, and frame construction are interconnected, and all must be equally effective. If any single link is weak, the system will break down. The Medeco Guide for Developing and Managing Key Control states the following:[24]

"The following represents the basic and most critical elements of key control and shall be included, as a minimum, in the key control specification.

2.1 "Facility shall appoint a Key Control Authority or Key Control Manager to implement, execute, and enforce key control policies and procedures.

2.2 "A policy and method for the issuing and collecting of all keys shall be implemented.

2.3 "Keys and key blanks shall be stored in a locked cabinet or container, in a secured area.

2.4 "A key control management program shall be utilized. A dedicated computer software application is preferred.

2.5 "All keys shall remain the property of the issuing facility.

2.6 "A key should be issued only to individuals who have a legitimate and official requirement for the key.

    2.6.1 "A requirement for access alone, when access can be accomplished by other means (such as unlocked doors, request for entry, intercoms, timers, etc.), shall not convey automatic entitlement to a key.

2.7 "All keys shall be returned and accounted for.

2.8 "Employees must ensure that keys are safeguarded and properly used."

Securing Communications and Server Rooms

Communication rooms or closets must maintain a high level of security. Access must be controlled into this area, and only authorized personnel should be allowed to work on this equipment. No matter what transmission mode or media is selected, it is important that a method for securing communications be included. This includes physical protection, such as providing a rigid metallic conduit for all conductors, as well as technical protection, such as encrypting communication transmissions.

What Is Cable Plant Management?

Cable plant management is the design, documentation, and management of the lowest layer of the OSI network model—the physical layer. The physical layer is the foundation of any network, whether it is data, voice, video, or alarms, and it defines the physical media upon which signals or data is transmitted through the network.

Approximately 70% of your network is composed of passive devices such as cables, cross-connect blocks, and patch panels. Documenting these network components is critical to keeping a network finely tuned. The physical medium can be copper cable (e.g., cat 6), coaxial cable, optical fiber (e.g., single or multimode), wireless, or satellite. The physical layer defines the specifics of implementing a particular transmission medium. It defines the type of cable, frequency, terminations, etc. The physical layer is relatively static. Most change in the network occurs at the higher levels in the OSI model.

Key components of the cable plant include the entrance facility, equipment room, backbone cable, backbone pathway, telecommunication room, and horizontal distribution system.

Entrance Facility

The service entrance is the point at which the network service cables enter or leave a building. It includes the penetration through the building wall and continues to the entrance facility. The entrance facility can house both public and private network service cables. The entrance facility provides the means for terminating the backbone cable. The entrance facility generally includes electrical protection, ground, and demarcation point.

Equipment Room

The equipment room serves the entire building and contains the network interfaces, uninterruptible power supplies, computing equipment (e.g., servers, shared peripheral devices, and storage devices), and telecommunication equipment (e.g., PBX). It may be combined with the entrance facility.

Backbone Distribution System

A backbone distribution system provides connection between entrance facilities, equipment rooms, and telecommunication rooms. In a multi-floor building, the backbone distribution system is composed of the cabling and pathways between floors and between multiple telecommunication rooms. In a campus environment, the backbone distribution system is composed of the cabling and pathways between buildings.

Telecommunication Room

The telecommunication room (TR) typically serves the needs of a floor. The TR provides space for network equipment and cable terminations (e.g., cross-connect blocks and patch panels). It serves as the main cross-connect between the backbone cabling and the horizontal distribution system.

Horizontal Distribution System

The horizontal distribution system distributes the signals from the telecommunication room to the work areas. The horizontal distribution system consists of

- Cables
- Cross-connecting blocks
- Patch panels
- Jumpers
- Connecting hardware
- Pathways (supporting structures such as cable trays, conduits, and hangers that support the cables from the telecommunication room to the work areas)

Protection from Lightning

A lightning strike to a grounding system produces an elevated ground or ground potential rise (GPR). Any equipment bonded to this grounding system and also connected to wire-line communications will most likely be damaged from outgoing currents seeking remote ground. Personnel working at this equipment are susceptible to harm because they will be in the current path of this outgoing current. The equipment damage from a lightning strike may not be immediate. Sometimes the equipment is weakened by stress and primed for failure at some future time. This is called latent damage and leads to premature *mean time before failure* (MTBF) of the equipment.

The best engineering design, for open-ended budgets, is the use of dielectric fiber optic cable for all communications. Obviously, a fiber-optic cable is non-conductive, provided that it is an all dielectric cable with no metallic strength members or shield, making isolation no longer a requirement. This is because physical isolation is inherent in the fiber-optic product itself. This dielectric fiber-optic cable must be placed in a PVC conduit to protect it from rodents.

However, if budgets are tight, the engineering design solution to protect this equipment is to isolate the wire-line communications from remote ground. This is accomplished using optical isolators or isolation transformers. This equipment is housed together, mounted on a non-conducting surface in a non-conducting cabinet, and is called the high voltage interface (HVI).

The HVI isolates the equipment during a GPR and prevents any current flow from a higher potential grounding system to a lower potential grounding system. This totally protects any equipment from damage or associated working personnel from harm. No ground shunting device ever made, no matter how fast acting, will ever completely protect equipment from a GPR. Ground shunting devices are connected to the elevated ground and during a GPR offer an additional current path in the reverse direction from which they were intended to operate. Obviously, this flow of current, even away from the equipment, will immediately cause equipment damage and harm to working personnel.

Server Rooms

A server room needs a higher level of security than the rest of the facility. This should encompass a protected room with no windows and only one controlled entry into the area. Remember that once servers are compromised, the entire network is at risk. While some server attacks are merely annoying, others can cause serious damage. In order to protect the organization, it is paramount to protect your servers. Physical access to a system is almost a guaranteed compromise if performed by a motivated attacker.[25] Therefore, server room security must be comprehensive and constantly under review.

Rack Security

It would be unusual for everyone in a room full of racks to have the need to access every rack; rack locks can ensure that only the correct people have access to servers and only telecommunications people have access to telecommunications gear. "Manageable" rack locks that can be remotely configured to allow access only when needed—to specific people at specific times—reduce the risk of an accident, sabotage, or unauthorized installation of additional equipment that could cause a potentially damaging rise in power consumption and rack temperature.

Restricted and Work Area Security

Depending on the configuration and operations structure of the data center, administrators and operators can be within the secured portion of the data center or can be in an auxiliary area. In most cases the latter is true, for the simple fact that there just isn't enough room within the data center to maintain equipment and personnel. Additionally, server rooms are noisy and cold, not ideal conditions for human beings.

Individuals who maintain sensitive information must present the commonsense attitude of being security minded within the confines of the facility. Not everyone who works on sensitive information needs to be inside a secured room. For areas not considered a high security area, there are still requirements to maintain a responsible profile. Store and maintain sensitive information in security containers, which can be a filing cabinet with locking bars and a padlock. Maintain a clean desk approach, which encourages personnel to lock up information when they are finished for the day.

Maintain strong password protection for workstations. Never have computer screens facing toward the window without blinds or some type of protective film. Privacy filters and screen protectors keep prying eyes off sensitive work. Have a shredding company destroy trash containing all proprietary and customer confidential information. This will eliminate outsiders from obtaining confidential information through dumpster diving.

In highly restricted work areas such as government SCIFs, there is a requirement to increase the security blanket to ensure tighter access to these areas. The physical security protection for a SCIF is intended to prevent as well as detect visual, acoustical, technical, and physical access by unauthorized persons. An organization may not be required to maintain government-classified information; however, the company's livelihood and your employment are tied to proprietary information that requires the same level of security.

SCIF walls will consist of 3 layers of 5/8-inch drywall and will be from true floor to true ceiling. There will typically be only one SCIF entrance door, which will have an X-09 combination lock along with access control systems. According to the United States Director of Central Intelligence Directive 1/21 DCID1-21, "all SCIF perimeter doors must be plumbed in their frames and the frame firmly affixed to the surrounding wall. Door frames must be of sufficient strength to preclude distortion that could cause improper alignment of door alarm sensors, improper door closure, or degradation of audio security. All SCIF primary entrance doors must be equipped with an automatic door closer."[26]

Basic HVAC requirements have any duct penetration into the secured area that is over 96 square inches include man bars to prevent a perpetrator from climbing through the ducts.

White noise or sound masking devices need to be placed over doors, in front of plenum, or pointed toward windows to keep an adversary from listening to classified conversations. Some SCIFs use music or noise that sounds like a constant flow of air to mask conversation. All access control must be managed from within the SCIF. Intrusion detection is sent out to a central station with the requirement that a response force will respond to the perimeter of the SCIF within 15 minutes.

Data Center Security

When discussing the need to secure the data center, security professionals immediately think of sabotage, espionage, or data theft. While the need is obvious for protection against intruders and the harm caused by intentional infiltration, the hazards from the ordinary activity of personnel working in the data center present a greater day-to-day risk for most facilities. For example, personnel within the organization need to be segregated from access areas where they have no "need to know" for that area. The security director would typically have physical access to most of the facility but has no reason to access financial or HR data. The head of computer operations might have access to computer rooms and operating systems but not the mechanical rooms that house power and HVAC facilities. It comes down to not allowing wandering within the organization.

As data centers and web hosting sites grow, the need for physical security at the facility is every bit as great as the need for cybersecurity of networks. The data center is the brains of the operation, and as such only specific people should be granted access. The standard scenario for increased security at a data center would consist of the basic security-in-depth: progressing from the outermost (least sensitive) areas to the innermost (most sensitive) areas. Security will start with entry into the building, which will require passing a receptionist or guard and then using a proximity card to gain building entry. For access into the computer room or data center, it will now require the same proximity card along with a PIN, plus a biometric device (Figure 2.20). Combining access control methods at an entry control point will increase the reliability of access for authorized personnel only. Using different methods for each access level significantly increases security at inner levels because each is secured by its own methods plus those of outer levels that must be entered first. This would also include internal door controls.

For a data center, the use of an internal mantrap or portal would provide increased entry and exit control. A portal (Figure 2.21) will open the inner door only once the outer door is closed. The portal can have additional biometrics within the device that must be activated before the secured side door opens.

FIGURE 2.21 A secure portal will only open the inner door once the outer door is closed.
PHOTO OF SECURE EXIT LANE COURTESY OF HORTON AUTOMATICS

FIGURE 2.20 A card reader with biometric features for additional security.
PHOTO OF BOSCH ARD-FPBEPXX-OC BIOENTRY PLUS WITH CARD READER COURTESY OF BOSCH SECURITY SYSTEMS, INC.

The *two-person* rule is a strategy where two people must be in an area together, making it impossible for a person to be in the area alone. Two-man rule programming is optional with many access control systems. It prevents an individual cardholder from entering a selected empty security area unless accompanied by at least one other person. Use of the two-person rule can help eliminate insider threats to critical areas by requiring at least two individuals to be present at any time. It is also used for life safety within a security area; if one person has a medical emergency, there will be assistance present.

Utilities and HVAC Considerations

Beyond the human component, there are other important facets of securing data centers. These include power, HVAC, air purity, and water.

Utilities and Power

Because they often host mission-critical servers, data centers are built with both battery and generator backups. If the power cuts out, the batteries take over, just as they might in a home user's uninterruptible power supply. The generators also begin and start producing power before the batteries fail. Areas that contain backup generators and power supplies need similar protection. This area can be controlled with key access or a card access reader, and electric door strikes can be installed for entry into this area. This area is also a person-specific area; there is no need to give everyone access to the generator room. This room will maintain backup power for the entire facility in the event of a power outage emergency. Two key aspects of power are the UPS and generator:

Uninterruptible Power Supply (UPS)   This is a battery backup system, which maintains a continuous supply of electric power to connected equipment by supplying power from a separate source when utility power is not available. A UPS has internal batteries to guarantee that continuous power is provided to the equipment even if the power source stops providing power. Of course, the UPS can provide power only for a while, typically a few minutes, but that is often enough to ride out power company glitches or short outages. Even if the outage is longer than the battery lifetime of the UPS, this provides the opportunity to execute an orderly shutdown of the equipment.

Generator   Generator power should be activated automatically in the event of a utility failure by the transfer switch. The data center load is maintained by the UPS units; however, often this is a short time as the generator should be active and up to speed within 10 seconds of a power failure. A generator (Figure 2.22) is typically run on diesel fuel and can be located outside of the facility or inside a parking garage. The generator room needs to be protected from unauthorized access by either access control devices or key-locked doors. The generator will operate as long as fuel is supplied. Some generators have a 300-gallon capacity, and a facilities manager will have a contract with a local distributor to supply fuel. Most operation centers have more than one generator and test them once a month. If it is located outside, it needs protective barriers placed around it to protect it from a vehicle running into it.

HVAC

HVAC stands for heating, ventilation, and air-conditioning. Heat can cause extensive damage to computer equipment by causing processors to slow down and stop execution or even cause solder connections to loosen and fail. Excessive heat degrades network performance and causes downtime. Data centers and server rooms need an uninterrupted cooling system. Generally, there are two types of cooling: latent and sensible.

FIGURE 2.22 A backup generator is activated automatically in the event of a utility failure by the transfer switch. PHOTO OF COMMERCIAL GENERAC UNIT (22-150KW) COURTESY OF GENERAC POWER SYSTEMS

Latent cooling is the ability of the air-conditioning system to remove moisture. This is important in typical comfort-cooling applications, such as office buildings, retail stores, and other facilities with high human occupancy and use. The focus of latent cooling is to maintain a comfortable balance of temperature and humidity for people working in and visiting such a facility. These facilities often have doors leading directly to the outside and a considerable amount of entrance and exit by occupants.

Sensible cooling is the ability of the air-conditioning system to remove heat that can be measured by a thermometer. Data centers generate much higher heat per square foot than typical comfort-cooling building environments, and they are typically not occupied by large numbers of people. In most cases, they have limited access and no direct means of egress to the outside of the building except for seldom used emergency exits.

Data centers have a minimal need for latent cooling and require minimal moisture removal. Sensible cooling systems are engineered with a focus on heat removal rather than moisture removal and have a higher sensible heat ratio; they are the most useful and appropriate choice for the data center. Cooling systems are dove tailed into the power supply overhead. If there is a power interruption, this will affect the cooling system. For the computers to continue operation, they need to be cooled. Portable air-conditioning units can be used as a backup in case of HVAC failure, but good design should ensure cooling systems are accounted for as backup devices.

Air Contamination

Over the past several years, there has been an increasing awareness dealing with anthrax and airborne attacks. Harmful agents introduced into the HVAC systems can rapidly spread throughout the structure and infect all persons exposed to the circulated air.

To avoid air contamination, place intakes at the highest practical level in the facility. For protection against malicious acts, the intakes should also be covered by screens so that objects cannot be tossed into the intakes or into air wells from the ground. Such screens should be sloped to allow thrown objects to roll or slide off the screen, away from the intake. Many existing buildings have air intakes that are located at or below ground level. For those that have wall-mounted or below-grade intakes close to the building, the intakes can be elevated by constructing a plenum or external shaft over the intake.

The following is a list of guidelines necessary to enhance security in this critical aspect of facility operations:

- Restrict access to main air intake points to persons who have a work-related reason to be there.

- Maintain access rosters of pre-approved maintenance personnel authorized to work on the system.

- Escort all contractors with access to the system while on site.

- Ensure that all air intake points are adequately secured with locking devices.

All buildings have air intake points that either are roof-mounted, exterior wall-mounted, or in a free-standing unit on the ground outside of the building. Due to "sick building syndrome," where one person infects several with a cold or flu through a building HVAC system, many governments require all new buildings to mix a certain percentage of fresh air in with re-circulated air in the HVAC system. The volume of fresh air taken in is based on the square footage of the building and the number of employees working inside.

One method of reducing the risk of biological agents circulating throughout a building is installation of UV light filters in the HVAC system's supply and return ducts. UV light inhibits the growth and reproduction of germs, bacteria, viruses, fungi, and mold. UV light is the portion of the electromagnetic spectrum that lies beyond the "purple" or visible edge of the spectrum. The sun acts as a natural outdoor air purification system, controlling airborne bacteria with UV rays. UV light penetrates the microorganism and breaks down molecular bonds causing cellular or genetic damage. The germs are either killed or sterilized, leaving them unable to reproduce. In either case, live bacterial counts can be significantly reduced and kept under control.

Water Issues

Along with excessive heat, water is a detriment to computer equipment. A data center may have a gas suppression fire system, but what about the floors above? Are they on a standard water sprinkler system, and what would happen if the sprinklers are activated or begin leaking? Proper planning moves equipment away from water pipes that might burst, basements that might flood, or roofs that might leak. However, there are other water leaks that are more difficult to recognize and detect. Blocked ventilation systems can cause condensation if warm, moist air is not removed quickly. If vents are located above or behind machines, condensation can form small puddles that no one sees. Stand-alone air conditioners are especially vulnerable to water leaks if condensation is not properly removed. Even small amounts of water near air intakes will raise humidity levels and fill servers with moisture.

Fire Detection and Suppression

To protect the server room from fire, the organization needs to have smoke detectors installed and linked to a panel with enunciators that will warn people that there is smoke in the room. Also, it should be linked to a fire suppression system that can help put out the fire with no damage to equipment from the gas itself.

Fire Detection

A smoke detector is one of the most important devices to have due to its ability to warn of a pending fire, coupled with a good signaling device.

A detector in proper working condition will sound an alarm and give all occupants a chance to make it out alive. There are two main categories of smoke detectors: optical detection (photoelectric) and physical process (ionization). Photoelectric detectors are classified as either beam or refraction. Beam detectors operate on the principle of light and a receiver. Once enough smoke enters the room and breaks the beam of light, the alarm is sounded. The refraction type has a blocker between the light and the receiver. Once enough smoke enters the room, the light is deflected around the beam to the signal. Finally, we have the ionization type detector; these detectors monitor the air around the sensors constantly. Once there is enough smoke in the room, the alarm will sound.

There are three main types of fire detectors: flame detectors, smoke detectors, and heat detectors. There are two main types of flame detectors, and they are classified as infrared (IR) and ultraviolet (UV) detectors. IR detectors primarily detect a large mass of hot gases that emit a specific spectral pattern in the location of the detector; these patterns are sensed with a thermographic camera and an alarm is sounded. Additional hot surfaces in the room may trigger a false response with this alarm. UV flame detectors detect flames at speeds of 3–4 milliseconds due to the high-energy radiation emitted by fires and explosions at the instant of their ignition. Some of the false alarms of this system include random UV sources such as lightning, radiation, and solar radiation that may be present in the room.

There are heat detectors, which include fixed temperature or rate of rise detectors. The user will set a predetermined temperature level for the alarm to sound. If the room temperature rises to that setting, the alarm will sound. Rate of rise temperature will detect a sudden change of temperature around the sensor. Usually this setting is at around 10–15 degrees per minute. Nothing more is required of the consumer except routine checks for battery life and operation status. Heat detectors should not be used to replace smoke detectors; each component in fire safety serves its purpose and should be taken seriously. The combination of devices and the knowledge of procedures are the only way to achieve success during a possible fire.

Fire Suppression

All buildings should be equipped with an effective fire suppression system, providing the building with around the clock protection. Traditionally, fire suppression systems employed arrays of water sprinklers that would douse a fire and surrounding areas. Sprinkler systems are classified into four different groups: wet, dry, pre-action, and deluge.

- **Wet Systems**—Have a constant supply of water in them at all times; once activated, these sprinklers will not shut off until the water source is shut off.
- **Dry Systems**— Do not have water in them. The valve will not release until the electric valve is stimulated by excess heat.
- **Pre-Action Systems**—Incorporate a detection system, which can eliminate concerns of water damage due to false activations. Water is held back until detectors in the area are activated.
- **Deluge Systems**—Operate in the same function as the pre-action system except all sprinkler heads are in the open position.

Water may be a sound solution for large physical areas such as warehouses, but it is entirely inappropriate for computer equipment. A water spray can irreparably damage hardware more quickly than encroaching smoke or heat. Gas suppression systems operate to starve the fire of oxygen. In the past, Halon was the choice for gas suppression systems; however, Halon leaves residue, depletes the ozone layer, and can injure nearby personnel.[27]

There are several gas suppression systems that are recommended for fire suppression in a server room or anywhere electronic equipment is employed:

- **Aero-K**—Uses an aerosol of microscopic potassium compounds in a carrier gas released from small canisters mounted on walls near the ceiling. The Aero-K generators are not pressurized until fire is detected. The Aero-K system uses multiple fire detectors and will not release until a fire is "confirmed" by two or more detectors (limiting accidental discharge). The gas is non-corrosive, so it does not damage metals or other materials. It does not harm electronic devices or media such as tape or discs. More important, Aero-K is nontoxic and does not injure personnel.

- **FM-200**—Is a colorless, liquefied compressed gas. It is stored as a liquid and dispensed into the hazard as a colorless, electrically non-conductive vapor that is clear and does not obscure vision. It leaves no residue and has acceptable toxicity for use in occupied spaces at design concentration. FM-200 does not displace oxygen and, therefore, is safe for use in occupied spaces without fear of oxygen deprivation.

SUMMARY

The SSCP must spend time to become comfortable with the intricacies of the organization's security operations. There are many aspects from the need to understand confidentiality, integrity, and availability, to non-repudiation and the separation of duties and defense-in-depth concepts. In addition, the SSCP is expected to have a firm understanding of the (ISC)² code of ethics, and as a result, knowledge of the actions required to be compliant. Further, the need to be able to document and operate security controls effectively within the organization is also a key responsibility that the SSCP is expected to undertake. An information security practitioner must have a thorough understanding of fundamental risk, response, and recovery concepts. By understanding each of these concepts, the security practitioner will have the knowledge required to protect the security practitioner's organization and professionally execute the security practitioner's job responsibilities.

SAMPLE QUESTIONS

1. Security awareness training aims to educate users on:
   a. What they can do to maintain the organization's security posture
   b. How to secure their home computer systems
   c. The work performed by the information security organization
   d. How attackers defeat security safeguards

2. Which of the following are operational aspects of configuration management (CM)?
   a. Identification, documentation, control, and auditing
   b. Documentation, control, accounting, and auditing
   c. Control, accounting, auditing, and reporting
   d. Identification, control, accounting, and auditing

3. The systems certification process can best be described as a:
   a. Process for obtaining stakeholder signoff on system configuration
   b. Method of validating adherence to security requirements
   c. Means of documenting adherence to security standards
   d. Method of testing a system to assure that vulnerabilities have been addressed

4. Which of the following is a degausser used to do?
   a. Render media that contain sensitive data unusable.
   b. Overwrite sensitive data with zeros so that it is unreadable.
   c. Eliminate magnetic data remanence on a disk or tape.
   d. Reformat a disk or tape for subsequent reuse.

5. A web application software vulnerability that allows an attacker to extract sensitive information from a backend database is known as a:
   a. Cross-site scripting vulnerability
   b. Malicious file execution vulnerability
   c. Injection flaw
   d. Input validation failure

6. The security practice that restricts user access based on need to know is called:
   a. Mandatory access control
   b. Default deny configuration

c. Role-based access control

   d. Least privilege

7. A security guideline is a:

   a. Set of criteria that must be met to address security requirements

   b. Tool for measuring the effectiveness of security safeguards

   c. Statement of senior management expectations for managing the security program

   d. Recommended security practice

8. A security baseline is a:

   a. Measurement of security effectiveness when a control is first implemented

   b. Recommended security practice

   c. Minimum set of security requirements for a system

   d. Measurement used to determine trends in security activity

9. An antifraud measure that requires two people to complete a transaction is an example of the principle of:

   a. Separation of duties

   b. Dual control

   c. Role-based access control

   d. Defense in depths

10. The waterfall model is a:

   a. Development method that follows a linear sequence of steps

   b. Iterative process used to develop secure applications

   c. Development method that uses rapid prototyping

   d. Extreme programming model used to develop web application

11. Code signing is a technique used to:

   a. Ensure that software is appropriately licensed for use

   b. Prevent source code tampering

   c. Identify source code modules in a release package

   d. Support verification of source code authenticity

12. The role of information owner in the system security plan includes:

    a. Maintaining the system security plan

    b. Determining privileges that will be assigned to users of the system

    c. Assessing the effectiveness of security controls

    d. Authorizing the system for operation

13. What are the mandatory tenets of the ISC2 Code of Ethics? (Choose all that apply.)

    a. Protect society, the commonwealth, and the infrastructure.

    b. Act honorably, honestly, justly, responsibly, and legally.

    c. Promote and preserve public trust and confidence in information and systems.

    d. Advance and protect the profession.

14. What principle does confidentiality support?

    a. Due diligence

    b. Due care

    c. Least privilege

    d. Collusion

15. What two things are used to accomplish non-repudiation?

    a. Proofing and provisioning

    b. Encryption and authorization

    c. Monitoring and private keys

    d. Digital signatures and public key infrastructure

16. What are the elements that make up information security risks?

    a. Requirements, threats, and exposures

    b. Threats, vulnerabilities, and impacts

    c. Assessments, vulnerabilities, and expenses

    d. Impacts, probabilities, and known errors

17. What is an example of a compensating control?

    a. A fence

    b. Termination

    c. Job rotation

    d. Warning banner

18. What is remote attestation?

   a. A form of integrity protection that makes use of a hashed copy of hardware and software configuration to verify that configurations have not been altered

   b. A form of confidentiality protection that makes use of a cached copy of hardware and software configuration to verify that configurations have not been altered

   c. A form of integrity protection that makes use of a cached copy of hardware and software configuration to verify that configurations have not been altered

   d. A form of confidentiality protection that makes use of a hashed copy of hardware and software configuration to verify that configurations have not been altered

19. With regards to the Change Control Policy document and Change Management, where should Analysis/Impact Assessment take place?

   a. After the decision making and prioritization activities, but before approval

   b. After the recording of the proposed change(s), but before decision making and prioritization activities

   c. After the approval, but before status tracking activities

   d. After the request submission, but before recording of the proposed change(s)

NOTES

[1] http://www.isc2.org

[2] https://books.google.com/books?id=XwUyn2rZUHkC&lpg=PA84&ots=u9B_5_XipV&dq=donn%20b%20parker%20Informed%20consent&pg=PA84#v=onepage&q=donn%20b%20parker%20Informed%20consent&f=false

[3] http://nvlpubs.nist.gov/nistpubs/SpecialPublications/NIST.SP.800-57Pt3r1.pdf

[4] https://www.cippguide.org/2010/07/01/generally-accepted-privacy-principles-gapp/

[5] http://www.oecd.org/sti/ieconomy/oecd_privacy_framework.pdf

[6] http://www.oecd.org/sti/ieconomy/oecdguidelinesontheprotectionofprivacyandtransborderflowsofpersonaldata.htm

[7] See the following for more information:

OCTAVE: http://www.cert.org/resilience/products-services/octave/

NIST SP 800-30 R1: http://csrc.nist.gov/publications/nistpubs/800-30-rev1/sp800_30_r1.pdf

[8] http://csrc.nist.gov/publications/fips/fips200/FIPS-200-final-march.pdf

[9] http://nvlpubs.nist.gov/nistpubs/SpecialPublications/NIST.SP.800-53r4.pdf (Chapter 2, page 9)

[10] See the following for more information: http://www.tutorialspoint.com/sdlc/sdlc_waterfall_model.htm

[11] See the following for more information: https://www.owasp.org/index.php/Category:OWASP_Top_Ten_Project

[12] http://owasptop10.googlecode.com/files/OWASP%20Top%2010%20-%202013.pdf

[13] See the following: https://www.us-cert.gov/sites/default/files/cdm_files/Intro_to_HWAM.pdf

[14] See the following: http://www.dhs.gov/sites/default/files/publications/FY13%20IG%20metrics.pdf.pdf

[15] See the following: https://www.us-cert.gov/sites/default/files/cdm_files/Intro_to_HWAM.pdf

[16] *The DAMA Guide to the Data Management Body of Knowledge* (DAMA-DMBOK), 1st Edition 2009, p.4

[17] If interested, the SSCP can find out additional information about secure shredding standards be examining DIN 32757, a shredding standard developed by the German Institute for Standardization, which is the de facto standard used by the shredding industry to classify equipment into hierarchical security levels based on the residue produced by shredding. Government and certain private applications may require use of shredders certified and labeled at a specific maximum security level for paper documents containing classified information. Security levels (with general applicability) are:

Level 1–Least secure, cuts paper into 12-mm strips. Not suitable for classified information.

Level 2–Cuts paper into 6-mm strips. Not suitable for classified information.

Level 3–Cuts paper into 2-mm strips. Limited suitability for confidential information.

Level 4–Cuts paper into particles 2 x 15 mm particles. Suitable for Sensitive but Unclassified or Business Proprietary information.

Level 5–Cuts paper into 0.8 x 12 mm particles. Suitable for Classified information.

Level 6-Cuts paper into 0.8 x 4 mm particles. Suitable for Top Secret information.

[18] http://csrc.nist.gov/publications/nistpubs/800-88/NISTSP800-88_with-errata.pdf

[19] See the following as examples: *Hack Attacks Denied: A Complete Guide to Network Lockdown*, John Chirillo, NIST Security Handbook—Technical Controls—Computer Security http://www.moct.gov.sy/ICTSandards/en/12/index.htm#6_Technical_Controls.htm, and *Cyber Terrorism: A Guide for Facility Managers*, Joseph F. Gustin

[20] The definition for interoperability was originally defined in the ISO/IEC 2382-01:1993 standard. The standard has been updated as of April 2015, and is now referenced as ISO/IEC 2382:2015. The definition for interoperability has not changed. The new standard may be examined online here: https://www.iso.org/obp/ui/#iso:std:iso-iec:2382:ed-1:v1:en

[21] See the following for more information: https://www.bis.org/publ/bcbsca07.pdf

[22] http://www.nfpa.org/codes-and-standards/document-information-pages?mode=code&code=101&DocNum=101&cookie_test=1

[23] http://www.nist.gov/standardsgov/upload/UL.pdf (page 8)

[24] http://www.medeco.com/Other/Medeco/Downloads/Key_Control/Key_Control.pdf (pg. 3)

[25] See the following for a discussion of the Ten Immutable Laws of Security V2.0: http://technet.microsoft.com/en-us/library/hh278941.aspx

[26] See the following: http://www.fas.org/irp/offdocs/dcid1-21.pdf

[27] The "Montreal Protocol on Substances that Deplete the Ozone Layer" was designed to reduce the production and consumption of ozone depleting substances in order to reduce their abundance in the atmosphere and thereby protect the earth's fragile ozone layer. The original Montreal Protocol was agreed on 16 September 1987 and entered into force on 1 January 1989. See the following: http://ozone.unep.org/new_site/en/Treaties/treaties_decisions-hb.php?sec_id=5

DOMAIN 3

Risk Identification, Monitoring, and Analysis

ORGANIZATIONS FACE A WIDE range of challenges today, including ever-expanding risks to organizational assets, intellectual property, and customer data. Understanding and managing these risks are integral components of organizational success. The security practitioner is expected to participate in organizational risk management process, assist in identifying risks to information systems, and develop and implement controls to mitigate identified risks. As a result, the security practitioner must have a firm understanding of risk, response, and recovery concepts and best practices.

TOPICS

The following topics are addressed in this chapter:

- ❏ Understand the risk management process

    - Risk management concepts (e.g., impacts, threats, vulnerabilities)

    - Risk assessment

    - Risk treatment (accept, transfer, mitigate, avoid)

    - Risk visibility and reporting (e.g., risk register, sharing threat intelligence)

    - Audit findings

- ❏ Perform security assessment activities

    - Participation in security and testing results

    - Penetration testing

    - Internal and external assessment (e.g., audit, compliance)

    - Vulnerability scanning

    - Interpretation and reporting of scanning and testing results

- ❏ Operate and maintain monitoring systems (e.g., continuous monitoring)

    - Events of interest

    - Logging

    - Source systems

- ❏ Analyze and report monitoring results

    - Security analytics, metrics, and trends (e.g., baseline)

    - Visualization

    - Event data analysis (e.g., log, packet dump, machine data)

    - Communicate findings

OBJECTIVES

Effective incident response allows organizations to respond to threats that attempt to exploit vulnerabilities to compromise the confidentiality, integrity, and availability of organizational assets.

A Systems Security Certified Practitioner (SSCP) plays an integral role in incident response at any organization. The security practitioner must

- Understand the organization's incident response policy and procedures
- Perform security assessments
- Operate and maintain monitoring systems
- Be able to execute the correct role in the incident response process

INTRODUCTION TO RISK MANAGEMENT

The security practitioner will be expected to be a key participant in the organizational risk management process. As a result, it is imperative that the security practitioner have a strong understanding of the responsibilities in the risk management process. To obtain this understanding, we will define key risk management concepts and then present an overview of the risk management process. We will then present real-world examples to reinforce key risk management concepts.

Risk Management Concepts

While you are reviewing risk management concepts, it is critical to remember that the ultimate purpose of information security is to reduce risks to organizational assets to levels that are deemed acceptable by senior management. Information security should not be performed using a "secure at any cost" approach. The cost of controls should never exceed the loss that would result if the confidentiality, integrity, or availability of a system were compromised. Risks, threats, vulnerabilities, and potential impacts should be assessed. Only after assessing these factors can cost-effective information security controls be selected and implemented that eliminate or reduce risks to acceptable levels.

We will reproduce the National Institute of Standards and Technology (NIST) Special Publication 800-30 R1, "Risk Management Guide for Information Systems,"[1] to establish definitions of key risk management concepts.

- **Risk**—A risk is a function of the likelihood of a given threat source's exercising a potential vulnerability, and the resulting impact of that adverse event on the organization.

- **Likelihood**—The probability that a potential vulnerability may be exercised within the construct of the associated threat environment.

- **Threat Source**—Either intent and method targeted at the intentional exploitation of a vulnerability or a situation or method that may accidentally trigger a vulnerability.

- **Threat**—The potential for a threat source to exercise (accidentally trigger or intentionally exploit) a specific vulnerability.

- **Vulnerability**—A flaw or weakness in system security procedures, design, implementation, or internal controls that could be exercised (accidentally triggered or intentionally exploited) and result in a security breach or a violation of the system's security policy.

- **Impact**—The magnitude of harm that could be caused by a threat's exercise of a vulnerability.

- **Asset**—Anything of value that is owned by an organization. Assets include both tangible items such as information systems and physical property and intangible assets such as intellectual property.

These basic risk management concepts merge to form a model for risk as seen in the NIST diagram in Figure 3.1.

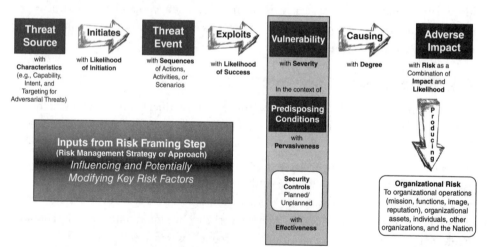

FIGURE 3.1 Determining likelihood of organizational risk

Now that we have established definitions for basic risk management concepts, we can proceed with an explanation of the risk management process. It is important to keep these definitions in mind when reviewing the risk management process because these concepts will be continually referenced.

Risk Management Process

Risk management is the process of identifying risks, assessing their potential impacts to the organization, determining the likelihood of their occurrence, communicating findings to management and other affected parties, and developing and implementing risk mitigation strategies to reduce risks to levels that are acceptable to the organization. The first step in the risk management process is conducting a risk assessment.

Risk Assessment

Risk assessments assess threats to information systems, system vulnerabilities, and weaknesses, and the likelihood that threats will exploit these vulnerabilities and weaknesses to cause adverse effects. For example, a risk assessment could be conducted to determine the likelihood that an un-patched system connected directly to the Internet would be compromised. The risk assessment would determine that there is almost 100% likelihood that the system would be compromised by a number of potential threats such as casual hackers and automated programs. Although this is an extreme example, it helps to illustrate the purpose of conducting risk assessments.

The security practitioner will be expected to be a key participant in the risk assessment process. The security practitioner's responsibilities may include identifying system, application, and network vulnerabilities or researching potential threats to information systems. Regardless of the security practitioner's role, it is important that the security practitioner understand the risk assessment process and how it relates to implementing controls, safeguards, and countermeasures to reduce risk exposure to acceptable levels.

When performing a risk assessment, an organization should use a methodology that uses repeatable steps to produce reliable results. Consistency is vital in the risk assessment process, as failure to follow an established methodology can result in inconsistent results. Inconsistent results prevent organizations from accurately assessing risks to organizational assets and can result in ineffective risk mitigation, risk transference, and risk acceptance decisions.

Although a number of risk assessment methodologies exist, they generally follow a similar approach. NIST Special Publication 800-30 R1, "Risk Management Guide for Information Technology Systems," details a four-step risk assessment process. The risk assessment process described by NIST is composed of the steps shown in Figure 3.2.

Although a complete discussion of each step described within the NIST Risk Assessment Process is outside the scope of this text, we will use the methodology as a guideline to explain the typical risk assessment process. A brief description of a number of the steps is provided to help the security practitioner understand the methodology and functions that the security practitioner will be expected to perform as an SSCP.

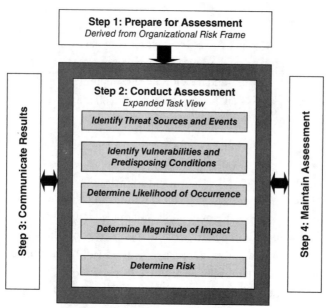

FIGURE 3.2 The NIST Risk Assessment Process

Step 1: Preparing for the Assessment

The first step in the risk assessment process is to prepare for the assessment. The objective of this step is to establish a context for the risk assessment. This context is established and informed by the results from the risk framing step of the risk management process. Risk framing identifies, for example, organizational information regarding policies and requirements for conducting risk assessments, specific assessment methodologies to be employed, procedures for selecting risk factors to be considered, scope of the assessments, rigor of analyses, degree of formality, and requirements that facilitate consistent and repeatable risk determinations across the organization. Preparing for a risk assessment includes the following tasks:

- Identify the purpose of the assessment.
- Identify the scope of the assessment.
- Identify the assumptions and constraints associated with the assessment.
- Identify the sources of information to be used as inputs to the assessment.
- Identify the risk model and analytic approaches (i.e., assessment and analysis approaches) to be employed during the assessment.

Step 2: Conducting the Assessment

The second step in the risk assessment process is to conduct the assessment. The objective of this step is to produce a list of information security risks that can be prioritized by risk level and used to inform risk response decisions. To accomplish this objective, organizations analyze threats and vulnerabilities, impacts and likelihood, and the uncertainty associated with the risk assessment process. This step also includes the gathering of essential information as a part of each task and is conducted in accordance with the assessment context established in the prepare step of the risk assessment process (Step 1). The expectation for risk assessments is to adequately cover the entire threat space in accordance with the specific definitions, guidance, and direction established during the prepare step. However, in practice, adequate coverage within available resources may dictate generalizing threat sources, threat events, and vulnerabilities to ensure full coverage and assessing specific, detailed sources, events, and vulnerabilities only as necessary to accomplish risk assessment objectives. Conducting risk assessments includes the following specific tasks:

- Identify threat sources that are relevant to organizations.
- Identify threat events that could be produced by those sources.
- Identify vulnerabilities within organizations that could be exploited by threat sources through specific threat events and the predisposing conditions that could affect successful exploitation.
- Determine the likelihood that the identified threat sources would initiate specific threat events and the likelihood that the threat events would be successful.
- Determine the adverse impacts to organizational operations and assets, individuals, other organizations, and the Nation resulting from the exploitation of vulnerabilities by threat sources (through specific threat events).
- Determine information security risks as a combination of likelihood of threat exploitation of vulnerabilities and the impact of such exploitation, including any uncertainties associated with the risk determinations.

The specific tasks are presented in a sequential manner for clarity. Depending on the purpose of the risk assessment, the SSCP may find reordering the tasks advantageous. Whatever adjustments the SSCP makes to the tasks, risk assessments should meet the stated purpose, scope, assumptions, and constraints established by the organizations initiating the assessments.

Step 2a: Identifying Threat Sources

As mentioned previously, a threat is the potential for a particular threat source to successfully exercise a specific vulnerability. During the threat identification stage, potential threats to information resources are identified. Threat sources can originate from natural threats, human threats, or environmental threats. Natural threats include earthquakes, floods, tornadoes, hurricanes, tsunamis, and the like. Human threats are events that either are caused through employee error or negligence or are events that are caused intentionally by humans via malicious attacks that attempt to compromise the confidentiality, integrity, and availability of IT systems and data. Environmental threats are those issues that arise because of environmental conditions such as power failure, HVAC failure, or electrical fire.

For the SSCP, the first step of a risk assessment involves understanding the threats that may target an organization. This step considers both adversarial threats and non-adversarial threats such as natural disasters. During this step, the security practitioner may

- Determine sources for obtaining threat information
- Determine what threat taxonomy may be used
- Provide input or determine what threat information will be used in the overall assessment

Several threat sources may be referenced as part of the threat identification. Honey pots and honey nets provide targeted and specific threat information in near–real time, but they require expert operation, interpretation, and analysis and therefore can be cumbersome and expensive for smaller organizations. Incorrectly configured and deployed honey pots/nets can also provide a staging ground for further attacks against an organization. Organizations may also consider threat catalogs such as Appendix D of NIST SP 800-30 R1 or the German BSI Threats Catalogue.[2]

An organization can subscribe to threat source information services. These services scan the Internet and the globe to determine active threats and how they may be targeting a specific industry, business, or economy. The more an organization is willing to pay, the more specific threat intelligence the organization may be able to maintain. Some programs such as the United States' FBI Infraguard are designed to provide threat information from the government to businesses and non-governmental organizations.

Since threat information is volatile yet crucial for the risk management process, organizations in similar economies or sectors may band together to share threat information between them. These collations often exist within a "no attribution" environment where confidentiality of the source of the threat information is the norm. While some areas, such as government, have done well in collaborating, other industries have been slow to adopt threat sharing for fear of losing competitive advantage over rivals.

After the threat identification process has been completed, a threat statement should be generated. A threat statement lists potential threat sources that could exploit system vulnerabilities. Successfully identifying threats coupled with vulnerability identification are prerequisites for selecting and implementing information security controls.

Step 2b: Identifying Potential Threat Events

Threat events are characterized by the threat sources that could initiate the events. The SSCP needs to define these threat events with sufficient detail to accomplish the purpose of the risk assessment. Multiple threat sources can initiate a single threat event.

Conversely, a single threat source can potentially initiate any of multiple threat events. Therefore, there can be a many-to-many relationship among threat events and threat sources that can potentially increase the complexity of the risk assessment. For each threat event identified, organizations need to determine the relevance of the event. The values selected by organizations have a direct linkage to organizational risk tolerance. The more risk averse, the greater the range of values considered. Organizations accepting greater risk or having a greater risk tolerance are more likely to require substantive evidence before giving serious consideration to threat events. If a threat event is deemed to be irrelevant, no further consideration is given. For relevant threat events, organizations need to identify all potential threat sources that could initiate the events.

Step 2c: Identifying Vulnerabilities and Predisposing Conditions

Identifying vulnerabilities is an important step in the risk assessment process. The step allows for the identification of both technical and nontechnical vulnerabilities that, if exploited, could result in a compromise of system or data confidentiality, integrity, and availability. A review of existing documentation and reports is a good starting point for the vulnerability identification process. This review can include the results of previous risk assessments. It can also include a review of audit reports from compliance assessments, a review of security bulletins and advisories provided by vendors, and data made available via personal and social networking. NIST SP 800-30 R1 Appendix F provides a set of tables for using in identifying predisposing conditions and vulnerabilities.

Vulnerability identification and assessment can be performed via a combination of automated and manual techniques. Automated techniques such as system scanning allow a security practitioner to identify technical vulnerabilities present in assessed IT systems. These technical vulnerabilities may result from failure to apply operating system and application patches in a timely manner, architecture design problems, or configuration errors. By using automated tools, systems can be rapidly assessed and vulnerabilities can be quickly identified.

Although a comprehensive list of vulnerability assessment tools is outside the scope of this text, an SSCP should spend a significant amount of time becoming familiar with the various tools that could be used to perform automated assessments. Although many commercial tools are available, there are also many open-source tools equally as effective in performing automated vulnerability assessments. Figure 3.3 is a screenshot of Nessus, a widely used vulnerability assessment tool, showing the progress of a network host scan.

Manual vulnerability assessment techniques may require more time to perform when compared to automated techniques. Typically, automated tools will initially be used to identify vulnerabilities. Manual techniques can then be used to validate automated findings. By performing manual techniques, one can eliminate false positives. False positives are potential vulnerabilities identified by automated tools that are not actual vulnerabilities.

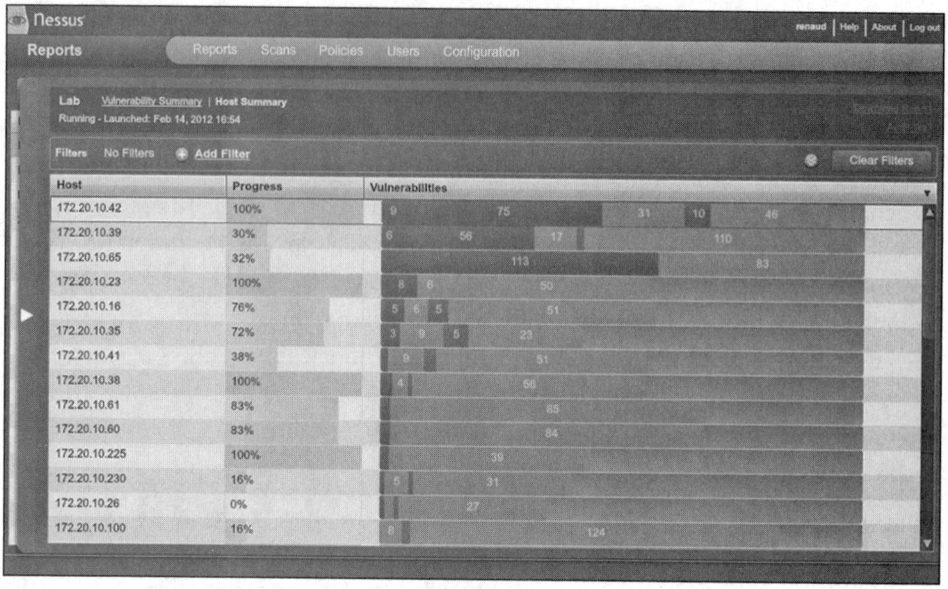

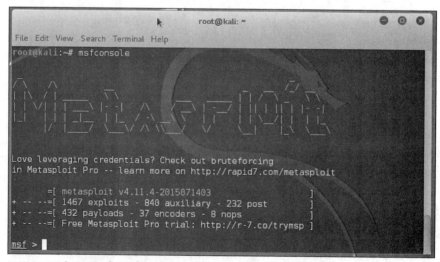

FIGURE 3.3 A screenshot of policy configuration using Nessus

Manual techniques may involve attempts to actually exploit vulnerabilities. When approved personnel attempt to exploit vulnerabilities to gain access to systems and data, it is referred to as penetration testing. Although vulnerability assessments merely attempt to identify vulnerabilities, penetration testing actually attempts to exploit vulnerabilities. Penetration testing is performed to assess security controls and to determine if vulnerabilities can be successfully exploited. Figure 3.4 is a screenshot of the Metasploit console, a widely used penetration-testing tool.

FIGURE 3.4 A screenshot of the Metasploit console

Step 2d: Determining Likelihood

Likelihood determination attempts to define the likelihood that a given vulnerability could be successfully exploited within the current environment. Likelihood is often the most difficult to determine in the risk framework. Factors that must be considered when assessing the likelihood of a successful exploit include

- The nature of the vulnerability, including factors such as:
    - The operating system, application, database, or device affected by the vulnerability
    - Whether local or remote access is required to exploit the vulnerability
    - The skills and tools required to exploit the vulnerability
- The threat source's motivation and capability, including factors such as:
    - Threat source motivational factors (e.g., financial gain, political motivation, revenge)
    - Capability (skills, tools, and knowledge required to exploit a given vulnerability)
- The effectiveness of controls deployed to prevent exploit of the given vulnerability

Step 2e: Determining Impact

An impact analysis defines the impact to an organization that would result if a vulnerability were successfully exploited. An impact analysis cannot be performed until system mission, system and data criticality, and system and data sensitivity have been obtained and assessed. The system mission refers to the functionality provided by the system in terms of business or IT processes supported. System and data criticality refer to the system's importance to supporting the organizational mission. System and data sensitivity refer to requirements for data confidentiality and integrity.

In many cases, system and data criticality and system and data sensitivity can be assessed by determining the adverse impact to the organization that would result from a loss of system and data confidentiality, integrity, or availability. Remember that confidentiality refers to the importance of restricting access to data so that they are not disclosed to unauthorized parties. Integrity refers to the importance that unauthorized modification of data is prevented. Availability refers to the importance that systems and data are available when needed to support business and technical requirements. When a person assesses each of these factors individually and aggregates the individual impacts resulting from a loss of confidentiality, integrity, and availability, the overall adverse impact from a system compromise can be assessed.

Impact can be assessed in either quantitative or qualitative terms. A quantitative impact analysis assigns a dollar value to the impact. The dollar value can be calculated based on an assessment of the likelihood of a threat source exploiting a vulnerability, the loss resulting from a successful exploit, and an approximation of the number of times that a threat source will exploit a vulnerability over a defined period. To understand how a dollar value can be assigned to an adverse impact, one must review some fundamental concepts. An explanation of each of these concepts is provided here:

- **Single Loss Expectancy (SLE)**—SLE represents the expected monetary loss to an organization from a threat to an asset. SLE is calculated by determining the value of a particular asset (AV) and the approximated exposure factor (EF). EF represents the portion of an asset that would be lost if a risk to the asset was realized. EF is expressed as a percentage value where 0% represents no damage to the asset and 100% represents complete destruction of the asset. SLE is calculated by multiplying the AV by the EF as indicated by the formula:

$$\text{Single Loss Expectancy} = \text{Asset Value} \times \text{Exposure Factor}$$

- **Annualized Loss Expectancy (ALE)**—ALE represents the expected annual loss because of a risk to a specific asset. ALE is calculated by determining the SLE and then multiplying it by the Annualized Rate of Occurrence (ARO) as indicated by the formula:

$$\text{Annual Loss Expectancy} = \text{Single Loss Expectancy} \times \text{Annualized Rate of Occurrence}$$

- **Annualized Rate of Occurrence**—ARO represents the expected number of exploitations by a specific threat of a vulnerability to an asset in a given year.

Organizations can use the results of annual loss expectancy calculations to determine the quantitative impact to an organization if an exploitation of a specific vulnerability were successful. In addition to the results of quantitative impact analysis, organizations should evaluate the results of qualitative impact analysis.

A qualitative impact analysis assesses impact in relative terms such as high impact, medium impact, and low impact without assigning a dollar value to the impact. A qualitative assessment is often used when it is difficult or impossible to accurately define loss in terms of dollars. For example, a qualitative assessment may be used to assess the impact resulting from a loss of customer confidence, from negative public relations, or from brand devaluation.

Organizations generally find it most helpful to use a blended approach to impact analysis. When they evaluate both the quantitative and qualitative impacts to an organization, a complete picture of impacts can be obtained. The results of these impact assessments provide required data for the risk determination process.

▶▶ **REAL WORLD EXAMPLE:**
Impact vs. Countermeasures

ABC Corp. has been experiencing increased hacking activity as indicated by their firewall and IPS logs. The logs also indicate that they have experienced at least one successful breach in the last 30 days. Upon further analysis of the breach, the security team has reported to senior management that the dollar value impact of the breach appears to be $10,000.

Senior management has asked the security team to come up with a recommendation to fix the issues that led to the breach. The recommendation from the team is that the countermeasures required to address the root cause of the breach will cost $30,000.

Senior management has asked you, as the SSCP, to evaluate the recommendation of the security team and ensure that the $30,000 expense to implement the countermeasures is justified.

Taking the loss encountered of $10,000 per a month, we can determine the annual loss expectancy as $120,000 assuming the frequency of attack and loss are consistent. Thus, the mitigation would pay for itself after three months ($30,000) and would provide a $10,000 loss prevention for each month after. Therefore, this would be a sound investment.

Step 2f: Risk Determination

In the risk determination step, the overall risk to an IT system is assessed. Risk determination uses the outputs from previous steps in the risk assessment process to assess overall risk. Risk determination results from the combination of

- The likelihood of a threat source attempting to exploit a specific vulnerability
- The magnitude of the impact that would result if an attempted exploit were successful
- The effectiveness of existing and planned security controls in reducing risk

A risk-level matrix can be created that analyzes the combined impact of these factors to assess the overall risk to a given IT system. The exact process for creating a risk-level matrix is outside the scope of this text. For additional information, refer to NIST Special Publication 800-30 R1, "Risk Management Guide for Information Technology Systems."

The result of creating a risk-level matrix is that overall risk level may be expressed in relative terms of high, medium, and low risk. Figure 3.5 provides an example of a risk matrix.

Threat Likelihood	Impact		
	Low (10)	Moderate (50)	High (100)
High (1.0)	10 × 1.0 = 10	50 × 1.0 = 50	100 × 1.0 = 100
Moderate (0.5)	10 × 0.5 = 5	50 × 0.5 = 25	100 × 0.5 = 50
Low (0.1)	10 × 0.1 = 1	50 × 0.1 = 5	100 × 0.1 = 10

Risk Scale: High (>50 to 100)   Moderate (>10 to 50)   Low (>1 to 10)   01527a

FIGURE 3.5 A risk-level matrix

A description of each risk level and recommended actions:

- **High Risk**—Significant risk to the organization and to the organizational mission exists. There is a strong need for corrective actions that include reevaluation of existing controls and implementation of additional controls. Corrective actions should be implemented as soon as possible to reduce risk to an acceptable level.

- **Medium Risk**—A moderate risk to the organization and to the organizational mission exists. There is a need for corrective actions that include reevaluation of existing controls and may include implementation of additional controls. Corrective actions should be implemented within a reasonable time frame to reduce risk to an acceptable level.

- **Low Risk**—A low risk to the organization exists. An evaluation should be performed to determine if the risk should be reduced or if it will be accepted. If it is determined that the risk should be reduced, corrective actions should be performed to reduce risk to an acceptable level.

Step 3: Communicating and Sharing Risk Assessment Information

The third step in the risk assessment process is to communicate the assessment results and share risk-related information. The objective of this step is to ensure that decision makers across the organization have the appropriate risk-related information needed to inform and guide risk decisions. Communicating and sharing information consists of the following specific tasks:

- Communicate the risk assessment results.

- Share information developed in the execution of the risk assessment to support other risk management activities.

Step 4: Maintaining the Risk Assessment

The fourth step in the risk assessment process is to maintain the assessment. The objective of this step is to keep current the specific knowledge of the risk organizations incur. The results of risk assessments inform risk management decisions and guide risk responses. To support the ongoing review of risk management decisions (e.g., acquisition decisions, authorization decisions for information systems and common controls, connection decisions), organizations maintain risk assessments to incorporate any changes detected through risk monitoring. Risk monitoring provides organizations with the means to, on an ongoing basis:

1. Determine the effectiveness of risk responses.

2. Identify risk-impacting changes to organizational information systems and the environments in which those systems operate.

3. Verify compliance.

Maintaining risk assessments includes the following specific tasks:

- Monitor risk factors identified in risk assessments on an ongoing basis and understand subsequent changes to those factors.

- Update the components of risk assessments reflecting the monitoring activities carried out by organizations.

✔ Risk Identification Exercise

Please see the section "Going Hands-on—Risk Identification Exercise" at the end of this domain for an interactive approach at learning to identify risk. This exercise will take the reader through the process of performing a basic vulnerability scan against a known vulnerable system using freely available tools.

Risk Treatment

Risk treatment is the next step in the risk assessment process. The goal of risk treatment is to reduce risk exposure to levels that are acceptable to the organization. Risk treatment can be performed using a number of different strategies. These strategies include

1. Risk mitigation

2. Risk transference

3. Risk avoidance

4. Risk acceptance

Risk Mitigation

Risk mitigation reduces risks to the organization by implementing technical, managerial, and operational controls. Controls should be selected and implemented to reduce risk to acceptable levels. When controls are selected, they should be selected based on their cost, effectiveness, and ability to reduce risk. Controls restrict or constrain behavior to acceptable actions. To help understand controls, look at some examples of security controls.

A simple control is the requirement for a password to access a critical system. When an organization implements a password control, unauthorized users would theoretically be prevented from accessing a system. The key to selecting controls is to select controls that are appropriate based on the risk to the organization. Although we noted that a password is an example of a control, we did not discuss the length of the password.

If a password is implemented that is one character long and must be changed on an annual basis, a control is implemented; however, the control will have almost no effect on reducing the risk to the organization because the password could be easily cracked. If the password is cracked, unauthorized users could access the system and, as a result, the control has not effectively reduced the risk to the organization.

On the other hand, if a password that is 200 characters long that must be changed on an hourly basis is implemented, it becomes a control that will effectively prevent authorized access. The issue in this case is that a password with those requirements will have an unacceptably high cost to the organization. End-users would experience a significant productivity loss because they would be constantly changing their passwords.

The key to control selection is to implement cost-effective controls that reduce or mitigate risks to levels that are acceptable to the organization. By implementing controls based on this concept, organizations will reduce risk but not totally eliminate it.

Controls can be categorized in technical, managerial, or operational control categories. Managerial controls are controls that dictate how activities should be performed. Policies, procedures, standards, and guidelines are examples of managerial controls. These controls provide a framework for managing personnel and operations. They also can establish requirements for systems operations. An example of a managerial control is the requirement that information security policies should be reviewed on an annual basis and updated as necessary to ensure that they accurately reflect the environment and remain valid.

Technical controls are designed to control end-user and system actions. They can exist within operating systems, applications, databases, and network devices. Examples of technical controls include password constraints, access control lists, firewalls, data encryption, antivirus software, and intrusion prevention systems.

Technical controls help to enforce requirements specified within administrative controls. For example, an organization could have implemented a malicious code policy as an administrative control. The policy could require that all end-users' systems have antivirus software installed. Installation of the antivirus software would be the technical control that provides support to the administrative control.

In addition to being categorized as technical, administrative, or operational, controls can be simultaneously categorized as either preventative or detective. Preventative controls attempt to prevent adverse behavior and actions from occurring. Examples of preventative controls include firewalls, intrusion prevention systems, and segregation of duties. Detective controls are used to detect actual or attempted violations of system security. Examples of detective controls include intrusion detection systems and audit logging.

Although implementing controls will reduce risk, some amount of risk will remain even after controls have been selected and implemented. The risk that remains after risk reduction and mitigation efforts are complete is referred to as *residual risk*. Organizations must determine how to treat this residual risk. Residual risk can be treated by *risk transference, risk avoidance*, or *risk acceptance*.

Risk Transference

Risk transference transfers risk from an organization to a third party. Some types of risk such as financial risk can be reduced by transferring it to a third party via a number of methods. The most common risk transference method is insurance. An organization can transfer its risk to a third party by purchasing insurance. When an organization purchases insurance, it effectively sells its risk to a third party. The insurer agrees to accept the risk in exchange for premium payments made by the insured. If the risk is realized, the insurer compensates the insured party for any incurred losses.

Organizations must be cautious when relying on risk transference because some risk cannot be transferred. Outsourcing sensitive information processing may seem like outsourcing the risk of personnel data breaches. If a breach occurs, surely those affected would understand that the outsourced processor caused the breach and focus their rage there, right? Unfortunately, this is rarely the case. In most instances, the victims seek damages against the organization that originally collected the information in the first place. Organizations must ensure they conduct their due diligence when transferring operations and data to third parties when the organization is still responsible for the protection of the data.

Finally, organizations must be aware of risk that cannot be transferred. While financial risk is easy to transfer to a third party through insurance, reputational damage and customer loyalty is almost impossible to transfer. When an information security risk affects these aspects of an organization, the organization must go on the defensive and engage public relations teams to try to maintain the goodwill of their customers and protect the reputation of their organization.

Risk Avoidance

Another alternative to mitigate risk is to avoid the risk. Risk can be avoided by eliminating the entire situation causing the risk. This could involve disabling system functionality or preventing risky activities when risk cannot be adequately reduced. In drastic measures, it can involve shutting down entire systems or parts of a business.

Risk Acceptance

Residual risk can also be accepted by an organization. A risk acceptance strategy indicates that an organization is willing to accept the risk associated with the potential occurrence of a specific event. It is important that when an organization chooses risk acceptance, it clearly understands the risk that is present, the probability that the loss related to the risk will occur, and the cost that would be incurred if the loss were realized. Organizations may determine that risk acceptance is appropriate when the cost of implementing controls exceeds the anticipated losses.

Risk Visibility and Reporting

Once assessed and quantified or qualified, risk should be reported and recorded. Organizations should have a way to aggregate risk in a centralized function that combines information security risk with other risk such as market risk, legal risk, human capital risk, and financial risk. The organizational risk executive function serves as a way to understand total risk to the organization. Risk is aggregated in a system called a risk register or, in some cases, a risk dashboard. The SSCP must ensure only risk information (not vulnerability or threat information) is reported to the risk register. The risk register serves as a way for the organization to know their possible exposure at a given time.

The risk register will generally be shared with stakeholders, allowing them to be kept aware of issues and providing a means of tracking the response to issues. It can be used to flag new risks and to make suggestions on what course of action to take to resolve any issues. The risk register is there to help with the decision-making process and enables managers and stakeholders to handle risk in the most appropriate way. The risk register is a document that contains information about identified risks, analysis of risk severity, and evaluations of the possible solutions to be applied. Presenting this in a spreadsheet is often the easiest way to manage things so that key information can be found and applied quickly and easily.

The SSCP should be familiar with how to create a risk register for the organization. If you are unsure how to create a risk register, the following is a brief guide on how to get started in just a few steps:

1. **Create the risk register**—Use a spreadsheet to document necessary information, as shown in Figure 3.6.

Risk Register

Functional Activity _____

Compiled By _____ Date _____

Reviewed By _____ Date _____

Ref	The Risk: What Can Happen and How It Can Happen	The Consequences of an Event Happening		Adequacy of Existing Controls	Consequence Rating	Likelihood Rating	Level of Risk	Risk Priority
		Consequences	Likelihood					

FIGURE 3.6 **Sample risk register**

2. **Record active risks**—Keep track of active risks by recording them in the risk register along with the date identified, date updated, target date, and closure date. Other useful information to include is the risk identification number, a description of the risk, type and severity of risk, its impact, possible response action, and the current status of risk.

3. **Assign a unique number to each risk element**—This will help to identify each unique risk so that you know what the status of the risk is at any given time.

The risk register addresses risk management in four key steps:

1. Identifying the risk

2. Evaluating the severity of any identified risks

3. Applying possible solutions to those risks

4. Monitoring and analyzing the effectiveness of any subsequent steps taken

Security Auditing Overview

A security audit is an evaluation of how well the objectives of a security framework are met and a verification to ensure the security framework is appropriate for the organization. Nothing that comes out of an audit should surprise security practitioners if they have been doing their continuous monitoring. Think of it this way. Monitoring is an ongoing evaluation of a security framework done by the folks who manage the security day-to-day, while an audit is an evaluation of the security framework performed by someone outside of the day-to-day security operations. Security audits serve two purposes for the security practitioner. First, they point out areas where security controls are lacking, policy is not being enforced, or ambiguity exists in the security framework. The second benefit of security audits is that they emphasize security things that are being done right. Auditors, in general, should not be perceived as the "bad guys" that are out to prove what a bad job the organization is doing. On the contrary, auditors should be viewed as professionals who are there to assist the organization in driving the security program forward and to assist security practitioners in making management aware of what security steps are being correctly taken and what more needs to be done.

So, who audits and why? There are two categories of auditors; the first type is an internal auditor. These people work for the company, and these audits can be perceived as an internal checkup. The other type of auditor is an external auditor. These folks either are under contract with the company to perform objective audits or are brought in by other external parties. Audits can be performed for several reasons. This list is by no means inclusive of all the reasons that an audit may be performed, but it covers most of them.

- **Annual Audit**—Most businesses perform a security audit on an annual basis as dictated by policy.

- **Event-Triggered Audit**—These audits are often conducted after a particular event occurs, such as an intrusion incident. They are used both to analyze what went wrong and, as with all audits, to confirm due diligence if needed.

- **Merger/Acquisition Audit**—These audits are performed before a merger/acquisition to give the purchasing company an idea of where the company they are trying to acquire stands on security in relation to their own security framework.

- **Regulation Compliance Audit**—These audits are used to confirm compliance with the IT security–related portions of legislated regulations such as Sarbanes–Oxley and HIPAA.

- **Ordered Audit**—Although rare, there are times when a company is ordered by the courts to have a security audit performed.

What are the auditors going to use as a benchmark to test against? Auditors should use the organization's security framework as a basis for them to audit against; however, to ensure that everything is covered, they will first compare the organization's framework against a well-known and accepted standard. What methodology will the auditors use for the audit? There are many different methodologies used by auditors worldwide. Here are a few of them:

- **ISO/IEC 27001:2013 (formerly BS 7799-2:2002)**—"Specification for Information Security Management." ISO/IEC 27001:2013 specifies the requirements for establishing, implementing, maintaining, and continually improving an information security management system within the context of the organization. It also includes requirements for the assessment and treatment of information security risks tailored to the needs of the organization. The requirements set out in ISO/IEC 27001:2013 are generic and are intended to be applicable to all organizations, regardless of type, size, or nature.

- **ISO/IEC 27002:2013 (previously named ISO/IEC 17799:2005)** — "Code of Practice for Information Security Management." ISO/IEC 27002:2013 gives guidelines for organizational information security standards and information security management practices including the selection, implementation, and management of controls taking into consideration the organization's information security risk environment(s). It is designed to be used by organizations that intend to

  - Select controls within the process of implementing an Information Security Management System based on ISO/IEC 27001

  - Implement commonly accepted information security controls

  - Develop their own information security management guidelines

- **NIST SP 800-37 R1** — "Guide for Applying the Risk Management Framework to Federal Information Systems," which can be retrofitted for private industry. This publication provides guidelines for applying the Risk Management Framework (RMF) to federal information systems. The six-step RMF includes security categorization, security control selection, security control implementation, security control assessment, information system authorization, and security control monitoring. The RMF promotes the concept of near real-time risk management and ongoing information system authorization through the implementation of robust continuous monitoring processes; provides senior leaders the necessary information to make cost-effective, risk-based decisions with regard to the organizational information systems supporting their core missions and business functions; and integrates information security into the enterprise architecture and system development life cycle. Applying the RMF within enterprises links risk management processes at the information system level to risk management processes at the organization level through a risk executive (function) and establishes lines of responsibility and accountability for security controls deployed within organizational information systems and inherited by those systems (i.e., common controls).

- **CobIT (Control Objectives for Information and related Technology)** — From the Information Systems Audit and Control Association (ISACA). With COBIT 5, ISACA introduced a framework for information security. It includes all aspects of ensuring reasonable and appropriate security for information resources. Its foundation is a set of principles upon which an organization should build and test security policies, standards, guidelines, processes, and controls:

  - Meeting stakeholder needs

  - Covering the enterprise end-to-end

  - Applying a single integrated framework

- Enabling a holistic approach
- Separating governance from management

Auditors may also use a methodology of their own design or one that has been adapted from several guidelines. What difference does it make to you as a security practitioner which methodology they use? From a technical standpoint, it does not matter; however, it is a good idea to be familiar with the methodology they are going to use to understand how management will be receiving the audit results.[3]

What Does an Auditor Do?

Auditors collect information about your security processes. Auditors are responsible for

- Providing independent assurance to management that security systems are effective
- Analyzing the appropriateness of organizational security objectives
- Analyzing the appropriateness of policies, standards, baselines, procedures, and guidelines that support security objectives
- Analyzing the effectiveness of the controls that support security policies
- Stating and explaining the scope of the systems to be audited

What Is the Audit Going to Cover?

Before auditors begin an audit, they define the audit scope that outlines what they are going to be looking at. One way to define the scope of an audit is to break it down into eight domains of security responsibility, that is, to break up the IT systems into manageable areas upon which audits may be based. For example, an audit may be broken into eight domains such as:

1. **User Domain**—The users themselves and their authentication methods
2. **Workstation Domain**—Often considered the end-user systems
3. **System/Application Domain**—Applications that you run on your network, such as e-mail, database, and web applications
4. **LAN Domain**—Equipment required to create the internal LAN
5. **LAN-to-WAN Domain**—The transition area between your firewall and the WAN, often where your DMZ resides
6. **WAN Domain**—Usually defined as things outside of your firewall
7. **Remote Access Domain**—How remote or traveling users access your network
8. **Cloud and Outsourced Domain**—In what areas has the organization outsourced data, processing, or transmission to other entities?

Auditors may also limit the scope by physical location, or they may just choose to review a subset of your security framework.

The security practitioner will be asked to participate in the audit by helping the auditors collect information and interpret the findings for the auditors. Having said that, there may be times when IT will not be asked to participate. They might be the reason for the audit, and the auditors need to get an unbiased interpretation of the data. There are several areas the security practitioner will be asked to participate in. Before participating in an audit, ensure controls, policies, and standards are in place to support target areas and be sure they are working up to the level prescribed. An audit is not the place to realize that logging or some other function is not working.

Documentation

As part of an audit, the auditors will want to review system documentation. This can include

- **Disaster/Business Recovery Documentation**—While some IT practitioners and auditors do not see this as part of a security audit, others feel that because the recovery process involves data recovery and system configuration, it is an important and often overlooked piece of information security.

- **Host Configuration Documentation**—Auditors are going to want to see the documentation on how hosts are configured on the organization's network both to see that everything is covered and to verify that the configuration documentation actually reflects what is being done.

- **Baseline Security Configuration Documentation for Each Type of Host**—As with the host configuration, this documentation does not just reflect the standard configuration data but specifically what steps are being done related to security.

- **Acceptable Use Documentation**—Organizations often spell out acceptable use policies under the user responsibilities policy and the administrator use policy. Some also include it for particular hosts. For example, a company may say that there is to be no transfer of business confidential information over the FTP (File Transfer Protocol) server within the user policies and reiterate that policy both in an acceptable use policy for the FTP server as well as use it as a login banner for FTP services. As long as the message is the same, there is no harm in repeating it in several places.

- **Change Management Documentation**—There are two different types of change management documentation needed to produce for auditors. The first one would be the policy outlining the change management process. The other would be documentation reflecting changes made to a host.

- **Data Classification Documentation** — How are data classified? Are there some data the organization should spend more effort on securing than others? Having data classification documentation comes in handy for justifying why some hosts have more security restrictions than others do.

- **Business Flow Documentation** — Although not exactly related to IT security, documentation that shows how business data flows through the network can be a great aid to auditors trying to understand how everything works. For example, how does order entry data flow through the system from when the order is taken until it is shipped out to the customer? What systems do data reside on, and how do data move around the network?

RESPONDING TO AN AUDIT

Once the security practitioner has finished helping the auditors gather the required data and finished assisting them with interpreting the information, the practitioner's work is not over. There are still a few more steps that need to be accomplished to complete the audit process.

Exit Interview

After an audit is performed, an exit interview will alert personnel to glaring issues they need to be concerned about immediately. Besides these preliminary alerts, an auditor should avoid giving detailed verbal assessments, which may falsely set the expectation level of the organization with regard to security preparedness in the audited scope.

Presentation of Audit Findings

After the auditors have finished tabulating their results, they will present the findings to management. These findings will contain a comparison of the audit findings versus the company's security framework and industry standards or "best practices." These findings will also contain recommendations for mitigation or correction of documented risks or instances of noncompliance.

Management Response

Management will have the opportunity to review the audit findings and respond to the auditors. This is a written response that becomes part of the audit documentation. It outlines plans to remedy findings that are out of compliance, or it explains why management disagrees with the audit findings.

The security practitioner should be involved in the presentation of the audit findings and assist with the management response. Even if input is not sought for the management response, the security practitioner needs to be aware of what issues were presented and what the management's responses to those issues were.

Once all these steps are completed, the security cycle starts over again. The findings of the audit need to be fixed, mitigated, or introduced into the organization's security framework.

SECURITY ASSESSMENT ACTIVITIES

The security practitioner will be expected to perform security assessment activities including but not limited to vulnerability scanning, penetration testing, internal-external assessment, and interpreting the outcomes of the results.

Vulnerability Scanning and Analysis

Vulnerability scanning is simply the process of checking a system for weaknesses. These vulnerabilities can take the form of applications or operating systems that are missing patches, misconfiguration of systems, unnecessary applications, or open ports. While these tests can be conducted from outside the network, as an attacker would, it is advisable to do a vulnerability assessment from a network segment that has unrestricted access to the host the security practitioner is conducting the assessment against. Why is this? If the security practitioner tests a system only from the outside world, the security practitioner will identify any vulnerability that can be exploited from the outside. However, what happens if an attacker gains access inside the target network? Now there are vulnerabilities exposed to the attacker that could have easily been avoided. Unlike a penetration test, which is discussed later in this domain, a vulnerability tester has access to network diagrams, configurations, login credentials, and other information needed to make a complete evaluation of the system. The goal of a vulnerability assessment is to study the security level of the systems, identify problems, offer mitigation techniques, and assist in prioritizing improvements.

The benefits of vulnerability testing include the following:

- It identifies system vulnerabilities.
- It allows for the prioritization of mitigation tasks based on system criticality and risk.
- It is considered a useful tool for comparing security posture over time, especially when done consistently each period.

The disadvantages of vulnerability testing include

- It may not effectively focus efforts if the test is not designed appropriately. Sometimes testers bite off more than they can chew.

- It has the potential to crash the network or host being tested if dangerous tests are chosen. (Innocent and noninvasive tests have been known to cause system crashes.)

Note that vulnerability testing software is often placed into two broad categories:

- General vulnerability
- Application-specific vulnerability

General vulnerability software probes hosts and operating systems for known flaws. It also probes common applications for flaws. Application-specific vulnerability tools are designed specifically to analyze certain types of application software. For example, database scanners are optimized to understand the deep issues and weaknesses of Oracle databases, Microsoft SQL Server, etc., and they can uncover implementation problems therein. Scanners optimized for web servers look deeply into issues surrounding those systems.

Vulnerability scanning software, in general, is often referred to as V/A (vulnerability assessment) software and sometimes combines a port mapping function to identify which hosts are where and the applications they offer with further analysis that assigns vulnerabilities to applications. Good vulnerability software will offer mitigation techniques or links to manufacturer websites for further research. This stage of security testing is often an automated software process. It is also beneficial to use multiple tools and cross-reference the results of those tools for a more accurate picture. As with any automated process, the security practitioner needs to examine the results closely to ensure that they are accurate for the organization's environment.

Vulnerability testing usually employs software specific to the activity and tends to have the following qualities:

- **OS Fingerprinting**—This technique is used to identify the operating system in use on a target. OS fingerprinting is the process where a scanner can determine the operating system of the host by analyzing the TCP/IP stack flag settings. These settings vary on each operating system from vendor to vendor or by TCP/IP stack analysis and banner grabbing. Banner grabbing is reading the response banner presented for several ports such as FTP, HTTP, and Telnet. This function is sometimes built into mapping software and sometimes into vulnerability software.

- **Stimulus and Response Algorithms**—These are techniques to identify application software versions and then reference these versions with known vulnerabilities. Stimulus involves sending one or more packets at the target. Depending on the response, the tester can infer information about the target's applications. For example, to determine the version of the HTTP server, the vulnerability testing software might send an HTTP GET request to a web server, just like a browser would (the stimulus), and read the reply information it receives back (the response) for information that details the fact that it is Apache version X, IIS version Y, etc.

- **Privileged Logon Ability**—The ability to automatically log onto a host or group of hosts with user credentials (administrator-level or other level) for a deeper "authorized" look at systems is desirable.

- **Cross-Referencing**—OS and applications/services (discovered during the port-mapping phase) should be cross-referenced to identify possible vulnerabilities. For example, if OS fingerprinting reveals that the host runs Red Hat Linux 8.0 and that portmapper is one of the listening programs, any pre-8.0 portmapper vulnerabilities can likely be ruled out. Keep in mind that old vulnerabilities have resurfaced in later versions of code even though they were patched at one time. While these instances may occur, the filtering based on OS and application fingerprinting will help the security practitioner better target systems and use the security practitioner's time more effectively.

- **Update Capability**—Scanners must be kept up to date with the latest vulnerability signatures; otherwise, they will not be able to detect newer problems and vulnerabilities. Commercial tools that do not have quality personnel dedicated to updating the product are of reduced effectiveness. Likewise, open-source scanners should have a qualified following to keep them up to date.

- **Reporting Capability**—Without the ability to report, a scanner does not serve much purpose. Good scanners provide the ability to export scan data in a variety of formats, including viewing in HTML or PDF format or to third-party reporting software, and are configurable enough to give the ability to filter reports into high-, mid-, and low-level detail depending on the intended audience for the report. Reports are used as basis for determining mitigation activities later. Additionally, many scanners are now feeding automated risk management dashboards using application portal interfaces.

Problems that may arise when using vulnerability analysis tools include

- **False Positives**—When scanners use generalized tests or if the scanner does not have the ability to deeply scan the application, it might not be able to determine whether the application actually has vulnerability. It might result in information that says the application might have vulnerability. If it sees that the server is running a remote control application, the test software may indicate that the security practitioner has a "High" vulnerability. However, if the security practitioner has taken care to implement the remote control application to a high standard, the organization's vulnerability is not as high.

- **Crash Exposure**—V/A software has some inherent dangers because much of the vulnerability testing software includes denial-of-service test scripts (as well as other scripts), which, if used carelessly, can crash hosts. Ensure that hosts being tested have proper backups and that the security practitioner tests during times that will have the lowest impact on business operations.

- **Temporal Information**—Scans are temporal in nature, which means that the scan results the security practitioner has today become stale as time moves on and new vulnerabilities are discovered. Therefore, scans must be performed periodically with scanners that are up to date with the latest vulnerability signatures.

Scanner Tools

A variety of scanner tools are available:

- Nessus open source scanner—`http://www.tenable.com/products/nessus`
- eEye Digital Security's Retina—`http://www.beyondtrust.com/Products/ RetinaNetworkSecurityScanner/`
- SAINT—`http://www.saintcorporation.com/`
- For a more in-depth list, see `http://sectools.org/web-scanners.html`

Weeding Out False Positives

Even if a scanner reports a service as vulnerable or missing a patch that leads to vulnerability, the system is not necessarily vulnerable. Accuracy is a function of the scanner's quality, that is, how complete and concise the testing mechanisms are built (better tests equal better results), how up to date the testing scripts are (fresher scripts are more likely to spot a fuller range of known problems), and how well it performs OS fingerprinting (knowing which OS the host runs helps the scanner pinpoint issues for applications that run on that OS). Double-check the scanner's work. Verify that a claimed vulnerability is an actual vulnerability. Good scanners will reference documents to help the security practitioner learn more about the issue.

Host Scanning

Organizations serious about security create hardened host configuration procedures and use policy to mandate host deployment and change. There are many ingredients to creating a secure host, but the security practitioner should always remember that what is secure today might not be secure tomorrow, because conditions are ever changing. There are several areas to consider when securing a host or when evaluating its security. These are discussed in the following sections.

Disabling Unneeded Services

Services that are not critical to the role the host serves should be disabled or removed as appropriate for that platform. For the services the host does offer, make sure it is using server programs considered secure, make sure the security practitioner fully understands them, and tighten the configuration files to the highest degree possible. Unneeded services are often installed and left at their defaults, but since they are not needed, administrators ignore or forget about them. This may draw unwanted data traffic to the host from other hosts attempting connections, and it will leave the host vulnerable to weaknesses in the services. If a host does not need a particular host process for its operation, do not install it. If software is installed but not used or intended for use on the machine, it may not be remembered or documented that software is on the machine and therefore will likely not be patched. Port mapping programs use many techniques to discover services available on a host. These results should be compared with the policy that defines this host and its role. One must continually ask the critical questions, for the less a host offers as a service to the world while still maintaining its job, the better for its security (because there is less chance of subverting extraneous applications).

Disabling Insecure Services

Certain programs used on systems are known to be insecure, cannot be made secure, and are easily exploitable; therefore, use only secure alternatives. These applications were developed for private, secure LAN environments, but as connectivity proliferated worldwide, their use has been taken to insecure communication channels. Their weakness falls into three categories:

- They usually send authentication information unencrypted. For example, FTP and Telnet send username and passwords in the clear.
- They usually send data unencrypted. For example, HTTP sends data from client to server and back again entirely in the clear. For many applications, this is acceptable; however, for some it is not.
- SMTP also sends mail data in the clear unless it is secured by the application (e.g., the use of Pretty Good Privacy [PGP] within Outlook).

Common services are studied carefully for weaknesses by people motivated to attack the organization's systems. Therefore, to protect hosts, one must understand the implications of using these and other services that are commonly hacked. Eliminate them when necessary or substitute them for more secure versions. For example:

- To ensure privacy of login information as well as the contents of client to server transactions, use SSH (secure shell) to log in to hosts remotely instead of Telnet.

- Use SSH as a secure way to send insecure data communications between hosts by redirecting the insecure data into an SSH wrapper. The details for doing this are different from system to system.

- Use SCP (Secure Copy) instead of FTP (File Transfer Protocol).

Ensuring Least Privilege File System Permissions

Least privilege is the concept that describes the minimum number of permissions required to perform a particular task. This applies to services/daemon processes as well as user permissions. Often systems installed out of the box are at minimum security levels. Make an effort to understand how secure newly installed configurations are, and take steps to lock down settings using vendor recommendations.

Making Sure File System Permissions Are as Tight as Possible

For UNIX-based systems, remove all unnecessary SUID (set used ID) and SGID (set group ID) programs that embed the ability for a program running in one user context to access another program. This ability becomes even more dangerous in the context of a program running with root user permissions as a part of its normal operation. For Windows-based systems, use the Microsoft Management Center (MMC) "security configuration and analysis" and "security templates" snap-ins to analyze and secure multiple features of the operation system, including audit and policy settings and the registry.

Establishing and Enforcing a Patching Policy

Patches are pieces of software code meant to fix a vulnerability or problem that has been identified in a portion of an operating system or in an application that runs on a host. Keep the following in mind regarding patching:

- Patches should be tested for functionality, stability, and security. You should also ensure that the patch does not change the security configuration of the organization's host. Some patches might reinstall a default account or change configuration settings back to a default mode. You need a way to test whether new patches will break a system or an application running on a system. When you are patching highly critical systems, it is advised to deploy the patch in a test environment that mimics the real environment. If the security practitioner does not have this luxury, only deploy patches at noncritical times, have a back-out plan, and apply patches in steps (meaning one by one) to ensure that each one was successful and the system is still operating.

- Use patch reporting systems that evaluate whether systems have patches installed completely and correctly and which patches are missing. Many vulnerability analysis tools have this function built into them, but be sure to understand how often the V/A tool vendor updates this list versus another vendor who specializes in patch analysis systems. Oftentimes, some vendors have better updating systems than others.

- Optimally, tools should test to see if once a patch has been applied to remove a vulnerability, the vulnerability does not still exist. Patch application sometimes includes a manual remediation component like a registry change or removing a user, and if the IT person applied the patch but did not perform the manual remediation component, the vulnerability may still exist.

Examining Applications for Weakness

In a perfect world, applications are built from the ground up with security in mind. Applications should prevent privilege escalation and buffer overflows and a myriad of other threatening problems. However, this is not always the case, and applications need to be evaluated for their ability not to compromise a host. Insecure services and daemons that run on hardened hosts may by nature weaken the host. Applications should come from trusted sources. Similarly, it is inadvisable to download executables from websites the security practitioner knows nothing about. Executables should be hashed and verified with the publisher. Signed executables also provide a level of assurance regarding the integrity of the file. Some programs can help evaluate a host's applications for problems. In particular, these focus on web-based systems and database systems:

- Nikto (`http://www.cirt.net`) evaluates web CGI systems for common and uncommon vulnerabilities in implementation.
- Web Inspect (`http://www.purehacking.com.au`) is an automated web server scanning tool.
- Trustwave (`https://www.trustwave.com`) evaluates applications, especially various types of databases, for vulnerabilities.

The SSCP should do the following:

- Ensure that antivirus and antimalware software is installed and is up to date with the latest scan engine and pattern file offered by the vendor.

- Use products that encourage easy management and updates of signatures; otherwise, the systems may fail to be updated, rendering them ineffective to new exploits.

- Use products that centralize reporting of problems to spot problem areas and trends.

- Use system logging. Logging methods are advisable to ensure that system events are noted and securely stored, in the event they are needed later.

- Subscribe to vendor information. Vendors often publish information regularly, not only to keep their name in front of the security practitioner but also to inform the security practitioner of security updates and best practices for configuring their systems. Other organizations such as Security Focus (`http://www.securityfocus.com`) and CERT (`http://www.cert.org`) publish news of vulnerabilities. Some tools also specialize in determining when a system's software platform is out of compliance with the latest patches.

Firewall and Router Testing

Firewalls are designed to be points of data restriction (choke points) between security domains. They operate on a set of rules driven by a security policy to determine what types of data are allowed from one side to the other (point A to point B) and back again (point B to point A). Similarly, routers can also serve some of these functions when configured with access control lists (ACLs). Organizations deploy these devices to not only connect network segments together but also to restrict access to only those data flows that are required. This can help protect organizational data assets. Routers with ACLs, if used, are usually placed in front of the firewalls to reduce the noise and volume of traffic hitting the firewall. This allows the firewall to be more thorough in its analysis and handling of traffic. This strategy is also known as layering or defense in depth.

Changes to devices should be governed by change control processes that specify what types of changes can occur and when they can occur. This prevents haphazard and dangerous changes to devices that are designed to protect internal systems from other potentially hostile networks, such as the Internet or an extranet to which the organization's internal network connects. Change control processes should include security testing to ensure the changes were implemented correctly and as expected.

Configuration of these devices should be reflected in security procedures, and the rules of the access control lists should be engendered by organizational policy. The point of testing is to ensure machine configurations match approved policy.

▶▶ REAL WORLD EXAMPLE:
Internet Perimeter Systems

A sample baseline for the Internet perimeter systems is given below.

Edge routers will have the following qualities:

- For management—Telnet disabled; SSH enabled.
- An authentication system that verifies that the person logging onto the router (for managing it) is who they say they are; accomplished with one-time password system.
- An authorization system that verifies that the logged on administrator has the privileges to perform the management routines they are attempting to invoke.
- An accounting system that tracks the commands that were invoked; this forms the audit trail.
- Basic intrusion detection signature recognition functionality.
- Syslog event reporting to an internal host.
- Blocking of RFC1918 (non-routable addresses) and packets sourced from 0.0.0.0 inbound and outbound.
- Blocking of inbound MS networking, MS SQL communication, TFTP, Oracle SQL*Net, DHCP, all types of ICMP packets except for path MTU and echo replies. It should be noted that some of these ports may be necessary for business operations, and they must be examined on a case-by-case basis before blocking.

Firewalls will have the following qualities:

- For management—Telnet disabled; SSH or SSL enabled.
- An authentication system that verifies that the person logging onto the firewall (for managing it) is who they say they are; accomplished with one-time password system.
- An authorization system that verifies that the logged on administrator has the privileges to perform the management routines they are attempting to invoke.
- An accounting system that tracks the commands that were invoked (this forms the audit trail).
- Event report logging to an internal host.

CONTINUES

- Network address translation functionality, if required, is working properly.
- Enabling inbound transmissions from anywhere to the organizational web server, FTP server, SMTP mail server, and e-commerce server (for example).
- Enabling inbound transmissions back to internal users that originally established the connections.
- Enabling outbound HTTP, HTTPS, FTP, and DNS from anyone on the inside (if approved in the policy).
- Enabling outbound SMTP from the mail server to any other mail server.
- Blocking all other outbound access.

With this sample baseline in mind, port scanners and vulnerability scanners can be leveraged to test the choke point's ability to filter as specified. If internal (trusted) systems are reachable from the external (untrusted) side in ways not specified by policy, a mismatch has occurred and should be assessed. Likewise, internal to external testing should conclude that only the allowed outbound traffic could occur. The test should compare a device's logs with the tests dispatched from the test host.

Advanced firewall testing will test a device's ability to perform the following (this is a partial list and is a function of the firewall's capabilities):

- Limit TCP port scanning reconnaissance techniques (explained earlier in this domain) including SYN, FIN, XMAS, and NULL via the firewall.
- Limit ICMP and UDP port scanning reconnaissance techniques.
- Limit overlapping packet fragments.
- Limit half-open connections to trusted side devices. Attacks like these are called SYN attacks, when the attacker begins the process of opening many connections but never completes any of them, eventually exhausting the target host's memory resources.

Advanced firewall testing can leverage a vulnerability or port scanner's ability to dispatch denial-of-service and reconnaissance tests. A scanner can be configured to direct, for example, massive amounts of SYN packets at an internal host. If the firewall is operating properly and effectively, it will limit the number of these half-open attempts by intercepting them so that the internal host is not adversely affected. These tests must be used with care because there is always a chance that the firewall will not do what is expected and the internal hosts might be affected.

Security Monitoring Testing

IDS systems are technical security controls designed to monitor for and alert on the presence of suspicious or disallowed system activity within host processes and across networks. Device logging is used for recording many types of events that occur within hosts and network devices. Logs, whether generated by IDS or hosts, are used as audit trails and permanent records of what happened and when. Organizations have a responsibility to ensure that their monitoring systems are functioning correctly and alerting on the broad range of communications commonly in use. Documenting this testing can also be used to show due diligence. Likewise, the security practitioner can use testing to confirm that IDS detects traffic patterns as claimed by the vendor.

With regard to IDS testing, methods should include the ability to provide a stimulus (i.e., send data that simulate an exploitation of a particular vulnerability) and observe the appropriate response by the IDS. Testing can also uncover an IDS's inability to detect purposeful evasion techniques that might be used by attackers. Under controlled conditions, stimulus can be crafted and sent from vulnerability scanners. Response can be observed in log files generated by the IDS or any other monitoring system used in conjunction with the IDS. If the appropriate response is not generated, investigation of the causes can be undertaken.

With regard to host logging tests, methods should also include the ability to provide a stimulus (i.e., send data that simulates a "log-able" event) and observe the appropriate response by the monitoring system. Under controlled conditions, stimulus can be crafted in many ways depending on the security practitioner's test. For example, if a host is configured to log an alert every time an administrator or equivalent logs on, the security practitioner can simply log on as the "root" user to the organization's UNIX system. In this example, the response can be observed in the system's log files. If the appropriate log entry is not generated, investigation of the causes can be undertaken.

The overall goal is to make sure the monitoring is configured to the organization's specifications and that it has all of the features needed.

The following traffic types and conditions are those the security practitioner should consider testing for in an IDS environment, as vulnerability exploits can be contained within any of them. If the monitoring systems the security practitioner uses do not cover all of them, the organization's systems are open to exploitation:

- **Data Patterns That Are Contained within Single Packets**—This is considered a minimum functionality because the IDS need only search through a single packet for an exploit.
- **Data Patterns Contained within Multiple Packets**—This is considered a desirable function because there is often more than one packet in a data stream between two hosts. This function, stateful pattern matching, requires the IDS to

"remember" packets it saw in the past to reassemble them as well as perform analysis to determine if exploits are contained within the aggregate payload.

- **Obfuscated Data**—This refers to data that is converted from ASCII to Hexadecimal or Unicode characters and then sent in one or more packets. The IDS must be able to convert the code among all of these formats. If a signature that describes an exploit is written in ASCII but the exploit arrives at the organization's system in Unicode, the IDS must convert it back to ASCII to recognize it as an exploit.

- **Fragmented Data**—IP data can be fragmented across many small packets, which are then reassembled by the receiving host. Fragmentation occasionally happens in normal communications. In contrast, overlapping fragments is a situation where portions of IP datagrams overwrite and supersede one another as they are reassembled on the receiving system (a teardrop attack). This can wreak havoc on a computer, which can become confused and overloaded during the reassembly process. IDS must understand how to reassemble fragmented data and overlapping fragmented data so it can analyze the resulting data. These techniques are employed by attackers to subvert systems and to evade detection.

- **Protocol Embedded Attacks**—IDS should be able to decode (i.e., break apart, understand, and process) commonly used applications (DNS, SSL, HTTP, FTP, SQL, etc.), just like a host would, to determine whether an attacker has manipulated code that might crash the application or host on which it runs. Therefore, testing should employ exploits embedded within application data.

- **Flooding Detection**—An IDS should be able to detect conditions indicative of a denial-of-service flood, when too many packets originate from one or more sources to one or more destinations. Thresholds are determined within the configuration. For example, an IDS should be able to detect if more than 10 half-open connections are opened within 2 seconds to any one host on the organization's network.

Intrusion Prevention Systems (IPS) Security Monitoring

IPSs are technical security controls designed to monitor and alert for the presence of suspicious or disallowed system activity within host processes and across networks and then take action on suspicious activities. Likewise, the security practitioner can use testing to confirm that IPS detects traffic patterns and reacts as claimed by the vendor. When one is auditing an IPS, its position in the architecture is slightly different from that of an IDS; an IPS needs to be positioned inline of the traffic flow so the appropriate action can be taken. Some of the other key differences are as follows: The IPS acts on issues and handles the problems, while an IDS only reports on the traffic and requires some other party to react to the situation. The negative consequence of the IPS is that it is possible to reject good traffic and there will only be the logs of the IPS to show why the good traffic is getting rejected. Many times, the networking staff may not have access to those logs and may find network troubleshooting more difficult.

Security Gateway Testing

Some organizations use security gateways or web proxies to intercept certain communications and examine them for validity. Gateways perform their analysis on these communications based on a set of rules supplied by the organization—rules driven by policy—and pass them along if they are deemed appropriate and exploitation-free, or block them if they are not. Security gateway types include the following:

- **Antivirus Gateways**—These systems monitor for viruses contained within communications of major application types like web traffic, e-mail, and FTP.

- **Java/ActiveX Filters**—These systems screen communications for these components and block or limit their transmission.

- **Web Traffic Screening**—These systems block web traffic to and from specific sites or sites of a specific type (gambling, pornography, games, travel and leisure, etc.).

Security testing should encompass these gateway devices to ensure their proper operation. Depending on the device, the easiest way to test to ensure that it is working is try to perform the behavior that it is supposed to block. There are "standard" antivirus (AV) test files available on the Internet that do not contain a virus but have a signature that will be discovered by all major AV vendors. While this file will not ensure that the organization's AV will catch everything, it will at least confirm that the gateway is looking into the traffic for virus patterns.

Wireless Networking Testing

With the proliferation of wireless access devices comes the common situation where they are not configured for even minimal authentication and encryption because the people deploying them generally have no knowledge of the ramifications. Therefore, periodic wireless testing to spot unofficial access points is needed.

Adding 802.11-based wireless access points (APs) to networks increases overall convenience for users, mostly because of the new mobility that is possible. Whether using hand-held wireless PDA devices, laptop computers, or the newly emerging wireless voice over IP telephones, users are now able to flexibly collaborate outside of the office confines—ordinarily within the building and within range of an AP—while still remaining connected to network-based resources. To enable wireless access, one can procure an inexpensive wireless access point and plug it into the network. Communication takes place from the unwired device to the AP. The AP serves (usually) as a bridge to the wired network.

The problem with this from a security perspective is that allowing the addition of one or more AP units onto the network infrastructure will likely open a large security hole. Therefore, no matter how secure the organization's wired network is, adding one AP with no configured security is like adding a network connection to the parking lot, which allows anyone with the right tools and motivation to access the network. The implication here is that many APs as originally implemented in the 802.11b/g/n standard have easily breakable security. Security testers should have methods to detect rogue APs that have been added by employees or unauthorized persons so these wireless security holes can be examined. The following wireless networking high points discuss some of the issues surrounding security of these systems:

- Wireless-enabled devices (e.g., laptops) can associate with wireless access points or other wireless devices to form a bridged connection to the wired network.

- Without some form of authentication, rogue devices can attach to the wireless network.

- Without some form of encryption, data transferring between the wired and the wireless network can be captured.

With this information, a security tester can test for the effectiveness of wireless security in the environment using specialized tools and techniques as presented here.

To search for rogue (unauthorized) access points, the security practitioner can use some of the following techniques:

- Use a network vulnerability scanner with signatures that specifically scan for MAC addresses (of the wired port) of vendors that produce AP units, and then attempt to connect to that interface on an HTTP port. If the unit responds, analyze the web code to determine if it is a webpage related to the management of the AP device. This requires periodic scanning and will leave the server vulnerable until the next scan.

- Use a laptop or handheld unit loaded with software that analyzes 802.11x radio frequency (RF) transmissions for SSIDs and WAP wired side MAC addresses that do not belong to the company or are not authorized. Make sure discovery tools pick up all bands and 802.11x types; that is, if the security practitioner only tests for 802.11b, the security practitioner may miss rogue 802.11a units. This requires periodic scanning by physically walking through the organization's grounds and will leave the organization vulnerable until the next scan.

- Up and coming solutions allow for authorized APs and wireless clients to detect unauthorized RF transmissions and "squeal" on the rogue access point. This information can be used to automatically disable an infrastructure switch port to which a rogue has connected.

To lock down the enterprise from the possibility of rogue APs, the security practitioner can do the following:

- Enable MAC address filtering on the infrastructure switches. This technique matches each port to a known MAC address. If someone plugs in an unapproved MAC to a switch port expecting another MAC address, the AP will never be able to join the network from the wired side unless it has its MAC changed.

To gauge security effectiveness of authorized APs:

- Discover authorized APs using the tools described herein and ensure they require encryption.

- Ensure discovered APs meet other policy requirements such as the type of authentication (802.1x or other), SSID naming structure, and MAC address filtering.

- Ensure APs have appropriate layer 2 Ethernet type filters, layer 3 protocol filters, and layer 4 port filters (to match the organization's configuration procedures) so that untrusted wireless traffic coming into the AP is limited to only that which is needed and required.

Wireless Tools

There are a variety of useful wireless tools available:

- **Netstumbler** (http://www.netstumbler.com)—Windows software that detects 802.11b information through RF detection including SSID, whether communication is encrypted, and signal strength.

- **Kismet** (http://www.kismetwireless.net)—Linux software that detects 802.11b and 802.11a information through RF detection including SSID, whether communication is encrypted, and signal strength. It features the ability to rewrite the MAC address on select wireless cards.

- **Wellenreiter** (http://sourceforge.net/projects/wellenreiter/?source=directory)—Linux software that detects wireless networks. It runs on Linux-based handheld PDA computers.

- **Nessus** (http://www.nessus.org)—Linux software for vulnerability assessment that includes 30-plus signatures to detect WAP units.

- **Aircrack-NG** (http://www.aircrack-ng.org/doku.php)—Aircrack-ng is an 802.11 WEP and WPA-PSK keys cracking program that can recover keys once enough data packets have been captured. It implements the standard FMS attack along with some optimizations like KoreK attacks, as well as the PTW attack, thus making the attack much faster compared to other WEP cracking tools. In fact, Aircrack-ng is a set of tools for auditing wireless networks.

War Dialing

War dialing attempts to locate unauthorized, also called *rogue*, modems connected to computers that are connected to networks. Attackers use tools to sequentially and automatically dial large blocks of numbers used by the organization in the hopes that rogue modems or modems used for out-of-band communication will answer and allow them to make a remote asynchronous connection to it. With weak or nonexistent authentication, these rogue modems may serve as a back door into the heart of a network, especially when connected to computers that host remote control applications with lax security. Security testers can use war dialing techniques as a preventative measure and attempt to discover these modems for subsequent elimination. Although modems and war dialing have fallen out of favor in the IT world, a security practitioner still needs to check for the presence of unauthorized modems connected to their network.

War Driving

War driving is the wireless equivalent of war dialing. While war dialing involves checking banks of numbers for a modem, war driving involves traveling around with a wireless scanner looking for wireless access points. Netstumbler was one of the original products that people used for war driving. From the attacker perspective, war driving gives them a laundry list of access points where they can attach to a network and perform attacks. The best ones in a hacker's eye are the unsecured wireless access points that allow unrestricted access to the corporate network. The hacker will not only compromise the corporate network but will then use the corporate Internet access to launch attacks at other targets that are then untraceable back to the hacker. From a security standpoint, war driving enables the security practitioner to detect rogue access points in and around the physical locations. Is an unsecured wireless access point that is not on the network a security threat to the network? It certainly is. If a user can connect their workstation to an unknown and unsecured network, they introduce a threat to the security of the network.

Penetration Testing

Penetration testing takes vulnerability assessment one step further. It does not stop at identifying vulnerabilities; it also uses those vulnerabilities to expose other weaknesses in the network. Penetration testing consists of five different phases:

- **Phase 1**—Preparation
- **Phase 2**—Information gathering
- **Phase 3**—Information evaluation and risk analysis
- **Phase 4**—Active penetration
- **Phase 5**—Analysis and reporting

Penetration testing also has three different modes, which will be explored in more detail later in the domain. Those modes are

- **White box**—Tester has complete knowledge of the systems and infrastructure being tested.
- **Grey box**—A hybrid between white and black box. This mode can vary greatly.
- **Black box**—Assumes no prior knowledge of the systems or infrastructure being tested.

White Box

These testers perform tests with the knowledge of the security and IT staff. They are given physical access to the network and sometimes even a normal username and password. Qualities include

- Full cooperation of organization
- Planned test times
- Network diagrams and systems configurations are supplied

There are several pros and cons to consider with the white box approach:

- **Pros**—The security practitioner should get good reaction and support from the organization being tested, and fixes can occur more rapidly. It is also good to use as a dry run for testing the organization's incident response procedures.
- **Cons**—An inaccurate picture of the organization's network response capabilities may appear because the organization is prepared for the "attack."

Grey Box

Grey box testing involves giving some information to the penetration testing team. Sometimes this may involve publically discoverable information, and it may also include some information about systems inside the protective boundaries of the organization. Grey box testing allows the penetration testing team to focus on attacking the organization and trying to get access and reducing time on discovery. Organizations who feel they have a good grasp on what is publically available about them often use this approach to maximize the resources focused on specific system attacks.

There are several pros and cons to consider with the grey box approach:

- **Pros**—The grey box approach provides the combined benefits of white and black box testing techniques and allows for the creation of really focused testing scenarios.
- **Cons**—Test coverage may be limited due to the level of access granted.

Black Box

These testers generally perform unannounced tests that even the security and IT staff may not know about. Sometimes these tests are ordered by senior managers to test their staff and the systems for which the staff are responsible. Other times, the IT staff will hire covert testers under the agreement that the testers can and will test at any given time, such as four times per year. The objective is generally to see what they can see and get into whatever they can get into, without causing harm, of course. Qualities include:

- Play the role of hostile attacker
- Perform testing without warning
- Receive little to no guidance from the organization being tested

There are several pros and cons to consider with the black box approach:

- **Pros**—The security practitioner can get a better overall view of the network's real responses without someone being prepared for the testing.
- **Cons**—The staff may take the findings personally and show disdain to the testing team and management.

Phase 1: Penetration Testing Goals

Without defined goals, security testing can be a meaningless and costly exercise. The following are examples of some high-level goals for security testing, thereby providing value and meaning for the organization:

- Anyone directly or indirectly sanctioned by the organization's management to perform testing should be doing so to identify vulnerabilities that can be quantified and placed in a ranking for subsequent mitigation.
- Since a security test is merely the evaluation of security on a system at a point in time, the results should be documented and compared to the results at other points in time. Analysis that compares results across times paints a picture of how well or poorly the systems are being protected across those periods (otherwise known as base lining).
- Security testing can be a form of self-audit by the IT staff to prepare them for the "real" audits performed by internal and external auditors.
- In the case of covert testing, testers aim to actually compromise security, penetrate systems, and determine if the IT staff notices the intrusion and an acceptable response has occurred.

It is extremely important as a security practitioner to ensure that the security practitioner has business support and authorization (in accordance with a penetration testing policy) before conducting a penetration test. It is advisable to get this support and permission in writing before conducting the testing.

Penetration Test Software Tools

Software tools exist to assist in the testing of systems from many angles. Tools help the security practitioner to interpret how a system functions for evaluating its security. This section presents some tools available on the commercial market and in the open source space as a means to the testing end. Do not interpret the listing of a tool as a recommendation for its use. Likewise, just because a tool is not listed does not mean it is not worth considering. Choosing a tool to test a particular aspect is a personal or organizational choice.

Some points to consider regarding the use of software tools in the security testing process:

- Do not let tools drive the security testing. Develop a strategy and pick the right tool mix for discovery and testing based on the overall testing plan.

- Use tools specific to the testing environment. For example, if the aim is to test the application of operating system patches on a particular platform, analyze the available ways the security practitioner might accomplish this process by seeing what the vendor offers and compare this against third-party tools. Pick tools that offer the best performance tempered with the budget constraints.

- Tool functions often overlap. The features found on one tool may be better than those on another.

- Security testing tools can make mistakes, especially network-based types that rely on circumstantial evidence of vulnerability. Further investigation is often necessary to determine if the tool interpreted an alleged vulnerability correctly.

- Placement of probes is critical. When possible, place them on the same segment the security practitioner is testing so that filtering devices and intrusion detection systems do not alter the results (unless the security practitioner is planning to test how intrusion detection systems react).

- Network tools sometimes negatively affect uptime; therefore, these tests should often be scheduled for off-hours execution due to the fact that they can potentially cause the following to occur:
  - Increasing network traffic load
  - Affecting unstable platforms that react poorly to unusual inputs

Be aware that the models for detection of vulnerabilities are inconsistent among different toolsets; therefore, results should be studied and made reasonably consistent among different tools.

Analyzing Testing Results

It is often easier to understand the testing results by creating a graphical depiction in a simple matrix of vulnerabilities, ratings for each, and an overall vulnerability index derived as the product of vulnerability and system criticality. More complicated matrices may include details describing each vulnerability and sometimes ways to mitigate it or ways to confirm the vulnerability.

Tests should conclude with a report and matrices detailing the following:

- Information derived publicly
- Information derived through social engineering or other covert ways
- Hosts tested and their addresses
- Services found
- Possible vulnerabilities
- Vulnerability ratings for each
- System criticality
- Overall vulnerability rating
- Vulnerabilities confirmation
- Mitigation suggestions

Testers often present findings matrices that list each system and the vulnerabilities found for each with a "high, medium, low" ranking. The intent is to provide the recipient a list of what should be fixed first. The problem with this method is that it does not take into account the criticality of the system in question. You need a way to differentiate among the urgency for fixing "high" vulnerabilities across systems. Therefore, reports should rank true vulnerabilities by seriousness, taking into account how the organization views the asset's value. Systems of high value may have their medium and low vulnerabilities fixed before a system of medium value has any of its vulnerabilities fixed. This criticality is determined by the organization, and the reports and matrices should help reflect a suggested path to rectifying the situation. For example, the organization has received a testing report listing the same two high vulnerabilities for a print server and an accounting database server. The database server is certainly more critical to the organization; therefore, its problems should be mitigated before those of the print server.

As another example, assume the organization has assigned a high value to the database server that houses data for the web server. The web server itself has no data but is considered medium value. In contrast, the FTP server is merely for convenience and is assigned a low value. A security testing matrix may show several high vulnerabilities for the low-value FTP server. It may also list high vulnerabilities for both the database server and the web server. The organization will likely be interested in fixing the high vulnerabilities first on the database server, then the web server, and then the FTP server. This level of triage is further complicated by trust and access between systems. If the web server gets the new pages and content from the FTP server, this may increase the priority of the FTP server issues over that of the usually low-value FTP server issues.

Phase 2: Reconnaissance and Network Mapping Techniques

Basic security testing activities include reconnaissance and network mapping.

- **Reconnaissance**—Collecting information about the organization from publicly available sources, social engineering, and low-tech methods. This information forms the test attack basis by providing useful information to the tester.

- **Network Mapping**—Collecting information about the organization's Internet connectivity and available hosts by (usually) using automated mapping software tools. In the case of internal studies, the internal network architecture of available systems is mapped. This information further solidifies the test attack basis by providing even more information to the tester about the services running on the network and is often the step before vulnerability testing, which is covered in the next section.

NOTE Penetration testing is an art. This means that different IT security practitioners have different methods for testing. This domain attempts to note the highlights to help the security practitioner differentiate among the various types and provides information on tools that assist in the endeavor. Security testing is an ethical responsibility. Testing must always be authorized, and the techniques should never be used for malice. This information on tools is presented for the purpose of helping the security practitioner spot weaknesses in the systems the security practitioner is authorized to test so that they may be improved.

Reconnaissance

Often reconnaissance is needed by a covert penetration tester who has not been granted regular access to perform a cooperative test. These testers are challenged with having little to no knowledge of the system and must collect it from other sources to form the basis of the test attack.

Reconnaissance is necessary for these testers because they likely have no idea what they will be testing at the commencement of the test. Their orders are usually "see what the security practitioner can find and get into but do not damage anything."

Once the security practitioner thinks they know what should be tested based on the information collected, they must always check with the persons who have hired them to ensure that the systems the security practitioner intends to penetrate are actually owned by the organization. Doing otherwise may put delicate systems in harm's way, or the tester may test something not owned by the organization ordering the test (leading to possible legal repercussions and financial exposure). These parameters should be defined before the test.

Social Engineering and Low-Tech Reconnaissance

Social engineering is an activity that involves the manipulation of persons or physical reconnaissance to get information for use in exploitation or testing activities. Low-tech reconnaissance uses simple technical means to obtain information.

Before attackers or testers make an attempt on the organization's systems, they can learn about the target using low-technology techniques such as:

- Directly visiting a target's web server and searching through it for information.

- Viewing a webpage's source for information about what tools might have been used to construct or run it.

- Accessing employee contact information.

- Obtaining corporate culture information to pick up internally used lingo and product names.

- Identifying business partners.

- Googling a target. Attackers perform reconnaissance activity by using search engines that have previously indexed a target site. The attacker can search for files of a particular type that may contain information they can use for further attacks. Google and other search engines can be very powerful tools to a cracker because of the volume of data the search engines are able to organize. Example: Search a particular website for spreadsheet files containing the word "employee" or "address" or "accounting."

- Dumpster diving to retrieve improperly discarded computer media and paper records for gleaning private information about an organization. Besides paper, this can include the following hardware:

  - Computer hard drives and removable media (floppies, USB drives, CDs, etc.) thrown away or sold without properly degaussing to remove all private information.

  - Equipment (routers, switches, and specialized data processing devices) discarded without configuration data being removed without a trace.

- Shoulder surfing, which means furtively collecting information by standing within view of a person typing a password or sensitive information (e.g., someone else's password).

- Engaging in social engineering using the telephone. Attackers often pose as an official technical support person or fellow employee and attempt to build a rapport with a user through small talk. The attacker may ask for the user's assistance with (false) troubleshooting "tests" aimed at helping the attacker collect information about the system. If the attacker finds a particularly "helpful" user, he might be bold enough to ask for their username and password because "we've been having trouble with the router gateway products interfacing with the LDAP directories where the username and password are stored, and we think it is getting corrupted as it passes over the network… So if you could just tell me what it is, that would be great," or some such nonsense aimed at gaining the user's confidence. The other possible scenarios that can be used with social engineering to gain information are limited only by the security practitioner's imagination.

- Conducting Usenet searches. Usenet postings can give away information about a company's internal system design and problems that exist within systems. For example: "I need advice on my firewall. It is an XYZ brand system, and I have it configured to do this, that, and the other thing. Can anyone help me?—signed joe@big_company_everyone_knows.com."

Mid-Tech Reconnaissance

Mid-tech reconnaissance includes several ways to get information that can be used for testing.

- Whois Information—Whois is a system that records Internet registration information, including the company that owns the domain, administrative contacts, technical contacts, when the record of domain ownership expires, and DNS servers authoritative for maintaining host IP addresses and their associated friendly names for the domains the security practitioner is testing. With this information, the security practitioner can use other online tools to dig for information about the servers visible on the Internet without ever sending a single probing packet at the Internet connection. The contact information provided by Whois can also be used for social engineering and war dialing.

The following are example attacks:

- Using Whois, collect information about DNS servers authoritative for maintaining host IP addresses for a particular domain.

- Using Whois, identify the administrative contact and his telephone number. Use social engineering on that person or security-unaware staff at the main telephone number to obtain unauthorized information.

- Using Whois, identify the technical contact and her area code and exchange (telephone number). Using war dialing software against the block of phone numbers in that exchange, the security practitioner attempts to make an unauthorized connection with a modem for the purpose of gaining backdoor entry to the system.

There are many sources for Whois information and tools, including:

- http://www.internic.net
- http://www.networksolutions.com

DNS Zone Transfers

In an effort to discover the names and types of servers operating inside or outside a network, attackers may attempt zone transfers from DNS servers. A zone transfer is a special type of query directed at a DNS server that asks the server for the entire contents of its zone (the domain that it serves). Information that is derived is useful only if the DNS server is authoritative for that domain. To find a DNS server authoritative for a domain, one can refer to the Whois search results, which often provide this information. Internet DNS servers will often restrict which servers are allowed to perform transfers, but internal DNS servers usually do not have these restrictions.

Secure systems should lock down DNS. Testers should see how the target does this by keeping the following in mind:

- Attackers will attempt zone transfers; therefore, configure DNS servers to restrict zone transfers to only approved hosts.

- Attackers will look for host names that may give out additional information— accountingserver.bigfinancialcompany.com.

- Avoid using Host Information Records (HINFOs) when possible. HINFO is the Host Information Record of a DNS entry. It is strictly informational in nature and serves no function. It is often used to declare the computer type and operating system of a host.

- Use a split DNS model with internal DNS and external DNS servers. Combining internal and external functions on one server is potentially dangerous. Internal DNS will serve the internal network and can relay externally bound queries to the external DNS servers that will do the lookup work by proxy. Incoming Internet-based queries will only reveal external hosts because the external hosts only know these addresses.

There are varieties of free programs available that will resolve DNS names, attempt zone transfers, and perform a reverse lookup of a specified range of IPs. Major operating systems also include the "nslookup" program, which can also perform these operations.

Network Mapping

Network mapping is a process that paints the picture of which hosts are up and running externally or internally and what services are available on the system. Commonly, the security practitioner may see mapping in the context of external host testing and enumeration in the context of internal host testing, but this is not necessarily ironclad, and mapping and enumeration often seem to be used interchangeably. They essentially accomplish similar goals, and the terms can be used in similar ways.

When performing mapping of any kind, the tester should limit the mapping to the scope of the project. Testers may be given a range of IP addresses to map, so the testers should limit the query to that range. Overt and covert testing usually includes network mapping, which is the activity that involves techniques to discover the following:

- Which hosts are up and running or "alive"?

- What is the general topology of the network (how are things interconnected)?

- What ports are open and serviceable on those hosts?

- What applications are servicing those ports?

- What operating system is the host running?

Mapping is the precursor to vulnerability testing and usually defines what will be tested more deeply at that next stage. For example, consider a scenario where the security practitioner discovers that a host is listening on TCP port 143. This probably indicates the host is running application services for the IMAP mail service. Many IMAP implementations have vulnerabilities. During the network mapping phase, the security practitioner learns that host 10.1.2.8 is listening on this port. Network mapping may provide insight about the operating system the host is running, which may in turn narrow the possible IMAP applications. For example, it is unlikely that the Microsoft Exchange IMAP process will be running on a Solaris computer; therefore, if network mapping shows a host with telltale Solaris "fingerprints" as well as indications that the host is listening on TCP port 143, the IMAP server is probably not being provided by Microsoft Exchange. As such, when the security practitioner is later exploring vulnerabilities, they can likely eliminate Exchange IMAP vulnerabilities for this host.

Mapping results can be compared to security policy to discover rogue or unauthorized services that appear to be running. For example, an organization may periodically run mapping routines to match results with what should be expected. If more services are running than one would expect to be running, the systems may have been accidentally misconfigured (therefore opening up a service not approved in the security policy) or the host(s) may have been compromised.

When performing mapping, make sure the security practitioner is performing the mapping on a host range owned by the organization. For example, suppose an nslookup DNS domain transfer for bobs-italianbookstore.com showed a mail server at 10.2.3.70 and a web server at 10.19.40.2. Assuming the security practitioner does not work for bobs-italianbookstore.com and does not have intimate knowledge of their systems, the security practitioner might assume that they have two Internet connections. In a cooperative test, the best course of action is to check with their administrative staff for clarification. They may tell the security practitioner that the mail is hosted by another company and that it is outside of the scope of the test. However, the web server is a host to be tested. You should ask which part of the 10.0.0.0 bobsbookstore.com controls. Let us assume they control the class-C 10.19.40.0 range. Therefore, network mapping of 10.19.40.1 through 10.19.40.254 is appropriate and will not interfere with anyone else's operations. Even though only one host is listed in the DNS, there may be other hosts up and running.

Depending on the level of stealth required (i.e., to avoid detection by IDS systems or other systems that will "notice" suspected activity if a threshold for certain types of communication is exceeded), network mapping may be performed very slowly over long periods of time. Stealth may be required for covert penetration tests.

Network mapping can involve a variety of techniques for probing hosts and ports. Several common techniques are

- **ICMP Echo Requests (ping)** — If the security practitioner pings a host and it replies, it is alive (i.e., up and running). This test does not show what individual services are running. Be aware that many networks block incoming echo requests. If the requests are blocked and the security practitioner pings a host and it does not reply, the security practitioner has no way of knowing if it is actually running or not because the request is blocked before it gets to the destination.

- **TCP Connect Scan** — A connect scan can be used to discover TCP services running on a host even if ICMP is blocked. This type of scan is considered "noisy" (noticeable to logging and intrusion detection systems) because it goes all the way through the connection process. This basic service discovery scan goes all the way through a TCP session setup by sending a SYN packet to a target, receiving the SYN/ACK from the target when the port is listening, and then sending a final ACK back to the target to establish the connection. At this point, the test host is "connected" to the target. Eventually the connection is torn down because the tester's goal is not to communicate with the port but only to discover whether it is available.

- **TCP SYN Scan**—SYN scanning can be used to discover TCP services running on a host even if ICMP is blocked. SYN scanning is considered less noisy than connect scans. It is referred to as "half-open" scanning because unlike a connect scan (above), the security practitioner does not open a full TCP connection. Your test host directs a TCP SYN packet on a particular port as if it were going to open a real TCP connection to the target host. A SYN/ACK from the target indicates the host is listening on that port. An RST from the target indicates that it is not listening on that port. If a SYN/ACK is received, the test host immediately sends an RST to tear down the connection to conserve resources on both the test and target host sides. Firewalls often detect and block these scan attempts.

- **TCP FIN Scan**—FIN scanning can be used to discover TCP services running on a host even if ICMP is blocked. FIN scanning is considered a stealthy way to discover if a service is running. The test host sends a TCP packet with the FIN bit on to a port on the target host. If the target responds with an RST packet, the security practitioner may assume that the target host is not using the port. If the host does not respond, it may be using the port that was probed. Caveats to this technique are Microsoft, Cisco, BSDI, HP/UX, MVS, and IRIX-based hosts that implement their TCP/IP software stack in ways not defined by the standard. These hosts may not respond with an RST when probed by a FIN. However, if the security practitioner follows up a nonreply to one of these systems with, for example, a SYN scan to that port and the host replies, the security practitioner has determined that the host is listening on the port being tested and a few possible operating systems (see OS fingerprinting).

- **TCP XMAS Scan**—XMAS scans are similar to a FIN scan (and similarly stealthy), but they additionally turn on the URG (urgent) and PSH (push) flags. The goal of this scan is the same as a TCP FIN scan. The additional flags might make a packet be handled differently than a standard packet, so the security practitioner might see different results.

- **TCP NULL Scan**—NULL scans are similar to a FIN scan (also stealthy), but they turn off all flags. The NULL scan is similar to the others noted earlier; however, by turning off all TCP flags (which should never occur naturally), the packet might be handled differently, and the security practitioner may see a different result.

- **UDP Scans**—A UDP scan determines which UDP service ports are opened on a host. The test machine sends a UDP packet on a port to the target. If the target sends back an ICMP port unreachable message, the target does not use that port. A potential problem with this methodology is the case where a router or firewall at the target network does not allow ICMP port unreachable messages to leave the network, making the target network appear as if all UDP ports are open (because no ICMP messages are getting back to the test host). Another problem is that many systems limit the number of ICMP messages allowed per second, which can make for a very slow scanning rate.

Available mapping tools include

- **Nmap**—`http://www.insecure.org`
- **Solarwinds**—`http://www.solarwinds.net`
- **Superscan**—`http://www.mcafee.com/us/downloads/free-tools/index.aspx`
- **Lanspy**—`http://lantricks.com/lanspy` (only available for Windows 2000/XP/2003)

Another technique for mapping a network is commonly known as "firewalking," which uses traceroute techniques to discover which services a filtering device like a router or firewall will allow through. These tools generally function by transmitting TCP and UDP packets on a particular port with a time to live (TTL) equal to at least one greater than the targeted router or firewall. If the target allows the traffic, it will forward the packets to the next hop. At that point, the traffic will expire as it reaches the next hop, and an ICMP_TIME_EXCEEDED message will be generated and sent back out of the gateway to the test host. If the target router or firewall does not allow the traffic, it will drop the packets and the test host will not see a response.

Available firewalking tools include

- **Hping**—`http://www.hping.org/`
- **Firewalk**—`http://www.tucows.com/preview/8046`

By all means, do not forget about the use of basic built-in operating system commands for discovering hosts and routes. Basic built-in and other tools include

- **Traceroute** (Windows calls this tracert)—Uses ICMP or TCP depending on the implementation of a path to a host or network.
- **Ping**—See if a host is alive using ICMP echo request messages.
- **Telnet**—Telnetting to a particular port is a quick way to find out if the host is servicing that port in some way.
- **Whois**—Command-line Whois can provide similar information to the web-based Whois methods previously discussed.

Another useful technique is system fingerprinting. System fingerprinting refers to testing techniques used by port scanners and vulnerability analysis software that attempt to identify the operating system in use on a network device and the versions of services running on the host. Why is it important to identify a system? By doing so, the security practitioner knows what they are is dealing with and, later on, what vulnerabilities are likely for that system. As mentioned previously, Microsoft-centric vulnerabilities are (usually) not going to show up on Sun systems and vice versa.

One final resource to keep in mind is web repositories for vulnerabilities are extremely useful for the security practitioner. Websites such as shodan (`www.shodanhq.com`) actively compile vulnerable online devices in a searchable format. Additionally, organizations such as NIST compile centralized vulnerability databases such as the National Vulnerability Database (`http://nvd.nist.gov/`).

Phase 3: Information Evaluation and Risk Analysis

Before active penetration, the security practitioner needs to evaluate the findings and perform risk analysis on the results to determine which hosts or services the security assessor is going to try to actively penetrate. The security practitioner should not perform an active penetration on every host until the organization has fully completed Phase 2. The security practitioner must also identify the potential business risks associated with performing a penetration test against particular hosts. The security practitioner can and probably will interrupt normal business processes if they perform a penetration test on a production system. The business leaders need to be made aware of that fact, and they need to be involved in making the decision on which devices to actively penetrate.

Phase 4: Active Penetration

This bears repeating. Think twice before attempting to exploit a possible vulnerability that may harm the system. For instance, if the system might be susceptible to a buffer overflow attack, it might be enough to identify the vulnerability without actually exploiting it and bringing down the system. Weigh the benefits of succinctly identifying vulnerabilities against potentially crashing the system. Here are some samples:

- Vulnerability testing shows that a web server may be vulnerable to crashing if it is issued a very long request with dots (i.e., ../../../../../../../../ 1000 times). The security practitioner can either try to actually crash the server using the technique (although this may have productivity loss consequences) or alternatively and perhaps for the better they can note it for further investigation, perhaps on a test server. Make sure permission is explicitly granted before attempting this type of actual exploitation.

- Vulnerability testing shows that a UNIX host has a root account with the password set to root. You can easily test this find to determine whether this is a false positive.

- Vulnerability testing shows that a router may be susceptible to an SSH attack. You can either try the attack with permission or note it for further investigation.

Phase 5: Analysis and Reporting

As with any security testing, documentation of the test, analysis of the results, and reporting those results to the proper managers are imperative. Many different methods can be utilized when reporting the results of a vulnerability scan. A comprehensive report will have separate sections for each management/technical level involved in the test. An overview of the results with a summary of the findings might be ideal for management, while a technical review of specific findings with remediation recommendations would be appropriate for the device administrators. As with any report that outlines issues, it is always best to offer solutions for fixing the issues as well as reporting their existence.

Penetration Testing High-Level Steps

The following outline provides a high-level view of the steps that could be taken to exploit systems during a penetration test. It is similar in nature to a vulnerability test but goes further to perform an exploit.

1. Obtain a network address (usually center on internal testing when the security practitioner is physically onsite). With the advent DHCP on the network, a tester can often plug in and get an IP address right away. DHCP-assigned addresses usually come with gateway and name server addresses. If the tester does not get a DHCP address, the system may be set up for static addresses. You can sniff the network for communications that detail the segment the security practitioner is on and guess at an unused address.

2. Reconnaissance—Verify target information:
   - DNS information obtained via DHCP
   - DNS zone transfer when allowed by the server
   - Whois
   - Browsing an internal domain
   - Using Windows utilities to enumerate servers
   - Pings sweeps
   - Traceroute
   - Port scans (TCP connect, SYN scans, etc.)
   - OS fingerprinting
   - Banner grabbing
   - Unix RPC discovery

3. Target vulnerability analysis and enumeration:

   - Using techniques that are less likely to be logged or reported in an IDS system (i.e., less "noisy" techniques) evaluates the vulnerability of ports on a target.

   - For Windows systems, gather user, group, and system information with null sessions (NT), "net" commands, nltest utility.

   - For UNIX systems, gather RPC information.

4. Exploitation—Identify and exploit the vulnerabilities:

   - Buffer overflows

   - Brute force

   - Password cracking

   - Vulnerability chaining

   - Data access

OPERATING AND MAINTAINING MONITORING SYSTEMS

Continuous monitoring represents the desire to have real-time risk information available at any time to make organizational decisions. Continuous monitoring systems are comprised of sensor networks, input from assessments, logging, and risk management. When implemented correctly, continuous monitoring systems can provide organizations with a sense of information security risk; when not configured correctly, they can lead an organization to false panic or a false sense of security.

Security Monitoring Concepts

The security practitioner should assume that all systems are susceptible to attack and at some point will be attacked. This mindset helps prepare for inevitable system compromises. Comprehensive policies and procedures and their effective use are excellent mitigation techniques for stemming the effectiveness of attacks. Security monitoring is a mitigation activity used to protect systems, identify network patterns, and identify potential attacks.

Monitoring Terminology

Monitoring terminology can seem arcane and confusing. The purpose of this list is to define by example and reinforce terminology commonly used when discussing monitoring technology.

   - **Safeguard**—A built-in proactive security control implemented to provide protection against threats.

- **Countermeasure**—An added-on reactive security controls.
- **Vulnerability**—A system weakness.
- **Exploit**—A particular attack. It is named this way because these attacks exploit system vulnerabilities.
- **Signature**—A string of characters or activities found within processes or data communications that describes a known system attack. Some monitoring systems identify attacks by means of a signature.
- **False Positive**—Monitoring triggered an event, but nothing was actually wrong, and in doing so, the monitoring has incorrectly identified benign communications as a danger.
- **False Negative**—The monitoring system missed reporting an exploit event by not firing an alarm. This is bad.
- **True Positive**—The monitoring system recognized an exploit event correctly.
- **True Negative**—The monitoring system has not recognized benign traffic as cause for concern. In other words, it does nothing when nothing needs to be done. This is good.
- **Tuning**—Customizing a monitoring system to your environment.
- **Promiscuous Interface**—A network interface that collects and processes all of the packets sent to it regardless of the destination MAC address.

IDS and IDPS

What is an IDS and an IDPS and how do they differ? IDS stands for intrusion detection system. It is a passive system that detects security events but has limited ability to intervene on the event. Intrusion prevention is the process of performing intrusion detection and attempting to stop detected possible incidents. Intrusion detection and prevention systems (IDPS) are primarily focused on identifying possible incidents, logging information about them, attempting to stop them, and reporting them to security administrators.[4]

There are two types of IDS/IDPS devices. Network-based IDS or NIDS generally connect to one or more network segments. It monitors and interprets traffic and identifies security events by anomaly detection or based on the signature of the event. Host-based IDS, or HIDS, usually reside as a software agent on the host. Most of the newer NIDS are IDPS devices and not IDS. Active HIDS can do a variety of activities to protect the host from intercepting system calls and examining them for validity to stopping application access to key system files or parameters. Active HIDS would be considered an IDP. Passive HIDS (IDS) take a snapshot of the file system in a known clean state and then compare that against the current file system on a regular basis. They can then flag alerts based on file changes.

Where Should HIDS and NIDS Be Deployed?

Business data flow diagrams and data classification policies are a good starting point. HIDS and NIDS need to be deployed where they can best protect critical organizational assets. Of course, in a perfect world with unlimited budget, all devices would be protected by HIDS and NIDS, but most IT security staff has to deal with limited personnel and limited budget. Protect critical assets first and protect the most possible with the fewest devices. A good starting point would be to place HIDS on all systems that contain financial data, HR data, PII, research, and any other data for which protection is mandated. NIDS should be placed on all ingress points into your network and on segments separating critical servers from the rest of the network. There used to be some debate among security practitioners as to whether NIDS should be placed outside your firewall to identify all attacks against your network or inside your firewall to only identify those that made it past your firewall rules. The general practice now appears to be to not worry if it is raining outside; only worry about what is dripping in your living room. In other words, keep the NIDS inside the firewall.

Both HIDS and NIDS are notoriously noisy out of the box and should be tuned for specific environments. They also need to be configured to notify the responsible people via the approved method if they identify a potential incident. These, like the alerts themselves, must be configured properly to ensure that when something really does happen, the designated people know to take action. For the most part, low-priority events can send alerts via e-mail, while high-priority events should page or call the security personnel on call.

Implementation Issues for Monitoring

The security practitioner should remember the security tenets *confidentiality*, *integrity*, and *availability*. IDS can alert to these conditions by matching known conditions (signatures) with unknown but suspect conditions (anomalies).

- **Confidentiality**—Unauthorized access may breach confidentiality.
- **Integrity**—Corruption due to an attack destabilizes integrity.
- **Availability**—Denial of service keeps data from being available.

The security practitioner must make decisions concerning the deployment of monitoring systems. What types to deploy and where to deploy are functions of budget and system criticality. Implementation of monitoring should be supported by policy and justified by the risk assessment. The actual deployment of the sensors will depend on the value of the assets.

Monitoring control deployment considerations should include

- Choose one or more monitoring technique types—HIDS, NIDS, or logging.

- Choose an analysis paradigm—statistical anomaly or signature.

- Choose a system that meets timeliness objectives—real-time or scheduled (non-real-time).

- Choose a reporting mechanism for incident response—push or pull; that is, does a management system query the monitoring devices for data or does the device push the data to a repository where it is stored or analyzed?

- Make the update mechanisms part of policy with well-defined procedures, especially for signature-based devices.

- Tune monitoring systems to reflect the environment they support.

- Choose automatic response mechanisms wisely.

- Maintenance and tuning—For the long-term use and effectiveness of the monitoring controls, systems should be cared for like any other mission-critical component.

- Keep IDS signatures (if applicable) current—Signature-based IDS must be kept up to date as previously unknown vulnerabilities are revealed. Take, for example, the ineffectiveness of a host antivirus system with virus signatures that are a year old. Since several new viruses emerge each week, a system with old signatures may be effective for the old exploits, but the system is defenseless for new viruses. IDS systems operate on the same principle. IDS vendors often have notification systems to alert you about new signature definitions or the capability for automatic update.

- Keep IDS subsystems current—As new generations of IDS subsystems (the operating systems and software engines that drive the system) become available, consider testing and then deploying these to know if they add to your capability to detect exploits, but do not introduce instability.

- Tune IDS—NIDS systems have limitations on how much processing they can handle; therefore, limit what the NIDS must monitor based on your environment. For example, if you do not have any Windows-based hosts, consider disabling monitoring for Windows-based exploits. Conversely, if you have a UNIX environment and UNIX-based signatures are not enabled, you will likely miss these events.

As system changes are made, the security systems that protect them should be considered. During the change control process, new changes should factor in how the security systems will handle them. Some sample questions that the security practitioner should consider are as follows:

- Will the host configuration change require a reconfiguration of the HIDS component?
- Will the addition of a database application of a host require the HIDS agent to be configured to screen database transactions for validity?
- Will the network change require alterations to the way the NIDS collects data?
- Will the new services offered on a host require the NIDS to be tuned to have the appropriate active or passive responses to exploits that target those new services?
- Will the DMZ to management network firewall rules need to be changed to accommodate the logging stream from the new web server placed on the DMZ?

Collecting Data for Incident Response

Organizations must have a policy and plan for dealing with events as they occur and the corresponding forensics of incidents.

The security practitioner should consider asking the following questions:

- **How does the organization plan to collect event and forensic information from the IDS/IPS?**—Organizations cannot expect IDS/IPS to be a "set it and forget it" technology. Human interaction is required to interpret events and high-level responses. IDS can organize events by priority and can even be set to react in a certain way to an observed event, but humans will periodically need to decide if the IDS is doing its job properly.
- **How will the organization have the IDS/IPS respond to events?**—Depending on the IDS/IPS capabilities, the organization will need to decide how it wants the IPS to react to an observed event. The next section discusses active versus passive IDS response.
- **How will the organization respond to incidents?**—What investigative actions will the security staff take based on singular or repeated incidents involving one or more observed events? This is a function of your security policy.

When organizations suffer attacks, logging information, whether generated by a host, network device, IDS/IPS, or other device, may be at some point considered evidence by law enforcement personnel. Preserving a chain of custody for law enforcement is important so as not to taint the evidence for use in criminal proceedings.

Monitoring Response Techniques

If unauthorized activity is detected, IDS/IPS systems can take one or both of the following actions:

- **Passive Response**—Notes the event at various levels but does not take any type of evasive action. The response is by definition passive because the event is merely noted.

- **Active Response**—Notes the event and performs a reaction to protect systems from further exploitation.

The following is a list of examples of passive IDS/IPS response:

- Logging the event to a log file
- Displaying an alert on the console of an event viewer or security information management system
- Logging the details of a packet flow that was identified to be associated with an unauthorized event for a specified period of time, for the purpose of subsequent forensic analysis
- Sending an alert page, text message, or e-mail to an administrator

The following is a list of examples of active IPS response:

- In the case of an unauthorized TCP data flow on a network, initiate a NIDS reset of the connection (with a TCP reset) between an attacker and the host being attacked. This works only with TCP-based attacks because they are connection oriented.

- In the case of any IP data flow (TCP, UDP, ICMP), initiate a NIDS, and instruct a filtering device like a firewall or router to dynamically alter its access control list to preclude further communications with the attacker, either indefinitely or for a specified period.

- In the case of a disallowed system call or application-specific behavior, initiate the HIDS agent to block the transaction.

- With TCP resets, often the IDS will send a TCP packet with the FIN flag set in the TCP header to both the attacker and the attacked host to gracefully reset the connection from both hosts' perspective. By resetting the attacker, the SSCP practitioner discourages future attacks (if they keep getting resets). By resetting the attacked host, the SSCP practitioner frees up system resources that may have been allocated because of the attack.

- With system calls, if a process that does not normally need to access the web server's data tries to access the data, the HIDS agent can disallow this access.

Response Pitfalls

Active IDS response pitfalls include

- Cutting off legitimate traffic due to false positives
- Self-induced denial of service

Many monitoring systems provide the means to specify some sort of response if a particular signature fires, although doing so may have unintended consequences.

Entertain the notion that a signature has been written that is too generic in nature. This means that it sometimes fires because of exploit traffic and is a true positive but sometimes fires because of innocent traffic and is a false positive. If the signature is configured to send TCP resets to an offending address and does so in a false-positive situation, the IDS may be cutting off legitimate traffic.

Self-induced denial of service can also be a problem with active response systems. If an attacker decided to spoof the IP address of a business partner and sends attacks with the partner's IP address and the organization's IDS reacted by dynamically modifying the edge router configuration, it would cut off communications with the business partner.

Take note that active response mechanisms should be used carefully and be limited to the types of actions listed earlier. Some organizations take it upon themselves to implement systems that actively counterattack systems they believe have attacked them as a response. This is highly discouraged and may result in legal issues for the organization. It is irresponsible to counterattack any system for any reason.

Attackers

Attackers are threats generally thought of as persons who perform overt and covert intrusions or attacks on systems, which are often motivated a combination of motive, means, and opportunity. Motivations typically fall into one of the following types:

- **Notoriety, Ego, or Sport**—Exemplifies the attacker's "power" to his or her audience, whether to just a few people or to the world. To the attacker, the inherent challenge is "I want to see if I can do it, and I want everyone to know about it."

- **Greed and Profit**—The attacker is attempting personal financial gain or financial gain of a client; that is, an attacker might have been hired by a business to furtively damage a competitor's system or gain unauthorized access to the competitor's data. An attacker may use or resell information found on systems, such as credit card numbers.

- **Political Agenda**—Attacking a political nemesis physically or electronically is seen as a way to further one's own agenda or ideals or call attention to a cause.

- **Revenge**—The overriding motivation behind revenge in the attacker's eyes is "I've been wronged, and I am going to get you back." Revenge is often exacted by former employees or those who were at one point in time trusted by the organization that is now being attacked.

- **Curiosity**—They do not really want to do any damage. They just want to see how it works.

There is one category of "attacker" that is often overlooked by security professionals, and while it may seem unfair to some to lump them in with attackers, organizations avoid them at their peril. These are the individuals within an organization who either through ignorance, ego, or stress cause unintended intrusions to occur. They could be the IT system administrator who finds it easier to grant everyone administrative rights to a server rather than take the time to define access controls correctly, or they could be the administrative assistant who uses someone else's login to get into the HR system just because it was already logged in. These individuals can cause as much damage to a company as someone who is trying to attack it, and the incidents they create need to be addressed like any other intrusion incident.

Intrusions

Intrusions are acts by persons, organizations, or systems that violate the security framework of the recipient. In some instances, it is easier to identify an intrusion as a violation. For example, you have a policy that prohibits users from using computing resources while logged in as someone else. While in the true sense of the definition, the event is an intrusion, it is more acceptable to refer to the event as a violation. Intrusions are considered attacks but are not just limited to computing systems. If something is classified as an intrusion, it will fall into one of following two categories:

- Intrusions can be overt and are generally noticeable immediately. Examples of overt intrusion include the following:
  - Someone breaking into your building and stealing computing hardware
  - Two people robbing a bank
  - Someone stealing copper wiring out of the electrical closet
  - Flooding an e-commerce site with too much data from too many sources, thereby rendering the site useless for legitimate customers
  - Attackers defacing a website

- Intrusions can be covert and not always noticeable right away, if at all. These, by their nature, are the most difficult to identify. Examples of covert intrusions include the following:

  - A waiter stealing a credit card number after the customer has paid his or her bill and using it on the Web that evening
  - An accounting department employee manipulating financial accounts for illegal and unauthorized personal financial gain
  - An authorized user who improperly obtains system administrator login credentials to access private company records to which he is not authorized
  - An attacker who poses as an authorized computer support representative to gain the trust of an unknowing user, to obtain information for use in a computer attack
  - A hacker who gets hired as IT staff so he can gain access to organizational systems

Events

An event is a single occurrence that may or may not indicate an intrusion. All intrusions contain events, but not all events are intrusions. For example, a user account is locked for bad password attempts. That is a security event. If it was just the user forgetting what she changed her password to last Friday, it is not an intrusion; however, if the user claims that they did not try to log in before their account was locked, it might be an intrusion.

Types of Monitoring

There are two basic classes of monitoring devices: real-time and non-real-time.

- **Real-Time Monitoring**—Real-time monitoring devices provide a means for immediately identifying and sometimes stopping (depending on the type of system used) overt and covert events. They include some types of network and host intrusion detection systems. These systems keep watch on systems and (can) alert administrators as unauthorized activity is happening. They can also log events for subsequent analysis if needed. A real-time monitor for computers is like the burglar alarm for your home. When someone breaks in, it sounds the alarm.

- **Non-Real-Time Monitoring**—Non-real-time monitoring systems provide a means for saving important information about system events and possibly monitoring the integrity of system configurations after the fact. These technologies include application logging, system logging, and integrity monitoring. Logging and integrity systems might tell you that a burglar was at your home, but he is likely gone by the time you find out. This does not mean that non-real-time systems are not as good as real-time systems. Each fulfills a different niche in monitoring. These system logs would be more like the footprints or fingerprints a burglar would leave behind.

Monitoring should be designed to positively identify actual attacks (true positive) but not identify regular communications as a threat (false positive) or do everything possible to increase the identification of actual attacks and decrease the false-positive notifications.

Monitoring event information can provide considerable insight about possible attacks perpetrated within your network. This information can help organizations make necessary modifications to security policies and the supporting safeguards and countermeasures for improved protection.

Monitoring technology needs to be "tuned," which is the process of customizing the default configuration to the unique needs of your systems. To tune out alarms that are harmless (false positives), the organization must know what types of data traffic are considered acceptable. If security framework, data classification documentation, and business flow documentation exist, the organization should have a good idea of what information should be on its network and how it should be moving between devices.

Deploying monitoring systems is one part of a multilayer security strategy comprised of several types of security controls. By itself, it will not prevent intrusions or give an organization all the information it needs to analyze an intrusion.

File Integrity Checkers

When a system is compromised, an attacker will often alter certain key files to provide continued access and prevent detection. By applying a message digest (cryptographic hash) to key files and then checking the files periodically to ensure the hash has not been altered, one can maintain a degree of assurance. On detecting a change, an alert will be triggered. Furthermore, following an attack, the same files can have their integrity checked to assess the extent of the compromise.

Some examples include

- Cimtrak—http://www.cimcor.com/products
- Advanced Intrusion Detection Environment (AIDE)—http://sourceforge .net/projects/aide/
- Verisys—http://www.ionx.co.uk/

Continuous/Compliance Monitoring

Monitoring is the ongoing, near-time analysis of traditional and non-traditional data sources, related to targeted business activities and controls, to proactively identify, trend, and respond to potential compliance signals and to be predictive of user behavior. Monitoring is considered distinct from auditing, which is typically retrospective and often limited by time, frequency, and scope. Monitoring results inform corrective action plans, including full-scale compliance investigations, policy changes, enhanced training and communications, additional monitoring, focused audits, and other programmatic responses.

Continuous monitoring represents the desire to have real-time risk information available at any time to make organizational decisions. Continuous monitoring systems are comprised of sensor networks, input from assessments, logging, and risk management. When implemented correctly, continuous monitoring systems can provide organizations with a sense of information security risk; when not configured correctly, they can lead an organization to false panic or a false sense of security.

Log Files

Log files can be cumbersome and unwieldy. They can also contain critical information within them that can document compliance with an organization's security framework. Your security framework should have the policies and procedures to cover log files; namely, they need to spell out the following:

- What devices and hosts might contain critical log data
- What information gets logged
- Where and how the log files are going to be stored
- Retention schedule for log files
- What security measures are going to be employed to ensure the integrity of the log files in storage and in transit
- Who has access to modify or delete log files

Reviewing Host Logs

Auditors are going to want to review host logs as part of the audit process. Security practitioners regularly review host log files as part of the organization's security program. As part of the organization's log processes, guidelines must be established for log retention and followed. If the organizational policy states to retain standard log files for only six months, that is all the organization should have. During normal log reviews, it is acceptable to use live log files as long as the review does not disrupt the normal logging process.

Reviewing Incident Logs

Any time an incident occurs, the security practitioner should save the log files of all devices that have been affected or are along the network path the intruder took. These files need to be saved differently than your standard log retention policy. Since it is possible that these log files might be used in a court case against the intruder, the security practitioner must follow sound forensic chain of custody principles when obtaining and preserving the logs.

- Document who saved the files, where they were saved, and who has access to them.

- The data retention rules might change for potential legal evidence, so ensure the organization's legal department has determined how long to retain incident logs.

- During an audit, auditors might want to review these files both to check on the organization's incident response policy and to identify any trends in the intrusions.

Log Anomalies

Identifying log anomalies is often the first step in identifying security-related issues both during an audit and during routine monitoring. What constitutes an anomaly? A log anomaly is anything out of the ordinary. Some will be glaringly obvious, for example, gaps in date/time stamps or account lockouts. Others will be harder to detect, such as someone trying to write data to a protected directory. While it would seem logging everything so that you would not miss any important data is the best approach, most would soon drown under the amount of data collected.

Log Management

Log files can grow beyond the organization's means to gather meaningful data from them if they are not managed properly. How can the organization ensure they are getting the data needed without overburdening the organization's resources with excessive log events? The first thing to remember is start with the organization's most critical resources. Then be selective in the amount of data received from each host. Finally, get the data somewhere easily accessible for analysis.

Clipping Levels

Clipping levels are a predefined criteria or threshold that sets off an event entry. For example, a security operations center does not want to be notified on every failed login attempt because everyone mistypes their password occasionally. Thus, set the clipping level to only create a log entry after two failed password attempts. Clipping levels usually have a time property associated with them. For the logging process to not have to keep track of every single failed password attempt in the off chance that the next time that account is logged in the password is mistyped, set the time limit to a reasonable amount of time, for example, 30 minutes. Now the system only has to keep track of an invalid login attempt on a particular account for 30 minutes. If another invalid attempt does not come in on that account, the system can disregard the first one. Clipping levels are great for reducing the amount of data accumulating in log files. Care must be taken to ensure important data is not skipped, and like everything else, the clipping levels need to be documented and protected because an attacker would gain an advantage knowing them.

Filtering

Log filtering usually takes place after the log files have been written. Clipping reduces the amount of data in the log; filtering reduces the amount of data viewed. Filters come in extremely handy when trying to isolate a particular host, user account, or event type. For example, you could filter a log file to only look at invalid login attempts or for all entries within a certain time window. Care must be taken when filtering so that you do not filter out too much information and miss what you are looking for.

Log Consolidation

Log consolidation gives one-stop shopping for log file analysis. Log file consolidation is usually done on a separate server from the one that actually generates the log files. These servers are called security information and event management (SIEM) systems. Most systems have the ability to forward log messages to another server. Thus, the entry not only appears in the log file of the server but it also appears in the consolidated log on the SIEM. Log consolidation is extremely useful when you are trying to track a user or event that reaches across multiple servers or devices. Log consolidation is discussed further in the "Centralized Logging (Syslog and Log Aggregation)" section.

Log Retention

Now that all the organization's systems are being logged and they are being reviewed for anomalies, how long is the organization required to keep the logs? How should they be storing the logs?

Automated Log Tools   Automation is one of the keys to successful log file management. There are many different tools, both commercial and open source, that can automate different phases of log file retention. Scripts are available on the Internet or can be written in-house, which can automate some of the processes needed in log management. Some key areas an organization might want to research for log file automation tools include

- **Log Consolidation Tools**—Tools that automatically copy log entries to a central server.

- **Log Retention Tools**—Tools that will move old log files to separate folders for backup and purge old data from log files.

Business and Legal Requirements Business and legal requirements for log reten- tion will vary among economies, countries, and industries. Some businesses will have no requirements for data retention. Others are mandated by the nature of their business or by business partners to comply with certain retention data. For example, the Payment Card Industry (PCI) Data Security Standard requires that businesses retain one year of log data in support of PCI with a minimum of three months' worth of data available online. Some federal regulations have requirements for data reten- tion as well. If unsure if a business has any requirements for log file retention, check with auditors and the organization's legal team. They should know for sure. So, if a business has no business or legal requirements to retain log data, how long should the organization keep it? The first people asked should be the legal department. Most legal departments have very specific guidelines for data retention, and those guidelines may drive the log retention policy. If legal does not provide guidance on how long to keep logs, try this technique.

Maintain three months' worth of logs online. Once the three-month threshold has passed, move the log files off to tape or other backup media. Keep offline backup files for a year; at the end of the year, see how far back the longest time was required to look for data, add three months to that time, document as the organizational stan- dard, and utilize it for the maximum length of time to retain offline log files.

Centralized Logging (Syslog and Log Aggregation)

Logs are a critical part of any system. They provide insight into what a system is doing, as well as what happened. Virtually every process running on a system generates logs in some form or another. Usually these logs are written to files on local disks. When your system grows to multiple hosts, managing the logs and accessing them can get compli- cated. Searching for a particular error across hundreds of log files on hundreds of servers is difficult without good tools. A common approach to this problem is to set up a central- ized logging solution so that multiple logs can be aggregated in a central location.

Syslog

Another option that you probably already have installed is syslog. Most people use rsyslog or syslog-ng, which are two syslog implementations. These daemons allow processes to send log messages to them, and the syslog configuration determines how they are stored. In a centralized logging setup, a central syslog daemon is set up on your network, and the client logging daemons are set up to forward messages to the central daemon.

Find syslog-ng at `http://www.balabit.com/network-security/syslog-ng`.

Distributed Log Collectors

All of these have their specific features and differences, but their architectures are fairly similar. They generally consist of logging clients and agents on each specific host. The agents forward logs to a cluster of collectors, which in turn forward the messages to a scalable storage tier. The idea is that the collection tier is horizontally scalable to grow with the increased number of logging hosts and messages. Similarly, the storage tier is also intended to scale horizontally to grow with increased volume. Some examples include

- **Scribe**—Scribe is a scalable and reliable log aggregation server used and released by Facebook as open source. Scribe is written in C++ and uses Thrift for the protocol encoding. Since it uses Thrift, virtually any language can work with it. (`https://github.com/facebookarchive/scribe`)

- **Flume**—Flume is an Apache project for collecting, aggregating, and moving large amounts of log data. It stores all this data on HDFS. (`https://cwiki.apache.org/confluence/display/FLUME/Home%3bjsessionid=611F9B1C12E6CD0ED777FD01A91C77DB`)

- **logstash**—logstash lets you ship, parse, and index logs from any source. It works by defining inputs (files, syslog, etc.), filters (grep, split, multiline, etc.), and outputs (elasticsearch, mongodb, etc.). It also provides a UI for accessing and searching your logs. (`https://www.elastic.co/products/logstash`)

- **Chukwa**—Chukwa is another Apache project that collects logs onto HDFS. (`http://wiki.apache.org/hadoop/Chukwa`)

- **Graylog2**—Graylog2 provides a UI for searching and analyzing logs. Logs are stored in MongoDB and elasticsearch. Graylog2 also provides the GELF logging format to overcome some issues with syslog message: 1024-byte limit and unstructured log messages. If you are logging long stacktraces, you may want to look into GELF. (`http://docs.graylog.org/en/stable/`)

- **Splunk**—Splunk is a commercial product that has been around for several years. It provides a whole host of features for not only collecting logs but also analyzing and viewing them. (`http://www.splunk.com/`)

Hosted Logging Services

There are also several hosted "logging as a service" providers as well. The benefit of them is that you only need to configure your syslog forwarders or agents, and they manage the collection, storage, and access to the logs. All of the infrastructure that you have to set up and maintain is handled by them, freeing you up to focus on your application. Each service provides a simple setup (usually syslog forwarding based), an API, and a UI to support search and analysis. Some examples include

- **Loggly**—`https://www.loggly.com/`
- **Papertrail**—`https://papertrailapp.com/`
- **Logentries**—`https://logentries.com/`

Configuring Event Sources (Cisco NetFlow and sFlow)

Both NetFlow and sFlow are used to provide visibility into an organization's network. Typically, NetFlow and sFlow are used to

- Analyze network and bandwidth usage by users and applications
- Measure WAN traffic and generate statistics for creating network policies
- Detect unauthorized network usage
- Diagnose and troubleshoot network problems

Cisco NetFlow

According to Cisco, NetFlow is an embedded instrumentation within Cisco IOS Software to characterize network operation. Netflow allows for the collection and monitoring of network traffic, which can then be analyzed to create a picture of the network traffic flow and its volume across the network. The netflow solution is implemented using a netflow collector, which is a centralized server used to gather up netflow Information from monitored systems and then allow for analysis of the data captured.[5]

sFlow

sFlow, short for "sampled flow," is an industry standard for packet export at layer 2 of the OSI model. It provides a means for exporting truncated packets, together with interface counters. Maintenance of the protocol is performed by the sFlow.org consortium, the authoritative source of the sFlow protocol specifications.

sFlow is a technology for monitoring traffic in data networks containing switches and routers. It is described in RFC 3176 (`https://www.ietf.org/rfc/rfc3176.txt`).

The sFlow monitoring system consists of a sFlow Agent (embedded in a switch or router or in a standalone probe) and a central data collector, or sFlow Analyzer. The sFlow Agent uses sampling technology to capture traffic statistics from the device it is monitoring. sFlow Datagrams are used to immediately forward the sampled traffic statistics to an sFlow Analyzer for analysis.

Event Correlation Systems (Security Information and Event Management [SIEM])

SIEM technology is used in many enterprise organizations to provide real-time reporting and long-term analysis of security events. SIEM products evolved from two previously distinct product categories, namely, security information management (SIM) and security event management (SEM).

- **Security Event Management (SEM)**—Analyzes log and event data in real time to provide threat monitoring, event correlation, and incident response. Data can be collected from security and network devices, systems, and applications.

- **Security Information Management (SIM)**—Collects, analyzes, and reports on log data (primarily from host systems and applications, but also from network and security devices) to support regulatory compliance initiatives, internal threat management, and security policy compliance management.

SIEM combines the essential functions of SIM and SEM products to provide a comprehensive view of the enterprise network using the following functions:

- Log collection of event records from sources throughout the organization provides important forensic tools and helps to address compliance reporting requirements.

- Normalization maps log messages from different systems into a common data model, enabling the organization to connect and analyze related events, even if they are initially logged in different source formats.

- Correlation links logs and events from disparate systems or applications, speeding detection of and reaction to security threats.

- Aggregation reduces the volume of event data by consolidating duplicate event records.

- Reporting presents the correlated, aggregated event data in real-time monitoring and long-term summaries.

The SIEM market is evolving towards integration with business management tools, internal fraud detection, geographical user activity monitoring, content monitoring, and business critical application monitoring. SIEM systems are implemented for compliance reporting, enhanced analytics, forensic discovery, automated risk assessment, and threat mitigation.

Compliance

Compliance with monitoring and reporting regulations is often a significant factor in the decision to deploy a SIEM system. Other policy requirements of a specific organization may also play a role. Examples of regulatory requirements include the Health Insurance

Portability and Accountability Act (HIPAA) for healthcare providers in the United States or the Payment Card Industry's Data Security Standard (PCI-DSS) for organizations that handle payment card information. A SIEM can help the organization to comply with monitoring mandates and document their compliance to auditors.

Enhanced Network Security and Improved IT/Security Operations

Attacks against network assets are a daily occurrence for many organizations. Attack sources can be inside or outside the organization's network. As the boundaries of the enterprise network expand, the role of network security infrastructure must expand as well. Typically, security operations staff deploys many security measures, such as firewalls, IDS sensors, IPS appliances, web and e-mail content protection, and network authentication services. All of these can generate significant amounts of information, which the security operations staff can use to identify threats that could harm network security and operations.

For example, when an employee's laptop becomes infected by malware, it may discover other systems on the corporate network and then attempt to attack those systems, spreading the infection. Each system under attack can report the malicious activity to the SIEM. The SIEM system can correlate those individual reports into a single alert that identifies the original infected system and its attempted targets. In this case, the SIEM's ability to collect and correlate logs of failed authentication attempts allows security operations personnel to determine which system is infected so that it can be isolated from the network until the malware is removed. In some cases, it may be possible to use information from a switch or other network access device to automatically disable the network connection until remediation takes place. The SIEM can provide this information in both real-time alerts and historical reports that summarize the security status of the enterprise network over a large data collection, typically on the order of months rather than days. This historical perspective enables the security administrators to establish a baseline for normal network operations, so they can focus their daily effort on any new or abnormal security events.

Full Packet Capture

Full packet capture devices typically sit at the ingress and egress points of an organization's network. These devices capture every single information packet that flows across the border. These devices are indispensable tools for the security practitioner as they capture the raw packet data, which can be analyzed later should an incident occur. As full packet capture devices capture every packet, they require an organizational network architecture that consolidates traffic to as few points as possible for collection. Many organizations use VPN tunnels and mandatory routing configurations for hosts to ensure all traffic is sent through a full packet capture device.

Full packet capture devices can consume tremendous amounts of storage. As every packet that flows into or out of the organization is captured, the security practitioner must be mindful of the storage capacities needed to maintain a useful packet capture. Knowing a breach occurred three months ago and having only one month of packet capture is not going to be helpful.

Most full capture packet devices also come with the ability to do a *packet dump* or extract a certain cross-section of the traffic as defined by criteria such as IP, protocol, or time of day. This traffic can then be analyzed using specialized tools or even played in a simulated browser if the traffic is web traffic. Full packet capture is indispensable in collecting evidence of workplace misconduct and understanding an attack. Often signatures for IDS/IPS systems come from the analysis and understanding of packet dumps from full packet capture systems.

While full packet capture systems are extremely useful, it is important to note what they do not do. Most if not all are not IDS or IPS systems. Additionally, they may not include the native ability to break encrypted transmissions such as SSL and HTTPS communications. Therefore, the security practitioner must understand how full packet capture fits with other information security technologies.

Source Systems

Monitoring of information and system state is one of the most important activities that the security practitioner can engage in to ensure that the infrastructure under their care is optimized and secured in a proactive manner. Monitoring can be focused on many different systems, from applications to operating systems to middleware and infrastructure.

Hyperic

According to VMware, VMware's vRealize Hyperic monitors operating systems, middleware, and applications running in physical, virtual, and cloud environments. Hyperic provides proactive performance management with complete and constant visibility into applications and infrastructure. It produces more than 50,000 performance metrics on more than 75 technologies at every layer of the stack. At startup, Hyperic automatically discovers and adds new servers and VMs to inventory; configures monitoring parameters; and collects performance metrics and events. Hyperic helps reduce operations workload, increases a company's IT management maturity level, and drives improvements in availability and infrastructure health.[6]

Operations Manager

Microsoft also provides complete management and monitoring capabilities with their System Center Suite of products. Operations Manager, a component of Microsoft System Center 2012/2012 R2, is software that helps the security practitioner monitor services, devices, and operations for many computers from a single console.

Using Operations Manager in the environment makes it easier to monitor multiple computers, devices, services, and applications. The Operations Manager console, shown in Figure 3.7, enables you to check the health, performance, and availability for all monitored objects in the environment and helps you identify and resolve problems.

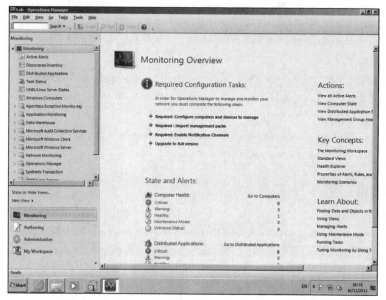

FIGURE 3.7 Microsoft System Center Operations Manager Console

Operations Manager will tell you which monitored objects are not healthy, send alerts when problems are identified, and provide information to help you identify the cause of a problem and possible solutions.[7]

Security Analytics, Metrics, and Trends

Effective network security demands an integrated defense-in-depth approach. The first layer of a defense-in-depth approach is the enforcement of the fundamental elements of network security. These fundamental security elements form a security baseline, creating a strong foundation on which more advanced methods and techniques can subsequently be built.

A security baseline defines a set of basic security objectives that must be met by any given service or system. The objectives are chosen to be pragmatic and complete and do not impose technical means. Therefore, details on how these security objectives are fulfilled by a particular service/system must be documented in a separate security implementation document. These details depend on the operational environment a service/system is deployed into, and might, thus, creatively use and apply any relevant security measure. Derogations from the baseline are possible and expected and must be explicitly marked.

Developing and deploying a security baseline can, however, be challenging due to the vast range of features available. For instance, a network security baseline is designed to assist in this endeavor by outlining those key security elements that should be addressed in the first phase of implementing defense-in-depth. The main focus of a network security baseline is to secure the network infrastructure itself: the control and management planes. The network security baseline presents the fundamental network security elements that are key to developing a strong network security baseline. The focus is primarily on securing the network infrastructure itself, as well as critical network services, and addresses the following key areas of baseline security:

- Infrastructure device access
- Routing infrastructure
- Device resiliency and survivability
- Network telemetry
- Network policy enforcement
- Switching infrastructure

Unless these baseline security elements are addressed, additional security technologies and features are typically useless. For example, if a default access account and password are active on a network infrastructure device, it is not necessary to mount a sophisticated attack because attackers can simply log in to the device and perform whatever actions they choose.

The use of metrics and analysis (MA) is a sophisticated practice in security management that takes advantage of data to produce usable, objective information and insights that guide decisions.

Analytics is the discovery and communication of meaningful patterns in data. Especially valuable in areas rich with recorded information, analytics relies on the simultaneous application of statistics, computer programming, and operations research to quantify performance. Risk analytics involves reporting on metrics from various areas that point out which businesses, processes, or systems are most at risk and require immediate attention.

Through MA, a CSO or other security professional can better understand risks and losses, discern trends, and manage performance. Software designed specifically for the security field can make the gathering of security and risk-significant data orderly, convenient, and accurate while holding the data in a format that facilitates analysis. Security and risk-focused incident management software offers both the standardization and consolidation of data. Such software also automates the task of analysis through trending and predictive analysis and the generation of customized statistical reports.

Carnegie Mellon University created the Systems Security Engineering Capability Maturity Model (SSE-CMM), which provides valuable metrics for security practitioners. Security metrics are a quantifiable measurement of actions that organizations take to manage and reduce security risks such as information theft, damage to reputation, financial theft, and business discontinuity. Administrators and other stakeholders use metrics to address concerns such as:

- Determining resources to allocate for security
- Figuring out which system components to prioritize
- Deciding how to effectively configure the system
- Gauging return on investment for security expenditures
- Identifying how to reduce exposure to risk[8]

For example, the use of metrics and analysis at the Massachusetts Port Authority (Massport) to solve the specific problem of security door alarms is illustrative. Massport was able to greatly reduce such alarms through the analysis of alarm metrics. That analysis helped security management determine the cause of each type of alarm and develop solutions to eliminate or reduce them. Analysis of detailed door transaction data, including video, showed the causes of alarms. That understanding led to a variety of corrective actions, including maintenance and user training being implemented.

The security practitioner can use MA not only to identify security problems but also to gauge the effectiveness of the various security measures used to counteract those problems.

Visualization

Data visualization is a general term that describes any effort to help people understand the significance of data by placing it in a visual context. Patterns, trends, and correlations that might go undetected in text-based data can be exposed and recognized easier with data visualization software. Data visualization tools go beyond the standard charts and graphs used in Excel spreadsheets, displaying data in more sophisticated ways such as infographics, dials and gauges, geographic maps, sparklines, heat maps, and detailed bar, pie, and fever charts. The images may include interactive capabilities, enabling users to manipulate them or drill into the data for querying and analysis. Indicators designed to alert users when data has been updated or predefined conditions occur can also be included. Some examples of data visualization tools include

- **Dygraphs** (`http://dygraphs.com/`)—A fast, flexible open source JavaScript charting library that allows users to explore and interpret dense data sets. It's highly customizable, it works in all major browsers, and you can even pinch to zoom on mobile and tablet devices.

- **ZingChart** (`http://www.zingchart.com/`)—ZingChart is a JavaScript charting library and feature-rich API set that lets you build interactive Flash or HTML5 charts. It offers over 100 chart types to fit your data.

- **InstantAtlas** (`http://www.instantatlas.com/`)—Enables you to create highly interactive dynamic and profile reports that combine statistics and map data to create engaging data visualizations.

- **Visual.ly** (`http://create.visual.ly/`)—Visual.ly is a combined gallery and infographic generation tool. It offers a simple toolset for building stunning data representations, as well as a platform to share your creations.

Event Data Analysis

According to the NIST Guide to Computer Security Log Management (SP 800-92), a log is a record of the events that occur in a system. The challenge that security practitioners face today is the increasing complexity of the systems that we are asked to manage, and as a result of that complexity, the increasing volumes of information generated by these systems. In order to be able to make sense of the day-to-day, moment-to-moment operation of systems, the security practitioner needs to be able to balance the continuous flow of information being gathered in logs with the ability to monitor and manage. Implementing the following NIST security log management recommendations should assist the security practitioner in facilitating more efficient and effective log management for the organization:

"**A. Organizations should establish policies and procedures for log management.**

To establish and maintain successful log management activities, an organization should develop standard processes for performing log management. As part of the planning process, an organization should define its logging requirements and goals. Based on those, an organization should then develop policies that clearly define mandatory requirements and suggested recommendations for log management activities, including log generation, transmission, storage, analysis, and disposal. An organization should also ensure that related policies and procedures incorporate and support the log management requirements and recommendations. The organization's management should provide the necessary support for the efforts involving log management planning, policy, and procedures development.

Requirements and recommendations for logging should be created in conjunction with a detailed analysis of the technology and resources needed to implement and maintain them, their security implications and value, and the regulations and laws to which the organization is subject (e.g., HIPAA, SOX). Generally, organizations should require logging and analyzing the data that is of greatest importance, and they should also have non-mandatory recommendations for which other types and sources of data should be logged and analyzed if time and resources permit. In some cases, organizations choose to have all or nearly all log data generated and stored for at least a short period of time in case it is needed, which favors security considerations over usability and resource usage, and also allows for better decision-making in some cases. When establishing requirements and recommendations, organizations should strive to be flexible since each system is different and will log different amounts of data than other systems.

The organization's policies and procedures should also address the preservation of original logs. Many organizations send copies of network traffic logs to centralized devices as well as use tools that analyze and interpret network traffic. In cases where logs may be needed as evidence, organizations may wish to acquire copies of the original log files, the centralized log files, and interpreted log data in case there are any questions regarding the fidelity of the copying and interpretation processes. Retaining logs for evidence may involve the use of different forms of storage and different processes, such as additional restrictions on access to the records.

B. Organizations should prioritize log management appropriately throughout the organization.

After an organization defines its requirements and goals for the log management process, it should then prioritize the requirements and goals based on the organization's perceived reduction of risk and the expected time and resources needed to perform log management functions. An organization should also define roles and responsibilities for log management for key personnel throughout the organization, including establishing log management duties at both the individual system level and the log management infrastructure level.

C. Organizations should create and maintain a log management infrastructure.

A log management infrastructure consists of the hardware, software, networks, and media used to generate, transmit, store, analyze, and dispose of log data. Log management infrastructures typically perform several functions that support the analysis and security of log data. After establishing an initial log management policy and identifying roles and responsibilities, an organization should next develop one or more log management infrastructures that effectively support the policy and roles. Organizations should consider implementing log management infrastructures that include centralized log servers and log data storage. When designing infrastructures, organizations should plan for both the current and future needs of the infrastructures and the individual log sources throughout the organization. Major factors to consider in the design include the volume of log data to be processed, network bandwidth, online and offline data storage, the security requirements for the data, and the time and resources needed for staff to analyze the logs.

D. Organizations should provide proper support for all staff with log management responsibilities.

To ensure that log management for individual systems is performed effectively throughout the organization, the administrators of those systems should receive adequate support. This should include disseminating information, providing training, designating points of contact to answer questions, providing specific technical guidance, and making tools and documentation available.

E. Organizations should establish standard log management operational processes.

The major log management operational processes typically include configuring log sources, performing log analysis, initiating responses to identified events, and managing long-term storage. Administrators have other responsibilities as well, such as the following:

- Monitoring the logging status of all log sources
- Monitoring log rotation and archival processes

- Checking for upgrades and patches to logging software, and acquiring, testing, and deploying them

- Ensuring that each logging host's clock is synched to a common time source

- Reconfiguring logging as needed based on policy changes, technology changes, and other factors

- Documenting and reporting anomalies in log settings, configurations, and processes"[9]

▶▶ REAL WORLD EXAMPLE:
Potential Uses of Server Log Data

IT organizations use server log analysis to answer questions about

- **Security**—For example, if we suspect a security breach, how can we use server log data to identify and repair the vulnerability?

- **Compliance**—Large organizations are bound by regulations such as HIPAA and Sarbanes-Oxley. How can IT administrators prepare for system audits?

✔ Try It for Yourself—Creating a Network Trace Using Wireshark or tcpdump

A network trace, also called a packet dump, sometimes must be generated to analyze packet traffic between systems to troubleshoot difficult application or networking problems. These are the steps to be taken to generate a network trace. Select your platform where the packet trace will be initiated, and follow the steps.

Windows and Mac OS X

WireShark is the recommended application for generating network traces on Windows and Mac OS X platforms. From a machine involved in the transmission of data, download WireShark (https://www.wireshark.org/) and install it (including the WinPcap application, if applicable). Follow these steps to create the trace:

1. From within Wireshark, click Capture Options.

2. In the Interface field, select the network card that connects to the remote system involved in the network transmission.

3. In the Capture Filter field, type **host** followed by the IP address of the remote system:

```
host xxx.xxx.xxx.xxx
```

where xxx.xxx.xxx.xxx is the IP address of the remote machine.

4. Click the Browse button next to the File field and select Desktop in the Save In Folder field.

5. Type a file name, such as **problem.cap**, in the Name field and click OK.

6. Click the Start button, or from the Capture menu, select Start.

7. Perform the network connection that displays the problem.

8. When the network operation is complete, click the Stop button or, from the Capture menu, select Stop.

9. Analyze and examine your captured data. See the following for a how-to on analyzing captured data using the WireShark toolsets:

```
https://www.wireshark.org/docs/wsug_html_chunked/
ChapterWork.html
```

Linux

`tcpdump` is the recommended application for generating network traces and is already installed on most Linux platforms. Here are the basic steps for creating a trace using the `tcpdump` command-line application:

1. Open a Terminal session and log in as the `root` user. To start the network trace, type the following:

```
tcpdump -s 0 -w /problem.cap -f host xxx.xxx.xxx.xxx
```

where xxx.xxx.xxx.xxx is the IP address of the remote machine, such as 192.168.200.201.

2. Perform the network connection that displays the problem.

3. When the network operation is complete, type **ctrl-c** in the Terminal to stop `tcpdump`.

4. Analyze and examine your captured data using the `problem.cap` file. See the following for the Linux man page for `tcpdump`:

```
http://www.tcpdump.org/manpages/tcpdump.1.html
```

Communication of Findings

Findings are most effectively communicated in reports embracing five key elements:

- Solid substance
- Sound logic
- Balanced tone
- Visual clarity
- Good mechanics

✔ Experience It!

The following checklist is handy for report writers and reviewers.

- **Solid Substance:** Does the report have all the attributes of a finding? The attributes of a finding are
    - **Criteria**—"What should be?"
    - **Condition**—"What is?"
    - **Cause**—"Why the condition happened?"
    - **Effect**—"What is the difference between the 'what is' and the 'what should be?'"
    - **Recommendation**—"What actions are needed to correct the cause?"
- **Sound Logic:** Does the report make sense, and is it easily readable?
- **Balanced Tone:** Does the report present a balanced tone, one that is respectful?
- **Visual Clarity:** Does the report's appearance guide the reader through the logic of the material?
- **Good Mechanics:** Do the report's words and sentences clearly and effectively communicate the message?

GOING HANDS-ON—RISK IDENTIFICATION EXERCISE

This exercise will take the reader through the process of performing a basic vulnerability scan against a known vulnerable system using freely available tools. As part of risk identification, the security practitioner should be versed in using vulnerability detection and scanning tools. This exercise assumes the security practitioner has experience with virtual environments and basic networking.

Virtual Testing Environment

The security practitioner should never conduct testing on any system without authorization and without assurance they will not cause damage or undesired impacts. Therefore, the security professional should be familiar with the operation of virtual test environments.

Setting Up VirtualBox

This exercise relies on virtual machines. VirtualBox will be the virtual environment used throughout this exercise. VirtualBox is freely available on the Internet at `https://www.virtualbox.org/wiki/Downloads`.

To install VirtualBox on a chosen system, ensure the downloaded software matches the target system's specifications and follow the directions for the specific platform found at `https://www.virtualbox.org/manual/ch01.html#intro-installing`.

Once VirtualBox is installed, two virtual machines will be downloaded for this exercise. The first is Kali Linux. Kali Linux is a staple in the security practitioner's toolkit and comes preloaded with numerous vulnerability scanning and exploitation tools.

Downloading Kali and Metasploitable

Download the Kali Virtual 32 bit machine from `http://www.offensive-security.com/kali-linux-vmware-arm-image-download/`.

NOTE The root password for the images is `toor`.

Next, download the Metasploitable virtual machine available at `https://information.rapid7.com/metasploitable-download.html?LS=1631875&CS=web`.

NOTE The provider does request some marketing information.

NOTE The default login/password is: `msfadmin:msfadmin`.

Alternatively, to create a new Metasploitable VM, download the image from here and build: `http://sourceforge.net/projects/metasploitable/files/Metasploitable2/`.

NOTE Both virtual machines will need to be unpacked since they have both been zipped. One of the files is packed using 7zip. 7zip can unzip both files and can be downloaded from http://www.7-zip.org/.

Creating the Environment

The goal in creating the virtual environment is to ensure all malicious activity is contained within the virtual environment. When one is creating this environment, it is vitally important the networks for all virtual machines be configured for a private subnet using the "host-only" option found in the network settings of the VirtualBox settings for each virtual machine. Next, the downloaded virtual machines need to be loaded.

Metasploitable Configuration

Follow these steps to configure Metasploitable:

1. In VirtualBox, choose Machine and then New.

2. Choose Linux, Debian (32 bit), and name the machine Metasploitable, as shown in Figure 3.8.

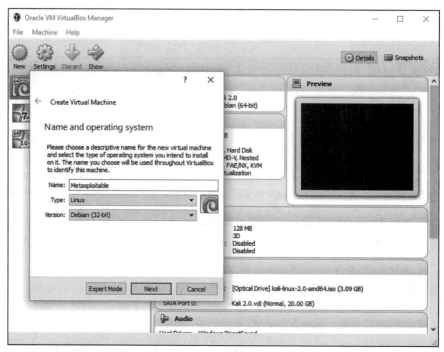

FIGURE 3.8 **Setting up a new machine in VirtualBox**

3. Choose at least 2 GB (2048 MB) of memory, as shown in Figure 3.9.

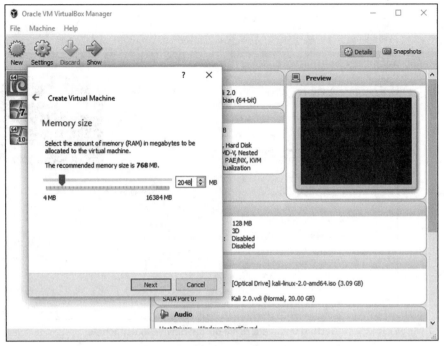

FIGURE 3.9 **Selecting memory size for the new virtual machine**

4. Choose to use an existing hard drive and navigate to the downloaded and unpacked Metasploitable folder. Choose the Metasploitable.vmdk file, as shown in Figure 3.10.

5. Choose Create, and the VM will be created.

6. Next, click the Settings button to open the Metasploitable settings. Ensure under System, Processor, that the option for Enable PAE/NX is checked, as shown in Figure 3.11.

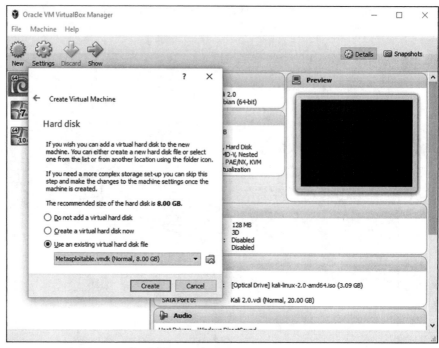

FIGURE 3.10 Setting up a hard drive on the new virtual machine

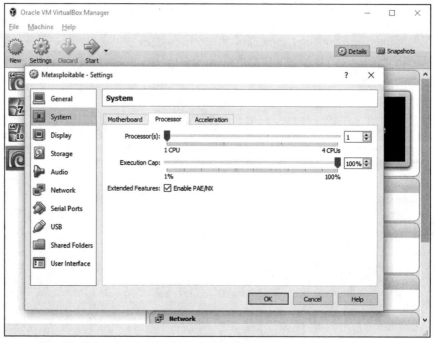

FIGURE 3.11 Verifying that PAE/NX (Physical Address Extension and Processor Bit) is enabled

7. Now, click Network and choose Host Only, as shown in Figure 3.12.

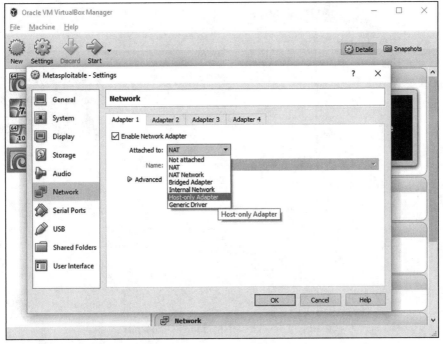

FIGURE 3.12 **Enabling the network adapter**

8. Next, click OK, and this will complete the configuration of the Metasploitable machine.

Kali Linux Configuration

Follow these steps to configure Kali Linux:

1. Start VirtualBox and choose Machine and then New, as shown in Figure 3.13.

2. Name the machine Kali and choose Linux and Debian (32bit), as shown in Figure 3.14.

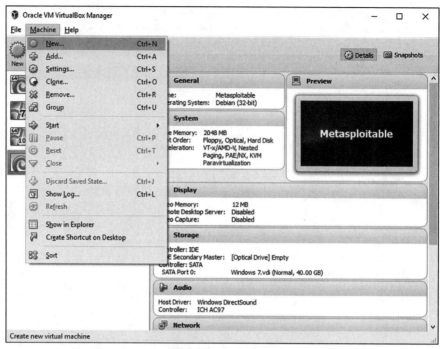

FIGURE 3.13 Creating a new virtual machine in Kali Linux

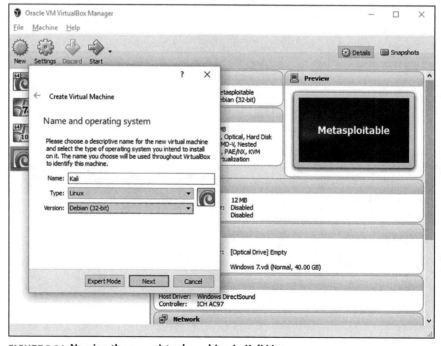

FIGURE 3.14 Naming the new virtual machine in Kali Linux

3. Next, set at least 4 GB (4096 MB) of memory, as shown in Figure 3.15.

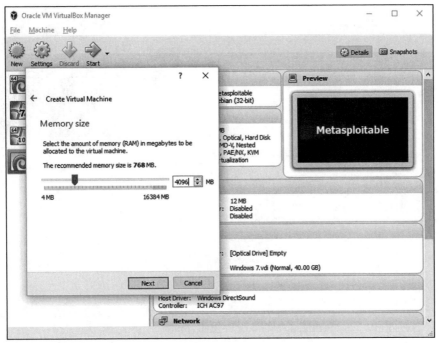

FIGURE 3.15 **Selecting memory size (Kali Linux)**

4. Next, choose the virtual hard drive from the unpacked Kali virtual machine files, as shown in Figure 3.16.

5. Click Create and the Kali VM should be created.

6. Next, click Network and ensure Host-only is chosen for the adapter, as is shown in Figure 3.17.

7. Click OK to complete the configuration of the Kali virtual machine.

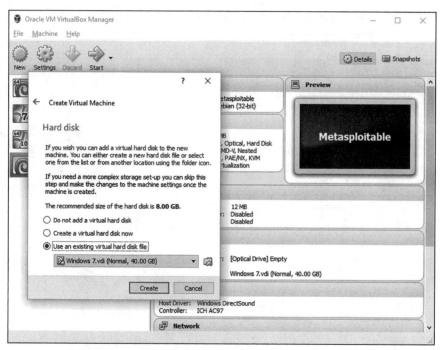

FIGURE 3.16 Setting up a hard drive (Kali Linux)

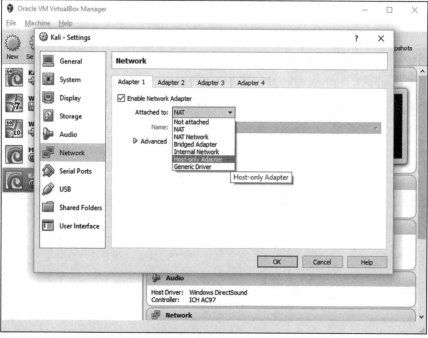

FIGURE 3.17 Enabling network adapter (Kali Linux)

Setting Up the Virtual Environment

Now that both virtual machines are created, they both need to be started.

1. To start them, simply click the desired virtual machine and then click the green start arrow on the top of the screen. Start both the Kali and the Metasploitable virtual machines. A new window will open for each of the virtual machines.

2. The IP addresses for each of the systems will be necessary for this exercise. First, log in to the Metasploitable virtual machine using the username and password combination of msfadmin/msfadmin.

3. Next, open a terminal command window, type **ifconfig**, and then press Enter to get the IP address of the virtual machine. See Figure 3.18.

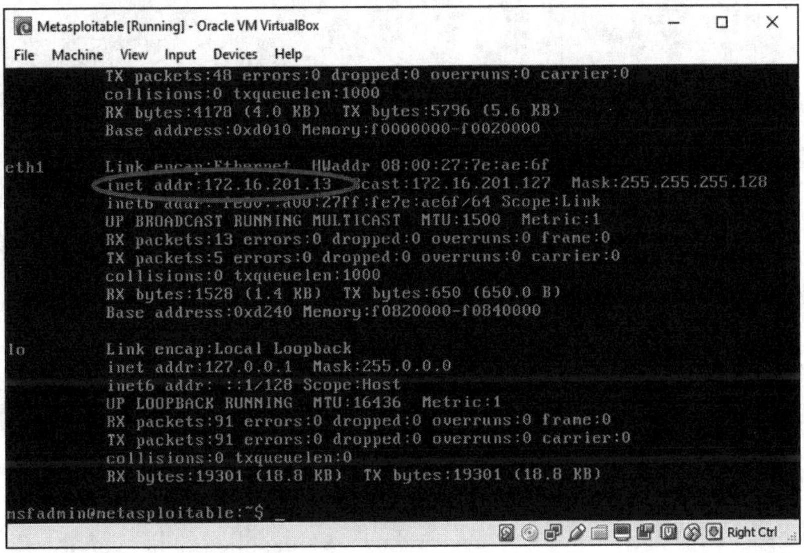

FIGURE 3.18 **Discovering the target IP address**

NOTE The IP address may be different than noted in Figure 3.18. Take note of the IP address listed. This is the target's IP address.

Launching a Scan

Follow these steps to launch a scan:

1. Go to the Kali virtual machine.

2. Log in using **root** as the username and **toor** as the password.

3. Once in, start Zenmap by clicking the following menus and submenus: Applications ⇨ Information Gathering ⇨ Zenmap. See Figure 3.19.

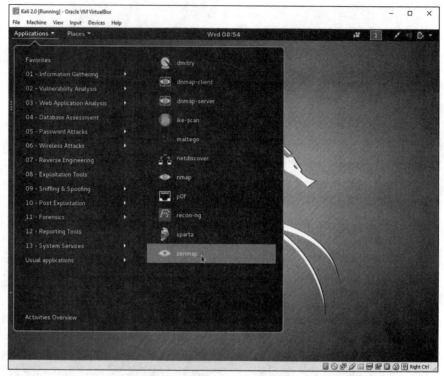

FIGURE 3.19 **Starting Zenmap to launch a scan**

4. Zenmap will start. Zenmap is a graphical tool used to perform basic network scanning, system scanning, detection of open ports, open services, and possible vulnerabilities.

5. Once started, type the IP address of the target identified earlier into the Target section of the Zenmap. See Figure 3.20.

Note that Zenmap automatically generates the command that a user would type should they decide to launch the scan from a terminal. Select Intense Scan from the profile drop-down menu. The types of scans and their meanings can be found at `http://www.securesolutions.no/zenmap-preset-scans/`.

The intense scan selected scans the most common TCP ports and makes an attempt to identify the operating system and services of the target.

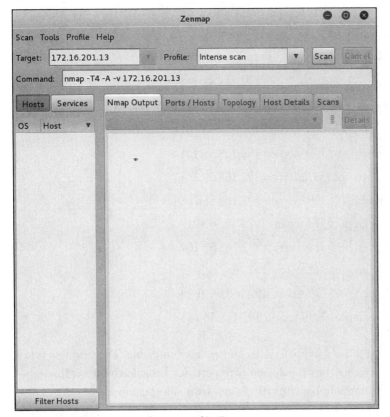

FIGURE 3.20 **Autogenerated command in Zenmap**

Reviewing the Results

Once the scan is complete, review Nmap Output and note that the scan discovered the following open ports:

- Scanning 192.168.56.101 [1000 ports]
- Discovered open port 3306/tcp on 192.168.56.101
- Discovered open port 23/tcp on 192.168.56.101
- Discovered open port 25/tcp on 192.168.56.101
- Discovered open port 80/tcp on 192.168.56.101
- Discovered open port 53/tcp on 192.168.56.101
- Discovered open port 5900/tcp on 192.168.56.101
- Discovered open port 445/tcp on 192.168.56.101
- Discovered open port 22/tcp on 192.168.56.101
- Discovered open port 139/tcp on 192.168.56.101

- Discovered open port 111/tcp on 192.168.56.101
- Discovered open port 21/tcp on 192.168.56.101
- Discovered open port 6000/tcp on 192.168.56.101
- Discovered open port 8009/tcp on 192.168.56.101
- Discovered open port 8180/tcp on 192.168.56.101
- Discovered open port 6667/tcp on 192.168.56.101
- Discovered open port 1524/tcp on 192.168.56.101
- Discovered open port 5432/tcp on 192.168.56.101
- Discovered open port 1099/tcp on 192.168.56.101
- Discovered open port 514/tcp on 192.168.56.101
- Discovered open port 2121/tcp on 192.168.56.101
- Discovered open port 512/tcp on 192.168.56.101
- Discovered open port 513/tcp on 192.168.56.101
- Discovered open port 2049/tcp on 192.168.56.101

Just because a port is listed as open doesn't mean it is vulnerable. The next step is to determine what services may be available on each port. Scrolling down further through the results will yield information about services and basic information about vulnerable configurations. See Figure 3.21.

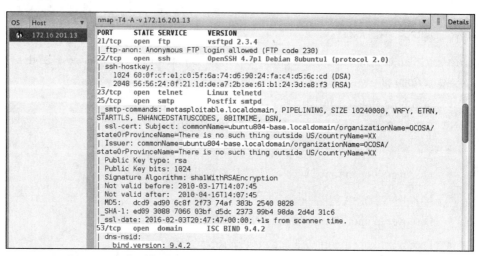

FIGURE 3.21 **Ports recognized by Zenscan**

Notice how Zenmap located services on port 21 and identified them as FTP services. Zenmap then attempted to log in with an anonymous account and was able to do so. Zenmap also identified the bind version the target is running as 9.4.2. There are also others, but for the sake of this exercise, the FTP and the BIND services are of interest.

Vulnerability to Risk

Having a vulnerability on the system does not equate to risk. If there is no actual sensitive information on the system and the system is in test, there is no risk because there is no risk when losing the information. For the sake of this exercise, assume the target system has sensitive information on it and is vital to the organization.

Risk must always be determined through the dimensions of impact, vulnerability, and threat. The scanner has provided vulnerability information. The last step is to determine the threat information. Threat information is sourced from a variety of services and systems. For the sake of this exercise, assume there is a highly motivated and capable threat.

The question the security professional must answer is "How would a threat exploit the vulnerabilities I've discovered to impact the organization?" In this scenario, the anonymous FTP access could allow access to sensitive information on the server if not properly secured and logically separated from the FTP server. Additionally, when researching the BIND service, the security professional discovers CVE-2014-3859 (`http://cve.mitre .org/cgi-bin/cvename.cgi?name=CVE-2014-3859`), which states this version of BIND used may be vulnerable to denial-of-service attacks. This information is combined with organizational risk information to determine the best mitigation approach.

Further Exercises

The virtual setup provided here can be used for numerous tests of attacking a vulnerable system. Several tutorials are available online for additional research and training.

SUMMARY

An information security practitioner must have a thorough understanding of fundamental risk, response, and recovery concepts. By understanding each of these concepts, the security practitioner will have the knowledge required to protect the security practitioner's organization and professionally execute the security practitioner's job responsibilities.

SAMPLE QUESTIONS

1. Which of the following terms refers to a function of the likelihood of a given threat source exercising a potential vulnerability, and the resulting impact of that adverse event on the organization?

   a. Threat

   b. Risk

   c. Vulnerability

   d. Asset

2. The process of an authorized user analyzing system security by attempting to exploit vulnerabilities to gain access to systems and data is referred to as:

   a. Vulnerability assessment

   b. Intrusion detection

   c. Risk management

   d. Penetration testing

3. The process for assigning a dollar value to anticipated losses resulting from a threat source successfully exploiting a vulnerability is known as:

   a. Qualitative risk analysis

   b. Risk mitigation

   c. Quantitative risk analysis

   d. Business impact analysis

4. When initially responding to an incident, it is critical for the SSCP to:

   a. Notify executive management.

   b. Restore affected data from backup.

   c. Follow organizational incident response procedures.

   d. Share information related to the incident with everyone in the organization.

5. Which of the following are threat sources to information technology systems? (Choose all that apply.)

   a. Natural threats

   b. Human threats

   c. Environmental threats

   d. Software bugs

6. The expected monetary loss to an organization from a threat to an asset is referred to as:

   a. Single loss expectancy

   b. Asset value

   c. Annualized rate of occurrence

   d. Exposure factor

7. Which risk-mitigation strategy would be appropriate if an organization decided to implement additional controls to decrease organizational risk?

   a. Risk avoidance

   b. Risk reduction

   c. Risk transference

   d. Risk acceptance

8. During which phase of the risk assessment process is technical settings and configuration documented?

   a. Risk determination

   b. Results documentation

   c. System characterization

   d. Control analysis

9. What is the correct order of steps for the NIST risk assessment process?

   a. Communicate, prepare, conduct, and maintain

   b. Prepare, conduct, communicate, and maintain

   c. Conduct, communicate, prepare, and maintain

   d. Maintain, communicate, prepare, and conduct

10. Cross-referencing and stimulus response algorithms are qualities of what associated with what activity?

    a. Vulnerability testing

    b. Penetration testing

    c. Static application security testing

    d. Dynamic application security testing

11. What is the correct order for the phases of penetration testing?

   a. Information gathering, preparation, information evaluation and risk analysis, active penetration, and analysis and reporting

   b. Preparation, information gathering, active penetration and analysis, information evaluation, and risk analysis and reporting

   c. Preparation, active penetration and analysis, information gathering, information evaluation, and risk analysis and reporting

   d. Preparation, information gathering, information evaluation and risk analysis, active penetration, and analysis and reporting

12. Where do the details as to how the security objectives of a security baseline are to be fulfilled come from?

   a. The system security plan

   b. A security implementation document

   c. The enterprise system architecture

   d. Authorization for the system to operate

13. Shoulder surfing, Usenet searching, and dumpster diving are examples of what kind of activity?

   a. Risk analysis

   b. Social engineering

   c. Penetration testing

   d. Vulnerability assessment

14. What is the most important reason to analyze event logs from multiple sources?

   a. They will help you obtain a more complete picture of what is happening on your network and how you go about addressing the problem.

   b. The log server could have been compromised.

   c. Because you cannot trust automated scripts to capture everything.

   d. To prosecute the attacker once he can be traced.

15. Security testing includes which of the following activities? (Choose all that apply.)

   a. Performing a port scan to check for up-and-running services

   b. Gathering publicly available information

   c. Counterattacking systems determined to be hostile

   d. Posing as technical support to gain unauthorized information

16. Why is system fingerprinting part of the security testing process?

    a. It is one of the easiest things to determine when performing a security test.

    b. It shows what vulnerabilities the system may be subject to.

    c. It tells an attacker that a system is automatically insecure.

    d. It shows the auditor whether a system has been hardened.

NOTES

[1] http://csrc.nist.gov/publications/nistpubs/800-30-rev1/sp800_30_r1.pdf

[2] https://www.bsi.bund.de/SharedDocs/Downloads/EN/BSI/Grundschutz/download/threats_catalogue.pdf?__blob=publicationFile

[3] Source: © 2012 ISACA. All rights reserved. Used by permission

[4] For more information, see the following: http://csrc.nist.gov/publications/drafts/800-94-rev1/draft_sp800-94-rev1.pdf

[5] See the following two documents for a detailed discussion of netflow: http://www.cisco.com/c/en/us/products/collateral/ios-nx-os-software/ios-netflow/prod_white_paper0900a-ecd80406232.html

http://www.cisco.com/en/US/products/sw/netmgtsw/ps1964/products_implementation_design_guide09186a00800d6a11.html

[6] https://support.hyperic.com/display/DOCS46/Introduction+to+Hyperic+Monitoring

[7] https://technet.microsoft.com/en-us/library/Hh230741.aspx

[8] George Campbell, Measures and Metrics in Corporate Security: Communicating Business Value (The Security Executive Council. 2006)

[9] See the following: http://csrc.nist.gov/publications/nistpubs/800-92/SP800-92.pdf

[10] Scanning methodology and input from Justin Warner.

Incident Response and Recovery

ORGANIZATIONS MUST PLAN FOR the worst and be prepared to act during an incident, breach, or disaster. Incident response and business continuity planning are designed to move an organization through an unforeseen event and back to normal business operations. Incident response and business continuity are complementary to each other. An incident such as a denial-of-service attack may lead an organization to *fail over* to an alternate provider, which is a process detailed in the organization's business continuity plans. During a continuity exercise, an alternate site firewall may have not been patched to the latest version of operating system and has now been exploited. This incident will have to be handled with the organization's incident response processes while operating in a contingency mode. Proper contingency planning and incident response are vital for an organization's survival.

TOPICS

The following topics are addressed in this chapter:

- ❏ Incident handling
    - ◼ Discovery
    - ◼ Escalation
    - ◼ Reporting and feedback loops
    - ◼ Incident response
    - ◼ Implementation of countermeasures
- ❏ Forensic investigations
- ❏ Business continuity planning (BCP) and disaster recovery planning (DRP)
    - ◼ Emergency response plans and procedures
    - ◼ Interim or alternate processing strategies
    - ◼ Restoration planning
    - ◼ Backup and redundancy implementation
    - ◼ Testing and drills

OBJECTIVES

The security practitioner is expected to participate in the following areas of incident response and business continuity:

- Incident handling
- The support of forensic investigations
- The support of business continuity plans (BCPs) and disaster recovery planning (DRP)

INCIDENT HANDLING

Incident response is the process of responding in an organized manner to a compromise or attempted compromise of organizational information technology assets. As an SSCP, the security practitioner will be actively involved with the incident response process. The security practitioner may be the first person to identify that an incident has occurred or may identify an active attempt to compromise system security. In any case, it is important that the security practitioner understand incident response best practices so the organization can react in a timely manner. It is equally important that the security practitioner does not perform any activities that may make the situation worse or that may compromise evidence required to investigate the incident and provide court-acceptable results.

The incident response process generally follows a phased approach, as shown in Figure 4.1.[1]

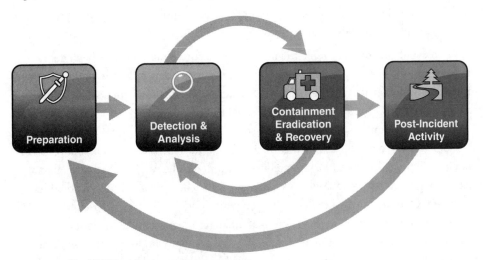

FIGURE 4.1 The NIST incident response process

Phases of the incident response process include

1. Preparation
2. Detection and analysis
3. Containment, eradication, and recovery
4. Post-incident activity

Before we begin explaining the phases of the incident response process, some definitions should be established. NIST Special Publication 800-61 Rev. 2, "Computer Security Incident Handling Guide," provides an excellent source of guidance in this area. Per SP 800-61:

> An event is any observable occurrence in a system or network. Events include a user connecting to a file share, a server receiving a request for a Web page, a user sending electronic mail (e-mail), and a firewall blocking a connection attempt.
>
> Adverse events are events with a negative consequence, such as system crashes, network packet floods, unauthorized use of system privileges, deface-ment of a Web page, and execution of malicious code that destroys data.
>
> The definition of a computer security incident has evolved. In the past, a computer security incident was thought of as a security-related adverse event in which there was a loss of confidentiality, disruption of data or system integrity, or disruption or denial of availability. New types of computer security incidents have emerged since then, necessitating an expanded definition of an incident. An incident can be thought of as a violation or imminent threat of violation of computer security policies, acceptable use policies, or standard security practices.

As an event, an adverse event, and a computer security incident have been defined, the background necessary to explore each phase of the incident response process is now in place. Remember that incident response is focused on dealing with a subset of all adverse effects that could occur within the organization.

Effective incident response is a critical security function that an SSCP should be able to perform. To perform this function, the SSCP must be aware of incident response policies and procedures and be prepared to act immediately. An SSCP must be able to analyze potential security incidents and determine if an actual security incident has transpired. Once a security incident has been confirmed, it is imperative that the SSCP follows the defined procedure to ensure that incidents are contained and eradicated in accordance with organizational requirements. It is equally important that while an organization is recovering from an incident, evidence is handled appropriately and that a chain of custody is maintained. Finally, post-incident activities must be performed, incident reports finalized, and procedures and policies updated where appropriate to reflect lessons learned from the incident response process.

Preparation

For an organization to have effective and efficient incident handling, a solid foundation must exist. In this instance, the foundation is comprised of a corporate incident handling and response policy, clearly articulated procedures and guidelines that take into consideration the various legal implications of reacting to incidents, and the management and handling of evidence (digital, physical, and document-based). The policy must be clear, be concise, and provide a mandate for the incident response/handling team to deal with any and all incidents. The policy must also provide direction for employees on the escalation process to follow when a potential incident is discovered and how various notifications, contacts, and liaisons with third-party entities, the media, government, and law enforcement authorities are to be notified, by whom, and in what manner.

A properly staffed and trained response team is also required; the team can be virtual or permanent depending on the requirements of the organization. Virtual teams usually consist of individuals that, while assigned to the response team, have other regular duties and are called upon only if there is some need to start the incident handling capability. Some organizations have teams whose members are permanently assigned to the incident team and work in this capacity on a full-time basis. A third model can be described as a hybrid of the virtual and permanent, with certain core members permanently assigned to the incident team and others called up as necessary.

The Incident Response Policy

It is important to note that the key to successful incident response is to have an established incident response policy and procedure. The incident response policy and related incident response procedures should clearly indicate who the members of the incident response team are and should define incident response responsibilities for each team member. The incident response policy should establish a phased approach to incident response, which mirrors, or is similar to, the process detailed earlier. Incident response procedures should describe the exact steps that should be performed during each phase of incident response.

Once an incident response policy and related procedures have been documented, reviewed, and approved, it is important that all personnel receive training related to their responsibilities. All personnel should understand the activities that they must perform. Of equal importance, personnel should understand activities that they must not perform. Training should include simulations to ensure that all personnel are prepared to act.

Simulations also help to validate that the incident response procedures are effective and not missing vital details that will be needed when an incident occurs.

In addition to ensuring that the incident response policy and procedure are well documented, organizations must ensure that incident response tools have been acquired. Specific software may be needed for incident handling activities such as forensics analysis. This type of software should be evaluated and purchased so that it is available when needed. Preparation is the key to incident response.

An incident response policy is the first mandatory step in ensuring appropriate incident response. The SSCP may be called on to develop the policy or hold a major role in the policy depending on the size and complexity of the organization. The policy should minimally contain the following elements:

- Statement of management support and endorsement
- Statement of alignment with the organization's strategy, mission, vision, objectives, and goals
- Objectives of the policy
- Scope and limitations
- Definitions of terms
- Roles and responsibilities
- Prioritization of risk when discovered
- Metrics and performance measures
- Communications planning
- Mandatory adherence to incident response plans, processes, and procedures
- How the policy complies with laws, regulations, or standards the organization must adhere to

The policy should reference an incident response plan or procedure that all employees will follow depending on their role in the incident response process. The plan may contain several procedures and standards related to incident response. The plan is a living instantiation of the organization's incident response policy. The plan covers with greater specificity all areas of the policy and may include areas covering the maturation of the incident response process and how the incident response process fits with other areas such as risk management and external communications. The organization's vision, strategy, and mission should shape the incident response process. Ultimately, the incident response policy is an important administrative control.

Communication Planning

Communication planning is an essential part of incident response planning. During an incident, the public, news media, government, and business partners may all be in need of accurate, thorough, and timely updates. The SSCP must be aware as to how they fit into the communications process. Figure 4.2 describes a typical communications web for an organization's incident response plan, which is referenced in NIST SP 800-61 Rev2.[2]

FIGURE 4.2 **A typical communications web for an organization's incident response plan**

Media and Public Relations

The SSCP must be aware that the media may become involved in a breach should the public be impacted or the breach is of national or local interest. The incident handling team should work with existing organizational communications teams such as external affairs, legal, or the office of communications to ensure the incident response process includes appropriate involvement of those parties. The incident response policy and plan should be consistent with any organizational standards or procedures for interaction with the media. As part of incident response plan training and testing, the SSCP must ensure all members of the incident response process are aware of how to handle interactions with the media and other communication partners. The training and testing should focus on the unapproved release of pre-decisional, deliberative, or sensitive information.

The whole domain of public relations and communications is an extremely sensitive issue at the best of times. When an event becomes an incident, the proper handling of public disclosure can either compound the negative impact or, if handled correctly, provide an opportunity to engender public trust in the organization. This is why communications, human resources, and only properly trained and authorized individuals should handle the communications and external notifications. In some countries or jurisdictions, legislation exists (or is being contemplated) that requires organizations to publicly disclose when they reasonably believe there has been an incident that may have jeopardized someone's private or financial information. Obviously, denial and "no comment" are not an effective public relations strategy in today's information culture.

Once an incident has occurred that the public or media is interested in, it is crucial the organization maintain the status of the incident and provide accurate and timely updates to the media. Failure to do so can lead to the spread of speculation and inaccurate assumptions. Mock interviews and press conferences as part of incident response testing are an excellent way to help train staff in the appropriate handling of media affairs.

Law Enforcement

Law enforcement reporting will vary by country, state, economy, and jurisdiction, but in general, the SSCP must be aware of the drivers that may necessitate law enforcement involvement. Many criminal actions that started as incidents are often not prosecuted because law enforcement was not involved early enough in the process, or the incident response team damaged evidence. In the United States, the Federal Bureau of Investigation, state and local law enforcement, and the district attorney offices may be involved in an incident. U.S. federal agencies also have the Office of Inspector General that is responsible for investigating fraud, waste, and abuse. Regardless of location, the incident response team should become familiar with relevant law enforcement agencies and know who the contacts are ahead of an incident.

In developing relationships with law enforcement agencies, the incident response team should understand under what conditions the law enforcement agency should be contacted, how the contact should occur, what evidence if any the incident response team should collect, and any standards or processes around collections. The organization's forensics policy, standards, and procedures should contain requirements as noted by the law enforcement partner. The organization must be collectively exhaustive and mutually exclusive in contacting law enforcement. The incident response plan or communications plan must clearly delineate who may contact a law enforcement organization and when. This avoids multiple agencies being contacted concurrently and creating confusion.

Official Organizations and Agencies

In addition to law enforcement, many organizations may also have an obligation to report to other organizations when certain types of incidents occur. For example, in the United States, federal agencies must report incidents to the United States Computer Emergency Readiness Team (US-CERT). In the case of the US-CERT, it does not replace any agency reporting function, but rather it exists as a coordinating organization with subject-matter expertise and a global view of incident response. Another example from the United States is the Department of Health and Human Services (HHS) Office of Civil Rights. Should a healthcare provider fall under the jurisdiction of the Health Information Portability and Accountability Act, they must report certain breaches to individuals, the media, the Secretary of HHS, and possibly the U.S. Federal Trade Commission. In addition to the parties noted prior, organizations may need to inform their Internet service providers, other incident response teams, software developers, owners of attacking systems (if suspected compromised), and affected parties.

The Incident Response Team

Although the actual makeup of the response team depends upon the structure of the organization, there are core areas that need to be represented: legal department (in lieu of in-house legal counsel, arrangements should be made with external counsel), human resources, communications, executive management, physical/corporate security, internal audit, information security (IS), and IT. Obviously, there needs to be representation by other pertinent business units as well as systems administrators and anyone else who can assist in the recovery and investigation of an incident. Once the team has been established, it must be trained and stay current with its training. This sounds easy enough at first glance, but the initial and ongoing training requires a budget and resources to cover for team members who are away at training; more than one organization has been stymied in its attempt to establish a response team because of the failure to anticipate realistic costs associated with training and education.

An organization's incident response team can be developed in a centralized or decentralized matter. Each approach has benefits and drawbacks. A centralized incident response team provides a consistent approach for incident response throughout the organization, but it is often feasible only for small or mid-sized organizations, as larger organizations may be more geographically dispersed and have more compliance drivers. A decentralized response team, on the other hand, may be divided by function such as physical and logical, geographic area, or division. These teams often are able to react to specific incidents within their specific incident response area with speed and specialization. The key to ensuring distributed teams are successful is the use of thorough communications and reporting structures. If teams cannot coordinate across the organization, teams may double report with partial information, creating confusion and conflict among the team and reporting entities.

The incident response team may be constructed of full-time employees, outsourced operations, or a hybrid. There are advantages to each approach. Having full-time employees often provides the best coverage and organizational knowledge for incident response. The trade-off is that full-time employees can be expensive to maintain for an around-the-clock incident response capability. The fully outsourced solution can often manage and support the need for around-the-clock incident response. The trade-off is most outsourced incident response teams may not have in-depth organizational knowledge about systems, sensitive information, and how the organization conducts business. The hybrid approach can bridge the best of both worlds, allowing an employee staff to maintain organizational knowledge and response while allowing the outsourced provider to focus on monitoring and reporting. Regardless of the approach, communication is essential to ensure incidents and important events are routed to the appropriate function or party.

NIST SP 800-61 R2 clearly states that incident response teams perform best when the following conditions are met:[3]

- Budget enough funding to maintain, enhance, and expand proficiency in technical areas and security disciplines, as well as less technical topics such as the legal aspects of incident response. This should include sending staff to conferences and encouraging or otherwise incentivizing participation in conferences, ensuring the availability of technical references that promote deeper technical understanding, and occasionally bringing in outside experts (e.g., contractors) with deep technical knowledge in needed areas as funding permits.

- Give team members opportunities to perform other tasks, such as creating educational materials, conducting security awareness workshops, and performing research.

- Consider rotating staff members in and out of the incident response team, and participate in exchanges in which team members temporarily trade places with others (e.g., network administrators) to gain new technical skills.

- Maintain sufficient staffing so that team members can have uninterrupted time off work (e.g., vacations).

- Create a mentoring program to enable senior technical staff to help less experienced staff learn incident handling.

- Develop incident handling scenarios and have the team members discuss how they would handle them.

The incident response team should be focused on service delivery to their organization. The team should strive to minimally provide near real-time continuous monitoring of information systems and be proactive through the distribution of advisories and threat notices. The incident response team should also be available to provide education and awareness for the organization's partners and employees.

NIST SP 800-61 R2 also clearly states that other important considerations[4] for the incident response team include but are not limited to

- Contact information for team members and others within and outside the organization (primary and backup contacts), such as law enforcement and other incident response teams; information may include phone numbers, e-mail addresses, public encryption keys (in accordance with the encryption software described below), and instructions for verifying the contact's identity.

- On-call information for other teams within the organization, including escalation information.

- Incident reporting mechanisms, such as phone numbers, e-mail addresses, online forms, and secure instant messaging systems that users can use to report suspected incidents; at least one mechanism should permit people to report incidents anonymously.

- Issue tracking system for tracking incident information, status, etc.

- Smartphones to be carried by team members for off-hour support and onsite communications.

- Encryption software to be used for communications among team members, within the organization and with external parties; for federal agencies, consider software that supports FIPS-validated encryption algorithms for extra assurance.

- "War room" for central communication and coordination; if a permanent war room is not necessary or practical, the team should create a procedure for procuring a temporary war room when needed.

- Secure storage facility for securing evidence and other sensitive materials.

- Incident analysis hardware and software.
  - Digital forensic workstations and backup devices to create disk images, preserve log files, and save other relevant incident data
  - Laptops for activities such as analyzing data, sniffing packets, and writing reports
  - Spare workstations, servers, and networking equipment, or the virtualized equivalents, which may be used for many purposes, such as restoring backups and trying out malware
  - Blank removable media

- Portable printer to print copies of log files and other evidence from non-networked systems
- Packet sniffers and protocol analyzers to capture and analyze network traffic
- Digital forensic software to analyze disk images
- Removable media with trusted versions of programs to be used to gather evidence from systems
- Evidence-gathering accessories, including hard-bound notebooks, digital cameras, audio recorders, chain of custody forms, evidence storage bags and tags, and evidence tape, to preserve evidence for possible legal actions
- Port lists, including commonly used ports and Trojan horse ports
- Documentation for OSs, applications, protocols, and intrusion detection and anti-virus products
- Network diagrams and lists of critical assets, such as database servers
- Current baselines of expected network, system, and application activity
- Cryptographic hashes of critical files to speed incident analysis, verification, and eradication
- Access to images of clean OS and application installations for restoration and recovery purposes

Detection and Analysis

An SSCP will be presented with a myriad of events during the course of normal business operations. Many events occur normally because of business operations. Examples of these events are authorized logon events, authorized access to files, and normal network usage. The SSCP should be able to identify normal events and realize that these events have no adverse effect on the environment.

Of the many events that occur on a daily basis, some of the events will be adverse. That is, the events will adversely affect the operation of information technology systems, network devices, applications, and services. Although these events may have a negative impact, they will not necessarily be classified as security incidents. For example, although a system may crash due to a hardware failure, this would not be considered a security incident because the failure was related to hardware and was not the result of a malicious activity that violated security policies.

Attacks and incidents may spawn from a variety of sources. The incident response team must be aware of not only technical attacks such as web and e-mail attacks but also physical attacks such as loss of sensitive information through portable media and social engineering attacks. Detecting an incident is one of the most challenging aspects of incident response. Incident detection is often hampered by a "noise floor" of false or unimportant events. For example, an organization's external firewall may be scanned thousands of times every day by hundreds of organizations, countries, and individuals. This does not mean each of the scanning events is an incident. However, one or some of the scans could be an attacker actually determined to break into the organization. An *indicator* is an event that means an incident is actually occurring or has occurred (like a workstation reaching out to a command and control network), while a *precursor* is an event that may signal an incident in the future (for example, a scanner continues to scan the organization's network persistently using different scope and criteria each time).

NIST SP 800-62 Rev2 provides the information provided in Table 4.1.

TABLE 4.1 **Common Sources of Precursors and Indicators**

SOURCE	DESCRIPTION
Alerts	
IDPS	IDPS products identify suspicious events and record pertinent data regarding them, including the date and time the attack was detected, the type of attack, the source and destination IP addresses, and the username (if applicable and known). Most IDPS products use attack signatures to identify malicious activity; the signatures must be kept up to date so that the newest attacks can be detected. IDPS software often produces false positives—alerts that indicate malicious activity is occurring, when in fact there has been none. Analysts should manually validate IDPS alerts either by closely reviewing the recorded supporting data or by getting related data from other sources.
SIEM	Security Information and Event Management (SIEM) products are similar to IDPS products, but they generate alerts based on analysis of log data (see the next page).
Antivirus and Anti-spam Software	Antivirus software detects various forms of malware, generates alerts, and prevents the malware from infecting hosts. Current antivirus products are effective at stopping many instances of malware if their signatures are kept up to date. Antispam software is used to detect spam and prevent it from reaching users' mailboxes. Spam may contain malware, phishing attacks, and other malicious content, so alerts from anti-spam software may indicate attack attempts.
File Integrity Checking Software	File integrity checking software can detect changes made to important files during incidents. It uses a hashing algorithm to obtain a cryptographic checksum for each designated file. If the file is altered and the checksum is recalculated, an extremely high probability exists that the new checksum will not match the old checksum. By regularly recalculating checksums and comparing them with previous values, one can detect changes to files.

CONTINUES

SOURCE	DESCRIPTION
Third-Party Monitoring Services	Third parties offer a variety of subscription-based and free monitoring services. An example is fraud detection services that will notify an organization if its IP addresses, domain names, etc., are associated with current incident activity involving other organizations. There are also free real-time blacklists with similar information. Another example of a third-party monitoring service is a CSIRC notification list; these lists are often available only to other incident response teams.
Logs	
Operating System, Service, and Application Logs	Logs from operating systems, services, and applications (particularly audit-related data) are frequently of great value when an incident occurs, such as recording which accounts were accessed and what actions were performed. Organizations should require a baseline level of logging on all systems and a higher baseline level on critical systems. Logs can be used for analysis by correlating event information. Depending on the event information, an alert can be generated to indicate an incident. Section 3.2.4 discusses the value of centralized logging.
Network Device Logs	Logs from network devices such as firewalls and routers are not typically a primary source of precursors or indicators. Although these devices are usually configured to log blocked connection attempts, they provide little information about the nature of the activity. Still, they can be valuable in identifying network trends and in correlating events detected by other devices.
Network Flows	A network flow is a particular communication session occurring between hosts. Routers and other networking devices can provide network flow information, which can be used to find anomalous network activity caused by malware, data exfiltration, and other malicious acts. There are many standards for flow data formats, including NetFlow, sFlow, and IPFIX.
Publicly Available Information	
Information on New Vulnerabilities and Exploits	Keeping up with new vulnerabilities and exploits can prevent some incidents from occurring and assist in detecting and analyzing new attacks. The National Vulnerability Database (NVD) contains information on vulnerabilities. Thirty-two organizations such as US-CERT33 and CERT®/CC periodically provide threat update information through briefings, web postings, and mailing lists.

SOURCE	DESCRIPTION
People	
People from within the Organization	Users, system administrators, network administrators, security staff, and others from within the organization may report signs of incidents. It is important to validate all such reports. One approach is to ask people who provide such information how confident they are of the accuracy of the information. Recording this estimate along with the information provided can help considerably during incident analysis, particularly when conflicting data is discovered.
People from Other Organizations	Reports of incidents that originate externally should be taken seriously. For example, the organization might be contacted by a party claiming a system at the organization is attacking its systems. External users may also report other indicators, such as a defaced webpage or an unavailable service. Other incident response teams also may report incidents. It is important to have mechanisms in place for external parties to report indicators and for trained staff to monitor those mechanisms carefully; this may be as simple as setting up a phone number and e-mail address, configured to forward messages to the help desk.

4

INCIDENT RESPONSE AND RECOVERY

Intrusion detection and prevention systems are used to identify and respond to suspected security-related events in real-time or near-real-time. Intrusion detection systems (IDSs) will use available information to determine if an attack is underway, send alerts, and provide limited response capabilities. Intrusion prevention systems (IPSs) will use available information to determine if an attack is underway, send alerts, but also block the attack from reaching its intended target.

Network-based intrusion systems focus on the analysis of network traffic, while host-based intrusion systems focus on audit logs and processes inside a single system.

The distinction between IDS and IPS is very important since it materially affects both how the system must be deployed and its effect on the systems it is monitoring. If an IDS is used, it may be deployed out-of-band, meaning that it is not deployed in the middle of the communications path and will not affect normal processing or cause latency. Any attacks, however, will likely reach their intended target. If an IPS is used, it must be deployed in-line (also known as in-band), meaning that it is deployed in the middle of the communications path. Because it is in-line, it will cause some latency and slow down normal processing to a slight extent. Detected attacks, however, will not likely reach their intended targets. On many modern systems, both IDS and IPS techniques can be used within the same device, allowing the security practitioner to decide whether to use one technique or the other.

Intrusion systems use a number of techniques to determine whether an attack is underway:

- **Signature or Pattern Matching Systems**—Examine the available information (logs or network traffic) to determine if it matches a known attack.

- **Protocol Anomaly-Based Systems**—Examine network traffic to determine if what it sees conforms to the defined standard for that protocol; for example, as it is defined in a Request for Comment or RFC.

- **Statistically Anomaly-Based Systems**—Establish a baseline of normal traffic patterns over time and detect any deviations from that baseline. Some also use heuristics to evaluate the intended behavior of network traffic to determine if it intended to be malicious or not. Most modern systems combine two or more of these techniques together to provide a more accurate analysis before it decides whether it sees an attack or not.

In most cases, there will continue to be problems associated with false-positives as well as false-negatives. False-positives occur when the IDS or IPS identifies something as an attack, but it is in fact normal traffic. False-negatives occur when it failed to interpret something as an attack when it should have. In these cases, intrusion systems must be carefully tuned to ensure that these are kept to a minimum. An IDS requires frequent to constant attention. An IDS requires the response of a human who is knowledgeable enough with the system and types of normal activity to make an educated judgment about the relevance and significance of the event. Alerts need to be investigated to determine if they represent an actual event.

Anti-Malware Systems

Today, anti-malware systems may be deployed at various points throughout the enterprise. They are installed on individual hosts, on key systems such as e-mail servers, and even at key points in the network in e-mail and web gateways as well as unified threat management (UTM) devices, which combine anti-malware with other functions (such as firewall, intrusion detection/prevention, and content filtering).

To remain effective, anti-malware solutions require continual updates and must be monitored to ensure they are still active and effective. Each implementation should be monitored to ensure that updates are received and active. Likewise, the anti-malware engines should be configured to take advantage of automatic scanning for new media and e-mail attachments. Scanning should be scheduled and accomplished on a regular basis. It is best for the scanning to be done automatically during nonpeak usage times.

Security Information and Event Management (SIEM)

Few solutions are more important to security operations than one that provides the ability to get a view into security-related events in real time. System audit logs collect valuable information on the operation of the system, but logs do not alert security professionals. They also do not provide ways to collate audit logs across multiple systems.

Security-related audit logs will typically log access attempts (including successes and failures), the use of privileges, service failures, and the like. Even on a single system, these logs can get to be very large. They may need to be tuned to ensure that you are only collecting the logs that you want using appropriate clipping levels. For example, successful login attempts may not be required for analysis and may be filtered out.

One disadvantage of system logs is that they provide a view into that single system. They do not provide a view into events that may be affecting multiple systems or where multiple systems have some information that may be required to detect an incident and track it back to its sources. SIEM solutions are intended to provide a common platform for log collection, collation, and analysis in real time to allow for more effective and efficient response. They can also provide reports on historical events using log information from multiple sources. Log management systems are similar: They also collect logs and provide the ability to report against them, although their focus tends to be on historical analysis of log information rather than real-time analysis. They may be combined with SIEM solutions to provide both historical and real-time functions.

In both cases, log information must be carefully managed, and security operations must maintain a disciplined practice of log storage and archiving. For most SIEM or log management systems, there is a practical limit to the amount of information they can analyze at once or generate reports against. For most systems, only a fraction of the logs will be stored online with the remaining logs moved into longer-term storage or archival solutions. These solutions store online logs for 30 to 180 days, shift them into an online or near-line archive for up to a year, and then move any logs into longer-term backup to cover the remainder of the retention period. At the end of that period, security operations are responsible for ensuring that old log information is properly disposed of using defined data disposal procedures and tools. Modern reporting tools can also be used to transform security event information into useful business intelligence. Rather than focusing on basic log analysis, they tend to focus on higher-level reporting on service metrics as well as reporting for compliance purposes.

Incident Analysis

Incident analysis focuses on understanding what constitutes an incident in the organization instead of drive-by scans, abnormal behavior, or new system configurations. The incident response team must be able to understand what "normal" behavior is for an organization. The team must be aware that normal behavior is based not only on day-to-day activities but also on business cycles and events that affect the business behavior such as mergers and acquisitions. For example, if an organization has a quarterly reporting requirement to outside entities, normal behavior would include increased traffic to those entities during the reporting cycles. Similarly, e-commerce sites experience an increase in traffic and transactions during holidays. While studying alerts and logs throughout time is useful, understanding the business and the mission of the organization will greatly help the incident response team understand what is normal.

Incident analysis also relies on a sound understanding of the organization's technology. The incident response team should profile each system and understand the critical system files and sensitive information each contains. They should then develop ways of comparing the established profiles against expected behaviors. One way to do this is using integrity checking software. The incident response team must work with the information system owner and in some cases the information owner to determine which files and information are the most critical and then place those files under integrity monitoring. The incident response team should then participate in the change management process of the organization to ensure any changes to the system and information are noted. Should a critical file or information change outside of authorized processes, the integrity software should send an alert to the incident response team for action.

Incident analysis also depends on the ability to accurately and thoroughly coordinate events between different systems. This necessitates the use of synchronized host clocks. All host systems should have their clocks synchronized to a common time source through Network Time Protocol (NTP). From an evidence standpoint, this ensures consistent timestamps in the logs rather than having to explain how each system had a slightly different clock. Event correlation may be based on numerous indicators such as username, IP address used, or attack signature. Having the ability to reach across all hosts to search for indicators is invaluable.

Once hosts have been identified and correlation has pieced together a partial event, packet sniffers are an invaluable tool to pull additional data. Packet sniffers (also called full-packet capture devices) keep a copy of every packet that crosses a specified point in the network. The most common locations for packet sniffers are on the consolidated ingress/egress network locations and in some cases on local hosts. Sniffers are limited by their amount of storage, so pulling packet capture related to specific hosts should be started as soon as possible once an incident is discovered. Incident responders must also be aware of the privacy implications of packet sniffing. Since all packet traffic is captured, the SSCP may be able to view personal sensitive information unrelated to the incident. To avoid privacy complications, incident response teams should consult with appropriate legal counsel regarding the use of the technology and any checks and balances that may need to be in place.

Another important consideration is encrypted traffic. While a packet sniffer works well for capturing raw packet data, it will not help the SSCP understand the data if it is encrypted. SSL encryption and encrypted files will be captured using a packet sniffer, but they will not be able to be opened unless the incident response team can decrypt the traffic. One way to eliminate SSL encryption concerns is using an inline SSL decryption device. These devices perform an operational man-in-the-middle attack and intercept SSL-encrypted traffic for full packet capture and analysis. As with packet inspection, due to the privacy concerns involved, the SSCP should ensure the organization's legal counsel has reviewed any SSL decryption practices.

Incident analysis includes thorough incident documentation. Minimally, the *who, what, why, where, and when* of the incident should be covered. A centralized incident management system enables multiple incident responders to work on the same incident and received updated information. Organizations may use the ticketing system as their help desk in some cases as long as it meets the requirements of the organization and the incident response team. Documentation may also include audio logs, video logs, and written narratives describing the impact of the incident on the system and the organization. Should an incident lead to a criminal or civil action, often this information will be brought in as evidence. As stated in NIST SP 800-61 R2, the records should minimally contain the following:[5]

- The current status of the incident (new, in progress, forwarded for investigation, resolved, etc.)
- Summary of the incident
- Indicators related to the incident
- Other incidents related to this incident
- Actions taken by all incident handlers on this incident
- Chain of custody, if applicable
- Impact assessments related to the incident
- Contact information for other involved parties (e.g., system owners, system administrators)
- A list of evidence gathered during the incident investigation
- Comments from incident handlers
- Next steps to be taken (e.g., rebuild the host, upgrade an application)

The next step in the analysis is to determine the risk of the incident. Not all incidents warrant immediate action, and not all incidents warrant a notification. The incident response team must work with relevant stakeholders such as the information system owner, the information owner, the CISO, the CIO, and legal counsel to determine the impact of a breach. If a breach involves personally identifiable information (PII), notifications may need to be sent out. Incident risk is often reported as high, moderate, or low. The impact of the incident should be determined using a predefined risk assessment methodology such as the NIST risk analysis approach shown in Domain 3 (Figure 3.1 — Determining likelihood of organizational risk).

Risk is then used to prioritize organizational resources toward response and mitigation. Higher risks are prioritized over moderate and low risks. The security practitioner should also be aware that risk can aggregate. This means several moderate and low risks independently may not seem like a high risk, but when taken together, they constitute a high risk. For example, losing a key to a home in a busy intersection may not be that great of a risk, but if an attacker who found the key also knows the person who lives in the home, the risk is much higher.

Incident Response

When an incident is detected, a containment strategy must be decided. Containment may include disconnecting devices from the network, shutting systems down, or redirecting traffic around an affected area of the network. The containment strategy should be driven by several criteria including the following:

- The need to preserve forensic evidence for possible legal action
- The availability of services the affected component provides
- The potential damage leaving the affected component in place may cause
- The time required for the containment strategy to be effective
- The resources required to contain the affected component

Delaying containment when a system is comprised by a suspected attacker is often a poor choice as it can lead to further attacks on more information systems. Arguments may be made that the security professional could observe the attacker to learn more about what is happening; however, that is best left to honeypots and experienced security engineers. There may also be legal implications if the organization knows about the compromised system and then the compromised system is used to attack another system.

The team should instead focus on obtaining a forensic image of the RAM and hard drive of the compromised system and then determine how to mitigate the vulnerability that caused the compromise. The security professional should consult an organization's legal team to determine if the image gathered must be suitable for law enforcement or be admissible in court. If it is needed for law enforcement or court, the security professional must avoid violating the chain of custody and is best assisted by law enforcement or an experienced forensics team while creating an image.

The initial incident and as much relevant information as possible should be documented in an incident management system. The incident should be updated as more information becomes available until the incident is deemed resolved by the security operations team. The documented incident is often one of the most important parts of reconstructing the attack and explaining what happened to third parties.

Only a subset of all adverse events will be classified as security incidents. It is the responsibility of the SSCP to review adverse events and determine if the event is actually a security incident. Making this determination and acting appropriately is one of the SSCP's key responsibilities.

When an issue is identified, identification may result from a preventative control, but generally, it results from a detective control. Preventative controls are security controls that are designed to prevent an incident from occurring. Examples of preventative controls include firewalls, access control lists, and intrusion prevention systems. Detective controls are controls that help detect when an incident has occurred. Examples of detective controls include intrusion detection systems, network monitoring systems, and event logging.

Reports from end users also provide an important method for identifying security incidents. End users may submit complaints to a help desk about virus warnings, poor system performance, or suspect results from standard business processes and related data outputs. Subsequent research into issues reported by end users may identify issues that would have been otherwise undiscovered.

Once a determination has been made that a security incident has occurred, the incident must be triaged to determine systems and data affected. An analysis of the incident must be performed to determine the overall impact. Impact can vary depending on both the number of systems affected as well as the sensitivity of the data affected. The assessed impact level of the incident will dictate the actions that should be taken as detailed within the incident response policy.

After a security incident has been identified and triaged, a determination must be made regarding who, if anyone, should be notified. Notification requirements may be explicitly stated within the incident response policy, or the security practitioner may be required to provide notification based on the security practitioner's best judgment. Generally, notification requirements will be based on the severity of the security event. For example, identification and correction of a virus affecting a single host may not require the security practitioner to provide notification to anyone. On the other hand, if an incident affects a significant number of hosts, affects a critical system, exposes critical data, or could result in revenue loss, immediate notification should be provided. In some situations, businesses must report any breach of health information no matter how small.

When in doubt, the best course of action is to escalate the security incident. The security practitioner may escalate the incident to a senior technical staff member, the security practitioner's manager, or the information security officer, depending on the security practitioner's position and the structure of the security practitioner's organization. Regardless, it is critical that timely notification is provided to all parties who should be aware of the incident or are directly involved in the incident response process.

Containment, Eradication, and Recovery

Once notification has been provided, a decision should be made regarding whether the incident should be contained or eradicated. Normally, the SSCP will not make this decision directly but rather will receive guidance from a manager or executive within the organization. Based on the magnitude of the incident, a decision from legal counsel may be required.

Containment

The goal of containment is to limit the damage caused by the security incident. Containment is required for most types of security incidents, including those that spread naturally. Some types of incidents, such as worms, spread rapidly and must be contained quickly to prevent affecting other systems. Other events, such as successful hacking attempts, should be contained by restricting access to the affected system or by ensuring that the affected system is unable to connect to additional systems or network resources that may not be compromised.

It is important that incident response procedures include containment instructions. Responders need to know the exact steps that they should perform to contain security incidents. If containment instructions are not included in incident response procedures, responders will either be forced to respond rapidly using a "best guess" approach or wait for containment instructions to be provided to them. In either case, critical steps in the containment process are likely to be missed. Missing steps will result in increased response and recovery times.

The steps taken during the containment process will vary depending on the type of security incident. For example, the steps taken when containing a virus outbreak would be different from the steps taken if credit card data were compromised. Incident response procedures should include a variety of containment strategies based on the type of security incident being contained.

Although a variety of containment strategies could be utilized based on the nature of the incident, some containment activities are commonly performed regardless of the strategy employed. Keep in mind that a complete system image or backup should be taken before altering the system. Forensics will be discussed later within this domain, but it must be noted that if a complete system backup is not taken, valuable forensic data may be lost during the containment process. Common containment activities include

- Backing up the affected system for subsequent forensic analysis

- Disconnecting the affected system from the network

- Changing system, application, and user passwords

- Analyzing network traffic with packet sniffers or network monitoring tools to identify the source of security incidents

- Modifying firewall rules to restrict access to affected systems

- Reviewing system, application, and security logs for additional data that may be useful in the containment process

Eradication

Once a security incident has been contained, the next step is to eradicate the incident. Eradication is performed to remove malicious code such as viruses, worms, and Trojan horses. Eradication can also be performed to remove tools and backdoors that may have been used to compromise affected hosts.

Antivirus software is generally effective in removing malicious code from affected systems. Keep in mind that antivirus software signature definition files must be routinely updated. Antivirus signature files are used by antivirus software to identify malicious code infections. Routine updates ensure that antivirus software is able to identify and remove newly released malicious code.

Recovery

In many cases, eradication will not be required. This is true when systems are rebuilt from an image or restored from backup. Reimaging end-user workstations may prove to be a quicker and more reliable option for recovering from a security incident than trying to eradicate the incident. By reimaging the system, one can ensure that it can be restored to a known good configuration with minimal downtime. As an SSCP, the security practitioner may be required to determine if eradication or reimaging is the more appropriate solution based on the nature of the incident. This decision may also be made by the system administrator of the affected system.

Administrators may decide that they prefer to restore affected systems from backup rather than attempting to eradicate the security incident. If it is not possible to validate that a security incident has been fully eradicated, restoration is the only viable choice. The system may be either rebuilt from scratch or restored from backup based on the nature of the system, the amount of time required, and the complexity of the process.

Post-Incident Activity

Once security incident recovery has been completed, post-incident activities should be performed. A post-incident report should be prepared that documents the security incident and all activities performed to recover from the incident. The report should include a technical section that details the root cause of the security incident that can generally be determined via a forensic analysis, actions taken to contain the incident, eradication and recovery steps, and the final restoration or recovery point that data were restored to. The report should also contain a management section that summarizes losses to the organization, residual risks, lessons learned, and methods for improving security incident response. Post-incident reports should be distributed to appropriate parties and collaboratively reviewed.

The incident response policy and related procedures should be updated, as necessary, based on lessons learned during the incident response process. By updating these documents, organizations can continually improve their incident response process. This will result in reduced recovery times and thus provide financial savings to the organization.

Implementation of Countermeasures

Countermeasures need to be implemented in a strategic manner that shows results both immediately and over the longer term. In doing so, particular attention should be paid to the key elements that underlie and increase risk. Furthermore, there are important differences between the various countermeasures in terms of their impact, their costs, and the timelines within which they can be implemented, which will condition the options for action.

The following is a suggested step-by-step implementation of countermeasures:

1. **Increase user awareness of the problem.** This could involve undertaking information campaigns, based on well-researched information, sensitizing users to the nature of the risk, and encouraging changes in attitudes and behavior. In itself, it is not expected to yield high reductions in risk, but it is a prerequisite for achieving greater understanding of the problem and encouraging acceptance of other countermeasures. Furthermore, the combination of other countermeasures, particularly enforcement, with communication can bring about changes in attitudes towards risk over the longer term.

2. **Implement overall improvements that address risk.** This includes ensuring the existence of appropriate policies and rigorous enforcement of standards, focusing on areas where risk is especially high. There will be important costs, in the form of resources used for enforcement. Effective communication will thus be required to gain user support. However, user resistance may be expected, particularly with regards to enforcement.

3. **Provide effective disincentives for inappropriate behavior.** Enforcement will be effective only if it is backed up with concrete repercussions for non-compliance.

4. **Improve user training, including a stronger focus on self-awareness and understanding the circumstances that lead to safer interaction with/usage of systems.** Such changes will require considerable prior analysis, meaning that they will require time for implementation. While this measure is important, it is not likely to have the same impact as countermeasures that effectively limit exposure to risk.

5. **Understand the benefits of "new" technological solutions for monitoring and enforcement, and selectively implement these where they prove to be effective.** This is a longer-term initiative, particularly as it will involve research and development. While the potential is high, the actual gains to be achieved from new technologies are unknown. These solutions will initially generate new costs for implementing technology, which could cause resistance from users. Concerns regarding the legal side effects of new technologies will also need to be addressed, particularly if they are perceived to relinquish the users of responsibility for operating a system.

Forensic Investigations

Once containment and eradication activities have been completed, a number of post-incident activities should be completed. Obviously, one of the most important activities to perform is to identify the root cause of the security incident. Root-cause analysis is a critical step in the process of determining how a security incident occurred. A security incident may have occurred due to the exploitation of an unpatched application vulnerability, as a result of a malicious internal user, by an inadvertent visit to a website containing drive-by malware, or through a myriad of other possibilities. Performing a forensic investigation helps to determine the root cause of security incidents.

One area that has traditionally been lacking in most organizations is proper evidence handling and management. The exact name given to this area ranges from computer forensics, digital forensics, and network forensics to electronic data discovery, cyber forensics, and forensic computing. For the sake of clarity, the term *digital investigations* will be used to encompass all the components expressed in the other terms mentioned; thus, no one definition will be provided. Instead, digital investigations will include all domains in which the evidence or potential evidence exists in a digital or electronic form, whether in storage or on the wire. Unlike the media depiction, computer forensics/digital investigations are not some piece of software or hardware. They are based on a methodical, verifiable, and auditable set of procedures and protocols.

Digital investigations fall under the larger domain of digital forensic science. In 2008, the American Academy of Forensic Sciences (AAFS) in the United States formally recognized digital forensic science as a discipline under the category of Digital and Multimedia Sciences; it was the first time in 28 years that a new section has been recognized by the AAFS. The Digital Forensic Science Research Workshop (DFRWS) defines digital forensic science as:

> The use of scientifically derived and proven methods toward the preservation, collection, validation, identification, analysis, interpretation, documentation and presentation of digital evidence derived from digital sources for the purpose of facilitating or furthering the reconstruction of events found to be criminal, or helping to anticipate unauthorized actions shown to be disruptive to planned operations.[6]

As a forensic discipline, this area deals with evidence and the legal system and is really the marriage of computer science, information technology, and engineering with law. The inclusion of the law introduces concepts that may be foreign to many information security practitioners. These include crime scene, chain of custody, best evidence, admissibility requirements, rules of evidence, etc. It is extremely important that anyone who may potentially be involved in an investigation be familiar with the basics of dealing with and managing evidence. There is nothing worse than finding the proverbial "smoking gun" only to learn that the evidence cannot be used, will be suppressed, or, even worse, the information security practitioner has violated the rights of the individuals in question and is now in worse trouble than the "bad guys." Although different countries and legal systems have slight variations in determining how evidence and the digital crime scene should be handled, there are enough commonalities that a general discussion is possible.

Like incident response, there are various computer forensics guidelines (e.g., International Organization of Computer Evidence [IOCE], Scientific Working Group on Digital Evidence [SWGDE], Association of Chief Police Officers [ACPO]). These guidelines formalize the computer forensic processes by breaking them into numerous phases or steps. A generic guideline includes

- **Identifying evidence**—Correctly identifying the crime scene, evidence, and potential containers of evidence.

- **Collecting or acquiring evidence**—Adhering to the criminalistic principles and ensuring that the contamination and the destruction of the scene are kept to a minimum. Using sound, repeatable collection techniques that allow for the demonstration of the accuracy and integrity of evidence, or copies of evidence.

- **Examining or analyzing the evidence**—Using sound scientific methods to determine the characteristics of the evidence, conducting comparison for individuation of evidence, and conducting event reconstruction.

- **Presentation of findings**—Interpreting the output from the examination and analysis based on findings of fact and articulating these in a format appropriate for the intended audience (e.g., court brief, executive memo, report).

Crime Scenes

Before one can identify evidence, the larger crime scene needs to be dealt with. A crime scene is nothing more than the environment in which potential evidence may exist. The same holds for a digital crime scene. The principles of criminalistics apply in both cases: Identify the scene, protect the environment, identify evidence and potential sources of evidence, collect evidence, and minimize the degree of contamination. With digital crime scenes, the environment consists of both the physical and the virtual, or cyber. The physical (e.g., server, workstation, laptop, smartphone, digital music device) is relatively straightforward to deal with; the virtual is more complicated because it is often more difficult to determine the exact location of the evidence (e.g., data on a cluster or GRID, data in a cloud, or storage area networks [SANs]) or acquire the evidence, as is the case with *live* systems.

Live evidence is data that are very dynamic and exist in running processes or other volatile locations (e.g., RAM) that disappear in a relatively short time once the system is powered down. It is also more difficult to protect the virtual scene. The crime scene can provide additional information related to whom or what might be responsible for the attack or incident.

Locard's principle of exchange states that when a crime is committed, the perpetrators leave something behind and take something with them, hence the exchange. This principle allows us to identify aspects of the persons responsible, even with a purely digital crime scene. As with traditional investigations, understanding the means, opportunity, and motives (MOM), as well as the modus operandi (method of operation [MO] or the way the crime was committed), allows for a more thorough investigation or root-cause analysis. As was mentioned in the "Incident Response" section, identifying the root cause correctly and quickly is extremely important when dealing with an incident, whether it is criminal or not.

Criminologists, sociologists, and psychologists generally agree that behavior is intentional and serves to fulfill some purpose (e.g., need fulfillment). Criminal behavior is no different, and thus neither is criminal computer behavior. Computer criminals and hackers rarely have significant differences related to motivation for attacking systems. Like traditional criminals, computer criminals have specific MOs (e.g., hacking software, type of system or network attacked) and leave behind signature behaviors (e.g., programming syntax, e-mail messages, bragging notices) that can be used to identify the attacker (or at least the tool), link other criminal behaviors together, and provide insight into the thought processes of the attackers. This information can be extremely useful in the event of an insider attack because it can be used during the interview process to solicit more accurate responses from the accused. With an external attack, the information can assist law enforcement in piecing together other offenses by the same individual, assist in the interview and interrogation process, and provide strategies at trial when the accused will be the most defensive.

Given the importance of the evidence that is available at a crime scene, only those individuals with knowledge of basic crime scene analysis should be allowed to deal with the scene. The logical choice is members of the incident response or handling team. The need for a formal approach to this task, coupled with very thorough documentation, is essential. So too is the ability to deal with a scene in a manner that minimizes the amount of disruption, contamination, or destruction of evidence. Once a scene has been contaminated, there is no undo or redo button to push; the damage is done. In many jurisdictions, the accused or opposing party has the right to conduct its own examination and analysis, requiring as original a scene as possible.

General Guidelines

Most seasoned digital investigators have mixed emotions regarding detailed guidelines for dealing with an investigation. The common concern is that too much detail and formalism will lead to rigid checklists and negatively affect the creative aspects of the analysis and examination. Too little formalism and methodology leads to sloppiness, difficulty in re-creating the investigative process, and the lack of an auditable process that can be examined by the courts. In response to this issue, several international entities (e.g., Scientific Working Group on Digital Evidence [SWGDE]) have devised general guidelines that are based on the IOCE/Group of 8 Nations (G8) principles for computer forensics and digital/electronic evidence. Common guidelines include the following:

- Anyone who accesses original digital evidence needs to be properly trained for the purpose.

- Anyone who possesses digital evidence is responsible for all actions taken with it.

- You need to ensure that that seized digital evidence will not be changed no matter what subsequent actions are taken.

- You must fully document, preserve, and keep available for review any and all activity regarding the seizure, storage, access, and transfer of digital evidence.

- Anyone who is responsible for seizing, accessing, storing, or transferring digital evidence is also responsible for complying with these forensic and procedural principles.

These principles form the foundation for the current international models most prominent today (e.g., United States National Institute of Standards and Technology [NIST], United States Department of Justice [DOJ]/Federal Bureau of Investigations [FBI] *Search and Seizure Manual*, NIST SP 800-86: "Computer Forensic Guidelines," "SWGDE Best Practices for Computer Forensics," "ACPO Good Practices Guide for Computer Based Evidence," IACIS forensic examination procedures). These models are also responsive to the prevailing requirements of the court systems and updated on a frequent basis.

The sagest advice that can be given to anyone involved in a computer forensics investigation or any form of incident response is to act ethically, in good faith, attempt to do no harm, and do not exceed one's knowledge, skills, and abilities. The following rules of thumb are quoted directly from the Australian Computer Emergency Response Team (AusCERT) guidelines and should be a part of an investigator's methodology:

- Minimize handling/corruption of original data.
- Account for any changes and keep detailed logs of your actions.
- Comply with the five rules of evidence.
- Do not exceed your knowledge.
- Follow your local security policy and obtain written permission.
- Capture as accurate an image of the system as possible.
- Be prepared to testify.
- Ensure your actions are repeatable.
- Work fast.
- Proceed from volatile to persistent evidence.
- Do not run any programs on the affected system.

As an information security practitioner, it is incumbent to stay current on the latest techniques, tools, processes, and requirements for admissibility of evidence. The entire area of computer forensics is coming under increased scrutiny by both the courts and the public and will undergo significant changes in the next few years as the field matures and develops, as did other more traditional forensic disciplines, such as DNA and latent fingerprint analysis.

Evidence Gathering

Evidence gathering is a critical component of the incident response process and forensic analysis. During the course of investigating a security incident, evidence related to the incident will be discovered and accumulated. This evidence may exist in many different formats such as a disk image, log files, memory contents, or physical evidence. When evidence is gathered, it must be done in a method that does not compromise data. Data gathering must be done using industry-accepted tools that are widely recognized and that have been independently evaluated and validated to produce consistent results.

When evidence is gathered, steps should be performed to ensure that data could not be subsequently altered. If evidence exists on disk, a disk image should be taken. The imaging tool should ensure that no additional data can be written to the compromised device nor should the tool change any data on the compromised device. After the image is taken, a cryptographic hash should be calculated and recorded. Calculating a hash ensures that any alterations to data that occur after imaging can be easily detected.

Hash algorithms take a file or disk image as input and then use mathematical computations to produce a unique value of a fixed length, which is referred to as a message digest. Examples of hash algorithms include SHA-1 and SHA-2. The SHA-1 hash algorithm produces a 160-bit message digest. Hash algorithms are one-way functions, which means that a message digest cannot be reversed to determine the original input.

To ensure that no changes have been made to the original disk image, a practitioner can calculate the hash value for an image and compare it to the original hash value. If the two values match, the practitioner can validate that no changes have been made to the image. On the other hand, if a different hash value result is produced, the practitioner will know that changes have been made to the disk image since the image was originally taken. Even a minor change to an image or file such as a change to a single character within a file would cause a different hash value to be produced.

Some security incidents will be severe enough that criminal charges may be filed against the incident perpetrator. For the evidence collected during the investigation to be admissible in a prosecution, the evidence must be handled properly. A chain of custody must be established that clearly details how evidence was obtained and handled so that evidence maintains its admissibility. If any action is taken that taints the evidence, it will no longer be admissible and thus cannot be used during prosecution. To establish a chain of custody for evidence, maintain documentation throughout the evidence handling process.

The documentation must include, at a minimum, the following information:

- What is the evidence?
- How was the evidence obtained?
- When was the evidence obtained?
- Who obtained the evidence?
- Who has handled the evidence since it was obtained?
- Why was the evidence handled by anyone who handled it after it was obtained?
- Where has the evidence traveled since it was obtained?

The SSCP must understand that as an incident unfolds it may turn into a criminal matter as more is discovered. Therefore, it is imperative that the practitioner ensures forensically sound processes and that documentation is used throughout the incident handling process. Discovering a crime that cannot be successfully prosecuted due to poor incident handling procedures will quickly erode the image of the security practitioner.

Forensic Procedures

The exact requirements for the admissibility of evidence vary across legal systems and between different cases (e.g., criminal versus tort). At a more generic level, evidence should have some probative value, be relevant to the case at hand, and meet the following criteria (often called the five rules of evidence):

- Be authentic
- Be accurate
- Be complete
- Be convincing
- Be admissible

Digital or electronic evidence, although more fragile or volatile, must meet these criteria as well. What constitutes digital/electronic evidence is dependent on the investigation; do not rule out any possibilities until they can be positively discounted. With evidence, it is better to have and not need than vice versa. Given the variance that is possible, the axiom to follow here is check with the respective judiciary, attorneys, or officer of the court for specific admissibility requirements.

The dynamic nature of digital electronic evidence bears further comment. Unlike more traditional types of evidence (e.g., fingerprints, hair, fibers, bullet holes), digital/electronic evidence can be very fragile and can be erased, partially destroyed, or contaminated very easily, and, in some circumstances, without the investigator knowing this has occurred. This type of evidence may also have a short life span and must be collected very quickly (e.g., cache memory, primary/random access memory, swap space) and by order of volatility (i.e., most volatile first). Sufficient care must also be taken not to disturb the timeline or chronology of events. Although time stamps are best considered relative and easily forged, the investigator needs to ensure that any actions that could alter the chronology (e.g., examining a live file system or accessing a drive that has not been write protected) are recorded or, if possible, completely avoided.

Media Analysis

Media analysis involves the recovery of information or evidence from information media such as hard drives, USB drives, DVDs, CD-ROMs, or portable memory devices. This media may have been damaged, overwritten, degaussed, or reused to aid in hiding evidence or useful information. Numerous tools and techniques exist that can recover information from the media with differing success. Should a forensic image be required, the information security practitioner may need to enlist the help of a media recovery specialist. These specialists often work in clean rooms and can rebuild a drive if needed and maintain a chain of custody while doing it if needed. However, they are very expensive, so unless a forensically sound image is required, several other tools and techniques should be considered.[8]

Network Analysis

The term *network forensics* (analysis) was coined in 1997 by Markus Ranum[9] and refers to the analysis and examination of data from network logs and network activity for use as potential evidence. (The original definition used the term *investigation*, but later authors amended this to *evidence* to emphasize the forensic aspect.) Like software forensics/analysis, network analysis or network forensics is now encompassed under the larger category of digital evidence.

The analysis of network activity is an innate function of any incident response situation, and the process model is identical to what has been previously discussed in the "Incident Response" section of this domain. The critical features are proper evidence management and handling (i.e., chain of custody) with the concern that any derived evidence will be admissible in a legal proceeding.

Software Analysis

With the move toward a more generic term for investigations related to digital evidence, many of the historical sub areas have been subsumed under the category of "digital evidence." However, the field of software analysis or software forensics bears further discussion.

Software analysis or forensics refers to the analysis and examination of program code. The code being analyzed can take the form of source code, compiled code, or machine code (binaries). Decompiling and reverse engineering techniques are often used as part of the process. Software analysis encompasses such investigative activities as malware analysis, intellectual property disputes, copyright infringements, etc. The objectives of the analysis include author identification, content analysis (payload), and context analysis.

Author identification, or more precisely author attribution, involves attempts to determine who created or authored the software/program in question (Was it an individual or group effort?). The code is examined for clues to programming style, program language, development toolkits used, embedded comments and addresses, etc. The underlying theory here is that writing code is similar to writing prose and each author has a unique style and eccentricities that allow the investigator to discriminate between various potential suspects. This is very similar to the scientific field of questioned document analysis, and both areas use many of the same techniques.

Content analysis involves the systematic analysis of the purpose of the code. In the case of Trojan horse programs, for example, the focus would be on determining what the actual attack was meant to do, what and where files were installed or altered on the infected systems, what communications channels were opened (ingress and egress), the identification of any upstream destination addresses, what information was being sent or stored locally for batch uploads, etc.

Content analysis is also used in cases related to intellectual property disputes. In these instances, a painstaking examination of the source code or decompiled binary is used to determine the similarity between two programs. The investigator is often asked to provide an expert opinion on how similar the programs are and on what basis the opinion is based.

Context analysis deals with developing a meta view of the impact of the suspicious software relative to the case or the environment it was found in. Understanding context can assist with the analysis and can be used to develop a realistic rating of the risk to the organization or victim.

Hardware/Embedded Device Analysis

The analysis of hardware and embedded devices often involves the analysis of mobile devices such as smartphones or personal digital assistants (PDAs). The standard hardware and firmware found in a laptop or a desktop computer's motherboard, such as the CMOS chip used to control basic functions, will also need to be forensically imaged and then examined. Special tools and techniques are required to image embedded devices. The information security practitioner must understand that many embedded devices cannot be read or copied without altering the very information they wish to obtain. The U.S. National Institute of Standards and Technology recommendations are reproduced here:[10]

- No actions performed by investigators should change data contained on digital devices or storage media.

- Individuals accessing original data must be competent to do so and have the ability to explain their actions.

- An audit trail or other record of applied processes, suitable for independent third-party review, must be created and preserved, accurately documenting each investigative step.

- The person in charge of the investigation has overall responsibility for ensuring the previously mentioned procedures are followed and in compliance with governing laws.

- When one seizes digital evidence, actions taken should not change that evidence.

- When it is necessary for a person to access original digital evidence, that person must be forensically competent.

- All activity relating to the seizure, access, storage, or transfer of digital evidence must be fully documented, preserved, and available for review.

- An individual is responsible for all actions taken with respect to digital evidence while the digital evidence is in their possession.

- Any agency that is responsible for seizing, accessing, storing, or transferring digital evidence is responsible for compliance with these principles.

Incident response, or more precisely incident handling, has become one of the primary functions of today's information security department, and thus of those practitioners working in this capacity. This increased importance is a direct result of the fact that attacks against networks and information systems are evolving—total volume of attacks appear to be decreasing, yet the sophistication and attack vectors are changing. Although statistics related to the exact increase in volumes of attacks and the corresponding economic costs are impossible to calculate given the lack of universal reporting, the gross trends indicate significant changes in the last few years. The types of attacks seem to undergo almost continuous modifications. Today spam, phishing scams, worms, spyware, distributed denial-of-service attacks (DDoS), botnets, and other imaginative yet malicious attacks and mutations inundate personal computers, networks, and corporate systems on a daily basis.

Historically, incident response has been precisely that, a reaction to a trigger event. Incident response in its simplest form is the practice of detecting a problem, determining its cause, minimizing the damage it causes, resolving the problem, and documenting each step of the response for future reference. Although reactive controls are obviously necessary, lessons learned from the various attacks against information systems worldwide make it painfully obvious that preventive controls as well as detective controls are also required if we are to have any hope of recovering or maintaining business operations. Although various entities have developed detailed models for incident handling (e.g., Computer Emergency Response Team Coordination Center [CERT/CC], AusCERT, Forum of Incident Response Teams [FIRST], NIST, British Computing Society, and Canadian Communications Security Establishment [CSE]), there is a common framework to these models as noted prior. The information security practitioner should ensure they understand the industry, relevant regulations, and prevalent incident response methodologies used by the organization they support.

RECOVERY AND BUSINESS CONTINUITY

As an SSCP, the security practitioner will be expected to play a key role in business continuity and disaster recovery operations performed by the organization. The security practitioner may be involved directly in strategic planning efforts related to business continuity and disaster recovery, or the security practitioner may serve as a team member responsible for executing specific recovery tasks. As a result, it is important that the security practitioner have a firm understanding of both business continuity planning and disaster recovery planning. The security practitioner must understand both of these activities, how they are related, and how to professionally perform the associated responsibilities.

Organizations are threatened by a myriad of issues that could potentially impact the continuity of business operations. These issues include natural disasters such as hurricanes, tornadoes, floods, and earthquakes; man-made disasters such as fires, chemical spills, and airplane crashes; health-related issues such as pandemic flu; loss of key personnel or vendors; and miscellaneous other issues that may be unique to the organization's location or business operations.

No matter what type of issue affects the security practitioner's organization, it is critical that the security practitioner has plans in place to recover and restore operations. These plans must be developed with the input of key representatives from business units within the security practitioner's organization and must have the support of executive management. Key personnel must receive training related to their business continuity and disaster recovery responsibilities. Plans must be tested to ensure that they can be effectively executed. Finally, plans must be constantly reviewed and updated to maintain their effectiveness.

Although business continuity planning and disaster recovery planning are related, there are some key differences between the two. Disaster recovery planning is focused on recovery of information technology infrastructure, applications, communications equipment, and data after a disaster. Business continuity planning focuses on the continuity and recovery of critical business functions during and after a disaster. Both disaster recovery planning and business continuity planning will be discussed in detail.

Business Continuity Planning

Developing a business continuity plan (BCP) requires a significant organizational commitment in terms of both personnel and financial resources. For one to gain this commitment, organizational support for business continuity planning efforts must be provided by executive management or an executive sponsor. Without the proper support, business continuity planning efforts have only a minimal chance of success.

Business continuity planning is the proactive development of a plan that can be executed to restore business operations within predetermined times after a disaster or other significant disruption to the organization. For one to gain a thorough understanding of business continuity planning, it is first necessary to explain some key continuity planning concepts. After we have defined these concepts, we will then have a proper foundation of knowledge on which to build our BCP.

The first step in developing a BCP is to establish the business continuity program and the directly related business continuity policy. When a business continuity program is developed, a strategy is defined and overall responsibility for BCP development is formally assigned to a specific individual or department. Key participants from various business units are identified, and program goals are established.

The business continuity policy normally includes a policy statement that sets program expectations and establishes management support for the program. The policy also documents BCP participant roles and responsibilities, program objectives, and key metrics. The policy should be reviewed and updated on an annual basis to ensure that it remains accurate.

The second step in developing a BCP is conducting a business impact analysis (BIA). BIA is performed to assess the financial and nonfinancial impacts to an organization that would result from a business disruption. Conducting a BIA aids in the identification of critical organizational functions and helps determine recovery time objectives, which are both prerequisites for developing the business continuity strategy and related DRP.

Before the process of performing a BIA is detailed, some key concepts should be defined. Once the security practitioner has a clear understanding of important BIA concepts, it will be easy to understand the inputs required for the BIA process and the resulting outputs that allow us to develop an appropriate continuity and recovery strategy.

All organizations perform critical business functions as well as numerous support functions. Critical business functions are those functions that are integral to the success of an organization, without which the organization is incapable of operating. Critical functions vary depending on the nature of the organization as well as the types of goods or services provided by the organization. When one is constructing a BCP, it is imperative that each organizational function is identified. A criticality level should then be assigned to each function based on the impact to organization that would result if the function was unavailable.

A function's criticality level helps to determine the function's *maximum tolerable downtime* (MTD), also referred to as the *maximum tolerable period of disruption* (MTPOD). The MTD is the maximum amount of time that a business function can be unavailable before the organization is harmed to a degree that puts the survivability of the organization at risk. When a business function is unavailable for longer than the MTD, the organization may suffer irreparable damages, either as a direct financial result or as an indirect result from loss of customer confidence or damage to organizational reputation.

Related to the concept of MTD is the *recovery time objective* or RTO concept. Recovery time objectives can be specified for business functions as well as information systems and supporting infrastructure and communications components. The recovery time objective indicates the period of time within which a business function or information system must be restored after a disruption. Recovery time objectives may be expressed in terms of hours, days, or weeks depending on the criticality of the affected business function or supporting information system. The recovery time objective is set less than MTD/MTPOD.

Another related concept is that of the *recovery point objective* or RPO. During a disaster, there will typically be a loss of data. The recovery point objective specifies the point in time to which data could be restored in the event of a business continuity disruption. Recovery point objectives will vary depending on data backup and system availability strategies utilized. For example, if the security practitioner's organization takes daily backups at the end of each business day, the security practitioner's recovery point objective would be the end of the previous day. If the security practitioner's organization uses real-time data mirroring to an alternate location, the security practitioner's recovery point objective could be to restore data to the exact state it was in before the business continuity event.

Although it should be quite evident, it is understood that recovery time objectives for specific functions, services, and systems must be less than the related MTD. An organization must not consider any recovery strategy with a length that exceeds the MTD as the results to the organization would be catastrophic. All effort should be focused on selecting a recovery strategy that allows functions and related information systems to be recovered to defined recovery point objectives and within recovery time objectives.

As mentioned previously, a BIA is performed to assess the financial and nonfinancial impacts to an organization that would result from a business disruption. By assessing the organizational impact that would result from a disruption in various business functions and related information systems, the security practitioner can evaluate business continuity and disaster recovery strategies to be selected and implemented.

When one is conducting a BIA, it is important that stakeholders understand that their responses serve as vital input into the development of business continuity and recovery strategies. Stakeholders must understand that the BCP can be successful only if they provide accurate and timely information to the BIA process. Stakeholders must also understand that failure to provide comprehensive information may result in either an extended delay or complete inability to recover business functions.

Conducting a BIA requires participation from stakeholders in all organizational business units. As a result, executive sponsorship is normally necessary to ensure that stakeholders are involved throughout the process. Without participation from stakeholders, it is difficult to validate that all business functions have been identified and properly categorized according to relative criticality levels.

Many approaches should be considered when determining how to obtain BIA information from stakeholders. Popular choices for obtaining this information include direct interviews with stakeholders, BIA questionnaires, review of organizational policies and procedures, and reviews of organizational contractual requirements and service level agreements.

An approach used by many practitioners is to initially review documentation, including policies, procedures, contracts, and service level agreements. The initial review provides an understanding of business functions and assists in defining recovery time objectives. The review also helps to define questions that should be asked of business unit personnel via questionnaires or via interview.

The documentation review is generally followed up by providing BIA questionnaires to project stakeholders. Stakeholders should complete BIA questionnaires related to functions in their areas of responsibility. Once they are completed, stakeholders should submit their completed questionnaires to the BIA coordinator. The coordinator should review the forms for completeness.

When one is performing a BIA, a defined process should be followed that ensures consistency throughout the analysis. For example, NIST SP 800-34, *Contingency Planning Guide for Information Technology Systems*, suggests that when conducting a BIA as part of contingency planning for information technology systems, project stages should include

- Identification of critical IT resources
- Identification of disruption impacts and allowable outage times
- Development of recovery priorities

For the practitioner to support the identification of critical IT resources, it is first necessary to identify critical business functions. Once each critical business function is identified, it should then be relatively easy to identify the critical IT resources that are required to support each business function. Critical IT resources include IT systems and the applications residing on those systems, as well as supporting network connectivity and security devices and applications.

Once critical business functions and related information technology resources have been identified, the next step is to determine the potential impacts that could result if the functions or supporting resources were unavailable because of a business disruption. When you are identifying disruption impacts, it is important to identify the potential range of impacts that could result from a disruption.

Business disruption impacts may have tangible or intangible results to the organization. Tangible results from a business disruption are those results that can be measured and that can have a direct cost to the organization assigned. Examples of tangible results include increased processing time, loss of revenue, decreased employee productivity, and potential financial losses resulting from a failure to meet established service level agreements. Intangible results are those results that, although not easily measured, have a negative impact on the organization. Examples of intangible impact results include loss of customer confidence, effects on employee morale, and negative public relations.

Only by carefully evaluating the potential range of tangible and intangible results can allowable outage times be accurately established. *Allowable outage time* indicates the amount of time that an IT system can be unavailable before there is a significant or critical impact to business functions that rely on the system. When conducting a BIA, establish an allowable outage time for each IT system.

Allowable outage times are directly related to the MTD of critical business functions. As business functions rely on IT systems, IT practitioners must ensure that outage times do not exceed MTD thresholds. In most cases, allowable outage times should be established that are well below the MTD of related business functions. This helps ensure that systems can be recovered and related business functions can be resumed before approaching the MTD threshold. This also helps to create a time buffer, which may be necessary if unforeseen circumstances that delay recovery efforts arise.

The establishment of allowable outage times for all information systems and related resources is required to prioritize the recovery of these systems. Assigning recovery priorities to systems allows an organization to determine the order that systems should be restored or recovered after a business disruption event. By setting recovery priority levels for systems, organizations can ensure that information systems supporting critical business functions are restored before systems that support less critical functions.

Establishing recovery priorities, recovery time objectives, and recovery point objectives allows an organization to evaluate alternative recovery strategies and select an appropriate recovery strategy. When an organization is selecting a recovery strategy, it is imperative to select one that meets organizational requirements.

✔ Try It for Yourself: Business Continuity Exercise

Business continuity is a standard strategy and operations element of any successful organization. Part of business continuity involves understanding critical business functions and prioritizing them for restoration and protection. This exercise guides you through a business impact assessment.

CONTINUES

CONTINUED

Gathering Information and Determining Value

Using the following table, consider an organization you may be familiar with. Determine the data most critical to the functioning of the organization and the organization's goals. List the type of information in the following table and indicate who normally has access to the data and the systems responsible for the information.

PRIORITY	TYPE OF INFO	WHO HAS ACCESS?	ON WHICH SYSTEM?
1			
2			
3			
4			
5			

Next, for each data type listed, determine the value of the data to the organization by filling in the following information about the data.

COSTS	IF DATA IS MODIFIED	IF DATA IS RELEASED	DATA IS MISSING
Cost of Revelation			
Cost to Verify Information			
Cost of Lost Availability			
Cost of Lost Work			
Legal Costs			
Loss of Confidence Costs			
Cost to Repair Problem			
Fines and Penalties			
Other Costs			

Next, consider the overall cost and priority of the data and determine which data or services are most critical for the organization. These services and data should be prioritized above the rest.

Recovery Point Objective and Recovery Time Objective

For each data point identified, the Recovery Point Objective (RPO) and Recovery Time Objective (RTO) must be established. The RPO represents how much of the data could be lost without impact. RTO is the amount of time a system or data could be unavailable before it affects the organization. For each data type, determine the RPO and RTO in the following table.

DATA OR SERVICE	RECOVER POINT OBJECTIVES	RECOVERY TIME OBJECTIVES

Mapping Systems to Criticality and Recovery Objectives

For each system identified in the first table, determine which data elements are present, the impact the data or services have on the organization, and the desired recovery objectives. Remember the system must support the lowest recovery point objective and the lowest recovery time objective.

SYSTEM	DATA TYPE OR SERVICES	RECOVERY POINT OBJECTIVES	RECOVERY TIME OBJECTIVES

CONTINUES

> ### Final Analysis
>
> Consider the business continuity requirements for each system. Is the system capable of meeting the stated objectives through contingency controls? If not, what resources or changes to the system will be required to meet the recovery objectives? If the system cannot meet the requirements, is there another system or cloud provider that could? Deficiencies identified through the BIA should be entered into the organization's risk register or plan of actions and milestones for follow-up actions. Residual risk identified should be conveyed to appropriate stakeholders for action.

Disaster Recovery Planning

While business continuity planning focuses on providing continuity of critical business operations, disaster recovery planning focuses on the restoration of IT functions after a business disruption event. A DRP is a document that details the steps that should be performed to restore critical IT systems in the event of a disaster. As an SSCP, the security practitioner will be expected to be a participant in disaster recovery planning efforts. The security practitioner will also be a valuable participant in the disaster recovery process in the event that a disaster occurs and the plan is activated.

Due to the heavy reliance on information technology, it is critical that a well-defined DRP exists to allow the organization to continue or resume operations in acceptable periods and with minimal impact. As mentioned previously, critical IT systems will be identified during the BIA. The information technology group must ensure that a DRP is developed, which allows for the restoration of these systems to defined recovery point objectives and within established recovery time objectives.

Disaster Recovery Considerations

When one is creating a DRP, it is important to identify different types of disasters that could threaten the organization and then try to assess the likelihood of each event occurring. Many different types of disasters could affect the organization, including natural disasters such as hurricanes, floods, earthquakes, and tornadoes; health- and wellness-related disasters such as the avian flu and swine flu; intentional acts of sabotage such as arson and hacking; as well as an untold number of potential threats that could result from geographic, industrial, political, and personnel factors that apply to the security practitioner's organization. By identifying potential threats and assessing the likelihood of their occurrence, the security practitioner can implement business continuity and recovery solutions that reduce organizational risk to acceptable levels.

Because of the variety of threats an organization faces and the resulting losses that may occur, DRPs need to account for the potential loss of a variety of assets. These assets include

- Data
- Information systems
- Network devices
- Telecommunications equipment
- Facilities
- Personnel
- Cloud providers
- Other assets unique to the security practitioner's organization

Recovery strategies and contingency plans for these assets, including data backup strategies and alternative processing facilities, must be considered. Regardless of the strategy that is selected, the strategy should be documented within the DRP.

Although it is important to document data recovery and alternate facility strategies, it is equally important to ensure the organization can recover from the loss of key IT personnel. Personnel may have unique skills or knowledge that is not widely available within the organization. To mitigate the risk associated with the loss of key personnel, backup personnel should be assigned within the DRP. Cross-training should be performed to ensure that backup personnel are prepared to complete their responsibilities should they be called upon.

DRPs can either directly include or reference additional policies, procedures, and other related documents. When an organization references these documents within the DRP, they can be located quickly in the event of a disaster. Personnel will be able to easily determine actions that should be performed and can avoid wasting critical time that could be used to perform recovery activities. Referencing related documents is especially important if key personnel are unavailable and recovery tasks must be performed by backup personnel or third parties.

Procedures are documents that list a series of steps that should be taken to perform a task. For example, a backup restoration procedure may be included in the DRP that indicates the steps that must be taken to restore a specific system from backup. It is critical that procedures for the backup and restoration of IT systems are well documented, reviewed on a periodic basis, and updated as needed based on technological or procedural changes.

Examples of other documents that may be included or referenced within the DRP include documents such as network topology maps, third-party contracts, and vendor contact lists. Although stated previously, the importance of including or referencing relevant information cannot be stressed enough as it is imperative that time is not wasted performing unnecessary tasks or searching for documentation when a disaster strikes.

Recovery Strategy Alternatives

Many recovery strategy alternatives exist, which vary in cost and complexity. These alternatives support different recovery time objectives and allow organizations to restore data to various recovery point objectives. The SSCP should have knowledge of these recovery alternatives and be able to assist in selecting an appropriate alternative based on organizational requirements. Remember when selecting a recovery strategy that the cost of the recovery strategy should never exceed the loss that an organization would incur if a business disruption occurred. Recovery alternatives include

- Cold site
- Warm site
- Hot site
- Multiple processing sites
- Mobile sites

Cold Site

A cold site is a facility that could be utilized as an alternative processing site for recovering IT operations. The cold site is generally preconfigured with necessary infrastructure components such as electrical, water, and communications access. The cold site does not contain any provisional equipment such as computer hardware, telecommunications, and network devices. The site is merely available such that equipment could be acquired and installed at the location in the event of disaster.

The cold site recovery alternative has a longer recovery time than any other recovery alternative. This is because the cold site requires that equipment is provisioned, installed, and configured at the cold site after the disaster has occurred. Once equipment and communications have been installed and configured, data must be restored from backup. Testing must then be performed to validate that systems and equipment operate as expected.

As no inventory of hardware or communications equipment is maintained at the cold site, the cold site alternative is far less costly than that of either the warm or hot site. The cold site should be considered when recovery time objectives do not require the immediate availability of information systems and related data housed on those systems. Cold site recovery normally requires days or weeks of recovery time to restore business operations.

The cold site alternative is not an appropriate recovery strategy when immediate recovery is required.

Warm Site

A warm site recovery alternative is similar to the cold site alternative; however, at a warm site, computer hardware and related communications and networking equipment is available. Generally, at a warm site, equipment has been installed and configured, but systems do not have current data. Restoration of data from backup is required before the warm site can function as a processing alterative. Depending on the recovery strategy selected, data backups may be stored at the warm site or may need to be recalled from an offsite data storage provider.

The warm site is a more expensive alternative than the cold site as equipment must be installed and configured at the warm site to ensure its availability during a disaster. As equipment has already been provisioned, installed, and configured, the warm site supports faster recovery of operations than the cold site alternative.

Hot Site

The hot site alternative provides a redundant processing environment that closely matches the production environment. The hot site contains all of the hardware and related communications and networking equipment required to provide continuity of operations. Data is maintained at the hot site, which is either a mirror of data at the production environment or a very close replica to that which is maintained at the production site. Technical solutions are utilized to provide real-time mirroring or synchronization of data between the production environment and the test environment. As a result, business operations can be transitioned from the production site to the hot site while minimizing downtime.

The hot site recovery alternative provides a shorter recovery time window than the warm site recovery strategy alternative. Although the hot site provides a shorter recovery time window, it is more expensive than the warm site recovery alternative. This results from the duplication of equipment and the real-time mirroring of data from the production environment to the hot site.

Multiple Processing Sites

A multiple processing site supports 100% availability because data are processed simultaneously at the alternate site. The alternate site is a redundant configuration of the primary facility and is fully operational at all times. Data are constantly synchronized between the primary facility and the multiple processing facility using data mirroring or synchronization technologies. This type of site is always staffed by organizational personnel and is always under organizational control. The multiple processing site provides the shortest recovery time alternative.

Because multiple processing sites permanently house organizational personnel, determining the costs allocation associated with this alternative may become complicated. These complications may arise if the personnel and equipment are used to perform support functions for the organization in addition to their business continuity responsibilities. It then becomes more complex to determine costs associated with business continuity when compared to costs associated with functions performed by personnel as part of normal day-to-day business operations.

Mobile Sites

Mobile recovery sites vary from traditional recovery alternatives in that a mobile recovery site can be deployed to any location based on the circumstances of the disaster. Traditional recovery alternatives exist in brick-and-mortar facilities and require that personnel are deployed from the disaster site to the alternate location. A mobile recovery site is a self-contained data processing facility. The mobile facility may be transported to an appropriate location by truck after a disaster situation. Due to the limited size of the mobile facility, this recovery alternative is most appropriate for recovery of individual departments within an organization.

For the mobile site alternative to be effective, the mobile site must be configured with necessary equipment and supplies. Mobile site alternatives are generally provided by a third party that specializes in this service. Therefore, it is important when considering this alternative to validate that any contract established between the security practitioner's organization and a mobile site provider includes a service level agreement that ensures that the mobile site will be available when needed.

Plan Testing

Once BCPs and DRPs have been developed, they must be tested to validate that they are accurate. They must also be tested to ensure that critical business functions can be recovered within defined recovery time objectives to established recovery point objectives. Several types of tests exist, which vary in complexity and thoroughness. Each test type will be detailed, and a comparison of each type will be provided. Test types include

- Checklist test
- Structured walkthrough test
- Simulation test
- Parallel test
- Full interruption test

Checklist Test

A checklist test should be routinely performed by the business continuity coordinator and appropriate business unit personnel. In a checklist test, each participant reviews his or her section of the plan to validate that it still contains accurate information. Specifically, participants review the plan to ensure that the contact information for each participant in their area of responsibility is still correct and that the criticality levels assigned to various business functions described within the plan are still appropriate. Participants also validate that new business functions are accounted for within the plan and that business functions that no longer exist are removed from the plan.

Structured Walkthrough Test

In a structured walkthrough test, representatives from each business unit gather together to review the BCP. Each team presents their section of the BCP to the group. The participants validate that the plan is correct and that the responsibilities of each participant are understood. Additionally, the scope of the plan and plan assumptions are reviewed to ensure that they are still correct.

The walkthrough should be conducted before more in-depth testing is performed. When an organization performs the walkthrough first, plan deficiencies can be identified and corrected early in the testing process. It is not uncommon for multiple walkthroughs to be performed before advancing to more thorough testing techniques. This is especially true with the initial development of BCPs as multiple iterations of design, documentation, and testing are common with new BCPs.

Simulation Test

Simulation testing is a more in-depth testing technique than either checklist or structured walkthrough testing. In a simulation test, an actual disaster situation is simulated. The disaster is simulated so that business operations are not actually interrupted. Participants' responses to the simulated disaster are measured to evaluate the accuracy of response actions as well as response times.

While previous test techniques, including checklist testing and structured walkthrough testing, are paper-based tests, the simulation test is the first testing technique that may involve testing actual recovery techniques such as file restoration from backup or failover from primary to secondary systems. As simulation testing is an advanced testing technique compared to previously discussed test types, it is important that simulation testing is not performed until the results of checklist and walkthrough tests have been validated and resulting modifications have been incorporated into the plan.

Simulation testing involves more personnel than the checklist or walkthrough testing techniques and may be the first exposure that new personnel have to the BCP. As a result, it is likely that new issues will be encountered when executing simulation testing. These issues and any resulting plan modifications should be documented and reviewed at the conclusion of testing. Although issues may be encountered, testing should continue until the simulation has been completed. Simulation testing should only be ended prematurely if it becomes impossible to continue.

Parallel Testing

Parallel testing involves performing processing at an alternate site. Parallel testing is an operational test and generally does not include representatives from departments that do not have direct involvement in operations such as human resources, public relations, or marketing. Although processing is performed at an alternate site, processing at production facilities is not interrupted or otherwise disrupted.

Because parallel testing is performed at an alternate site, this type of testing generally involves a significant cost to the organization. Due to the cost involved, senior management approval must be obtained before considering this testing approach. It is critical that parallel testing scenarios and desired outcomes are clearly defined and communicated to all participants.

During parallel testing, historical transactions are processed against data backups that have been restored at the alternate site. Transaction results are compared against results from the production facility to validate accuracy. Results may be compared by running typical business reports and validating that report output is consistent between data at the production facility and data restored at the alternate site.

External auditors or designated observers are often present during parallel test execution. This allows an independent party to observe parallel test execution, document observations, and generate a report of test results. The report can then be used by the BCP team to create a gap analysis, identify plan deficiencies, and implement plan corrections and improvements.

Full Interruption Testing

Full interruption testing is performed when business operations are actually interrupted at the primary processing facility. Processing is performed at the alternate site, and processing is ceased at the primary facility for the duration of the test. This type of testing is highly disruptive and may result in an actual disaster if processing cannot be returned to the original status after testing.

Therefore, it is critical that this type of testing is performed only after all previous testing techniques have been executed successfully. Senior management must be fully informed of the risks of full interruption testing. Executive approval must be obtained before executing this testing. Executives should be provided with real-time updates throughout full interruption testing and must be immediately notified of test results and issues arising from the testing process.

During the BCP testing process, the SSCP will be expected to fulfill a number of important roles, including providing technical support during the process as well as ensuring that appropriate security controls are enabled. SSCP participation is particularly important when performing simulation, parallel, and full interruption testing because these tests involve the actual restoration of processing at an alternate site.

Although the SSCP understands the importance of implementing security controls at the alternate processing site, the organization's primary focus is restoring business operations within defined recovery time objectives. When possible, the SSCP should validate that security controls are in place and operational, which provide an equivalent level of security as that which exists at the primary processing facility.

Though security controls should be implemented, the controls implemented at the alternate site may not mirror those that exist in the primary processing facility due to financial resource constraints. When an equivalent level is not possible due to resource constraints, the SSCP should assist in defining and implementing additional manual controls. Additional controls could include increased monitoring and logging so that unusual activities can be identified and investigated.

Plan Review and Maintenance

Both BCPs and DRPs should be reviewed on an annual basis, at a minimum, or after significant changes to business operations or information technology infrastructure. This review is important to ensure that the plan is continually up to date and that it can be relied upon if disaster strikes. Just like initial plan development, plan review should involve participants from all business units.

When making modifications to the BCP, the business continuity team should track and approve all modifications. A summary of changes made to the BCP should be provided to all participants. This ensures that all participants are aware of changes to the plan and prepared to fulfill their responsibilities.

The BCP should contain a section that documents important version control data. Data tracked within the version control section should include the current BCP version number, a summary of changes made to the BCP, the review date, and the approver or approvers. Tracking BCP version information allows BCP participants to verify they have the most recent version of the plan, which is vital to successful execution of the plan. A periodic review of the BCP is also a requirement of many compliance regulations. When an organization tracks the review and approval dates within the BCP, evidence of periodic review can easily be provided to internal and external auditors.

Data Backup and Restoration

Many approaches exist to perform both data backup and restoration. Backup solutions vary in cost and complexity and allow data recovery within a wide array of time frames. An SSCP should be familiar with various alternatives for data backup and restoration and be able to recommend appropriate solutions based on recovery time objectives and recovery point objectives. In some cases, the SSCP will also be expected to utilize data backup and restoration procedures to restore data in the event of disaster. In other cases, data backup and restoration functions may be performed by a server or database administration team.

When evaluating backup solutions, remember that the security practitioner must first evaluate what needs to be backed up. Solutions may vary depending on whether operating systems, file data, databases, applications, or utilities are to be backed up and subsequently restored. The security practitioner should take time to familiarize himself or herself with available alternatives. Selecting the appropriate data backup solution is a critical component of implementing successful business continuity and DRPs. Only by understanding available alternatives can the security practitioner ensure the most appropriate choices are being made.

Several backup alternatives exist when selecting the frequency and amount of data to back up. These backup alternatives include *full backups, incremental backups*, and *differential backups*. Data are normally backed up to tape but can be backed up to other media, including CD, DVD, and disk. An explanation of each backup type is presented here:

Full Backup   When a full backup is performed, the entire system is copied to backup media. This is the slowest type of backup to perform as more data is copied to backup media when compared to incremental or differential backups. Due to this fact, full system backups are generally performed on an infrequent basis, normally weekly.

Differential Backup   Differential backups record differences in data since the most recent full backup. For example, if a full backup was performed on the weekend, a differential backup may be performed each day of the week. The differential backup records all differences between the current system configuration and the system configuration taken at the time of full data backup.

Incremental Backup   Incremental backups record changes that are made to the system on a daily basis. Each day when the incremental backup is performed, changes from the previous day are recorded on the incremental backup. Incremental backups generally complete faster than any other type of backup as only daily changes are recorded by the backup process.

When we are evaluating backup alternatives, it is important to note that although it is faster to perform incremental backups when compared to performing differential backups, there is an offsetting cost when restoring from backup. When restoring a differential backup, the full backup is restored initially and then only the most recent differential backup is restored. When restoring incremental backups, each incremental backup taken after the most recent full backup must be restored before the system restoration process can be completed. This is because differential backups store all changes since the most recent full backup, whereas incremental backups only record daily changes. Table 4.2 compares the strengths of each backup type.

TABLE 4.2 **Backup Types**

BACKUP TYPES	DATA BACKED UP	TIME TO COMPLETE
Full Backup	All data are copied to backup media.	The full system backup takes the longest time to complete.
Differential Backup	All data that are different between the current system configuration and the system configuration at the time of the last full backup.	The differential backup takes less time than the full system backup but more time than an incremental backup.
Incremental Backup	Each incremental backup records changes in data from the previous incremental backup.	The incremental backup is the fastest backup type to perform when compared to full and differential backups.

Offsite Storage

When at all possible, backup tapes should be stored offsite at a secure location. By storing backups offsite, we can ensure that they are available for restoration at an alternate location should the primary facility become unavailable. If backups are stored at the primary facility and a disaster strikes, the backup will likely also be damaged by the same event and thus will be useless for disaster recovery purposes.

Strong consideration should be given to using a secure, bonded courier service for transporting backup media to an offsite storage vendor. By using a bonded courier and a secure storage service, organizations can guarantee that data are stored at an offsite location that provides equivalent security controls to their own.

Any time that data are stored offsite, strong controls should be in place related to access to backup media. Access to backup media should be restricted to authorized personnel. Transfer of backup media to a third party should be tracked via an inventory control system that records barcodes of tapes entering and exiting the facility. Data back-ups should be encrypted to prevent access to data by unauthorized parties in the event that backup media is lost, misplaced, or stolen.

It is important to note that when data backups are encrypted and stored offsite, encryption key management procedures must be implemented to ensure that data can be accessed and restored should access to the original keys become unavailable. The keys should not be stored directly with the data backups, but rather they should be stored separately in a secure manner. Access to encryption keys should be restricted to appropriate personnel. As key rotation occurs, it is important to ensure that offsite keys are updated to match those in use in the production environment. In addition to performing backups locally and then transferring them offsite, data backup can be performed directly to an offsite location. Backups to an offsite location can either be performed directly to another site that is owned by the security practitioner's organization, or they can be performed to a vendor location. When an organization performs backups directly to an offsite location, data loss can be reduced in the event that there is a disaster that renders the primary facility unavailable. Electronic vaulting and remote journaling are methods for performing data backup to an offsite location.

Electronic Vaulting

Electronic vaulting is another method of performing data backup. This method allows data backup across a WAN connection or the Internet to an offsite location. With many electronic vaulting solutions, an appliance sits at the source location, which collects data backups from individual systems and then transmits them to the vendor location. The backup is encrypted in transit to preserve confidentiality and eliminate the risk of data being intercepted in transit. Data backups may be restored directly from the electronic vault to the source system should data be lost because of human or technical error.

Remote Journaling

Remote journaling is a similar concept to electronic vaulting. In remote journaling, journals and database transaction logs are transmitted electronically to an offsite location. Transaction logs can then be applied against a copy of the database at the offsite location. In the event of a processing interruption at the primary site, the offsite copy can be restored quickly from the offsite location to the primary site.

System and Data Availability

Although a number of different methods for backing up and restoring critical systems have been discussed, methods for preventing system downtime have yet to be covered. In addition to the numerous methods for recovering data, there are also numerous methods available to enhance system and data redundancy and resiliency. Redundant configurations can be established for both individual system components as well as complete systems. Examples of redundant system components include redundant hard drives, power supplies, and network interfaces. Redundant system configuration options include standby servers and clusters.

Clustering

Clustering refers to a method of configuring multiple computers so that they effectively operate as a single system. Clustering can be performed for several reasons, including high availability, load balancing, increasing computational performance, and grid computing. For purposes of our discussion, we will focus on high availability clusters and load-balancing clusters, which are the clustering methods that provide redundancy to the information technology environment.

High Availability Clustering

High availability clustering is a clustering method that uses multiple systems to reduce the risk associated with a single point of failure. In a high availability cluster, systems may be configured in an active/passive configuration. In this configuration, a primary system is considered the active system, and a secondary system with an identical configuration operates as a passive server. The passive system does not process any transactions, but rather it stands by in case it must take over processing for the primary system.

Failure monitoring is implemented through a heartbeat, which is a communications link between the active and passive server. The secondary server is configured to monitor the "health" of the active server via the heartbeat. In the event that the secondary server detects an issue with the primary server, automatic failover occurs. When failover occurs, the secondary system begins performing all processing activities in place of the primary server.

Automatic failover provides service redundancy and allows system administrators to investigate and correct issues with the primary server. After the issues have been corrected, the primary system can be reactivated. Once the primary system has been reactivated, the secondary system returns to its passive state and continues to monitor the heartbeat for additional issues.

IT systems that provide support for critical business functions are prime candidates for high availability clustering if clustering is supported by the operating system and application. When evaluating high availability clustering, the security practitioner should determine the overall cost of implementing high availability and then compare the cost to the cost associated with system downtime. Performing this comparison will allow the security practitioner to determine if the costs associated with implementing high availability can be justified.

Load-Balancing Clustering

In addition to the active/passive high availability configuration, an active/active configuration is also available. This configuration is referred to as a load-balancing configuration. In a load-balancing cluster, all cluster nodes are active. Load balancing provides redundancy because multiple systems are simultaneously active. If a single system fails, the remaining systems continue to provide the service.

Load balancing can be implemented through a number of algorithms that determine how to allocate processing and network traffic. The *round-robin* algorithm allocates service requests by distributing them to each server based on a rotation regardless of processing load. For example, in a three-server configuration, the first request would be processed by the first server, the second request by the second server, the third request by the third server, and the fourth request would be directed back to the first server.

Other load-balancing algorithms exist that allocate service requests based on server load, geographic location, ping response times, and a number of other factors. Although a description of these algorithms is outside the scope of this text, the SSCP should be aware that implementing load balancing is an effective method for improving system redundancy that should be evaluated when designing a redundancy and recovery strategy.

Redundant Array of Independent Disks

A method that may be used to provide data redundancy is via a RAID (*Redundant Array of Independent Disks*) implementation. In a RAID implementation, data are written across a series of disks. RAID can be implemented via either software or hardware. Although multiple disks are used in the RAID array, they are seen as a single disk by the operating system and by the end user. Also, RAID provides disk redundancy; it does not provide for redundancy of other system components.

RAID is based on three different data redundancy techniques that can be applied in multiple combinations to achieve varying results. Different RAID levels exist, which are used to describe each combination. The data redundancy techniques employed by RAID include parity, striping, and mirroring. The following excerpt from NIST Special Publication 800-34, "Contingency Planning Guide for Information Technology Systems," provides a thorough explanation of the concepts of parity, striping, and mirroring:[11]

- **Mirroring**—With this technique, the system writes data simultaneously to separate hard drives or drive arrays. The advantages of mirroring are minimal downtime, simple data recovery, and increased performance reading from disk. If one hard drive or disk array fails, the system can operate from the working hard drive or disk array, or the system can use one disk to process a read request and another disk for a different processing request. The disadvantage of mirroring is that both drives or disk arrays are processing in the writing-to-disks function, which can hinder system performance. Mirroring has a high fault tolerance and can be implemented through a hardware RAID controller or through the operating system.

- **Parity**—Parity refers to a technique of determining whether data had been lost or overwritten. Parity has a lower fault tolerance than mirroring. The advantage of parity is that data can be protected without having to store a copy of the data, as is required with mirroring.

- **Striping**—Striping improves the performance of the hardware array controller by distributing data across all drives. In striping, a data element is broken into multiple pieces, and a piece is distributed to each hard drive. Data transfer performance is increased using striping because the drives may access each data piece simultaneously. Striping can be implemented in bytes or blocks. Byte-level striping breaks the data into bytes and stores the bytes sequentially across the hard drives. Block-level striping breaks the data into a given-size block, and each block is distributed to a disk.

RAID uses a numeric-level system to represent different data redundancy techniques. It is important to note that although some RAID levels provide data redundancy, not all do. An SSCP should be familiar with available RAID configuration choices and be able to recommend and configure an appropriate RAID configuration based on the needs of the organization. The RAID levels include

- **RAID 0**—A RAID 0 configuration, also known as a striped set, is a configuration that relies on striping data across multiple disks. In a RAID 0 configuration, data are striped across multiple disks, but no parity information is included. As a result, although performance is improved, RAID 0 provides no data redundancy. Because no redundancy is provided by a RAID 0 configuration, it is not a viable solution for disaster recovery.

- **RAID 1**—In a RAID 1 configuration, data mirroring is used. Identical copies of data are stored on two separate drives. In the event that one disk fails, an exact duplicate of the data resides on the other disk. RAID 1 is a simple solution to implement; however, 50% of total disk space is lost because all data is duplicated on both disks.

- **RAID 2**—In a RAID 2 configuration, striping is performed at the bit level. RAID 2 configuration is costly, difficult to implement, and, therefore, not used in practice.

- **RAID 3**—In a RAID 3 configuration, striping is performed at the byte level and uses a dedicated parity disk. RAID 3 is not used in practice.

- **RAID 4**—RAID 4 configurations implement striping at the block level and use a dedicated parity disk. RAID 4 is not used in practice.

- **RAID 5**—RAID 5 uses block-level striping with parity information that is distributed across multiple disks. In the event that a single disk fails, the data on the disk can be re-created based on the data stored on the remaining disks.

In addition to the RAID levels detailed here, RAID levels can be combined to gain the benefits of both levels. For example, a RAID 10 (1+0) configuration would be a configuration with mirrored disks, which are then striped. In a RAID 01 (0+1) configuration, a striped data set exists, which is then mirrored.

SUMMARY

As more attacks are launched on systems, the synthesis of incident response and handling with digital evidence management and handling will become increasingly more important. One of the artifacts of having more and better detective/investigative controls has been the increase in the volume of incidents that need to be dealt with. As incidents end up in the various court systems, care must be taken to ensure that from the very start of the incident, evidence is handled and managed properly (i.e., forensically sound practices). Digital evidence is coming under increased scrutiny, and what was allowable and admissible yesterday may not be tomorrow.

BC and DR are comprised of the processes for determining risks, adopting counter measures to mitigate those risks, and developing real, tested, and executable plans for continuing the organization if the disaster occurs. BC and DR is more than just planning; it is executing, integrating with change management, and using BC as part of routine operations. Organizations with well-defined and executed contingency programs are much more likely not only to survive during adverse events but also to outperform other organizations due to process maturity.

SAMPLE QUESTIONS

1. Creating incident response policies for an organization would be an example of:

    a. A technical control

    b. An administrative control

    c. A logical control

    d. A physical control

2. A security audit is best defined as:

    a. A covert series of tests designed to test network authentication, hosts, and perimeter security

    b. A technical assessment that measures how well an organization uses strategic security policies and tactical security controls for protecting its information assets

    c. Employing intrusion detection systems (IDSs) to monitor anomalous traffic on a network segment and logging attempted break-ins

    d. Hardening systems before deploying them on the corporate network

3. What is the primary purpose of testing an intrusion detection system?

    a. To observe that the IDS is observing and logging an appropriate response to a suspicious activity

    b. To determine if the IDS is capable of discarding suspect packets

    c. To analyze processor utilization to verify whether hardware upgrades are necessary

    d. To test whether the IDS can log every possible event on the network

4. Which of the following is true regarding computer intrusions?

    a. Covert attacks such as a distributed denial-of-service (DDoS) attack harm public opinion of an organization.

    b. Overt attacks are easier to defend against because they can be readily identified.

    c. Network intrusion detection systems (NIDSs) help mitigate computer intrusions by notifying personnel in real time.

    d. Covert attacks are less effective because they take more time to accomplish.

5. This documents the steps that should be performed to restore IT functions after a business disruption event:

   a. Critical business function

   b. Business continuity plan

   c. Disaster recovery plan

   d. Crisis communications plan

6. During which phase of incident response are the results of incident response activities documented and communicated to the appropriate parties?

   a. Post-incident activity

   b. Detection and analysis

   c. Containment, eradication, and recovery

   d. Preparation

7. What is the first type of disaster recovery testing that should be performed when initially testing a disaster recovery plan?

   a. Simulation

   b. Structured walkthrough

   c. Parallel

   d. Full interruption

8. This concept refers to the point in time to which data could be restored in the event of a business disruption:

   a. Recovery time objective (RTO)

   b. Business impact analysis (BIA)

   c. Recovery point objective (RPO)

   d. Maximum tolerable downtime (MTD)

9. Which RAID level uses block-level striping with parity information distributed across multiple disks?

   a. RAID 0

   b. RAID 1

   c. RAID 4

   d. RAID 5

10. The type of data backup that only backs up files that have been changed since the last full backup is called:

   a. Full backup

   b. Incremental backup

   c. Partial backup

   d. Differential backup

11. Selecting this type of alternate processing site would be appropriate when an organization needs a low-cost recovery strategy and does not have immediate system recovery requirements:

   a. Cold site

   b. Warm site

   c. Hot site

   d. Mobile site

12. What are the phases of the incident response process? (Choose all that apply.)

   a. Preparation

   b. Detection and analysis

   c. Assessment and recovery

   d. Authorization

13. Phases of the incident response process include:

   a. Preparation

   b. Detection and analysis

   c. Containment, eradication, and recovery

   d. Post-incident activity

14. This data backup strategy allows data backup to an offsite location via a WAN or Internet connection:

   a. Remote journaling

   b. Electronic vaulting

   c. RAID

   d. Clustering

NOTES

[1] http://nvlpubs.nist.gov/nistpubs/SpecialPublications/NIST.SP.800-61r2.pdf (page 21)

[2] http://nvlpubs.nist.gov/nistpubs/SpecialPublications/NIST.SP.800-61r2.pdf (page 10)

[3] http://nvlpubs.nist.gov/nistpubs/SpecialPublications/NIST.SP.800-61r2.pdf (page 17)

[4] http://nvlpubs.nist.gov/nistpubs/SpecialPublications/NIST.SP.800-61r2.pdf (page 22)

[5] http://nvlpubs.nist.gov/nistpubs/SpecialPublications/NIST.SP.800-61r2.pdf (page 31)

[6] Gary Palmer, "A Road Map for Digital Forensic Research." Technical Report DTR-T0010-01, DFRWS, November 2001. Report from the First Digital Forensic Research Workshop (DFRWS). http://www.dfrws.org/2001/dfrws-rm-final.pdf

[7] Australian Computer Emergency Response Team: Collecting Electronic Evidence After a System Compromise (https://www.google.com/url?sa=t&rct=j&q=&esrc=s&source=web&cd=4&cad=rja&uact=8&ved=0CCQQFjADahUKEwiulcWN-fbHAhWKOIAKHel1CpY&url=https%3A%2F%2Fwww.auscert.org.au%2Fdownload.html%3Ff%3D22&usg=AFQjCNFntZ9JvAyjPrw2IOj_cEcxfCuDyQ&bvm=bv.102537793,d.dmo)

[8] Read more about Media Analysis here: http://www.cscjournals.org/download/issuearchive/IJS/Volume3/IJS_V3_I2.pdf

[9] Simson Farfinkel, and Gene Spafford, *Web Security, Privacy & Commerce*, (O'Reilly Media, 2001) http://archive.oreilly.com/network/2002/04/26/nettap.html (accessed July 31, 2012).

[10] Read more about hardware and embedded forensics here: http://csrc.nist.gov/publications/nistpubs/800-72/sp800-72.pdf

[11] NIST Special Publication 800-34 "Contingency Planning Guide for Information Technology Systems"

Cryptography

CRYPTOGRAPHY IS ONE OF the most common and effective tools the security practitioner has to meet the security objectives of an organization. This chapter explains the key foundational concepts the security practitioner will need to understand and apply the fundamental concepts of cryptography.

TOPICS

The following topics are addressed in this chapter:

- ☐ Fundamental concepts of cryptography

  - ■ Evaluation of algorithms

  - ■ Hashing

  - ■ Salting

  - ■ Symmetric/asymmetric cryptography

  - ■ Digital signatures

  - ■ Non-repudiation

- ☐ Requirements for cryptography

- ☐ Secure protocols

- ☐ Cryptographic systems

  - ■ Fundamental key management concepts

  - ■ Public key infrastructure

  - ■ Administration and validation

  - ■ Web of Trust

  - ■ Implementation of secure protocols

OBJECTIVES

The security practitioner is expected to participate in the following areas related to cryptography:

- ■ Understand and apply fundamental concepts of cryptography
- ■ Understand requirements for cryptography
- ■ Understand and support secure protocols
- ■ Operate and implement cryptographic systems

ENCRYPTION CONCEPTS

The whole of the cryptographic universe revolves around a few key concepts and definitions. Mastering these is fundamental to gaining the understanding necessary to obtain the SSCP certification. A successful candidate must understand how cryptography plugs into the overall framework of confidentiality, integrity, and availability. Confidentiality is the most obvious use for cryptography. A message or data stream that is encrypted with even the most basic of techniques is certainly more confidential than one left alone in plaintext. Integrity is the next great area of contribution for cryptography. Hashes and cryptographic hashes are often used to verify the integrity of message as we will learn shortly.

However, if cryptography provides so many benefits, why is it that everything is not encrypted at all times? The answer is unfortunately, availability. Availability is adversely impacted by cryptography through the introduction of extra risk from the loss, distribution, or mismanagement of cryptographic keys. Data that are encrypted must at some point be unencrypted, so losing a decryption key becomes a real problem with the passage of time. In addition, key distribution (the method of getting a key from where it was generated to where it needs to be used) adds another layer of risk and complexity should a key not be transported in time for its use. On top of all of this, cryptography can add a measure of processing overhead and lag time to a data stream or message decryption that may make the data obsolete or unusable. A successful implementer and operator of cryptographic solutions must keep the balance of these three critical aspects in mind at all times to effectively exercise the strengths and minimize the weaknesses involved with this domain.

Key Concepts and Definitions

Before exploring encryption in more depth, it is important to understand the key concepts and definitions:

- *Key clustering* is when different encryption keys generate the same ciphertext from the same plaintext message.
- *Synchronous* is a term used to refer to when each encryption or decryption request is performed immediately.
- *Asynchronous* refers to when encrypt/decrypt requests are processed in queues. A key benefit of asynchronous cryptography is utilization of hardware devices and multiprocessor systems for cryptographic acceleration.
- A *hash function* is a one-way mathematical operation that reduces a message or data file into a smaller fixed length output, or hash value. By comparing the hash

value computed by the sender with the hash value computed by the receiver over the original file, unauthorized changes to the file can be detected, assuming they both used the same hash function. Ideally there should never be more than one unique hash for a given input and one hash exclusively for a given input.

■ *Digital signatures* provide authentication of a sender and integrity of a sender's message. A message is input into a hash function. Then the hash value is encrypted using the private key of the sender. The result of these two steps yields a digital signature. The receiver can verify the digital signature by decrypting the hash value using the signer's public key, then perform the same hash computation over the message, and then compare the hash values for an exact match. If the hash values are the same, then the signature is valid.

■ *Asymmetric* is a term used in cryptography in which two different but mathematically related keys are used where one key is used to encrypt and another is used to decrypt. This term is most commonly used in reference to *public key infrastructure* (PKI).

■ A *digital certificate* is an electronic document that contains the name of an organization or individual, the business address, the digital signature of the certificate authority issuing the certificate, the certificate holder's public key, a serial number, and the expiration date. The certificate is used to identify the certificate holder when conducting electronic transactions.

■ *Certificate authority* (CA) is an entity trusted by one or more users as an authority in a network that issues, revokes, and manages digital certificates.

■ *Registration authority* (RA) performs certificate registration services on behalf of a CA. The RA, a single-purpose server, is responsible for the accuracy of the information contained in a certificate request. The RA is also expected to perform user validation before issuing a certificate request.

■ *Plaintext* or *cleartext* is the message in its natural format. Plaintext is readable to anyone and is extremely vulnerable from a confidentiality perspective.

■ *Ciphertext* or *cryptogram* is the altered form of a plaintext message, so as to be unreadable for anyone except the intended recipients. An attacker seeing ciphertext would be unable to easily read the message or to determine its content.

■ The *cryptosystem* represents the entire cryptographic operation. This includes the algorithm, the key, and key management functions.

■ *Encryption* is the process of converting the message from its plaintext to ciphertext. It is also referred to as enciphering. The two terms are used interchangeably in the literature and have similar meanings.

- *Decryption* is the reverse process from encryption. It is the process of converting a ciphertext message into plaintext through the use of the cryptographic algorithm and key that was used to do the original encryption. This term is also used interchangeably with the term *decipher*.

- The *key* or *cryptovariable* is the input that controls the operation of the cryptographic algorithm. It determines the behavior of the algorithm and permits the reliable encryption and decryption of the message. There are both secret and public keys used in cryptographic algorithms.

- *Nonrepudiation* is a security service by which evidence is maintained so that the sender and the recipient of data cannot deny having participated in the communication. Individually, it is referred to as the "nonrepudiation of origin" and "nonrepudiation of receipt."

- An *algorithm* is a mathematical function that is used in the encryption and decryption processes. It may be quite simple or extremely complex.

- *Cryptanalysis* is the study of techniques for attempting to defeat cryptographic techniques and, more generally, information security services.

- *Cryptology* is the science that deals with hidden, disguised, or encrypted communications. It embraces communications security and communications intelligence.

- *Collision* occurs when a hash function generates the same output for different inputs.

- *Key space* represents the total number of possible values of keys in a cryptographic algorithm or other security measure, such as a password. For example, a 20-bit key would have a key space of 1,048,576.

- *Work factor* represents the time and effort required to break a protective measure.

- An *initialization vector (IV)* is a non-secret binary vector used as the initializing input algorithm for the encryption of a plaintext block sequence to increase security by introducing additional cryptographic variance and to synchronize cryptographic equipment.

- *Encoding* is the action of changing a message into another format through the use of a code. This is often done by taking a plaintext message and converting it into a format that can be transmitted via radio or some other medium and is usually used for message integrity instead of secrecy. An example would be to convert a message to Morse code.

- *Decoding* is the reverse process from encoding—converting the encoded message back into its plaintext format.

- *Transposition* or *permutation* is the process of reordering the plaintext to hide the message.

- *Substitution* is the process of exchanging one letter or byte for another.

- The *SP-network* is the process described by Claude Shannon used in most block ciphers to increase their strength. SP stands for *substitution and permutation* (transposition), and most block ciphers do a series of repeated substitutions and permutations to add confusion and diffusion to the encryption process. An SP-network uses a series of S-boxes to handle the substitutions of the blocks of data. Breaking a plaintext block into a subset of smaller S-boxes makes it easier to handle the computations.

- *Confusion* is provided by mixing (changing) the key values used during the repeated rounds of encryption. When the key is modified for each round, it provides added complexity that the attacker would encounter.

- *Diffusion* is provided by mixing up the location of the plaintext throughout the ciphertext. Through transposition, the location of the first character of the plaintext may change several times during the encryption process, and this makes the cryptanalysis process much more difficult.

- The *avalanche effect* is an important consideration in all cryptography used to design algorithms where a minor change in either the key or the plaintext will have a significant change in the resulting ciphertext. This is also a feature of a strong-hashing algorithm.

Foundational Concepts

The information security practitioner must also be familiar with the fundamental concepts and methods related to cryptography. Methods and concepts range from different ways of using cryptographic technologies to encrypt information to different standard encryption systems used in industry.

High Work Factor

The average amount of effort or work required to break an encryption system, that is to say, decrypt a message without having the entire encryption key or to find a secret key given all or part of a ciphertext, is referred to as the *work factor* of the cryptographic system. This is measured in some units such as hours of computing time on one or more given computer systems or a cost in dollars of breaking the encryption.

If the work factor is sufficiently high, the encryption system is considered to be practically or economically unbreakable and is sometimes referred to as "economically infeasible" to break. Communication systems using encryption schemes that are economically infeasible to break are generally considered secure.

The work factor required to break a given cryptographic system can vary over time due to advancements in technology, such as improvements in the speed and capacity of computers. For example, while a 40-bit secret key encryption scheme can currently be broken by a fast personal computer in less than a year or by a room full of personal computers in a short amount of time, future advances in computer technology will likely substantially reduce this work factor.

Stream-Based Ciphers

There are two primary methods of encrypting data: the stream and block methods. When a cryptosystem performs its encryption on a bit-by-bit basis, it is called a stream-based cipher. This is the method most commonly associated with streaming applications, such as voice or video transmission. Wireless Equivalent Privacy, or WEP, uses a streaming cipher, RC4, but is not considered secure due to number of weaknesses that expose the encryption key to an attacker and weak key size, among other well-known vulnerabilities in WEP implementation. Newer wireless cryptography implements block ciphers such as Advanced Encryption Standard (AES), which provide stronger security. The cryptographic operation for a stream-based cipher is to mix the plaintext with a keystream that is generated by the cryptosystem. The mixing operation is usually an exclusive-or (XOR) operation—a very fast mathematical operation.

As seen in Table 5.1, the plaintext is XORed with a seemingly random keystream to generate ciphertext. It is seemingly random because the generation of the keystream is usually controlled by the key. If the key could not produce the same keystream for the purposes of decryption of the ciphertext, then it would be impossible to ever decrypt the message.

TABLE 5.1 **Plaintext being xored to generate ciphertext**

PLAINTEXT	ENCRYPTION KEYSTREAM	CIPHERTEXT
A	XOR randomly generated keystream	$
0101 0001	0111 0011	0010 0010

The exclusive-or process is a key part of many cryptographic algorithms. It is a simple binary operation that adds two values together. If the two values are the same, $0 + 0$ or $1 + 1$, then the output is always a 0; however, if the two values are different, $1 + 0$ or $0 + 1$, then the output is a 1.

From the previous example, the following operation is the result:

Input plaintext + keystream = output of XOR

or

$$0101\ 0001 + 0111\ 0011 = 0010\ 0010$$

A stream-based cipher relies primarily on substitution—the substitution of one character or bit for another in a manner governed by the cryptosystem and controlled by the cipher key. For a stream-based cipher to operate securely, it is necessary to follow certain rules for the operation and implementation of the cipher:

1. The keystream should not be linearly related to the cryptovariable. Knowledge of the keystream output value does not disclose the cryptovariable (encryption/decryption key).

2. It should be statistically unpredictable. Given n successive bits from the keystream, it is not possible to predict the $n + 1$st bit with a probability different from 1/2.

3. It should be statistically unbiased. There should be as many 0s as 1s, as many 00s as 01s, 10s, 11s, etc.

4. There should be long periods without repetition.

5. It should have functional complexity. Each keystream bit should depend on most or all of the cryptovariable bits.

The keystream must be strong enough to not be easily guessed or predictable. In time, the keystream will repeat, and that period (or length of the repeating segment of the keystream) must be long enough to be difficult to calculate. If a keystream is too short, then it is susceptible to frequency analysis or other language-specific attacks.

The implementation of the stream-based cipher is probably the most important factor in the strength of the cipher—this applies to nearly every crypto product and, in fact, to security overall. Some important factors in the implementation are to ensure that the key management processes are secure and cannot be readily compromised or intercepted by an attacker.

Block Ciphers

A block cipher operates on blocks or chunks of text. As plaintext is fed into the cryptosystem, it is divided into blocks of a preset size—often a multiple of the ASCII character size—64, 128, 192 bits, etc. Most block ciphers use a combination of substitution and transposition to perform their operations. This makes a block cipher relatively stronger than most stream-based ciphers, but more computationally intensive and usually more expensive to implement. This is also why many stream-based ciphers are implemented in hardware, whereas a block-based cipher is implemented in software.

Initialization Vectors (IVs)

Because messages may be of any length and because encrypting the same plaintext using the same key always produces the same ciphertext as described next, several "modes of operation" have been invented, which allow block ciphers to provide confidentiality for messages of arbitrary length. (See Table 5.2 for block cipher mode descriptions.) The use of various modes answers the need for unpredictability into the keystream such that even if the same key is used to encrypt the same message, the ciphertext will still be different each time.

TABLE 5.2 Basic block cipher modes

MODE	HOW IT WORKS	USAGE
Electronic Code Book (ECB)	In ECB mode, each block is encrypted independently, allowing randomly accessed files to be encrypted and still accessed without having to process the file in a linear encryption fashion.	Any file with non-repeating blocks (less than 64 bits in length), such as transmission of a DES key or short executables.
Cipher Block Chaining (CBC)	In CBC mode, the result of encrypting one block of data is fed back into the process to encrypt the next block of data.	Data at rest, such as stand-alone encrypted files on users' hard drives.
Cipher Feedback (CFB)	In CFB mode, the cipher is used as a keystream generator rather than for confidentiality. Each block of keystream comes from encrypting the previous block of ciphertext.	Retired due to the delay imposed by encrypting each block of keystream before proceeding.
Output Feedback (OFB)	In OFB mode, the keystream is generated independently of the message	Retired due to Avalanche problems. Was used in Pay-Per-View applications.
Counter (CTR)	Uses the formula Encrypt (Base+N) as a keystream generator where Base is a starting 64 bit number and N is a simple incrementing function.	Used where high speed or random access encryption is needed. Examples are WPA2 and the Content Scrambling System.

Source: Tiller, J.S., "Message authentication," Information Security Management Handbook, 5th ed., Tipton, H.F. and Krause, M., Eds., Auerbach Publications, New York, 2004. With permission.

To illustrate why an initialization vector (IV) is needed when using block ciphers, consider how they are used in various modes of operation using block ciphers. The simplest mode is the Electronic Code Book (ECB) mode where the plaintext is divided into blocks and each block is encrypted separately. However, in the Cipher-Block Chaining (CBC) mode, each block of plaintext is XORed with the previous ciphertext block before being encrypted. In the ECB mode, the same plaintext will encrypt to same ciphertext for the same key. This reveals patterns in the code.

In the CBC mode, each block is XORed with the result of the encryption of the previous block. This hides patterns. However, two similar plaintexts that have been encrypted using the same key will yield the same ciphertext up to the block containing the first difference. This problem can be avoided by adding an IV block, which starts the keystream randomization process for the first real block, to the plaintext. This will make each ciphertext unique, even when similar plaintext is encrypted with the same key in the CBC mode. There is no need for the IV to be secret, in most cases, but it is important that it is never reused with the same key. Reusing an IV leaks some information about the first block of plaintext and about any common prefix shared by the two messages. Therefore, the IV must be randomly generated at encryption time.

Key Length

Key length is another important aspect of key management to consider when generating cryptographic keys. Key length is the size of a key, usually measured in bits or bytes, which a cryptographic algorithm used in ciphering or deciphering protected information. As discussed earlier, keys are used to control how an algorithm operates so that only the correct key can decipher the information. The resistance to successful attack against the key and the algorithm, aspects of their cryptographic security, is of concern when choosing key lengths. An algorithm's key length is distinct from its cryptographic security.

Cryptographic security is a logarithmic measure of the fastest known computational attack on the algorithm, also measured in bits. The security of an algorithm cannot exceed its key length. Therefore, it is possible to have a very long key that still provides low security. As an example, three-key (56 bits per key) Triple DES (i.e., Triple Data Encryption Algorithm, aka TDEA) can have a key length of 168 bits but, due to the meet-in-the-middle attack, the effective security that it provides is at most 112 bits. However, most symmetric algorithms are designed to have security equal to their key length.

A natural inclination is to use the longest key possible, which may make the key more difficult to break. However, the longer the key, the more computationally expensive the encrypting and decrypting process can be. The goal is to make breaking the key cost more (in terms of effort, time, and resources) than the worth of the information or mission being protected and, if possible, not a penny more (to do more would not be economically sound).

Block Size

The block size of a block cipher, like key length, has a direct bearing on the security of the key. Block ciphers produce a fixed-length block of ciphertext. However, since the data being encrypted is an arbitrary number of bytes, the ciphertext block size may not come out to be a full block. This is solved by padding the plaintext up to the block size before encryption and unpadding after decryption. The padding algorithm is to calculate the smallest nonzero number of bytes, say n, which must be suffixed to the plaintext to bring it up to a multiple of the block size.[1]

Evaluation of Algorithms

Many encryption algorithms are available for information security. The two main categories of encryption algorithms are symmetric (private) and asymmetric (public) keys encryption. Symmetric keys encryption (also known as secret key encryption) uses only one key to both encrypt and decrypt data. The key is distributed before transmission between entities begins. The size of the key will determine how strong it is.

Asymmetric key encryption (also known as public key encryption) is used to solve the problem of key distribution. Asymmetric keys use two keys, one private and the other public. The public key is used for encryption, and the private key is used for decryption. Users tend to use two keys: a public key, which is known to the public, and a private key, which is known only to the user.

Some common encryption techniques include the following:

- **DES (Data Encryption Standard)** was the first encryption standard recommended by NIST. DES has a 64-bit key size and a 64-bit block size. Due to a history of successful attacks, DES is now considered to be an insecure block cipher.

- **3DES** is an enhancement of DES with a 64-bit block size and a 192-bit key size. This uses an encryption method similar to that of DES but applies it three times to increase the encryption level and the average safe time. 3DES is slower than other block cipher methods.

- **RC2** uses a 64-bit block cipher and a variable key size that ranges from 8 to 128 bits. Unfortunately, RC2 can be exploited using a related-key attack.

- **Blowfish** is another block cipher with a 64-bit block. It uses a variable-length key that ranges from 32 bits to 448 bits. The default is 128 bits. Blowfish is unpatented, license-free, and free.

- **AES (Advanced Encryption Standard)** is a block cipher with a variable key length of 128, 192, or 256 bits. The default is 256 bits. AES encrypts 128-bit data blocks in 10, 12, or 14 rounds depending on the key size. AES is fast and flexible- and has been tested for many security applications.

- **RC6** is a block cipher derived from RC5. RC6 has a block size of 128 bits and key sizes of 128, 192, or 256 bits.

Encryption algorithm characteristics that could be considered for the development of metrics include

- Type
- Functions
- Key size
- Rounds
- Complexity
- Attack
- Strength

The security practitioner can use some or all of the items mentioned to engage in the evaluation of algorithms for deployment and use within the organization. Best known methods of attack include brute force, factoring, linear, and differential cryptanalysis (qualified with whether known or chosen plaintext is provided). Strength is an assessment of the algorithm, based on key length, algorithm complexity, and the best methods of attack.

As a first step towards *any* evaluation process, the security practitioner would need to understand and document the business requirements that will be used to create the baseline functionality profile for the deployment and use of the algorithm to be evaluated. Once this has been done, then the evaluation process can proceed.

Hashing

A cryptographic hash function is a hash function that is considered practically impossible to *invert*, that is, to re-create the input data from its hash value alone. The input data is often called the *message*, and the hash value is often called the *message digest* or simply the *digest*.

The ideal cryptographic hash function has four main properties:

- It is easy to compute the hash value for any given message.
- It is infeasible to generate a message that has a given hash.
- It is infeasible to modify a message without changing the hash.
- It is infeasible to find two different messages with the same hash.

Cryptographic hash functions have many information security applications, notably in digital signatures, message authentication codes (MACs), and other forms of authentication. They can also be used as ordinary hash functions, to index data in hash tables, for fingerprinting, to detect duplicate data or uniquely identify files, and as checksums to detect accidental data corruption.

The general idea of a cryptographic hash function can be summarized with the following formula:

Variable data input + hashing algorithm = fixed bit size data output (the digest)

The security practitioner needs to understand the use of a cryptographic hash with regards to the formula and how it allows for the validation of data integrity. Figure 5.1 illustrates this point.

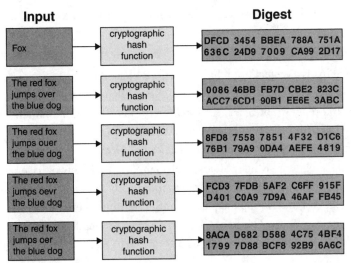

FIGURE 5.1 **Cryptographic hashing function** SOURCE: https://en.wikipedia.org/wiki/File:Cryptographic_Hash_Function.svg

Specific Hashes

Up until now we have been discussing the concepts of hashing at a high level, focusing on how hashing works theoretically. In the following sections, we will turn our attention to some specific examples of hashing algorithms, their use, and implementation details.

Message Digest 2, 4, and 5

Message Digest (MD) 2, 4, and 5 are hash functions used to create message digests for digital signatures. MD2 was first created in 1989 and forms a 128-bit message digest using a 128-bit block through 18 rounds of operation. Although it is considered to be older than is ideal, MD2 is still used in certain PKI environments where it is used in the generation of digital certificates. MD4 was created in 1990 and also generates a 128-bit message digest using a 512-bit block, but does so through only three rounds of operation. MD4 is a popular choice among file sharing and synchronization applications, although there are several well-published compromises that severely limit the nonrepudiation qualities of an MD4 hash. MD5 uses a 512-bit block and generates a 128-bit message digest as well, but does so over four rounds of operation along with several mathematical tweaks including a unique additive constant that is used during each round to provide an extra level of nonrepudiation assurance. That being said, there are numerous easy and well-published exploits available for creating hash collisions in an MD5-enabled environment.

Secure Hash Algorithm 0, 1, and 2

Secure Hash Algorithm (SHA) is a collection of hash functions created by the U.S. government starting in the early mid-1990s. SHA-0 was the first of these hash standards but was quickly removed and replaced by SHA-1 in 1995 due to some rather fundamental flaws in the original SHA-0. SHA-1 uses a block size of 512 bits to create a message digest of 160 bits through 80 rounds of operation. SHA-1 does not provide a great deal of protection against attacks such as a birthday attack, and so the SHA-2 family of hash functions was created. With SHA-2, the often employed naming convention is to use the size of the created message digest to describe the particular SHA-2 implementation. In SHA-2, the possible message digests are 224, 256, 384, and 512 bits in length. SHA-224 and SHA-256 use a block length of 512 bits while SHA-384 and SHA-512 use a block length of 1024 bits.

HAVAL

HAVAL was created in the in the mid-1990s as a highly flexible and configurable hash function. With HAVAL, the implementer can create hashes of 128, 160, 192, 224, and 256 bits in length, using a fixed block size of 128 bits and 3, 4, or 5 rounds of operation.

RIPEMD-160

Research and Development in Advanced Communications Technologies in Europe (RACE) Integrity Primitives Evaluation Message Digest (RIPEMD) is a hash function that produces 160-bit message digests using a 512-bit block size. RIPEMD was produced by a collaborative effort of European cryptographers and is not subject to any patent restrictions.

Attacks on Hashing Algorithms and Message Authentication Codes

There are two primary ways to attack hash functions: through brute-force attacks and cryptanalysis. Over the past few years, research has been done on attacks on various hashing algorithms, such as MD-5 and SHA-1. Both cases are susceptible to cryptographic attacks. A brute-force attack relies on finding a weakness in the hashing algorithm that would allow an attacker to reconstruct the original message from the hash value (defeat the one-way property of a hash function), find another message with the same hash value, or find any pair of messages with the same hash value (which is called collision resistance). Oorschot and Weiner developed a machine that could find a collision on a 128-bit hash in about 24 days.[2]

Cryptanalysis is the art and science of defeating cryptographic systems and gaining access to encrypted messages even when the keys are unknown. Side-channel attacks are examples of cryptanalyses. These attacks do not attack the algorithms but rather the implementation of the algorithms. Cryptanalysis is responsible for the development of *rainbow tables*, which are used to greatly reduce the computational time and power needed to break a cipher at the expense of storage. A freely available password cracking program called Cain and Abel comes with rainbow tables preloaded.[3]

Rainbow tables are pre-computed tables or lists used in cracking password hashes. Tables are designed for specific algorithms such as MD5 and SHA-1 and can be purchased on the open market. *Salted* hashes provide a defense against rainbow tables. In cryptographic terms, "salt" is made of random bits and is an input to the one-way hash function with target plaintext as the only other input. The salt is stored with the resulting hash so hashing will use the same salt and get the same results. As the rainbow table did not include the salt when it was created, its values will never match the salted values.

The Birthday Paradox

The birthday paradox has been described in textbooks on probability for several years. It is a surprising mathematical condition that indicates the ease of finding two people with the same birthday in a group of people. If one considers that there are 365 possible birthdays (not including leap years and assuming that birthdays are spread evenly across all possible dates), then one would expect to need to have roughly 183 people together to have a 50% probability that two of those people share the same birthday. In fact, once there are more than 23 people together, there is a greater than 50% probability that two of them share the same birthday. Consider that in a group of 23 people, there are 253 different pairings (n(n − 1)/2). Once 100 people are together, the chance of two of them having the same birthday is greater than 99.99%.

So why is a discussion about birthdays important in the middle of hashing attacks? Because the likelihood of finding a collision for two messages and their hash values may be a lot easier than may have been believed.

It would be very similar to the statistics of finding two people with the same birthday. One of the considerations for evaluating the strength of a hash algorithm must be its resistance to collisions. The probability of finding a collision for a 160-bit hash can be estimated at either 2160 or 2160/2, depending on the level of collision resistance needed.

This approach is relevant because a hash is a representation of the message and not the message itself. Obviously, the attacker does not want to find an identical message; he wants to find out how to (1) change the message contents to what he wants it to read or (2) cast some doubt on the authenticity of the original message by demonstrating that another message has the same value as the original. The hashing algorithm must be resistant to a birthday-type attack that would allow the attacker to feasibly accomplish his goals.

Salting

In cryptography, a *salt* is random data that is used as an additional input to a one-way function that hashes a password or passphrase. The primary function of salts is to defend against dictionary attacks and against pre-computed rainbow table attacks. A new salt is randomly generated for each password. In a typical setting, the salt and the password are concatenated and processed with a cryptographic hash function, and the resulting output (but not the original password) is stored with the salt in a database. Hashing allows for later authentication while defending against compromise of the plaintext password in the event that the database is somehow compromised.

Salts also combat the use of rainbow tables for cracking passwords. A rainbow table is a large list of pre-computed hashes for commonly used passwords. For a password file without salts, an attacker can go through each entry and look up the hashed password in the rainbow table. Salts protect against the use of rainbow tables as they, in effect, extend the length and potentially the complexity of the password. If the rainbow tables do not have passwords matching the length (e.g., an 8-byte password and 2-byte salt is effectively a 10-byte password) and complexity (non-alphanumeric salt increases the complexity of strictly alphanumeric passwords) of the salted password, then the password will not be found. If found, one will have to remove the salt from the password before it can be used.

Encryption and Decryption

Encryption is the process of transforming information so it is unintelligible to anyone but the intended recipient. Decryption is the process of transforming encrypted information so that it is intelligible again. A cryptographic algorithm, also called a cipher, is a mathematical function used for encryption or decryption. In most cases, two related functions are employed, one for encryption and the other for decryption.

With most modern cryptography, the ability to keep encrypted information secret is based not on the cryptographic algorithm, which is widely known, but on a number called a key that must be used with the algorithm to produce an encrypted result or to decrypt previously encrypted information. Decryption with the correct key is simple. Decryption without the correct key is very difficult and in some cases impossible for all practical purposes.

Symmetric Cryptography

There are two primary forms of cryptography in use today, symmetric and asymmetric cryptographies. Symmetric algorithms operate with a single cryptographic key that is used for both encryption and decryption of the message. For this reason, it is often called single, same, or shared key encryption. It can also be called secret or private key encryption because the key factor in secure use of a symmetric algorithm is to keep the cryptographic key secret.

Some of the most difficult challenges of symmetric key ciphers are the problems of key management. Because the encryption and decryption processes both require the same key, the secure distribution of the key to both the sender (or encryptor) of the message and the receiver (or decryptor) is a key factor in the secure implementation of a symmetric key system. The cryptographic key cannot be sent in the same channel (or transmission medium) as the data, so out-of-band distribution must be considered. *Out of band* means using a different channel to transmit the keys, such as courier, fax, phone, or some other method (Figure 5.2).

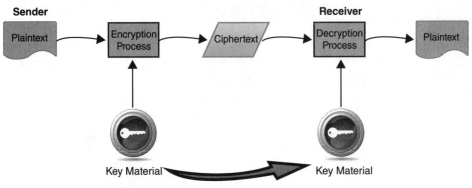

FIGURE 5.2 **Out-of-band key distribution**

The advantages of symmetric key algorithms are that they are usually very fast, secure, and cheap. There are several products available on the Internet at no cost to the user who uses symmetric algorithms.

The disadvantages include the problems of key management, as mentioned earlier, but also the limitation that a symmetric algorithm does not provide many benefits beyond confidentiality, unlike most asymmetric algorithms, which also provide the ability to establish nonrepudiation, message integrity, and access control. Symmetric algorithms can provide a form of message integrity—the message will not decrypt if changed. Symmetric algorithms also can provide a measure of access control—without the key, the file cannot be decrypted.

This limitation is best described by using a physical security example. If 10 people have a copy of the key to the server room, it can be difficult to know who entered that room at 10 p.m. yesterday. There is limited access control in that only those people with a key are able to enter; however, it is unknown which one of those 10 actually entered. The same with a symmetric algorithm; if the key to a secret file is shared between two or more people, then there is no way of knowing who the last person to access the encrypted file was. It would also be possible for a person to change the file and allege that it was changed by someone else. This would be most critical when the cryptosystem is used for important documents such as electronic contracts. If a person that receives a file can change the document and allege that that was the true copy he had received, repudiation problems arise.

Algorithms and systems such as the Caesar cipher, the Spartan Scytale, and the Enigma machine are all examples of symmetric algorithms. The receiver needed to use the same key to perform the decryption process as he had used during the encryption process. The following sections cover many of the modern symmetric algorithms.

The Data Encryption Standard (DES)

When looking at a Data Encryption Standard (DES) key, it is 64 bits in length; however, every eighth bit (used for parity) is ignored. Therefore, the effective length of the DES key is 56 bits. Because every bit has a possible value of either 1 or 0, it can be stated that the effective key space for the DES key is 2^{56}. This gives a total number of keys for DES to be 7.2×10^{16}. However, the modes of operation discussed next are used by a variety of other block ciphers, not just in DES. Originally there were four modes of DES accepted for use by the U.S. federal government (NIST); in later years, the CTR mode was also accepted.

Basic Block Cipher Modes

The following basic block cipher modes operate in a block structure:[4]

- **Electronic Codebook Mode**—The electronic codebook mode (ECB) is the most basic block cipher mode (Figure 5.3). It is called codebook because it is similar to having a large codebook containing every piece of 64-bit plaintext input and all possible 64-bit ciphertext outputs. In a manual sense, it would be the same as looking up the input in a book and finding what the output would be depending on which key was used. When a plaintext input is received by ECB, it operates on that block independently and produces the ciphertext output. If the input was more than 64 bits long and each 64-bit block was the same, then the output blocks would also be the same. Such regularity would make cryptanalysis simple. For that reason, ECB is only used for very short messages (less than 64 bits in length), such as transmission of a key. As with all Feistel ciphers, the decryption process is the reverse of the encryption process.

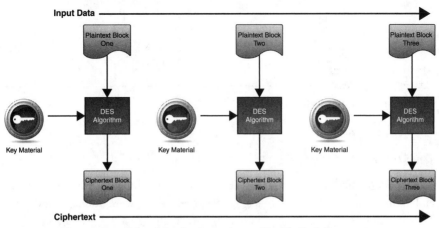

FIGURE 5.3 **Electronic codebook is a basic mode used by block ciphers.**

- **Cipher Block Chaining Mode**—The cipher block chaining mode (CBC) mode is stronger than ECB in that each input block will produce a different output—even if the input blocks are identical. This is accomplished by introducing two new factors in the encryption process—an IV and a chaining function that XORs each input with the previous ciphertext. (Note: Without the IV, the chaining process applied to the same messages would create the same ciphertext.) The IV is a randomly chosen value that is mixed with the first block of plaintext. This acts just like a seed in a stream-based cipher. The sender and the receiver must know the IV so that the message can be decrypted later. The function of CBC can be seen in Figure 5.4.

The initial input block is XORed with the IV, and the result of that process is encrypted to produce the first block of ciphertext. This first ciphertext block is then

XORed with the next input plaintext block. This is the chaining process, which ensures that even if the input blocks are the same, the resulting outputs will be different.

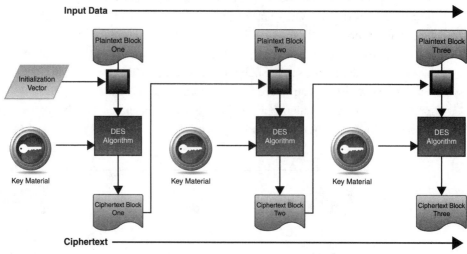

FIGURE 5.4 Cipher block chaining mode

The Stream Modes of DES

The following modes of DES operate as a stream; even though DES is a block mode cipher, these modes attempt to make DES operate as if it were a stream mode algorithm. A block-based cipher is subject to the problems of latency or delay in processing. This makes them unsuitable for many applications where simultaneous transmission of the data is desired. In these modes, DES tries to simulate a stream to be more versatile and provide support for stream-based applications.

- **Cipher Feedback Mode**—In the cipher feedback mode (CFB) mode, the input is separated into individual segments, the size of which can be 1-bit, 8-bit, 64-bit, or 128-bit (the four sub-modes of CFB)—usually of 8 bits, because that is the size of one character (Figure 5.5). When the encryption process starts, the IV is chosen and loaded into a shift register. It is then run through the encryption algorithm. The first 8 bits that come from the algorithm are then XORed with the first 8 bits of the plaintext (the first segment). Each 8-bit segment is then transmitted to the receiver and also fed back into the shift register. The shift register contents are then encrypted again to generate the keystream to be XORed with the next plaintext segment. This process continues until the end of the input. One of the drawbacks of this, however, is that if a bit is corrupted or altered, all of the data from that point onward will be damaged. It is interesting to note that because of the nature of the operation in CFB, the decryption process uses the encryption operation rather than operate in reverse like CBC.

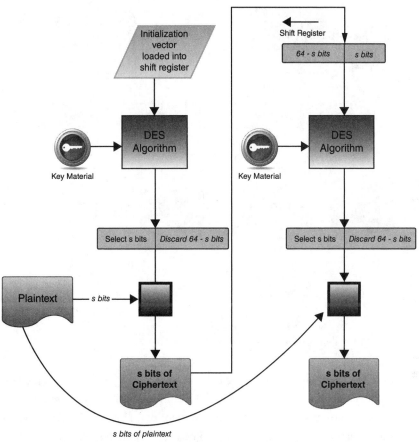

FIGURE 5.5 Cipher feedback mode of DES

- **Output Feedback Mode**—The output feedback mode (OFB) mode is very similar in operation to the CFB except that instead of using the ciphertext result of the XOR operation to feed back into the shift register for the ongoing keystream, it feeds the encrypted keystream itself back into the shift register to create the next portion of the keystream (Figure 5.6).

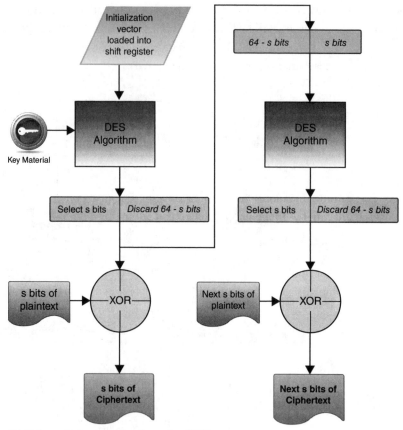

FIGURE 5.6 **Output feedback mode of DES**

Because the keystream and message data are completely independent (the keystream itself is chained, but there is no chaining of the ciphertext), it is now possible to generate the entire keystream in advance and store it for later use. However, this does pose some storage complications, especially if it were to be used in a high-speed link.

- **Counter Mode**—The counter mode (CTR) mode is used in high-speed applications such as IPSec and ATM (Figure 5.7). In this mode, a counter—a 64-bit random data block—is used as the first IV. A requirement of CTR is that the counter must be different for every block of plaintext, so for each subsequent block, the counter is incremented by 1. The counter is then encrypted just as in OFB, and the result is used as a keystream and XORed with the plaintext. Because the keystream is independent from the message, it is possible to process several blocks of data at the same time, thus speeding up the throughput of the algorithm. Again, because of the characteristics of the algorithm, the encryption process is used at both ends of the process—there is no need to install the decryption process.

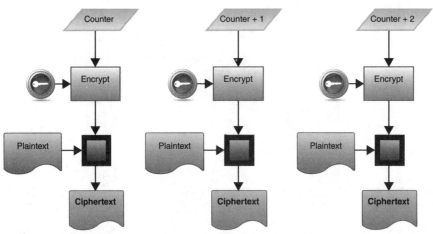

FIGURE 5.7 Counter mode is used in high-speed applications such as IPSec and ATM.

Advantages and Disadvantages of DES

DES is a strong, fast algorithm that has endured the test of time; however, it is not suitable for use for very confidential data due to the increase in computing power over the years. Initially, DES was considered unbreakable, and early attempts to break a DES message were unrealistic. (A computer running at one attempt per millisecond would still take more than 1,000 years to try all possible keys.) However, DES is susceptible to a brute-force attack. Because the key is only 56 bits long, the key may be determined by trying all possible keys against the ciphertext until the true plaintext is recovered. The Electronic Frontier Foundation (`www.eff.org`) demonstrated this several years ago. However, it should be noted that they did the simplest form of attack—a known plaintext attack; they tried all possible keys against a ciphertext knowing what they were looking for (they knew the plaintext). If they did not know the plaintext (if they did not know what they were looking for), the attack would have been significantly more difficult.

Regardless, DES can be deciphered using today's computing power and enough stubborn persistence. There have also been criticisms of the structure of the DES algorithm. The design of the S-boxes used in the encryption and decryption operations was secret, and this can lead to claims that they may contain hidden code or untried operations.

Double DES

The primary complaint about DES was that the key was too short. This made a known plaintext brute-force attack possible. One of the first alternatives considered to create a stronger version of DES was to double the encryption process, as shown in Figure 5.8. The first DES operation created an intermediate ciphertext, which will be referred to as "m" for discussion purposes.

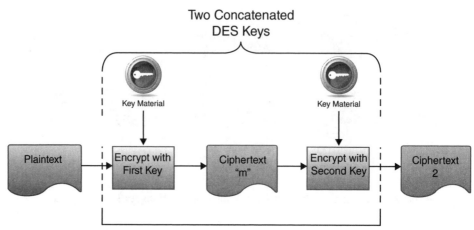

FIGURE 5.8 **Operations within double DES cryptosystems**

This intermediate ciphertext, m, was then re-encrypted using a second 56-bit DES key for greater cryptographic strength. Initially there was a lot of discussion as to whether the ciphertext created by the second DES operation would be the same as the ciphertext that would have been created by a third DES key.

Ciphertext created by double DES is the result of the plaintext encrypted with the first 56-bit DES key and then re-encrypted with the second 56-bit DES key.

Would the result of two operations be the same as the result of one operation using a different key? This is not the case as more serious vulnerabilities in double DES have emerged. The intention of double DES was to create an algorithm that would be equivalent in strength to a 112-bit key (two 56-bit keys). Unfortunately, this was not the case because of the "meet in the middle" attack, which is why the lifespan of double DES was very short.

Meet in the Middle

The most effective attack against double DES was just like the successful attacks on single DES, based on doing a brute-force attack against known plaintext[5] (Figure 5.9). The attacker would encrypt the plaintext using all possible keys and create a table containing all possible results. This intermediate cipher is referred to as "m" for this discussion.

This would mean encrypting using all 2^{56} possible keys. The table would then be sorted according to the values of m. The attacker would then decrypt the ciphertext using all possible keys until he found a match with the value of m. This would result in a true strength of double DES of approximately 2^{56} (twice the strength of DES, but not strong enough to be considered effective), instead of the 2^{112} originally hoped for.[6]

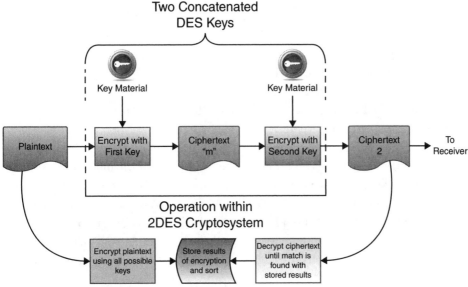

FIGURE 5.9 **Meet-in-the-middle attack on 2DES**

Triple DES (3DES)

The defeat of double DES resulted in the adoption of triple DES as the next solution to overcome the weaknesses of single DES. Triple DES was designed to operate at a relative strength of 2^{112} using two different keys to perform the encryption.

The ciphertext is created by encrypting the plaintext with key 1, re-encrypting with key 2, and then encrypting again with key 1.

This would have a relative strength of 2^{112} and be unfeasible for attack using either the known plaintext or differential cryptanalysis attacks. This mode of 3DES would be referred to as EEE2 (encrypt, encrypt, encrypt using two keys).

The plaintext was encrypted using key 1, then decrypted using key 2, and then encrypted using key 1.

Doing the decrypt operation for the intermediate step does not make a difference in the strength of the cryptographic operation, but it does allow backward compatibility through permitting a user of triple DES to also access files encrypted with single DES. This mode of triple DES is referred to as EDE2. Originally, the use of triple DES was primarily done using two keys as shown earlier, and this was compliant with ISO 8732 and ANS X9.17; however, some users, such as Pretty Good Privacy (PGP) and Secure/Multipurpose Internet Mail Extension (S/MIME), are moving toward the adoption of triple DES using three separate keys.

The Advanced Encryption Standard (AES)

In 1997, the National Institute of Standards and Technology (NIST) in the United States issued a call for a product to replace DES and 3DES. The requirements were that the new algorithm would be at least as strong as DES, have a larger block size (because a larger block size would be more efficient and more secure), and overcome the problems of performance with DES. DES was developed for hardware implementations and is too slow in software. 3DES is even slower and thus creates a serious latency in encryption as well as significant processing overhead.

After considerable research, the product chosen to be the new advanced encryption standard (AES) was the Rijndael algorithm, created by Dr. Joan Daemon and Dr. Vincent Rijmen of Belgium. The name Rijndael was merely a contraction of their surnames. Rijndael beat out the other finalists: Serpent, of which Ross Anderson was an author; MARS, an IBM product; RC6, from Ron Rivest and RSA; and TwoFish, developed by Bruce Schneier. The AES algorithm was obliged to meet many criteria, including the need to be flexible, implementable on many types of platforms, and free of royalties.

Counter Mode with Cipher Block Chaining Message Authentication Code Protocol (CCMP)

Counter Mode with Cipher Block Chaining Message Authentication Code Protocol (CCMP) is an encryption protocol that forms part of the 802.11i standard for wireless local area networks. The CCMP protocol is based on AES encryption using the CTR with CBC-MAC (CCM) mode of operation. CCMP is defined in the IETF RFC 3610 and is included as a component of the 802.11i IEEE standard.[7]

AES processing in CCMP must use AES 128-bit key and 128-bit block size. Per United States' Federal Information Processing Standard (FIPS) 197 standard, the AES algorithm (a block cipher) uses blocks of 128 bits, cipher keys with lengths of 128, 192, and 256 bits, as well as a number of rounds—10, 12, and 14, respectively. CCMP use of 128-bit keys and a 48-bit IV minimizes vulnerability to replay attacks. The CTR component provides data privacy. The Cipher Block Chaining Message Authentication Code component produces a message integrity code (MIC) that provides data origin authentication and data integrity for the packet payload data.

The 802.11i standard includes CCMP. AES is often referred to as the encryption protocol used by 802.11i; however, AES itself is simply a block cipher. The actual encryption protocol is CCMP. It is important to note here that, although the 802.11i standard allows for TKIP encryption, Robust Security Network (RSN) is part of the 802.11i IEEE standard and negotiates authentication and encryption algorithms between access points and wireless clients. This flexibility allows new algorithms to be added at any time and supported alongside previous algorithms. The use of AES-CCMP is mandated for RSNs. AES-CCMP introduces a higher level of security from past protocols by providing protection for the MAC protocol data unit (MPDU) and parts of the 802.11 MAC headers. This protects even more of the data packet from eavesdropping and tampering.

Rijndael

The Rijndael algorithm can be used with block sizes of 128, 192, or 256 bits. The key can also be 128, 192, or 256 bits, with a variable number of rounds of operation depending on the key size. Using AES with a 128-bit key would do 10 rounds, whereas a 192-bit key would do 12, and a 256-bit key would do 14. Although Rijndael supports multiple block sizes, AES supports only one block size (subset of Rijndael). AES is reviewed below in the 128-bit block format. The AES operation works on the entire 128-bit block of input data by first copying it into a square table (or array) that it calls state. The inputs are placed into the array by column so that the first four bytes of the input would fill the first column of the array.

Following is input plaintext when placed into a 128-bit state array:

1st byte	5th byte	9th byte	13th byte
2nd byte	6th byte	10th byte	14th byte
3rd byte	7th byte	11th byte	15th byte
4th byte	8th byte	12th byte	16th byte

The key is also placed into a similar square table or matrix. The Rijndael operation consists of four major operations.

1. **Substitute Bytes**—Use of an S-box to do a byte-by-byte substitution of the entire block.

2. **Shift Rows**—Transposition or permutation through offsetting each row in the table.

3. **Mix Columns**—A substitution of each value in a column based on a function of the values of the data in the column.

4. **Add Round Key**—XOR each byte with the key for that round; the key is modified for each round of operation.

These four major operations of the Rijndael operation deserve more examination:

Substitute Bytes   The substitute bytes operation uses an S-box that looks up the value of each byte in the input and substitutes it with the value in the table. The S-box table contains all possible 256 8-bit word values and a simple cross-reference is done to find the substitute value using the first half of the byte (4-bit word) in the input table on the x-axis and the second half of the byte on the y-axis. Hexadecimal values are used in both the input and S-box tables.

Shift Row Transformation   The shift row transformation step provides blockwide transposition of the input data by shifting the rows of data as follows. If one starts with the input table described earlier, the effect of the shift row operation can be observed. Please note that by this point the table will have been subjected to the substitute bytes operation, so it would not look like this any longer, but this table will be used for the sake of clarity.

COLUMNS			
ROWS 1st byte	5th byte	9th byte	13th byte
2nd byte	6th byte	10th byte	14th byte
3rd byte	7th byte	11th byte	15th byte
4th byte	8th byte	12th byte	16th byte

The first row is not shifted.

1st byte	5th byte	9th byte	13th byte

The second row of the table is shifted one place to the left.

6th byte	10th byte	14th byte	2nd byte

The third row of the table is shifted two places to the left.

11th byte	15th byte	3rd byte	7th byte

The fourth row of the table is shifted three places to the left.

16th byte	4th byte	8th byte	12th byte

The final result of the shift rows step would look as follows:

1	5	9	13
6	10	14	2
11	15	3	7
16	4	8	12

Mix Column Transformation   The mix column transformation is performed by multiplying and XORing each byte in a column together, according to the table in Figure 5.10.

1	5	9	13
6	10	14	2
11	15	3	7
16	4	8	12

02	03	01	01
01	02	03	01
01	01	02	03
03	01	01	01

State table   Exclusive OR   Mix Columns table

FIGURE 5.10 Mix column transformation

The table in Figure 5.10 is the result of the previous step, so when the first column (shaded in the state table), is worked using use multiplication and XOR with the first row in the mix column table (shaded), the computation of the mix columns step for the first columns would be

$$(1\times02)\ (6\times03)\ (11\times01)\ (16\times01)$$

The second byte in the column would be calculated using the second row in the mix columns table as

$$(6\times01)\ (11\times02)\ (16\times03)\ (1\times01)$$

Add Round Key   The key is modified for each round by first dividing the key into 16-bit pieces (four 4-bit words) and then expanding each piece into 176 bits (44 4-bit words). The key is arrayed into a square matrix, and each column is subjected to rotation (shifting the first column to the last [1, 2, 3, 4 would become 2, 3, 4, 1]) and then the substitution of each word of the key using an S-box. The result of these first two operations is then XORed with a round constant to create the key to be used for that round. The round constant changes for each round, and its values are predefined. Each of the previous steps (except for the mix columns, which is done only for nine rounds) is done for 10 rounds to produce the ciphertext. AES is a strong algorithm that is not considered breakable at any time in the near future and is easy to deploy on many platforms with excellent throughput.

Other Symmetric Algorithm Approaches

Besides DES and AES, a number of other approaches to encryption algorithms have been developed over the years.

International Data Encryption Algorithm (IDEA)

International Data Encryption Algorithm (IDEA) was developed as a replacement for DES by Xuejai Lai and James Massey in 1991. IDEA uses a 128-bit key and operates on 64-bit blocks. IDEA does eight rounds of transposition and substitution using modular addition and multiplication and bitwise exclusive-or (XOR). The patents on IDEA expired in 2011.

CAST

CAST was developed in 1996 by Carlisle Adams and Stafford Tavares. CAST-128 can use keys between 40 and 128 bits in length and will do between 12 and 16 rounds of operation, depending on key length. CAST-128 is a Feistel-type block cipher with 64-bit blocks. CAST-256 was submitted as an unsuccessful candidate for the new AES. CAST-256 operates on 128-bit blocks and with keys of 128, 192, 160, 224, and 256 bits. It performs 48 rounds and is described in RFC 2612.

Secure and Fast Encryption Routine (SAFER)

All of the algorithms in Secure and Fast Encryption Routine (SAFER) are patent-free. The algorithms were developed by James Massey and work on either 64-bit input blocks (SAFER-SK64) or 128-bit blocks (SAFER-SK128). A variation of SAFER is used as a block cipher in Bluetooth.

Blowfish

Blowfish is a symmetrical algorithm developed by Bruce Schneier. It is an extremely fast cipher and can be implemented in as little as 5K of memory. It is a Feistel-type cipher in that it divides the input blocks into two halves and then uses them in XORs against each other. However, it varies from the traditional Feistel cipher in that Blowfish does work against both halves, not just one. The Blowfish algorithm operates with variable key sizes, from 32 up to 448 bits on 64-bit input and output blocks. One of the characteristics of Blowfish is that the S-boxes are created from the key and are stored for later use. Because of the processing time taken to change keys and recompute the S-boxes, Blowfish is unsuitable for applications where the key is changed frequently or in applications on smart cards or with limited processing power. Blowfish is currently considered unbreakable (using today's technology), and in fact, because the key is used to generate the S-boxes, it takes over 500 rounds of the Blowfish algorithm to test any single key.

Twofish

Twofish was one of the finalists for the AES. It is an adapted version of Blowfish developed by a team of cryptographers led by Bruce Schneier. It can operate with keys of 128, 192, or 256 bits on blocks of 128 bits. It performs 16 rounds during the encryption/decryption process.

RC5

RC5 was developed by Ron Rivest of RSA and is deployed in many of RSA's products. It is a very adaptable product useful for many applications, ranging from software to hardware implementations. The key for RC5 can vary from 0 to 2040 bits, the number of rounds it executes can be adjusted from 0 to 255, and the length of the input words can also be chosen from 16-, 32-, and 64-bit lengths. The algorithm operates on two words at a time in a fast and secure manner.

RC5 is defined in RFC 2040 for four different modes of operation:

- RC5 block cipher is similar to DES ECB producing a ciphertext block of the same length as the input.

- RC5-CBC is a cipher block chaining form of RC5 using chaining to ensure that repeated input blocks would not generate the same output.

- RC5-CBC-Pad combines chaining with the ability to handle input plaintext of any length. The ciphertext will be longer than the plaintext by at most one block.

- RC5-CTS is called ciphertext stealing and will generate a ciphertext equal in length to a plaintext of any length.

RC4

RC4, a stream-based cipher, was developed in 1987 by Ron Rivest for RSA Data Security and has become the most widely used stream cipher, being deployed, for example, in WEP and SSL/TLS. RC4 uses a variable-length key ranging from 8 to 2048 bits (1 to 256 bytes) and a period of greater than 10^{100}. In other words, the keystream should not repeat for at least that length.

The key is used to initialize a state vector that is 256 bytes in length and contains all possible values of 8-bit numbers from 0 through 255. This state is used to generate the keystream that is XORed with the plaintext. The key is only used to initialize the state and is not used thereafter. Because no transposition is done, RC4 is considered by some cryptographers to be theoretically weaker. The U.S. federal government through the NIST bans its use for protecting sensitive data for federal agencies and their contractors. If RC4 is used with a key length of at least 128 bits, there are currently no practical ways to attack it; the published successful attacks against the use of RC4 in WEP applications are related to problems with the implementation of the algorithm, not the algorithm itself.

Advantages and Disadvantages of Symmetric Algorithms

Symmetric algorithms are very fast and secure methods of providing confidentiality and some integrity and authentication for messages being stored or transmitted. Many algorithms can be implemented in either hardware or software and are available at no cost to the user.

However, there are serious disadvantages to symmetric algorithms—key management is very difficult, especially in large organizations. The number of keys needed grows rapidly with every new user according to the formula $n(n - 1)/2$, where n is the number of users. An organization with only 10 users, all wanting to communicate securely with one another, requires 45 keys ($10 \times 9/2$). If the organization grows to 1000 employees, the need for key management expands to nearly a half million keys.

Symmetric algorithms also are not able to provide nonrepudiation of origin, access control, and digital signatures, except in a very limited way. If two or more people share a symmetric key, then it is impossible to prove who altered a file protected with a symmetric key. Selecting keys is an important part of key management. There needs to be a process in place that ensures that a key is selected randomly from the entire key space and that there is some way to recover a lost or forgotten key.

Because symmetric algorithms require both users (the sender and the receiver) to share the same key, there can be challenges with secure key distribution. Often the users must use an out-of-band channel such as mail, fax, telephone, or courier to exchange secret keys. The use of an out-of-band channel should make it difficult for an attacker to seize both the encrypted data and the key. The other method of exchanging the symmetric key is to use an asymmetric algorithm.

Asymmetric Cryptography

Due to the practical limitations of symmetric cryptography, asymmetric cryptography attempts to provide the best of all worlds. While initially more key management is required, the fundamentals of asymmetric cryptography provide an extensible and elastic framework in which to deploy cryptographic functions for integrity, confidentiality, authentication, and nonrepudiation.

Asymmetric Algorithms

Unlike symmetric algorithms, which have been in existence for several millennia, the use of asymmetric (or public key) algorithms is relatively new. These algorithms became commonly known when Drs. Whit Diffie and Martin Hellman released a paper in 1976 called "New Directions in Cryptography."[8] The Diffie–Hellman paper described the concept of using two different keys (a key pair) to perform the cryptographic operations. The two keys would be linked mathematically but would be mutually exclusive. For most asymmetric algorithms, if one half of this key pair was used for encryption, then the other key half would be required to decrypt the message.

When a person wishes to communicate using an asymmetric algorithm, she would first generate a key pair. Usually this is done by the cryptographic application or the PKI without user involvement to ensure the strength of the key generation process. One half of the key pair is kept secret, and only the key holder knows that key. For this reason, it is often called the private key. The other half of the key pair can be given freely to anyone that wants a copy. In many companies, it may be available through the corporate website or access to a key server. That is why this half of the key pair is often referred to as the public key. Asymmetric algorithms are one-way functions, that is, a process that is much simpler to go in one direction (forward) than to go in the other direction (backward or reverse engineering). The process to generate the public key (forward) is fairly simple, and providing the public key to anyone who wants it does not compromise the private key because the process to go from the public key to the private key is computationally infeasible.

Confidential Messages

Because the keys are mutually exclusive, any message that is encrypted with a public key can only be decrypted with the corresponding other half of the key pair, the private key. Therefore, as long as the key holder keeps her private key secure, there exists a method of transmitting a message confidentially. The sender would encrypt the message with the public key of the receiver. Only the receiver with the private key would be able to open or read the message, providing confidentiality. See Figure 5.11.

Open Messages

Conversely, when a message is encrypted with the private key of a sender, it can be opened or read by anyone who possesses the corresponding public key. When a person needs to send a message and provide proof of origin (nonrepudiation), he can do so by encrypting it with his own private key. The recipient then has some guarantee that, because she opened it with the public key from the sender, the message did, in fact, originate with the sender. See Figure 5.12.

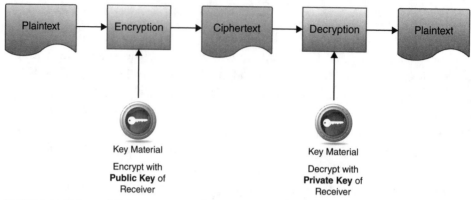

FIGURE 5.11 Using public key cryptography to send a confidential message

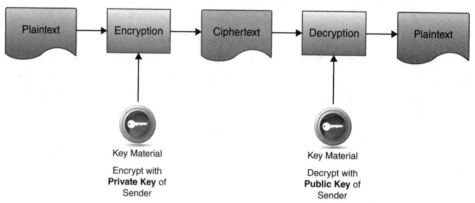

FIGURE 5.12 Using public key cryptography to send a message with proof of origin

Confidential Messages with Proof of Origin

By encrypting a message with the private key of the sender and the public key of the receiver, the ability exists to send a message that is confidential and has proof of origin. See Figure 5.13.

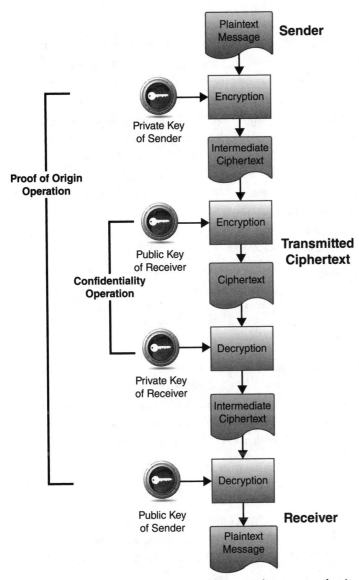

FIGURE 5.13 Using public key cryptography to send a message that is confidential and has a proof of origin

RSA

RSA was developed in 1978 by Ron Rivest, Adi Shamir, and Len Adleman when they were at MIT. RSA is based on the mathematical challenge of factoring the product of two large prime numbers. A prime number can only be divided by 1 and itself. Some prime numbers include 2, 3, 5, 7, 11, 13, and so on. Factoring is defined as taking a number and finding the numbers that can be multiplied together to calculate that number. For example, if the product of a×b = c, then c can be factored into a and b. As 3×4 = 12, then 12 can be factored into 3, 4 and 6, 2 and 12, 1. The RSA algorithm uses large prime numbers that when multiplied together would be incredibly difficult to factor. Successful factoring attacks have been executed against 512-bit numbers (at a cost of approximately 8000 MIPS years), and since successful attacks against 1024-bit numbers appeared increasingly possible in the near term, the U.S. government organization, NIST recommended moving away from 1024-bit RSA key size by the end of 2010.[9]

The three primary approaches to attack the RSA algorithm are to use brute force, trying all possible private keys; mathematical attacks, factoring the product of two prime numbers; and timing attacks, measuring the running time of the decryption algorithm.

Diffie–Hellmann Algorithm

Diffie–Hellmann is a key exchange algorithm. It is used to enable two users to exchange or negotiate a secret symmetric key that will be used subsequently for message encryption. The Diffie–Hellmann algorithm does not provide for message confidentiality but is extremely useful for applications such as public key infrastructure. Diffie–Hellmann is based on discrete logarithms. This is a mathematical function based first on finding the primitive root of a prime number.

El Gamal

The El Gamal cryptographic algorithm is based on the work of Diffie–Hellmann, but it included the ability to provide message confidentiality and digital signature services, not just session key exchange. The El Gamal algorithm was based on the same mathematical functions of discrete logs.

Elliptic Curve Cryptography (ECC)

One branch of discrete logarithmic algorithms is based on the complex mathematics of elliptic curves. These algorithms, which are too complex to explain in this context, are advantageous for their speed and strength. The elliptic curve algorithms have the highest strength per bit of key length of any of the asymmetric algorithms. The ability to use much shorter keys for Elliptic Curve Cryptography (ECC) implementations provides savings on computational power and bandwidth. This makes ECC especially beneficial for implementation in smart cards, wireless, and other similar application areas. Elliptic curve algorithms provide confidentiality, digital signatures, and message authentication services.

Advantages and Disadvantages of Asymmetric Key Algorithms

The development of asymmetric key cryptography revolutionized the cryptographic community. Now it was possible to send a message across an untrusted medium in a secure manner without the overhead of prior key exchange or key material distribution. It allowed several other features not readily available in symmetric cryptography, such as the nonrepudiation of origin, access control, data integrity, and the nonrepudiation of delivery.

The problem was that asymmetric cryptography is extremely slow compared to its symmetric counterpart. Asymmetric cryptography was a product that was extremely problematic in terms of speed and performance and would be impractical for everyday use in encrypting large amounts of data and frequent transactions. This is because asymmetric is handling much larger keys and computations—making even a fast computer work harder than if it were only handling small keys and less complex algebraic calculations. The ciphertext output from asymmetric algorithms may be much larger than the plaintext. This means that for large messages, they are not effective for secrecy; however, they are effective for message integrity, authentication, and nonrepudiation.

Hybrid Cryptography

The solutions to many of the problems with symmetric encryption lies in developing a hybrid technique of cryptography that combined the strengths of both symmetric cryptography, with its great speed and secure algorithms, and asymmetric cryptography, with its ability to securely exchange session keys, message authentication, and nonrepudiation. Symmetric cryptography is best for encrypting large files. It can handle the encryption and decryption processes with little impact on delivery times or computational performance.

Asymmetric cryptography can handle the initial setup of the communications session through the exchange or negotiation of the symmetric keys to be used for this session. In many cases, the symmetric key is only needed for the length of this communication and can be discarded following the completion of the transaction, so the symmetric key in this case will be referred to as a session key. A hybrid system operates as shown in Figure 5.14. The message itself is encrypted with a symmetric key, SK, and is sent to the recipient. The symmetric key is encrypted with the public key of the recipient and sent to the recipient. The symmetric key is decrypted with the private key of the recipient. This discloses the symmetric key to the recipient. The symmetric key can then be used to decrypt the message.

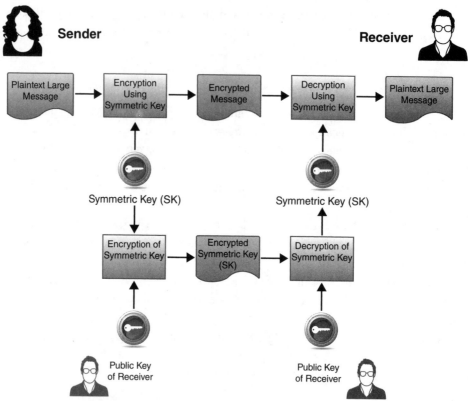

FIGURE 5.14 Hybrid system using asymmetric algorithm for bulk data encryption and an asymmetric algorithm for distribution of the symmetric key

Message Digests

A message digest is a small representation of a larger message. Message digests are used to ensure the authentication and integrity of information, not the confidentiality.

Message Authentication Code

A message authentication code (MAC, also known as a *cryptographic checksum*) is a small block of data that is generated using a secret key and then appended to the message. When the message is received, the recipient can generate her own MAC using the secret key and thereby know that the message has not changed either accidentally or intentionally in transit. Of course, this assurance is only as strong as the trust that the two parties have that no one else has access to the secret key. A MAC is a small representation of a message and has the following characteristics:

- A MAC is much smaller than the message generating it.

- Given a MAC, it is impractical to compute the message that generated it.
- Given a MAC and the message that generated it, it is impractical to find another message generating the same MAC.

In the case of DES-CBC, a MAC is generated using the DES algorithm in CBC mode, and the secret DES key is shared by the sender and the receiver. The MAC is actually just the last block of ciphertext generated by the algorithm. This block of data (64 bits) is attached to the unencrypted message and transmitted to the far end. All previous blocks of encrypted data are discarded to prevent any attack on the MAC itself. The receiver can just generate his own MAC using the secret DES key he shares to ensure message integrity and authentication. He knows that the message has not changed because the chaining function of CBC would significantly alter the last block of data if any bit had changed anywhere in the message. He knows the source of the message (authentication) because only one other person holds the secret key. If the message contains a sequence number (such as a TCP header or X.25 packet), he knows that all messages have been received and not duplicated or missed.

HMAC

A MAC based on DES is one of the most common methods of creating a MAC; however, it is slow in operation compared to a hash function. A hash function such as MD5 does not have a secret key, so it cannot be used for a MAC. Therefore, RFC 2104 was issued to provide a hashed MACing (HMAC) system that has become the process used now in IPSec and many other secure Internet protocols, such as SSL/TLS. Hashed MACing implements a freely available hash algorithm as a component (black box) within the HMAC implementation. This allows ease of the replacement of the hashing module if a new hash function becomes necessary. The use of proven cryptographic hash algorithms also provides assurance of the security of HMAC implementations. HMACs work by adding a secret key value to the hash input function along with the source message. The HMAC operation provides cryptographic strength similar to a hashing algorithm, except that it now has the additional protection of a secret key, and still operates nearly as rapidly as a standard hash operation.

Digital Signatures

Tamper detection and related authentication techniques rely on a mathematical function called a one-way hash (also called a message digest). A one-way hash is a number with fixed length that has the following characteristics:

- The value of the hash is unique for the hashed data. Any change in the data, even deleting or altering a single character, results in a different value.

- The content of the hashed data cannot, for all practical purposes, be deduced from the hash—which is why it is called "one-way."

It is possible to use your private key for encryption and your public key for decryption. Although this is not desirable when you are encrypting sensitive information, it is a crucial part of digitally signing any data. Instead of encrypting the data itself, the signing software creates a one-way hash of the data and then uses your private key to encrypt the hash. The encrypted hash, along with other information, such as the hashing algorithm, is known as a *digital signature*.

The recipient of some signed data will get two items: the original data and the digital signature, which is a one-way hash (of the original data) that has been encrypted with the signer's private key. To validate the integrity of the data, the receiving software first uses the signer's public key to decrypt the hash. It then uses the same hashing algorithm that generated the original hash to generate a new one-way hash of the same data. Information about the hashing algorithm used is sent with the digital signature. Finally, the receiving software compares the new hash against the original hash. If the two hashes match, the data has not changed since it was signed. If they do not match, the data may have been tampered with since it was signed, or the signature may have been created with a private key that does not correspond to the public key presented by the signer.

If the two hashes match, the recipient can be certain that the public key used to decrypt the digital signature corresponds to the private key used to create the digital signature. Confirming the identity of the signer, however, also requires some way of confirming that the public key really belongs to a particular person or other entity.

The significance of a digital signature is comparable to the significance of a handwritten signature. Once you have signed some data, it is difficult to deny doing so later—assuming that the private key has not been compromised or out of the owner's control. This quality of digital signatures provides a high degree of nonrepudiation—that is, digital signatures make it difficult for the signer to deny having signed the data. In some situations, a digital signature may be as legally binding as a handwritten signature.

Non-repudiation

Non-repudiation is a service that ensures the sender cannot deny a message was sent and the integrity of the message is intact. NIST's SP 800–57 "Recommendation for Key Management—Part 1: General" (Revision 3) defines non-repudiation as:

> A service that is used to provide assurance of the integrity and origin of data in such a way that the integrity and origin can be verified by a third party as having originated from a specific entity in possession of the private key of the claimed signatory. In a general information security context, assurance that the sender of information is provided with proof of delivery

and the recipient is provided with proof of the sender's identity, so neither can later deny having processed the information.

Non-repudiation can be accomplished with digital signatures and PKI. The message is signed using the sender's private key. When the recipient receives the message, they may use the sender's public key to validate the signature. While this proves the integrity of the message, it does not explicitly define the ownership of the private key. A certificate authority must have an association between the private key and the sender (meaning only the sender has the private key) for the non-repudiation to be valid.

Methods of Cryptanalytic Attack

Any security system or product is subject to compromise or attack. The following explains common attacks against cryptography systems that the security practitioner needs to be aware of.

Chosen Plaintext

To execute the chosen attacks, the attacker knows the algorithm used for the encrypting, or even better, he may have access to the machine used to do the encryption and is trying to determine the key. This may happen if a workstation used for encrypting messages is left unattended. Now the attacker can run chosen pieces of plaintext through the algorithm and see what the result is. This may assist in a known plaintext attack. An adaptive chosen plaintext attack is where the attacker can modify the chosen input files to see what effect that would have on the resulting ciphertext.

Social Engineering for Key Discovery

This is the most common type of attack and usually the most successful. All cryptography relies to some extent on humans to implement and operate. Unfortunately, this is one of the greatest vulnerabilities and has led to some of the greatest compromises of a nation's or organization's secrets or intellectual property. Through coercion, bribery, or befriending people in positions of responsibility, spies or competitors are able to gain access to systems without having any technical expertise.

Brute Force

Brute force is trying all possible keys until one is found that decrypts the ciphertext. This is why key length is such an important factor in determining the strength of a cryptosystem. Because DES only had a 56-bit key, in time the attackers were able to discover the key and decrypt a DES message. This is also why SHA-256 is considered stronger than MD5, because the output hash is longer, and, therefore, more resistant to a brute-force attack. Graphical processor units (GPUs) have revolutionized brute-force hacking methods. Where a standard CPU might take 48 hours to crack an eight-character mixed password, a modern GPU can crack it in less than ten minutes. GPUs have a large number of Arithmetic/Logic Units (ALUs) and are designed to perform repetitive tasks continuously. These characteristics make them ideal for performing brute-force attack processes. Due to the introduction of GPU-based brute-force attacks, many security professionals are evaluating password length, complexity, and multifactor considerations.

Differential Cryptanalysis

Also called a side channel attack, this more complex attack is executed by measuring the exact execution times and power required by the crypto device to perform the encryption or decryption. By measuring this, it is possible to determine the value of the key and the algorithm used.

Linear Cryptanalysis

This is a known plaintext attack that uses linear approximations to describe the behavior of the block cipher. Linear cryptanalysis is a known plaintext attack and uses a linear approximation to describe the behavior of the block cipher. Given sufficient pairs of plaintext and corresponding ciphertext, bits of information about the key can be obtained and increased amounts of data will usually give a higher probability of success.

There have been a variety of enhancements and improvements to the basic attack. For example, there is an attack called differential-linear cryptanalysis, which combines elements of differential cryptanalysis with those of linear cryptanalysis.

Algebraic

Algebraic attacks are a class of techniques that rely for their success on block ciphers exhibiting a high degree of mathematical structure. For instance, it is conceivable that a block cipher might exhibit a group structure. If this were the case, it would then mean that encrypting a plaintext under one key and then encrypting the result under another key would always be equivalent to single encryption under some other single key. If so, then the block cipher would be considerably weaker, and the use of multiple encryption cycles would offer no additional security over single encryption.

Rainbow Table

Hash functions map plaintext into a hash. Since the hash function is a one-way process, one should not be able to determine the plaintext from the hash itself. To determine a given plaintext from its hash, there are two ways to do that:

- Hash each plaintext until a matching hash is found.
- Hash each plaintext but store each generated hash in a table that can be used as a lookup table so hashes do not need to be generated again.

A rainbow table is a lookup table of sorted hash outputs. The idea here is that storing pre-computed hash values in a rainbow table that one can later refer to saves time and computer resources when attempting to decipher the plaintext from its hash value.

Ciphertext-Only Attack

The ciphertext-only attack is one of the most difficult because the attacker has so little information to start with. All the attacker starts with is some unintelligible data that he suspects may be an important encrypted message. The attack becomes simpler when the attacker is able to gather several pieces of ciphertext and thereby look for trends or statistical data that would help in the attack. Adequate encryption is defined as encryption that is strong enough to make brute-force attacks impractical because there is a higher work factor than the attacker wants to invest into the attack. Moore's law states that available computing power doubles every 18 months.[11] Experts suggest this advance may be slowing; however, encryption strength considered adequate today will probably not be sufficient a few years from now due to advances in CPU and GPU technology and new attack techniques. Security professionals should consider this when defining encryption requirements.

Known Plaintext

For a known plaintext attack, the attacker has access to both the ciphertext and the plaintext versions of the same message. The goal of this type of attack is to find the link—the cryptographic key that was used to encrypt the message. Once the key has been found, the attacker would then be able to decrypt all messages that had been encrypted using that key. In some cases, the attacker may not have an exact copy of the message—if the message was known to be an e-commerce transaction, the attacker knows the format of such transactions even though he does not know the actual values in the transaction.

Frequency Analysis[12]

This attack works closely with several other types of attacks. It is especially useful when attacking a substitution cipher where the statistics of the plaintext language are known. In English, for example, some letters will appear more often than others will, allowing an attacker to assume that those letters may represent an E or S.

Chosen Ciphertext

This is similar to the chosen plaintext attack in that the attacker has access to the decryption device or software and is attempting to defeat the cryptographic protection by decrypting chosen pieces of ciphertext to discover the key. An adaptive chosen ciphertext would be the same, except that the attacker can modify the ciphertext prior to putting it through the algorithm. Asymmetric cryptosystems are vulnerable to chosen ciphertext attacks. For example, the RSA algorithm is vulnerable to this type of attack. The attacker would select a section of plaintext, encrypt it with the victim's public key, and then decrypt the ciphertext to get the plaintext back. Although this does not yield any new information to the attacker, the attacker can exploit properties of RSA by selecting blocks of data that when processed using the victim's private key, yields information that can be used in cryptanalysis. The weakness with asymmetric encryption in chosen ciphertext attacks can be mitigated by including a random padding in the plaintext before encrypting the data. Security vendor RSA Security recommends modifying the plaintext using process called *optimal asymmetric encryption padding* (OAEP). RSA encryption with OAEP is defined in PKCS #1 v2.1.[13]

Birthday Attack

Because a hash is a short representation of a message, given enough time and resources, another message would give the same hash value. However, hashing algorithms have been developed with this in mind so that they can resist a simple birthday attack. (This is described in more detail in the "The Birthday Paradox" section earlier in this domain.) The point of the birthday attack is that it is easier to find two messages that hash to the same message digest than to match a specific message and its specific message digest. The usual countermeasure is to use a hash algorithm with twice the message digest length as the desired work factor (e.g., use 160 bit SHA-1 to have it resistant to 280 work factor).

Dictionary Attack

The dictionary attack is used most commonly against password files. It exploits the poor habits of users who choose simple passwords based on natural words. The dictionary attack merely encrypts all of the words in a dictionary and then checks whether the resulting hash matches an encrypted password stored in the SAM file or other password file.

Replay Attack

This attack is meant to disrupt and damage processing by the attacker sending repeated files to the host. If there are no checks or sequence verification codes in the receiving software, the system might process duplicate files.

Factoring Attacks

This attack is aimed at the RSA algorithm. Because that algorithm uses the product of large prime numbers to generate the public and private keys, this attack attempts to find the keys through solving the factoring of these numbers.

Reverse Engineering

This attack is one of the most common. A competing firm buys a crypto product from another firm and then tries to reverse engineer the product. Through reverse engineering, it may be able to find weaknesses in the system or gain crucial information about the operations of the algorithm.

Attacking the Random Number Generators

This attack was successful against the SSL installed in Netscape several years ago. Because the random number generator was too predictable, it gave the attackers the ability to guess the random numbers so critical in setting up initialization vectors or a nonce. With this information in hand, the attacker is much more likely to run a successful attack.

Temporary Files

Most cryptosystems will use temporary files to perform their calculations. If these files are not deleted and overwritten, they may be compromised and lead an attacker to the message in plaintext.

Implementation Attacks

Implementation attacks are some of the most common and popular attacks against cryptographic systems due to their ease and reliance on system elements outside of the algorithm. The main types of implementation attacks include

- Side-channel analysis
- Fault analysis
- Probing attacks

Side-channel attacks are passive attacks that rely on a physical attribute of the implementation such as power consumption/emanation. These attributes are studied to determine the secret key and the algorithm function. Some examples of popular side-channels include timing analysis and electromagnetic differential analysis.

Fault analysis attempts to force the system into an error state to gain erroneous results. By forcing an error, gaining the results, and comparing them with known good results, an attacker may learn about the secret key and the algorithm.

Probing attacks attempt to watch the circuitry surrounding the cryptographic module in hopes that the complementary components will disclose information about the key or the algorithm. Additionally new hardware may be added to the cryptographic module to observe and inject information.

DATA SENSITIVITY AND REGULATORY REQUIREMENTS

Some data is subject to various laws and regulations and requires notification in the event of a disclosure. Beyond that, some data requires special handling, especially particularly to protect against penalties, identity theft, financial loss, invasion of privacy, or unauthorized access. Data should be assigned a level of sensitivity based on who has access to it and the risk of potential harm that is involved. This assignment of sensitivity is sometimes referred to as "data classification." The data classification process is often context-sensitive. Incidents involving data in the organization's custody should be judged on a case-by-case basis. Some common examples of data classifications include the following:[14]

- Regulated data such as credit card numbers, bank accounts, medical information, and employee data are all protected by laws and regulations. This data should be accessible only by users who are granted specific authorization. If this data is compromised, the harm to finances and reputation can be extreme. This should have the highest data classification.

- Confidential data such as contracts, NDA-protected data, financial data, personnel data, and sensitive research are generally protected by legally binding contractual obligations. This information should be accessible only by individuals who have a designated, business-based need to know. If this data is compromised, the harm to reputation and finances can be serious but generally not as bad as with regulated data. This should have a high data classification.

- Public data such as public web sites, navigational maps, and press releases are generally at the discretion of the content provider. This information should be accessible by a large number of people (possibly everyone). This data presents little risk of harm to privacy, finances, and reputation and generally has a low data classification.

Legislative and Regulatory Compliance

Organizations operate in environments where laws, regulations, and compliance requirements must be met. Security professionals must understand the laws and regulations of the country and industry they are working in. An organization's governance and risk management processes must take into account these requirements from an implementation and risk perspective. These laws and regulations often offer specific actions that must be met for compliance or, in some cases, that must be met for a *safe harbor* provision. A safe harbor provision is typically a set of "good faith" conditions that, if met, may temporarily or indefinitely protect the organization from the penalties of a new law or regulation.

For example, in the United States, federal executive agencies are required to adhere to the Federal Information Security Management Act (FISMA).[15] FISMA mandates the use of specific actions, standards, and requirements for agencies to ensure sensitive information and vital mission services are not disrupted, distorted, or disclosed to improper individuals. Agencies often take the requirements from FISMA and use them as the baseline for their information security policy and adopt the standards required by FISMA as their own. In doing so, they not only meet the requirements of the law but can also provide proof to external parties that they are making a good faith effort to comply with the requirements of the law.

Compliance stemming from legal or regulatory requirements is best addressed by ensuring an organization's policies, procedures, standards, and guidance are consistent with any laws or regulations that may govern it. Furthermore, it is advisable that specific laws and their requirements are sited in an organization's governance program and information security training programs. As a general rule, laws and regulations represent a "moral minimum," which must be adhered to and should never be considered wholly adequate for an organization without a thorough review. Additional requirements and specificity can be added to complement the requirements of law and regulation, but they should never conflict with them. For example, a law may require sensitive financial information to be encrypted, and an organization's policy could state that in accordance with the law all financial information will be encrypted. Furthermore, the agency may specify a standard strength and brand of encryption software to be used in order to achieve the required level of compliance with the law, while also providing for the additional layers of protection that the organization wants in place.

Privacy Requirements Compliance

Privacy laws and regulations pose confidentially challenges for the security practitioner. Personally identifiable information is becoming an extremely valuable commodity for marketers, as demonstrated by the tremendous growth of social networking sites based on demography and the targeted marketing activities that come with them. While valuable, this information can also become a liability for an organization which runs afoul of information privacy regulations and laws.

For example, the European Data Protection Directive only allows for the processing of personal data under specific circumstances such as:

- When processing is necessary for compliance with a legal action
- When processing is required to protect the life of the subject
- When the subject of the personal data has provided consent
- When the processing is performed within the law and scope of "public interest"

The four requirements listed reflect only a small portion of the directive. The directive further states what rights the subject has, such as objecting at any time to the processing of their personal data if the use is for direct marketing purposes. Recently, several Internet search companies and social media companies have been cited for not complying with this law. These organizations have been accused of using the personal data of the subject for direct marketing efforts without the subject's permission. The information security professional working in a marketing firm in the European Union must understand the impact of these requirements on how information will be processed, stored, and transmitted in their organization.

The "Directive 95/46 of the European Parliament and the Council of 24 October 1995 on the protection of individuals with regard to the processing of personal data and on the free movement of such data" (Data Protection Directive 95/46/EC) was established to provide a regulatory framework to guarantee secure and free movement of personal data across the national borders of the EU member countries, in addition to setting a baseline of security around personal information wherever it is stored, transmitted or processed.[16] The Directive contains 33 articles in 8 chapters. The Directive went into effect in October, 1998. This general Data Protection Directive has been complemented by other legal instruments, such as the e-Privacy Directive (Directive 2002/58/EC) for the communications sector.[17] There are also specific rules for the protection of personal data in police and judicial cooperation in criminal matters (Framework Decision 2008/977/JHA).[18]

The Data Protection Directive 95/46/EC clarifies the data protection elements that EU states must transpose into law. Each EU state regulates data protection and enforcement within its own jurisdiction. Additionally, data protection commissioners from the EU states participate in a working group together.

The Data Protection Directive 95/46/EC defines personal data as any information related to an "identified or identifiable natural person." The data controller must ensure compliance with the principles relating to data quality and legitimate reasons for data processing. Whenever personal data is collected, the data controller has information duties toward the data subject. The data controller also must implement appropriate technical and organizational measures against unlawful destruction, accidental loss, or unauthorized access, alteration, or disclosure.

The Directive establishes data subjects' rights as the following: the right to know who the data controller is, who the recipient of the data is, and the purpose of the processing; the right to have inaccurate data rectified; a right of recourse in the event of unlawful processing; and the right to withhold permission to use data in some circumstances. The EU Data Protection Directive also strengthens protections regarding the use of sensitive personal data such as health, sex life, and religious beliefs.

The regulatory framework can be enforced through either judicial remedies or administrative proceedings of the supervisory authority. EU member states' supervisory authorities are given investigative and intervening powers. These include the power to issue a ban on processing or to order blocking, erasure, and destruction of data. Any individual who has suffered damage resulting from an unlawful processing operation is entitled to receive compensation from the liable controller. The Data Protection Directive provides a mechanism by which transfers of personal data outside of the EU have to meet a processing level adequate to the degree prescribed by the directive's provisions.

In January 2012, after the Lisbon Treaty gave the EU the explicit competence to legislate on the protection of individuals with regard to the processing of their personal data, the Commission proposed a reform package comprising a general data protection regulation to replace Directive 95/46/EC and a directive to replace Framework Decision 2008/977/JHA.

The Parliament's committee on Civil Liberties, Justice, and Home Affairs adopted its reports on the basis of 4,000 amendments (to the Regulation) and 768 amendments (to the Directive). The Parliament adopted a position at first reading in March 2014. The key points of the Parliament's position as regards the Regulation are directly reproduced here:[19]

- A comprehensive approach to data protection, with a clear, single set of rules, which applies within and outside the Union

- A clarification of the concepts used (personal data, informed consent, data protection by design and default) and a strengthening of individuals' rights (e.g., as regards inter alia the right of access or the right to object to data processing)

- A more precise definition of the rules concerning the processing of personal data relating to some sectors (health, employment, and Social Security) or for some specific purposes (historical, statistical, scientific research or archives-related purposes)

- A clarification and a strengthening of the regime of sanctions
- A better and consistent enforcement of data protection rules (strengthened role of the corporate data protection officers, setting up of a European Data Protection Board, unified framework for all Data Protection Authorities, creation of a one-stop shop mechanism)
- A strengthening of the criteria for assessing the adequacy of protection offered in a third country

The proposed directive deals with the processing of personal data in the context of prevention, investigation, or prosecution, of criminal offences or the execution of criminal penalties. Parliament's position on the directive contains the key elements reproduced here:

- A clear definition of the data protection principles (the exceptions that have to be duly justified)
- The conditions to be complied with as regards the processing (e.g., lawful, fair, transparent and legitimate processing, and explicit purposes) and the transmission of personal data
- The setting up of an evaluation mechanism and of a data protection impact assessment
- A clear definition of profiling
- A strengthening of the regime for transferring personal data to third countries
- A clarification of the monitoring and enforcement powers of the Data Protection Authorities
- A new article on genetic data

The security practitioner needs to stay up to date on the latest developments such as those being pursued by the Parliament with regards to processing and handling of personal information in order to ensure that the compliance activities that they engage in are directed towards to support the required laws and regulations that are in force within the geographies that the enterprise operates within and that they are responsible for.

End-User Training

Security awareness is the knowledge and attitude members of an organization possess regarding the protection of the physical and, especially, information assets of that organization. Many organizations require formal security awareness training for all workers when they join the organization and periodically thereafter, usually annually.

SANS, through their Securing The Human project, offers online security awareness training that is free. It is comprised of approximately 43 modules averaging 3 minutes in length each, and is available in 28 languages. The content can be accessed at `http://www.securingthehuman.org/enduser`.

Topics covered in security awareness training traditionally will include

- The nature of sensitive material and physical assets such as trade secrets, privacy concerns, and classified government information

- The responsibilities of contractors and employees when handling sensitive information, which includes NDAs

- The requirements for properly handling sensitive material in physical form, including marking, transmission, storage, and destruction

- The proper techniques for protecting sensitive computer data, including password policy and two-factor authentication

- Understanding computer-based security concerns such as phishing, malware, and social engineering

- Workplace security, including building access, wearing of security badges, reporting of incidents, forbidden articles, etc.

- Knowing the repercussions of failing to properly protect information, including potential loss of employment, economic harm to the company, damage to individuals whose private records are divulged, and possible civil and criminal penalties

Public Key Infrastructure (PKI)

A public key infrastructure (PKI) is a set of system, software, and communication protocols required to use, manage, and control public key cryptography. It has three primary purposes: publish public keys/certificates, certify that a key is tied to an individual or entity, and provide verification of the validity of a public key.

The certificate authority (CA) "signs" an entity's digital certificate to certify that the certificate content accurately represents the certificate owner. There can be different levels of assurance implied by the CA signing the certificate, similar to forms of the physical identification of an individual can imply differing levels of trust. In the physical world, a credit card with a name on it has a differing level of authentication value than, say, a government-issued ID card. Any entity can claim to be anything it wants, but if the entity wants to provide a high level of assurance, it should provide identifying content in its certificate that is easily confirmed by third parties that are trusted by all parties involved. In the digital world, a Dun and Bradstreet number, credit report, or perhaps another form of trusted third party reference would be provided to the CA before certifying by signing the entity's certificate with a marking indicating the CA asserts a high level of trust of the entity. Now all the entities that trust the CA can now trust that the identity provided by a certificate is trustworthy.

The functions of a CA may be distributed among several specialized servers in a PKI. For example, server registration authorities (RAs) may be used to provide scalability and reliability of the PKI. RA servers provide the facility for entities to submit requests for certificate generation. The RA service is also responsible for ensuring the accuracy of certificate request content.

The CA can revoke certificates and provide an update service to the other members of the PKI via a certificate revocation list (CRL), which is a list of non-valid certificates that should not be accepted by any member of the PKI. The use of public key (asymmetric) cryptography has enabled more effective use of symmetric cryptography as well as several other important features, such as greater access control, nonrepudiation, and digital signatures.

So often, the biggest question is "who can be trusted?" How does one know that the public key being used to verify Terry's digital signature truly belongs to Terry or that the public key being used to send a confidential message to Pat is truly Pat's and not that of an attacker who has set himself up in the middle of the communications channel?

Public keys are by their very nature public. Many people include them on signature lines in e-mails, or organizations have them on their web servers so that customers can establish confidential communications with the employees of the organization, who they may never even meet. How does one know an imposter or attacker has not set up a rogue web server and is attracting communications that should have been confidential to his site instead of the real account, as in a phishing attack?

Setting up a trusted public directory of keys is one option. Each user must register with the directory service, and a secure manner of communications between the user and the directory would be set up. This would allow the user to change keys—or the directory to force the change of keys. The directory would publish and maintain the list of all active keys and also delete or revoke keys that are no longer trusted. This may happen if a person believes that her private key has been compromised or she leaves the employ of the organization. Any person wanting to communicate with a registered user of the directory could request the public key of the registered user from the directory.

An even higher level of trust is provided through the use of public key certificates. This can be done directly. Pat would send a certificate to Terry, or through a CA, which would act as a trusted third party and issue a certificate to both Pat and Terry containing the public key of the other party. This certificate is signed with the digital signature of the CA and can be verified by the recipients. The certification process binds identity information and a public key to an identity. The resultant document of this process is the public key certificate. A CA will adhere to the X.509 standards. This is part of the overall X.500 family of standards applying to directories. X.509 version 3 of the standard is the most common. Table 5.3 shows an example of an X.509 certificate issued by VeriSign.

TABLE 5.3 A X.509 certification issued by VeriSign

FIELD	DESCRIPTION OF CONTENTS
Algorithm used for the signature	Algorithm used to sign the certificate
Issuer name	X.500 name of CA
Period of Validity	
Start Date/End Date	
Subject's name	Owner of the public key
Subject's Public Key Information (algorithm, parameters, key)	Public key and algorithm used to create it
Issuer unique identifier	Optional field used in case the CA used more than one X.500 name
Subject's unique identifier	Optional field in case the public key owner has more than one X.500 name
Extensions	
Digital signature of CA	Hash of the certificate encrypted with the private key of the CA

Fundamental Key Management Concepts

Perhaps the most important part of any cryptographic implementation is key management. Control over the issuance, revocation, recovery, distribution, and history of cryptographic keys is of utmost importance to any organization relying on cryptography for secure communications and data protection. The information security practitioner should know the importance of Kerckhoff's law. Auguste Kerckhoff wrote: "a cryptosystem should be secure even if everything about the system, except the key, is public knowledge."[20] The key, therefore, is the true strength of the cryptosystem. The size of the key and the secrecy of the key are perhaps the two most important elements in a crypto implementation.

Advances in Key Management

Key management has become increasingly important due to critical business requirements for secure information sharing and collaboration in high-risk environments. As a result, developers are seeing the need to embed security, particularly cryptography, directly into the application or network device. However, the complexity and specialized nature of cryptography means increased risk if not implemented properly. To meet this challenge, a number of standardized key management specifications are being developed and implemented for use as a sort of key management "plug-in" for such products.

XML (Extensible Markup Language), the flexible data framework that allows applications to communicate on the Internet, has become the preferred infrastructure for e-commerce applications. All of those transactions require trust and security, making it mission-critical to devise common XML mechanisms for authenticating merchants, buyers, and suppliers to each other, and for digitally signing and encrypting XML documents such as contracts and payment transactions. XML-based standards and specifications have been in development for use in the field of key management systems. Such specifications and standards are then implemented within web services libraries, provided by vendors or by open source collaborative efforts.

One such specification is the XML Key Management Specification 2.0 (XKMS).[21] This specification defines protocols for distributing and registering public keys, suitable for use in conjunction with XML Digital Signatures[22] and XML Encryption.[23] XKMS, while very focused on key management, works in conjunction with other specifications that define protocols and services necessary to establishing and maintaining the trust needed for secure web transactions.[24] These basic mechanisms can be combined in various ways to accommodate building a wide variety of security models using a variety of cryptographic technologies. A goal of XKMS implementation is based on the assumption that simplicity helps developers avoid mistakes and, as such, increases the security of applications. The XKMS protocol consists of pairs of requests and responses. XKMS protocol messages share a common format that may be carried within a variety of protocols. However, XKMS messages transported via SOAP over HTTP is recommended for interoperability.

The two parts of the XML Key Management Specification 2.0 are the XML Key Information Service Specification (X-KISS) and the XML Key Registration Service Specification (X-KRSS). First, X-KISS describes a syntax that allows a client (i.e., application) to delegate part or all of the tasks required to process XML Signature `< ds:KeyInfo >` elements to a trust service. A key objective of the protocol design is to minimize the complexity of applications that use XML Digital Signatures. By becoming a client of the trust service, the application is relieved of the complexity and syntax of the underlying PKI used to establish trust relationships, which may be based upon a different specification such as X.509/PKIX, SPKI, PGP, Diffie–Hellman, or Elliptic Curve, and can be extended for other algorithms. The `< ds:KeyInfo >` element in an XML Digital Signature is an optional element that enables the recipient to obtain cryptography key-related data needed to validate the signature. The `< ds:KeyInfo >` element may contain the key itself, a key name, X.509 certificate, a PGP key identifier, chain of trust, revocation list info, in-band key distribution or key agreement data, and so on. As an option, a link to the location where the full `< ds:KeyInfo >` data set can be found can also be provided.

For example, if using certificates, DSA, RSA, X.509, PGP, and SPKI are values that can be used in the `< ds:KeyInfo >` element of an XML Digital Signature. An application (client of the XKMS) would learn what public key cryptographic algorithm is being used for the transaction by reading from a directory server the `< ds:KeyInfo >` element of an XML Digital Signature using the X-KISS protocol of XKMS 2.0.

Second, X-KRSS describes a protocol for registration of public key information. The key material can be generated by the X-KRSS, on request to support easier key recovery, or manually. The registration service can also be used to subsequently recover a private key. An application may request that the registration service (X-KRSS) bind information to a public key. The information bound may include a name, an identifier, or other attributes defined by the implementation. After first registering a key pair, the key pair is then usable along with the X-KISS or a PKI such as X.509v3.

The XKMS service shields the client application from the complexities of the underlying PKI such as:

- Handling of complex syntax and semantics (e.g., X.509v3)
- Retrieval of information from directory/data repository infrastructure
- Revocation status verification
- Construction and processing of trust chains

Additional information about the signer's public signing key (`< ds:KeyInfo >`) can be included inside the signature block, which can be used to help the verifier determine which public key certificate to select.

Information contained in the `< ds:KeyInfo >` element may or may not be cryptographically bound to the signature itself. Therefore, `< ds:KeyInfo >` element data can be replaced or extended without invalidating the digital signature. For example, Valerie signs a document and sends it to Jim with a `< ds:KeyInfo >` element that specifies only the signing key data. On receiving the message, Jim retrieves additional information required to validate the signature and adds this information into the `< ds:KeyInfo >` element when he passes the document on to Yolanda (see Figure 5.15).

The X-KISS Locate service resolves a `< ds:KeyInfo >` element but does not require the service to make an assertion concerning the validity of the binding between the data in the `< ds:KeyInfo >` element. The XKMS service can resolve the `< ds:KeyInfo >` element using local information store or may relay the request to other directory servers. For example, the XKMS service might resolve a `< ds:RetrievalMethod >` element (Figure 5.16) or act as a gateway to an underlying PKI based on a non-XML syntax (e.g., X.509v3).

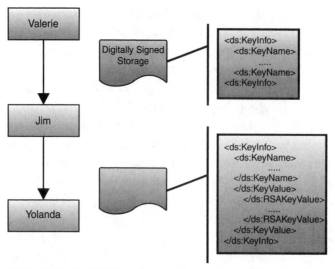

FIGURE 5.15 The XKMS service shields the client application from the complexities of the underlying PKI.

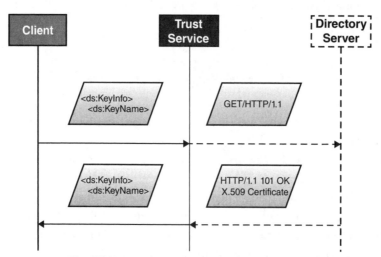

FIGURE 5.16 The SKMS service might resolve a <ds: Retrieval Method> element.

Encryption

Terry wants to send an encrypted e-mail to Pat but does not know Pat's encryption key. Terry can use both the S/MIME and PGP secure e-mail formats. Terry's client uses distinguished names (DNs) to locate the XKMS service that provides a locate service for keys bound to the domain example.com and then sends an XKMS locate request to the discovered XKMS service for a key bound to Pat@example.com and the S/MIME or PGP protocol. The application then verifies that the certificate obtained meets its trust criteria by standard certificate validation to a trusted root.

Pat receives the signed document from Terry, which specifies Terry's X.509v3 certificate but not the key value. Pat's e-mail client is not capable of processing X.509v3 certificates but can obtain the key parameters from the XKMS service by means of the locate service. Pat's e-mail client sends the < ds:Keyinfo > element to the location service requesting that the corresponding < KeyValue > element be returned. The location service does not report the revocation status or the trust level of the certificate. However, the service takes the X.509v3 certificate from the < ds:Keyinfo> element and sends the key values.

Standards for Financial Institutions

ANSI X9.17 was developed to address the need of financial institutions to transmit securities and funds securely using an electronic medium. Specifically, it describes the means to ensure the secrecy of keys. The ANSI X9.17 approach is based on a hierarchy of keys. At the bottom of the hierarchy are data keys (DKs). Data keys are used to encrypt and decrypt messages. They are given short lifespans, such as one message or one connection. At the top of the hierarchy are master key-encrypting keys (KKMs).

KKMs, which must be distributed manually, are afforded longer lifespans than data keys. Using the two-tier model, the KKMs are used to encrypt the data keys. The data keys are then distributed electronically to encrypt and decrypt messages. The two-tier model may be enhanced by adding another layer to the hierarchy. In the three-tier model, the KKMs are not used to encrypt data keys directly but to encrypt other key-encrypting keys (KKs). The KKs, which are exchanged electronically, are used to encrypt the data keys.

Segregation of Duties

Another aspect of key management is maintaining control over sensitive cryptographic keys that enforce the need-to-know principle as part of a business process. For example, in many business environments, employees are required to maintain separation or segregation of duties. In other words, in such environments no one person is allowed to have full control over all phases of an entire transaction without some level of accountability enforcement. The more negotiable the asset under protection, the greater the need for the proper segregation of duties is. Especially in the area of cryptography, this is a business concern. Imagine the damage that could be done by a single dishonest person if allowed unchecked access to cryptographic keys that, for example, unlock high risk, high value, or high liquidity information such as customer financial accounts.

The segregation of duties is used as a cross-check to ensure that misuse and abuse of assets, due to innocent mistake or malicious intent, can be efficiently detected and prevented. This is an important confidentiality and integrity principle that is often misunderstood, judging by news reports of embezzlement schemes, primarily by employee insiders, that go undetected for long amounts of time. The segregation of duties is primarily a business policy and access control issue. However, it may not be possible for smaller organizations, due to personnel constraints, to perform the segregation of all duties, so other compensating controls may have to be used to achieve the same control objective. Such compensating controls include monitoring of activities, audit trails, and management supervision. Two mechanisms necessary to implement high-integrity cryptographic operations environments where separation of duties is paramount are dual control and split knowledge.

Dual Control   *Dual control* is implemented as a security procedure that requires two or more persons to come together and collude to complete a process. In a cryptographic system the two (or more) persons would each supply a unique key that, when taken together, performs a cryptographic process. Split knowledge is the other complementary access control principle to dual control.

Split Knowledge   *Split knowledge* is the unique "what each must bring" and joined together when implementing dual control. To illustrate, a box containing petty cash is secured by one combination lock and one keyed lock. One employee is given the combination to the combo lock and another employee has possession of the correct key to the keyed lock. In order to get the cash out of the box, both employees must be present at the cash box at the same time. One cannot open the box without the other. This is the aspect of dual control.

On the other hand, split knowledge is exemplified here by the different objects (the combination to the combo lock and the correct physical key), both of which are unique and necessary, that each brings to the meeting. Split knowledge focuses on the uniqueness of separate objects that must be joined together. Dual control has to do with forcing the collusion of at least two or more persons to combine their split knowledge to gain access to an asset. Both split knowledge and dual control complement each other and are necessary functions that implement the segregation of duties in high-integrity cryptographic environments (see Table 5.4).

In cryptographic terms, one could say dual control and split knowledge are properly implemented if no one person has access to or knowledge of the content of the complete cryptographic key being protected by the two processes. The sound implementation of dual control and split knowledge in a cryptographic environment necessarily means that the quickest way to break the key would be through the best attack known for the algorithm of that key. The principles of dual control and split knowledge primarily apply to access to plaintext keys. Access to cryptographic keys used for encrypting and decrypting data or access to keys that are encrypted under a master key (which may or may not be maintained under dual control and split knowledge) do not require dual control and split knowledge.

TABLE 5.4 **Split knowledge and dual control complement each other and are necessary functions that implement segregation of duties in high-integrity cryptographic environments.**

BAD EXAMPLES	PROBLEM	HOW TO MAKE DUAL CONTROL/SPLIT KNOWLEDGE COMPLIANT
Splitting a key "in half" to form two parts.	Dual control but no split knowledge (assuming two people each with a unique key half). One person could determine the key by brute forcing the other key half space.	Each person maintains control of his or her half of the key. Protect each half with a unique PIN or passphrase.
Storing key components on two cryptographic tokens with no further user authentication.	No enforcement of split knowledge (i.e., no unique authentication method for individual accountability).	Each person maintains control of his individual token/smartcard. Protect each smartcard with unique PIN/passphrase.
Storing a key on a single smartcard (or cryptographic token) that requires one or more passphrases to access.	No dual control enforcement. Single card cannot be maintained by two or more persons.	Distribute cryptographic token to each person. Protect token with unique PIN/passphrase.

Dual control and split knowledge can be summed up as the determination of any part of a key being protected must require the collusion between two or more persons with each supplying unique cryptographic materials that must be joined together to access the protected key. Any feasible method to violate the axiom means that the principles of dual control and split knowledge are not being upheld.

There are a number of applications that implement aspects of dual control and split knowledge in a scalable manner. For example, a PGP commercial product based on the OpenPGP standard has features for splitting public keys that are not part of the OpenPGP standard.[25] These features use Blakely–Shamir secret sharing. This is an algorithm that allows the user to take a piece of data and break it into N shares, of which K of them are needed to retrieve the original data. Using a simple version of this approach, the user could break the data into three shares, two of which are needed to get the data back. In a more complex version, the user could require 3 of 6 or even 5 of 12 shares to retrieve the original data, with each key share protected with a unique passphrase known only to the key holder.

Such a solution uses the basic form of secret sharing and shares the private key. This process permits a key pair to be controlled by a group of people, with some subgroup required to reconstitute and use the key. Other systems are based on key holders answering a series of questions in order to recover passwords needed to unlock a protected plaintext key.

To re-create the key under protection, a user can create a set of questions that contain some information only the user would know. The key is split to those questions, with some set of them being required to synthesize the key. Not only does the user provide individualized security questions that are unique to each key holder but also decides how many of the questions need to be answered correctly to retrieve the key under protection, by having it reconstructed from the split parts.

Management and Distribution of Keys

The details of key creation using various algorithms were discussed earlier in this domain in the "Foundational Concepts" section. However, from a key management perspective there are a number of issues that pertain to scalability and cryptographic key integrity.

Automated Key Generation

Mechanisms used to automatically generate strong cryptographic keys can be used to deploy keys as part of key lifecycle management. Effective automated key generation systems are designed for user transparency as well as complete cryptographic key policy enforcement.

Truly Random

For a key to be truly effective, it must have an appropriately high work factor. That is to say, the amount of time and effort (work by an attacker) needed to break the key must be sufficient so that it at least delays its discovery for as long as the information being protected needs to be kept confidential. One factor that contributes to strong keys, which have a high work factor, is the level of randomness of the bits that make up the key.

Random

As discussed earlier, cryptographic keys are essentially strings of numbers. The numbers used in making up the key need to be unpredictable so that an attacker cannot easily guess the key and then expose the protected information. Thus, the randomness of the numbers that comprise a key plays an important role in the lifecycle of a cryptographic key. In the context of cryptography, randomness is the quality of lacking predictability. Randomness intrinsically generated by a computer system is also called pseudo randomness. Pseudo randomness is the quality of an algorithm for generating a sequence of numbers that approximates the properties of random numbers. Computer circuits and software libraries are used to perform the actual generation of pseudo random key values. Computers and software libraries are well known as weak sources of randomness.

Computers are inherently designed for predictability, not randomness. Computers are so thoroughly deterministic that they have a hard time generating high-quality randomness. Therefore, special-purpose-built hardware and software called *random number generators*, or RNGs, are needed for cryptography applications. The U.S. federal government provides recommendations on deterministic random number generators through the NIST.[26] An international standard for random number generation suitable for cryptographic systems is sponsored by the International Organization for Standardization as ISO 18031.[27] A rigorous statistical analysis of the output is often needed to have confidence in such RNG algorithms. A random number generator based solely on deterministic computation done solely by computer cannot be regarded as a true random number generator sufficient in lack of predictability for cryptographic applications, since its output is inherently predictable.

There are various methods for ensuring the appropriate level of randomness in pseudo random keys. The approach found in most business-level cryptographic products uses computational algorithms that produce long sequences of apparently random results, which are in fact completely determined by a shorter initial value, known as a seed or key. The use of initialization vectors and seed values that are concatenated onto computer-generated keys increases the strength of keys by adding additional uniqueness to a random key material. The seed value or initialization vector is the number input as a starting point for an algorithm. The seed or IV can be created either manually or by an external source of randomness, such as radio frequency noise, randomly sampled values from a switched circuit, or other atomic and subatomic physical phenomenon. To provide a degree of randomness intermediate between specialized hardware on the one hand and algorithmic generation on the other, some security-related computer software requires the user to input a lengthy string of mouse movements or keyboard input.

Regarding manually created seed or initialization values, many may be familiar with this process if they have ever set up a wireless network with encryption using a WEP/WPA key. In most cases, when configuring wireless encryption on a wireless adapter or router, the user is asked to enter a password or variable-length "key" that is used by the wireless device to create cryptographic keys for encrypting data across the wireless network. This "key" is really a seed or initialization value that will be concatenated to the computer-generated key portion that together comprise the keying material to generate a key consisting of appropriate amount of pseudo-randomness to make it hard for an attacker to easily guess and thus "breaking" the key.

The important role randomness plays in key creation is illustrated by the following example. One method of generating a two-key encryption key set making a private component and a public component is comprised of the following steps:

1. Generate a first pseudo-random prime number.

2. Generate a second pseudo-random prime number.

3. Produce a modulus by multiplying the first pseudo-random number by the second pseudo-random prime number.

4. Generate a first exponent by solving a first modular arithmetic equation.

5. Generate a second exponent that is a modular inverse to the first exponent, by solving a second modular arithmetic equation and securely storing either the first exponent or the second exponent in at least one memory location.

Key Length

Key length is another important aspect of key management to consider when generating cryptographic keys. Key length is the size of a key, usually measured in bits or bytes, which a cryptographic algorithm uses in ciphering or deciphering protected information. Keys are used to control how an algorithm operates so that only the correct key can decipher the information. The resistance to successful attack against the key and the algorithm, aspects of their cryptographic security, is of concern when choosing key lengths. An algorithm's key length is distinct from its cryptographic security. Cryptographic security is a logarithmic measure of the fastest known computational attack on the algorithm, also measured in bits.

The security of an algorithm cannot exceed its key length. Therefore, it is possible to have a very long key that still provides low security. As an example, three-key (56 bits per key) Triple DES can have a key length of 168 bits but, due to the meet-in-the-middle attack, the effective security that it provides is at most 112 bits. However, most symmetric algorithms are designed to have security equal to their key length. A natural inclination is to use the longest key possible, which may make the key more difficult to break. However, the longer the key, the more computationally expensive the encrypting and decrypting process can be. The goal is to make breaking the key cost more (in terms of effort, time, and resources) than the worth of the information being protected and, if possible, not a penny more (to do more would not be economically sound).

The effectiveness of asymmetric cryptographic systems depends on the hard-to-solve nature of certain mathematical problems such as prime integer factorization. These problems are time-consuming to solve but usually faster than trying all possible keys by brute force. Thus, asymmetric algorithm keys must be longer for equivalent resistance to attack than symmetric algorithm keys.

RSA Security claims that 1024-bit RSA keys are equivalent in strength to 80-bit symmetric keys, 2048-bit RSA keys to 112-bit symmetric keys, and 3072-bit RSA keys to 128-bit symmetric keys. RSA claims that 2048-bit keys are sufficient until 2030. An RSA key length of 3072 bits should be used if security is required beyond 2030.[28] NIST key management guidelines further suggest that 15,360-bit RSA keys are equivalent in strength to 256-bit symmetric keys.[29]

ECC can secure with shorter keys than those needed by other asymmetric key algorithms. NIST guidelines state that elliptic curve keys should be twice the length of equivalent strength symmetric key algorithms. For example, a 224-bit elliptic curve key would have roughly the same strength as a 112-bit symmetric key. These estimates assume no major breakthroughs in solving the underlying mathematical problems that ECC is based on.

Key Wrapping and Key Encrypting Keys

One role of key management is to ensure that the same key used in encrypting a message by a sender is the same key used to decrypt the message by the intended receiver. Thus, if Terry and Pat wish to exchange encrypted messages, each must be equipped to decrypt received messages and to encrypt sent messages. If they use a cipher, they will need appropriate keys. The problem is how to exchange whatever keys or other information are needed so that no one else can obtain a copy.

One solution is to protect the session key with a special purpose long-term use key called a key encrypting key (KEK). KEKs are used as part of key distribution or key exchange. The process of using a KEK to protect session keys is called *key wrapping*. Key wrapping uses symmetric ciphers to securely encrypt (thus encapsulating) a plaintext key along with any associated integrity information and data. One application for key wrapping is protecting session keys in untrusted storage or when sending over an untrusted transport. Key wrapping or encapsulation using a KEK can be accomplished using either symmetric or asymmetric ciphers. If the cipher is a symmetric KEK, both the sender and the receiver will need a copy of the same key. If using an asymmetric cipher, with public/private key properties, to encapsulate a session key, both the sender and the receiver will need the other's public key.

Protocols such as SSL, PGP, and S/MIME use the services of KEKs to provide session key confidentiality, integrity, and sometimes to authenticate the binding of the session key originator and the session key itself to make sure the session key came from the real sender and not an attacker.

Key Distribution

Keys can be distributed in a number of ways. For example, two people who wish to perform key exchange can use a medium other than that through which secure messages will be sent. This is called *out-of-band* key exchange. If the two or more parties will send secure messages via e-mail, they may choose to meet up with each other or send via courier. The concept of out of band key exchange is not very scalable beyond a few people. A more scalable method of exchanging keys is through the use of a PKI key server. A key server is a central repository of public keys of members of a group of users interested in exchanging keys to facilitate electronic transactions. Public key encryption provides a means to allow members of a group to conduct secure transactions spontaneously. The receiver's public key certificate, which contains the receiver's public key, is retrieved by the sender from the key server and is used as part of a public key encryption scheme, such as S/MIME, PGP, or even SSL to encrypt a message and send it. The digital certificate is the medium that contains the public key of each member of the group and makes the key portable, scalable, and easier to manage than an out-of-band method of key exchange.

Key Distribution Centers

Recall the formula used before to calculate the number of symmetric keys needed for users: $n(n - 1)/2$. This necessitates the setup of directories, public key infrastructures, or key distribution centers.

The use of a key distribution center (KDC) for key management requires the creation of two types of keys. The first are master keys, which are secret keys shared by each user and the KDC. Each user has his own master key, and it is used to encrypt the traffic between the user and the KDC. The second type of key is a session key, created when needed, used for the duration of the communications session, and then discarded once the session is complete. When a user wants to communicate with another user or an application, the KDC sets up the session key and distributes it to each user for use. An implementation of this solution is found in Kerberos. A large organization may even have several KDCs, and they can be arranged so that there are global KDCs that coordinate the traffic between the local KDCs.

Because master keys are integral to the trust and security relationship between the users and hosts, such keys should never be used in compromised situations or where they may become exposed. For encrypting files or communications, separate non-master keys should be used. Ideally, a master key is never visible in the clear; it is buried within the equipment itself, and it is not accessible to the user.

Key Storage and Destruction

The proper storing and changing of cipher keys are important aspects of key management and are essential to the effective use of cryptography for security. Ultimately, the security of information protected by cryptography directly depends on the protection afforded by the keys. All keys need to be protected against modification, and secret and private keys need to be protected against unauthorized disclosure. Methods for protecting stored keying material include trusted, tamperproof hardware security modules, passphrase protected smart cards, key wrapping the session keys using long-term storage KEKs, splitting cipher keys and storing in physically separate storage locations, protecting keys using strong passwords/passphrases, key expiry, and the like.

In order to guard against a long-term cryptanalytic attack, every key must have an expiration date after which it is no longer valid. The key length must be long enough to make the chances of cryptanalysis before key expiration extremely small. The validity period for a key pair may also depend on the circumstances in which the key is used. A signature verification program should check for expiration and should not accept a message signed with an expired key. The fact that computer hardware continues to improve makes it prudent to replace expired keys with newer, longer keys every few years. Key replacement enables one to take advantage of any hardware improvements to increase the security of the cryptosystem. According to NIST's "Guideline for Implementing Cryptography In the Federal Government," additional guidance for storage of cipher keys include the following:[30]

- All centrally stored data that is related to user keys should be signed or have a MAC applied to it (MACed) for integrity and encrypted if confidentiality is required (all user secret keys and CA private keys should be encrypted). Individual key records in a database—as well as the entire database—should be signed or MACed and encrypted. To enable tamper detection, each individual key record should be signed or MACed so that its integrity can be checked before allowing that key to be used in a cryptographic function.

- Backup copies should be made of central/root keys, since the compromise or loss of those components could prevent access to keys in the central database and possibly deny system users the ability to decrypt data or perform signature verifications.

- Provide key recovery capabilities. There must be safeguards to ensure that sensitive records are neither irretrievably lost by the rightful owners nor accessed by unauthorized individuals. Key recovery capabilities provide these functions.

- Archive user keys for a sufficiently long crypto period. A crypto period is the time during which a key can be used to protect information; it may extend well beyond the lifetime of a key that is used to apply cryptographic protection (where the lifetime is the time during which a key can be used to generate a signature or perform encryption). Keys may be archived for a lengthy period (on the order of decades) so that they can be used to verify signatures and decrypt ciphertext.

Among the factors affecting the risk of exposure are the following:[31]

- The strength of the cryptographic mechanisms (e.g., the algorithm, key length, block size, and mode of operation)

- The embodiment of the mechanisms (e.g., FIPS 140−2 Level 4 implementation, or software implementation on a personal computer)

- The operating environment (e.g., secure limited access facility, open office environment, or publicly accessible terminal)

- The volume of information flow or the number of transactions

- The security life of the data

- The security function (e.g., data encryption, digital signature, key production or derivation, key protection)

- The re-keying method (e.g., keyboard entry, re-keying using a key loading device where humans have no direct access to key information, remote re-keying within a PKI)

- The key update or key derivation process

- The number of nodes in a network that share a common key

- The number of copies of a key and the distribution of those copies

- The threat to the information (e.g., whom the information is protected from and what are their perceived technical capabilities and financial resources to mount an attack).

In general, short crypto periods enhance security. For example, some cryptographic algorithms might be less vulnerable to cryptanalysis if the adversary has only a limited amount of information encrypted under a single key. Caution should be used when deleting keys that are no longer needed. A simple deletion of the keying material might not completely obliterate the information. For example, erasing the information might require overwriting that information multiple times with other non-related information, such as random bits or all zero or one bits. Keys stored in memory for a long time can become "burned in." This can be mitigated by splitting the key into components that are frequently updated, as shown in Figure 5.17.

Key Type	Crypto Period	
	Originator Usage Period (OUP)	Recipient Usage Period
1. Private Signature Key	1-3 Years	
2. Public Signature Key	Several Years (Depends on Key Size)	
3. Symmetric Authentication Key	≤ 2 Years	≤ OUP + 3 Years
4. Private Authentication Key	1-2 Years	
5. Public Authentication Key	1-2 Years	
6. Symmetric Data Encryption Keys	≤ 2 Years	≤ OUP + 3 Years
7. Symmetric Key Wrapping Keys	≤ 2 Years	≤ OUP + 3 Years
8. Symmetric and Asymmetric RNG Keys	Upon Reseeding	
9. Symmetric Master Key	About 1 Year	
10. Private Transport Key	≤ 2 Years	
11. Public Key Transport Key	1-2 Years	

FIGURE 5.17 Recommended crypto periods for key types

On the other hand, where manual key distribution methods are subject to human error and frailty, more frequent key changes might actually increase the risk of exposure. In these cases, especially when very strong cryptography is employed, it may be more prudent to have fewer, well-controlled manual key distributions rather than more frequent, poorly controlled manual key distributions. Secure automated key distribution, where key generation and exchange are protected by appropriate authentication, access, and integrity controls, may be a compensating control in such environments.

Users with different roles should have keys with lifetimes that take into account the different roles and responsibilities, the applications for which the keys are used, and the security services that are provided by the keys (user/data authentication, confidentiality, data integrity, etc.). Reissuing keys should not be done so often that it becomes excessively burdensome; however, it should be performed often enough to minimize the loss caused by a possible key compromise.

Handle the deactivation/revocation of keys so that data signed prior to a compromise date (or date of loss) can be verified. When a signing key is designated as "lost" or "compromised," signatures generated prior to the specified date may still need to be verified in the future. Therefore, a signature verification capability may need to be maintained for lost or compromised keys. Otherwise, all data previously signed with a lost or compromised key would have to be re-signed.

Cost of Certificate Replacement/Revocation

In some cases, the costs associated with changing digital certificates and cryptographic keys are painfully high. Examples include decryption and subsequent re-encryption of very large databases, decryption and re-encryption of distributed databases, and revocation and replacement of a very large number of keys, e.g., where there are very large numbers of geographically and organizationally distributed key holders. In such cases, the expense of the security measures necessary to support longer crypto periods may be justified, e.g., costly and inconvenient physical, procedural, and logical access security; and use of cryptography strong enough to support longer crypto periods even where this may result in significant additional processing overhead.

In other cases, the crypto period may be shorter than would otherwise be necessary; for example, keys may be changed frequently in order to limit the period of time the key management system maintains status information. On the other hand, a user losing their private key would require that the lost key be revoked so that an unauthorized user cannot use it. It would be a good practice to use a master decryption key (additional decryption key in PGP) or another key recovery mechanism to guard against losing access to the data encrypted under the lost key. Another reason to revoke a certificate is when an employee leaves the company or, in some cases, when changing job roles, as in the case of someone moving to a more trusted job role, which may require a different level of accountability, access to higher risk data, and so on.

Key Recovery

A lost key may mean a crisis to an organization. The loss of critical data or backups may cause widespread damage to operations and even financial ruin or penalties. There are several methods of key recovery, such as common trusted directories or a policy that requires all cryptographic keys to be registered with the security department. Some people have even been using steganography to bury their passwords in pictures or other locations on their machine to prevent someone from finding their password file. Others use password wallets or other tools to hold all of their passwords.

One method is multiparty key recovery. A user would write her private key on a piece of paper and then divide the key into two or more parts. Each part would be sealed in an envelope. The user would give one envelope each to trusted people with instructions that the envelope was only to be opened in an emergency where the organization needed access to the user's system or files (disability or death of the user). In case of an emergency, the holders of the envelopes would report to human resources, where the envelopes could be opened and the key reconstructed. The user would usually give the envelopes to trusted people at different management levels and different parts of the company to reduce the risk of collusion.

Key recovery should also be conducted with the privacy of the individual in mind. If a private individual used encryption to protect the confidentiality of some information, it may be legally protected according to local laws. In some situations, a legal order may be required to retrieve the key and decrypt the information.

Key Escrow

Key escrow is the process of ensuring a third party maintains a copy of a private key or key needed to decrypt information. Key escrow also should be considered mandatory for most organizations' use of cryptography, as encrypted information belongs to the organization and not the individual; however, often an individual's key is used to encrypt the information. There must be explicit trust between the key escrow provider and the parties involved as the escrow provider now holds a copy of the private key and could use it to reveal information. Conditions of key release must be explicitly defined and agreed upon by all parties.

Web of Trust

In cryptography, a *web of trust* is a concept used in PGP, GnuPG, and other OpenPGP-compatible systems to establish the authenticity of the binding between a public key and its owner. Its decentralized trust model is an alternative to the centralized trust model of a public key infrastructure (PKI), which relies exclusively on a certificate authority (or a hierarchy of such). As with computer networks, there are many independent webs of trust, and any user (through their identity certificate) can be a part of, and a link between, multiple webs. The web of trust concept was first put forth by PGP creator Phil Zimmermann in 1992 in the manual for PGP version 2.0:

> As time goes on, you will accumulate keys from other people that you may want to designate as trusted introducers. Everyone else will each choose their own trusted introducers. And everyone will gradually accumulate and distribute with their key a collection of certifying signatures from other people, with the expectation that anyone receiving it will trust at least one or two of the signatures. This will cause the emergence of a decentralized fault-tolerant web of confidence for all public keys.

Secure Protocols

IP Security (IPSec) is a suite of protocols for communicating securely with IP by providing mechanisms for authenticating and encryption. Implementation of IPSec is mandatory in IPv6, and many organizations are using it over IPv4. Further, IPSec can be implemented in two modes, one that is appropriate for end-to-end protection and one that safeguards traffic between networks. Standard IPSec only authenticates hosts with each other. If an organization requires users to authenticate, they must employ a nonstandard proprietary IPSec implementation or use IPSec over L2TP (Layer 2 Tunneling Protocol). The latter approach uses L2TP to authenticate the users and encapsulate IPSec packets within an L2TP tunnel. Because IPSec interprets the change of IP address within packet headers as an attack, NAT does not work well with IPSec. To resolve the incompatibility of the two protocols, NAT-Transversal (aka NAT-T) encapsulates IPSec within UDP port 4500 (see RFC 3948 for details).[32]

Authentication Header (AH)

The authentication header (AH) is used to prove the identity of the sender and ensure that the transmitted data has not been tampered with. Before each packet (headers + data) is transmitted, a hash value of the packet's contents (except for the fields that are expected to change when the packet is routed) based on a shared secret is inserted in the last field of the AH. The endpoints negotiate which hashing algorithm to use and the shared secret when they establish their security association. To help thwart replay attacks (when a legitimate session is retransmitted to gain unauthorized access), each packet that is transmitted during a security association has a sequence number, which is stored in the AH. In transport mode, the AH is shimmed between the packet's IP and TCP header. The AH helps ensure integrity, not confidentiality. Encryption is implemented through the use of encapsulating security payload (ESP).

Encapsulating Security Payload (ESP)

The encapsulating security payload (ESP) encrypts IP packets and ensures their integrity. ESP contains four sections:

- **ESP Header**—Contains information showing which security association to use and the packet sequence number. Like the AH, the ESP sequences every packet to thwart replay attacks.

- **ESP Payload**—The payload contains the encrypted part of the packet. If the encryption algorithm requires an initialization vector (IV), it is included with the payload. The endpoints negotiate which encryption to use when the security association is established. Because packets must be encrypted with as little overhead as possible, ESP typically uses a symmetric encryption algorithm.

- **ESP Trailer**—May include padding (filler bytes) if required by the encryption algorithm or to align fields.

- **Authentication**—If authentication is used, this field contains the integrity check value (hash) of the ESP packet. As with the AH, the authentication algorithm is negotiated when the endpoints establish their security association.

Security Associations

A security association (SA) defines the mechanisms that an endpoint will use to communicate with its partner. All SAs cover transmissions in one direction only. A second SA must be defined for two-way communication. Mechanisms that are defined in the SA include the encryption and authentication algorithms and whether to use the AH or ESP protocol. Deferring the mechanisms to the SA, as opposed to specifying them in the protocol, allows the communicating partners to use the appropriate mechanisms based on situational risk.

Transport Mode and Tunnel Mode

Endpoints communicate with IPSec using either transport or tunnel mode. In transport mode, the IP payload is protected. This mode is mostly used for end-to-end protection, for example, between client and server. In tunnel mode, the IP payload and its IP header are protected. The entire protected IP packet becomes a payload of a new IP packet and header. Tunnel mode is often used between networks, such as with firewall-to-firewall VPNs.

Internet Key Exchange (IKE)

Internet key exchange allows communicating partners to prove their identity to each other and establish a secure communication channel, and is applied as an authentication component of IPSec. IKE uses two phases:

Phase 1   In this phase, the partners authenticate with each other, using one of the following:

- **Shared Secret**—A key that is exchanged by humans via telephone, fax, encrypted e-mail, etc.

- **Public Key Encryption**—Digital certificates are exchanged.

- **Revised Mode of Public Key Encryption**—To reduce the overhead of public key encryption, a nonce (a cryptographic function that refers to a number or bit string used only once, in security engineering) is encrypted with the communicating partner's public key, and the peer's identity is encrypted with symmetric encryption using the nonce as the key.

Next, IKE establishes a temporary security association and secure tunnel to protect the rest of the key exchange.

Phase 2   The peers' security associations are established, using the secure tunnel and temporary SA created at the end of phase 1.

High Assurance Internet Protocol Encryptor (HAIPE)

Based on IPSec, High Assurance Internet Protocol Encryptor (HAIPE) possesses additional restrictions and enhancements, for instance, the ability to encrypt multicast data using high-assurance hardware encryption, which requires that the same key be manually loaded on all communicating devices. HAIPE is an extension of IPSec that would be used for highly secure communications such as those employed by military applications.

Secure Sockets Layer/Transport Layer Security (SSL/TLS)

Secure sockets layer/transport layer security (SSL/TLS) is primarily used to encrypt confidential data sent over an insecure network such as the Internet. In the HTTPS protocol, the types of data encrypted include URL, HTTP header, cookies, and data submitted through forms. A web page secured with SSL/TLS has a URL that begins with `https://`.

According to the Microsoft TechNet site, "the SSL/TLS security protocol is layered between the application protocol layer and TCP/IP layer, where it can secure and then send application data to the transport layer. Because it works between the application layer and the TCP/IP layer, SSL/TLS can support multiple application layer protocols.

"The SSL/TLS protocol can be divided into two layers. The first layer is the handshake protocol layer, which consists of three sub-protocols: the handshake protocol, the change cipher spec protocol, and the alert protocol. The second layer is the record protocol layer. Figure 5.18 illustrates the various layers and their components.

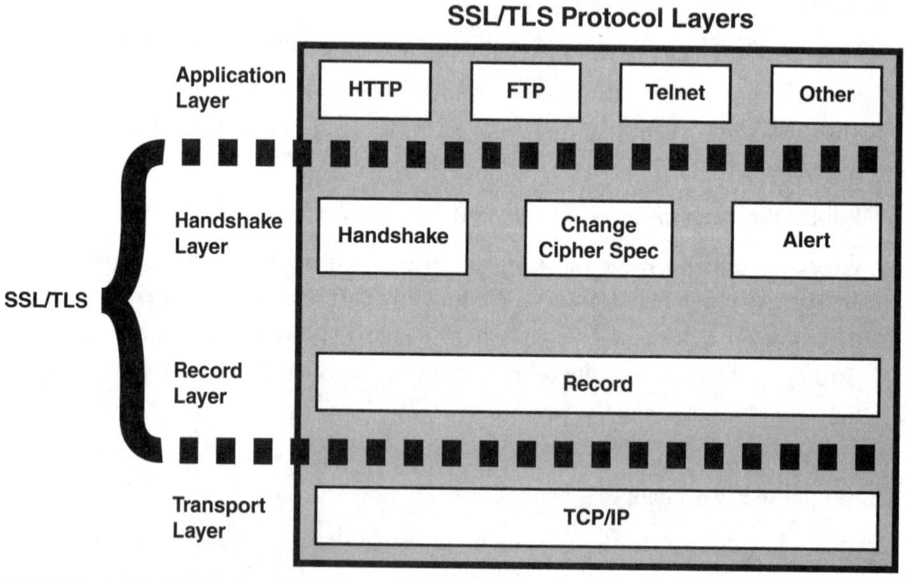

FIGURE 5.18 SSL/TLS protocol layers

"SSL/TLS uses both symmetric key and asymmetric key encryption. SSL/TLS uses public key encryption to authenticate the server to the client, and optionally the client to the server. Public key cryptography is also used to establish a session key. The session key is used in symmetric algorithms to encrypt the bulk of the data. This combines the benefit of asymmetric encryption for authentication with the faster, less processor-intensive symmetric key encryption for the bulk data."[33]

Secure/Multipurpose Internet Mail Extensions (S/MIME)[34]

According to the Microsoft TechNet site, "Secure/Multipurpose Internet Mail Extensions (S/MIME) is a widely accepted method, or more precisely a protocol, for sending digitally signed and encrypted messages. S/MIME allows you to encrypt e-mails and digitally sign them. When you use S/MIME with an e-mail message, it helps the people who receive that message to be certain that what they see in their inbox is the exact message that started with the sender. It will also help people who receive messages to be certain that the message came from the specific sender and not from someone pretending to be the sender. To do this, S/MIME provides for cryptographic security services such as authentication, message integrity, and non-repudiation of origin (using digital signatures). It also helps enhance privacy and data security (using encryption) for electronic messaging."[35]

GOING HANDS-ON WITH CRYPTOGRAPHY— CRYPTOGRAPHY EXERCISE

Cryptography is a modern cornerstone of secure information storage and transmission. This exercise is designed to provide the security practitioner with an overview of public key infrastructure using Gnu Privacy Guard (GPG).

Requirements

The following items are necessary to perform this exercise:

- An Internet-accessible system capable of running the following software programs:
  - Claws Mail (`http://www.claws-mail.org/downloads.php?section=downloads`)
  - Thunderbird Mail (`https://www.mozilla.org/en-US/thunderbird/`)
- Free e-mail accounts from Yahoo!, Gmail, or any other provider that has a web-mail interface.

Be sure to use different random account names than those listed in the exercise.

Setup

For this exercise two simulated users will be present. Andy will be the first user, and Rae will be the second. They both have a need to communicate securely through e-mail with each other. They have never met in person and therefore have never had a chance to exchange a synchronous encryption key with each other. They suspect PKI might be able to help them.

Set up the first user account by setting up a free e-mail account. (Andy will use Gmail [andysscp@gmail.com] for this example, and Rae will use Hotmail [raesscp@outlook.com] for each user.) You'll notice they used addresses that do not include their real names. They have a need for discretion and confidentiality in their work!

Once that is completed, download each software package (Claws and Thunderbird) from the download sites.

First User E-mail Setup

For this example the fictitious Andy account (andysscp@gmail.com) is going to use the Claws e-mail client. Since Andy is using Claws, he will need to ensure he has installed the GnuPG core package first. (See Figure 5.19.) Download the system-appropriate GnuPG package from `https://www.gnupg.org/download/index.html`.

NOTE The Windows version of GnuPG is found at `http://gpg4win.org/download.html`, and the Full version contains Claws already. If installing the Windows version, ensure Claws is selected as part of the default settings for install.

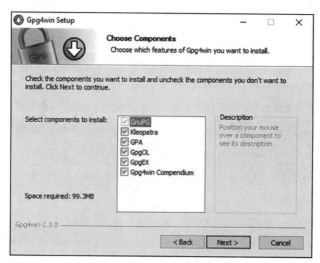

FIGURE 5.19 **Choosing components during GnuPG setup**

---

1. During the first launch of Claws, it will ask for account information. Choose IMAP and auto-configure. See Figure 5.20.

2. Next configure the SMTP settings. See Figure 5.21.

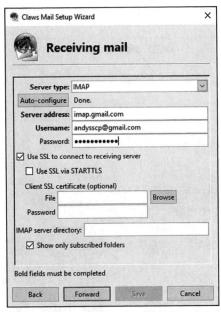

FIGURE 5.20 Setting up Claws account information

FIGURE 5.21 SMTP server setup in Claws

3. Click Forward and then Save. Depending on the e-mail provider, an SSL certificate error may be present. Since this is simply an exercise, click Accept and Save to continue to the main mailbox.

4. Once you open that mailbox, a message warning about keys should pop up, as shown in Figure 5.22.

FIGURE 5.22 **No PGP key warning**

5. Click Yes to create a new key pair. On the screen that follows, create a new passphrase for the encryption keys. See Figure 5.23. This should be different than the passphrase developed for the e-mail account.

6. Once the password is confirmed, a key creation dialog box will prompt the user to randomly move the mouse to help create entropy for the encryption key pair. Once complete, the user is given the option to publish the public key to a keyserver. Click Yes and upload Andy's public key to a key server.

In Windows you may get an error stating the key cannot be exported. If this error comes up, perform steps 7 through 9 to publish the public key. Otherwise, skip to step 10.

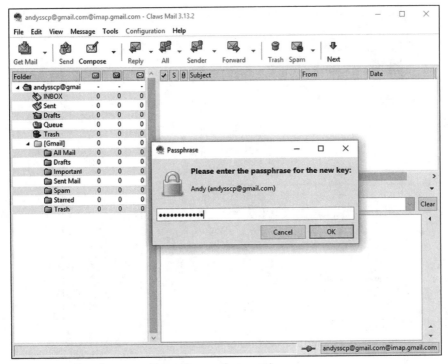

FIGURE 5.23 Entering a passphrase for new key creation

7. Click Start ➪ All Apps, then locate and click on Gpg4win, and then click GPA. See Figure 5.24.

FIGURE 5.24 Accessing GPA from the Windows Start menu

8. Andy's Key should be listed in the key manager. Right-click the entry for Andy and choose Send Keys. See Figure 5.25.

9. A warning will be provided regarding sending the private key to a server. See Figure 5.26. Choose Yes, and a confirmation should appear. This concludes the additional information necessary should the automatic key upload for Windows fail.

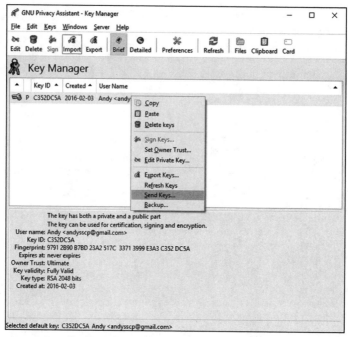

FIGURE 5.25 Finding a key in the key manager

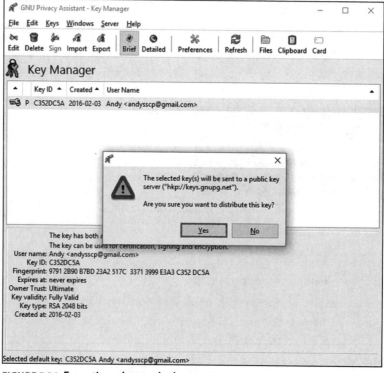

FIGURE 5.26 Exporting a key to the key server

10. Next, proper plugins should be installed for Claws. Click Configuration and then Plugins. See Figure 5.27.

11. Ensure the three plugins shown in Figure 5.28 are present, and if not, click the Load button, select them, and then click Open.

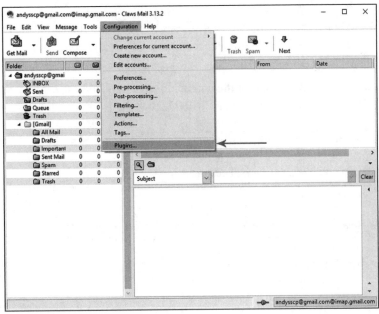

FIGURE 5.27 Accessing the plug-ins menu

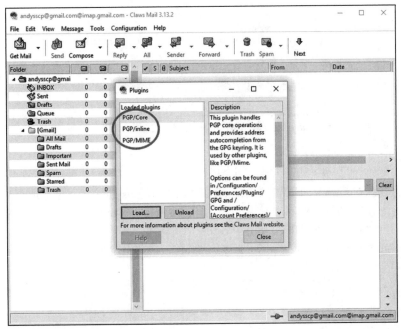

FIGURE 5.28 Selecting and loading plug-ins

12. Once it's loaded, click Close.

The first e-mail user is now configured with a public and private key along with an e-mail account and an e-mail client.

Second User E-mail Setup

The second user, Rae (raesscp@outlook.com), uses Outlook.com mail and Mozilla Thunderbird for her e-mail. To set up her account, install Thunderbird from the download file. When Thunderbird first launches, it will prompt for account creation.

1. Thunderbird may prompt for the creation of an e-mail address. Choose Skip This and Use My Existing E-mail. See Figure 5.29.

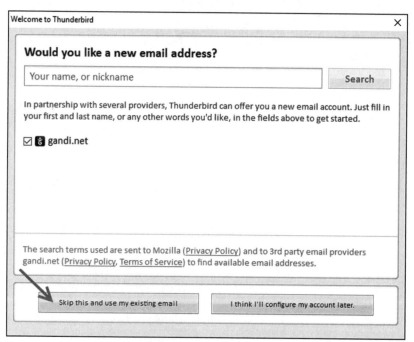

FIGURE 5.29 **Setting up a user in Thunderbird**

2. Next enter the e-mail information for the second user. See Figure 5.30.
3. Click Continue. Thunderbird automatically detects the majority of major e-mail providers. If it detects the settings for the selected account, simply click Done. If it doesn't detect the settings, review the e-mail service provider's self-help for information regarding server settings and manually configure the client. See Figure 5.31.

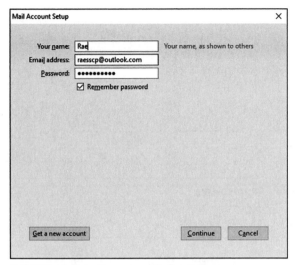

FIGURE 5.30 Entering account information

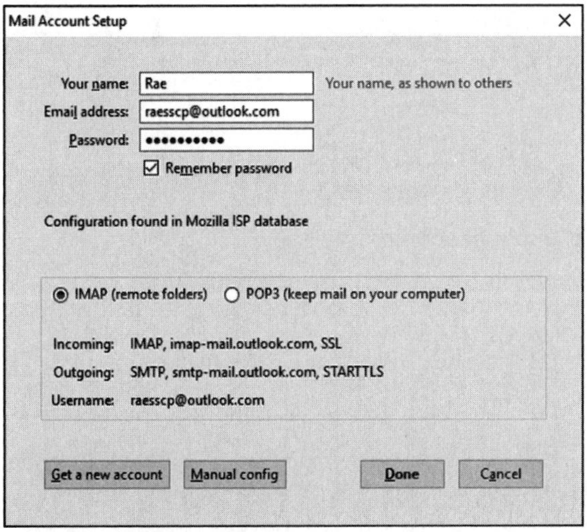

FIGURE 5.31 Mail account setup

4. Once that's completed, the next step is to set up the public and private key for the second user. Doing this in Thunderbird requires an additional plugin called Enigmail. To enable Enigmail, click the Thunderbird menu and choose Add-ons. See Figure 5.32.

5. In the Add-ons Manager, type **enigmail** in the search box and hit the Search button. See Figure 5.33.

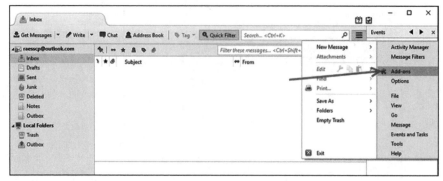

FIGURE 5.32 Accessing the Add-ons menu

FIGURE 5.33 Searching for a specific add-on

6. When the search results return, click Install for Enigmail. See Figure 5.34.

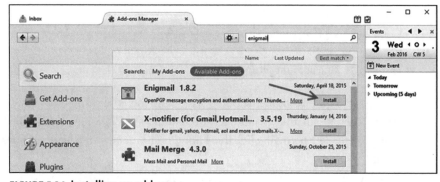

FIGURE 5.34 Installing an add-on

7. Once the install is complete, choose Restart Now. See Figure 5.35.

FIGURE 5.35 **Restarting machine after add-on installation is complete**

8. When Thunderbird restarts, the Enigmail wizard will start as well. See Figure 5.36.

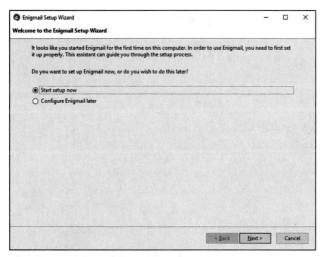

FIGURE 5.36 **Enigmail Setup Wizard**

9. Select Start Setup Now, and then click Next.
10. Select "I prefer a standard configuraton (recommended for beginners)," and then click Next.

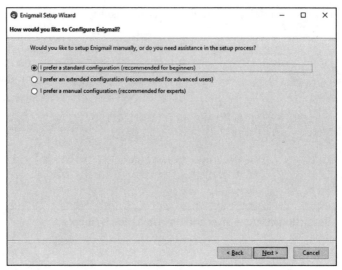

FIGURE 5.37 **Configuring Enigmail**

11. On the next screen there may be a prompt to use the first user's certificates. For this exercise, do not choose the first user (as they are going to use the Claws client). Instead, choose to create a new key pair and click Next. See Figure 5.38.

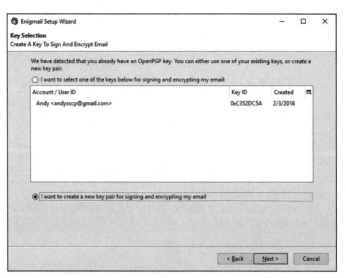

FIGURE 5.38 **Creating a key to sign and encrypt e-mail**

12. Next create a passphrase for the second user (Rae) key pair, confirm it, and then click Next. See Figure 5.39.

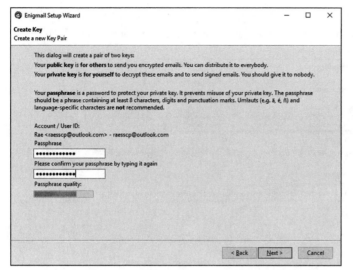

FIGURE 5.39 Configuring a passphrase to be used to protect the private key

13. The key creation process will start for the second user (Rae). See Figure 5.40.

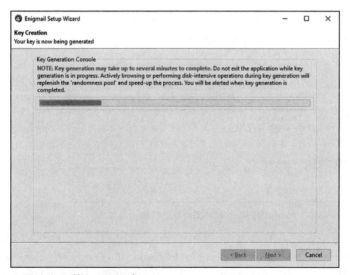

FIGURE 5.40 Key generation

14. When completed, an option to generate a revocation certificate is offered. Generate the certificate and store it in a known location. See Figure 5.41.

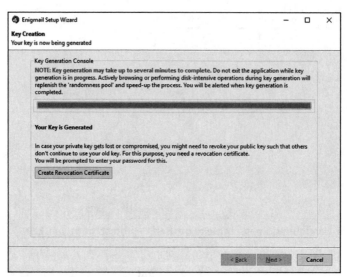

FIGURE 5.41 **Revocation certificate creation**

15. Next there will be a prompt to enter the key pair password for the second user (Rae). Enter the password created when generating the keys. See Figure 5.42.

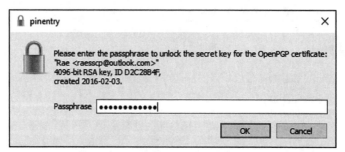

FIGURE 5.42 **Passphrase entry to unlock the secret key**

16. A notice will appear regarding the use of the revocation certificate. See Figure 5.43. Click OK, then Next, and then Finish. If the Add-ons Manager tab is still open, close it and return to the main mail window. See Figure 5.44.

FIGURE 5.43 Save your revocation certificate in a safe place.

FIGURE 5.44 Close the Add-ons Manager.

Both users (Andy and Rae) now have secure e-mail clients and key pairs for PKI.

Key Exchange and Sending Secure E-mail

This section explains how Andy and Rae exchange keys and how they securely send each other e-mail. If the e-mail clients and GPA are still open, close them before starting this section.

Since Andy and Rae have never seen each other and don't trust many people, they would not want to use a "shared secret" like a single password that they could both use to encrypt e-mails to each other. With PKI they don't need a secret shared key. All they need is each other's public key!

First User (Andy) Gets the Public Key of the Second User (Rae)

Now that the PKI is set up, Andy and Rae are excited to start sharing secure e-mails between them. To look up Rae's public key, Andy needs to pull it off the public key server. To do that he will need Rae's e-mail address. He asks Rae what e-mail address she is using and she replies with jennifersscp@hotmail.com.

1. Now that Andy knows Rae's e-mail address, he can look up her public key automatically using his e-mail client (Claws). He opens his e-mail client and clicks the Compose button. See Figure 5.45.

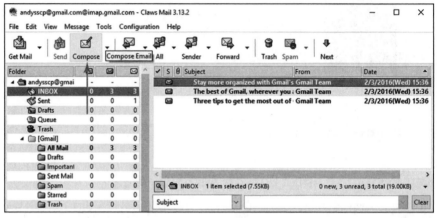

FIGURE 5.45 **Composing a message**

2. In the blank message window, he clicks Options, then Privacy System, then PGP Inline. He then checks the Encrypt option in the Options menu for the message. This means the body of the message will be encrypted.

3. In the To line, he types Rae's address (raesscp@outlook.com) and then types a subject and a test message, and when he is done, he clicks Send. See Figure 5.47.

4. A warning message will come up and explain that only the body of the message is encrypted. Click Continue.

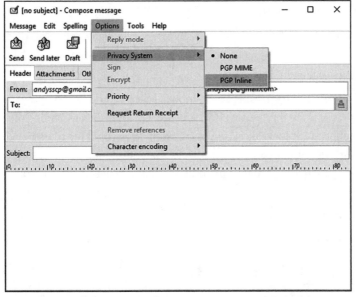

FIGURE 5.46 **Accessing the privacy system and encryption options**

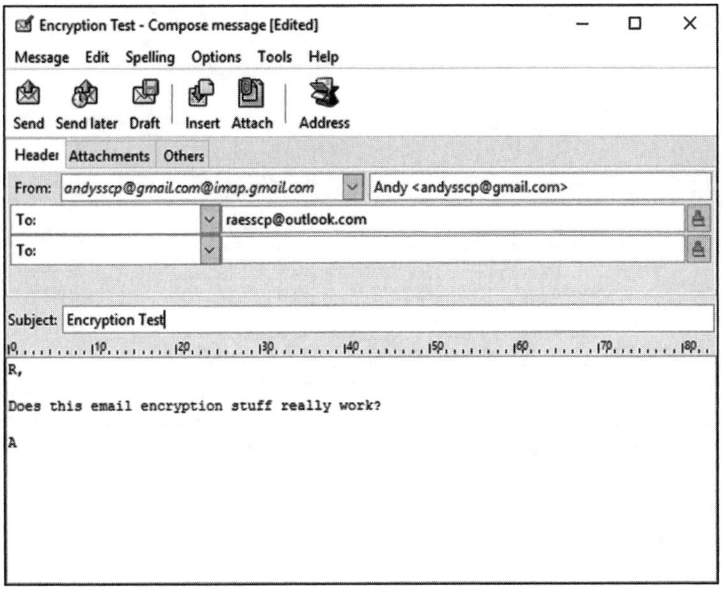

FIGURE 5.47 **Sending a message**

The message will be sent to Rae, and it will be encrypted. The plugins automatically search for the e-mail address provided (jennifersscp@hotmail.com) and use the appropriate public key if it is available on the server.

Rae Receives the Message and Responds

Once the message is sent, Rae can check her e-mail and see if Andy's message is indeed encrypted.

1. Close Claws and open Thunderbird.

2. When Thunderbird opens, check the Inbox. There should be a message there from Andy. Clicking the message will provide a preview below. Notice the preview is ciphertext! It looks like Andy successfully encrypted the message! Clicking the message will prompt for Rae's password. Rae must enter her password to unlock her private key (which is the only key that can decrypt the message).

3. Enter Rae's private key password. (It is the same password generated when the key pair was created.) See Figure 5.48.

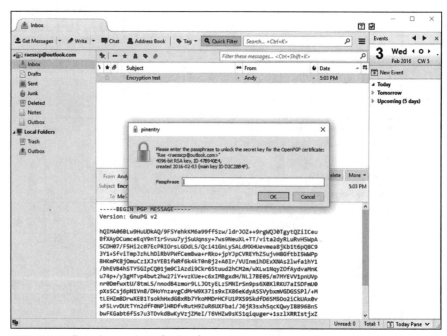

FIGURE 5.48 **Entering a private key to decrypt a message**

Once the password is entered, the message decrypts into its original form. See Figure 5.49.

Rae is worried that the message might actually be unencrypted on the server as well. So she logs into the webmail site to see what the message looks like on the server. To her relief, it is encrypted on the server because the encryption and decryption take place locally! See Figure 5.50.

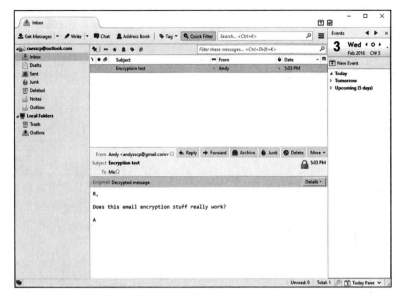

FIGURE 5.49 Decrypted message

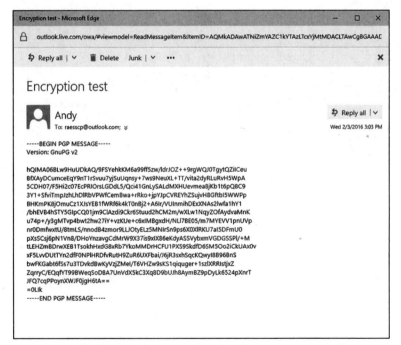

FIGURE 5.50 Checking on the encryption of mail message on e-mail server

Rae decides to send Andy an encrypted response.

4. First she needs to look up his public key. In Thunderbird she clicks the Thunderbird menu, then Enigmail, then Key Management. See Figure 5.51.

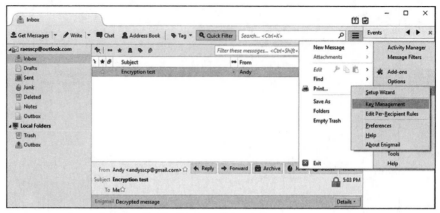

FIGURE 5.51 Accessing Thunderbird Enigmail Key Management menu

5. In the Key Management menu, she picks Key Server and then Search. She puts Andy's e-mail address into the Search box and hits the Search key. See Figure 5.52.

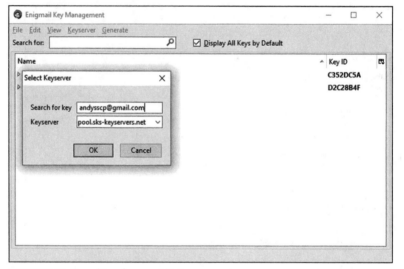

FIGURE 5.52 Searching for a public key

6. Andy's public key is found through the search. Rae clicks OK to import the public key and OK once more on the confirmation screen. Now that Rae has Andy's public key, she can send him an encrypted response.

7. She clicks Reply on the message in Thunderbird and creates a quick response. She then looks at the Enigmail toolbar above the To line to see the statement "This message will be encrypted." See Figure 5.53.

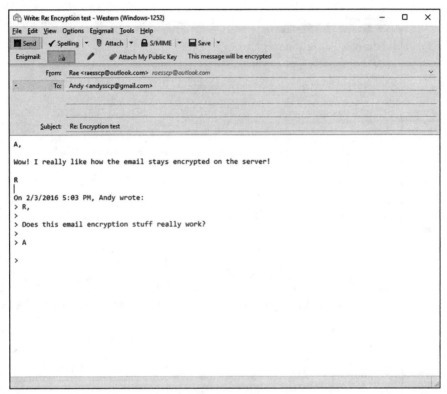

FIGURE 5.53 Enigmail encryption and signing settings

8. Rae reviews her short reply and hits Send. Rae closes Thunderbird.

9. Andy opens Claws and sees he has a new message from Rae. When he clicks the message, he is prompted for his private key passphrase to complete the decryption. See Figure 5.54.

The message decrypts, and Andy is able to read Rae's response. See Figure 5.55.

FIGURE 5.54 Entering the passphrase to unlock the secret key for the OpenPGP certificate

FIGURE 5.55 Reading the decrypted message

Andy is impressed but wants to ensure the message is encrypted on the server. He logs into the webmail interface of his e-mail provider and views the message there. See Figure 5.56.

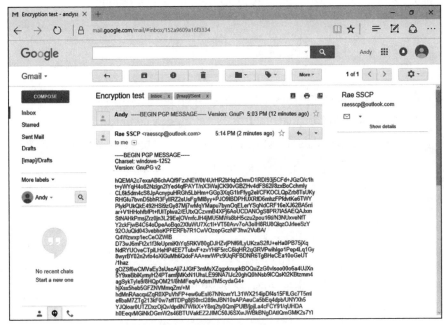

FIGURE 5.56 **Viewing the encrypted message on the e-mail server**

Andy is pleased to see the messages are indeed encrypted on the server. Andy and Rae continue to send encrypted messages back and forth. Each has fewer worries about an e-mail server breach since they each control their own encryption.

Conclusion

The e-mail encryption tools illustrated as part of this exercise can be easily deployed by anyone. The exercise provided two different e-mail clients and an open source PGP encryption suite that is suitable for a variety of platforms and systems. While digital signatures were not explicitly covered as part of this exercise, they may also be performed using the tools demonstrated.

SUMMARY

The areas touched on in the cryptography domain include the fundamental concepts of cryptography such as hashing, salting, digital signatures, and symmetric/asymmetric cryptographic systems. In addition, the need to understand and support secure protocols to help operate and implement cryptographic systems was also discussed. The SSCP needs to be aware of the importance of cryptography and its impact on the ability to ensure both confidentiality and integrity within the organization.

SAMPLE QUESTIONS

1. Applied against a given block of data, a hash function creates:
   a. A chunk of the original block used to ensure its confidentiality
   b. A block of new data used to ensure the original block's confidentiality
   c. A chunk of the original block used to ensure its integrity
   d. A block of new data used to ensure the original block's integrity

2. In symmetric key cryptography, each party should use:
   a. A publicly available key
   b. A previously exchanged secret key
   c. A randomly generated value unknown to everyone
   d. A secret key exchanged with the message

3. Nonrepudiation of a message ensures that the message:
   a. Can be attributed to a particular author
   b. Is always sent to the intended recipient
   c. Can be attributed to a particular recipient
   d. Is always received by the intended recipient

4. In Electronic Code Book (ECB) mode, data is encrypted using:
   a. A cipher-based on the previous block of a message
   b. A user-generated variable-length cipher for every block of a message
   c. A different cipher for every block of a message
   d. The same cipher for every block of a message

5. In Cipher Block Chaining (CBC) mode, the key is constructed by:
   a. Generating new key material completely at random
   b. Cycling through a list of user defined choices
   c. Modifying the previous block of ciphertext
   d. Reusing the previous key in the chain of message blocks

6. Stream ciphers are normally selected over block ciphers because of:

   a. The high degree of strength behind the encryption algorithms

   b. The high degree of speed behind the encryption algorithms

   c. Their ability to use large amounts of padding in encryption functions

   d. Their ability to encrypt large chunks of data at a time

7. A key escrow service is intended to allow for the reliable:

   a. Recovery of inaccessible private keys

   b. Recovery of compromised public keys

   c. Transfer of inaccessible private keys between users

   d. Transfer of compromised public keys between users

8. The correct choice for encrypting the entire original data packet in a tunneled mode for an IPSec solution is:

   a. Generic Routing Encapsulation (GRE)

   b. Authentication Header (AH)

   c. Encapsulating Security Payload (ESP)

   d. Point-to-Point Tunneling Protocol (PPTP)

9. When implementing an MD5 solution, what randomizing cryptographic function should be used to help avoid collisions?

   a. Multistring concatenation

   b. Modular addition

   c. Message pad

   d. Salt

10. Key clustering represents the significant failure of an algorithm because:

    a. A single key should not generate different ciphertext from the same plaintext, using the same cipher algorithm.

    b. Two different keys should not generate the same ciphertext from the same plaintext, using the same cipher algorithm.

    c. Two different keys should not generate different ciphertext from the same plaintext, using the same cipher algorithm.

    d. A single key should not generate the same ciphertext from the same plaintext, using the same cipher algorithm.

11. Asymmetric key cryptography is used for the following:

   a. Asymmetric key cryptography is used for the following:

   b. Encryption of data, nonrepudiation, access control

   c. Nonrepudiation, steganography, encryption of data

   d. Encryption of data, access control, steganography

12. Which of the following algorithms supports asymmetric key cryptography?

   a. Diffie-Hellman

   b. Blowfish

   c. SHA-256

   d. Rijndael

13. A certificate authority (CA) provides which benefit to a user?

   a. Protection of public keys of all users

   b. History of symmetric keys

   c. Proof of nonrepudiation of origin

   d. Validation that a public key is associated with a particular user

14. What is the output length of a RIPEMD-160 hash?

   a. 150 bits

   b. 128 bits

   c. 160 bits

   d. 104 bits

15. ANSI X9.17 is concerned primarily with:

   a. Financial records and retention of encrypted data

   b. The lifespan of master key-encrypting keys (KKM's)

   c. Formalizing a key hierarchy

   d. Protection and secrecy of keys

16. What is the input that controls the operation of the cryptographic algorithm?

   a. Decoder wheel

   b. Encoder

   c. Cryptovariable

   d. Cryptographic routine

17. AES is a block cipher with variable key lengths of?

    a. 128, 192, or 256 bits

    b. 32, 128, or 448 bits

    c. 8, 64, 128 bits

    d. 128, 256, or 448 bits

18. A Hashed Message Authentication Code (HMAC) works by:

    a. Adding a non-secret key value to the input function along with the source message

    b. Adding a secret key value to the output function along with the source message

    c. Adding a secret key value to the input function along with the source message

    d. Adding a non-secret key value to the output function along with the source message

19. The main types of implementation attacks include which of the following? (Choose all that apply.)

    a. Linear

    b. Side-channel analysis

    c. Fault analysis

    d. Probing

20. What is the process of using a key encrypting key (KEK) to protect session keys called?

    a. Key distribution

    b. Key escrow

    c. Key generation

    d. Key wrapping

END NOTES

1. http://www.ibimapublishing.com/journals/CIBIMA/volume8/v8n8.pdf

2. Read more about Oorschot and Weiner at http://people.scs.carleton.ca/~paulv/papers/JoC97.pdf

3. More information about Cain and Abel may be found at http://www.oxid.it/cain.html

4. See the following for a current list of block cipher modes approved by the U.S. government: `http://csrc.nist.gov/groups/ST/toolkit/BCM/current_modes.html`

5. In a known plaintext attack, the attacker has both the plaintext and the ciphertext, but he does not have the key, and the brute-force attack was an attack trying all possible keys.

6. Note that most cryptographers consider the strength of single DES to be 2^{55}, not 2^{56} as might be expected. Because double DES is approximately twice the strength of DES, it would be considered to be 2^{56}.

7. See the following: `http://tools.ietf.org/html/rfc3610`

8. Whit Diffie and Martin Hellman, "New directions in cryptography," *IEEE Transactions on Information Theory*, IT-22, 1976.

   See chart on page 5, NIST SP 800—131A "Transitions: Recommendation for Transitioning the Use of Cryptographic Algorithms and Key Lengths," `http://csrc.nist.gov/publications/nistpubs/800-131A/sp800-131A.pdf`

9. `http://csrc.nist.gov/publications/nistpubs/800-57/sp800-57_part1_rev3_general.pdf` (page 25 & 32).

10. In 1965, Gordon Moore made the following observation: "The complexity for minimum component costs has increased at a rate of roughly a factor of two per year. Certainly over the short term this rate can be expected to continue, if not to increase. Over the longer term, the rate of increase is a bit more uncertain, although there is no reason to believe it will not remain nearly constant for at least 10 years. That means by 1975, the number of components per integrated circuit for minimum cost will be 65,000."

    His reasoning was based on an empirical relationship between device complexity and time, observed over three data points. He used this to justify that by 1975, devices with as many as 65,000 components would become feasible on a single silicon chip occupying an area of only about one-fourth of a square inch. This projection turned out to be accurate with the fabrication of a 16K CCD memory with about 65,000 components in 1975. In a subsequent paper in 1975, Moore attributed the relationship to exponential behavior of die sizes, finer minimum dimensions, and "circuit and device cleverness." He went on to state that:

    "There is no room left to squeeze anything out by being clever. Going forward from here we have to depend on the two size factors—bigger dies and finer dimensions."

    He revised his rate of circuit complexity doubling to 18 months and projected from 1975 onwards at this reduced rate. This curve came to be known as "Moore's Law". Formally, Moore's Law states that circuit complexity doubles every eighteen months. By relating component density and increases in die-size to the computing power of a device, Moore's law has been extended to state that the amount of computing power available at a given cost doubles approximately every 18 months.

11. Read more about the slowing of Moore's law here: http://news.cnet.com/8301-10784_3-9780752-7.html

12. Read more about Frequency Analysis and Claude Shannon's work at: https://www.schneier.com/crypto-gram/archives/1998/1215.html

13. See the following: http://www.emclink.net/emc-plus/rsa-labs/standards-initiatives/pkcs-rsa-cryptography-standard.htm

14. https://ist.mit.edu/security/data_sensitivity

15. See the following:

    http://csrc.nist.gov/groups/SMA/fisma/

    http://www.whitehouse.gov/sites/default/files/omb/memoranda/2014/m-14-04.pdf

16. See the following for the full text of Directive 95/46/EC: http://eur-lex.europa.eu/legal-content/EN/TXT/?uri=CELEX:31995L0046

17. See the following for the full text of Directive 2002/58/EC: http://eur-lex.europa.eu/legal-content/EN/ALL/?uri=CELEX:32002L0058

18. See the following for the full text of Directive 2008/977/JHA: http://eur-lex.europa.eu/legal-content/EN/TXT/?qid=1405188191230&uri=CELEX:32008F0977

19. See the following for the full text of the adopted 12 March, 2014 by the Parliament, including all of the proposed amendments:

    http://www.europarl.europa.eu/sides/getDoc.do?type=TA&language=EN&reference=P7-TA-2014-0212

    http://ec.europa.eu/prelex/detail_dossier_real.cfm?CL=en&DosId=201286

20. See the following: https://www.schneier.com/crypto-gram/archives/2002/0515.html

21. "XML Key Management Specification (XKMS 2.0)," W3C, 28 June 2005, available online: http://www.w3.org/TR/xkms2/

22. "XML Signature Syntax and Processing (Second Edition)," W3C, 10 June 2008, Available online: http://www.w3.org/TR/xmldsig-core/

23. "XML Encryption Syntax and Processing", W3C, 10 December 2002, available online: http://www.w3.org/TR/xmlenc-core/

24. For example, Security Assertion Markup Language (SAML) for communicating user authentication, entitlement, and attribute information and WS-Security et al. For more details see: `http://www.oasis-open.org`

25. Callas, Jon, "OpenPGP Message Format," IETF, available online: `http://www.ietf.org/rfc/rfc2440.txt`

26. NIST, "Recommendation for Random Number Generation Using Deterministic Random Bit Generators, SP800—90," available online: `http://csrc.nist.gov/publications/nistpubs/800-90A/SP800-90A.pdf`

27. "Security Techniques—Random Bit Generation, ISO/IEC 18031:2005," ISO, available online: `http://www.iso.org/iso/catalogue_detail.htm?csnumber=54945`

28. Kaliski, Burt, "TWIRL and RSA Key Size, RSA Labs," available online: `http://www.emc.com/emc-plus/rsa-labs/historical/twirl-and-rsa-key-size.htm`

29. "Recommendation for Key Management-SP800—57," NIST, available online: `http://csrc.nist.gov/publications/nistpubs/800-57/sp800-57_part1_rev3_general.pdf`

30. "Guideline for Implementing Cryptography In the Federal Government," NIST, available online: `http://csrc.nist.gov/publications/nistpubs/800-21-1/sp800-21-1_Dec2005.pdf`

31. "Recommendations for Key Management, SP800—57",NIST, Available Online: `http://csrc.nist.gov/publications/nistpubs/800-57/sp800-57-Part1-revised2_Mar08-2007.pdf`

32. `http://tools.ietf.org/html/rfc3948`

33. See the following: `https://technet.microsoft.com/en-us/library/cc781476(v=ws.10).aspx`

34. See the following for the RFC for S/MIME version 3.1: `http://www.ietf.org/rfc/rfc3851.txt`

35. See the following for a thorough overview of S/MIME and its functionality: `https://technet.microsoft.com/en-us/library/aa995740(v=exchg.65).aspx`

Networks and Communications Security

IN THE NETWORKS AND Communications Security domain, students will learn about the network structure, data transmission methods, transport formats, and the security measures used to maintain integrity, availability, authentication, and confidentiality of the information being transmitted. Concepts for both public and private communication networks will be discussed.

TOPICS

The following topics are addressed in this chapter:

❏ Security issues related to networks

- OSI and TCP/IP models

- Network topographies and relationships (e.g., ring, star, bus, mesh, tree)

- Commonly used ports and protocols

❏ Telecommunications technologies

- Converged communications

- VoIP

- POTS, PBX

- Cellular

- Attacks and countermeasures

❏ Network access

- Access control and monitoring (e.g., NAC, remediation, quarantine, admission)

- Access control standards and protocols (e.g., IEEE 802.1X, RADIUS, TACACS)

- Remote Access operation and configuration (e.g., thin client, SSL VPN, IPSec VPN)

- Attacks and countermeasures

❏ LAN-based security

- Separation of data plane and control plane

- Segmentation (e.g., VLAN, ACLs)

- MACsec (e.g., IEEE 802.1AE)

❏ Secure device management

❏ Network-based security devices

- Firewalls and proxies

- Network intrusion detection/prevention systems

- ■ Routers and switches

- ■ Traffic shaping devices (e.g., WAN optimization)

- ■ Frameworks for data sharing (e.g., trusted computing groups IF-MAP)

- ❏ Wireless technologies

  - ■ Transmission security (e.g., WPA, WPA2/802.11i, AES, TKIP)

  - ■ Wireless security devices (e.g., integrated/dedicated WIPS, WIDS)

  - ■ Common vulnerabilities and countermeasures (e.g., management protocols)

OBJECTIVES

The security practitioner is expected to participate in the following areas related to network and telecommunications security:

- ■ Describe network related security issues.

- ■ Identify protective measures for telecommunication technologies.

- ■ Define processes for controlling network access.

- ■ Identify processes for managing LAN-based security.

- ■ Describe procedures for operating and configuring network-based security devices.

- ■ Define procedures to implement and operate wireless technologies.

SECURITY ISSUES RELATED TO NETWORKS

There are many issues that the SSCP will need to address as part of a comprehensive approach to network security. Areas such as the OSI model, network topologies, ports, and protocols all play an important part in network security. As we begin our discussions in these areas, the SSCP should keep in mind the operational concept of defense in depth, which specifies that a secure design will incorporate multiple overlapping layers of protection mechanisms to ensure that the concerns regarding confidentiality, integrity, and availability are addressed.

OSI and TCP/IP Models

Network communication is usually described in terms of layers. Several layering models exist; the most commonly used are

- The OSI reference model, structured into seven layers (physical layer, data-link layer, network layer, transport layer, session layer, presentation layer, application layer)[1]

- The TCP/IP or Department of Defense (DoD) model (not to be confused with the TCP/IP protocols), structured into four layers (link layer, network layer, transport layer, application layer)[2]

One feature that is common to both models and highly relevant from a security perspective is encapsulation. This means that not only do the different layers operate independently from each other, but they are also isolated on a technical level. Short of technical failures, the contents of any lower- or higher-layer protocol are inaccessible from any particular layer. This function of the models allows the security architect to ensure that their designs can provide both confidentiality and integrity. It also allows the security practitioner to implement those designs and operate them effectively, knowing that data flowing up and down the model's layers is being safeguarded.

OSI Model

The seven-layer Open System Interconnect (OSI) model was defined in 1984 and published as an international standard, ISO/IEC 7498—1.[3] The last revision to this standard was in 1994. Although sometimes considered complex, it has provided a practical and widely accepted way to describe networking. In practice, some layers have proven to be less crucial to the concept (such as the presentation layer), while others (such as the network layer) have required more specific structure, and applications overlapping and transgressing layer boundaries exist. See Figure 6.1.[4]

Layer 1: Physical Layer

Physical topologies are defined at this layer. Because the required signals depend on the transmitting media (e.g., required modem signals are not the same as ones for an Ethernet network interface card), the signals are generated at the physical layer. Not all hardware consists of layer 1 devices. Even though many types of hardware, such as cables, connectors, and modems, operate at the physical layer, some operate at different layers. Routers and switches, for example, operate at the network and data link layers, respectively.

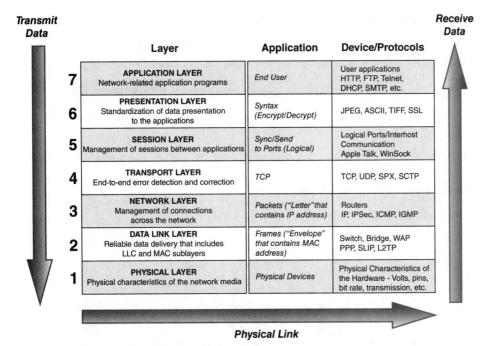

Transmit Data → | Layer | Application | Device/Protocols

Layer	Application	Device/Protocols
7 APPLICATION LAYER — Network-related application programs	End User	User applications HTTP, FTP, Telnet, DHCP, SMTP, etc.
6 PRESENTATION LAYER — Standardization of data presentation to the applications	Syntax (Encrypt/Decrypt)	JPEG, ASCII, TIFF, SSL
5 SESSION LAYER — Management of sessions between applications	Sync/Send to Ports (Logical)	Logical Ports/Interhost Communication Apple Talk, WinSock
4 TRANSPORT LAYER — End-to-end error detection and correction	TCP	TCP, UDP, SPX, SCTP
3 NETWORK LAYER — Management of connections across the network	Packets ("Letter" that contains IP address)	Routers IP, IPSec, ICMP, IGMP
2 DATA LINK LAYER — Reliable data delivery that includes LLC and MAC sublayers	Frames ("Envelope" that contains MAC address)	Switch, Bridge, WAP PPP, SLIP, L2TP
1 PHYSICAL LAYER — Physical characteristics of the network media	Physical Devices	Physical Characteristics of the Hardware - Volts, pins, bit rate, transmission, etc.

Receive Data

Physical Link

FIGURE 6.1 **The seven-layer OSI reference model**

Layer 2: Data Link Layer

The data link layer prepares the packet that it receives from the network layer to be transmitted as frames on the network. This layer ensures that the information that it exchanges with its peers is error free. If the data link layer detects an error in a frame, it will request that its peer resend that frame. The data link layer converts information from the higher layers into bits in the format that is expected for each networking technology, such as Ethernet, Token Ring, etc. Using hardware addresses, this layer transmits frames to devices that are physically connected only. As an analogy, consider the path between the end nodes on the network as a chain and each link as a device in the path. The data link layer is concerned with sending frames to the next link.

The Institute of Electrical and Electronics Engineers (IEEE) data link layer is divided into two sublayers:

- **Logical Link Control (LLC)**—Manages connections between two peers. It provides error and flow control and control bit sequencing.

- **Media Access Control (MAC)**—Transmits and receives frames between peers. Logical topologies and hardware addresses are defined at this sublayer. An Ethernet's 48-bit hardware address is often called a MAC address as a reference to the name of the sublayer.

Layer 3: Network Layer

It is important to clearly distinguish between the functions of the network and data link layers. The network layer moves information between two hosts that are not physically connected. On the other hand, the data link layer is concerned with moving data to the next physically connected device. Also, whereas the data link layer relies on hardware addressing, the network layer uses logical addressing that is created when hosts are configured.

Internet Protocol (IP) is part of the TCP/IP suite and is the most important network layer protocol. IP has two functions:

- **Addressing**—IP uses the destination IP address to transmit packets through networks until the packets' destination is reached.

- **Fragmentation**—IP will subdivide a packet if its size is greater than the maximum size allowed on a local network.

IP is a connectionless protocol that does not guarantee error-free delivery. Layer 3 devices, such as routers, read the destination layer 3 address (e.g., destination IP address) in received packets and use their routing table to determine the next device on the network (the next hop) to send the packet. If the destination address is not on a network that is directly connected to the router, it will send the packet to another router.

Routing tables are built either statically or dynamically. Static routing tables are configured manually and change only when updated. Dynamic routing tables are built automatically when routers periodically share information that reflects their view of the network, which changes as routers go on and offline. When traffic congestion develops, this allows the routers to effectively route packets as network conditions change. Some examples of other protocols that are traditionally considered to work at layer 3 are as follows:

Routing Information Protocol (RIP) Versions 1 and 2   The RIP v1 standard is defined in RFC 1058.[5] Routing Information Protocol (RIP) is a standard for exchange of routing information among gateways and hosts. RIP is most useful as an "interior gateway protocol." RIP uses distance vector algorithms to determine the direction and distance to any link in the internetwork. If there are multiple paths to a destination, RIP selects the path with the least number of hops. However, because hop count is the only routing metric used by RIP, it does not necessarily select the fastest path to a destination.

RIP v1 allows routers to update their routing tables at programmable intervals. The default interval is 30 seconds. The continual sending of routing updates by RIP v1 means that network traffic builds up quickly. To prevent a packet from looping infinitely, RIP allows a maximum hop count of 15. If the destination network is more than 15 routers away, the network is considered unreachable, and the packet is dropped.

The RIP v2 standard is defined in RFC 1723 and updated for cryptographic authentication by RFC 4822.[6] RIP v2 provides the following advances over RIP v1:

- Carries a subnet mask
- Supports password authentication security
- Specifies the next hop address
- Does not require that routes be aggregated on the network boundary

Open Shortest Path First (OSPF) Versions 1 and 2 The OSPF v1 standard is defined in RFC 1131.[7] Open Shortest Path First (OSPF) is an interior gateway routing protocol developed for IP networks based on the shortest path first or link-state algorithm. Routers use link-state algorithms to send routing information to all nodes in an internetwork by calculating the shortest path to each node based on a topography of the Internet constructed by each node. Each router sends that portion of the routing table (keeps track of routes to particular network destinations) that describes the state of its own links, and it also sends the complete routing structure (topography).

The advantage of shortest path first algorithms is that their use results in smaller, more frequent updates everywhere. They converge quickly, thus preventing such problems as routing loops and Count-to-Infinity (when routers continuously increment the hop count to a particular network). This makes for a more stable network. The disadvantage of shortest path first algorithms is that they require large amounts of CPU power and memory.

OSPF v2 is defined in RFC 1583 and updated by RFC 2328.[8] It is used to allow routers to dynamically learn routes from other routers and to advertise routes to other routers. Advertisements containing routes are referred to as *link state advertisements* (LSAs) in OSPF. OSPF routers keep track of the state of all the various network connections (links) between itself and a network it is trying to send data to. This is the behavior that makes it a link-state routing protocol.

OSPF supports the use of classless IP address ranges and is very efficient. OSPF uses areas to organize a network into a hierarchal structure; it summarizes route information to reduce the number of advertised routes and thereby reduce network load and uses a designated router (elected via a process that is part of OSPF) to reduce the quantity and frequency of link state advertisements.

OSPF selects the best routes by finding the lowest-cost paths to a destination. All router interfaces (links) are given a cost. The cost of a route is equal to the sum of all the costs configured on all the outbound links between the router and the destination network, plus the cost configured on the interface that OSPF received the link state advertisement on.

Internet Control Message Protocol (ICMP)   Internet Control Message Protocol (ICMP) is documented in RFC 792.[9] ICMP messages are classified into two main categories:

- ICMP error messages
- ICMP query messages

ICMP's goals are to provide a means to send error messages for non-transient error conditions and to provide a way to probe the network in order to determine general characteristics about the network. Some of ICMP's functions are to

- **Announce Network Errors**—Such as a host or entire portion of the network being unreachable, due to some type of failure. A TCP or UDP packet directed at a port number with no receiver attached is also reported via ICMP.

- **Announce Network Congestion**—When a router begins buffering too many packets, due to an inability to transmit them as fast as they are being received, it will generate ICMP Source Quench messages. Directed at the sender, these messages should cause the rate of packet transmission to be slowed.

- **Assist Troubleshooting**—ICMP supports an Echo function, which just sends a packet on a round trip between two hosts. Ping, a common network management tool, is based on this feature. Ping will transmit a series of packets, measuring average round-trip times and computing loss percentages.

- **Announce Timeouts**—If an IP packet's TTL field drops to zero, the router discarding the packet will often generate an ICMP packet announcing this fact. TraceRoute is a tool that maps network routes by sending packets with small TTL values and watching the ICMP timeout announcements.

Internet Group Management Protocol (IGMP)   Internet Group Management Protocol (IGMP) is used to manage multicasting groups, which are a set of hosts anywhere on a network that are interested in a particular multicast. Multicast agents administer multicast groups, and hosts send IGMP messages to local agents to join and leave groups. There are three versions of IGMP, as highlighted here:[10]

- **Version 1**—Multicast agents periodically send queries to a host on its network to update its database of multicast groups' membership. Hosts stagger their replies to prevent a storm of traffic to the agent. When replies no longer come from a group, agents will stop forwarding multicasts to that group.

- **Version 2**—This version extends the functionality of version 1. It defines two types of queries: a general query to determine membership of all groups and a group-specific query to determine the membership of a particular group. In addition, a member can notify all multicast routers that it wishes to leave a group.

- **Version 3**—This version further enhances IGMP by allowing hosts to specify from which sources they want to receive multicasts.

For a listing of protocols associated with layer 3 of the OSI model, see the following:

- **IPv4/IPv6**—Internet Protocol
- **DVMRP**—Distance Vector Multicast Routing Protocol
- **ICMP**—Internet Control Message Protocol
- **IGMP**—Internet Group Multicast Protocol
- **IPsec**—Internet Protocol Security
- **IPX**—Internetwork Packet Exchange
- **DDP**—Datagram Delivery Protocol
- **SPB**—Shortest Path Bridging

Layer 4: Transport Layer

The transport layer creates an end-to-end transport between peer hosts. User Datagram Protocol (UDP) and Transmission Control Protocol (TCP) are important transport layer protocols in the TCP/IP suite. UDP does not ensure that transmissions are received without errors, and therefore it is classified as a connectionless, unreliable protocol. This does not mean that UDP is poorly designed. Rather, the application will perform the error checking instead of the protocol.

Connection-oriented reliable protocols, such as TCP, ensure integrity by providing error-free transmission. They divide information from multiple applications on the same host into segments to be transmitted on a network. Because it is not guaranteed that the peer transport layer receives segments in the order that they were sent, reliable protocols reassemble received segments into the correct order. When the peer layer receives a segment, it responds with an acknowledgment. If an acknowledgment is not received, the segment is retransmitted. Lastly, reliable protocols ensure that each host does not receive more data than it can process without loss of data.

TCP data transmissions, connection establishment, and connection termination maintain specific control parameters that govern the entire process. The control bits are listed as follows:

- **URG**—Urgent Pointer field significant
- **ACK**—Acknowledgment field significant
- **PSH**—Push function
- **RST**—Reset the connection

- **SYN** — Synchronize sequence numbers
- **FIN** — No more data from sender

These control bits are used for many purposes; chief among them is the establishment of a guaranteed communication session via a process referred to as the TCP *three-way handshake*, as described here:

1. First, the client sends a SYN segment. This is a request to the server to synchronize the sequence numbers. It specifies its initial sequence number (ISN), which is incremented by 1, and that is sent to the server. To initialize a connection, the client and server must synchronize each other's sequence numbers.

2. Second, the server sends an ACK and a SYN in order to acknowledge the request of the client for synchronization. At the same time, the server is also sending its request to the client for synchronization of its sequence numbers. There is one major difference in this transmission from the first one. The server transmits an acknowledgment number to the client. The acknowledgment is just proof to the client that the ACK is specific to the SYN the client initiated. The process of acknowledging the client's request allows the server to increment the client's sequence number by one and uses it as its acknowledgment number.

3. Third, the client sends an ACK in order to acknowledge the request from the server for synchronization. The client uses the same algorithm the server implemented in providing an acknowledgment number. The client's acknowledgment of the server's request for synchronization completes the process of establishing a reliable connection.

For a listing of protocols associated with layer 4 of the OSI model, see the following:

- **FCP** — Fiber Channel Protocol
- **RDP** — Reliable Datagram Protocol
- **SCTP** — Stream Control Transmission Protocol
- **SPX** — Sequenced Packet Exchange
- **SST** — Structured Stream Transport
- **TCP** — Transmission Control Protocol
- **UDP** — User Datagram Protocol

Layer 5: Session Layer

This layer provides a logical, persistent connection between peer hosts. A session is analogous to a conversation that is necessary for applications to exchange information. The session layer is responsible for creating, maintaining, and tearing down the session. Three modes are offered:

- **Full Duplex**—Both hosts can exchange information simultaneously, independent of each other.

- **Half Duplex**—Hosts can exchange information but only one host at a time.

- **Simplex**—Only one host can send information to its peer. Information travels in one direction only.

For a listing of protocols associated with layer 5 of the OSI model, see the following:

- **H.245**—Call Control Protocol for Multimedia Communication

- **iSNS**—Internet Storage Name Service

- **PAP**—Password Authentication Protocol

- **PPTP**—Point-to-Point Tunneling Protocol

- **RPC**—Remote Procedure Call Protocol

- **RTCP**—Real-time Transport Control Protocol

- **SMPP**—Short Message Peer-to-Peer

Layer 6: Presentation Layer

The applications that are communicating over a network may represent information differently, such as using incompatible character sets. This layer provides services to ensure that the peer applications use a common format to represent data. For example, if a presentation layer wants to ensure that Unicode-encoded data can be read by an application that understands the ASCII character set only, it could translate the data from Unicode to a standard format. The peer presentation layer could translate the data from the standard format into the ASCII character set.

In many widely used applications and protocols, no distinction is made between the presentation and application layers. For example, Hypertext Transfer Protocol (HTTP), generally regarded as an application layer protocol, has presentation layer aspects such as the ability to identify character encoding for proper conversion, which is then done in the application layer.

Layer 7: Application Layer

This layer is the application's portal to network-based services, such as determining the identity and availability of remote applications. When an application or the operating system transmits or receives data over a network, it uses the services from this layer. Many well-known protocols, such as Hypertext Transfer Protocol (HTTP), File Transfer Protocol (FTP), and Simple Mail Transfer Protocol (SMTP), operate at this layer. It is important to remember that the application layer is not the application, especially when an application has the same name as a layer 7 protocol. For example, the FTP command on many operating systems initiates an application called FTP, which eventually uses the FTP protocol to transfer files between hosts. While some protocols are easily ascribed to a certain layer based on their form and function, others are very difficult to place precisely. An example of a protocol that falls into this category would be the Border Gateway Protocol.

Border Gateway Protocol (BGP)

Border Gateway Protocol (BGP) was created to replace the Exterior Gateway Protocol (EGP) to allow fully decentralized routing. This allowed the Internet to become a truly decentralized system. BGP performs inter-domain routing in Transmission Control Protocol/Internet Protocol (TCP/IP) networks. BGP is a protocol for exchanging routing information between gateway hosts (each with its own router) in a network of autonomous systems. BGP is often the protocol used between gateway hosts on the Internet. The routing table contains a list of known routers, the addresses they can reach, and a cost metric associated with the path to each router so that the best available route is chosen.

Hosts using BGP communicate using the Transmission Control Protocol (TCP) and send updated router table information only when one host has detected a change. Only the affected part of the routing table is sent. BGP-4, the latest version, lets administrators configure cost metrics based on policy statements.[11]

Many consider BGP an application that happens to affect the routing table. There are also those that would consider BGP a routing protocol as opposed to an application that affects the routing table. BGP creates and uses code attached to sockets. Does that mean that it should be considered an application? In the case of BGP, when viewed in a traffic sniffer, there is a layer 4 header between the IP Header and the Routing Protocol header. Does that mean that we can say that BGP is an application that transports routing information at layer 4?

Perhaps a more appropriate way to classify a protocol is to look at the services it provides. BGP clearly provides services to the network layer, not the traditional transport services, but rather, BGP provides control information about how the network layer operates. This could allow us to move BGP down to the network layer.

This perspective is especially useful for management, control, and supervisory protocols that can be seen as applications of other protocols, and yet providing the necessary control, management, and supervisory information to the managed infrastructure that is on lower layers than the application layer. From this viewpoint, while BGP is truly just an application running over TCP, it is intimately tied into the operation of the network layer because it provides the necessary information about how the network layer should operate. That means that we could say that BGP is implemented as an application layer protocol, but with respect to its function, it is a network layer protocol.

As a security practitioner, you should understand how BGP works in real networks. Following are several links to simulators that can be used to model BGP and demonstrate how it works:

- **BGPlay**, an HTML widget that presents a graphical visualization of BGP routes and updates for any real AS on the Internet. The link is:

  `https://stat.ripe.net/widget/bgplay`

- **SSFnet**, SSFnet network simulator includes a BGP implementation developed by BJ Premore. The link is:

  `http://www.ssfnet.org/homePage.html`

- **C-BGP**, a BGP simulator able to perform large scale simulation trying to model the ASes of the Internet or modelling ASes as large as Tier-1. The link is:

  `http://c-bgp.sourceforge.net/`

- **NetViews**, a Java application that monitors and visualizes BGP activity in real time. The link is:

  `http://netlab.cs.memphis.edu/projects_netviews.html`

For a listing of protocols associated with layer 7 of the OSI model, see the following:

- **DHCP**—Dynamic Host Configuration Protocol
- **DNS**—Domain Name System
- **HTTP**—Hypertext Transfer Protocol
- **IMAP**—Instant Message Access Protocol
- **LDAP**—Lightweight Directory Access Protocol
- **SMTP**—Simple Mail Transfer Protocol
- **FTP**—File Transfer Protocol

TCP/IP Reference Model

The U.S. Department of Defense developed the TCP/IP model, which is very similar to the OSI model but with fewer layers, as shown in Figure 6.2.

The link layer provides physical communication and routing within a network. It corresponds to everything required to implement an Ethernet. It is sometimes described as two layers, a physical layer and a link layer. In terms of the OSI model, it covers layers 1 and 2. The network layer includes everything that is required to move data between networks. It corresponds to the IP protocol, but also Internet Control Message Protocol (ICMP) and Internet Group Management Protocol (IGMP). In terms of the OSI model, it corresponds to layer 3.

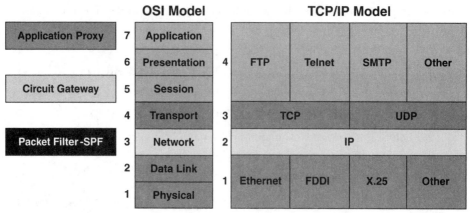

FIGURE 6.2 OSI model and TCP/IP model

The transport layer includes everything required to move data between applications. It corresponds to TCP and UDP. In terms of the OSI model, it corresponds to layer 4. The application layer covers everything specific to a session or application, in other words, everything relating to the data payload. In terms of the OSI model, it corresponds to layers 5 through 7. Owing to its coarse structure, it is not well suited to describe application-level information exchange.

As with the OSI model, data that is transmitted on the network enters the top of the stack, and each of the layers, with the exception of the physical layer, encapsulates information for its peer at the beginning and sometimes the end of the message that it receives from the next highest layer. On the remote host, each layer removes the information that is peer encapsulated before the remote layer passes the message to the next higher layer. Also, each layer processes messages in a modular fashion, without concern for how the other layers on the same host process the message.

IP Networking

Internet Protocol (IP) is responsible for sending packets from the source to the destination hosts. Because it is an unreliable protocol, it does not guarantee that packets arrive error free or in the correct order. That task is left to protocols on higher layers. IP will subdivide packets into fragments when a packet is too large for a network.

Hosts are distinguished by the IP addresses of their network interfaces. The address is expressed as four octets separated by a dot (.), for example, 216.12.146.140. Each octet may have a value between 0 and 255. However, 0 and 255 are not used for hosts. The latter is used for broadcast addresses, and the former's meaning depends on the context in which it is used. Each address is subdivided into two parts: the network number and the host. The network number, assigned by an external organization, such as the Internet

Corporation for Assigned Names and Numbers (ICANN), represents the organization's network. The host represents the network interface within the network.

Originally, the part of the address that represented the network number depended on the network's class. As shown in Table 6.1, a Class A network used the leftmost octet as the network number, Class B used the leftmost two octets, etc.

TABLE 6.1 **Network Classes**

CLASS	RANGE OF FIRST OCTET	NUMBER OF OCTETS FOR NET-WORK NUMBER	NUMBER OF HOSTS IN NETWORK
A	1–126	1	16,777,214
B	128–191	2	65,534
C	192–223	3	254
D	224–239	Multicast	
E	240–255	Reserved	

The part of the address that is not used as the network number is used to specify the host. For example, the address 216.12.146.140 represents a Class C network. Therefore, the network portion of the address is represented by the 216.12.146, and the unique host address within the network block is represented by 140.

127 is reserved for a computer's loopback address. Usually the address 127.0.0.1 is used. The loopback address is used to provide a mechanism for self-diagnosis and trouble-shooting at the machine level. This mechanism allows a network administrator to treat a local machine as if it were a remote machine and ping the network interface to establish whether or not it is operational.

The explosion of Internet utilization in the 1990s caused a shortage of unallocated IPv4 addresses. To help remedy the problem, Classless Inter-Domain Routing (CIDR) was implemented. CIDR does not require that a new address be allocated based on the number of hosts in a network class. Instead, addresses are allocated in contiguous blocks from the pool of unused addresses.

To ease network administration, networks are typically subdivided into subnets. Because subnets cannot be distinguished with the addressing scheme discussed so far, a separate mechanism, the subnet mask, is used to define the part of the address that is used for the subnet. Bits in the subnet mask are 1 when the corresponding bits in the address are used for the subnet. The remaining bits in the mask are 0. For example, if the leftmost three octets (24 bits) are used to distinguish subnets, the subnet mask is 11111111 11111111 11111111 00000000. A string of 32 1s and 0s is very unwieldy, so the mask is usually converted to decimal notation: 255.255.255.0. Alternatively, the mask is expressed with a slash (/) followed by the number of 1s in the mask. The previous mask would be written as /24.

IPv6

After the explosion of Internet usage in the mid-1990s, IP began to experience serious growing pains. It was obvious that the phenomenal usage of the Internet was stretching the protocol to its limit. The most obvious problems were a shortage of unallocated IP addresses and serious shortcomings in security. IPv6 is a modernization of IPv4 that includes

- **A much larger address field:** IPv6 addresses are 128 bits, which supports 2 hosts. Suffice it to say that we will not run out of addresses.

- **Improved security:** As we will discuss next, IPSec must be implemented in IPv6. This will help ensure the integrity and confidentiality of IP packets and allow communicating partners to authenticate with each other.

- **A more concise IP packet header:** Hosts will require less time to process each packet, which will result in increased throughput.

- **Improved quality of service:** This will help services obtain an appropriate share of a network's bandwidth.

Transmission Control Protocol (TCP)

The Transmission Control Protocol provides connection-oriented data management and reliable data transfer. TCP and UDP map data connections through the association of port numbers with services provided by the host. TCP and UDP port numbers are managed by the Internet Assigned Numbers Authority (IANA). A total of 65,536 (2^{16}) ports exist. These are broken into three ranges:

- **Well-Known Ports**—Ports 0 through 1023 are considered to be well known. Ports in this range are assigned by IANA and, on most systems, can only be used by privileged processes and users.

- **Registered Ports**—Ports 1024 through 49151 can be registered with IANA by application developers but are not assigned by them. The reason for choosing a registered instead of a well-known port can be that on most systems the user may not have the privileges to run an application on a well-known port.

- **Dynamic or Private Ports**—Ports 49152 through 65535 can be freely used by applications; one typical use for these ports is initiation of return connections for requested data or services.

Attacks against TCP include sequence number attacks, session hijacking, and SYN floods. More information about attacks can be found later in this domain.

User Datagram Protocol (UDP)

The User Datagram Protocol (UDP) provides a lightweight service for connectionless data transfer without error detection and correction. For UDP, the same considerations for port numbers as described for TCP in the section on Transmission Control Protocol apply. A number of protocols within the transport layer have been defined on top of UDP, thereby effectively splitting the transport layer into two. Protocols stacked between layers 4 and 5 include Real-time Protocol (RTP) and Real-time Control Protocol (RTCP) as defined in RFC 3550, MBone, a multicasting protocol, Reliable UDP (RUDP), and Stream Control Transmission Protocol (SCTP) as defined in RFC 2960. As a connectionless protocol, UDP services are easy prey for spoofing attacks.

Internet—Intranet

The Internet, a global network of independently managed, interconnected networks, has changed life on Earth. People from anywhere on the globe can share information almost instantaneously using a variety of standardized tools such as web technologies or e-mail.

An *intranet*, on the other hand, is a network of interconnected internal networks within an organization, which allows information to be shared within the organization and sometimes with trusted partners and suppliers. For instance, during a project, staff in a global company can easily access and exchange documents, thereby working together almost as if they were in the same office. As with the Internet, the ease with which information can be shared comes with the responsibility to protect it from harm. Intranets will typically host a wide range of organizational data. For this reason, access to these resources is usually coupled with existing internal authentication services even though they are technically on an internal network, such as a directory service coupled with multi-factor authentication.

Extranet

An extranet differs from a DMZ (demilitarized network zone) in the following way: An extranet is made available to authenticated connections that have been granted an access account to the resources in the extranet. Conversely, a DMZ will host publicly available resources that must support unauthenticated connections from just about any source, such as DNS servers and e-mail servers. Due to the need for companies to share large quantities of information, often in an automated fashion, typically one company will grant the other controlled access to an isolated segment of its network to exchange information through the use of an extranet.

Granting an external organization access to a network comes with significant risk. Both companies have to be certain that the controls, both technical and nontechnical (e.g., operational and policy), effectively minimize the risk of unauthorized access to information. Where access must be granted to external organizations, additional controls such as deterministic routing can be applied upstream by service providers. This sort of safeguard is relatively simple to employ and has significant advantages because the ability for malicious entities to target an extranet for compromise leading to internal network penetration is abbreviated.

Companies that access extranets often treat the information within these networks and their servers as "trusted," confidential, and possessing integrity (uncorrupted and valid). However, these companies do not have control of each other's security profile. Who knows what kind of trouble a user can get into if he or she accesses supposedly trusted information through an extranet from an organization whose network has been compromised? To mitigate this potential risk, security architects and practitioners need to demand that certain security controls are in place before granting access to an extranet.

Dynamic Host Configuration Protocol (DHCP)

System and network administrators are busy people and hardly have the time to assign IP addresses to hosts and track which addresses are allocated. To relieve administrators from the burden of manually assigning addresses, many organizations use the Dynamic Host Configuration Protocol (DHCP) to automatically assign IP addresses to workstations (servers and network devices usually are assigned static addresses).

Dynamically assigning a host's IP configuration is fairly simple. When a workstation boots, it broadcasts a DHCPDISCOVER request on the local LAN, which could be forwarded by routers. DHCP servers will respond with a DHCPOFFER packet, which contains a proposed configuration, including an IP address. The DHCP client selects a configuration from the received DHCPOFFER packets and replies with a DHCPRE-QUEST. The DHCP server replies with a DHCPACK (DHCP acknowledgment), and the workstation adapts the configuration. Receiving a DHCP-assigned IP address is referred to as receiving a lease.

A client does not request a new lease every time it boots. Part of the negotiation of IP addresses includes establishing a time interval for which the lease is valid and timers that reflect when the client must attempt to renew the lease. This timer is referred to as a Time to Live counter, or just simply as the TTL. As long as the timers have not expired, the client is not required to ask for a new lease. Within the DHCP servers, administrators create address pools from which addresses are dynamically assigned when requested by a client. In addition, they can assign specific hosts to have static (i.e., permanent) addresses through the use of client reservations.

Because the DHCP server and client do not always authenticate with each other, neither host can be sure that the other is legitimate. For example, in a DHCP network, an attacker can plug his or her workstation into a network jack and receive an IP address, without having to obtain one by guessing or through social engineering. Also, a client cannot be certain that a DHCPOFFER packet is from a DHCP server instead of an intruder masquerading as a server.

To counteract these concerns, in June 2001 the IETF published RFC 3118, which specifies how to implement Authentication for DHCP Messages.[12] This standard describes an enhancement that replaces the normal DHCP messages with authenticated ones. Clients and servers check the authentication information and reject messages that come from invalid sources. The technology involves the use of a new DHCP option type, the Authentication option, and operating changes to several of the leasing processes to use this option. Although these vulnerabilities are not trivial, the ease of administration of IP addresses usually makes the risk from the vulnerabilities acceptable, except in very high security environments. Ultimately, the security architect will need to weigh the risks associated with using DHCP without an authentication option and decide how best to proceed.

Internet Control Message Protocol (ICMP)

The Internet Control Message Protocol (ICMP) is used for the exchange of control messages between hosts and gateways and is used for diagnostic tools such as ping and traceroute. ICMP can be leveraged for malicious behavior, including man-in-the-middle and denial-of-service attacks.

Ping of Death[13]

Ping is a diagnostic program used to determine if a specified host is on the network and can be reached by the pinging host. It sends an ICMP echo packet to the target host and waits for the target to return an ICMP echo reply. Amazingly, an enormous number of operating systems would crash or become unstable upon receiving an ICMP echo greater than the legal packet limit of 65,536 bytes. Before the ping of death became famous, the source of the attack was difficult to find because many system administrators would ignore a seemingly harmless ping in their logs.

ICMP Redirect Attacks[14]

A router may send an ICMP redirect to a host to tell it to use a different, more effective default route. However, an attacker can send an ICMP redirect to a host telling it to use the attacker's machine as a default route. The attacker will forward all of the redirected traffic to a router so that the victim will not know that his or her traffic has been intercepted. This is a good example of a man-in-the-middle attack. Some operating systems will crash if they receive a storm of ICMP redirects. The security practitioner should have several tools in his or her toolbox to be able to model and interact with attacks such as the ICMP redirect attack in order to better understand them. One such tool that will be very effective is called Scapy.

Scapy is a powerful interactive packet manipulation program. It is able to forge or decode packets of a wide number of protocols, send them on the wire, capture them, match requests and replies, and much more. It can easily handle most classical tasks like scanning, tracerouting, probing, unit tests, attacks, or network discovery. (It can replace hping, 85% of nmap, arpspoof, arp-sk, arping, tcpdump, tethereal, p0f, etc.) It also performs very well at a lot of other specific tasks that most other tools cannot handle, like sending invalid frames, injecting your own 802.11 frames, and combining techniques (VLAN hopping+ARP cache poisoning, VOIP decoding on WEP encrypted channel, etc.). You can find Scapy here: `http://www.secdev.org/projects/scapy/`.

Ping Scanning

Ping scanning is a basic network mapping technique that helps narrow the scope of an attack. An attacker can use one of many tools such as Very Simple Network Scanner for Windows-based platforms and NMAP for Linux- and Windows-based platforms to ping all of the addresses in a range.[15] If a host replies to a ping, then the attacker knows that a host exists at that address.

Traceroute Exploitation

Traceroute is a diagnostic tool that displays the path a packet traverses between a source and destination host. Traceroute can be used maliciously to map a victim network and learn about its routing. In addition, there are tools, such as Firewalk, that use techniques similar to those of traceroute to enumerate a firewall rule set.[16] The Firewalk tool stopped being actively developed and maintained as of version 5.0 in 2003. The functionality of the Firewalk tool has been subsumed into NMAP as part of the rule set that can be configured for use.[17]

What the Firewalk host rule tries to do is to discover firewall rules using an IP TTL expiration technique known as firewalking. To determine a rule on a given gateway, the scanner sends a probe to a metric located behind the gateway, with a TTL one higher than the gateway. If the probe is forwarded by the gateway, then we can expect to receive an ICMP_TIME_EXCEEDED reply from the gateway next hop router, or eventually the metric itself if it is directly connected to the gateway. Otherwise, the probe will time out.

Remote Procedure Calls

Remote procedure calls (RPCs) represent the ability to allow for the executing of objects across hosts, with a client sending a set of instructions to an application residing on a different host on the network. Generically, several (mutually incompatible) services in this category exist, such as distributed computing environment RPC (DCE RPC) and Sun's Open Network Computing RPC (ONC RPC, also referred to as SunRPC or simply RPC). It is important to note that RPC does not in fact provide any services on its own; instead, it provides a brokering service by providing (basic) authentication and a way to address the actual service. Common Object Request Broker Architecture (CORBA) and Microsoft Distributed Component Object Model (DCOM) can be viewed as RPC-type protocols. Security problems with RPC include its weak authentication mechanism, which can be leveraged for privilege escalation by an attacker.

Network Topographies and Relationships

There are many network topographies and relationships. It is important for the SSCP to understand the merits of each of them. The following sections explore all of the major topographies and related important information.

Bus

A bus topology is a LAN with a central cable (bus) to which all nodes (devices) connect. All nodes transmit directly on the central bus. Each node listens to all of the traffic on the bus and processes only the traffic that is destined for it. This topology relies on the data-link layer to determine when a node can transmit a frame on the bus without colliding with another frame on the bus. A LAN with a bus topology is shown in Figure 6.3.

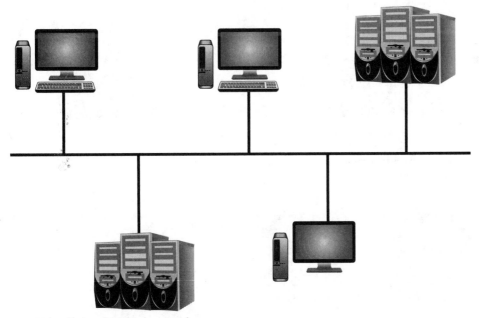

FIGURE 6.3 **Network with a bus topology**

Advantages of buses include

- Adding a node to the bus is easy.
- A node failure will not likely affect the rest of the network.

Disadvantages of buses include

- Because there is only one central bus, a bus failure will leave the entire network inoperable.

Tree

A tree topology is similar to a bus. Instead of all of the nodes connecting to a central bus, the devices connect to a branching cable. Like a bus, every node receives all of the transmitted traffic and processes only the traffic that is destined for it. Furthermore, the data-link layer must transmit a frame only when there is not a frame on the wire. A network with a tree topology is shown in Figure 6.4.

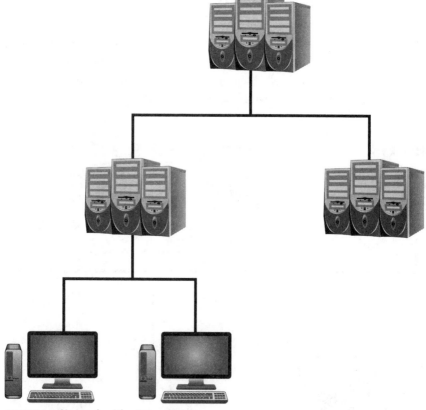

FIGURE 6.4 **Network with a tree topology**

Advantages of a tree include

- Adding a node to the tree is easy.
- A node failure will not likely affect the rest of the network.

Disadvantages of a tree include

- A cable failure could leave the entire network inoperable.

Ring

A ring is a closed-loop topology. Data is transmitted in one direction only, based on the direction that the ring was initialed to transmit in, either clockwise or counter-clockwise. Each device receives data from its upstream neighbor only and transmits data to its downstream neighbor only. Typically, rings use coaxial cables or fiber optics. A Token Ring network is shown in Figure 6.5.

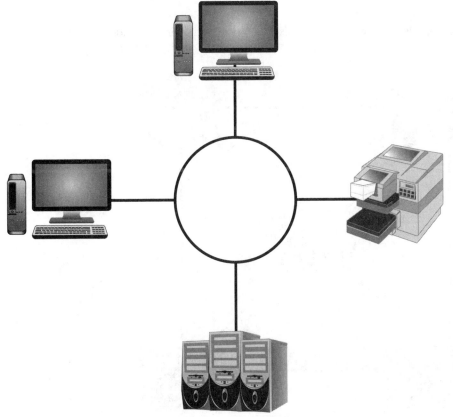

FIGURE 6.5 Network with a ring topology

Advantages of rings include

- Because rings use tokens, one can predict the maximum time that a node must wait before it can transmit (i.e., the network is deterministic).

- Rings can be used as a LAN or network backbone.

Disadvantages of rings include

- Simple rings have a single point of failure. If one node fails, the entire ring fails. Some rings, such as fiber distributed data interface (FDDI), use dual rings for failover.

Mesh

In a mesh network, all nodes are connected to every other node on the network. A full mesh network is usually too expensive because it requires many connections. As an alternative, a partial mesh can be employed in which only selected nodes (typically the most critical) are connected in a mesh, and the remaining nodes are connected to a few devices. As an example, core switches, firewalls, and routers and their hot standbys are often all connected to ensure as much availability as possible. A mesh network is shown in Figure 6.6.

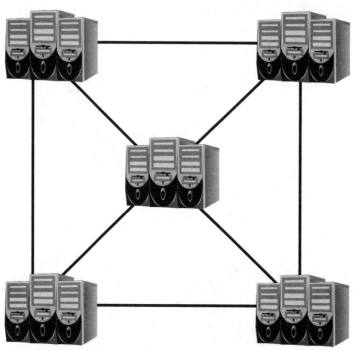

FIGURE 6.6 **Network with a mesh topology**

Advantages of a mesh include

■ Mesh networks provide a high level of redundancy.

Disadvantages of a mesh include

■ Mesh networks are very expensive because of the enormous number of cables that are required.

Star

All nodes in a star network are connected to a central device, such as a hub, switch, or router. Modern LANs usually employ a star typology. A star network is shown in Figure 6.7.

FIGURE 6.7 Network with a star topology

Advantages of a star include

■ Star networks require fewer cables than full or partial mesh.

■ Star networks are easy to deploy, and nodes can be easily added or removed.

Disadvantages of a star include

■ The central connection device is a single point of failure. If it is not functional, all of the connected nodes lose network connectivity.

There are many points that the security architect and practitioner must consider about transmitting information from sender to receiver. For example, will the information be expressed as an analog or digital wave? How many recipients will be there? If the transmission media will be shared with others, how can one ensure that the signals will not interfere with each other?

Unicast, Multicast, and Broadcast Transmissions

Most communication, especially that directly initiated by a user, is from one host to another. For example, when a person uses a browser to send a request to a web server, he or she sends a packet to the web server. A transmission with one receiving host is called a unicast transmission.

A host can send a broadcast to everyone on its network or sub-network. Depending on the network topology, the broadcast could have anywhere from one to tens of thousands of recipients. Like a person standing on a soapbox, this is a noisy method of communication. Typically, only one or two destination hosts are interested in the broadcast; the other recipients waste resources to process the transmission. However, there are productive uses for broadcasts. Consider a router that knows a device's IP address but must determine the device's MAC address. The router will broadcast an Address Resolution Protocol (ARP) request asking for the device's MAC address.

Notice how one broadcast could result in hundreds or even thousands of packets on the network. Intruders often leverage this fact in denial-of-service attacks.

Public and private networks are used more often than ever for streaming transmissions, such as movies, videoconferences, and music. Given the intense bandwidth needed to transmit these streams and that the sender and recipients are not necessarily on the same network, how does one transmit the stream to only the interested hosts? The sender could send a copy of the stream via unicast to each receiver. Unless there is a very small audience, unicast delivery is not practical because the multiple simultaneous copies of the large stream on the network at the same time could cause congestion. Delivery with broadcasts is another possibility, but every host would receive the transmission, even if they were not interested in the stream.

Multicasting was designed to deliver a stream to only interested hosts. Radio broadcasting is a typical analogy for multicasting. To select a specific radio show, you tune a radio to the broadcasting station. Likewise, to receive a desired multicast, you join the corresponding multicast group.

Multicast agents are used to route multicast traffic over networks and administer multicast groups. Each network and sub-network that supports multicasting must have at least one multicast agent. Hosts use Internet Group Management Protocol (IGMP) to tell a local multicast agent that it wants to join a specific multicast group. Multicast agents also route multicasts to local hosts that are members of the multicast's group and relay multicasts to neighboring agents.

When a host wants to leave a multicast group, it sends an IGMP message to a local multicast agent. Multicasts do not use reliable sessions. Therefore, the multicasts are transmitted as best effort, with no guarantee that datagrams are received. As an example, consider a server multicasting a videoconference to desktops that are members of the same multicast group as the server. The server transmits to a local multicast agent. Next, the multicast agent relays the stream to other agents. All of the multicast agents transmit the stream to local hosts that are members of the same multicast group as the server.

Circuit-Switched Networks

Circuit-switched networks establish a dedicated circuit between endpoints. These circuits consist of dedicated switch connections. Neither endpoint starts communicating until the circuit is completely established. The endpoints have exclusive use of the circuit and its bandwidth. Carriers base the cost of using a circuit-switched network on the duration of the connection, which makes this type of network only cost-effective for a steady communication stream between the endpoints. Examples of circuit-switched networks are the plain old telephone service (POTS), Integrated Services Digital Network (ISDN), and Point-to-Point Protocol (PPP).

Packet-Switched Networks

Packet-switched networks do not use a dedicated connection between endpoints. Instead, data is divided into packets and transmitted on a shared network. Each packet contains meta-information so that it can be independently routed on the network. Networking devices will attempt to find the best path for each packet to its destination. Because network conditions could change while the partners are communicating, packets could take different paths as they transverse the network and arrive in any order. It is the responsibility of the destination endpoint to ensure that the received packets are in the correct order before sending them up the stack.

Switched Virtual Circuits (SVCs) and Permanent Virtual Circuits (PVCs)

Virtual circuits provide a connection between endpoints over high-bandwidth, multiuser cable or fiber that behaves as if the circuit were a dedicated physical circuit. There are two types of virtual circuits, based on when the routes in the circuit are established. In a permanent virtual circuit, the carrier configures the circuit's routes when the circuit is purchased. Unless the carrier changes the routes to tune the network, responds to an outage, etc., the routes do not change. On the other hand, the routes of a switched virtual circuit are configured dynamically by the routers each time the circuit is used.

Carrier Sense Multiple Access

As the name implies, Carrier Sense Multiple Access (CSMA) is an access protocol that uses the absence/presence of a signal on the medium that it wants to transmit on as permission to speak. Only one device may transmit at a time; otherwise, the transmitted frames will be unreadable. Because there is not an inherent mechanism that determines which device may transmit, all of the devices must compete for available bandwidth. For this reason, CSMA is referred to as a contention-based protocol. Also, because it is impossible to predict when a device may transmit, CSMA is also nondeterministic.

There are two variations of CSMA based on how collisions are handled. LANs using Carrier Sense Multiple Access with Collision Avoidance (CSMA/CA) require devices to announce their intention to transmit by broadcasting a jamming signal. When devices detect the jamming signal, they know not to transmit; otherwise, there will be a collision. After sending the jamming signal, the device waits to ensure that all devices have received that signal, and then it broadcasts the frames on the media. CSMA/CA is used in the IEEE 802.11 wireless standard.

Devices on a LAN using Carrier Sense Multiple Access with Collision Detection (CSMA/CD) listen for a carrier before transmitting data. If another transmission is not detected, the data will be transmitted. It is possible that a station will transmit before another station's transmission had enough time to propagate. If this happens, two frames will be transmitted simultaneously, and a collision will occur. Instead of all stations simply retransmitting their data, which will likely cause more collisions, each station will wait a randomly generated interval before retransmitting. CSMA/CD is part of the IEEE 802.3 standard.[18]

Polling

A network that employs polling avoids contention by allowing a device (a slave) to transmit on the network only when it is asked to by a master device. Polling is used mostly in mainframe protocols, such as Synchronous Data Link. The point coordination function, an optional function of the IEEE standard, uses polling as well.

Token Passing

Token passing takes a more orderly approach to media access. With this access method, only one device may transmit on the LAN at a time, thus avoiding retransmissions.

A special frame, known as a token, circulates through the ring. When a device wishes to transmit on the network, it must possess the token. The device replaces the token with a frame containing the message to be transmitted and sends the frame to its neighbor. When each device receives the frame, it relays it to its neighbor if it is not the recipient. The process continues until the recipient possesses the frame. That device will copy the message, modify the frame to signify that the message was received, and transmit the frame on the network.

When the modified frame makes a trip back to the sending device, the sending device knows that the message was received. Token passing is used in Token Ring and FDDI networks. An example of a LAN using token passing can be seen in Figure 6.8.

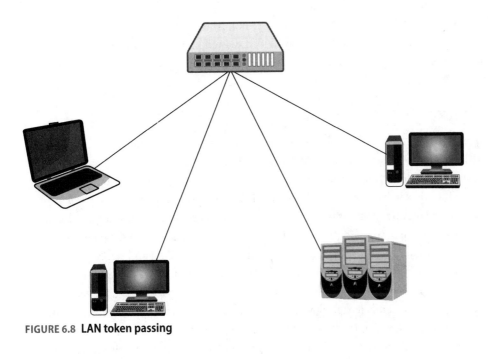

FIGURE 6.8 LAN token passing

Ethernet (IEEE 802.3)

Ethernet, which is defined in IEEE 802.3, played a major role in the rapid proliferation of LANs in the 1980s. The architecture was flexible and relatively inexpensive, and it was easy to add and remove devices from the LAN. Even today, for the same reasons, Ethernet is the most popular LAN architecture. The physical topologies that are supported by Ethernet are bus, star, and point to point, but the logical topology is the bus.

With the exception of full-duplex Ethernet (which does not have the issues of collisions), the architecture uses CSMA/CD. This protocol allows devices to transmit data with a minimum of overhead (compared to Token Ring), resulting in an efficient use of bandwidth. However, because devices must retransmit when more than one device attempts to send data on the medium, too many retransmissions due to collisions can cause serious throughput degradation.

The Ethernet standard supports coaxial cable, unshielded twisted pair, and fiber optics as transmission media.

Ethernet was originally rated at 10 Mbps, but like 10-megabyte disk drives, users quickly figured out how to use and exceed its capacity and needed faster LANs. To meet the growing demand for more bandwidth, 100 Base-TX (100 Mbps over twisted pair) and 100 Base-FX (100 Mbps over multimode fiber optics) were defined. When the demand grew for even more bandwidth over unshielded twisted pair, 1000 Base-T was defined, and 1000 Base-SX and 1000 Base-LX were defined for fiber optics. These standards support 1,000 Mbps.

Token Ring (IEEE 802.5)

Originally designed by IBM, Token Ring was adapted with some modification by the IEEE as IEEE 802.5. Despite the architecture's name, Token Ring uses a physical star topology. The logical topology, however, is a ring. Each device receives data from its upstream neighbor and transmits to its downstream neighbor. Token Ring uses ring passing to mediate which device may transmit. As mentioned in the section on token passing, a special frame, called a token, is passed on the LAN. To transmit, a device must possess the token.

To transmit on the LAN, the device appends data to the token and sends it to its next downstream neighbor. Devices retransmit frames whenever the token is not the intended recipient. When the destination device receives the frame, it copies the data, marks the frame as read, and sends it to its downstream neighbor. When the packet returns to the source device, it confirms that the packet has been read. It then removes the frame from the ring. Token ring is now considered a "legacy" technology that is rarely seen and on those rare occasions, it is only because there has been no reason for an organization to upgrade away from it. Token ring has almost entirely been replaced with Ethernet technology.

Fiber Distributed Data Interface (FDDI)

Fiber Distributed Data Interface (FDDI) is a token-passing architecture that uses two rings. Because FDDI employs fiber optics, FDDI was designed to be a 100-Mbps network backbone. Only one ring (the primary) is used; the other one (secondary) is used as a backup. Information in the rings flows in opposite directions from each other. Hence, the rings are referred to as counter rotating. FDDI is also considered a legacy technology and has been supplanted by more modern transport technologies; initially Asynchronous Transfer Mode (ATM) but more recently Multiprotocol Label Switching (MPLS).

Multiprotocol Label Switching (MPLS)[19]

Multiprotocol Label Switching (MPLS) has attained a significant amount of popularity at the core of the carrier networks as of late because it manages to couple the determinism, speed, and QoS controls of established switched technologies like ATM and Frame Relay with the flexibility and robustness of the Internet Protocol world. (MPLS is developed and propagated through the Internet Engineering Task Force [IETF].) Additionally, the once faster and higher-bandwidth ATM switches are being outperformed by Internet backbone routers. Equally important, MPLS offers simpler mechanisms for packet-oriented traffic engineering and multi-service functionality with the added benefit of greater scalability.

MPLS is often referred to as *IP VPN* because of the ability to couple highly deterministic routing with IP services. In effect, this creates a VPN-type service that makes it logically impossible for data from one network to be mixed or routed over to another network without compromising the MPLS routing device itself. MPLS does not include encryption services; therefore, any MPLS service called "IP VPN" does not in fact contain any cryptographic services. The traffic on these links would be visible to the service providers. The following guidelines should be considered by the network and security architects during the negotiation of MPLS bandwidth and associated service level agreements (SLAs) to ensure that services live up to the assurance requirements for the assets relying upon the network:

- **Site Availability**—Make certain MPLS is available for all desired locations; i.e., all the planned remote connections (offices) have MPLS service available in that area.

- **End-to-End Network Availability**—Inquire about peering relationships for MPLS for network requirements that cross Tier 1 carrier boundaries.

- **Provisioning**—How fast can new links in new sites be provisioned?

Local Area Network (LAN)

Local Area Networks (LANs) service a relatively small area, such as a home, office building, or office campus. In general, LANs service the computing needs of their local users. LANs consist of most modern computing devices, such as workstations, servers, and peripherals connected in a star topology or internetworked stars. Ethernet is the most popular LAN architecture because it is inexpensive and very flexible. Most LANs have connectivity to other networks, such as dial-up or dedicated lines to the Internet, access to other LANs via WANs, and so on.

Commonly Used Ports and Protocols

When the SSCP considers the protocols and ports to be used to drive secure communication in the network, they will need to ensure that they are making wise choices. Having an understanding of name resolution through the use of DNS and directory services through the use of LDAP are two examples of areas that the SSCP will want to ensure they focus on.

Domain Name System (DNS) [20]

The Domain Name System (DNS) is a hierarchical distributed naming system for computers, services, or any resource connected to the Internet or a private network.[21] DNS associates various pieces of information with domain names assigned to each of the participating entities. It translates domain names to the numerical IP addresses needed for the purpose of locating computer services and devices worldwide. By providing a worldwide, distributed keyword-based redirection service, the Domain Name System is an essential component of the functionality of the Internet. The security practitioner can think of the Domain Name System as the phone book for the Internet, allowing people all over the world to find resources by translating human-friendly computer hostnames into IP addresses. For example, the domain name www.isc2.org translates to the addresses 209.188.91.140, 0:0:0:0:0:ffff:d1bc:5b8c (6to4 address), and 2002:d1bc:5b8c:0:0:0:0:0 (IPv4-mapped IPv6 address). DNS can be quickly updated, allowing a service's location on the network to change without affecting the end users, who continue to use the same host name. Users take advantage of this when they use meaningful Uniform Resource Locators (URLs) and e-mail addresses without having to know how the computer actually locates the services.

DNS is a globally distributed, scalable, hierarchical, and dynamic database that provides a mapping between hostnames, IP addresses (both IPv4 and IPv6), text records, mail exchange information (MX records), name server information (NS records), and security key information defined in Resource Records (RRs). The information defined in RRs is grouped into zones and maintained locally on a DNS server so it can be retrieved globally through the distributed DNS architecture. DNS can use either the User Datagram Protocol (UDP) or Transmission Control Protocol (TCP) and uses a destination port of 53. When the DNS protocol uses UDP as the transport, it has the ability to deal with UDP retransmission and sequencing.

DNS is composed of a hierarchical domain name space that contains a tree-like data structure of linked domain names (nodes). Domain name space uses RRs to store information about the domain. The tree-like data structure for the domain name space starts at the root zone ".", which is the topmost level of the DNS hierarchy. Although it is not typically displayed in user applications, the DNS root is represented as a trailing dot in a fully qualified domain name (FQDN). For example, the right-most dot in www.isc2 .org. represents the root zone. From the root zone, the DNS hierarchy is then split into sub-domain (branches) zones.

Each domain name is composed of one or more labels. Labels are separated with "." and may contain a maximum of 63 characters. A FQDN may contain a maximum of

255 characters, including the ".". Labels are constructed from right to left, where the label at the far right is the top-level domain (TLD) for the domain name. Figure 6.9 shows how to identify the TLD for a domain name.

org is the TLD for www.isc2.org as it is the label furthest to the right.

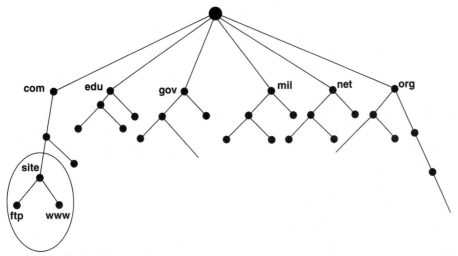

FIGURE 6.9 **The DNS database structure**

DNS's central element is a set of hierarchical name (domain) trees, starting from a so-called top-level domain (TLD). A number of so-called root servers manage the authoritative list of TLD servers. To resolve any domain name, each Domain Name System in the world must hold a list of these root servers.

To understand DNS, security practitioners should be familiar with the following terms:

- **Resolver**—A DNS client that sends DNS messages to obtain information about the requested domain name space.

- **Recursion**—The action taken when a DNS server is asked to query on behalf of a DNS resolver.

- **Authoritative Server**—A DNS server that responds to query messages with information stored in RRs for a domain name space stored on the server.

- **Recursive Resolver**—A DNS server that recursively queries for the information asked in the DNS query.

- **FQDN**—A Fully Qualified Domain Name is the absolute name of a device within the distributed DNS database.

- **RR**—A Resource Record is a format used in DNS messages that is composed of the following fields: NAME, TYPE, CLASS, TTL, RDLENGTH, and RDATA.

- **Zone**—A database that contains information about the domain name space stored on an authoritative server.

DNS primarily translates hostnames to IP addresses or IP addresses to hostnames. This translation process is accomplished by a DNS resolver; this could be a client application such as a web browser or an e-mail client, or a DNS application such as BIND, sending a DNS query to a DNS server requesting the information defined in a RR. Some examples of the DNS resolution process are listed here:

- If the DNS server is configured only as an authoritative server and it receives a DNS query message asking about information that the server is authoritative for, it will cause the server to inspect locally stored RR information and return the value of the record in the Answer Section of a DNS response message. If the requested information for the DNS query message does not exist, the DNS server will respond with a NXDOMAIN (Non-Existent Domain) DNS response message or a DNS Referral Response message.

- If the DNS server is authoritative, not configured as a recursive resolver, and it receives a DNS query message asking about information that the server is not authoritative for, it will cause the server to issue a DNS response message containing RRs in the Authority Section and the address mapping for the FQDN from that section may be present in the Additional Section. This informs the DNS resolver where to send queries in order to obtain authoritative information for the question in the DNS query. This is also known as a DNS Referral Response message.

- If the DNS server is not authoritative but is configured as a recursive resolver and it receives a DNS query asking about information, it will cause the server to recursively query the DNS architecture for the authoritative DNS server of the information included in the DNS request. Once the recursive DNS resolver has obtained this information, it will provide that information to the original DNS resolver using a DNS response message, and the RR will be non-authoritative (since the recursive DNS resolver is not authoritative for the requested information). The recursive DNS resolver may also have knowledge about the requested information stored in DNS cache. If the requested information is present in the DNS cache, then the recursive DNS resolver will respond with that RR information.

To understand DNS security, security practitioners should be familiar with the following attack types:

- **DNS Denial-of-Service (DoS) attacks**—Reflector attacks are examples of exploits of denial-of-service vulnerabilities in default DNS configurations. A reflector attack is launched when an attacker delivers traffic to the victim of their attack by reflecting it off of a third party so that the origin of the attack is concealed from the victim.

■ **DNS Distributed Denial-of-Service (DDoS) attacks**—Amplification attacks are examples of attacks that combine reflection with amplification to achieve an attack that causes the byte count of traffic received by the victim to be substantially greater than the byte count of traffic sent by the attacker, thus amplifying or multiplying the sending power of the attacker. To perform a DNS amplification attack, an attacker begins by identifying a large set of resolvers that can be used as reflectors. Then, from one or more machines the attacker causes UDP DNS queries to be sent to the reflecting resolvers, with the source IP addresses for the queries set to the address of the target/victim. The reflecting servers process the recursive query and send the response to the IP address from which they believe the queries originated. Because of the spoofed origin, the replies are actually sent to the target. The unrequested DNS responses are discarded when they reach the target machine, but by the time they have done so, they have consumed network resources and a small portion of CPU time on the target machine.

■ **Query or Request Redirection**—Request redirection occurs when the DNS query is intercepted and modified in transit to the DNS server. If the request is redirected on the path to the caching name server, this indicates that the interception occurred on the LAN. This is significant because the mitigation technique differs from redirection that occurs outside of the local network. Query interception can also occur on recursive queries outside of the local network. Query redirection that occurs outside of the local network can be mitigated through the use of Domain Name System Security Extensions (DNSSEC).[22] The recursive resolver must turn on the DNSSEC enables flag in the name daemon configuration file. DNSSEC-enabled validation checks work when the zone data is signed. The problem is that not all public zones are signed. In the case of a LAN interception, or an unsigned response, traffic monitoring is needed to address the attack. New addresses should be minimally compared against black lists and whois registrations in order to attempt to validate them.

■ **DNS Cache-Poisoning Attack**—Attackers inject malicious DNS data into the recursive DNS servers operated by Internet service providers (ISPs). The damage caused by this attack is localized to specific users connecting to the compromised servers. One of the most famous cache poisoning attacks is the Kaminsky bug. Discovered by researcher Dan Kaminsky, the bug resulted when the random values for transaction ID and source port were easily guessed, thereby, allowing the attacker to insert a "poisoned" value.[23] When the Kaminsky attack was first discovered, it was noted that sites running DNSSEC with DNSSEC validation enabled were immune to the attack. This led to an increase in the number of DNSSEC deployments. The patch for this problem made the random number for the return port a stronger number to crack.

- **Zone Enumeration** — Enumeration of zone data occurs when a user invokes DNS diagnostic commands, such as dig or nslookup, against a site in an attempt to gain information about the site's network architecture. Oftentimes this behavior precedes an attempt at an attack. Mitigating zone-enumeration threats requires the site administrator to determine what DNS information the site wishes to make available. Many sites will use "split brain" DNS views by running internal and external DNS servers.

- **Tunnels** — Most of the attention paid to DNS security focuses on the DNS query and response transaction. This transaction is a UDP transaction; however, DNS utilizes both UDP and TCP transport mechanisms. DNS TCP transactions are used for secondary zone transfers and for some DNSSEC traffic. Mitigating DNS tunneling traffic relies on a combination of traffic monitoring and server configuration. Zone transfers should only occur between an authoritative server and the secondary server. This should be fairly straightforward, since the secondary server is a known entity and should be listed in the whitelist. The quantity of DNS transactions should also be monitored, since this could be an indication of DNS misuse.

- **DNS fast Flux** — Fast flux represents the ability to quickly move the location of a web, e-mail, DNS, or any Internet or distributed service from one or more computers connected to the Internet to a different set of computers to delay or evade detection.[24] Defending against fast flux sites requires monitoring and blocking techniques. In some cases, there are known IP address ranges that are associated with fast flux behavior, so these addresses can be blocked. However, the dynamic nature of these sites makes monitoring as important as blocking. A sudden appearance of new destination addresses requires investigation in order to determine if the site is legitimate or a potential fast flux site. Phishing and pharming are big business in cybercrime and rely in part on DNS exploits. Phishing utilizes fast flux behavior when a link to a fast flux address is inserted in a targeted email. Pharming is associated with poisoned DNS cache records or DNS redirection, which occurs when a user enters a legitimate destination address, but the request is redirected to a malicious site.

- **Taking over the Registration of a Domain** — Attackers take over the registration of a domain and change the authoritative DNS servers. This was the type of attack used by the Syrian Electronic Army. They gained access to the domain registration accounts operated by Melbourne IT and changed the authoritative DNS servers to `ns1.syrianelectronicarmy.com` and `ns2.syrianarmyelectronicarmy.com`.[25] Such an attack allows hackers to redirect email and other services provided to clients. The changes created by this attack are globally cached on recursive DNS servers for a full day. Unless they are purged, it can take a full day or longer for the effects to be reversed.

Table 6.2 provides a DNS quick reference of ports and definitions.

TABLE 6.2 DNS Quick Reference

Ports	53/TCP, 53/UDP
Definition	RFC 882
	RC 1034
	RFC 1035

Various extensions to DNS have been proposed, to enhance its functionality and security, for instance, by introducing authentication through the use of DNSSEC, multicasting, or service discovery.[26]

Lightweight Directory Access Protocol (LDAP)[27]

Lightweight Directory Access Protocol (LDAP) is a client/server-based directory query protocol loosely based upon X.500, commonly used for managing user information. As opposed to DNS, for instance, LDAP is a front end and not used to manage or synchronize data per se. Back ends to LDAP can be directory services, such as NIS (see the section "Network Information Service [NIS], NIS +"), Microsoft's Active Directory Service, Sun's iPlanet Directory Server (renamed to Sun Java System Directory Server), and Novell's eDirectory. LDAP provides only weak authentication based on host name resolution. It would therefore be easy to subvert LDAP security by breaking DNS (see the section "Domain Name System [DNS]").

Table 6.3 provides an LDAP quick reference of ports and definitions.

TABLE 6.3 LDAP Quick Reference

Ports	389/TCP, 389/UDP
Definition	RFC 1777

LDAP communication is transferred in cleartext and therefore is easily intercepted. One way for the security architect to address the issues of weak authentication and cleartext communication would be through the deployment of LDAP over SSL, providing authentication, integrity, and confidentiality.

Network Basic Input Output System (NetBIOS)

The Network Basic Input Output System (NetBIOS) application programming interface (API) was developed in 1983 by IBM. NetBIOS was later ported to TCP/IP (NetBIOS over TCP/IP, also known as NetBT). Under TCP/IP, NetBIOS runs over TCP on ports 137 and 138 and over UDP on port 139. In addition, it uses port 135 for remote procedure calls (see the section "Remote Procedure Calls").

Table 6.4 provides a NetBIOS quick reference of ports and definitions.

TABLE 6.4 NetBIOS Quick Reference

Ports	135/UDP
	137/TCP
	138/TCP
	139/UDP
Definition	RFC 1001
	RFC 1002

Network Information Service (NIS), NIS +

Network Information Service (NIS) and NIS + are directory services developed by Sun Microsystems and are mostly used in UNIX environments. They are commonly used for managing user credentials across a group of machines, for instance, a UNIX workstation cluster or client/server environment, but they can be used for other types of directories as well.

NIS

NIS uses a flat namespace in so-called domains. It is based on RPC and manages all entities on a server (NIS server). NIS servers can be set up redundantly through the use of slave servers. NIS is known for a number of security weaknesses. The fact that NIS does not authenticate individual RPC requests can be used to spoof responses to NIS requests from a client. This would, for instance, enable an attacker to inject fake credentials and thereby obtain or escalate privileges on the target machine. Retrieval of directory information is possible if the name of a NIS domain has become known or is guessable, as any of the clients can associate themselves with a NIS domain. A number of guides have been published on how to secure NIS servers. The basic steps that the security architect and practitioner would need to take are the following: Secure the platform a NIS server is running on, isolate the NIS server from traffic outside of a LAN, and configure it so the probability for disclosure of authentication credentials, especially system privileged ones, is limited.

NIS +

NIS+ uses a hierarchical namespace. It is based on Secure RPC (see the section "Remote Procedure Calls"). Authentication and authorization concepts in NIS+ are more mature; they require authentication for each access of a directory object. However, NIS+ authentication in itself will only be as strong as authentication to one of the clients in a NIS+ environment, as NIS+ is built on a trust relationship between different hosts. The most relevant attacks against a correctly configured NIS+ network come from attacks against its cryptographic security. NIS+ can be run at different security levels; however, most levels available are irrelevant for an operational network.[28]

Common Internet File System (CIFS)/Server Message Block (SMB)

Common Internet File System (CIFS)/Server Message Block (SMB) is a file-sharing protocol prevalent on Windows systems. A UNIX/Linux implementation exists in the free Samba project. SMB was originally designed to run on top of the NetBIOS protocol (see the section "Network Basic Input Output System [NetBIOS]"); it can, however, be run directly over TCP/IP.

Table 6.5 provides a CIFS/SMB quick reference of ports and definitions.

TABLE 6.5 CIFS/SMB Quick Reference

Ports	445/TCP
	See also "Network Basic Input Output System (NetBIOS)"
Definition	Proprietary

CIFS is capable of supporting user-level and tree/object-level (share-level) security. Authentication can be performed via challenge/response authentication as well as by transmission of credentials in cleartext. This second provision has been added largely for backward compatibility in legacy Windows environments.

The main attacks against CIFS are based upon obtaining credentials, be it by sniffing for cleartext authentication or by cryptographic attacks.

Network File System (NFS)

Network File System (NFS) is a client/server file-sharing system common to the UNIX platform. It was originally developed by Sun Microsystems, but implementations exist on all common UNIX platforms, including Linux, as well as Microsoft Windows. NFS has been revised several times, including updates to NFS Versions 2 and 3. NFS version 2 was based on UDP, and version 3 introduced TCP support. Both are implemented on top of RPC (see the section "Remote Procedure Calls"). NFS versions 2 and 3 are stateless protocols, mainly due to performance considerations. As a consequence, the server must manage file locking separately.

Table 6.6 provides an NFS quick reference of ports and definitions.

TABLE 6.6 NFS Quick Reference

Ports	See the section "Remote Procedure Calls"
Definition	RFC 1094
	RFC 1813
	RFC 3010

Secure NFS (SNFS) offers secure authentication and encryption using Data Encryption Standard (DES) encryption. In contrast to standard NFS, secure NFS (or rather secure RPC) will authenticate each RPC request. This will increase latency for each request as the authentication is performed and introduces a light performance premium, mainly paid for in terms of computing capacity. Secure NFS uses DES-encrypted time stamps as authentication tokens. If server and client do not have access to the same time server, this can lead to short-term interruptions until server and client have resynchronized themselves.

NFS version 4 is a stateful protocol that uses TCP port 2049. UDP support (and dependency) has been discontinued. NFS version 4 implements its own encryption protocols on the basis of Kerberos and has discontinued use of RPC. Foregoing RPC also means that additional ports are no longer dynamically assigned, which enables use of NFS through firewalls. Another approach that the security architect could consider as part of his or her design is to plan for the securing of NFS where it must be deployed, by tunneling NFS through Secure Shell (SSH), which can be integrated with operating system authentication schemes.

Simple Mail Transfer Protocol (SMTP) and Enhanced Simple Mail Transfer Protocol (ESMTP)

Using port 25/TCP, Simple Mail Transfer Protocol (SMTP) is a client/server protocol utilized to route email on the Internet. Information on mail servers for Internet domains is managed through DNS, using mail exchange (MX) records. Although SMTP takes a simple approach to authentication, it is robust in the way it deals with unavailability; an SMTP server will try to deliver email over a configurable period.

From a protocol perspective, SMTP's main shortcomings are the complete lack of authentication and encryption. Identification is performed by the sender's e-mail address. A mail server will be able to restrict sending access to certain hosts, which should be on the same network as the mail server, as well as set conditions on the sender's email address, which should be one of the domains served by this particular mail server. Otherwise, the mail server may be configured as an open relay, although this is not a recommended practice traditionally because it poses a variety of security concerns and may get the server placed on ban lists of anti-spam organizations.

To address the weaknesses identified in SMTP, an enhanced version of the protocol, ESMTP, was defined. ESMTP is modular in that client and server can negotiate the enhancements used. ESMTP does offer authentication, among other things, and allows for different authentication mechanisms, including basic and several secure authentication mechanisms.

A quick summary comparison of SMTP and ESMTP can be seen in Table 6.7.

TABLE 6.7 Comparison between SMTP and EMTP

SMTP	ESMTP
Simple Mail Transfer Protocol	Extended Simple Mail Transfer Protocol
First command in SMTP session:	First command in ESMTP session:
HELO sayge.com	EHLO sayge.com
RFC 821	RFC 1869
SMTP MAIL FROM and RCPT TO allows size only of 512 characters including <CRLF>.	ESMTP MAIL FROM and RCPT TO allows size greater than 512 characters.
SMTP alone cannot be extended with new commands.	ESMTP is a framework that has enhanced capabilities, allowing it to extend existing SMTP commands.

File Transfer Protocol (FTP)

Before the advent of the World Wide Web and proliferation of Hypertext Transfer Protocol (HTTP), which is built on some of its features, File Transfer Protocol (FTP) was *the* protocol for publishing or disseminating data over the Internet.

Table 6.8 provides an FTP quick reference of ports and definitions.

TABLE 6.8 FTP Quick Reference

Ports	20/TCP (data stream)
	21/TCP (control stream)
Definition	RFC 959

Although this authentication weakness can be addressed through the use of encryption, this approach carries with it the need for additional requirements to be imposed on the client. These requirements and methods are briefly outlined here:

1. Secure FTP with TLS is an extension to the FTP standard that allows clients to request that the FTP session be encrypted. This is done by sending the "AUTH TLS" command. The server has the option of allowing or denying connections that do not request TLS. This protocol extension is defined in the proposed standard RFC 4217.

2. SFTP, the SSH File Transfer Protocol, is not related to FTP except that it also transfers files and has a similar command set for users. SFTP, or secure FTP, is a program that uses SSH to transfer files. Unlike standard FTP, it encrypts both commands and data. It is functionally similar to FTP, but because it uses a different protocol, standard FTP clients cannot be used to talk to an SFTP server.

3. FTP over SSH refers to the practice of tunneling a normal FTP session over an SSH connection. Because FTP uses multiple TCP connections, it is particularly difficult to tunnel over SSH. With many SSH clients, attempting to set up a tunnel for the control channel (the initial client-to-server connection on port 21) will protect only that channel; when data is transferred, the FTP software at either end will set up new TCP connections (data channels), which bypass the SSH connection and thus have no confidentiality or integrity protection.

Trivial File Transfer Protocol (TFTP)

Trivial File Transfer Protocol (TFTP) is a simplified version of FTP, which is used when authentication is not needed and quality of service is not an issue. TFTP runs on port 69 over UDP. It should therefore be used only in trusted networks with low latency.

Table 6.9 provides a TFTP quick reference of ports and definitions.

TABLE 6.9 **TFTP Quick Reference**

Ports	69/UDP
Definition	RFC 1350

In practice, TFTP is used mostly in LANs for the purpose of pulling packages, for instance, in booting up a diskless client or when using imaging services to deploy client environments.

Hypertext Transfer Protocol (HTTP)

Hypertext Transfer Protocol (HTTP) is the layer 7 foundation of the World Wide Web (WWW). HTTP, originally conceived as a stateless, stripped-down version of FTP, was developed at the European Organization for Nuclear Research (CERN) to support the exchange of information in Hypertext Markup Language (HTML).

Table 6.10 provides an HTTP quick reference of ports and definitions.

TABLE 6.10 **HTTP Quick Reference**

Ports	80/TCP; other ports are in use, especially for proxy services
Definition	RFC 1945
	RFC 2109
	RFC 2616

HTTP's popularity caused the deployment of an unprecedented number of Internet-facing servers; many were deployed with out-of-the-box, vendor-preset configurations. Often these settings were geared at convenience rather than security. As a result, numerous previously closed applications were suddenly marketed as "web enabled." By implication, not much time was spent on developing the web interface in a secure manner, and authentication was simplified to become a browser-based style.

Even though HTTP does not natively support quality of service or bidirectional communication, workarounds were quickly developed to deal with Quality of Service (QoS) concerns and bidirectional communication needs. Consequently, HTTP will work from within most networks, shielded or not, and thereby lends itself to tunneling an impressive number of other protocols.

HTTP does not natively support encryption and has a fairly simple authentication mechanism based on domains, which in turn are normally mapped to directories on a web server. Although HTTP authentication is extensible, it is most often used in the classic username/password style.

HTTP Proxying and Anonymizing Proxies

Because HTTP is transmitting data in cleartext and generates a slew of logging information on web servers and proxy servers, the resulting information can be readily used for illegitimate activities, such as industrial espionage. To address this significant concern, the security practitioner can use any of the commercial and free services available that allow for the anonymization of HTTP requests. These services are mainly geared at the privacy market but have also attracted a criminal element seeking to obfuscate activity. A relatively popular free service is Java Anonymous Proxy, or JAP, also referred to as project AN.ON, or Anonymity.Online. JAP is referred to as JonDo within the commercially available solution JonDonym anonymous proxy server.[29]

Open Proxy Servers

Like open mail relays, open proxy servers allow unrestricted access to GET commands from the Internet. They can therefore be used as stepping stones for launching attacks or simply to obscure the origin of illegitimate requests. More importantly, an open proxy server bears an inherent risk of opening access to protected intranet pages from the Internet. (A misconfigured firewall allowing inbound HTTP requests would need to be present on top of the open proxy to allow this to happen.)

As a general rule, HTTP proxy servers should not allow queries from the Internet. For the security architect, it is a best practice to separate application gateways (sometimes implemented as reverse proxies) from the proxy for web browsing because both have very different security levels and business importance. (It would be even better to implement the application gateway as an application proxy and not an HTTP proxy, but this is not always possible.)

Content Filtering

In many organizations, the HTTP proxy is used as a means to implement content filtering, for instance, by logging or blocking traffic that has been defined as or is assumed to be nonbusiness related for some reason. Although filtering on a proxy server or firewall as part of a layered defense can be quite effective to prevent virus infections (though it should never be the only protection against viruses), it will be only moderately effective in preventing access to unauthorized services (such as certain remote-access services or file sharing), as well as preventing the download of unwanted content.

HTTP Tunneling

HTTP tunneling is technically a misuse of the protocol on the part of the designer of such tunneling applications. It has become a popular feature with the rise of the first streaming video and audio applications and has been implemented into many applications that have a market need to bypass user policy restrictions. Usually, HTTP tunneling is applied by encapsulating outgoing traffic from an application in an HTTP request and incoming traffic in a response. This is usually not done to circumvent security but rather to be compatible with existing firewall rules and allow an application to function through a firewall without the need to apply special rules or additional configurations. Many of the most prevalent and successful malicious software packages, including viruses, worms, and especially botnets, will use HTTP as the means to transmit stolen data or control information from infected hosts through firewalls.

Suitable countermeasures that the security practitioner should consider include filtering on a firewall or proxy server and assessing clients for installations of unauthorized software. However, a security professional will have to balance the business value and effectiveness of these countermeasures with the incentive for circumvention that a restriction of popular protocols will create.

Implications of Multi-Layer Protocols

Multi-layer protocols have ushered in an era of new vulnerabilities that were once unthinkable. In the past, several "networked" solutions were developed to provide control and communications with industrial devices. These often proprietary protocols evolved over time and eventually merged with other networking technologies such as Ethernet and Token Ring. Several vendors now use the TCP/IP stack to channel and route their own protocols. These protocols are used to control coils, actuators, and machinery in multiple industries such as energy, manufacturing, construction, fabrication, mining, and farming, to name a few. Insecurities in these systems often have real-world visibility and impact. Given the fact that the life expectancy of many of the devices under control is 20 years or longer, it is easy to see how systems can become outdated. Often, critical infrastructure, such as power grids, is controlled using multi-layer protocols. Table 6.11 from the Idaho National Laboratory illustrates some of the differences and related challenges of control systems vs. standard information technology.[30]

TABLE 6.11 Differences and Challenges for Control Systems vs. Information Technology

SECURITY TOPIC	INFORMATION TECHNOLOGY	CONTROL SYSTEMS
Antivirus/Mobile Code	Common Widely used	Uncommon/impossible to deploy effectively
Support Technology Lifetime	2-3 years Diversified vendors	Up to 20 years Single vendor
Outsourcing	Common Widely used	Operations are often outsourced but not diverse to various providers
Application of Patches	Regular Scheduled	Rare, unscheduled Vendor specific
Change Management	Regular Scheduled	Highly managed and complex
Time Critical Content	Generally delays accepted	Delays are unacceptable
Availability	Generally delays accepted	24x7x365 (continuous)
Security Awareness	Moderate in both private and public sector	Poor except for physical
Security Testing/Audit	Part of a good security program	Occasional testing for outages
Physical Security	Secure (server rooms, etc.)	Remote/Unmanned Secure

SCADA

The term most often associated with multi-layer protocols is *supervisory control and data acquisition* (SCADA). Another term used in relation with multi-layer protocols is *industrial control system* or ICS. In general, SCADA systems are designed to operate with several different communication methods including modems, WANS, and various networking equipment. Figure 6.10 shows a general layout of a SCADA system.[31]

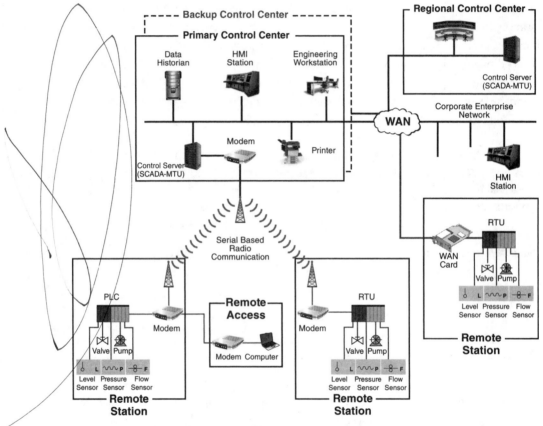

FIGURE 6.10 Diagram of a generic SCADA ICS

As Figure 6.10 demonstrates, a great complexity of devices and information exists in SCADA systems. Most SCADA systems minimally contain the following:

■ **Control Server**—A control server hosts the software and often the interfaces used to control actuators, coils, and PLCs through subordinate control modules across the network.

- **Remote Terminal Unit (RTU)** — The RTU supports SCADA remote stations often equipped with wireless radio interfaces and is used in situations where land-based communications may not be possible.

- **Human-Machine Interface (HMI)** — The HMI is the interface where the humans (operators) can monitor, control, and command the controllers in the system.

- **Programmable Logic Controller (PLC)** — The PLC is a small computer that controls relays, switches, coils, counters, and other devices.

- **Intelligent Electronic Devices (IED)** — The IED is a sensor that can acquire data and also provide feedback to the process through actuation. These devices allow for automatic control at the local level.

- **Input/Output (IO) Server** — The IO server is responsible for collecting process information from components such as IEDs, RTUs, and PLCs. They are often used to interface third-party control components such as custom dashboards with a control server.

- **Data Historian** — The data historian is like the security event and incident management (SEIM) for industrial control systems. It is typically a centralized database for logging process information from a variety of devices.

Given the unique design of SCADA systems and the critical infrastructures that they control, it is little wonder they are a new focus of attacks. Security architects and practitioners responsible for implementing or protecting SCADA systems should be aware of the following types of attacks:

- Network perimeter vulnerabilities

- Protocol vulnerabilities throughout the stack

- Database insecurities

- Session hijacking and man-in-the-middle attacks

- Operating system and server weaknesses

- Device and vendor "backdoors"

In late October of 2013, U.S.-based researchers identified 25 zero-day vulnerabilities in industrial control SCADA software from 20 suppliers that are used to control critical infrastructure systems. Attackers could exploit some of these vulnerabilities to gain control of electrical power and water systems. The vulnerabilities were found in devices that are used for serial and network communications between servers and substations. Serial communication has not been considered as an important or viable attack vector up until now, but breaching a power system through serial communication devices can be easier than attacking through the IP network because it does not require bypassing layers of firewalls. In theory, an intruder could exploit the vulnerabilities simply by breaching the wireless radio network over which the communication passes to the server.

Another issue that the security professional needs to contend with is the inability of antivirus software to address the threats facing SCADA/ICS environments. The Flame virus, for example, avoided detection from 43 different antivirus tools and took more than two years to detect. What the security practitioner needs to do, instead of continuing to rely on the traditional enterprise tools that may work well for desktops and servers, is to have tools in place that allow them to identify threats, respond, and expedite forensic analysis in real time within these complicated systems. For the security practitioner to achieve this, continuous monitoring of all log data generated by IT systems is required to automatically baseline normal, day-to-day activity across systems and identify any and all anomalous activity immediately.

It was announced in March of 2014 that more than 7,600 different power, chemical, and petrochemical plants may still be vulnerable to a handful of SCADA vulnerabilities. A researcher at Rapid 7, the Boston-based firm responsible for the popular pen testing software Metasploit, and an independent security researcher discovered three bugs in Yokogawa Electric's CENTUM CS3000 R3 product. The Windows-based software is primarily used by infrastructure in power plants, airports, and chemical plants across Europe and Asia. The vulnerabilities are essentially a series of buffer overflows, heap based and stack based, that could open the software up to attack. All of them affect computers where CENTUM CS 3000, software that helps operate and monitor industrial control systems, is installed. With the first one, an attacker could send a specially crafted sequence of packets to BKCLogSvr.exe and trigger a heap-based buffer overflow, which in turn could cause a DoS and allow the execution of arbitrary code with system privileges. The second would involve a similar situation; a special packet could be sent to BKHOdeq .exe and cause a stack-based buffer overflow, allowing execution of arbitrary code with the privileges of the CENTUM user. Lastly, another stack-based buffer overflow, this involving the BKBCopyD.exe service, could allow the execution of arbitrary code as well.[32]

In April of 2014, attackers were able to compromise a utility in the United States through an Internet-connected system that gave the attackers access to the utility's internal control system network. The utility had remote access enabled on some of its Internet-connected hosts, and the systems were protected only by simple passwords. Officials at the ICS-CERT, an incident response and forensics organization inside the Department of Homeland Security that specializes in ICS and SCADA systems, said that the public utility was compromised "when a sophisticated threat actor gained unauthorized access to its control system network." The attacker apparently used a simple brute-force attack to gain access to the Internet-facing systems at the utility and then compromised the ICS network. "After notification of the incident, ICS-CERT validated that the software used to administer the control system assets was accessible via Internet facing hosts. The systems were configured with a remote access capability, utilizing a simple password mechanism; however, the authentication method was susceptible to compromise via standard brute forcing techniques," ICS-CERT said in a published report.[33]

The security of industrial control systems and SCADA systems has become a serious concern in recent years as attackers and researchers have begun to focus their attention on them. Many of these systems, which control mechanical devices, manufacturing equipment, utilities, nuclear plants, and other critical infrastructure, are connected to the Internet, either directly or through networks, and this has drawn the attention of attackers looking to do reconnaissance or cause trouble on these networks. Researchers have been sharply critical of the security in the SCADA and ICS industries, saying it's "laughable" and has no formal security development lifecycle. The ICS-CERT report states that the systems in the compromised utility probably were the target of a number of attacks: "It was determined that the systems were likely exposed to numerous security threats and previous intrusion activity was also identified." The investigators were able to identify the issues and found that the attackers likely had not done any damage to the ICS system at the utility.

In the same report, ICS-CERT detailed a separate compromise at an organization that also had a control system connected to the Internet. Attackers were able to compromise the ICS system, which operates an unspecified mechanical device, but did not do any real damage. "The device was directly Internet accessible and was not protected by a firewall or authentication access controls. At the time of compromise, the control system was mechanically disconnected from the device for scheduled maintenance," the report says. "ICS-CERT provided analytic assistance and determined that the actor had access to the system over an extended period of time and had connected via both HTTP and the SCADA protocol. However, further analysis determined that no attempts were made by the threat actor to manipulate the system or inject unauthorized control actions."

The security architect and practitioner should familiarize themselves with the latest alerts released by the ICS-CERT. These can be found at `https://ics-cert.us-cert.gov/alerts/`.

Security professionals should also consider the following list as a starting point for defensive actions that can be used to help secure SCADA/ICS systems:

- Minimize network exposure for all control system devices. In general, locate control system networks and devices behind firewalls and isolate them from the business network.

- When remote access is required, employ secure methods, such as virtual private networks (VPNs), recognizing that VPNs may have vulnerabilities and should be updated to the most current version available. Also recognize that a VPN is only as secure as the connected devices.

- Remove, disable, or rename any default system accounts wherever possible.
- Implement account lockout policies to reduce the risk from brute-forcing attempts.
- Establish and implement policies requiring the use of strong passwords.
- Monitor the creation of administrator-level accounts by third-party vendors.
- Apply patches in the ICS environment, when possible, to mitigate known vulnerabilities.

Modbus and Fieldbus

Modbus and Fieldbus are standard industrial communication protocols designed by separate groups. The focus of the design around these protocols is not security; rather it is uptime and control of devices. Many of these protocols send information in cleartext across transmission media. Additionally, many of these protocols and the devices they support require little or no authentication to execute commands on a device. The security architect and practitioner need to work together to ensure that strict logical and physical controls are implemented to ensure these protocols are encapsulated and isolated from any public or open network.

TELECOMMUNICATIONS TECHNOLOGIES

The area of telecommunications technologies is a broad one that encompasses many things that the SSCP will need to know. IP convergence, VoIP, POTS, PBX, cellular, and attacks and countermeasures are all items that are important to understand fully. The SSCP will want to ensure that they have a good, broad understanding of the key enabling technologies in this area, as well as the use of these technologies within the enterprise in a secure manner.

Converged Communications

IP convergence can be defined as using the Internet Protocol (IP) to transmit all of the information that transits a network, such as voice, data, music, or video.

The benefits of IP convergence that the security architect and practitioner can bring to the enterprise through the design, deployment, and management of a converged network infrastructure are as follows:

- Excellent support for multimedia applications.
- A converged IP network is a single platform on which interoperable devices can be run in innovative ways.

- A converged IP network is easier to manage because of the uniform setup in which the system resources operate.

- An IP convergent network is capable of making use of the developments in class of service differentiation and QoS-based routing.

- A uniform environment requires fewer components in the network.

- Device integration has the potential to simplify end-to-end security management and at the same time make it more robust.

Fibre Channel over Ethernet (FCoE)

Now that 10 GbE is becoming more widespread, Fibre Channel over Ethernet (FCoE) is the next attempt to converge block storage protocols onto Ethernet. FCoE takes advantage of 10 GbE performance and compatibility with existing Fibre Channel protocols. It relies on an Ethernet infrastructure that uses the IEEE Data Center Bridging (DCB) standards. The DCB standards can apply to any IEEE 802 network, but most often the term DCB refers to enhanced Ethernet.

The DCB standards define four new technologies:[34]

1. **Priority-based Flow Control (PFC), 802.1Qbb**—Allows the network to pause different traffic classes.

2. **Enhanced Transmission Selection (ETS), 802.1Qaz**—Defines the scheduling behavior of multiple traffic classes, including strict priority and minimum guaranteed bandwidth capabilities. This should enable fair sharing of the link, better performance, and metering.

3. **Quantized Congestion Notification (QCN), 802.1Qau**—Supports end-to-end flow control in a switched LAN infrastructure and helps eliminate sustained, heavy congestion in an Ethernet fabric. Before the network can use QCN, you must implement QCN in all components in the Converged Enhanced Ethernet (CEE) data path. (This includes components such as Converged Network Adapters [CNAs], switches, and so on.) QCN networks must also use PFC to avoid dropping packets and ensure a lossless environment.

4. **Data Center Bridging Exchange Protocol (DCBX), 802.1Qaz**—Supports discovery and configuration of network devices that support PFC, ETS, and QCN.

FCoE is a lightweight encapsulation protocol and lacks the reliable data transport of the TCP layer. Therefore, FCoE must operate on DCB-enabled Ethernet and use lossless traffic classes to prevent Ethernet frame loss under congested network conditions. FCoE on a DCB network mimics the lightweight nature of native FC protocols and media. It does not incorporate TCP or even IP protocols. This means that FCoE is a layer 2 (non-routable) protocol just like FC. FCoE is only for short-haul communication within a data center.

iSCSI

iSCSI is Internet SCSI (Small Computer System Interface), an Internet Protocol (IP)-based storage networking standard for linking data storage facilities, developed by the Internet Engineering Task Force (IETF) as RFC 3720.[35] By carrying SCSI commands over IP networks, iSCSI is used to facilitate data transfers over intranets and to manage storage over long distances. Because of the ubiquity of IP networks, iSCSI can be used to transmit data over local area networks (LANs), wide area networks (WANs), or the Internet and can enable location-independent data storage and retrieval.

When an end user or application sends a request, the operating system generates the appropriate SCSI commands and data request, which then go through encapsulation and, if necessary, encryption procedures. A packet header is added before the resulting IP packets are transmitted over an Ethernet connection. When a packet is received, it is decrypted (if it was encrypted before transmission) and disassembled, separating the SCSI commands and request. The SCSI commands are sent on to the SCSI controller and from there to the SCSI storage device. Because iSCSI is bidirectional, the protocol can also be used to return data in response to the original request.

Multi-Protocol Label Switching (MPLS)

Multi-Protocol Label Switching (MPLS) is best summarized as a Layer 2.5 networking protocol. In a traditional IP network, each router performs an IP lookup ("routing"), determines a next-hop based on its routing table, and forwards the packet to that next-hop. Every router does the same, each making its own independent routing decisions, until the final destination is reached. MPLS does *label switching* instead. The first device does a routing lookup, just like before, but instead of finding a next-hop, it finds the final destination router. And it finds a pre-determined path from "here" to that final router. The router applies a "label" (or "shim") based on this information. Future routers use the label to route the traffic without needing to perform any additional IP lookups. At the final destination router, the label is removed, and the packet is delivered via normal IP routing.[36]

So why do security professionals still care about MPLS? Three reasons:

- **Implementing Traffic-Engineering**—The ability to control where and how traffic is routed on your network, manage capacity, prioritize different services, and prevent congestion.

- **Implementing Multi-Service Networks**—The ability to deliver data transport services, as well as IP routing services, across the same packet-switched network infrastructure.

- **Improving Network Resiliency**—With MPLS Fast Reroute.

VoIP

Voice over Internet Protocol (VoIP) is a technology that allows you to make voice calls using a broadband Internet connection instead of a regular (or analog) phone line. VoIP is simply the transmission of voice traffic over IP-based networks. VoIP is also the foundation for more advanced unified communications applications such as web and video conferencing. VoIP systems are based on the use of the Session Initiation Protocol (SIP), which is the recognized standard. Any SIP compatible device can talk to any other. Any SIP-based IP-phone can call another right over the Internet; you do not need any additional equipment or even a phone provider. Just plug your SIP phone into an Internet connection, configure it, and then dial the other person right over the Internet.

In all VoIP systems, your voice is converted into packets of data and then transmitted to the recipient over the Internet and decoded back into your voice at the other end. To make it quicker, these packets are compressed before transmission with certain codecs, almost like zipping a file on the fly. There are many codecs with different ways of achieving compression and managing bitrates; thus, each codec has its own bandwidth requirements and provides different voice quality for VoIP calls.

VoIP systems employ session control and signaling protocols to control the signaling, setup, and teardown of calls. They transport audio streams over IP networks using special media delivery protocols that encode voice, audio, video with audio codecs, and video codecs as digital audio by streaming media. Various codecs exist that optimize the media stream based on application requirements and network bandwidth; some implementations rely on narrowband and compressed speech, while others support high-fidelity stereo codecs. Some popular codecs include μ-law and a-law versions of G.711, G.722 (which is a high-fidelity codec marketed as HD Voice by Polycom), a popular open source voice codec known as iLBC, a codec that only uses 8 kbit/s each way called G.729, and many others.

Session Initiation Protocol (SIP)[37]

As its name implies, Session Initiation Protocol (SIP) is designed to manage multimedia connections. SIP is designed to support digest authentication structured by realms, similar to HTTP (basic username/password authentication has been removed from the protocol as of RFC 3261).[38] In addition, SIP provides integrity protection through MD5 hash functions. SIP supports a variety of encryption mechanisms, such as TLS. Privacy extensions to SIP, including encryption and caller ID suppression, have been defined in extensions to the original Session Initiation Protocol (RFC 3325).[39]

Packet Loss

A technique called packet loss concealment (PLC) is used in VoIP communications to mask the effect of dropped packets. There are several techniques that may be used by different implementations. Zero substitution is the simplest PLC technique that requires the least computational resources. These simple algorithms generally provide the lowest-quality sound when a significant number of packets are discarded. Waveform substitution is used in older protocols, and it works by substituting the lost frames with artificially generated, substitute sound. The simplest form of substitution simply repeats the last received packet. Unfortunately, waveform substitution often results in unnatural, "robotic" sound when a long burst of packets is lost.

Jitter

Unlike network delay, jitter does not occur because of the packet delay, but because of a variation of packet delays. As VoIP endpoints try to compensate for jitter by increasing the size of the packet buffer, jitter causes delays in the conversation. If the variation becomes too high and exceeds 150ms, callers notice the delay and often revert to a walkie-talkie style of conversation. By definition, reducing the delays on the network helps keep the buffer under 150ms even if a significant variation is present.

Sequence Errors

Some VoIP systems discard packets received out of order, while other systems discard out-of-order packets if they exceed the size of the internal buffer, which in turn causes jitter. Sequence errors can also cause significant degradation of call quality. Sequence errors may occur because of the way packets are routed. Packets may travel along different paths through different IP networks, causing different delivery times. As a result, lower-numbered packets may arrive at the endpoint later than higher numbered ones.

Codec Quality

A codec is software that converts audio signals into digital frames and vice versa. Codecs are characterized by different sampling rates and resolutions. Different codecs employ different compression methods and algorithms, using different bandwidth and computational requirements.

POTS and PBX

There are two standard phone systems used for telecommunications: POTS and PBX.

POTS

Plain old telephone service (POTS) is commonly found in the "last mile" of most residential and business telephone services. Once called "Post Office Telephone Service" in some countries, the name has mostly been retired due to the proliferation of phones in homes and businesses. POTS typically represents a bidirectional analog telephone interface that was designed to carry the sound of the human voice. POTS lacks the mobility of cellular phones and the bandwidth of several competing products; however, it is one of the most reliable systems available with an uptime close to or exceeding 99.999%. POTS is still often the telecom method of choice when high reliability is required and bandwidth is not. Typical applications include alarm systems and "out-of-band" command links for routers and other network devices.

PBX

A private branch exchange (PBX) is an enterprise-class phone system typically used in businesses or large organizations. A PBX often includes an internal switching network, and a controller that is attached to telecommunications trunks. Many PBXs had default manufacturer configuration codes, ports, and control interfaces that could be exploited if the security professional did not reconfigure them prior to deployment. A PBX is often targeted by war dialers who can then use the PBX to route long distance calling or eavesdrop on the organization. Analog POTS PBXs have largely been replaced with VoIP-based or VoIP-enabled PBXs.

Cellular

A cellular network or mobile network is a radio network distributed over land areas called cells, each served by at least one fixed-location transceiver, known as a *cell site* or *base station*. In a cellular network, each cell characteristically uses a different set of radio frequencies from all their immediate neighboring cells to avoid any interference. When joined together, these cells provide radio coverage over a wide geographic area. This enables a large number of portable transceivers (e.g., mobile phones, pagers, etc.) to communicate with each other and with fixed transceivers and telephones anywhere in the network, via base stations, even if some of the transceivers are moving through more than one cell during transmission.

Attacks and Countermeasures

DDoS affects many types of systems. Some have used the term TDoS to refer to DDoS or DoS attacks on telecommunications systems (Telecommunications Denial of Service). Typical motives can be anything from revenge, extortion, political/ideological, and distraction from a larger set of financial crimes. The Dirt Jumper bot has been used to create distractions by launching DDoS attacks upon financial institutions and financial infrastructure at the same time that fraud is taking place (with the Zeus Trojan, or other banking malware or other attack technique). See Figure 6.11. Similarly, DDoS aimed at telecommunications is being used to create distractions that allow other crimes to go unnoticed for a longer period.

FIGURE 6.11 Dirt Jumper Bot Malware screen capture

A successful cyber-attack on a telecommunications operator could disrupt service for thousands of phone customers, sever Internet service for millions of consumers, cripple businesses, and shut down government operations. And there's reason to worry: Cyber-attacks against critical infrastructure are soaring. For instance, in 2012, the U.S. Computer Emergency Readiness Team (US-CERT), a division of the Department of Homeland Security, processed approximately 190,000 cyber incidents involving U.S. government agencies, critical infrastructure, and the department's industry partners. This represents a 68% increase over 2011.[40]

Another issue is the DDoS "attack for hire" networks that exist in the wild today. For example, keyword searches discovered several DDoS-as-a-service (DaaS) sites like the ones pictured in Figures 6.12 and 6.13 offering DDoS attack services starting at $30 per month.

FIGURE 6.12 A DDoS attack for hire network ad

Prices depend on the individual and "complexity" of the order:

1 hour from $10
Day $30
Week $180
sms 1000 sms flood - a $20
phone numbers flood, flooding call 1- hour $30

Online, almost constantly

FIGURE 6.13 **Another DDoS attack for hire network ad**

SIP flooding attacks are another attack vector that the security practitioner needs to be aware of. Often, SIP flooding attacks take place because attackers are running brute-force password guessing scripts that overwhelm the processing capabilities of the SIP device, but pure flooding attacks on SIP servers also occur. Once the attackers obtain credentials into a VoIP or other PBX system, that system can become a pawn in their money-making scheme to perform DoS, Vishing, or other types of attacks. Default credentials are one of the security weaknesses that the attackers leverage to gain access to the VoIP/PBX systems, so organizations should ensure that their telecommunications systems credentials are strong enough to resist brute-force attack and that the ability to reach the telephone system is limited as much as possible in order to reduce the attack surface and convince the attacker to move on to the next victim.

Any system is subject to availability attacks at any point where an application layer or other processor-intensive operation exists as well as the networks that supply these systems via link saturation and state-table exhaustion. Telecommunications systems are no exception to this principle.

CONTROL NETWORK ACCESS

The best way to control access to anything is to monitor any and all routes that can be used to access the item in question. Through continuous monitoring of the known access pathways, any attempts to gain access will be observed and can then be managed. The same thought process is applied to network access. The SSCP will want to understand how to ensure that all identified pathways to gain access to a system are monitored and that the appropriate control mechanisms are deployed to secure them. These may include the use of secure routing, DMZs, and hardware such as firewalls.

Secure Routing/Deterministic Routing

While it is possible to establish corporate wide area networks (WANs) using the Internet and VPN technology, it is not desirable. Relying on the Internet to provide connectivity means that there is little ability to control the routes that traffic takes or to remedy performance issues. Deterministic routing means that WAN connectivity is supplied based upon a limited number of different routes, typically supplied by a large network provider. Deterministic routing means that traffic only travels by pre-determined routes that are known to be either secure or less susceptible to compromise. Similarly, deterministic routing from a large carrier will make it much easier to address performance issues and to maintain the service levels required by the applications on the WAN. If the WAN is supporting converged applications like voice (VOIP) or video (for security monitoring or video conferencing), then deterministic routing becomes even more essential to the assurance of the network.

Boundary Routers

Boundary routers primarily advertise routes that external hosts can use to reach internal ones. However, they should also be part of an organization's security perimeter by filtering external traffic that should never be allowed to enter the internal network. For example, boundary routers may prevent external packets from the Finger service from entering the internal network because that service is used to gather information about hosts.

A key function of boundary routers is the prevention of inbound or outbound IP spoofing attacks. In using a boundary router, spoofed IP addresses would not be routable across the network perimeter. Examples of IP spoofing attacks are

Non-Blind Spoofing   This type of attack takes place when the attacker is on the same subnet as the victim. The sequence and acknowledgement numbers can be sniffed, eliminating the potential difficulty of calculating them accurately. The biggest threat of spoofing in this instance would be session hijacking. This is accomplished by corrupting the data stream of an established connection and then re-establishing it based on correct sequence and acknowledgment numbers with the attack machine.

Blind Spoofing   This is a more sophisticated attack because the sequence and acknowledgment numbers are unattainable. Several packets are sent to the target machine in order to sample sequence numbers. While not the case today, machines in the past used basic techniques for generating sequence numbers. It was relatively easy to discover the exact formula by studying packets and TCP sessions. Today, operating systems implement random sequence number generation, making it difficult to predict sequence numbers accurately. If, however, the sequence number was compromised, data could be sent to the target.

Man-in-the-Middle Attack   Both types of spoofing are forms of a common security violation known as a man-in-the-middle (MITM) attack. In these attacks, a malicious party intercepts a legitimate communication between two friendly parties. The malicious host then controls the flow of communication and can eliminate or alter the information sent by one of the original participants without the knowledge of either the original sender or the recipient.

Security Perimeter

The security perimeter is the first line of protection between trusted and untrusted networks. In general, it includes a firewall and router that help filter traffic. Security perimeters may also include proxies and devices, such as an intrusion detection system (IDS), to warn of suspicious traffic. The defensive perimeter extends out from these first protective devices to include proactive defense such as boundary routers, which can provide early warning of upstream attacks and threat activities.

It is important to note that while the security perimeter is the first line of defense, it must not be the only one. If there are not sufficient defenses within the trusted network, then a misconfigured or compromised device could allow an attacker to enter the trusted network.

Network Partitioning

Segmenting networks into domains of trust is an effective way to help enforce security policies. Controlling which traffic is forwarded between segments will go a long way to protecting an organization's critical digital assets from malicious and unintentional harm.

Dual-Homed Host

A dual-homed host has two network interface cards (NICs), each on a separate network. Provided that the host controls or prevents the forwarding of traffic between NICs, this can be an effective measure to isolate a network.

Bastion Host

Bastion hosts serve as a gateway between a trusted and untrusted network that gives limited, authorized access to untrusted hosts. For instance, a bastion host at an Internet gateway could allow external users to transfer files to it via FTP. This permits files to be exchanged with external hosts without granting them access to the internal network in an uncontrolled manner.

If an organization has a network segment that has sensitive data, it can control access to that network segment by requiring that all access must be from the bastion host. In addition to isolating the network segment, users will have to authenticate to the bastion host, which will help audit access to the sensitive network segment. For example, if a firewall limits access to the sensitive network segment, allowing access to the segment from only the bastion host will eliminate the need for allowing many hosts access to that segment. For instance, terminal servers are a form of bastion host, which allow authenticated users deeper into the network.

A bastion host may also include functionality called a "data diode." In the world of electronics, a diode is a device that only allows current to flow in a single direction. A data diode only allows information to flow in a single direction; for instance, it enforces rules that allow information to be read, but nothing may be written (changed or created or moved).

A bastion host is a specialized computer that is deliberately exposed on a public network. From a secured network perspective, it is the only node exposed to the outside world and is therefore very prone to attack. It is placed outside the firewall in single firewall systems or, if a system has two firewalls, it is often placed between the two firewalls or on the public side of a demilitarized zone (DMZ).

The bastion host processes and filters all incoming traffic and prevents malicious traffic from entering the network, acting much like a gateway. The most common examples of bastion hosts are mail, domain name system, web, and File Transfer Protocol (FTP) servers. Firewalls and routers can also become bastion hosts.

The bastion host node is usually a very powerful server with improved security measures and custom software. It often hosts only a single application because it needs to be very good at what it does. The software is usually customized, proprietary, and not available to the public. This host is designed to be the strong point in the network to protect the system behind it. Therefore, it often undergoes regular maintenance and audit. Sometimes bastion hosts are used to draw attacks so that the source of the attacks may be traced.

For one to maintain the security of bastion hosts, all unnecessary software, daemons, and users are removed. The operating system is continually updated with the latest security updates, and an intrusion detection system is installed.[41]

Demilitarized Zone (DMZ)

A demilitarized zone (DMZ), also known as a screened subnet, allows an organization to give external hosts limited access to public resources, such as a company website, without granting them access to the internal network. See Figure 6.14. Typically, the DMZ is an isolated subnet attached to a firewall (when the firewall has three interfaces—internal, external, and DMZ—this configuration is sometimes called a three-legged firewall). Because external hosts by design have access to the DMZ (albeit controlled by the firewall), organizations should only place in the DMZ hosts and information that are not sensitive.

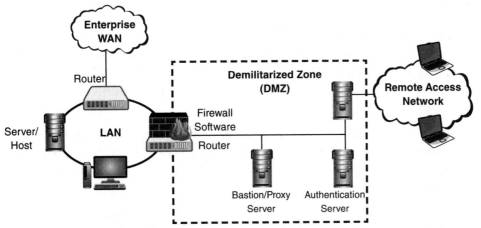

FIGURE 6.14 **A demilitarized zone (DMZ) allows an organization to give external hosts limited access to public resources, such as a company website, without granting them access to the internal network.**

Hardware

Networks use a vast array of hardware, including modems, concatenators, front-end processors, multiplexers, hubs, repeaters, bridges, switches, and routers.

Modems

Modems (modulator/demodulator) allow users remote access to a network via analog phone lines. Essentially, modems convert digital signals to analog and vice versa. A modem that is connected to the user's computer converts a digital signal to analog to be transmitted over a phone line. On the receiving end, a modem converts the user's analog signal to digital and sends it to the connected device, such as a server. Of course, the process is reversed when the server replies. The server's reply is converted from digital to analog and transmitted over the phone line, and so on.

In order to mitigate some of the risks that exist from the legacy analog work of communications, vendors have developed and taken to market *telephony firewalls*, which act not unlike IP firewalls but are designed specifically to focus on analog signals. These firewalls will sit at the demarcation point between the public switched telephone network (PSTN) and the internal organizational network, whether it is an IP phone system or an analog phone system. Telephony firewalls will monitor both incoming and outgoing analog calls to enforce rule-sets.

Concentrators

Concentrators multiplex connected devices into one signal to be transmitted on a network. For instance, a fiber distributed data interface (FDDI) concentrator multiplexes transmissions from connected devices to an FDDI ring.

Front-End Processors

Some hardware architectures employ a hardware front-end processor that sits between the input/output devices and the main computer. By servicing input/output on behalf of the main computer, front-end processors reduce the main computer's overhead.

Multiplexers

A multiplexer overlays multiple signals into one signal for transmission. Using a multiplexer is much more efficient than transmitting the same signals separately. Multiplexers are used in devices from simple hubs to very sophisticated dense-wave division multiplexers (DWDMs) that combine multi-optical signals on one strand of optical fiber.

Hubs and Repeaters

Hubs are used to implement a physical star topology. All of the devices in the star connect to the hub. Essentially, hubs retransmit signals from each port to all other ports. Although hubs can be an economical method to connect devices, there are several important disadvantages:

- All connected devices will receive each other's broadcasts, potentially wasting valuable resources processing irrelevant traffic.
- All devices can read and potentially modify the traffic of other devices.
- If the hub becomes inoperable, then the connected devices will not have access to the network.

Bridges and Switches

Bridges are layer 2 devices that filter traffic between segments based on media access control (MAC) addresses. In addition, they amplify signals to facilitate physically larger networks. A basic bridge filters out frames that are not destined for another segment. Bridges can connect LANs with unlike media types, such as connecting an unshielded twisted pair (UTP) segment with a segment that uses coaxial cable. Bridges do not reformat frames, such as converting a Token Ring frame to Ethernet. This means that only identical layer 2 architectures can be connected with a simple bridge (e.g., Ethernet to Ethernet, etc.). Network administrators can use encapsulating bridges to connect dissimilar layer

2 architectures, such as Ethernet to Token Ring. These bridges encapsulate incoming frames into frames of the destination's architecture. Other specialized bridges filter outgoing traffic based on the destination MAC address. Bridges do not prevent an intruder from intercepting traffic on the local segment. A common type of bridge for many organizations is a wireless bridge based upon one of the IEEE 802.11 standards. While wireless bridges offer compelling efficiencies, they can pose devastating security issues to organizations by effectively making all traffic crossing the bridge visible to anyone connected to the LAN. Wireless bridges must absolutely apply link-layer encryption and any other available native security features such as access lists to ensure secure operation.

Switches solve the same issues posed at the beginning of this section, except the solutions are more sophisticated and more expensive. Essentially, a basic switch is a multiport device to which LAN hosts connect. Switches forward frames only to the device specified in the frame's destination MAC address, which greatly reduces unnecessary traffic. Switches can perform more sophisticated functions to increase network bandwidth. Due to the increased processing speed of switches, models exist that can make forwarding decisions based on IP address and prioritization of types of network traffic. Similar to hubs and bridges, switches forward broadcasts.

Routers

Routers forward packets to other networks. They read the destination layer 3 address (e.g., destination IP address) in received packets, and based on the router's view of the network, it determines the next device on the network (the next hop) to send the packet. If the destination address is not on a network that is directly connected to the router, it will send the packet to another router. Routers can be used to interconnect different technologies. For example, connecting Token Ring and Ethernet networks to the same router would allow IP Ethernet packets to be forwarded to a Token Ring network.

Wired Transmission Media

When the SSCP considers wired transmission media, they should be thinking about items such as Ethernet network cables and fiber-optic cables. Both of these cable types are used to carry information and provide data transmission across the wired networks that make up the corporate LAN. In addition, understanding the differences in cable transmission speeds and distance based on the type of cable used is an important area of knowledge for the SSCP to focus on.

Here are some parameters that should be considered when selecting cables:

- **Throughput**—The rate that data will be transmitted.
- **Distance between Devices**—The degradation or loss of a signal (attenuation) in long runs of cable is a perennial problem, especially if the signal is at a high

frequency. Also, the time required for a signal to travel (propagation delay) may be a factor.

- **Data Sensitivity**—What is the risk of someone intercepting the data in the cables? Fiber optics, for example, makes data interception more difficult than copper cables.

- **Environment**—It is a cable-unfriendly world. Cables may have to be bent when installing, which contributes to degradation of conduction and signal distortion. The amount of electromagnetic interference is also a factor because cables in an industrial environment with a lot of interference may have to be shielded. Similarly, cables running through areas with wide temperature fluctuations and especially exposure to ultra-violet (sunlight) will degrade faster and be subject to degrading signals.

Twisted Pair[42]

Pairs of copper wires are twisted together to reduce electromagnetic interference and cross talk. Each wire is insulated with a fire-resistant material, such as Teflon. The twisted pairs are surrounded by an outer jacket that physically protects the wires. The quality of cable, and therefore its appropriate application, is determined by the number of twists per inch, the type of insulation, and conductive material. Cables are assigned into categories to help determine which cables are appropriate for an application or environment. See Table 6.12.

TABLE 6.12 Cable Categories

CABLE CATEGORIES	SPEED	APPLICATION OR ENVIRONMENT
Category 1	Less than 1 Mbps	Analog voice and basic interface rate (BRI) in Integrated Services Digital Network (ISDN)
Category 2	4 Mbps	4 Mbps IBM Token Ring LAN
Category 3	10 Mbps	10 Base-T Ethernet
Category 4	16 Mbps	16 Mbps Token Ring
Category 5	100 Mbps	100 Base-TX and Asynchronous Transfer Mode(ATM)
Category 5e	1,000 Mbps (1GB)	1000 Base-T Ethernet
Category 6	Up to 10,000 Mbps (10GB)	10BASE-T, 100BASE-TX, 1000BASE-TX, and 10GBASE-T
Category 6a	Up to 10,000 Mbps (10GB)	10BASE-T, 100BASE-TX, 1000BASE-TX, and 10GBASE-T

Unshielded Twisted Pair (UTP)

Unshielded Twisted Pair (UTP) has several drawbacks. Unlike shielded twisted-pair cables, UTP does not have shielding and is therefore susceptible to interference from external electrical sources, which could reduce the integrity of the signal. Also, to intercept transmitted data, an intruder can install a tap on the cable or monitor the radiation from the wire. Thus, UTP may not be a good choice when transmitting very sensitive data or when installed in an environment with much electromagnetic interference (EMI) or radio frequency interference (RFI). Despite its drawbacks, UTP is the most common cable type. UTP is inexpensive, it can be easily bent during installation, and, in most cases, the risk from the above drawbacks is not enough to justify more expensive cables.

Shielded Twisted Pair (STP)

Shielded twisted pair (STP) is similar to UTP. Pairs of insulated twisted copper are enclosed in a protective jacket. However, STP uses an electronically grounded shield to protect the signal. The shield surrounds each of the twisted pairs in the cable, surrounds the bundle of twisted pairs, or both. The shield protects the electronic signals from outside. Although the shielding protects the signal, STP has disadvantages over UTP. STP is more expensive and is bulkier and hard to bend during installation.

Coaxial Cable

Instead of a pair of wires twisted together, coaxial cable (or simply, coax) uses one thick conductor that is surrounded by a grounding braid of wire. A non-conducting layer is placed between the two layers to insulate them. The entire cable is placed within a protective sheath. The conducting wire is much thicker than the twisted pair and therefore can support greater bandwidth and longer cable lengths. The superior insulation protects coaxial cable from electronic interference, such as EMI and RFI. Likewise, the shielding makes it harder for an intruder to monitor the signal with antennae or install a tap. Coaxial cable has some disadvantages. The cable is expensive and is difficult to bend during installation. For this reason, coaxial cable is used in specialized applications, such as cable TV.

Patch Panels

As an alternative to directly connecting devices, devices are connected to the patch panel. Then, a network administrator can connect two of these devices by attaching a small cable, called a patch cord, to two jacks in the panel. To change how these devices are connected, network administrators only have to reconnect patch cords. Patch panels and wiring closets must be secured since they offer an excellent place to tap into the network and egress the product. Wiring must be well laid out, it must be neat, and the records must be kept in a secure location; otherwise, it is much easier to hide a tap in a mess of wires. Shared wiring closets should be avoided.

Fiber Optic

Fiber optics use light pulses to transmit information down fiber lines instead of using electronic pulses to transmit information down copper lines. At one end of the system is a transmitter. This is the place of origin for information coming on to fiber-optic lines. The transmitter accepts coded electronic pulse information coming from copper wire. It then processes and translates that information into equivalently coded light pulses. A light-emitting diode (LED) or an injection-laser diode (ILD) can be used for generating the light pulses. Using a lens, the light pulses are funneled into the fiber-optic medium where they travel down the cable.

There are three types of fiber-optic cable commonly used: single mode, multimode, and plastic optical fiber (POF). See Table 6.13.

TABLE 6.13 Fiber Types and Typical Specifications

CORE/CLADDING	ATTENUATION	BANDWIDTH	APPLICATIONS/NOTES
Multi-mode Graded-Index			
	@850/1300 nm	@850/1300 nm	
50/125 microns	3/1 dB/km	500/500 MHz-km	Laser-rated for GbE LANs
50/125 microns	3/1 dB/km	2000/500 MHz-km	Optimized for 850 nm VCSELs
62.5/125 microns	3/1 dB/km	160/500 MHz-km	Most common LAN fiber
100/140 microns	3/1 dB/km	150/300 MHz-km	Obsolete
Single-mode			
	@1310/1550 nm		
8-9/125 microns	0.4/0.25 dB/km	HIGH!	Telco/CATV/long high speed LANs
		~100 Terahertz	
Multi-mode Step-Index			
	@850 nm	@850 nm	
200/240 microns	4-6 dB/km	50 MHz-km	Slow LANs & links
POF (Plastic Optical Fiber)			
	@ 650 nm	@ 650 nm	
1 mm	~ 1 dB/m	~5 MHz-km	Short links & cars

WARNING   You cannot mix and match fibers! Trying to connect single-mode to multimode fibers can cause 20 dB loss—that's 99% of the power. Even connections between 62.5/125 and 50/125 can cause loss of 3 dB or more—over half the power.

Endpoint Security

Workstations should be hardened, and users should be using limited access accounts whenever possible in accordance with the concept of "least privilege." Workstations should minimally have

- Up-to-date antivirus and antimalware software
- A configured and operational host-based firewall
- A hardened configuration with unneeded services disabled
- A patched and maintained operating system

While workstations are clearly the endpoint most will associate with endpoint attacks, the landscape is changing. Mobile devices such as smartphones, tablets, and personal devices are beginning to make up more and more of the average organization's endpoints. With this additional diversity of devices, there becomes a requirement for the security architect to also increase the diversity and agility of an organization's endpoint defenses. For mobile devices such as smartphones and tablets, security practitioners should consider

- Encryption for the whole device, or if not possible, then at least encryption for sensitive information held on the device
- Remote management capabilities including:
  - Remote wipe
  - Remote geo-locate
  - Remote update
  - Remote operation
- User policies and agreements that ensure an organization can manage the device or seize it for legal hold

Voice Technologies

In the age of convergence, the area of voice technologies is an important one for the SSCP to consider when it comes to a discussion around the concepts of controlling network access. If voice technologies are not made a part of the plan that the SSCP will use to ensure that network communications enforce data confidentiality and integrity, then a defense-in-depth architecture cannot be fully realized. In that case, the SSCP is not exercising due care and due diligence with regard to the security of the network design and operation.

Modems and Public Switched Telephone Networks (PSTN)

The Public Switched Telephone Network (PSTN) is a circuit-switched network that was originally designed for analog voice communication. When a person places a call, a dedicated circuit is created between the two phones. Although it appears to the callers that they are using a dedicated line, they are actually communicating through a complex network. As with all circuit-switched technology, the path through the network is established before communication between the two endpoints begins, and barring an unusual event, such as a network failure, the path remains constant during the call. Phones connect to the PSTN with copper wires to a central office (CO), which services an area of about 1 to 10 km. The central offices are connected to a hierarchy of tandem offices (for local calls) and toll offices (toll calls), with each higher level of the hierarchy covering a larger area. Including the COs, the PSTN has five levels of offices. When both endpoints of a call are connected to the same CO, the traffic is switched within the CO. Otherwise, the call must be switched between a toll center and a tandem office. The greater the distance between the calls, the higher in the hierarchy the calls are switched. To accommodate the high volume of traffic, toll centers communicate with each other over fiber-optic cables.

War Dialing

Although modems allowed remote access to networks from almost anywhere, they could be used as a portal into the network by an attacker. Using automated dialing software, the attacker could dial the entire range of phone numbers used by the company to identify modems. If the host, to which the modem was attached, had a weak password, then the attacker would easily gain access to the network. Worse yet, if voice and data shared the same network, then both voice and data could be compromised.

The best defense against this attack is not to leave unattended modems turned on and keep an up-to-date inventory of all modems so none get orphaned and left to operate without the knowledge and oversight of the security professional. All modems should require some form of authentication, at least a single factor, although the industry standard has moved to two-factor authentication for modem connections due to the risks that use of these devices poses. If modems are necessary, then organizations must ensure that the passwords protecting the attached host are strong, preferably with the help of authentication mechanisms, such as RADIUS, one-time passwords, etc.

Multimedia Collaboration

The use of multimedia collaboration technologies is standard practice in the enterprise today. The need to understand and secure these technologies as part of a defense-in-depth approach to network security is part of the responsibilities that the SSCP has in their role as a security practitioner. Whether it is P2P, remote meeting technology, or instant messaging clients, the unrestricted usage of these applications and technologies can lead to vulnerabilities being exploited by bad actors to the detriment of the organization.

Peer-to-Peer Applications and Protocols

Peer-to-Peer (P2P) applications are often designed to open an uncontrolled channel through network boundaries (normally through tunneling). They therefore provide a way for dangerous content, such as botnets, spyware applications, and viruses, to enter an otherwise protected network. Because P2P networks can be established and managed using a series of multiple, overlapping master and slave nodes, they can be very difficult to fully detect and shut down. If one master node is detected and shut down, the "bot herder" who controls the P2P botnet can make one of the slave nodes a master and use that as a redundant staging point, allowing for botnet operations to continue unimpeded.

Remote Meeting Technology

Several technologies and services exist that allow organizations and individuals to meet virtually. These applications are typically web-based, and they install extensions in the browser or client software on the host system. These technologies also typically allow desktop sharing as a feature. This feature not only allows the viewing of a user's desktop but also control of the system by a remote user.

Some organizations use dedicated equipment such as cameras, monitors, and meeting rooms to host and participate in remote meetings. These devices are often a combination of VoIP and in some cases POTS technology. They are also subject to the same risks including but not limited to

- War dialing
- Vendor backdoors
- Default passwords
- Vulnerabilities in the underlying operating system or firmware

Instant Messaging

Instant messaging systems can generally be categorized in three classes: peer-to-peer networks, brokered communication, and server-oriented networks. All these classes will support basic "chat" services on a one-to-one basis and frequently on a many-to-many basis. Most instant messaging applications do offer additional services beyond their text messaging capability, for instance, screen sharing, remote control, exchange of files, and voice and video conversation. Some applications even allow command scripting. Instant messaging/chat is increasingly considered a significant business application used for office communications, customer support, and "presence" applications. Instant message capabilities will frequently be deployed with a bundle of other IP-based services such as VoIP and video conferencing support. It should be noted that many of the risks mentioned here apply also to online games, which today offer instant communication between participants. For instance, multiplayer role-playing games, such as multiuser domains (MUDs), rely heavily on instant messaging that is similar in nature to Internet Relay Chat (IRC), even though it is technically based on a variant of the TELNET protocol.

Open Protocols, Applications, and Services

In order to be able to properly secure network access, it is important to understand the traffic that is moving through the network at all times. The ability to monitor traffic is impacted by the types of traffic being created and used in a network. The SSCP should have an understanding of the protocols, applications, and services that are in use on the networks that they are charged with defending. For example, the use of Jabber should raise a red flag for a security professional, as Jabber may be a potential source of confidentiality concerns if not configured properly. This section will discuss these issues and concerns and help the SSCP to understand what they need to do to address them.

Extensible Messaging and Presence Protocol (XMPP) and Jabber

Jabber is an open instant messaging protocol for which a variety of open source clients exist. A number of commercial services based on Jabber exist. Jabber has been formalized as an Internet standard under the name Extensible Messaging and Presence Protocol (XMPP), as defined in RFC 3920 and RFC 3921.[43]

Jabber is a server-based application. Its servers are designed to interact with other instant messaging applications. As with IRC, anybody can host a Jabber server. The Jabber server network can therefore not be considered trusted. Although Jabber traffic can be encrypted via TLS, this does not prevent eavesdropping on the part of server operators. However, Jabber does provide an API to encrypt the actual payload data.[44] Jabber itself offers a variety of authentication methods, including cleartext and challenge/response authentication. To implement interoperability with other instant messaging systems from the server, however, the server will have to cache the user's credentials for the target network, enabling a number of attacks, mainly on behalf of the server operator but also for anyone able to break into a server.

Internet Relay Chat (IRC)[45]

Internet Relay Chat (IRC) is a client/server-based network. IRC is unencrypted and therefore an easy target for sniffing attacks. The basic architecture of IRC, founded on trust among servers, enables special forms of denial-of-service attacks. For instance, a malicious user can hijack a channel while a server or group of servers has been disconnected from the rest (net split). IRC is also a common platform for social engineering attacks, aimed at inexperienced or technically unskilled users.

Tunneling Firewalls and Other Restrictions

Control of HTTP tunneling can happen on the firewall or the proxy server. It should, however, be considered that in the case of peer-to-peer protocols, this would require a "deny by default" policy, and blocking instant messaging without providing a legitimate alternative is not likely to foster user acceptance and might give users incentive to utilize even more dangerous workarounds. It should be noted that inbound file transfers can also result in circumvention of policy or restrictions in place, in particular for the spreading of viruses. An effective countermeasure can be found in on-access antivirus scanning on the client, which should be enabled anyway.

Remote Access

Remote access technologies are an important area for the SSCP to focus on with regards to the ability to build a complete solution that addresses all aspects of controlling network access. Being able to balance the needs of users who will want to be able to work remotely and still maintain access to necessary corporate resources against the organization's needs to ensure the confidentiality, integrity, and availability of the same resources is difficult. The ability for remote access technologies to address the needs and concerns of both audiences hinges on the design, implementation, and operation of the technology solution being used. It is up to the SSCP to develop the level of knowledge required to ensure that remote access technologies such as VPNs and tunneling protocols such as L2TP are used properly to ensure availability of resources while also safeguarding the confidentiality and integrity of them as well.

Virtual Private Network (VPN)

A Virtual Private Network (VPN) is an encrypted tunnel between two hosts that allows them to securely communicate over an untrusted network, e.g., the Internet. Remote users employ VPNs to access their organization's network, and depending on the VPN's implementation, they may have most of the same resources available to them as if they were physically at the office. As an alternative to expensive dedicated point-to-point connections, organizations use gateway-to-gateway VPNs to securely transmit information over the Internet between sites or even with business partners.

Tunneling

A tunnel is a communications channel between two networks that is used to transport another network protocol by encapsulation of its packets. Protocols such as Point-to-Point Tunneling Protocol (PPTP) and Layer 2 Tunneling (L2TP) are used to create these tunnels and to allow for the secure transmission of data between two endpoints, whether they are on the same or different networks. Authentication protocols such as Remote Authentication Dial In User Service (RADIUS) are deployed alongside of tunneling protocols to ensure that user authentication is handled properly within these solutions.

Point-to-Point Tunneling Protocol (PPTP)

Point-to-Point Tunneling Protocol (PPTP) is a VPN protocol that runs over other protocols. PPTP relies on generic routing encapsulation (GRE) to build the tunnel between the endpoints. After the user authenticates, typically with Microsoft Challenge Handshake Authentication Protocol version 2 (MSCHAPv2), a Point-to-Point Protocol (PPP) session creates a tunnel using GRE. A key weakness of PPTP is the fact that it derives its encryption key from the user's password. This violates the cryptographic principle of randomness and can provide a basis for attacks. Password-based VPN authentication in general violates the recommendation to use two-factor authentication for remote access. The security architect and practitioner both need to consider known weaknesses, such as the issues identified with PPTP, when planning for the deployment and use of remote access technologies.

Layer 2 Tunneling Protocol (L2TP)

Layer 2 Tunneling Protocol (L2TP) is a hybrid of Cisco's Layer 2 Forwarding (L2F) and Microsoft's PPTP. It allows callers over a serial line using PPP to connect over the Internet to a remote network. A dial-up user connects to his ISP's L2TP access concentrator (LAC) with a PPP connection. The LAC encapsulates the PPP packets into L2TP and forwards it to the remote network's layer 2 network server (LNS). At this point, the LNS authenticates the dial-up user. If authentication is successful, the dial-up user will have access to the remote network. LAC and LNS may authenticate each other with a shared secret, but as RFC 2661 states, the authenticating is effective only while the tunnel between the LAC and LNS is being created.[46] L2TP does not provide encryption and relies on other protocols, such as tunnel mode IPSec, for confidentiality.

Remote Authentication Dial-in User Service (RADIUS)[47]

Remote Authentication Dial-in User Service (RADIUS) is an authentication protocol used mainly in networked environments, such as ISPs, or for similar services requiring single sign-on for layer 3 network access, for scalable authentication combined with an acceptable degree of security. On top of this, RADIUS provides support for consumption measurement such as connection time. RADIUS authentication is based on provision of simple username/password credentials. These credentials are encrypted by the client using a shared secret with the RADIUS server. Overall, RADIUS has the following issues:

- RADIUS has become the victim of a number of cryptographic attacks and can be successfully attacked with a replay attack.

- RADIUS suffers from a lack of integrity protection.

- RADIUS transmits only specific fields using encryption.

Simple Network Management Protocol (SNMP)[48]

Simple Network Management Protocol (SNMP) is designed to manage network infrastructure.

Table 6.14 provides an SNMP quick reference of ports and definitions.

TABLE 6.14 SNMP Quick Reference [49]

Ports	161/TCP, 161/UDP
	162/TCP, 162/UDP
Definition	RFC 1157

SNMP architecture consists of a management server (called the manager in SNMP terminology) and a client, usually installed on network devices such as routers and switches called an agent. SNMP allows the manager to retrieve "get" values of variables from the agent, as well as "set" variables. Such variables could be routing tables or performance-monitoring information.

Although SNMP has proven to be remarkably robust and scalable, it does have a number of clear weaknesses. Some of them are by design; others are subject to configuration parameters.

Probably the most easily exploited SNMP vulnerability is a brute-force attack on default or easily guessable SNMP passwords known as "community strings" often used to manage a remote device. Given the scale of SNMP v1 and v2 deployment, combined with a lack of clear direction from the security professional with regards to the risks associated with using SNMP without additional security enhancements to protect the community string, it is certainly a realistic scenario, and a potentially severe but easily mitigated risk.

Until version 2, SNMP did not provide any degree of authentication or transmission security. Authentication consists of an identifier called a community string, by which a manager will identify itself against an agent (this string is configured into the agent), and a password sent with a command. As a result, passwords can be easily intercepted, which could then result in commands being sniffed and potentially faked. Similar to the previous problem, SNMP version 2 did not support any form of encryption so that passwords (community strings) were passed as cleartext. SNMP version 3 addresses this particular weakness with encryption for passwords.[50]

Remote-Access Services

The services described under this section, TELNET and rlogin, while present in many UNIX operations and, when combined with NFS and NIS, provide the user with seamless remote working capabilities, do in fact form a risky combination if not configured and managed properly. Conceptually, because they are built on mutual trust, they can be misused to obtain access and to horizontally and vertically escalate privileges in an attack. Their authentication and transmission capabilities are insecure by design; they therefore have had to be retrofitted or replaced altogether, as TELNET and rlogin have been through the use of SSH.

TCP/IP Terminal Emulation Protocol (TELNET)[51]

TELNET is a command-line protocol designed to give command-line access to another host. Although implementations for Windows exist, TELNET's original domain was the UNIX server world, and in fact, a TELNET server is standard equipment for any UNIX server. (Whether it should be enabled is another question entirely, but in small LAN environments, TELNET is still widely used.)

- TELNET offers little security, and indeed, its use poses serious security risks in untrusted environments.

- TELNET is limited to username/password authentication.

- TELNET does not offer encryption.

Remote Log-in (rlogin), Remote Shell (rsh), Remote Copy (rcp)[52]

In its most generic form, remote log-in (rlogin) is a protocol used for granting remote access to a machine, normally a UNIX server. Similarly, remote shell (rsh) grants direct remote command execution, while rcp copies data from or to a remote machine. If an rlogin daemon (rlogind) is running on a machine, rlogin access can be granted in two ways, through the use of a central configuration file or through a user configuration. By the latter, a user may grant access that was not permitted by the system administrator. The same mechanism applies to rsh and remote copy (rcp), although they are relying on a different daemon (rshd). Authentication can be considered host/IP address based. Although rlogin grants access based on user ID, it is not verified; i.e., the ID a remote client claims to possess is taken for granted if the request comes from a trusted host. The rlogin protocol transmits data without encryption and is hence subject to eavesdropping and interception.

The rlogin protocol is of limited value—its main benefit can be considered its main drawback: remote access without supplying a password. It should be used only in trusted networks, if at all. A more secure replacement is available in the form of SSHv2 for rlogin, rsh, and rcp.

Screen Scraper

A screen scraper is a program that can extract data from output on a display intended for a human. Screen scrapers are used in a legitimate fashion when older technologies are unable to interface with modern ones. In a nefarious sense, this technology can also be used to capture images from a user's computer such as PIN pad sequences at a banking website when implemented by a virus or malware.

Virtual Network Terminal Services

Virtual terminal service is a tool frequently used for remote access to server resources. Virtual terminal services allow the desktop environment for a server to be exported to a remote workstation. This allows users at the remote workstation to execute desktop commands as though they were sitting at the server terminal interface in person. The advantage of terminal services such as those provided by Citrix, Microsoft, or public domain VNC services is that they allow for complex administrative commands to be executed using the native interface of the server rather than a command-line interface, which might be available through SSHv2 or telnet. Terminal services also allow for the authentication and authorization services integrated into the server to be leveraged for remote users, in addition to all the logging and auditing features of the server as well.

Telecommuting

Common issues such as visitor control, physical security, and network control are almost impossible to address with teleworkers. Strong VPN connections between the teleworker and the organization need to be established, and full device encryption should be the norm for protecting sensitive information. If the user works in public places or a home office, the following should also be considered:

- Is the user trained to use secure connectivity software and methods such as a VPN?
- Does the user know which information is sensitive or valuable and why someone might wish to steal or modify it?
- Is the user's physical location appropriately secure for the type of work and type of information they are using?
- Who else has access to the area?
- While a child may seem trusted, the child's friends may not be.

Data Communication

Data can be transmitted using analog communication or digital communication.

Analog Communication

Analog signals use electronic properties, such as frequency and amplitude, to represent information. Analog recordings are a classic example: A person speaks into a microphone, which converts the vibration from acoustical energy to an electrical equivalent. The louder the person speaks, the greater the electrical signal's amplitude. Likewise, the higher the pitch of the person's voice, the higher the frequency of the electrical signal. Analog signals are transmitted on wires, such as twisted pair, or with a wireless device.

Digital Communication

Whereas analog communication uses complex waveforms to represent information, digital communication uses two electronic states (on and off). By convention, 1 is assigned to the on state and 0 to off. Electrical signals that consist of these two states can be transmitted over a cable, converted to light and transmitted over fiber optics, and broadcasted with a wireless device. In all of the previously mentioned media, the signal would be a series of one of two states: on and off. It is easier to ensure the integrity of digital communication because the two states of the signal are sufficiently distinct. When a device receives a digital transmission, it can determine which digits are 0s and which are 1s (if it cannot, then the device knows the signal is erroneous or corrupted). On the other hand, analog complex waveforms make ensuring integrity very difficult.

LAN-BASED SECURITY

In order for the SSCP to be able to manage LAN-based security concerns effectively within the enterprise, they must understand the concept of separation between the data and control planes of a network. The control plane is where routing is handled, while the data plane is where commands are executed based on input from the control plane. In addition, the use of technologies such as logical segmentation of the network through the use of one or more VLANs is also important for the SSCP to be familiar with. The implementation of security solutions such as MACsec and secure device management are also important pieces of the LAN-based security puzzle that need to be considered carefully.

Separation of Data Plane and Control Plane

The control plane is where forwarding/routing decisions are made. Switches and routers have to figure out where to send frames (L2) and packets (L3). The switches and routers that run the network run as discrete components, but since they are in a network, they have to exchange information such as host reachability and status with neighbors. This is done in the control plane using protocols like spanning tree, OSPF, BGP, QoS enforcement, etc.

The data plane is where the action takes place. It includes things like the forwarding tables, routing tables, ARP tables, queues, tagging and re-tagging, etc. The data plane carries out the commands of the control plane. Figure 6.15 shows the control, data, and management plane as they would appear in a logical design diagram.

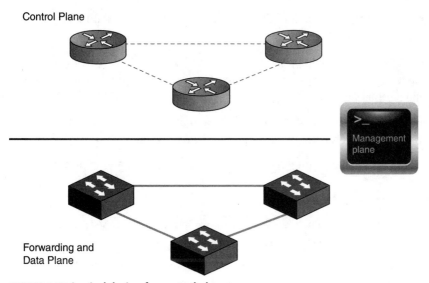

FIGURE 6.15 Logical design for control planes

For example, in the control plane, you set up IP networking and routing (routing protocols, route preferences, static routers, etc.) and connect hosts and switches/routers together. Each switch/router figures out what is directly connected to it and then tells its neighbor what it can reach and how it can reach it. The switches/routers also learn how to reach hosts and networks not attached to it. Once all of the routers/switches have a coherent picture—shared via the control plane—the network is converged.

In the data plane, the routers/switches use what the control plane built to dispose of incoming and outgoing frames and packets. Some get sent to another router, for example. Some may get queued up when congested. Some may get dropped if congestion gets bad enough.

Segmentation

In simple terms, a VLAN is a set of workstations within a LAN that can communicate with each other as though they were on a single, isolated LAN. What does it mean to say that they "communicate with each other as though they were on a single, isolated LAN"?

Among other things, it means that

- Broadcast packets sent by one of the workstations will reach all the others in the VLAN.

- Broadcasts sent by one of the workstations in the VLAN will not reach any workstations that are not in the VLAN.

- Broadcasts sent by workstations that are not in the VLAN will never reach workstations that are in the VLAN.

- The workstations can all communicate with each other without needing to go through a gateway. For example, IP connections would be established by ARPing for the destination.

- IP and sending packets directly to the destination workstation—there would be no need to send packets to the IP gateway to be forwarded on.

- The workstations can communicate with each other using non-routable protocols.

The Purpose of VLANs

The basic reason for splitting a network into VLANs is to reduce congestion on a large LAN. There are several advantages to using VLANs:

- **Performance**—Removing routers from the equation avoids the bottlenecks that can occur when data rates increase.

- **Flexibility**—Users can easily change locations within the VLAN without the restrictions that would otherwise be placed on them by routers in a physical LAN.

- **Virtual workgroups**—Workers can be joined together by simply changing the configuration of switches without worrying about all of the hardware connections that would be necessary in a physical system.

- **Partitioning resources**—You can place servers or other equipment on separate VLANs and easily control how much access to grant to each user for each VLAN.

Implementing VLANs/Port-Based VLANs

The act of creating a VLAN on a switch involves defining a set of ports and defining the criteria for VLAN membership for workstations connected to those ports. By far the most common VLAN membership criterion is port-based. With port-based VLANs, the ports of a switch are simply assigned to VLANs, with no extra criteria. All devices connected to a given port automatically become members of the VLAN to which that port was assigned. In effect, this just divides a switch up into a set of independent sub-switches.

It is important to remember that VLANs do not guarantee a network's security. At first glance, it may seem that traffic cannot be intercepted because communication within a VLAN is restricted to member devices. However, there are attacks that allow a malicious user to see traffic from other VLANs (so-called VLAN hopping). Therefore, a VLAN can be created so that engineers can efficiently share confidential documents, but the VLAN does not significantly protect the documents from unauthorized access. The following lists the most common attacks that could be launched against VLANs at the data link layer:

- **MAC Flooding Attack**—This is not properly a network "attack" but more a limitation of the way all switches and bridges work. They possess a finite hardware learning table to store the source addresses of all received packets: When this table becomes full, the traffic that is directed to addresses that cannot be learned anymore will be permanently flooded. Packet flooding, however, is constrained within the VLAN of origin; therefore, no VLAN hopping is permitted. This behavior can be exploited by a malicious user who wants to turn the switch he or she is connected to into a dumb pseudo-hub and sniff all the flooded traffic. This weakness can then be exploited to perform an actual attack, like the ARP poisoning attack.

- **802.1Q and Inter-Switch Link Protocol (ISL) Tagging Attack**—Tagging attacks are malicious schemes that allow a user on a VLAN to get unauthorized access to another VLAN.

- **Double-Encapsulated 802.1Q/Nested VLAN Attack**—While internal to a switch, VLAN numbers and identification are carried in a special extended format that allows the forwarding path to maintain VLAN isolation from end to end without any loss of information. Instead, outside of a switch, the tagging rules are dictated by standards such as Cisco's ISL or 802.1Q. When double-encapsulated 802.1Q packets are injected into the network from a device whose VLAN happens to be the native VLAN of a trunk, the VLAN identification of those packets cannot be preserved from end to end since the 802.1Q trunk would always modify the packets by stripping their outer tag. After the external tag is removed, the internal tag permanently becomes the packet's only VLAN identifier. Therefore, by double-encapsulating packets with two different tags, traffic can be made to hop across VLANs.

- **ARP Attacks**—In L2 devices that implement VLANs independently of MAC addresses, changing a device's identity in an ARP packet does not make it possible to affect the way it communicates with other devices across VLANs. As a matter of fact, any VLAN hopping attempts would be thwarted. On the other hand, within the same VLAN, the ARP poisoning or ARP spoofing attacks are a very effective way to fool end stations or routers into learning counterfeited device identities: This can allow a malicious user to pose as intermediary and perform a man-in-the-middle (MiM) attack. The MiM attack is performed by impersonating another device (for example, the default gateway) in the ARP packets sent to the attacked device; these packets are not verified by the receiver, and therefore they "poison" its ARP table with forged information.

- **Multicast Brute Force Attack**—This attack tries to exploit switches' potential vulnerabilities, or bugs, against a storm of L2 multicast frames. The correct behavior should be to constrain the traffic to its VLAN of origin; the failure behavior would be to leak frames to other VLANs.

- **Spanning-Tree Attack**—Another attack that tries to leverage a possible switch weakness is the STP attack. The attack requires sniffing for STP frames on the wire to get the ID of the port STP is transmitting on. Then, the attacker would begin sending out STP Configuration/Topology Change Acknowledgment BPDUs announcing that he was the new root bridge with a much lower priority.

- **Random Frame Stress Attack**—This last attack can have many incarnations, but in general it consists of a brute-force attack that randomly varies several fields of a packet while keeping only the source and destination addresses constant.

While many of these attacks are old and may not be effective unless certain circumstances or misconfiguration issues are allowed to go unchecked within the network, the security practitioner needs to be aware of these attack vectors and ensure that they understand how they operate and what appropriate countermeasures are available.

Media Access Control Security (IEEE 802.1AE)

Media Access Control Security (MACsec) provides point-to-point security on Ethernet links between directly connected nodes. MACsec identifies and prevents most threats, including denial of service, intrusion, man-in-the-middle, masquerading, passive wiretapping, and playback attacks. MACsec is standardized in IEEE 802.1AE. When combined with other security protocols such as IP Security (IPsec) and Secure Sockets Layer (SSL), MACsec can provide end-to-end network security.

How MACsec Works

MACsec uses secured point-to-point Ethernet links. Matching security keys are exchanged and verified between the interfaces at each end of the link. Ports, MAC addresses, and other user-configurable parameters are similarly verified. Data integrity checks are used to secure and verify all data that traverses the link. If the data integrity check detects anything irregular about the traffic, the traffic is dropped. MACsec can also be configured to encrypt all data on the Ethernet link to prevent if from being viewed by anyone who might be monitoring traffic on the link.[53]

Connectivity Associations and Secure Channels

MACsec is configured using connectivity associations. You can configure MACsec using static secure association key (SAK) security mode or static connective association key (CAK) mode. Both modes use secure channels that send and receive data on the MACsec-enabled link. When you use SAK security mode, you configure the secure channels, which also transmit the SAKS across the link to enable the MACsec. Typically, you configure two secure channels, one for inbound traffic and the other for outbound traffic. When you use CAK security mode, you create and configure the connectivity association. Your secure channels are automatically created and configured in the process of configuring the connectivity association. The secure channels are cannot be separately configured by users.[54]

Secure Device Management

Configuration Management/Monitoring (CM) is the application of sound program practices to establish and maintain consistency of a product's or system's attributes with its requirements and evolving technical baseline over its life. It involves interaction among systems engineering, hardware/software engineering, specialty engineering, logistics, contracting, and production in an integrated product team environment. A configuration management/monitoring process guides the system products, processes, and related documentation, and facilitates the development of open systems. Configuration management/monitoring efforts result in a complete audit trail of plans, decisions, and design modifications.

Automated CM tools can help the security practitioner to

- Record, control, and correlate configuration items (CIs), configuration units (CUs), and configuration components (CCs) within a number of individual baselines across the life cycle.
- Identify and control baselines.
- Track, control, manage, and report change requests for the baseline CIs, CCs, and CUs.

- Track requirements from specification to testing.
- Identify and control software versions.
- Track hardware parts.
- Enable rigorous compliance with a robust CM process.
- Conduct physical configuration audits (PCAs).
- Facilitate conduct of functional configuration audits.

Secure Shell (SSH)

Secure Shell's services include remote log-on, file transfer, and command execution. It also supports port forwarding, which redirects other protocols through an encrypted SSH tunnel. Many users protect less secure traffic of protocols, such as X Windows and virtual network computing (VNC), by forwarding them through an SSH tunnel. The SSH tunnel protects the integrity of communication, preventing session hijacking and other man-in-the-middle attacks.

There are two incompatible versions of the protocol, SSH-1 and SSH-2, though many servers support both. SSH-2 has improved integrity checks (SSH-1 is vulnerable to an insertion attack due to weak CRC-32 integrity checking) and supports local extensions and additional types of digital certificates such as Open PGP. SSH was originally designed for UNIX, but there are now implementations for other operating systems, including Windows, Macintosh, and OpenVMS.

DNSSEC

According to Nick Sullivan at Cloudfare, "The point of DNSSEC is to provide a way for DNS records to be trusted by whoever receives them. The key innovation of DNSSEC is the use of public key cryptography to ensure that DNS records are authentic. DNSSEC not only allows a DNS server to prove the authenticity of the records it returns. It also allows the assertion of "non-existence of records."

The DNSSEC trust chain is a sequence of records that identify either a public key or a signature of a set of resource records. The root of this chain of trust is the root key, which is maintained and managed by the operators of the DNS root. DNSSEC is defined by the IETF in RFCs 4033, 4034, and 4035.

There are several important new record types:

- **DNSKEY**—A public key, used to sign a set of resource records (RRset)
- **DS**—Delegation signer, a hash of a key
- **RRSIG**—A signature of an RRset that shares name/type/class

A DNSKEY record is a cryptographic public key; DNSKEYs can be classified into two roles, which can be handled by separate keys or a single key.

- **KSK (Key Signing Key)**—Used to sign DNSKEY records
- **ZSK (Zone Signing Key)**—Used to sign all other records in the domain that it is authoritative for

For a given domain name and question, there are a set of answers. For example, if you ask for the A record for ISC2.org, you get a set of A records as the answer:

```
ISC2.org.          IN    A    208.78.71.5

ISC2.org.          IN    A    208.78.70.5

ISC2.org.          IN    A    208.78.72.5

ISC2.org.          IN    A    208.78.73.5
```

The set of all records of a given type for a domain is called an RRset. A Resource Record SIGnature (RRSIG) is essentially a digital signature for an RRset. Each RRSIG is associated with a DNSKEY. The RRset of DNSKEYs is signed with the key signing key (KSK). All others are signed with the zone signing key (ZSK). Trust is conferred from the DNSKEY to the record though the RRSIG: If you trust a DNSKEY, then you can trust the records that are correctly signed by that key.

However, the domain's ZSK is signed by itself, making it difficult to trust. The way around this is to walk the domain up to the next/parent zone. To verify that the DNSKEY for ISC2.org is valid, you have to ask the .org authoritative server. This is where the DS record comes into play: It acts as a bridge of trust to the parent level of the DNS.

The DS record is a hash of a DNSKEY. The .org zone stores this record for each zone that has supplied DNSSEC keying information. The DS record is part of an RRset in the zone for .org and therefore has an associated RRSIG. This time, the RRset is signed by the .com ZSK. The .org DNSKEY RRset is signed by the .org KSK.

The ultimate root of trust is the KSK DNSKEY for the DNS root. This key is universally known and published.

Here is the DNSKEY root KSK that was published in August 2010 and will be used until sometime in 2015 or 2016 (encoded in base64):

```
AwEAAagAIK1VZrpC6Ia7gEzahOR+9W29euxhJhVVLOyQbSEWOO8gcC
jFFVQUTf6v58fLjwBd0YIOEzrAcQqBGCzh/RStIoO8gONfnfL2MTJR
kxoXbfDaUeVPQuYEhg37NZWAJQ9VnMVDxP/VHL496M/QZxkjf5/
Efu cp2gaDX6RS6CXpoY68LsvPVjR0ZSwzz1apAzvN9dlzEheX7ICJBBtuA
6G3LQpzW5hOA2hzCTMjJPJ8LbqF6dsV6DoBQzgul0sGIcGOY17OyQd
XfZ57relSQageu+ipAdTTJ25AsRTAoub8ONGcLmqrAmRLKBP1dfwhY
B4N7knNnulqQxA+Uklihz0=
```

By following the chain of DNSKEY, DS, and RRSIG records to the root, any record can be trusted.[55]

NETWORK-BASED SECURITY DEVICES

Key concepts for the security professional to consider regarding network-based security devices include

- **Definition of Security Domains**—This could be defined by level of risk or by organizational control. A prime example is the tendency of decentralized organizations to manage their IT—and thereby also their network security—locally, and as a result, with different degrees of success.

- **Segregation of Security Domains**—Control of traffic flows according to risk/benefit assessment, and taking into account formal models, such as the Bell–La Padula model, the Biba integrity model, or the Clark–Wilson model.

- **Incident Response Capability**—Including but not limited to

  - An inventory of business-critical traffic (this could, for instance, be e-mail or file and print servers but also DNS and DHCP, telephony traffic—VoIP,

building access control traffic, and facilities management traffic. Remember—
modern building controls, physical security controls, and process controls are
converging onto IP).

- An inventory of less critical traffic (such as HTTP or FTP).

- A way to quickly contain breaches (for instance, by shutting off parts of the
  network or blocking certain types of traffic).

- A process for managing the reaction.

- Contingency or network "diversity" in case of overload or failure of the primary
  network connection; alternate network connections are in place to absorb the
  load/traffic automatically without loss of services to applications and users.

Network Security Objectives and Attack Modes

It is a common misperception that network security is the endpoint for all other security
measures; i.e., that firewalls only will protect an organization. This is a flawed perception;
perimeter defense (defending the edges of the network) is merely part of the overall solution set or enterprise security architecture that the security professional needs to ensure is
in place in the enterprise. Perimeter defense is part of a wider concept known as *defense
in depth*, which simply holds that security must be a multi-layer effort including the edges
but also the hosts, applications, network elements (routers, switches, DHCP, DNS, wireless access points), people, and operational processes. Techniques associated with proac-
tivity can be undertaken independently by organizations with a willingness and resources
to do so. Others such as upstream intercession (assuming an external source of the threat
such as DDOS, spam/phish, or botnet attacks) can be accomplished fairly easily and
affordably through cooperation with telecommunications suppliers and Internet service
providers (ISP). Finally, the most effective proactive network defense is related to the
ability to disable attack tools before they can be deployed and applied against you.

Confidentiality

In the context of telecommunications and network security, confidentiality is the property
of nondisclosure to unauthorized parties. Attacks against confidentiality are by far the most
prevalent today because information can be sold or exploited for profit in a huge variety of
(mostly criminal) ways. The network, as the carrier of almost all digital information within
the enterprise, provides an attractive target to bypass access control measures on the assets
using the network and access information while it is in transit on the wire. Among the
information that can be acquired is not just the payload information but also credentials,
such as passwords. Conversely, an attacker might not even be interested in the information

transmitted but simply in the fact that the communication has occurred. An overarching class of attacks carried out against confidentiality is known as "eavesdropping."

Eavesdropping (Sniffing)

To access information from the network, an attacker must have access to the network itself in the first place. An eavesdropping computer can be a legitimate client on the network or an unauthorized one. It is not necessary for the eavesdropper to become a part of the network (for instance, having an IP address); it is often far more advantageous for an attacker to remain invisible (and un-addressable) on the network. This is particularly easy in wireless LANs, where no physical connection is necessary. Countermeasures to eavesdropping include encryption of network traffic on a network or application level, traffic padding to prevent identification of times when communication happens, rerouting of information to anonymize its origins and potentially split different parts of a message, and mandating trusted routes for data such that information is only traversing trusted network domains.

Integrity

In the context of telecommunications and network security, integrity is the property association with corruption or change (intentional or accidental). A network needs to support and protect the integrity of its traffic. In many ways, the provisions taken for protection against interception to protect confidentiality will also protect the integrity of a message. Attacks against integrity are often an interim step to compromising confidentiality or availability as opposed to the overall objective of the attack. Although the modification of messages will often happen at the higher network layers (i.e., within applications), networks can be set up to provide robustness or resilience against interception and change of a message (man-in-the-middle attacks) or replay attacks. Ways to accomplish this can be based on encryption or checksums on messages, as well as on access control measures for clients that would prevent an attacker from gaining the necessary access to send a modified message into the network in the first place. Conversely, many protocols, such as SMTP, HTTP, or even DNS, do not provide any degree of authentication. Consequently, it becomes relatively easy for the attacker to inject messages with fake sender information into a network from the outside through an existing gateway. The fact that no application can rely on the security or authenticity of underlying protocols has become a common design factor in networking.

Availability

In the context of telecommunications and network security, *availability* is the property of a network service related to its uptime, speed, and latency. Availability of the service is commonly the most obvious business requirement especially with highly converged networks, where multiple assets (data, voice, physical security) are riding on top of the same network. For this very reason, network availability has also become a prime target for attackers and a key business risk that security professionals need to be prepared to address. While a variety of availability threats and risks are addressed in this domain, an overarching class of attack against availability is known as *denial of service*.

Attacks on the transport layer of the OSI model (layer 4) seek to manipulate, disclose, or prevent delivery of the payload as a whole. This can, for instance, happen by reading the payload (as would happen in a sniffer attack) or changing it (which could happen in a man-in-the-middle attack). While disruptions of service can be executed at other layers as well, the transport layer has become a common attack ground via ICMP.

Domain Litigation

Domain names are subject to trademark risks, related to a risk of temporary unavailability or permanent loss of an established domain name. For the business in question, the consequences can be equivalent to the loss of its whole Internet presence in an IT-related disaster. Businesses should therefore put in place contingency plans if they are concerned with trademark disputes of any kind over a domain name used as their main web and e-mail address. Such contingency plans might include setting up a second domain unrelated to the trademark in question (based, for instance, on the trademark of a parent company) that can be advertised on short notice, if necessary. Cyber-squatting and the illegitimate use of similar domains, containing common misspellings or representing the same second-level domain under a different top-level domain, is occurring more frequently as the range of domains continues to expand. The only way to protect a business from this kind of fraud is the registration of the most prominent adjacent domains or by means of trademark litigation. A residual risk will always remain, relating not only to public misrepresentation but also to potential loss or disclosure of e-mail.

Open Mail Relay Servers

An open mail relay server is an SMTP service that allows inbound SMTP connections for domains it does not serve; i.e., for which it does not possess a DNS MX record. An open mail relay is generally considered a sign of bad system administration. Open mail relays are a principal tool for the distribution of spam because they allow an attacker to hide their identity. A number of blacklists for open mail relay servers exist that can be used for blacklisting open mail relays; i.e., a legitimate mail server would not accept any email from this host because it has a high likelihood of being spam. Although using blacklists as one indicator in spam filtering has its merits, it is risky to use them as an exclusive indicator. Generally, they are run by private organizations and individuals according to their own rules, they are able to change their policies on a whim, they can vanish overnight for any reason, and they can rarely be held accountable for the way they operate their lists.

Spam

By far the most common way of suppressing spam is e-mail filtering on an e-mail gateway. A large variety of commercial products exists, based on a variety of algorithms. Filtering based on simple keywords can be regarded as technically obsolete because this method is prone to generating false-positives, and spammers are able to easily work around this type of filter simply by manipulating the content and key words in their messages. More sophisticated filters, based, for instance, upon statistical analysis or analysis of e-mail traffic patterns, have come to market. Filtering can happen on an e-mail server (mail transfer agent [MTA]) or in the client (mail user agent [MUA]). The administrator of a mail server can configure it to limit or slow down an excessive number of connections (tar pit). A mail server can be configured to honor blacklists of spam sources either as a direct blocking list or as one of several indicators for spam.

Firewalls and Proxies

Firewalls and proxies are both considered to be gateway protection devices. They are deployed by the SSCP to help to support a defense-in-depth architecture design for the enterprise. A firewall is used to examine the flow of traffic entering and exiting a network and to match that traffic flow against a predetermined set of rules that are used to determine whether that traffic should be allowed or denied. A proxy device is used to manage the exchange of traffic between networks and can also be used to filter traffic, examining it for layer 7 protocols such as HTTP or FTP.

Firewalls

Firewalls are devices that enforce administrative security policies by filtering incoming traffic based on a set of rules. Often firewalls are thought of as protectors of an Internet gateway only. While a firewall should always be placed at Internet gateways, there are also internal network considerations and conditions where a firewall would be employed, such as network zoning. Additionally, firewalls are also threat management appliances with a variety of other security services embedded, such as proxy services and intrusion prevention services that seek to monitor and alert proactively at the network perimeter.

Firewalls will not be effective right out of the box. Firewall rules must be defined correctly in order to not inadvertently grant unauthorized access. Like all hosts on a network, administrators must install patches to the firewall and disable all unnecessary services. Also, firewalls offer limited protection against vulnerabilities caused by application flaws in server software on other hosts. For example, a firewall will not prevent an attacker from manipulating a database to disclose confidential information.

Filtering

Firewalls filter traffic based on a rule set. Each rule instructs the firewall to block or forward a packet based on one or more conditions. For each incoming packet, the firewall will look through its rule set for a rule whose conditions apply to that packet and block or forward the packet as specified in that rule. Here are two important conditions used to determine if a packet should be filtered:

By Address   Firewalls will often use the packet's source or destination address, or both, to determine if the packet should be filtered.

By Service   Packets can also be filtered by service. The firewall inspects the service the packet is using (if the packet is part of the TCP or UDP, the service is the destination port number) to determine if the packet should be filtered. For example, firewalls will often have a rule to filter the Finger service to prevent an attacker from using it to gather information about a host. Filtering by address and by service are often combined together in rules. If the engineering department wanted to grant anyone on the LAN access to its web server, a rule could be defined to forward packets whose destination address is the web server's and the service is HTTP (TCP port 80).

Network Address Translation (NAT)

Firewalls can change the source address of each outgoing (from trusted to untrusted network) packet to a different address. This has several applications, most notably to allow hosts with RFC 1918 addresses access to the Internet by changing their non-routable address to one that is routable on the Internet.[56] A non-routable address is one that will not be forwarded by an Internet router, and therefore remote attacks using non-routable internal addresses cannot be launched over the open Internet. Anonymity is another reason to use NAT. Many organizations do not want to advertise their IP addresses to an untrusted host and thus unnecessarily give information about the network. They would rather hide the entire network behind translated addresses. NAT also greatly extends the capabilities of organizations to continue using IPv4 address spaces.

Port Address Translation (PAT)

An extension to NAT is to translate all addresses to one routable IP address and translate the source port number in the packet to a unique value. The port translation allows the firewall to keep track of multiple sessions that are using PAT.

Static Packet Filtering

When a firewall uses static packet filtering, it examines each packet without regard to the packet's context in a session. Packets are examined against static criteria, for example, blocking all packets with a port number of 79 (Finger). Because of its simplicity, static packet filtering requires very little overhead, but it has a significant disadvantage. Static rules cannot be temporarily changed by the firewall to accommodate legitimate traffic. If a protocol requires a port to be temporarily opened, administrators have to choose between permanently opening the port and disallowing the protocol.

Stateful Inspection or Dynamic Packet Filtering

Stateful inspection examines each packet in the context of a session, which allows it to make dynamic adjustments to the rules to accommodate legitimate traffic and block malicious traffic that would appear benign to a static filter. Consider FTP. A user connects to an FTP server on TCP port 21 and then tells the FTP server on which port to transfer files. The port can be any TCP port above 1023. So, if the FTP client tells the server to transfer files on TCP port 1067, the server will attempt to open a connection to the client on that port. A stateful inspection firewall would watch the interaction between the two hosts, and even though the required connection is not permitted in the rule set, it would allow the connection to occur because it is part of FTP.

Static packet filtering, in contrast, would block the FTP server's attempt to connect to the client on TCP port 1067 unless a static rule was already in place. In fact, because the client could instruct the FTP server to transfer files on any port above 1023, a static rule would have to be in place to permit access to the specified port.

Personal Firewalls

Following the principle of security in depth, personal firewalls should be installed on workstations, which protect the user from all hosts on the network. It is critical for home users with DSL or cable modem access to the Internet to have a personal firewall installed on every PC, especially if they do not have a firewall protecting their network.

Proxies

A proxy firewall mediates communications between untrusted endpoints (servers/hosts/clients) and trusted endpoints (servers/hosts/clients). From an internal perspective, a proxy may forward traffic from known, internal client machines to untrusted hosts on the Internet, creating the illusion for the untrusted host that the traffic originated from the proxy firewall, thus hiding the trusted internal client from potential attackers. To the user, it appears that he or she is communicating directly with the untrusted server. Proxy servers are often placed at Internet gateways to hide the internal network behind one IP address and to prevent direct communication between internal and external hosts.

Circuit-Level Proxy

A circuit-level proxy creates a conduit through which a trusted host can communicate with an untrusted one. This type of proxy does not inspect any of the traffic that it forwards, which adds very little overhead to the communication between the user and untrusted server. The lack of application awareness also allows circuit-level proxies to forward any traffic to any TCP and UDP port. The disadvantage is that traffic will not be analyzed for malicious content.

Application-Level Proxy

An application-level proxy relays the traffic from a trusted endpoint running a specific application to an untrusted endpoint. The most significant advantage of application-level proxies is that they analyze the traffic that they forward for protocol manipulation and various sorts of common attacks such as buffer overflows. Application-level proxies add overhead to using the application because they scrutinize the traffic that they forward.

Web proxy servers are a very popular example of application-level proxies. Many organizations place one at their Internet gateway and configure their users' web browsers to use the web proxy whenever they browse an external web server (other controls are implemented to prevent users from bypassing the proxy server). The proxies typically include required user authentication, inspection of URLs to ensure that users do not browse inappropriate sites, logging, and caching of popular webpages. In fact, web proxies for internal users are one of the prime manners in which acceptable usage policies can be enforced because external sites can be blacklisted by administrators and logs of user traffic kept for later analysis if required for evidentiary purposes.

Network Intrusion Detection/Prevention Systems

It is important for the SSCP to understand the difference between intrusion detection and intrusion prevention. Intrusion detection technologies are considered "passive," only recording activity and potentially alerting an administrator that something unusual is occurring. Intrusion prevention technologies are considered "active," meaning that they will do everything that an intrusion detection device does, but they will also have the capacity to react to the unusual or suspicious behavior in preprogrammed ways. It is important for the SSCP to carefully consider which technology or mix of technologies will be the best for their organization's security needs.

Port Scanning

Port scanning is the act of probing for TCP services on a machine. It is performed by establishing the initial handshake for a connection. Although not in itself an attack, it allows an attacker to test for the presence of potentially vulnerable services on a target system. Port scanning can also be used for fingerprinting an operating system by evaluating its response characteristics, such as timing of a response, and details of the handshake. Protection from port scanning includes restriction of network connections, e.g., by means of a host-based or network-based firewall or by defining a list of valid source addresses on an application level.

FIN, NULL, and XMAS Scanning

In FIN scanning, a stealth scanning method, which is a request to close a connection, is sent to the target machine. If no application is listening on that port, a TCP RST or an ICMP packet will be sent. This attack commonly works only on UNIX machines, as Windows machines behave in a slightly different manner, deviating from RFC 793 (always responding to a FIN packet with an RST, thereby rendering recognition of open ports impossible) and thereby not being susceptible to the scan.[57] Firewalls that put a system into stealth mode (i.e., suppressing system responses to FIN packets) are available. In NULL scanning, no flags are set on the initiating TCP packet; in XMAS scanning, all TCP flags are set (or "lit," as in a Christmas tree). Otherwise, these scans work in the same manner as the FIN scan.

TCP Sequence Number Attacks

To detect and correct loss of data packets, TCP attaches a sequenced number to each data packet that is transmitted. If a transmission is not reported back as successful, a packet will be retransmitted. By eavesdropping on traffic, these sequence numbers can be predicted, and fake packets with the correct sequence number can be introduced into the data stream by a third party. This class of attacks can, for instance, be used for session hijacking. Protection mechanisms against TCP sequence number attacks have been proposed based on better randomization of sequence numbers as described in RFC 1948.[58]

Methodology of an Attack

Security attacks have been described formally as attack tree models. Attack trees are based upon the goal of the attacker, the risks to the defender, and the vulnerabilities of the defense systems. They are a specialized form of decision tree that can be used to formally evaluate system security. The following methodology describes not the attack tree itself (which is a defender's view) but the steps that an attacker would undergo to success-fully traverse the tree toward his or her target.

Target Acquisition An attack usually starts with intelligence gathering and sur-veillance to obtain a collection of possible targets, for instance, through evaluating directory services and network scanning. It is therefore important for the security architect and the security practitioner to work together to limit information avail-able on a network and make intelligence gathering as difficult as possible for the attacker. This would include installation of split network security zones (internal nodes are only visible on the inside of a network), network address translation, lim-iting access to directories of persons and assets, using hidden paths, nonstandard privileged usernames, etc. Importantly, not all of these obscurity measures have an inherent security value. They serve to slow the attacker down but will not in and of themselves provide any protection beyond this point; these measures are referred to as delaying tactics.

Target Analysis In a second step, the identified target is analyzed for security weak-nesses that would allow the attacker to obtain access. Depending on the type of attack, the discovery scan has already taken this into account, e.g., by scanning for servers sus-ceptible to a certain kind of buffer overflow attack. Tools available for the target acqui-sition phase are generally capable of automatically performing a first-target analysis. The most effective protection that the security professional can deploy is to minimize security vulnerabilities, for instance, by applying software patches at the earliest possi-ble opportunity and practicing effective configuration management. In addition, target analysis should be made more difficult for the attacker. For example, system adminis-trators should minimize the system information (e.g., system type, build, and release) that an attacker could glean, making it more difficult to attack the system.

Target Access In the next step, an attacker will obtain some form of access to the system. This can be access as a normal user or as a guest. The attacker could be exploiting known vulnerabilities or common tools for this or bypassing technical secu-rity controls altogether by using social engineering attacks. For one to mitigate the risk of unauthorized access, existing user privileges need to be well managed, access profiles need to be up to date, and unused accounts should be blocked or removed. Access should be monitored, and monitoring logs need to be regularly analyzed; how-ever, most malware will come with root kits ready to subvert basic operating system privilege management.

Target Appropriation As the last level of an attack, the attacker can then escalate his or her privileges on the system to gain system-level access. Again, exploitation of known vulnerabilities through existing or custom tools and techniques is the main technical attack vector; however, other attack vectors, such as social engineering, need to be taken into account.

Countermeasures against privilege escalation, by nature, are similar to the ones for gaining access. However, because an attacker can gain full control of a system through privilege escalation, secondary controls on the system itself (such as detecting unusual activity in log files) are less effective and reliable. Network (router, firewall, and intrusion detection system) logs can therefore prove invaluable to the security practitioner. Logs are so valuable, in fact, that an entire discipline within IT security has developed known as security event management (SEM) or sometimes security incident and event management (SIEM).

To detect the presence of unauthorized changes, which could indicate access from an attacker or backdoors into the system, the use of host-based or network-based intrusion detection systems can provide useful detection services. However, it is important to keep in mind that because an IDS relies on constant external input in the form of attack signature updates to remain effective, these systems are only as "good" as the quality and timeliness of the updates being applied to them. The output from the host-based IDS (such as regular snapshots or file hashes) needs to be stored in such a way that it cannot be overwritten from the source system in order to ensure integrity.

Finally, yet importantly, the attacker may look to remotely maintain control of the system to regain access at a later time or to use it for other purposes, such as sending spam or as a stepping stone for other attacks. To such an end, the attacker could avail himself of prefabricated "rootkits" to sustain and maintain control over time. Such a rootkit will not only allow access but also hide its own existence from traditional cursory inspection methods.

Bots and *botnets* are responsible for most of the activity leading to unauthorized, remote control of compromised systems today. Machines that have become infected and are now considered to be bots: essentially, zombies controlled by shadowy entities from the dark places on the Internet. Bots and botnets are the largest source of spam e-mail and can be coordinated by *bot herders* to inflict highly effective denial-of-services attacks, all without the knowledge of the system owners.

Network Security Tools and Tasks

Tools can make a security practitioner's job easier. Regardless of whether they are aids in collecting input for risk analysis or scanners to assess how well a server is configured, tools automate processes, which saves time and reduces error. Do not allow yourself to fall into the trap of reducing network security to collecting and using tools, however.

Intrusion Detection Systems

Intrusion detection systems (IDSs) monitor activity and send alerts when they detect suspicious traffic. (See Figure 6.16.) There are two broad classifications of IDS: host-based IDS, which monitors activity on servers and workstations, and network-based IDS, which monitors network activity. Network IDS services are typically stand-alone devices or at least independent blades within network chassis. Network IDS logs would be accessed through a separate management console that will also generate alarms and alerts.

Currently, there are two approaches to the deployment and use of intrusion detection systems. An appliance on the network can monitor traffic for attacks based on a set of signatures (analogous to antivirus software), or the appliance can watch the network's traffic for a while, learn what traffic patterns are normal, and send an alert when it detects an anomaly. Of course, the IDS can be deployed using a hybrid of the two approaches as well.

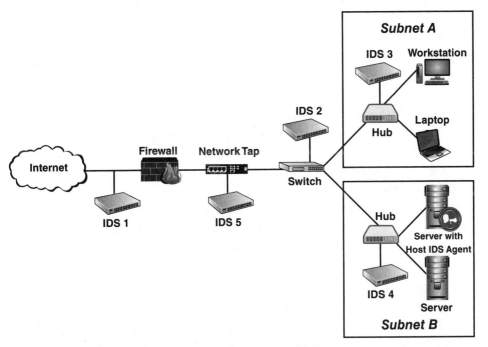

FIGURE 6.16 **Architecture of an intrusion detection system (IDS)**

Independent of the approach, how an organization uses an IDS determines whether the tool is effective. Despite its name, the IDS should not be used to detect intrusions because IDS solutions are not designed to be able to take preventative actions as part of their response. Instead, it should send an alert when it detects interesting, abnormal traffic that could be a prelude to an attack. For example, someone in the engineering department trying to access payroll information over the network at 3 a.m. is probably very interesting and not normal. Or perhaps a sudden rise in network utilization should be noted.

Security Event Management (SEM)/ Security Incident and Event Management (SIEM)

Security Event Management (SEM)/ Security Incident and Event Management (SIEM) is a solution that involves harvesting logs and event information from a variety of different sources on individual servers or assets and analyzing it as a consolidated view with sophisticated reporting. Similarly, entire IT infrastructures can have their logs and event information centralized and managed by large-scale SEM/SIEM deployments. SEM/SIEM will not only aggregate logs but will perform analysis and issue alerts (e-mail, pager, audible, etc.) according to suspicious patterns.

Aggregation and consolidation of logs and events will also potentially require additional network resources to transfer log and event data from distinct servers and arrays to a central location. This transfer will also need to occur in as close to real time as possible if the security information is to possess value beyond forensics. SEM/SIEM systems can benefit immensely from Security Intelligence Services (SIS). The output from security appliances is esoteric and lacks the real-world context required for predictive threat assessments. It falls short of delivering consistently relevant intelligence to businesses operating in a competitive marketplace. SIS uses all-source collection and analysis methods to produce and deliver precise and timely intelligence guiding not only the *business of security* but the *security of the business*. SIS services are built upon accurate security metrics (cyber and physical), market analysis, and technology forecasting, and are correlated to real-world events, giving business decision makers time and precision. SIS provides upstream data from proactive cyber defense systems monitoring darkspace and darkweb.

Scanners

A network scanner can be used in several ways by the security practitioner:

Discovery Scanning   Discovery scanning can be performed on devices and services on a network, for instance, to establish whether new or unauthorized devices have been connected. Conversely, this type of scan can be used for intelligence gathering on potentially vulnerable services. A discovery scan can be performed with very simple methods, for example, by sending a ping packet (ping scanning) to every address in a subnet. More sophisticated methods will also discover the operating system and services of a responding device.

Compliance Scanning   Compliance scanning can be used to test for compliance with a given policy, for instance, to ensure certain configurations (deactivation of services) have been applied. A compliance scan can be performed either from the network or on the device, for instance, as a security health check. If performed on the network, it will usually include testing for open ports and services on the device.

Vulnerability Scanning and Penetration Testing   Vulnerability scanning can be used to test for vulnerabilities, for instance, as part of a penetration test but also in preparation for an attack. A vulnerability scan tests for vulnerability conditions generally by looking at responding ports and applications on a given server and determining patch levels. A vulnerability scan will infer a threat based upon what might be available as an avenue of attack. When new vulnerabilities have been published or are exploited, targeted scanner tools often become available from software vendors, antivirus vendors, independent vendors, or the open-source community. Care must be taken when running scans in a corporate environment so that the load does not disrupt operations or cause applications and services to fail.

A penetration test is the follow-on step after a vulnerability scan, where the observed vulnerabilities are actually exploited or are attempted. It is often the case that an inferred vulnerability, when tested, is not actually a vulnerability. For instance, a service might be open on a port and appear un-patched, but upon testing it turns out that the security administrator has implemented a secure configuration that mitigates the vulnerabilities. Penetration tests always have an elevated risk potential to bring down the asset against which they are being performed and for this reason should never be conducted on operational systems unless the risks associated with the tests have been assessed and accepted by the systems owner. In addition, a clear waiver from the asset owner should be obtained prior to testing.

The following tools are commonly used scanning tools that are worth understanding:

- **Nessus**—A vulnerability scanner
- **Nmap**—A discovery scanner that will allow for determining the services running on a machine, as well as other host characteristics, such as a machine's operating system

Network Taps

A *network tap* or *span* is a device that has the ability to selectively copy all data flowing through a network in real time for analysis and storage. (See Figure 6.17.) Network taps may be deployed for the purposes of network diagnostics and maintenance or for purposes of forensic analysis related to incidents or suspicious events. Network taps will generally be fully configurable and will function at all layers from the physical layer up. In other words, a tap should be capable of copying everything from layer 1 (Ethernet, for instance) upward, including all payload information within the packets. Additionally, a tap can be configured to vacuum up every single packet of data or perhaps just focus on selected application traffic from selected sources.

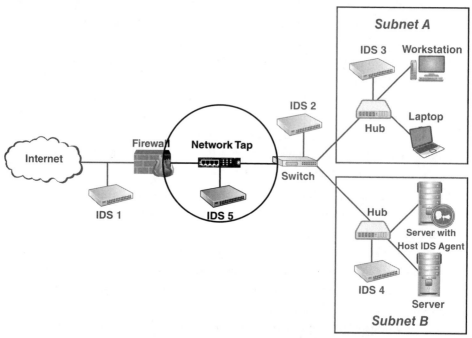

FIGURE 6.17 **A network tap is a device that simply sits on a network in "monitor" or "promiscuous" mode and makes a copy of all the network traffic, possibly right down to the Ethernet frames.**

IP Fragmentation Attacks and Crafted Packets

The Internet Protocol (IP) uses datagram fragmentation to split up the pieces of data being transmitted between two network interfaces so that they are able to be sized at or under the maximum transmission unit (MTU) value set for the network. When packets are fragmented, they can be used to hide attack data, obfuscating the attack from the monitoring devices designed to protect the network. The following sections discuss the details of these attacks and how they may be addressed.

Teardrop

In this attack, IP packet fragments are constructed so that the target host calculates a negative fragment length when it attempts to reconstruct the packet. If the target host's

IP stack does not ensure that fragment lengths are set within appropriate boundaries, the host could crash or become unstable. This problem is easily fixed with a vendor patch.

Overlapping Fragment Attack

Overlapping fragment attacks are used to subvert packet filters that only inspect the first fragment of a fragmented packet. The technique involves sending a harmless first fragment, which will satisfy the packet filter. Other packets follow that overwrite the first fragment with malicious data, thus resulting in harmful packets bypassing the packet filter and being accepted by the victim host. A solution to this problem is for TCP/IP stacks not to allow fragments to overwrite each other.

Source Routing Exploitation

Instead of only permitting routers to determine the path a packet takes to its destination, IP allows the sender to explicitly specify the path. An attacker can abuse source routing so that the packet will be forwarded between network interfaces on a multi-homed computer that is configured not to forward packets. This could allow an external attacker access to an internal network. Source routing is specified by the sender of an IP datagram, whereas the routing path would normally be left to the router to decide. The best solution is to disable source routing on hosts and to block source-routed packets.

Smurf and Fraggle Attacks

Both attacks use broadcasts to create denial-of-service attacks. A Smurf attack misuses the ICMP echo request to create denial-of-service attacks. In a Smurf attack, the intruder sends an ICMP echo request with a spoofed source address of the victim. The packet is sent to a network's broadcast address, which forwards the packet to every host on the network. Because the ICMP packet contains the victim's host as the source address, the victim will be overwhelmed by the ICMP echo replies, causing a denial-of-service attack.

The Fraggle attack uses UDP instead of ICMP. The attacker sends a UDP packet on port 7 with a spoofed source address of the victim. Like the Smurf attack, the packet is sent to a network's broadcast address, which will forward the packet to all of the hosts on the network. The victim host will be overwhelmed by the responses from the network.

NFS Attacks

The first step in setting up an NFS connection will be the publication (exporting) of file system trees from the server. These trees can be arbitrarily chosen by the administrator. Access privileges are granted based upon the client IP address and directory tree. Within the tree, the privileges of the server file system will be mapped to client users.

Several points of risk exist:

- **Export of parts of the file system that were not intended for publication or with inappropriate privileges.** This can be done by accident or through the existence of UNIX file system hard links (which can be generated by the user). This is of particular concern if parts of the server root file system are made accessible. One can easily imagine scenarios where a password file can be accessed and the encrypted passwords contained therein are subsequently broken by an off-the-shelf tool. Regular review of exported file system trees is an appropriate mitigation.

- **Using an unauthorized client.** Because NFS identifies the client by its IP address or (indirectly) a host name, it is relatively easy to use a different client than the authorized one, by means of IP spoofing or DNS spoofing. At the very least, resolution of server host names should therefore happen via a file (/etc/hosts on UNIX), not through DNS.

- **Incorrect mapping of user IDs between server and client.** Any machine not controlled by the server administrator can be used to propagate an attack, as NFS relies on user IDs as the only form of authorization credential. An attacker, having availed himself of administrative access to a client, could generate arbitrary user IDs to match those on the server. It is paramount that user IDs on server and client are synchronized, e.g., through the use of NIS/NIS+.

- **Sniffing and access request spoofing.** Because NFS traffic, by default, is not encrypted, it is possible to intercept it, either by means of network sniffing or by a man-in-the-middle attack. Because NFS does not authenticate each RPC call, it is possible to access files if the appropriate access token (file handle) has been obtained, for instance, through sniffing. NFS itself does not offer appropriate mitigation; however, the use of secure NFS may.[59]

- **SetUID files.** The directories accessed via NFS are used in the same way local directories are. On UNIX systems, files with the SUID bit can therefore be used for privilege escalation on the client. NFS should therefore be configured in such a way as to not respect SUID bits.

Network News Transport Protocol (NNTP) Security

From a security perspective, the main shortcoming in Network News Transport Protocol (NNTP) is authentication. One of the earlier solutions users found to this problem was signing messages with Pretty Good Privacy (PGP). However, this did not prevent impersonation or faked identities, as digital signatures were not a requirement, and indeed would be unsuitable for the repudiation problem implied. To make matters worse, NNTP offers a cancellation mechanism to withdraw articles already published. Naturally, the same authentication weakness applies to the control messages used for these cancellations, allowing users with even moderate skills to delete messages at will.

Finger User Information Protocol

Finger is an identification service that allows a user to obtain information about the last login time of a user and whether he or she is currently logged into a system. The "fingered" user has the possibility to have information from two files in their home directory displayed (the `.project` and `.plan` files). For all practical purposes, the Finger protocol has become obsolete. Its use should be restricted to situations where no alternatives are available.

Network Time Protocol (NTP)

Network Time Protocol (NTP) synchronizes computer clocks in a network. This can be extremely important for operational stability (for instance, under NIS) but also for maintaining consistency and coherence of audit trails, such as in log files. A variant of NTP exists in Simple Network Time Protocol (SNTP), offering a less resource-intensive but also less exact form of synchronization. From a security perspective, our main objective with NTP is to prevent an attacker from changing time information on a client or a whole network by manipulating its local time server. NTP can be configured to restrict access based upon IP address. From NTP version 3 onward, cryptographic authentication has become available, based upon symmetric encryption, but is to be replaced by public key cryptography in NTP version 4.

To make a network robust against accidental or deliberate timing inaccuracies, a network should have its own time server and possibly a dedicated, highly accurate clock. As a standard precaution, a network should never depend on one external time server alone, but it should synchronize with several trusted time sources. Thus, manipulation of a single source will have no immediate effect. To detect de-synchronization, one can use standard logging mechanisms with NTP to ensure synchronicity of time stamping.

DoS/DDoS

There are a number of different types of attacks that can be launched against a network, many of which we have already discussed. A special category is the denial-of-service and distributed denial-of-service attacks. Denial-of-service (DoS) attacks are carried out when an attacker sets out to attack a system through a set of activities designed to culminate in knocking the target offline and denying it ongoing access to the network for the duration of the attack. The key is that this attack is carried out by a single attacker. A distributed denial-of-service (DDoS) attack is designed to achieve the same end result as a DoS attack, but it is perpetrated by multiple attackers simultaneously coordinating their efforts.

Denial-of-Service Attack (DoS)

The easiest attack to carry out against a network, or so it may seem, is to overload it through excessive traffic or traffic that has been "crafted" to confuse the network into shutting down or slowing to the point of uselessness. Countermeasures include, but are not limited to, multiple layers of firewalls, careful filtering on firewalls, routers and switches, internal network access controls (NACs), redundant (diverse) network connections, load balancing, reserved bandwidth (quality of service, which would at least protect systems not directly targeted), and blocking traffic from an attacker on an upstream router. Bear in mind that malicious agents can and will shift IP address or DNS name to sidestep the attack, as well as employing potentially thousands of unique IP addresses during the execution of an attack. Enlisting the help of upstream service providers and carriers is ultimately the most effective countermeasure, especially if the necessary agreements and relationships have been established proactively or as part of agreed-on service levels.

It is instructive to note that many protocols contain basic protection from message loss that would at least mitigate the effects of denial-of-service attacks. This starts with TCP managing packet loss within certain limits, and it ends with higher-level protocols, such as SMTP, that will provide robustness against temporary connection outages (store and forward).[60]

Distributed Denial of Service (DDoS) Types

There are several tactics used to disrupt or deny service to a computer, such as congesting netflow traffic to a computer or attempting to overwhelm a server on the application level. Distributed denial-of-service (DDoS) attacks can be broadly divided in three types:

1. **Volume-Based Attacks**—Includes UDP floods, ICMP floods, and other spoofed-packet floods. The attack's goal is to saturate the bandwidth of the attacked site, and magnitude is measured in bits per second (Bps).

2. **Protocol Attacks**—Includes SYN floods, fragmented packet attacks, Ping of Death, Smurf DDoS, and more. This type of attack consumes actual server resources or those of intermediate communication equipment, such as firewalls and load balancers, and is measured in packets per second.

3. **Application Layer Attacks**—Includes Slowloris,[61] zero-day DDoS attacks, DDoS attacks that target Apache, Windows, or OpenBSD vulnerabilities, and more. Comprised of seemingly legitimate and innocent requests, these attacks have a goal to crash the web server, and the magnitude is measured in requests per second.

Security practitioners need to be aware of the impact of DDoS attacks against their networks. Perhaps because they are a convenient attack vector requiring little specialized expertise, DDoS attacks are increasing in scope to include bigger targets and more packets. During Q1 2013, the average DDoS attack bandwidth totaled 48.25 Gbps, a 718% increase over the previous quarter—and the average packet-per-second rate reached 32.4 million. "DDoS challenges have spiked for enterprises in 2013," noted Lawrence Orans of the research firm Gartner in a recent report. "Gartner estimates that its DDoS inquiry level quadrupled from September 2012 through September 2013. An increase of higher-volume and application-based DDoS attacks on corporate networks will force Chief Information Security Officers (CISOs) and security teams to find new, proactive solutions for reducing downtime."[62]

Some examples of DDoS attacks include the following:

- The Spamhaus DDoS attack in March 2013. This was not your typical hacktivist DDoS attack; rather, it was a massive, 300 gigabits-per-second traffic attack against volunteer spam filtering organization Spamhaus, which spread to multiple Internet exchanges and ultimately slowed traffic for users mainly in Europe at the end of March 2013. The attackers abused improperly configured or default-state DNS servers, also known as open DNS resolvers, in the attacks. This allowed for a bigger bandwidth attack with fewer machines since DNS servers are large and run on high-speed Internet connections, a recipe that led to the record-breaking DDoS bandwidth levels. Security experts estimate that there are around 21 million of these servers running on the Internet. Properly configured DNS servers only accept traffic from their own IP space or in the case of ISPs, from their customers, whereas "open" DNS resolvers can take requests from anyone on the Internet. This makes it possible to send these servers DNS queries from a spoofed address. The attackers basically sent traffic purportedly from Spamhaus, so when the weak DNS servers returned their DNS resolver responses, they all bombarded Spamhaus.[63]

- In April 2013, WordPress came under attack, as a DDoS botnet of almost 100,000 machines was used to brute-force account passwords.

- In May 2013, a large DNS reflection denial-of-service (DrDoS) attack was targeted against a real-time financial exchange platform. The attack peaked at 167 Gigabits per second (Gbps). In this kind of attack, the attacker makes large numbers of spoofed queries against many public DNS servers. The source IP address is forged to appear as the target of the attack. When a DNS server receives the forged request, it replies, but the reply is directed to the forged source address. This is the reflection component. The target of the attack receives replies from all the DNS servers that are used. This type of attack makes it very difficult to identify the malicious sources. If the queries, which are small packets, generate larger responses, then the attack is said to have an amplifying characteristic.

- On August 25, 2013, China faced the largest distributed denial-of-service (DDoS) attack in its history, leading to a two-to-four hour shutdown of swaths of IP addresses using .cn, China's country code top-level domain. The China Internet Network Information Center (CNNIC), which maintains the registry for .cn, issued an apology and a notice that at 2 and 4 a.m. Sunday local time, its National Nodes DNS was hit with two big attacks.[64] CloudFlare CEO Matthew Prince told the *Wall Street Journal* that his company saw a 32% drop in traffic for the thousands of Chinese domains on the company's network during the attack period, compared with the same timeframe 24 hours prior.

Countermeasures are similar to those of conventional denial-of-service attacks, but simple IP or port filtering might not work.

SYN Flooding

A SYN flood attack is a denial-of-service attack against the initial handshake in a TCP connection. Many new connections from faked, random IP addresses are opened in short order, overloading the target's connection table.

Countermeasures include tuning of operating system parameters such as the size of the backlog table according to vendor specifications. Another solution, which requires modification to the TCP/IP stack, is SYN cookies changing TCP numbers in a way that makes faked packets immediately recognizable.[65]

Daniel J. Bernstein, the primary inventor of this approach, defines them as "particular choices of initial TCP sequence numbers by TCP servers. The difference between the server's initial sequence number and the client's initial sequence number is:

- "**Top 5 bits**—t mod 32, where t is a 32 bit time counter that increases every 64 seconds;

- "**Next 3 bits**—An encoding of an MSS selected by the server in response to the client's MSS;

- "**Bottom 24 bits**—A server-selected secret function of the client IP address and port number, and the server IP address and port number.

"A server that uses SYN cookies does not have to drop connections when its SYN queue fills up. Instead it sends back a SYN+ACK, exactly as if the SYN queue had been larger. When the server receives an ACK, it checks that the secret function works for a recent value of t, and then rebuilds the SYN queue entry from the encoded MSS."

One of the most successful variants of SYN flooding can be carried out by the botnets discussed earlier. Botnets have the ability to direct potentially thousands of SYN requests to hosts at the same time, overwhelming not only the hosts but also the network connections that they rest upon. Under such circumstances, there are no host-configuration countermeasures available because a host without a network is as good as dead anyway. While SYN flooding might be the mode of attack, it is not being employed in any cunning manner with spoofed IP addresses from possibly a single malicious host; it is being applied as a pure brute-force form of attack.

Countermeasures include protecting the operating system through securing its network stack. This is not normally something the user or owner of a system has any degree of control over; it is a task for the vendor.

Finally, the network needs to be included in a corporation's disaster recovery and business contingency plans. For local area networks, one may set high recovery objectives and provide appropriate contingency, based upon the fact that any recovery of services is likely to be useless without at least a working local area network (LAN) infrastructure. As wide area networks are usually outsourced, contingency measures might include acquisition of backup lines from a different provider, procurement of telephone or digital subscriber loop (DSL) lines, etc.

Spoofing

Spoofing is defined as acting with the intent of impersonating someone or something, with the goal of attempting to get a target to accept you as the legitimate party, even though you are not. When spoofing is used by a bad actor to attempt to trick a target machine on the corporate network into accepting the traffic being sent to it from the machine that is controlled by the attacker, this can present a challenge to confidentiality, integrity, and availability. The SSCP needs to understand the intricacies of spoofing and the types of attacks that may be used with spoofing to gain access to the network.

IP Address Spoofing and SYN-ACK attacks

Packets are sent with a bogus source address so that the victim will send a response to a different host. Spoofed addresses can be used to abuse the three-way handshake that is required to start a TCP session. Under normal circumstances, a host offers to initiate a session with a remote host by sending a packet with the SYN option. The remote host responds with a packet with the SYN and ACK options. The handshake is completed when the initiating host responds with a packet with the ACK option.

An attacker can launch a denial-of-service attack by sending the initial packet with the SYN option with a source address of a host that does not exist. The victim will respond to the forged source address by sending a packet with the SYN and ACK options and then wait for the final packet to complete the handshake. Of course, that packet will never arrive because the victim sent the packet to a host that does not exist. If the attacker sends a storm of packets with spoofed addresses, the victim may reach the limit of uncompleted (half-open) three-way handshakes and refuse other legitimate network connections.

This scenario takes advantage of a protocol flaw. To mitigate the risk of a successful attack, vendors have released patches that reduce the likelihood of the limit of uncompleted handshakes being reached. In addition, security devices, such as firewalls, can block packets that arrive from an external interface with a source address from an internal network.

E-mail Spoofing

As SMTP does not possess an adequate authentication mechanism, e-mail spoofing is extremely simple. The most effective protection against this is a social one, whereas the recipient can confirm or simply ignore implausible e-mail. Spoofing e-mail sender addresses is extremely simple, and it can be done with a simple TELNET command to port 25 of a mail server and by issuing a number of SMTP commands. E-mail spoofing is frequently used as a means to obfuscate the identity of a sender in spamming, whereas the purported sender of a spam email is in fact another victim of spam, whose e-mail address has been harvested by or sold to a spammer.

DNS Spoofing

To resolve a domain name query, such as mapping a web server address to an IP address, the user's workstation will in turn have to undertake a series of queries through the Domain Name System hierarchy. Such queries can be either recursive (a name server receiving a request will forward it and return the resolution) or iterative (a name server receiving a request will respond with a reference).

An attacker aiming to poison a DNS server's (name server) cache (information related to previous queries, which is stored for reuse in future queries for speed and efficiency) by injecting fake records, and thereby falsifying responses to client requests, will need to send a query to this very name server. The attacker now knows that the name server will shortly send out a query for resolution.

In the first case, the attacker has sent a query for a domain, whose primary name server he controls. The response from this query will contain additional information that was not originally requested but that the target server will now cache. The second case is a dissimilar method that can also be used in iterative queries. Using IP spoofing, the attacker will send a response to his own query before the authoritative (correct) name server has a chance to respond.

In both cases, the attacker has used an electronic conversation to inject false information into the name server's cache. Not only will this name server now use the cached information, but the false information will propagate to other servers, making inquiries to this one. Due to the caching nature of DNS, attacks on DNS servers as well as countermeasures always have certain latency, determined by the configuration of a (domain) zone.

There are two principal vulnerabilities here, both inherent in the design of the DNS protocol: It is possible for a DNS server to respond to a recursive query with information that was not requested, and the DNS server will not authenticate information. Approaches to address or mitigate this threat have been only partly successful.

Later versions of DNS server software are programmed to ignore responses that do not correspond to a query. Authentication has been proposed, but attempts to introduce stronger (or even "any") authentication into DNS (for instance, through the use of DNSSEC) have not found wide acceptance. Authentication services have been delegated upward to higher protocol layers. Applications in need of guaranteeing authenticity cannot rely on DNS to provide such but will have to implement a solution themselves.

The ultimate solution to DNS security issues for many organizations is to establish DNS servers dedicated to their domains and vigorously monitor them. An "internal" DNS server will also be established, which only accepts queries from internal networks and users, and therefore it is considered to be substantially more difficult for outsiders to compromise and use as a staging point for penetrating internal networks.

Manipulation of DNS Queries

Technically, the following two techniques are only indirectly related to DNS weaknesses. However, it is worth mentioning them in the context of DNS because they seek to manipulate name resolution in other ways.

Pharming is the manipulation of DNS records, for instance, through the "hosts" file on a workstation. A hosts file (/etc/hosts on many UNIX machines, C:\Windows\System32\drivers\etc on a Windows machine) is the resource first queried before a DNS request is issued. It will always contain the mapping of the host name local host to the IP address 127.0.0.1 (loopback interface, as defined in RFC 3330) and potentially other hosts.[66] A virus or malware may add addresses of antivirus software vendors with invalid IP addresses to the hosts file to prevent download of virus pattern files. Alternately, Internet banking sites might have their IP addresses substituted for rogue, imposters' sites, which will attempt to trick the user into providing login information. A further form of DNS pharming is to compromise a DNS server itself and thereby re-direct all users of the DNS server to imposter websites even though their workstation itself may be free from compromise.

Social engineering techniques will not try to manipulate a query on a technical level but can trick the user into misinterpreting a DNS address that is displayed to him in a phishing email or in his web browser address bar. One way to achieve this in e-mail or Hypertext Markup Language (HTML) documents is to display a link in text where the actual target address is different from what is displayed. Another way to achieve this is the use of non-ASCII character sets (for instance, Unicode—ISO/IEC 10646:2012—characters) that closely resemble ASCII (i.e., Latin) characters to the user.[67] This may become a popular technique with the popularization of internationalized domain names.

Information Disclosure

Smaller corporate networks do not split naming zones; i.e., names of hosts that are accessible only from an intranet are visible from the Internet. Although knowing a server name will not enable anyone to access it, this knowledge can aid and facilitate preparation of a planned attack as it provides an attacker with valuable information on existing hosts (at least with regard to servers), network structure, and, for instance, details such as organizational structure or server operating systems (if the OS is part of the host name, etc.).

An organization should therefore operate split DNS zones wherever possible and refrain from using telling naming conventions for their machines. In addition, a domain registrar's database of administrative and billing domain contacts (whois database) can be an attractive target for information and e-mail harvesting.

Session Hijack

Session hijacking is the act of unauthorized insertion of packets into a data stream. It is normally based on sequence number attacks, where sequence numbers are either guessed or intercepted. Different types of session hijacking exist:

- **IP Spoofing**—Based on a TCP sequence number attack, the attacker would insert packets with a faked sender IP address and a guessed sequence number into the stream. The attacker would not be able to see the response to any commands inserted.

- **Man-in-the-Middle Attack**—The attacker would sniff or intercept packets, removing legitimate packets from the data stream and replacing them with his own. In fact, both sides of a communication would then communicate with the attacker instead of each other.

Countermeasures against IP spoofing can be executed at layer 3 (see the section "IP Address Spoofing and SYN-AcCKAttacks"). As TCP sessions only perform an initial authentication, application layer encryption can be used to protect against man-in-the-middle attacks.

SYN Scanning

As traditional TCP scans became widely recognized and were blocked, various stealth scanning techniques were developed. In TCP half scanning (also known as TCP SYN scanning), no complete connection is opened; instead, only the initial steps of the handshake are performed. This makes the scan harder to recognize; for instance, it would not show up in application log files. However, it is possible to recognize and block TCP SYN scans with an appropriately equipped firewall.

WIRELESS TECHNOLOGIES

The security practitioner needs to understand the common wireless technologies, networks, and methods. With that foundation, it is easier to understand common vulnerabilities and countermeasures.

Wireless Technologies, Networks, and Methodologies

There are several types of wireless technologies. They include the following:

Wi-Fi   Primarily associated with computer networking, Wi-Fi uses the IEEE 802.11 specification to create a wireless local-area network that may be secure, such as an office network, or public, such as a coffee shop. Usually a Wi-Fi network consists of a wired connection to the Internet, leading to a wireless router that transmits and receives data from individual devices, connecting them not only to the outside world but also to each other. Wi-Fi range is generally wide enough for most homes or small offices, and for larger campuses or homes, range extenders may be placed strategically to extend the signal. Over time, the Wi-Fi standard has evolved, with each new version faster than the last. Current devices usually use the 802.11n or 802.11ac versions of the spec, but backwards compatibility ensures that an older laptop can still connect to a new Wi-Fi router. However, in order for you to see the fastest speeds, both the computer and the router must use the latest 802.11 version.

Bluetooth   While both Wi-Fi and cellular networks enable connections to anywhere in the world, Bluetooth is much more local, with the stated purpose of "replacing the cables connecting devices," according to the official Bluetooth website. Bluetooth uses a low-power signal with a maximum range of 50 feet, but with sufficient speed to enable transmission of high-fidelity music and streaming video. As with other wireless technologies, Bluetooth speed increases with each revision of its standard but requires up-to-date equipment at both ends to deliver the highest possible speed. Also, the latest Bluetooth revisions are capable of using maximum power only when it's required, preserving battery life.

WiMAX   While over-the-air data is fast becoming the realm of cellular providers, dedicated wireless broadband systems also exist, offering fast web surfing without connecting to cable or DSL. One well-known example of wireless broadband is WiMAX. Although WiMAX can potentially deliver data rates of more than 30 megabits per second, providers offer average data rates of 6 Mbps and often deliver less, making the service significantly slower than hard-wired broadband.

Wireless technologies are used in a variety of wireless networks. Types of wireless networks include the following:

Wireless PAN   Wireless personal area networks (WPANs) interconnect devices within a relatively small area that is generally within a person's reach. Wi-Fi PANs are becoming commonplace as equipment designers start to integrate Wi-Fi into a variety of consumer electronic devices. Intel "My WiFi" and Windows 7 "virtual Wi-Fi" capabilities have made Wi-Fi PANs simpler and easier to set up and configure.

Wireless LAN   A wireless local area network (WLAN) links two or more devices over a short distance using a wireless distribution method, usually providing a connection through an access point for Internet access. The use of spread-spectrum or OFDM technologies may allow users to move around within a local coverage area and still remain connected to the network. It is often used in cities to connect networks in two or more buildings without installing a wired link.

Wireless Mesh Network   A wireless mesh network is a wireless network made up of radio nodes organized in a mesh topology. Each node forwards messages on behalf of the other nodes. Mesh networks can "self-heal," automatically re-routing around a node that has lost power.

Wireless MAN   Wireless metropolitan area networks are a type of wireless network that connects several wireless LANs. WiMAX is a type of Wireless MAN and is described by the IEEE 802.16 standard.

Wireless WAN   Wireless wide area networks are wireless networks that typically cover large areas, such as between neighboring towns and cities, or city and suburb. These networks can be used to connect branch offices of business or as a public Internet access system. The wireless connections between access points are usually point-to-point microwave links using parabolic dishes on the 2.4 GHz band, rather than omnidirectional antennas used with smaller networks. A typical system contains base station gateways, access points, and wireless bridging relays.

Cellular Network   A cellular network or mobile network is a radio network distributed over land areas called cells, each served by at least one fixed-location transceiver, known as a cell site or base station. In a cellular network, each cell characteristically uses a different set of radio frequencies from all their immediate neighboring cells to avoid any interference. When joined together, these cells provide radio coverage over a wide geographic area. This enables a large number of portable transceivers (e.g., mobile phones, pagers, etc.) to communicate with each other and with fixed transceivers and telephones anywhere in the network, via base stations, even if some of the transceivers are moving through more than one cell during transmission.

It is important to understand the principles and methodologies of delivering wireless information. These include the following:

Spread Spectrum   Spread spectrum is a method commonly used to modulate information into manageable bits that are sent over the air wirelessly. Essentially, spread spectrum refers to the concept of splitting information over a series of radio channels or frequencies. Generally, the number of frequencies is in the range of about 70, and the information is sent over all or most of the frequencies before being demodulated, or combined at the receiving end of the radio system.

Two kinds of spread spectrum are available:

- **Direct-Sequence Spread Spectrum (DSSS)**—Direct-sequence spread spectrum is a wireless technology that spreads a transmission over a much larger frequency band and with corresponding smaller amplitude. By spreading the signal over a wider band, the signal is less susceptible to interference at a specific frequency. In other words, the interference affects a smaller percentage of the signal. During transmission, a pseudorandom noise code (PN code) is modulated with the signal. The sender and receiver's PN code generators are synchronized, so that when the signal is received, the PN code can be filtered out.

- **Frequency-Hopping Spread Spectrum (FHSS)**—This wireless technology spreads its signal over rapidly changing frequencies. Each available frequency band is subdivided into sub-frequencies. Signals rapidly change (hop) among these sub-frequencies in an order that is agreed upon between the sender and receiver. The benefit of FHSS is that the interference at a specific frequency will affect the signal during a short interval. Conversely, FHSS can cause interference with adjacent DSSS systems.

Orthogonal Frequency Division Multiplexing (OFDM)   A signal is subdivided into sub-frequency bands or tones, and each of these bands is manipulated so that they can be broadcasted together without interfering with each other. In an Orthogonal Frequency Division Multiplexing (OFDM) system, each tone is considered to be orthogonal (independent or unrelated) to the adjacent tones and, therefore, does not require a guard band. Because OFDM is made up of many narrowband tones, narrowband interference will degrade only a small portion of the signal and has no or little effect on the remainder of the frequency components.

Vectored Orthogonal Frequency Division Multiplexing (VOFDM)   In addition to the standard OFDM principles, the use of spatial diversity can increase the system's tolerance to noise, interference, and multipath. This is referred to as vectored OFDM, or VOFDM. Spatial diversity is a widely accepted technique for improving performance in multipath environments. Because multipath is a function of the collection of bounced signals, that collection is dependent on the location of the receiver antenna. If two or more antennae are placed in the system, each would have a different set of multipath signals. The effects of each channel would vary from one antenna to the next, so carriers that may be unusable on one antenna may become usable on another.

Frequency Division Multiple Access (FDMA)   Frequency division multiple access (FDMA) is used in analog cellular only. It subdivides a frequency band into sub-bands and assigns an analog conversation to each sub-band. FDMA was the original "cellular" phone technology and has been de-commissioned in many locations in favor of GSM or CDMA-based technologies.

Time Division Multiple Access (TDMA)   Time division multiple access (TDMA) multiplexes several digital calls (voice or data) at each sub-band by devoting a small time slice in a round-robin to each call in the band. Two sub-bands are required for each call: one in each direction between sender and receiver.

Transmission Security and Common Vulnerabilities and Countermeasures

Wireless technologies rely on a variety of protocols and authentication systems that have vulnerabilities that can be exploited. Fortunately, there are wireless security devices and countermeasures that can be used to provide stronger security.

Wireless Security Issues

The protocols and authentication methods that wireless technologies employ are intrinsically related to how secure they are. It is important to understand both the strengths and vulnerabilities that come with them.

Open System Authentication

Open System Authentication (OSA) is the default authentication protocol for the 802.11 standard. It consists of a simple authentication request containing the station ID and an authentication response containing success or failure data. Upon successful authentication, both stations are considered mutually authenticated. It can be used with the Wired Equivalent Privacy (WEP) protocol to provide better communication security; however, it is important to note that the authentication management frames are still sent in cleartext during the authentication process. WEP is used only for encrypting data once the client is authenticated and associated. Any client can send its station ID in an attempt to associate with the AP. In effect, no authentication is actually done.

Shared Key Authentication

Shared Key Authentication (SKA) is a standard challenge and response mechanism that makes use of WEP and a shared secret key to provide authentication. Upon encrypting the challenge text with WEP using the shared secret key, the authenticating client will return the encrypted challenge text to the access point for verification. Authentication succeeds if the access point decrypts the same challenge text.

Ad-Hoc Mode

Ad-hoc mode is one of the networking topologies provided in the 802.11 standard. It consists of at least two wireless endpoints where there is no access point involved in their communication. Ad-hoc mode WLANs are normally less expensive to run, as no APs are needed for their communication. However, this topology cannot scale for larger networks and lacks some security features like MAC filtering and access control.

Infrastructure Mode

Infrastructure mode is another networking topology in the 802.11 standard. It consists of a number of wireless stations and access points. The access points usually connect to a larger wired network. This network topology can scale to form large networks with arbitrary coverage and complex architectures.

Wired Equivalent Privacy Protocol (WEP)

Wired Equivalent Privacy (WEP) protocol is a basic security feature in the IEEE 802.11 standard, intended to provide confidentiality over a wireless network by encrypting information sent over the network. A key-scheduling flaw has been discovered in WEP, so it is now considered to be insecure because a WEP key can be cracked in a few minutes with the aid of automated tools.

Wi-Fi Protected Access (WPA) and Wi-Fi Protected Access 2 (WPA2)

Wi-Fi Protected Access (WPA) provides users with a higher level of assurance that their data will remain protected by using the Temporal Key Integrity Protocol (TKIP) for data encryption. 802.1x authentication has been introduced in this protocol to improve user authentication. Wi-Fi Protected Access 2 (WPA2), based on IEEE 802.11i, is a wireless security protocol that allows only authorized users to access a wireless device, with features supporting stronger cryptography (e.g., Advanced Encryption Standard or AES), stronger authentication control (e.g., Extensible Authentication Protocol or EAP), key management, replay attack protection, and data integrity.

In July 2010, a security vendor claimed they discovered a vulnerability in the WPA2 protocol, named "Hole 196."[68] By exploiting the vulnerability, an internally authenticated

Wi-Fi user could decrypt the private data of other users and inject malicious traffic into the wireless network. After a thorough investigation, it turned out that such an attack cannot actually recover, break, or crack any WPA2 encryption keys (AES or TKIP). Instead, attackers could only masquerade as access points and launch a man-in-the-middle attack when clients attached to them. In addition, if the security architect does their job properly, such an attack would not be able to succeed in a properly configured environment in the first place. If the client isolation feature is enabled on all access points, wireless clients are not allowed to talk with each other when they are attached to the same access point. As a result of this simple security configuration setting being applied, an attacker is unable to launch a man-in-the-middle attack against other wireless users.

TKIP was initially designed to be used with WPA, while the stronger algorithm AES was designed to be used with WPA2. Some devices may allow WPA to work with AES, while some others may allow WPA2 to work with TKIP. In November 2008, a vulnerability in TKIP was uncovered that would allow an attacker to be able to decrypt small packets and inject arbitrary data into a wireless network. Thus, TKIP encryption is no longer considered to be secure. The security architect should consider using the stronger combination of WPA2 with AES encryption.

The design flaws in the security mechanisms of the 802.11 standard also give rise to a number of potential attacks, both passive and active. These attacks enable intruders to eavesdrop on, or tamper with, wireless transmissions.

A Parking Lot Attack

Access points emit radio signals in a circular pattern, and the signals almost always extend beyond the physical boundaries of the area they are intended to cover. Signals can be intercepted outside of buildings, or even through the floors in multi-story buildings. As a result, attackers can implement a "parking lot" attack, where they actually sit in the organization's parking lot and try to access internal hosts via the wireless network. If a network is compromised, the attacker has achieved a high level of penetration into the network. They are now through the firewall and have the same level of network access as trusted employees within the enterprise. An attacker may also fool legitimate wireless clients into connecting to the attacker's own network by placing an unauthorized access point with a stronger signal in close proximity to wireless clients. The aim is to capture end-user passwords or other sensitive data when users attempt to log on to these rogue servers.

Shared Key Authentication Flaw

Shared key authentication can easily be exploited through a passive attack by eavesdropping on both the challenge and the response between the access point and the authenticating client. Such an attack is possible because the attacker can capture both the plaintext (the challenge) and the ciphertext (the response). WEP uses the RC4 stream cipher as its encryption algorithm. A stream cipher works by generating a keystream, i.e., a sequence of pseudo-random bits, based on the shared secret key, together with an initialization vector (IV). The keystream is then XORed against the plaintext to produce the ciphertext. An important property of a stream cipher is that if both the plaintext and the ciphertext are known, the keystream can be recovered by simply XORing the plaintext and the ciphertext together, in this case the challenge and the response. The recovered keystream can then be used by the attacker to encrypt any subsequent challenge text generated by the access point to produce a valid authentication response by XORing the two values together. As a result, the attacker can be authenticated to the access point.

Service Set Identifier (SSID) Flaw

Access points come with vendor-provided default Service Set Identifiers (SSIDs) programmed into them. If the default SSID is not changed, it is very likely that an attacker will be able to successfully attack the device due to the use of the default configuration. In addition, SSIDs are embedded in management frames that will be broadcast in cleartext from the device, unless the access point is configured to disable SSID broadcasting or is using encryption. By conducting analysis on the captured network traffic from the air, the attacker could be able to obtain the network SSID and may be able to perform further attacks as a result.

The Vulnerability of Wired Equivalent Privacy Protocol (WEP)

Data passing through a wireless LAN with WEP disabled (which is the default setting for most products) is susceptible to eavesdropping and data modification attacks. However, even when WEP is enabled, the confidentiality and integrity of wireless traffic is still at risk because a number of flaws in WEP have been revealed, which seriously undermine its claims to security. In particular, the following attacks on WEP are possible:

- Passive attacks to decrypt traffic based on known plaintext and chosen ciphertext attacks
- Passive attacks to decrypt traffic based on statistical analysis of ciphertexts
- Active attacks to inject new traffic from unauthorized mobile stations
- Active attacks to modify data
- Active attacks to decrypt traffic, based on tricking the access point into redirecting wireless traffic to an attacker's machine

Attack on Temporal Key Integrity Protocol (TKIP)

The Temporal Key Integrity Protocol (TKIP) attack uses a mechanism similar to the WEP attack, in that it tries to decode data one byte at a time by using multiple replays and observing the response over the air. Using this mechanism, an attacker can decode small packets like ARP frames in about 15 minutes. If Quality of Service (QoS) is enabled in the network, the attacker can further inject up to 15 arbitrary frames for every decrypted packet. Potential attacks include ARP poisoning, DNS manipulation, and denial of service. Although this is not a key recovery attack and it does not lead to compromise of TKIP keys or decryption of all subsequent frames, it is still a serious attack and poses risks to all TKIP implementations on both WPA and WPA2 networks.

Wireless Security Devices

As wireless enterprise networks become more pervasive, increasingly sophisticated attacks are developed to exploit these networks. In response, many organizations consider the deployment of wireless intrusion protection and wireless intrusion detection systems (WIPS/WIDSs). These systems can offer sophisticated monitoring and reporting capabilities to identify attacks against wireless infrastructure while stopping multiple classes of attack before they are successful against a network.

Deployment Approaches

When selecting a WIDS vendor, it is important for the security practitioner to first understand the deployment methodologies supported by each system. The available WIDS deployment models include overlay, integrated, and hybrid.

Overlay Monitoring

In an overlay monitoring deployment, organizations augment their existing WLAN infrastructure with dedicated wireless sensors or *Air Monitors* (AMs). The AMs are connected to the network in a manner similar to access points (APs). They can be deployed in ceilings or on walls and supported by power over Ethernet (PoE) injectors in wiring closets. While APs are responsible for providing client connectivity, AMs are primarily passive devices that monitor the air for signs of attack or other undesired wireless activity. In an overlay WIDS system, the WIDS vendor provides a controller in the form of a server or appliance that collects and assesses information from the AMs that is monitored by an administrator. These devices do not otherwise participate with the rest of the wireless network and are limited to assessing traffic at the physical layer (layer 1) and the data-link layer (layer 2).

Integrated Monitoring

In an integrated monitoring deployment, organizations leverage existing access point hardware as dual-purpose AP/AM devices. APs are responsible for providing client connectivity in an infrastructure role and for analyzing wireless traffic to identify attacks and other undesired activity at the same time. This is often a less-costly approach compared to overlay monitoring because organizations use existing hardware for both monitoring and infrastructure access without the need for additional sensors or an overlay management controller.

Hybrid Monitoring

A hybrid monitoring approach leverages the strengths of both the overlay and integrated monitoring models. A hybrid approach uses both dual-purpose APs and dedicated AMs for intrusion detection and protection. Organizations can use an existing deployment of APs and augment that protection with dedicated AMs, or they can deploy a dedicated monitoring infrastructure consisting solely of AM devices. In either case, analysis is performed by a centralized controller similar to what is used with an overlay model, rather than the approach used in an integrated WIDS deployment, where processing is handled by distributed access points.

Powerful Attack Response

To mitigate attacks on the wireless network, WIDS vendors have augmented the analysis components of their products with reactive components, often known as Wireless Intrusion Prevention Services (WIPSs). When the analysis mechanism recognizes an attack, such as an attempt at accelerated WEP key cracking, the wireless device reacts to the event by reporting it to the administrator and by taking steps to prevent the attack from succeeding.

SUMMARY

Network and communications security can be a complex set of topics for the SSCP to understand. The need to be able to describe network-related security issues can involve multiple topics made up of many moving parts. The ability to identify protective measures for telecommunications technologies can be challenging, as the speed at which technology changes and evolves continues to increase. The SSCP needs to be able to also identify the processes best suited for managing LAN-based security at the same time, take into account the needs of the organization overall and the necessary procedures for operating and configuring network-based security devices such as IDS and IPS solutions. The security professional should be able to put all of these issues and concerns into context, understand their main goals, and apply a commonsense approach to typical scenarios. The focus here is to maintain operational resilience and protect valuable operational assets through a combination of people, processes, and technologies. At the same time, security services must be managed effectively and efficiently just like any other set of services in the enterprise.

SAMPLE QUESTIONS

1. Which of the following is typically deployed as a screening proxy for web servers?

   a. Intrusion prevention system

   b. Kernel proxies

   c. Packet filters

   d. Reverse proxies

2. A customer wants to keep cost to a minimum and has ordered only a single static IP address from the ISP. Which of the following must be configured on the router to allow for all the computers to share the same public IP address?

   a. Virtual Private Network (VPN)

   b. Port Address Translation (PAT)

   c. Virtual Local Area Network (VLAN)

   d. Power over Ethernet (PoE)

3. Sayge installs a new Wireless Access Point (WAP), and users are able to connect to it. However, once connected, users cannot access the Internet. Which of the following is the *most* likely cause of the problem?

   a. An incorrect subnet mask has been entered in the WAP configuration.

   b. Users have specified the wrong encryption type, and packets are being rejected.

   c. The signal strength has been degraded, and latency is increasing hop count.

   d. The signal strength has been degraded, and packets are being lost.

4. Which of the following devices should be part of a network's perimeter defense?

   a. Web server, host-based intrusion detection system (HIDS), and a firewall

   b. DNS server, firewall, and a boundary router

   c. Switch, firewall, and a proxy server

   d. Firewall, proxy server, and a host-based intrusion detection system (HIDS)

5. A Security Incident Event Management (SIEM) service performs which of the following function(s)? (Choose all that apply.)

   a. Coordinates software for security conferences and seminars

   b. Aggregates logs from security devices and application servers looking for suspicious activity

   c. Gathers firewall logs for archiving

   d. Reviews access control logs on servers and physical entry points to match user system authorization with physical access permissions

6. A botnet can be characterized as a:

    a. Type of virus

    b. Group of dispersed, compromised machines controlled remotely for illicit reasons

    c. Automatic security alerting tool for corporate networks

    d. Network used solely for internal communications

7. During a disaster recovery test, several billing representatives need to be temporarily set up to take payments from customers. It has been determined that this will need to occur over a wireless network, with security being enforced where possible. Which of the following configurations should be used in this scenario?

    a. WPA2, SSID disabled, and 802.11a

    b. WEP, SSID disabled, and 802.11g

    c. WEP, SSID enabled, and 802.11b

    d. WPA2, SSID enabled, and 802.11n

8. A new installation requires a network in a heavy manufacturing area with substantial amounts of electromagnetic radiation and power fluctuations. Which media is best suited for this environment is little traffic degradation is tolerated?

    a. Shielded twisted pair

    b. Coax

    c. Fiber

    d. Wireless

9. What is the network ID portion of the IP address 191.154.25.66 if the default subnet mask is used?

    a. 191

    b. 191.154.25

    c. 191.154

10. Given the address 192.168.10.19/28, which of the following are valid host addresses on this subnet? (Choose two.)

    a. 192.168.10.31

    b. 192.168.10.17

    c. 192.168.10.16

    d. 192.168.10.29

11. Circuit-switched networks do which of the following tasks?

   a. Divide data into packets and transmit it over a virtual network.

   b. Establish a dedicated circuit between endpoints.

   c. Divide data into packets and transmit it over a shared network.

   d. Establish an on-demand circuit between endpoints.

12. What is the biggest security issue associated with the use of a multiprotocol label switching (MPLS) network?

   a. Lack of native encryption services

   b. Lack of native authentication services

   c. Support for the Wired Equivalent Privacy (WEP) and Data Encryption Standard (DES) algorithms

   d. The need to establish peering relationships to cross Tier 1 carrier boundaries

13. The majority of DNS traffic is carried using User Datagram Protocol (UDP); what types of DNS traffic is carried using Transmission Control Protocol (TCP)? (Choose all that apply)

   a. Query traffic

   b. Response traffic

   c. DNNSEC traffic that exceeds single packet size maximum

   d. Secondary zone transfers

14. What is the command that a client would need to issue to initialize an encrypted FTP session using Secure FTP as outlined in RFC 4217?

   a. "ENABLE SSL"

   b. "ENABLE TLS"

   c. "AUTH TLS"

   d. "AUTH SSL"

15. What is the IEEE designation for Priority-based Flow Control (PFC) as defined in the Data Center Bridging (DCB) Standards?

   a. 802.1Qbz

   b. 802.1Qau

   c. 802.1Qaz

   d. 802.1Qbb

16. What is the integrity protection hashing function that the Session Initiation Protocol (SIP) uses?

   a. SHA-160

   b. MD4

   c. MD5

   d. SHA-256

17. Layer 2 Tunneling Protocol (L2TP) is a hybrid of:

   a. Cisco's Layer 2 Forwarding (L2F) and Microsoft's Point to Point Tunneling Protocol (PPTP)

   b. Microsoft's Layer 2 Forwarding (L2F) and Cisco's Point to Point Tunneling Protocol (PPTP)

   c. Cisco's Layer 2 Forwarding (L2F) and Point to Point Protocol (PPP)

   d. Microsoft's Layer 2 Forwarding (L2F) and Point to Point Protocol (PPP)

18. With regards to LAN-based security, what is the key difference between the control plane and the data plane?

   a. The data plane is where forwarding/routing decisions are made, while the control plane is where commands are implemented.

   b. The control plane is where APIs are used to monitor and oversee, while the data plane is where commands are implemented.

   c. The control plane is where forwarding/routing decisions are made, while the data plane is where commands are implemented.

   d. The data plane is where APIs are used to monitor and oversee, while the control plane is where commands are implemented.

19. There are several record types associated with the use of DNSSEC. What does the DS record type represent?

   a. A private key

   b. A public key

   c. A hash of a key

   d. A signature of an RRSet

20. MACsec (IEEE 802.1AE) is used to provide secure communication for all traffic on Ethernet links. How is MACsec configured?

   a. Through key distribution

   b. Using connectivity groups

   c. Using key generation

   d. Using connectivity associations

END NOTES

1. See the following for a high-level overview of the OSI reference model:

   http://en.wikipedia.org/wiki/OSI_model

2. See the following for a high-level overview of the TCP/IP model:

   http://en.wikipedia.org/wiki/TCP/IP_model

3. See the following:

   http://www.ecma-international.org/activities/Communications/TG11/s020269e.pdf

4. See the following for the original paper by Hubert Zimmermann that lays out the OSI Reference Model Architecture based on the work of the ISO SC16, the working group established to create the OSI model in 1977.

   "OSI Reference Model—The ISO Model of Architecture for Open Systems Interconnection"

   http://citeseerx.ist.psu.edu/viewdoc/download?doi=10.1.1.136.9497&rep=rep1&type=pdf

5. See the following: http://tools.ietf.org/html/rfc1058

6. See the following:

   http://tools.ietf.org/html/rfc1723

   http://tools.ietf.org/html/rfc4822

7. See the following: http://tools.ietf.org/pdf/rfc1131.pdf

8. See the following:

   RFC 1583: http://tools.ietf.org/html/rfc1583

   RFC 2328: http://tools.ietf.org/html/rfc2328

9. See the following: http://tools.ietf.org/html/rfc792

10. See the following for the RFC for IGMP Version 3:

    http://tools.ietf.org/html/rfc4604

11. See the following: http://tools.ietf.org/html/rfc4271

12. See the following: http://tools.ietf.org/html/rfc3118

13. See the following: http://insecure.org/sploits/ping-o-death.html

14. See the following: http://www.sans.org/reading-room/whitepapers/threats/icmp-attacks-illustrated-477

15. See the following to download:

    Very Simple Network Scanner for Windows:

    `http://www.softpedia.com/progDownload/Very-Simple-Network-Scanner-Download-112841.html`

    NMAP for Linux/Windows: `http://nmap.org/download.html`

16. See the following for the last available build (version 5.0) of firewalk: `http://packetfactory.openwall.net/projects/firewalk/`

17. See the following to download the Firewalk host rule script for NMAP: `http://nmap.org/nsedoc/scripts/firewalk.html`

18. See the following to download the latest version for the IEEE 802.3 Standard: `http://standards.ieee.org/about/get/802/802.3.html`

19. See the following for the IETF working Group on MPLS's homepage: `https://datatracker.ietf.org/wg/mpls/documents/`

20. See the following for a general overview video presentation of how the DNS system works: `http://www.youtube.com/watch?v=2ZUxoi7YNgs`

21. See the following for the RFC's that establish the Domain Name System:

    "Domain Names—Concepts and Facilities" [RFC-1034] `http://www.ietf.org/rfc/rfc1034.txt`

    "Domain Names—Implementation and Specification" [RFC-1035] `http://www.ietf.org/rfc/rfc1035.txt`

22. DNS Security Extensions (DNSSEC) adds security functions to the DNS protocol that can be used to prevent some of the attacks discussed such as DNS cache poisoning. DNSSEC adds data origin authentication and data integrity to the DNS protocol. DNSSEC specifications, implementation, and operational information are defined in multiple RFCs, as listed here:

    RFC4033: DNS Security Introduction and Requirements

    RFC4034: Resource Records for the DNS Security Extensions

    RFC4035: Protocol Modifications for the DNS Security Extensions

    RFC5155: DNS Security (DNSSEC) Hashed Authenticated Denial of Existence

    RFC4310: Domain Name System (DNS) Security Extensions Mapping for the Extensible Provisioning Protocol (EPP)

    RFC4641: DNSSEC Operational Practices

23. See the following for a historical account of the discovery of the Kaminsky bug: `http://www.seattlepi.com/local/article/Seattle-security-expert-helped-uncover-major-1281123.php`

24. See the following for ICANN Security and Stability Advisory Committee (SSAC) SAC 025: SSAC Advisory on Fast Flux Hosting and DNS http://www.icann.org/en/groups/ssac/documents/sac-025-en.pdf

25. See the following for a story that summarizes the attacks carried out by the SEA: http://rt.com/news/sea-hack-nyt-site-twitter-077/

    See the following for the SEA's official website: http://sea.sy/index/en

26. The following list of RFCs provides the details for all of the updated functionality that has been proposed for DNS:

    RFC 1101: DNS Encoding of Network Names and Other Types

    RFC 1183: New DNS RR Definitions

    RFC 1706: DNS NSAP Resource Records

    RFC 1982: Serial Number Arithmetic

    RFC 2181: Clarifications to the DNS Specification

    RFC 2308: Negative Caching of DNS Queries (DNS NCACHE)

    RFC 4033: DNS Security Introduction and Requirements

    RFC 4034: Resource Records for the DNS Security Extensions

    RFC 4035: Protocol Modifications for the DNS Security Extensions

    RFC 4470: Minimally Covering NSEC Records and DNSSEC On-line Signing

    RFC 4592: The Role of Wildcards in the Domain Name System

    RFC 5155: DNS Security (DNSSEC) Hashed Authenticated Denial of Existence

    RFC 5452: Measures for Making DNS More Resilient against Forged Answers

    RFC 6014: Cryptographic Algorithm Identifier Allocation for DNSSEC

    RFC 6604: xNAME RCODE and Status Bits Clarification

    RFC 6672: DNAME Redirection in the DNS

    RFC 6840: Clarifications and Implementation Notes for DNS Security (DNSSEC)

    RFC 6944: Applicability Statement: DNS Security (DNSSEC) DNSKEY Algorithm Implementation Status

27. See the following RFC's for LDAPv3 information:

    The technical specification detailing version 3 of the Lightweight Directory Access Protocol (LDAP), an Internet protocol, consists of this document and the following documents:

    LDAP: Lightweight Directory Access Protocol (LDAP): Technical Specification Road Map [RFC4510]

LDAP: The Protocol [RFC4511]

LDAP: Directory Information Models [RFC4512]

LDAP: Authentication Methods and Security Mechanisms [RFC4513]

LDAP: String Representation of Distinguished Names [RFC4514]

LDAP: String Representation of Search Filters [RFC4515]

LDAP: Uniform Resource Locator [RFC4516]

LDAP: Syntaxes and Matching Rules [RFC4517]

LDAP: Internationalized String Preparation [RFC4518]

LDAP: Schema for User Applications [RFC4519]

28. Because the services provided by NIS+ are security-critical, NIS+ is designed to operate securely. An aspect of this design is the concept of "security levels," which determine the amount of scrutiny given to incoming RPC NIS requests. There are three security levels, numbered 0 through 2. In level 0, the NIS+ server (rpc.nisd) performs no authentication to determine the legitimacy of incoming requests. This option is provided for debugging purposes. In level 1, RPC AUTH_ UNIX (client-presented UIDs and GIDs) are used to authenticate requests. In level 2, the most secure level, AUTH_DES is used to cryptographically authenticate incoming requests. Unfortunately, even when the system is operating in security level 2, which should mandate cryptographic authentication for all requests, the rpc.nisd daemon provides several RPC calls that are not authenticated. These calls allow a remote client to obtain sensitive system status information from the NIS+ server. The information available to a remote attacker includes NIS+ configuration information (including the security level of the server and a list of directory objects served by it), as well as the ability to determine valid process IDs on the NIS+ server. Additionally, one of the RPC calls available to remote clients can allow an attacker to disable logging on the NIS+ server, as well as to manipulate the NIS+ caches. This may allow attackers to degrade or deny service on NIS+ servers. The ability to use NIS+ to remotely ascertain valid process IDs is serious because it allows an attacker the ability to predict certain random numbers generated by Unix applications. Frequently, Unix applications generate random numbers using the process ID and the current time, either directly or as a seed to a random number generator.

29. See the following: http://jap.inf.tu-dresden.de/index_en.html

30. http://www.inl.gov/technicalpublications/Documents/3375141.pdf (Page 8)

31. http://csrc.nist.gov/publications/nistir/ir7442/NIST-IR-7442_2007CS-DAnnualReport.pdf

32. See the following for the full text of the Yokogawa Security Advisory Report: http://www.yokogawa.com/dcs/security/ysar/YSAR-14-0001E.pdf

33. `http://ics-cert.us-cert.gov/sites/default/files/Monitors/ICS-CERT_Monitor_%20Jan-April2014.pdf`

34. See the following:

    `http://www.cisco.com/c/dam/en/us/solutions/collateral/data-center-virtualization/ieee-802-1-data-center-bridging/at_a_glance_c45-460907.pdf`

35. See the following: `http://www.ietf.org/rfc/rfc3720.txt`

    Here is a list of the additional RFCs relating to iSCSI:

    RFC 3721—Internet Small Computer Systems Interface (iSCSI) Naming and Discovery

    RFC 3722—String Profile for Internet Small Computer Systems Interface (iSCSI) Names

    RFC 3723—Securing Block Storage Protocols over IP (Scope: The use of IPsec and IKE to secure iSCSI, iFCP, FCIP, iSNS and SLPv2.)

    RFC 3347—Small Computer Systems Interface protocol over the Internet (iSCSI) Requirements and Design Considerations

    RFC 3783—Small Computer Systems Interface (SCSI) Command Ordering Considerations with iSCSI

    RFC 3980—T11 Network Address Authority (NAA) Naming Format for iSCSI Node Names

    RFC 4018—Finding Internet Small Computer Systems Interface (iSCSI) Targets and Name Servers by Using Service Location Protocol version 2 (SLPv2)

    RFC 4173—Bootstrapping Clients using the Internet Small Computer System Interface (iSCSI) Protocol

    RFC 4544—Definitions of Managed Objects for Internet Small Computer System Interface (iSCSI)

    RFC 4850—Declarative Public Extension Key for Internet Small Computer Systems Interface (iSCSI) Node Architecture

    RFC 4939—Definitions of Managed Objects for iSNS (Internet Storage Name Service)

    RFC 5048—Internet Small Computer System Interface (iSCSI) Corrections and Clarifications

    RFC 5047—DA: Datamover Architecture for the Internet Small Computer System Interface (iSCSI)

    RFC 5046—Internet Small Computer System Interface (iSCSI) Extensions for Remote Direct Memory Access (RDMA)

36. See the following: MPLS Fundamentals, Luc De Ghein, Nov 21, 2006 (ISBN-10 1-58705-197-4)

    `http://www.cisco.com/c/en/us/support/docs/multiprotocol-label-switch-ing-mpls/mpls/4649-mpls-faq-4649.html`

37. See the following: `http://www.ietf.org/rfc/rfc2543.txt`

38. See the following: `http://www.ietf.org/rfc/rfc3261.txt`

39. See the following: `http://www.ietf.org/rfc/rfc3325.txt`

40. `http://www.dhs.gov/news/2013/05/16/written-testimony-nppd-house-home-land-security-subcommittee-cybersecurity-hearing`

41. "What is a Bastion Host?", accessed January 15, 2015, `http://www.techopedia.com/definition/6157/bastion-host`

42. TIA/EIA-568 is a set of telecommunications standards from the Telecommunications Industry Association (TIA), an offshoot of the Electronic Industries Alliance (EIA). The standards address commercial building cabling for telecommunications products and services. As of 2014, the standard is at revision C, replacing the 2001 revision B, the 1995 revision A, and the initial issue of 1991, which are now obsolete. Perhaps the best known features of TIA/EIA-568 are the pin/pair assignments for eight-conductor 100-ohm balanced twisted pair cabling. These assignments are named T568A and T568B. An IEC standard ISO/IEC 11801 provides similar standards for network cables.

43. See the following:

    `http://www.ietf.org/rfc/rfc3920`

    `http://www.ietf.org/rfc/rfc3921`

44. See the following for an overview of the Jabber development SDK and APIs: `https://developer.cisco.com/site/collaboration/jabber/overview.gsp`

45. `https://tools.ietf.org/html/rfc1459`

46. `http://tools.ietf.org/html/rfc2661`

47. See the following for the complete set of RFCs pertaining to RADIUS:

    `http://tools.ietf.org/html/rfc2865`

    `http://tools.ietf.org/html/rfc3575`

    `http://tools.ietf.org/html/rfc5080`

    `http://tools.ietf.org/html/rfc6929`

48. See the following for the RFCs pertaining to SNMP:

    `http://tools.ietf.org/html/rfc1157`

    `http://www.ietf.org/rfc/rfc3410`

6

NETWORKS AND COMMUNICATIONS SECURITY

http://www.ietf.org/rfc/rfc3411

http://www.ietf.org/rfc/rfc3412

http://www.ietf.org/rfc/rfc3413

http://www.ietf.org/rfc/rfc3414

http://www.ietf.org/rfc/rfc3415

http://www.ietf.org/rfc/rfc3416

http://www.ietf.org/rfc/rfc3417

http://www.ietf.org/rfc/rfc3418

http://www.ietf.org/rfc/rfc3584

49. See the following for the RFCs pertaining to SNMP:

http://tools.ietf.org/html/rfc1157

http://www.ietf.org/rfc/rfc3410

http://www.ietf.org/rfc/rfc3411

http://www.ietf.org/rfc/rfc3412

http://www.ietf.org/rfc/rfc3413

http://www.ietf.org/rfc/rfc3414

http://www.ietf.org/rfc/rfc3415

http://www.ietf.org/rfc/rfc3416

http://www.ietf.org/rfc/rfc3417

http://www.ietf.org/rfc/rfc3418

http://www.ietf.org/rfc/rfc3584

50. See the following for a good overall reference for SNMP across all versions:

http://www.ibr.cs.tu-bs.de/projects/snmpv3/

51. http://www.ietf.org/rfc/rfc854

http://www.ietf.org/rfc/rfc855

52. http://www.ietf.org/rfc/rfc1258

53. http://www.juniper.net/techpubs/en_US/junos14.1/topics/concept/macsec.html

54. http://www.juniper.net/techpubs/en_US/junos14.1/topics/concept/macsec.html

55. See the following: https://blog.cloudflare.com/dnssec-an-introduction/

56. See the following:

http://tools.ietf.org/html/rfc1918

http://tools.ietf.org/html/rfc6761

57. http://www.ietf.org/rfc/rfc793

58. http://www.ietf.org/rfc/rfc1948

59. Secure NFS (SNFS) offers secure authentication and encryption on the basis of secure RPC, which authenticates each RPC request.

60. The concept of store and forward allows for the reception of a data packet upstream from the endpoint, and the queuing of that data for a period of time if necessary, in order to ensure delivery of the data to the endpoint once it is located.

61. Slowloris is especially dangerous to hosts running Apache, dhttpd, Tomcat, and the GoAhead WebServer. Slowloris is a highly targeted attack, enabling one web server to take down another server, without affecting other services or ports on the target network. Slowloris does this by holding as many connections to the target web server open for as long as possible. It accomplishes this by creating connections to the target server but sending only a partial request. Slowloris constantly sends more HTTP headers but never completes a request. The targeted server keeps each of these false connections open. This eventually overflows the maximum concurrent connection pool, and leads to denial of additional connections from legitimate clients.

    See the following for overview information on Slowloris: https://en.wikipedia.org/wiki/Slowloris_(computer_security)

62. Gartner, "Prepare for 2020 by Owning Your Own Internet Security and Reliability," Lawrence Orans, October 17, 2013.

    See the following for the full Gartner report: https://www.gartner.com/doc/2608916

63. See the following for additional information on the attack, including the arrest of a 16-year-old boy in London for direct involvement in the attack: http://www.standard.co.uk/news/crime/london-schoolboy-secretly-arrested-over-worlds-biggest-cyber-attack-8840766.html

64. See the following for the original notice issued by the Chinese CNNIC in Chinese: http://www.cnnic.net.cn/gjymaqzx/aqgg/aqggaqsj/201308/t20130826_41325.htm

    The English translation of this notice follows:

    So at 0:00 on August 25, the State DNS nodes denial of service attacks, the China Internet Network Information Center, disposal, to 2 pm, the service returns to normal, 3:00 a notice through the official micro. At 4 pm, the National DNS nodes are again the largest ever denial of service attacks, some websites analytical

6

affected, leading to slow or interrupt access. To give notice when the attacker continues, the country has been gradually restored DNS service. Ministry of Industry and Information Technology launched the "Domain Name System Security special contingency plan" to further protect the national domain name resolution services. China Internet Network Information Center on the affected users to apologize for launching cyberattacks affect the stability of the Internet behavior condemned. China Internet Network Information Center will be coordinated with the national departments continue to enhance service capabilities.

65. Bernstein, Daniel J., "SYN cookies," N.P., 1996. Web. 30 June 2014. `http://cr.yp.to/syncookies.html`

66. `http://tools.ietf.org/html/rfc3330`

67. See the following to download the ISO/IEC 10646:2012 Standard: `http://standards.iso.org/ittf/PubliclyAvailableStandards/index.html`

68. See the following: `http://community.arubanetworks.com/t5/Community-Tribal-Knowledge-Base/Analysis-of-quot-Hole-196-quot-WPA2-Attack/ta-p/25382`

Systems and Application Security

MALCODE, ALSO KNOWN AS malicious code or malware, can be found running rampant on Windows and other operating systems today. System administrators are no longer protecting the perimeter of a network but managing an ever-porous network constantly under attack from within and by external actors.

In 2014, a major enterprise environment suffered a large-scale botnet attack with hundreds of infected hosts appearing within the network. Multiple acquisitions and merging of networks left the network vulnerable to attack. No clear chain of command and control (C&C) for security measures existed within the global network. The bot attack was able to significantly disrupt the business due to the most basic of procedures and safeguards not being implemented effectively and thoroughly across the entire network. As a result of lax patch management procedures, inadequate change management controls, and an "it can't happen to us" mindset, the attack was widespread, devastatingly effective, and proved to be very expensive with regards to the loss of productivity and mitigation expenses. System administrators were able to quickly reimage the affected computers and get them back online, but unfortunately they did not know how to protect against the original vector of the attack and were soon successfully attacked again. This is a lesson in properly understanding how to mitigate a threat.

In 2015, a Trojan was installed on a computer in a major network. It also installed a rootkit that was undetected by updated antivirus software. System administrators updated their antivirus and detected and removed the Trojan from multiple desktops using antivirus software. The rootkit remained undetected in the system. It also remained undetected over the network communicating with a remote C&C server through encrypted TCP port 80 communications. The integrity of the entire network was compromised for several months before the rootkit was discovered and mitigation actions were taken accordingly. This is a lesson in properly understanding the impact of an attack to restore integrity to an infected host.

TOPICS

The following topics are addressed in this chapter:

- ❏ Identify and analyze malicious code and activity

  - ▪ Malicious code (e.g., virus, worms, Trojan horses, logic bombs, malware, botnet)

  - ▪ Malicious code countermeasures (e.g., scanners, anti-malware, code signing, sandboxing)

  - ▪ Malicious activity (e.g., social engineering, insider threat, spoofing, phishing, spam, Botnets)

  - ▪ Malicious activity countermeasures (e.g., user awareness, system hardening, patching, sandboxing)

- ❏ Implement and operate end-point device security (e.g., virtualization, thin clients, thick clients, USB devices)

  - ▪ HIDS

  - ▪ Host-based firewalls

  - ▪ Application white listing

  - ▪ Endpoint encryption

  - ▪ Trusted platform module

  - ▪ Mobile device management (e.g., COPE, BYOD, telework)

  - ▪ Secure browsing (e.g., sandboxing)

- ❏ Operate and configure cloud security

  - ▪ Operation models (e.g., public, private, hybrid cloud)

  - ▪ Service models (e.g., DNS, e-mail, proxy, VPN)

  - ▪ Virtualization (e.g., hypervisor)

  - ▪ Legal and privacy concerns (e.g., surveillance, data ownership, jurisdiction, eDiscovery)

  - ▪ Data storage and transmission (e.g., archiving, recovery, resilience)

  - ▪ Third-party/outsourcing implications (e.g., SLA, data portability, data destruction, auditing)

- ❏ Secure big data systems
  - ■ Application vulnerabilities
  - ■ Architecture or design vulnerabilities
- ❏ Operate and secure virtual environments
  - ■ Software-defined network (SDN)
  - ■ Hypervisor
  - ■ Virtual appliances
  - ■ Continuity and resilience
  - ■ Attacks and countermeasures
  - ■ Shared storage

OBJECTIVES

The security practitioner is expected to participate in the following areas related to systems and application security:

- ■ Describe malicious code and the various countermeasures
- ■ Describe the processes for operating end-point device security
- ■ Define mobile device management processes
- ■ Describe the process for configuring cloud security
- ■ Explain the process for securing big data systems
- ■ Summarize the process for securing virtual environments

IDENTIFYING AND ANALYZING MALICIOUS CODE AND ACTIVITY

The role of the SSCP is broad ranging, covering many areas of system operations and the security requirements associated with them. One of the most important activities that the SSCP engages in on a daily basis is identifying and analyzing malicious code and activity within the network. The skills required to identify suspicious activity in a system that may indicate that malicious code is at work are not really complicated to acquire, as they are primarily focused around common sense, situational awareness, and the use of configuration management baselines. The challenging and unique skills that the SSCP has to work hard to acquire are those that speak to the analysis of malicious code once it has been discovered in a system. The skills required to engage in malicious code analysis cover areas such as forensic examinations, code analysis and decomposition, and system testing.

CIA TRIAD: APPLICABILITY TO MALCODE

The CIA triad shown in Figure 7.1 is the central component of all eight domains of computer security and especially pertinent to malcode risk. Table 7.1 gives examples of how all elements of the triad are applicable to malcode.

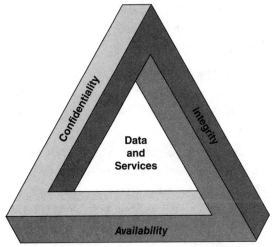

FIGURE 7.1 The CIA triad: confidentiality, integrity, and availability

TABLE 7.1 CIA Elements as They Apply to Malcode

Confidentiality	A Trojan infects a host and provides a remote attacker with access to sensitive documents, breaching confidentiality.
Integrity	A bot is installed on a computer and immediately installs several other files that are not detected through antivirus software. While the original file is later removed by a scan with updated antivirus software, the additional payloads remain intact on the system, leading to a compromise of systems integrity.
Availability	A computer that is infected with malicious code is instructed by a remote actor to perform a distributed denial-of-service (DDoS) attack against a web server. The web server becomes unavailable due to network congestion caused by the overloading of the server through the DDoS attack. The infected host also suffers degraded performance due to large volumes of egress traffic, leading to a lack of system availability.

Malcode Naming Conventions and Types

There is no international standard for malcode naming conventions. Some names, like the infamous Storm worm from 2007, StuxNet, Duqu, and Flame get traction in public media reports and become popularized over time. Others, such as Code Red, are assigned as a family name by individuals analyzing a new worm while staying up late at night drinking Code Red soda. In general, the antivirus industry follows CARO-like naming standards.

CARO-Like Naming Standards

CARO is short for the Computer Antivirus Research Organization and was established in the early 1990s to research malcode.[1] In 1991, a committee was formed to develop a naming convention to help organize the technical classifications of malicious code. What they came up with was a way to classify codes based on the following general structure:

```
Platform.Type.Family _Name.Variant[:Modifier]@Suffix
```

It is important to note that the previous syntax has been modified slightly to best reflect the combined usage and terms related to the original CARO naming standard proposed years ago. The previous syntax is how malcode is generally named today based on CARO discussions in the early 1990s and later.[2]

- **Platform**—Commonly denotes the operating system, such as W32 for a Windows 32-bit platform malicious code. It can also be an application specific to that threat, such as PPT for PowerPoint-based malicious code. Proposed prefixes from 1999 are listed here, taken from `http://members.chello.at/erikajo/vnc99b2.txt`:

  - BOOT—MBR, DOS-BR, Floppy-BR
  - DOS—DOS file
  - BAT—DOS batches
  - OS2—IBM's OS/2 viruses
  - MAC—Macintosh viruses
  - W3X—Windows 3.x files
  - W95—Windows 95 files
  - WNT—Windows NT files
  - W2K—Windows 2000 files
  - W32—Windows 95/98/NT/2K files

  - WM—Microsoft Winword Macro viruses
  - XM—Microsoft Excel Macro viruses
  - W97M—Microsoft Word 97 viruses
  - X97M—Microsoft Excel 97 viruses
  - PPT—Microsoft PowerPoint
  - WORK—Microsoft Works
  - AM—Microsoft Access
  - A97M—Microsoft Access 97
  - O97M—Microsoft Office 97
  - HLP—Microsoft Helpfile viruses

- VBS—Microsoft Visual Basic
- JS—JavaScript
- JAVA—Java viruses
- COR—CorelDRAW viruses
- AMI—AmiPro viruses
- ELF86—ELF x86 binary viruses
- BASH—Bash viruses
- PERL—Perl viruses

Obviously technology has changed since this original suggestion was made by CARO in the early 1990s. These platform rules are roughly followed by antivirus companies helping computer professionals to extract some meaning from the CARO-like name of a sample.

✔ Try It for Yourself— Using the CARO Naming Convention

Take a look at the naming convention for the following worm discovered in the wild on July 17, 2013.

W32.Waledac.D!gen5 [3]

Question 1: What does the "W32" portion of the name indicate?

Answer 1: The W32-portion of the name indicates that this is malcode that spreads on Windows 32-bit operating systems. Systems that would be affected by this worm include Windows 95, Windows 98, Windows Me, Windows NT, Windows 2000, Windows XP, Windows Vista, and Windows 7.

Question 2: What is the "Waledac" portion of the name?

Answer 2: Waledac is the family name for this worm.

Question 3: What does the "D" designation in the name represent?

Answer 3: "D" indicates that this is the fourth variant in this family to be reported.

- **Type** is the next major category that sometimes appears first in a malcode name, such as Trojan.FamilyName.Variant. Types correlate to the types seen in this domain, such as Trojan, worm, virus, joke, dropper, etc. Each antivirus company uses its own naming schemes or abbreviations that roughly follow this model.

- **Family Name** is the name given to the family. There is a "group name" that can also be assigned according to older proposed standards, but this is not used today. The family name is the area where antivirus companies have had great variance in the past. Family names vary based on how each company or reporter references a malcode. Family names are selected for a variety of reasons, such as a string seen in egress packets to a remote C&C, strings within the binary, text related to the author or target of attack, etc. In general, professionals try not to honor bad actor names for code or promote virus authoring group names to avoid any gratification for bad actors. To look at how family names can vary greatly, take a look at Backdoor.Win32.Breplibot.b (Kaspersky):

- **CA**—Win32.OutsBot.U
- **F-Secure**—Breplibot.b
- **Kaspersky**—Backdoor.Win32.Breplibot.b
- **McAfee**—W32/Brepibot!CME-589
- **Microsoft**—Backdoor:Win32/Ryknos.A!CME-589
- **Norman**—W32/Ryknos.A
- **Panda**—Bck/Ryknos.A
- **Sophos**—Troj/Stinx-E
- **Symantec**—Backdoor.Ryknos
- **Trend Micro**—BKDR_BREPLIBOT.C

Notice in the preceding example CARO-like naming standards. Unfortunately, naming conventions and family names vary greatly among antivirus companies. Some start with the operating system, such as W32, and others with the type, such as Backdoor or Troj (short for Trojan). Some spell out W32 to Win32, etc. Also notice that some use slashes instead of dots (or underscores and hashes), and some use an exclamation point to then include the common malware enumeration (CME) value assigned to the code, 589. Family names are even worse for this sample with names such as OutsBot, Breplibot, Brepibot (no L), Ryknos, and Stinx. This makes correlation of samples very difficult, if not impossible, with binaries in hand for proper comparisons.

- **Variants**, also referred to as identifiers and with major and minor classification possibilities, identify each unique member of a family. In some cases, antivirus companies use a .GEN signature for code to generically handle a certain code family. In other cases, especially with companies like Kaspersky, unique individual variant names are assigned to each variant of code within a family. Variants may be minor, like a small repacking of a Trojan, or major, like an upgrade from AgoBot to PhatBot code justifying an entire new family name. However, antivirus companies all handle such situations differently, resulting in some using one family name forever if the code is based on the same source code, such as AgoBot, while others differentiate based on major changes in functionality or similar malcode characteristics.

Variants are typically done with A–Z assignments, using the structure ".AAA. . ." as needed for variants of a family. For example, the first new variant of a family is ".A." The next variant is ".B." When the ".Z" variant is used, the next variant is ".AA," then ".AB," and so on. Numbers and symbols can also be used for the naming of malcode.

- **@Suffix** may be attached to some CARO-like naming conventions to identify how a malcode spreads. Common suffixes include @M for mailing virus or worm code by Symantec and @MM for a mass mailing virus or worm. Symantec defines a mailing malcode as one that only sends out malicious e-mails as the user sends out e-mails, appending or hijacking the mail code. A mass mailing malcode is one that sends messages to every e-mail found within the address book of the infected computer or addresses harvested from multiple other locations on the computer.

Cross-Referencing Malcode Names

This generally involves looking at multiscanner results, looking up available documentation on specific antivirus vendor sites, open source intelligence (OSINT) queries for incidents and data related to the threat, and more. To get started, refer to a few cross-referencing and documentation tools that exist on the Internet, which every professional should properly understand: CME, multiscanners, and VGrep.

Common Malware Enumeration

Common malware enumeration (CME) is yet one of many such failed efforts to coordinate naming conventions to date. A public site for the initiative first appeared in late 2005. The goal of the group was to reduce public confusion in referencing malcode threats, enhance communications between antivirus vendors, and improve communication and information sharing for the information security community at large. In short, many names and a lack of sharing lead to confusion during a malcode outbreak.

CME included a group of experts who submitted, analyzed, and shared threats to evaluate them for CME inclusion. If accepted, a CME number or identifier is assigned in a semirandom order (not 1, 2, 3, but 711, 416, etc.). Each participating vendor then assigns their unique name to that same sample shared within CME to help produce an authoritative laboratory-qualified correlation of names to a specific binary. A list of all the samples managed by the CME effort while still funded is available online at `http://cme.mitre.org/data/list.html`.

Unfortunately, the group lost funding and momentum by 2007. Today, CME is nonfunctional other than as a historical reference on their public website. This is sadly the reality when it comes to information sharing and especially code sharing within the antivirus industry to date. Competitive interests and costs associated with having to rename samples for standardization greatly hinder global coordination. For this reason, it is important to learn how to cross-correlate names for malcode to properly analyze code.

Public Multiscanners

Public multiscanners (multiple antivirus engines are deployed through a common web-based front end to scan the code) exist today that make it trivial for any user to upload and quickly identify names assigned to a specific binary. Analysts can then look up specific malcode names on each vendor site to identify any documentation related to the sample in question. If no specific information is available on a specific variant of a family, sometimes a family report may exist or a similar variant within the family (if you cannot find FamilyName.C, FamilyName.A may be documented). A partial list of public multiscanner sites is here:

https://www.virustotal.com/en/
(Figure 7.2)

http://virusscan.jotti.org/en

http://www.virscan.org/

https://www.metadefender.com/

FIGURE 7.2 **A multiscanner site**

These systems provide a valuable service, allowing individuals to upload suspicious files, scan them in a controlled environment, and share the results of that scan with the participating antivirus software vendors to enable them to glean intelligence directly from the wild in real time. However, there is also a dark side to this technology that the security practitioner needs to be aware of as they weigh the value of using this approach to gain insights into the kind of files that are transiting their networks.

The use of public cloud scanning platforms is not restricted to security practitioners today, as the BlackHat hacking community has also picked up on these tools as a way to achieve ongoing real-time validation of their exploit code and in the process has built a parallel "hidden" cloud infrastructure to allow members to carry out real-time validation of their exploit code without the concern of having that code sent to the AV software vendors, thus rendering its efficacy and impact as an exploit tool short-lived. These sites are often using the same exact technologies and AV engines as the public sites maintained by the AV vendors. The AV engines are "hijacked" versions of the official products and are maintained by the hackers in order to offer up-to-date scanning and detection capabilities to their users.

These sites warn users to not use public AV scanners because they maintain their own scanners and scan the file base every hour to ensure that it is up to date, clean, and always providing the latest exploit code for download. The entities behind these sites are typically using a pay per install (PPI) subscription model to allow members access to the scanned and validated source files for the various malware packages being hosted at any given time on the sites. The interesting thing about these services is that they also offer updates to member users and will alert them when scanning has picked up on the fact that the exploit package has been detected during a scan and as a result may be compromised. This alerting feature allows the authors to be notified and upload newer versions of their malware to keep the distributions up to date and stealthed for as long as possible. This also allows members who are actively deploying the malware in the wild to be alerted as soon as possible to the potential for exposure, thus giving them the opportunity to achieve and maintain deep, persistent access to the networks that they have infected by simply continuing to update and redeploy the newest binary exploit packages once they become available through the marketplace.

A specific example of software designed for these kinds of activities is called the Kim Multiscanner (up to version 1.2) and now goes by the name KIMS 2.0 Indetectables. Figure 7.3 shows the main screen from KIMS 2.0 in English. (The software is written in Spanish, but it can be used in a variety of languages that include English, French, Portuguese, and Turkish as well.)

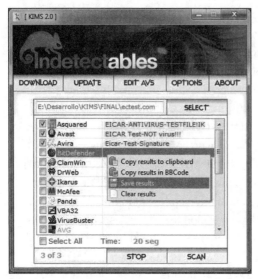

FIGURE 7.3 **KIMS Indetectables 2.0**

Figure 7.4 shows what is one of the most interesting and potentially dangerous features of the program, which is the ability to toggle on and off the use of the heuristic scanning capabilities of the various AV software packages being used by the tool, as well as setting the specific level for the heuristic scans. This capability combined with the capability to scan "offline" so that no data is uploaded to the AV vendors, and the ability to download and update the AV software for all supported vendors makes this tool, and others like it such as AntivirusMulti, a potent tool in the wrong hands.

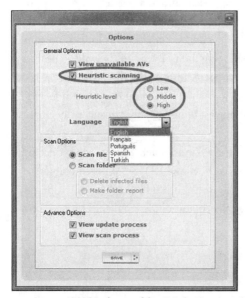

FIGURE 7.4 **KIMS Indetectables 2.0 Options settings**

vgrep

vgrep is another tool that has been used by antivirus professionals for many years that helps to correlate codes by name. Once registered on the site, users may freely use vgrep to correlate samples of interest.[4] Figure 7.5 is a screenshot of what it looks like when one searches for a common family name like "MyDoom," one of the most prolific mass mailing worm families in the history of computing.

Search results for 'MyDoom'

More than 400 results found

Vendor	1	2	3
AVG	not detected	I-Worm/Mydoom.N	I-Worm/Mydoom.AG
Avast	Win32:Mydoom-H [Wrm]	Win32:Mydoom-L [Wrm]	Win32:Mydoom-AB [Wrm]
Avira	Worm/Mydoom.H	Worm/Mydoom.L.1	Worm/Mydoom.AN
Bitdefender	Worm.Generic.63722		Win32.Mydoom.AL@mm
ClamAV	Worm.Mydoom.H	PUA.Win32.Packer.Upx-28	Worm.Mydoom.AN
Commtouch	not detected	W32/Mydoom.M@mm	W32/Mydoom.AO@mm
Dr.Web	not detected		Win32.HLLM.MyDoom.36
ESET	not detected	Win32/Mydoom.Q worm	not detected
Fortinet	not detected	W32/MyDoom.M@mm	W32/MyDoom.AH@mm
GFI VIPRE	not detected	Email-Worm.Win32.Mydoom.gen (v)	not detected
Ikarus	not detected	Email-Worm.Win32.Mydoom	Worm.Win32.Mydoom
K7 Computing	not detected	EmailWorm (0000439e1)	EmailWorm (ad9b925e0)
McAfee	not detected		W32/Mydoom.at@MM
Microsoft	not detected		Worm:Win32/Mydoom.AL@mm
Norman	not detected	MyDoom.I@mm (worm)	not detected
Panda	not detected	W32/Mydoom.DN.worm	W32/Mydoom.BF.worm
Quick Heal	not detected	W32.Mydoom.L	not detected
Rising	not detected	Worm.Mail.Win32.Mydoom.I	not detected
Sophos	not detected	W32/MyDoom-N	W32/MyDoom-AL
Symantec	W32.Mydoom.H@mm	W32.Mydoom.L@mm	W32.Mydoom.AL@mm
Total Defense	not detected	Win32/Mydoom.N	not detected
Trend Micro	not detected	WORM_MYDOOM.GEN	WORM_MYDOOM.AL
Vba32	not detected	Worm.Mydoom.I	not detected
VirusBuster	not detected	I-Worm.Mydoom.CR (iworm)	not detected

FIGURE 7.5 **vgrep search for MyDoom worm**

Today, vgrep also includes hyperlinks to vendor reports rendered with the vgrep results. This makes it easy to quickly correlate codes and look up information on multiple vendor sites related to a variant or family of code. Unfortunately, it is a database and may not include emergent threats of interest to a security practitioner. In short, it is a fantastic tool for looking at historical codes, but it may not help with the latest variants to be spread in the wild.

Malcode Types and Terminology

Classification schemes were heavily debated in the 1990s as the malcode scene significantly changed and matured. Shortly after 2000, the term *blended threats* became popularized through white papers and media. A blended threat is one that combines multiple characteristics of malcode (viruses, worms, Trojan, etc.) to initiate, transmit, and spread an attack. This means that lots of codes with varied functionality are used in an attack.

The days of a single backdoor Trojan attack on a computer quickly faded into the sunset as criminals sought financial gain. Within a few years attacks became increasingly large scale, automated by bad actors, including multiple minor variants and multiple codes in an incident. In some cases hundreds of files are installed on a computer for maximum financial gain and abuse. The advent of such attacks has quickly dissolved traditional classification schemes, largely rendering them useless. For example, what do you call a threat that includes a downloader Trojan horse, a mass mailing worm, a rootkit to conceal files and activity on a computer, ad/spyware illegally installed on the computer but has a legal end user license agreement included and a backdoor Trojan that steals sensitive information? Most companies have since moved to an itemized approach, naming and handling each threat individually. Unfortunately, this acts to hinder the security practitioner, who needs to understand the entire scope of the attack in order to be able to prevent, identify, and mitigate all the codes and vectors of vulnerability used in such an attack.

An excellent professional source for technical terms relating to malcode exists on the Virus Bulletin site.[5] Virus Bulletin is also a leading malcode research organization that should be considered a resource of interest for any security practitioner that specializes in malcode-related work.

The following sections explore types, aspects, and related terminology of malcode.

Vector

The vector of attack is how the transmission of malcode takes place, such as e-mail, a link sent to an instant messenger user, or a hostile website attempting to exploit vulnerable software on a remote host. This is one of the most important components of a malcode incident for a security practitioner to understand to properly protect against reinfection or additional attacks on the infrastructure of a corporate network.

Payload

A payload is the primary action of a malicious code attack. This generally refers to the end point or primary impact rather than smaller components of an attack.

Virus

A virus is malicious software that infects a host file in order to spread. It is commonly used in a general sense to refer to all sorts of malcode, but this is not technically accurate. Fred Cohen is credited with first using this term officially in 1983.[6] There are many lists and reports on all aspects of the history of the computer virus, tracking all the way back to its official naming by Fred Cohen. The following list represents some of the more interesting items found on the World Wide Web:

- The History of Computer Viruses (Infographic): `http://mashable.com/2011/03/16/history-of-computer-viruses/`

- 14 Infamous Computer Virus Snippets That Trace a History of Havoc: `http://gizmodo.com/14-infamous-computer-virus-snippets-that-trace-a-histor-601745022`

- Computer Virus Timeline: `http://www.infoplease.com/ipa/A0872842.html`

Logic Bomb

A logic bomb is a type of Trojan that typically executes a destructive routine when certain conditions are met, such as date and time. A logic bomb can be planted by a disgruntled employee within a network to then launch a destructive routine, such as overwriting or corrupting data, several weeks or months after the employee leaves the company.

Worm

A worm is malicious software that creates a copy of itself (or clones itself) in order to spread. For example, a mass-mailing worm sends out copies of itself via e-mail. It is possible for worms to even occur accidentally. One famous example of an accidental worm is the Morris worm, which was created to gauge the size of the Internet but due to an error actually resulted in denial-of-service attacks. (See Figure 7.6.)

Trojan

A Trojan is malicious software that masquerades as something it is not. It does not replicate. Up-to-date lists of Trojans being found in the wild are maintained by all of the major virus software vendors and research companies. Here is a small list of the most common sites:

- `http://www.symantec.com/security_response/landing/threats.jsp`
- `http://home.mcafee.com/virusinfo`
- `http://www.bitdefender.com/free-virus-removal/`

FIGURE 7.6 **The floppy disk that contains the complete source code for the Morris internet worm in the Computer History Museum.** Photo © Intel Free Press, http://www.intelfreepress.com/news/lessons-from-the-first-computer-virus-the-morris-worm/7223/

Dropper

A dropper is a malicious file used to install malicious code on a computer. Downloader Trojans are sometimes also called *droppers*.

Keylogger

A keylogger is a type of Trojan used to capture data keylogged on a system. It may also include sophisticated Trojans that can capture all keystrokes and take pictures of the screen at specific points in time to steal online credentials and other sensitive information. It may also refer to physical keylogger devices that can be placed in line between keyboards and a computer to steal sensitive information. An example of a physical keylogger device is KeyGhost, available at `http://www.keyghost.com/keylogger/`.

Bot

A bot is malicious code that acts like a remotely controlled "robot" for an attacker, with other Trojan and worm capabilities. This term may refer to the code itself or an infected computer, also known as a *drone* or *zombie*. Other related terms are bot herder or botmaster, for the bad actor that manages the bot herd or botnet (typically thousands of infected zombies). Some also refer to automation as a key component differentiating bots from other types of code. However, that definition then can be confused with worms that can be fully automated rather than carefully controlled like a bot. McAfee and Guardian Analytics released a report on June 26, 2012, that detailed a sophisticated type of bank fraud that originated in Italy and spread globally, initiating the transfer of at least $78 million from around 60 financial institutions. Banks in the Netherlands were hit the hardest, with fraudsters attempting to transfer over $44 million worth of funds.

The security firms said the attack was unique because it featured both off-the-shelf and custom malicious code to break into the banks' systems. The firms suggested that the creators of the code knew a lot about internal banking transactions. McAfee and Guardian called their investigation "Operation High Roller" because the fraudsters targeted high-worth individuals and businesses to disguise illegal transfers that were much larger than those in usual bank fraud.

"While at first consistent with other client-based attacks we have seen, this attack showed more automation. Instead of collecting the data and performing the transaction manually on another computer, this attack injected a hidden iFRAME tag and took over the victim's account—initiating the transaction locally without an attacker's active participation," according to the Operation High Roller white paper (PDF). In Italy, "the code used by the malware looked for the victim's highest value account, looked at the balance, and transferred either a fixed percentage (defined on a per campaign basis, such as three percent) or a relatively small, fixed €500 amount [roughly $625] to a prepaid debit card or bank account." [7]

Eventually, the money launderers were able to simulate a two-factor authentication. Where the victim would have to use a SIM card to authenticate a transfer in the system, the white paper notes that the thief's system was "able to capture and process the necessary extra information, representing the first known case of fraud being able to bypass this form of two-factor authentication." During the Netherlands attack, the criminals found that they could get around security and monitoring tools by enabling transfers on the server side of the bank accounts. In one instance where servers automating the attacks were found in Brea, California, a criminal was found logging in from Moscow, Russia.

The dynamics of a botnet attack can be very difficult to understand and defend against for the security practitioner. Understanding the underlying architecture of a botnet attack, the tools that are being used to build the components of these advanced persistent threats (APTs), and how they are deployed are skills that many security practitioners will need to build in real time as these threats continue to evolve and change to elude detection.

Some examples of financial botnets that have continued to wreak havoc in 2014 and 2015 are Zeus, Carberp, Citadel, and SpyEye, to name a few. Following is a list of several

YouTube videos that will give the security practitioner an overview of how to build, install, and manage several different botnets, including Zeus.[8]

- Nuke Portal Botnet: `http://www.youtube.com/watch?v=S81diy9-d28`

- ICE9 Botnet: `https://www.youtube.com/watch?v=oiB1klbKSvY`

- Zeus Botnet: `http://www.youtube.com/watch?v=QAQC8oT2w7g`

File Infector

File infector, mostly a historical term, generally refers to viruses that infect files. Perhaps the most well-known historical file-infecting virus is Jerusalem, which infects all executable files run except for command.com in DOS.

File-infecting viruses may prepend code to the front of the file, append code to the end of the file, or creatively inject into various locations of the file. File-infecting viruses that inject into various locations of the body are also known as *Cavity Viruses,* such as the infamous Elkern. Removal of such code can be quite difficult, and multiple file infections often corrupt files beyond repair.

Modern-day file-infecting viruses are rare but are sometimes included with blended threats that install Trojans, spreading as worms across the network and infecting specific files types of interest on the host, such as EXE or even web content such as HTML pages (with script injects).

Macro Viruses

Macro viruses first emerged with Concept in 1995, spreading within Microsoft Office software. They are created within Visual Basic for Applications or WordBasic and spread through Office documents such as DOC files. Macro viruses spread like wildfire for several years until changes in technology and security responses to the threat, in addition to a competitive criminal marketplace with Trojans and bots, essentially removed them from the wild as a prevalent threat shortly after the turn of the century.[9]

Boot Sector Virus

A boot sector virus is malcode that spreads in the wild by copying itself to the master boot record (MBR) of a hard disk and boot sectors of floppy disks. Brain, the first PC virus, is a boot sector virus. Other notable examples include Form, Joshi, and AntiCMOS. In 2007, a new threat emerged against the MBR called Mebroot, which modified the MBR of hard disks and installed into the slack space (unused space at the end of a drive) to load a kernel-level rootkit before the operating system even booted up. It is possible that such stealthy code would then be installed in available memory on hardware, pushing the boundaries of software-based threats on hardware loading before the operating system.

Removal of such threats required that the MBR be overwritten with new data in addition to reimaging or reinstalling of the operating system.

Windows Rootkit

The historical definition of a rootkit comes from UNIX computers that had been hacked, where the attacker wanted to maintain root or administrator privileges on a computer after a compromise. To accomplish this feat, the attacker installed a variety of modified UNIX tools to function as normal but not show the compromise, such as an open port to the attacker or malicious files installed on the computer. As a result the name *rootkit* makes sense, where a "kit" or suite of tools was used to maintain root.

Some have defined Windows rootkits as codes that mask intrusion as well as being used in the compromise of a system. Strictly speaking, rootkits are used to maintain elevated privileges on a system by being stealthy. In Windows the term *rootkit* is more generalized to identify malcode that attempts to conceal the presence of code (stealth techniques) on a system by injecting processes, concealing files on the system, hiding registry keys from users attempting to analyze keys on the system, and more. Windows rootkits are not necessarily a suite of tools but are often one or two files. There are four types of Windows rootkits: *persistent rootkits, memory-based rootkits, user-mode rootkits,* and *kernel-mode rootkits*.

- **Persistent-Mode Rootkits**—A persistent rootkit is one associated with malware that activates each time the system boots. Because such malware contains code that must be executed automatically each system start or when a user logs in, they must store code in a persistent store, such as the Registry or file system, and configure a method by which the code executes without user intervention.

- **Memory-Based Rootkits**—Memory-based rootkits are malware that has no persistent code and therefore does not survive a reboot.

- **User-Mode Rootkits**—User-mode rootkits involve system hooking in the user or application space. Whenever an application makes a system call, the execution of that system call follows a predetermined path and a Windows rootkit can hijack the system call at many points along that path.

- **Kernel-Mode Rootkits**—Kernel-mode rootkits are more powerful than user-mode rootkits because they have the same level of power as an administrator (root on Windows). Software attempting to identify and remove rootkits on a system is in a race condition to not be manipulated or controlled by hostile code operating on the same layer of access control and permissions. Kernel-level rootkits are typically installed as a SYS or VXD file type in the Windows or Windows System32 directories. Kernel-mode rootkits are considered to be more powerful than other kinds of rootkits because not only can they intercept the native API in kernel mode, but they can also directly manipulate kernel-mode data structures. A common technique for hiding the presence of a malware process is to remove the process from the kernel's list of active processes. Since process management APIs rely on the contents of the list, the malware process will not display in process management tools like Task Manager or Process Explorer. Another kernel-mode rootkit technique is to simply modify the data structures in kernel memory. For example, kernel memory must keep a list of all running processes, and a rootkit can simply remove themselves and other malicious processes they wish to hide from this list. This technique is known as *direct kernel object modification* (DKOM).

Adware, Spyware, and Potentially Unwanted Programs

Adware, spyware, and potentially unwanted programs are technically legal software, but they are frequently illegally installed without user consent to display advertisements or monitor behavior or sensitive data. These programs are technically legal, including an end user license agreement (EULA). However, affiliate abuse frequently involves such software being illegally installed by bad actors who seek financial rewards per install. As a result, the legal software is illegally installed on computers.

Adware is software funded for advertising, such as pop-up advertisements for porn sites.

Spyware is legal software that is used to report user information to a remote party. For example, the code used tracks user habits online such as search terms and then reports it to a remote agency. This is different from malicious Trojans, which keylog or steal sensitive information, because spyware includes a valid EULA agreement.

Rogue software, also known as goadware, is a new subset of this type of malcode that may or may not include a EULA. They are illegal due to their deceptive business practices and court cases to date. Rogue software is commonly installed illegally through exploitation or through deceitful user interaction procedures. Once installed, the software goads the user in an aggressive fashion, such as changing the desktop image and displaying frequent pop-ups and windows with no easy close options. It frequently masquerades as antivirus, ad/spyware software and performance-improving software programs, making it difficult for consumers to identify what is legitimate and what may be rogue software.

Polymorphic Polymorphic viruses assume many (poly) shapes and forms (morphic) by encrypting code differently with each infection. This term caught on in the mid-1990s with tools that emerged to generate thousands of new minor variants of code based on mutation routines to subvert signature technology used by antivirus software at the time.

Like an encrypted virus, a polymorphic virus includes a scrambled virus body and a decryption routine that first gains control of the computer and then decrypts the virus body. However, a polymorphic virus also adds a mutation engine that generates randomized decryption routines that change each time a virus infects a new program. In a polymorphic virus, the mutation engine and virus body are both encrypted. When a user runs a program infected with a polymorphic virus, the decryption routine first gains control of the computer and then decrypts both the virus body and the mutation engine. Next, the decryption routine transfers control of the computer to the virus, which locates a new program to infect. At this point, the virus makes a copy of both itself and the mutation engine in random access memory (RAM). The virus then invokes the mutation engine, which randomly generates a new decryption routine that is capable of decrypting the virus yet bears little or no resemblance to any prior decryption routine. Next, the virus encrypts this new copy of the virus body and mutation engine. Finally, the virus appends this new encryption routine, along with the newly encrypted virus and mutation engine, onto a new program. As a result, not only is the virus body encrypted, but the virus decryption routine varies from infection to infection. This confounds a virus scanner searching for the tell-tale sequence of bytes that identifies a specific decryption routine. With no fixed signature to scan for and no fixed decryption routine, no two infections look alike.[10]

Proof of Concept   A proof of concept (POC) is functional code that can be used in order to validate that an exploit actually works and to detail the specifics of how it functions. POCs are created by authors of exploits to prove that exploitation of a vulnerability is possible. POC malcode may also be created to show that malcode can be spread in new environments or across new platforms.

One example of the use of a proof of concept in order to validate and test a disclosed vulnerability took place in July 2013. A proof-of-concept exploit was built and released for a discovered application signature checking vulnerability on the Android platform. At the time that the vulnerability was discovered and disclosed, the potential existed to affect millions of devices on the Android platform, potentially allowing attackers exploiting the vulnerability to turn legitimate apps into Trojan programs capable of launching malware. Pau Oliva Fora, a mobile security engineer at the security firm ViaForensics, developed a proof-of-concept Linux shell script that could be used to modify an app in a way that exploited the flaw. The code made use of the APKTool program and was released on GitHub.[11]

The exploit takes advantage of the way Android handles APKs that have duplicate file names inside; the entry that is verified for signature is the second one inside the APK, and the entry that ends up being installed is the first one inside the APK—the injected one that can contain the malicious payload and is not checked for signature at all. Shortly after the release of this exploit, Google made changes to Google Play in order to detect apps modified in this way and issued a patch to device manufacturers. The remaining issue, which is a potentially serious one for security practitioners in this case, stems from behavior that would leave users who install applications from sources other than Google Play, a process known as sideloading, potentially vulnerable. If a business allows users to engage in sideloading of applications into their devices, then this vulnerability, and others like it, will go unchecked and unpatched, and as a result it will continue to present threats to the business that the security practitioner may or may not even be aware of. This vulnerability allows Android malware authors to add malicious code to legitimate app packages and have them properly update the original applications if they are installed on the targeted devices. Android malware authors are already distributing malicious apps that masquerade as popular games or applications through a variety of methods, including through third-party app stores. Vulnerabilities like this could make this social engineering technique more efficient.

Malicious Code Countermeasures

Malicious code is a type of software designed to take over or damage a computer's operating system, without the user's knowledge or approval. Malicious code protection is commonly provided at both the gateway and workstations that access information services. Because most data files are stored on networks or shared file systems, the constant protection of network connections at the gateway is crucial. Malicious code often enters networks by means of security loopholes, e-mail attachments, or protocols such as File Transfer Protocol (FTP), Hypertext Transfer Protocol (HTTP), and Simple Mail Transfer Protocol (SMTP) (e-mail).

Malicious Code Detection System Requirements

NSA's Information Assurance Technical Framework defines malicious code detection system requirements. This section is reproduced directly from that document.

The following have been identified as representative malicious code detection system requirements from a customer's perspective of needs.
The malicious code detection system shall

- Allow access to all services available on the wide area networks (WAN) using any of the existing and emerging networking technologies and applications.
- Be able to locate the source and type of an infection, be able to react to such intrusions, and be able to fully reconstitute the system following damage caused by intrusions.
- Have minimal operational effect on the user.
- Have minimal operational effect on performance of the associated components.
- Have appropriate documentation for its use and upgradability and contain all currently available references and resources.

- Allow automatic malicious code prevention programs to run in the background.

- Allow a disaster recovery plan to recover data if necessary.

- Provide adequate scanning tools to be able to contain an identified virus by isolating affected systems and media.

- Have appropriate means to trace all incoming and outgoing data, including e-mail, FTP transactions, and web information.

- Be able to, in the event the Internet is unavailable for any reason, still have access to virus updates from the manufacturer or vendor of the antivirus product.

- Monitor usage as required by the administrator.

- Scan for malicious software at the enclave boundary and at individual workstations.

- Log and analyze source-routed and other packets; react to or restrict malicious code attacks.

- Allow a rapid disconnect from the network in the event of a detected malicious code attack.

Configuration/Management Requirements

NSA's Information Assurance Technical Framework defines malicious code detection system configuration and management requirements. This section is reproduced directly from that document.

The following have been identified as representative configuration and/or management requirements for malicious code detection systems.

The malicious code detection system shall:

- Be updated with regard to relevant security issues (malicious code detection, system vulnerability) so maximum protection is provided.

- Be configured by the administrator to filter all incoming data, including e-mail, FTP transactions, and web information, for all types of malicious code.

- Allow the administrator to automatically create policy for network usage that details what sort of computing activity will and will not be allowed.

- Allow regular backups of all system data by the administrator.

- Provide adequate controls such as strong user authentication and access control mechanisms on network connections for the administrator.

- Be capable of setting additional passwords or authentication for select files and accounts accessed from network ports.

- Be capable of placing restrictions on types of commands used on networks and in select files.

- Deny access to system manager accounts from network ports, if possible.
- Monitor usage of the network during odd hours, if possible, and create a log of all activity for the system administrator.
- Provide no more than one administrator account (i.e., not give other users administrator privileges).

Common malware examples include the following:

Virus   A virus is a program that attempts to damage a computer system and replicate itself to other computer systems. A virus:

- Requires a host to replicate and usually attaches itself to a host file or a hard drive sector.
- Replicates each time the host is used.
- Often focuses on destruction or corruption of data.
- Usually attaches to files with execution capabilities such as .doc, .exe, and .bat extensions.
- Often distributes via e-mail. Many viruses can e-mail themselves to everyone in your address book.

Examples: Stoned, Michelangelo, Melissa, I Love You.

Worm   A worm is a self-replicating program that can be designed to do any number of things, such as delete files or send documents via e-mail. A worm can negatively impact network traffic just in the process of replicating itself. A worm:

- Can install a backdoor in the infected computer.
- Is usually introduced into the system through a vulnerability.
- Infects one system and spreads to other systems on the network.

Example: Code Red.

Trojan Horse   A Trojan horse is a malicious program that is disguised as legitimate software. Discretionary environments are often more vulnerable and susceptible to Trojan horse attacks because security is user focused and user directed. Thus the compromise of a user account could lead to the compromise of the entire environment. A Trojan horse:

- Cannot replicate itself.
- Often contains spying functions (such as a packet sniffer) or backdoor functions that allow a computer to be remotely controlled from the network.
- Often is hidden in useful software such as screen savers or games.

Examples: Back Orifice, NetBus, Whack-a-Mole.

Logic Bomb A logic bomb is malware that lies dormant until triggered. A logic bomb is a specific example of an asynchronous attack. A trigger activity may be a specific date and time, the launching of a specific program, or the processing of a specific type of activity. Logic bombs do not self-replicate.

Countermeasures for malware are as follows:

- Antivirus software on user machines. Update antivirus definition files as soon as they are released. Most antivirus software automatically checks for updated definition files each time the system starts. Update checks should be made daily. Antivirus software is the least effective protection against zero-day malicious code as the AV product will unlikely be able to detect the new malicious code. Only after the signature or pattern of malicious code is added to its database can an AV product reliably protect against it.

- Install and use several different antivirus software products on enterprise infrastructure.

- User awareness training to help with identifying suspicious e-mail.

- Disable scripts when previewing or viewing e-mail.

- Block attachments at network borders.

- Prevent download of software from the Internet.

- Strict software installation policies.

- Block the use of removable drives to prevent unauthorized software entering a system.

- Antivirus scanners on e-mail gateways are the most effective security measure against e-mail viruses.

Software exploitation involves taking advantage of known vulnerabilities in software and systems. The following are common exploitation methods:

Backdoor A backdoor attack exploits an unprotected access method or pathway. A backdoor:

- May be developer-installed for easier debugging or to simplify distribution of software updates.

- May be an intentionally placed vulnerability installed by a Trojan horse, a remote control tool, or utility.

- On devices, it could be console ports, maintenance modems, or open connection ports.

Countermeasures for a backdoor attack are as follows:

- Auditing.
- Antivirus and malware code scanning.
- For malicious user-installed backdoors, use access control management and controlled software deployment.
- For developer-installed backdoors, disable them, change the defaults, or block access.
- For device backdoors, maintain physical access control.

Buffer Overflow Attack   A buffer overflow attack exploits programs with poor buffer management. In the buffer overflow attack:

- The attacker identifies a system using an application with poor buffer management.
- The attacker determines where the next process pointer is in the stack.
- The attacker overflows the buffer and places a malicious application at location in the stack where the process pointer is pointing.
- The malicious application is launched when the process pointer is activated.

Countermeasures for buffer overflow attacks include:

- Limit user input to less than the size of the buffer.
- Validate input by looking for certain symbols that may be program instructions.
- Implement strict coding standards to eliminate the potential for weaknesses.

Pointer Overflow Attack   A pointer overflow attack is similar to a buffer overflow attack in that it exploits programs with poor buffer management. In the pointer overflow attack:

- The attacker identifies a system using an application with poor buffer management.
- The attacker determines where the next process pointer is in the stack.
- The attacker overflows the process pointer.
- The attacker changes the pointer to go to the location of the malicious application.

Countermeasures for pointer overflow attacks are the same as buffer overflow attacks.

Directory Traversal   A directory traversal exploits a lack of security in web applications and allows an attacker to access files. The directory traversal:

- Uses a common means of representing a parent directory, ./ (dot dot slash), to access files not intended to be accessed.
- Consists of adding the characters ./ to the right side of a URL, An example is: ././././<filename>.

Countermeasures include:

- Disable all services that are not explicitly required.
- Install security patches.
- Review audit logs.

Covert Channels   A covert channel is hidden use of bandwidth or storage to communicate or hide a message.

- Covert timing channels use the timing of occurrences of an activity to transfer information in an unintended manner.
- Covert storage channels store hidden data in unused portions of a file.
- A timing covert channel works by modulating utilization levels. The recipient needs only to monitor those levels in order to receive the communication.
- Covert channels have the potential for occurring when two or more subjects or objects share a common resource.
- Covert channels can involve saturating or not saturating a communications path in a timed fashion to transfer information to a receiver observing the communication path in synchronization with the sender.

Scanners

Different forms of malicious code can be detected and removed by special scanning software and integrity checkers. Scanners can work in offline or online modes. Online operation of a scanner provides active protection, i.e., detection (and possible removal), of malicious code before any infection takes place and damage is done to the IT system. Scanners are available for stand-alone computers, workstations, file servers, electronic mail servers, and firewalls. However, users and administrators should be made aware that scanners cannot be relied upon to detect all malicious code (or even all malicious code of a particular type) because new forms of malicious code are continually arising. There are four generations of antivirus scanning software:

- **First Generation**—Simple scanners
- **Second Generation**—Heuristic scanners
- **Third Generation**—Activity traps
- **Fourth Generation**—Full-featured protection

A first-generation scanner requires a malware signature to identify the malware. The signature may contain "wildcards" but matches essentially the same structure and bit pattern in all copies of the malware. Such signature-specific scanners are limited to the detection of known malware. Another type of first-generation scanner maintains a record of the length of programs and looks for changes in length as a result of virus infection.

A second-generation scanner does not rely on a specific signature. Rather, the scanner uses heuristic rules to search for probable malware instances. One class of such scanners looks for fragments of code that are often associated with malware. An example of this type of scanner would be a scanner that may look for the beginning of an encryption loop used in a polymorphic virus and discover the encryption key. Once the key is discovered, the scanner can decrypt the malware to identify it and then remove the infection and return the program to service. Another second-generation approach is integrity checking. A checksum can be appended to each program. If malware alters or replaces some program without changing the checksum, then an integrity check will catch this change. To counter malware that is sophisticated enough to change the checksum when it alters a program, an encrypted hash function can be used. The encryption key is stored separately from the program so that the malware cannot generate a new hash code and encrypt that. By using a hash function rather than a simpler checksum, the malware is prevented from adjusting the program to produce the same hash code as before.

Third-generation programs are memory-resident programs that identify malware by its actions rather than its structure in an infected program. Such programs have the advantage that it is not necessary to develop signatures and heuristics for a wide array of malware. Rather, it is necessary only to identify the small set of actions that indicate malicious activity is being attempted and then to intervene.

Fourth-generation products are packages consisting of a variety of antivirus techniques used in conjunction. These include scanning and activity trap components. In addition, such a package includes access control capability, which limits the ability of malware to penetrate a system and then limits the ability of a malware to update files in order to propagate.

Generic decryption (GD) technology enables the antivirus program to easily detect even the most complex polymorphic viruses and other malware while maintaining fast scanning speeds. Remember that when a file containing a polymorphic virus is executed, the virus must decrypt itself to activate. In order to detect such a structure, executable files are run through a GD scanner, which contains the following elements:

- **CPU Emulator**—A software-based virtual computer. Instructions in an executable file are interpreted by the emulator rather than executed on the underlying processor. The emulator includes software versions of all registers and other processor hardware so that the underlying processor is unaffected by programs interpreted on the emulator.

- **Virus Signature Scanner**—A module that scans the target code looking for known malware signatures.

- **Emulation Control Module**—Controls the execution of the target code.

At the start of each simulation, the emulator begins interpreting instructions in the target code, one at a time. Thus, if the code includes a decryption routine that decrypts and hence exposes the malware, that code is interpreted. In effect, the malware does the work for the antivirus program by exposing itself. Periodically, the control module interrupts interpretation to scan the target code for malware signatures. During interpretation, the target code can cause no damage to the actual personal computer environment because it is being interpreted in a completely controlled environment. The most difficult design issue with a GD scanner is to determine how long to run each interpretation. Typically, malware elements are activated soon after a program begins executing, but this need not be the case. The longer the scanner emulates a particular program, the more likely it is to catch any hidden malware. However, the antivirus program can take up only a limited amount of time and resources before users complain of degraded system performance.

Behavior-blocking software integrates with the operating system of a host computer and monitors program behavior in real time for malicious actions. The behavior blocking software then blocks potentially malicious actions before they have a chance to affect the system. Monitored behaviors can include:

- Attempts to open, view, delete, and modify files
- Attempts to format disk drives and other unrecoverable disk operations
- Modifications to the logic of executable files or macros
- Modification of critical system settings, such as start-up settings
- Scripting of e-mail and instant messaging clients to send executable content
- Initiation of network communications.

Because a behavior blocker can block suspicious software in real time, it has an advantage over the antivirus detection techniques like fingerprinting or heuristics. There are literally trillions of different ways to obfuscate and rearrange the instructions of a virus or worm, many of which will evade detection by a fingerprint scanner or heuristic. But eventually, malicious code must make a well-defined request to the operating system. Given that the behavior blocker can intercept all such requests, it can identify and block malicious actions regardless of how obfuscated the program logic appears to be. Behavior blocking alone has limitations. Because the malicious code must run on the target machine before all its behaviors can be identified, it can cause harm before it has been detected and blocked. For instance, a new item of malware might shuffle a number of seemingly unimportant files around the hard drive before modifying a single file and being blocked. Even though the actual modification was blocked, the user may be unable to locate his or her files, causing a loss to productivity or possibly worse.

Spyware-specific detection and removal utilities specialize in the detection and removal of spyware and provide more robust capabilities. Thus, they complement, and should be used along with, more general antivirus products.

Rootkits can be especially difficult to detect and neutralize, particularly so for kernel-level rootkits. Many of the administrative tools that could be used to detect a rootkit or its traces can be compromised by the rootkit precisely so that it is undetectable. Countering rootkits requires a variety of network- and computer-level security tools. Both network-based and host-based intrusion detection systems can look for the code signatures of known rootkit attacks in incoming traffic. Host-based antivirus software can also be used to recognize the known signatures.

The next location where antivirus software is used is on an organization's firewall and IDS. It is typically included in e-mail and web proxy services running on these systems. It may also be included in the traffic analysis component of an IDS. Antivirus software:

- Has access to malware in transit over a network connection to any of the organization's systems
- Gets a larger scale view of malware activity
- Can block the flow of any suspicious traffic.

However, this limits to scanning the malware content, and it does not have access to any behavior observed on an infected system. Two types of monitoring software may be used:

- **Ingress Monitors**—Located at the border between the enterprise network and the Internet. An example of a detection technique for an ingress monitor is to look for incoming traffic to unused local IP addresses.
- **Egress Monitors**—Located at the egress point of individual LANs on the enterprise network as well as at the border between the enterprise network and the Internet. The egress monitor is designed to catch the source of a malware attack by monitoring outgoing traffic for signs of scanning or other suspicious behavior.

Code Signing

A fundamental technique for protecting an agent system is signing code or other objects with a digital signature. A digital signature serves as a means of confirming the authenticity of an object, its origin, and its integrity. Typically, the code signer is either the creator of the agent, the user of the agent, or some entity that has reviewed the agent. Because an agent operates on behalf of an end-user or organization, mobile agent systems commonly use the signature of the user as an indication of the authority under which the agent operates.

Code signing involves public key cryptography, which relies on a pair of keys associated with an entity. One key is kept private by the entity, and the other is made publicly available. Digital signatures benefit greatly from the availability of a public key infrastructure because certificates containing the identity of an entity and its public key (i.e., a public key certificate) can be readily located and verified. Passing the agent's code through a non-reversible hash function, which provides a fingerprint or unique message digest of the code, and then encrypting the result with the private key of the signer forms a digital signature. Because the message digest is unique, and thus bound to the code, the resulting signature also serves as an integrity mechanism. The agent code, signature, and public key certificate can then be forwarded to a recipient, who can easily verify the source and authenticity of the code. Note that the meaning of a signature may be different depending on the policy associated with the signature scheme and the party who signs. For example, the author of the agent, either an individual or an organization, may use a digital signature to indicate who produced the code but not to guarantee that the agent performs without fault or error.

In fact, author-oriented signature schemes were originally intended to serve as digital shrink wrap, whereby the original product warranty limitations stated in the license remain in effect (e.g., manufacturer makes no warranties as to the fitness of the product for any particular purpose). Microsoft's Authenticode, a common form of code signing, enables Java applets or Active X controls to be signed, ensuring users that the software has not been tampered with or modified and that the identity of the author is verified.

Code signing certificates are digital certificates that will help protect users from downloading compromised files or applications. When a file or application signed by a developer is modified or compromised after publication, a pop-up browser warning will appear to let users know that the origin of the file or application cannot be verified.

Sandboxing

Dynamic analysis of malicious code has increasingly become an essential component of defense against Internet threats. By executing malware samples in a controlled environment, security practitioners and researchers are able to observe its malicious behavior, obtain its unpacked code, detect botnet C&C servers, and generate signatures for C&C traffic as well as remediation procedures for malware infections. Large-scale dynamic malware analysis systems (DMAS) based on tools such as Anubis and CWSandbox are operated by security researchers and companies. These services are freely available to the public and are widely used by security practitioners around the world. In addition to these public-facing services, private malware analysis sandboxes are operated by a variety of security companies such as antivirus vendors.

One way for malware to defeat dynamic analysis is to detect that it is running in an analysis sandbox rather than on a real user's system and refuse to perform its malicious function. For instance, code packers that include detection of virtual machines, such as Themida, will produce executables that exit immediately when run inside a virtual machine such as VMware. There are many characteristics of a sandbox environment that may be used to fingerprint it. Malware authors can detect specific sandboxes by taking advantage of identifiers such as volume serial numbers or IP addresses.

Sandboxes and Virtual Machines

A sandbox is a secluded environment on a computer where you can run untested code or malware to study the results without having any ill effects on the rest of your software. A virtual machine is the most commonly used example of a sandbox because it emulates a complete computer, called a guest operating system, on the main machine (called the host). Well-known examples include Microsoft Hyper-V, VMware ESXi, VirtualBox, Sandboxie, The Chromium Projects, and QEMU. Some even offer online sandboxes that present the analysis results in an organized way. Anubis, ThreatExpert, and GFI ThreatTrack are a few examples of services that offer online sandboxes.

How Malware Researchers Use VMs

In malware research, sandboxes are used to study the behavior of malware. It is not only safer, it's also a lot quicker to restore an image of a previous state of the guest machine as opposed to the worst-case scenario for a real computer, re-formatting and re-installing the software that you need, which could take hours.

How Malware Writers Try to Avoid Sandboxes

There are a few methods for a process to determine if it is running in a virtual environment. The most obvious one would be to check for running processes that a VM uses, like for example VBoxTray.exe (VirtualBox). A similar method is to compare the services that are running to a list of known services in use by virtualization software or check for drivers like vmmouse.sys (VMWare). Another approach would be to check for virtual hardware like a network interface. Like any network interface, they are assigned a unique MAC address that includes the manufacturer's identification number. Given the limited number of manufacturers, checking for these processes and interfaces does not require a lot of code. The same kind of checks can be done for GUIDs and other unique identifiers used by virtualization software. In addition, the malware can run a check for extra debuggers. The program that wants to avoid being debugged checks the port number for the debugger of the process. A value other than 0 indicates that the process is being run through a debugger handled by the user.

Reviewing Application Code

The Veracode State of Software Security Report states

> "Cryptographic issues affect a sizeable portion of Android (64%) and iOS (58%) applications.

Using cryptographic mechanisms incorrectly can make it easier for attackers to compromise the application. For example, cryptographic keys can be used to protect transmitted or stored data. However, practices such as hard-coding a cryptographic key directly into a mobile application can be problematic. Should these keys be compromised, any security mechanisms that depend on the privacy of the keys are rendered ineffective."[12]

The previous quoted passage illustrates several facts that the security practitioner needs to be aware of. First, security is not limited to a single platform in the enterprise, nor are the issues associated with security. Second, while good design and architecture is important, bad implementation can still render a system or an application insecure. Third, using shortcuts to design applications can lead to unintended consequences and can impact many systems, not just those that the application is running on top of. All of these issues lead the security practitioner to the need for clarity—clarity with regards to the application code running in the enterprise systems that they are being asked to operate. The big question for the security practitioner is "How do I develop an understanding of the application code running on my systems?" That is where tools such as SWAMP and static source code analyzers come in handy.

SWAMP

SWAMP is designed by researchers from the Morgridge Institute, the University of Illinois-Champaign/Urbana, Indiana University, and the University of Wisconsin-Madison. The SWAMP servers themselves are hosted at the Morgridge Institute in Madison, WI. At the institute, the clustered servers are kept at a secure facility. The SWAMP cluster currently has 700 cores, 5TB of RAM, and 100TB of storage to meet the continuous assurance needs of multiple software and tool development projects. SWAMP opened its services to the community in February 2014, offering open-source static analysis tools that analyze source code for possible security defects without having to execute the program. These tools currently are the following:

- **FindBugs:** Identifies errors in Java programs using Java bytecode rather than source code.
- **PMD:** Finds common programming flaws in Java, JavaScript, XML, and XSL applications.
- **Cppcheck:** Detects bugs usually missed by compilers in the C and C++ languages.
- **Clang Static Analyzer:** Finds bugs in C, C++, and Objective-C programs.
- **GCC:** The Gnu C compiler is used to ensure C and C++ code is syntactically correct.
- **CheckStyle:** Evaluates a wide variety of programming style rules for Java.
- **error-prone:** This tool finds violations in Java code using Google's best practice programming style.

In addition, SWAMP hosts almost 400 open source software packages to enable tool developers to add enhancements in both the precision and scope of their tools. On top of that, SWAMP provides developers with software packages from the National Institute for Standards and Technology's (NIST) Juliet Test Suite. The Juliet Test Suite is a collection of over 81,000 synthetic C/C++ and Java public domain programs with known flaws. These known flaws are used to test the effectiveness of static analyzers and other software assurance tools. The Juliet Test Suite covers 181 different common weakness enumerations (CWEs) and also includes similar, but non-flawed, code to test tool discrimination.[13] Tools such as SWAMP allow for the testing and review of application code in order to uncover potential vulnerabilities and threats in their design and implementation.

Static Analysis

Static source code analyzers attempt to find code sequences that, when executed, could result in buffer overflows, resource leaks, or many other security and reliability problems. Source code analyzers are effective at locating a significant class of flaws that are not detected by compilers during standard builds and often go undetected during runtime testing as well.

A typical compiler will issue warnings and errors for some basic potential code problems, such as violations of the language standard or use of implementation-defined constructs. In contrast, a static source code analyzer performs a full program analysis, finding bugs caused by complex interactions between pieces of code that may not even be in the same source file. The analyzer determines potential execution paths through code, including paths into and across subroutine calls, and how the values of program objects (such as standalone variables or fields within aggregates) could change across these paths. The objects could reside in memory or in machine registers.

The analyzer looks for many types of flaws. It looks for bugs that would normally compile without error or warning. The following is a list of some of the more common errors that a modern static source code analyzer will detect:

- Potential NULL pointer dereferences
- Access beyond an allocated area, otherwise known as a buffer overflow
- Writes to potentially read-only memory
- Reads of potentially uninitialized objects
- Resource leaks (e.g., memory leaks and file descriptor leaks)
- Use of memory that has already been deallocated
- Out-of-scope memory usage (e.g., returning the address of an automatic variable from a subroutine)

- Failure to set a return value from a subroutine
- Buffer and array underflows

The static analyzer also has knowledge about how many standard runtime library functions behave. The analyzer uses this information to detect errors in code that calls or uses the result of a call to these functions. The analyzer can also be taught about properties of user-defined subroutines. For example, if a custom memory allocation system is used, the analyzer can be taught to look for misuses of this system. By teaching the analyzer about properties of subroutines, users can reduce the number of false positives. A false positive is a potential flaw identified by the analyzer that would not actually occur during program execution. Of course, one of the major design goals of a static source code analyzer is to minimize the number of false positives so that developers can minimize time looking at them.

VECTORS OF INFECTION

The vector is where the malcode comes from, which can be a form of media transfer such as e-mail or peer-to-peer (P2P) networks, or exploitation combined with web browsing. Various techniques exist to trick users into executing code or revealing sensitive information. For example, the default view settings inside of the Windows Explorer do not show the true extension of a file. "report.doc" may only appear as "report" to the end user. Various methods exist to then trick users into thinking malicious files are safe, allowing the file to exploit this default behavior of Windows, when it is actually malicious.

An interesting new vector emerged around Christmas 2007, where digital frames were infected with malcode. These new gifts enabled users to transfer malcode through a USB-based thumb drive. One example of redirection and the abuse of default behavior can be seen in the following description, reproduced directly from the InfoSec Community Forums at `https://isc.sans.edu/forums/diary/More+on+Google+image+poisoning/10822/`, of how hackers were able to exploit Google's image search capability to serve up malware to unsuspecting users.

1. The attackers compromise a number of legitimate websites.
2. Once the source websites have been exploited, the attackers plant their PHP scripts. These scripts vary from simple to very advanced scripts that can automatically monitor Google trend queries and create artificial webpages based on current trending in Google's search results. These websites contain not only text but also images that are acquired from various websites. They embed links to pictures that are really related to the topic, so the automatically generated webpage contains convincing content.

3. Google now crawls through these websites. The scripts from the attackers will detect Google's bots either by their IP address or the User Agent and will deliver special pages back containing automatically generated content. Google will also parse links to images and, if appropriate, populate the image search database.

4. Now, when a user searches for something through the Google image search function, thumbnails of pictures are displayed. Depending on the automatically generated content created in step 3, as well as the number of links to the webpage and other parameters used by Google, the attacker's page will be shown at a certain position in the results webpage. The exploit happens when a user clicks the thumbnail. Google now shows a special page that shows the thumbnail in the center of the page, links to the original image on the right, and the original website in the background. This is where the "vulnerability" is. Google displays this in a simple iframe. The user's browser will automatically send a request to the bad page that has been made available through the compromise of legitimate websites in step 1, which runs the attacker's PHP script. This script checks the request's referrer field, and if it contains "Google," meaning this was a click the results page in Google, the script displays a small JavaScript script that causes the browser to be redirected to another site that is serving up malware.

By pairing malicious script actions with Google's default behavior, the hackers are able to touch thousands of people's machines and infect many of them without anyone's knowledge. This activity was very prevalent in 2011, and while Google was able to take steps to mark and eliminate bad or suspicious URLs being returned to users in search results, they were unable to eliminate this issue with their image browser results as quickly, and as a result, this behavior continued to infect unsuspecting users for several months.

At the end of 2013, another example emerged, although this time it was in the form of a Trojan purporting to be antivirus software. The Protector Rogue took its namesake from the filename `protector-xxx.exe` (where x's were random letters). This malware was very common until it was mostly eradicated in September 2012. This new version of the Protector Rogue has the filename `guard-xxx.exe` and the registry run value GuardSoftware. GuardSoftware's installer, or dropper, has a valid digital signature, which makes it appear to be trustworthy and which can bypass certain forms of heuristic detection. At the same time, GuardSoftware utilizes hijacking techniques not previously observed in comparable rogue programs. After installation, GuardSoftware restarts the computer and then essentially locks the desktop with a "scanning in progress" screen named Windows Cleaning Toolkit, as shown in Figure 7.7.

This screen is meant to fool users into trusting GuardSoftware, and it even goes as far as allowing the user to disable the scan through an options feature. This will unlock the desktop, but it will not stop the scan. Instead, the supposed scan will continue to run in the background, with constant pop-up reminders that the computer is infected, all aimed at persuading the user to purchase the full version of GuardSoftware by entering their credit card information into the purchase screen pop-up.

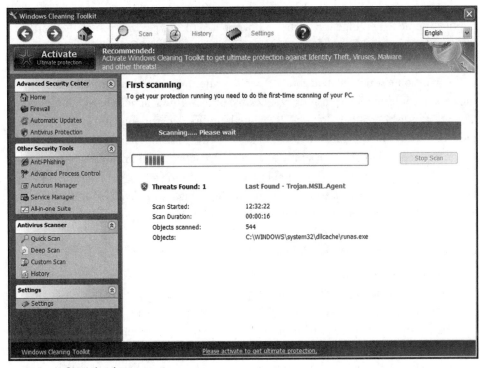

FIGURE 7.7 Scanning in progress

GuardSoftware is one of the first rogue programs to utilize such screen locking, which in the past has typically only been observed in ransomware. In the past, Protector Rogues would instead just scare users with frightening messages, such as "YOUR COMPUTER IS INFECTED" or "PROTECTOR FOUND 136 VIRUSES ON YOUR COMPUTER!!!" This rogue family uses a variety of names; some examples are Windows Expert Console, Windows Cleaning Toolkit, and Windows Active Hotspot. These are some SHA1 hashes listed for these variants:

- FAAB416D4423F08337707D6FC15FA4ACA143D9BE
- 2966D9B0B7B27C1CA2FA46F93E26E82FBB7FE64C
- CB8B40EACC05C5D34396D70C9B9C1D931A780517

The security practitioner needs to be aware of exploits such as the GuardSoftware Protector Rogue in order to be able to defend against them and to ensure that end users are educated about the types of exploits and threats that they face in the wild as well.

Malicious Activity

Social engineering is a term used to describe methods that bad actors can use to trick users or "con" them into engaging in behavior that they would not normally engage in. For instance, opportunistic attacks may make use of promising something sexual as a popular theme to get someone to click a link, open a file, or perform some other sort of desired action. Another common approach may be the use of fear, such as falsely claiming that the user's services have been or are about to be terminated or that there is a problem of some sort with an account or service, attempting to trick the user into revealing sensitive information (phishing-type scams) or performing actions to install malcode. The use of phishing attacks to target individuals, entire departments, and even companies continues to be a significant threat that the security practitioner needs to be aware of and be prepared to defend against. The many derivative attack vectors that have been spawned as a result of the modification of the basic phishing attack in recent years have led to a variety of attacks that are deployed relentlessly against individuals and networks in a never-ending stream of e-mails, phone calls, spam, instant messages, videos, file attachments, and many other delivery mechanisms.[14]

Here are five examples of additional social engineering attacks:

Baiting   Baiting involves dangling something that the target will want to entice them into taking an action that the criminal desires. It can be in the form of a music or movie download on a peer-to-peer site, or it can be a file on a USB flash drive with a company logo labeled "Financials Q2" left out in the open for you to find. Then, once the device is used or downloaded, the person or company's computer is infected with malicious software, allowing the criminal to take control of the targeted system.

Phone Phishing—Vishing   Phone phishing, or *vishing*, uses a rogue interactive voice response (IVR) system to re-create a legitimate-sounding copy of a bank or other institution's IVR system. The victim is prompted via a phishing e-mail to call in to the "bank" via a number provided in order to verify certain information such as account numbers, account access codes or a PIN, answers to security questions, as well as contact information and addresses. A typical system will reject logins continually, ensuring the victim enters PINs or passwords multiple times, often disclosing several different passwords. More advanced systems may be used to transfer the victim to the attacker posing as a customer service agent for further questioning.

Pretexting   Pretexting is the human equivalent of phishing, where someone impersonates an authority figure or someone you trust to gain access to your login information. It can take form as fake IT support needing to do maintenance or a false investigator performing a company audit. Someone might impersonate co-workers, the police, tax authorities, or other seemingly legitimate people in order to gain access to your computer and information.

Quid Pro Quo   Quid pro quo is a request for your information in exchange for some compensation. It could be the offer of a free item or access to an online game or service in exchange for your login credentials or a researcher asking for your password as part of an experiment in exchange for money. If it sounds too good to be true, it probably is quid pro quo.

Tailgating   Tailgating is when someone follows you into a restricted area or system. Traditionally, this is when someone asks you to hold the door open behind you because they forgot their company RFID card. However, this could also take the form of someone asking to borrow your phone or laptop to perform a simple action when they are actually installing some malicious software.

Security awareness training can be highly effective in helping those who may become the targets of social engineering attacks to not be taken advantage of easily. Simply training people to never trust unsolicited e-mails, instant messages, or other communications is an essential step but is only the beginning.[15] In addition to basic awareness, all users in a system must be provided training that is targeted toward situational specific awareness based on their roles and responsibilities within an organization. For instance, a senior-level executive within a bank must be given additional security awareness training focused around their situational awareness to educate them with regards to threats that they may face as they interact with peers and colleagues outside the bank in social settings such as conferences and while travelling. This training would be different in focus and content than the training that a teller in the bank would receive. However, an acceptable use policy and support from management must be in place to give any such training teeth and follow-up. With such a combination, the "user-to-keyboard" error risk can be lowered. Examples of this abound, such as the Storm worm of 2007/2008 as well as the highly publicized 2011 breach of RSA by a hacker using socially engineered e-mails and malware attachments.[16] Some additional well-known examples include the Facebook social engineering attacks against NATO in early 2012, the hack of a Wal-Mart store in Canada during a social engineering capture the flag contest at DefCon in August 2012, and the Francophoned social engineering attack carried out against a French-based multinational in April 2013.[17]

How to Do It for Yourself: Using the Social Engineer Toolkit (SET)

You can examine one of the toolkits that is being used by hackers to execute social engineering attacks against systems and, in so doing, gain insights into how these attacks are built and executed. The required tool and a step-by-step overview of the Social Engineer Toolkit (SET) are covered next.

What you will need:

- A Linux-based machine that is running KALI Linux (this can be either a physical or a virtual machine). The current distribution (distro) for KALI can be found here:

  `http://www.kali.org/`

- If you choose not to use KALI Linux, which has the Social Engineer Toolkit already built in, then the toolkit can be downloaded separately from here:

  `https://github.com/trustedsec/social-engineer-toolkit`

To open the SET in KALI Linux, go to Applications ➤ Exploitation Tools ➤ Social Engineering Toolkit, as shown in Figure 7.8.

FIGURE 7.8 **Social Engineering Toolkit in KALI Linux**

The SET is a menu-driven attack system. The SET menu is listed here:

1. Social-Engineering Attacks
2. Fast-Track Penetration Testing
3. Third Party Modules
4. Update the Social-Engineer Toolkit
5. Update SET configuration
6. Help, Credits, and About

The menu item that you will be interested in for this exercise will be 1, as shown in Figure 7.9.

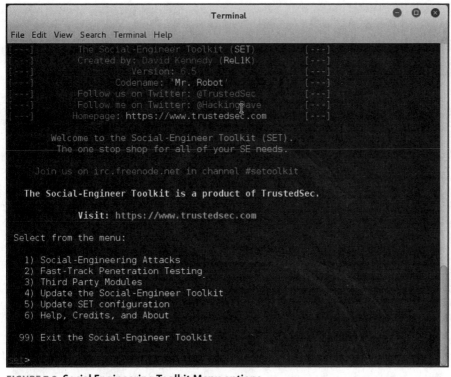

FIGURE 7.9 Social Engineering Toolkit Menu options

Now, you will select social engineering attacks from the menu. Once it is chosen, you will get the submenu list, which gives details about the type of attack, as shown in Figure 7.10.

1. Spear-Phishing Attack Vectors

2. Website Attack Vectors

3. Infectious Media Generator

4. Create a Payload and Listener

5. Mass Mailer Attack

6. Arduino-Based Attack Vector

7. Wireless Access Point Attack Vector

8. QRCode Generator Attack Vector

9. Powershell Attack Vectors

10. Third Party Modules

FIGURE 7.10 Social Engineering Toolkit sublist menu of attack options

Now, you will be able to select any of the listed options to explore the attacks by category and to gain a better understanding of the options available within each attack type. For instance, if you choose the website attack vectors from the menu, which is item 2, then you will get the submenu list, which gives details about the type of attacks available, as shown here:

1. Java Applet Attack Method

2. Metasploit Browser Exploit Method

3. Credential Harvester Attack Method

4. Tabnabbing Attack Method

5. Man Left in the Middle Attack Method

6. Web Jacking Attack Method

7. Multi-Attack Web Method

8. Create or Import a CodeSigning Certificate

SET will provide a small summary of the functionality of each attack when chosen, as the following example illustrates for the first three items listed in the menu:

■ The Java Applet Attack method will spoof a Java certificate and deliver a Metasploit-based payload. It uses a customized Java applet created by Thomas Werth to deliver the payload.

- The Metasploit Browser Exploit method will utilize select Metasploit browser exploits through an iframe and deliver a Metasploit payload.

- The Credential Harvester method will utilize web cloning of a website that has a username and password field and harvest all the information posted to the website.

WARNING   Please remember that this is an exercise designed to give you the opportunity to explore different attack types and to gain understanding of a tool that you, as a security practitioner, may have to face in the wild one day. At no time should you actually deploy any of these attacks against any live environments or any networks or users that could be damaged by them in any way.

Long File Extensions

Long file extensions have been around for many years. On Windows NTFS-based operating systems, the filename can be up to 255 characters long.[18] Filenames that are very long are abbreviated with three dots, ". . .", concealing the true extension of the file. The security practitioner needs to be familiar with how to view a full file name, including the extension of the file being examined, because this information can be very valuable in many circumstances.

Double File Extensions

The use of double file extensions is often combined with long file names to show only the first extension, such as Madonna.jpg followed by many spaces and then the real extension, such as .exe: Madonna.jpg.exe. The security practitioner needs to be aware of this kind of behavior because the information that is being hidden through the use of the double file extension will help to provide an understanding of the true nature of the file as well as its contents. See Figure 7.11 for an example of double file extensions.

Name		Date modified	Type	Size	
SSCP Test Document.docx.xls		2/3/2016 7:26 PM	Microsoft Excel 97-2003 Worksheet	12 KB	

FIGURE 7.11 A file that has been created using double file extensions

The "original" version of this file was created as a Microsoft Word file, using Office 2013. Once the second file extension was added to the file, two critical things happened. First, the file type, according to Windows Explorer, is now registered as being an Excel file of type version 97−2003, based on the file extension .xls being used for the file.

The second thing that has happened is that the file icon, the file association, and all of the metadata associated with the file have been modified and now reference Microsoft Excel, not Microsoft Word. When you try to open the file, this will result in a warning similar to the one shown in Figure 7.12.

FIGURE 7.12 Opening a file with a different version of a program

The security warning prompted by the system indicates another interesting behavior for the security practitioner to be aware of when dealing with double file extensions. The security warning indicates that this file is attempting to be opened in a different format by a program of a different type than the file extension would normally indicate should be opening the file. This is happening because the version of the file was set to `.xls` when saved, but the program being used to open the file is newer, specifically Excel 2013, and is expecting to see an `.xlsx` file extension. If the Yes button is clicked, the file would open with no trouble, even though the security warning indicated that the file could possibly be corrupt. The security practitioner needs to understand that file extensions can be used to alter file associations, as well as the default program that would be used by the operating system to open a file and, as a result, could potentially lead to a rogue program being launched without the prior knowledge of the end user once a modified file has been accessed.

The security practitioner cannot always rely on the operating system to provide a security prompt, or a warning of any kind for that matter, indicating that a modified file is being accessed. Figure 7.13 shows another file with double file extensions.

Name	Date modified	Type	Size
SSCP Test Document.docx.txt	2/3/2016 7:26 PM	Text Document	12 KB

FIGURE 7.13 File with double file extensions

The file, which was originally created as a Microsoft Office Word 2013 document and then "transformed" into a Notepad text file through the addition of the `.txt` file extension, opens with no security warning of any kind for the end user when accessed, as Figure 7.14 illustrates.

This kind of behavior can lead to an end user's system being compromised easily if the right type of modified file is accessed by the user under the guise of "legitimate" use.

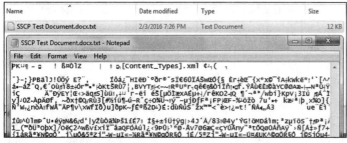

FIGURE 7.14 File opened without any security warning

Figure 7.15 shows one final issue that double file extensions can cause if left undiscovered in a system.

Name ▲	Date modified	Type	Size
📄 wmplayer.exe.txt	2/2/2015 10:30 PM	Text Document	164 KB

FIGURE 7.15 File renaming through extension manipulation

The file `wmplayer.exe.txt` was created by taking a copy of the legitimate `wmplayer.exe` file from a Windows 7 machine and renaming it by adding a `.txt` extension onto the end of the file name. This action allowed the file type to be registered by the Windows OS as a text document type, as can be seen at the top-right corner of the figure. When the file is accessed, it is now opened by the `notepad.exe` program, not by the Windows Media Player. This allows the underlying source code of the `wmplayer.exe` file to be examined, as shown in the lower portion of Figure 7.16.

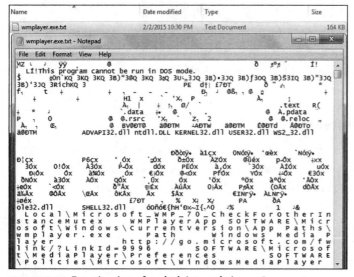

FIGURE 7.16 Examination of underlying code in `wmplayer.exe`

The reader should take notice of the fact that while a lot of the code is unreadable, there are also several pieces of information that may be of value for an attacker if he or she is looking to modify the functionality of this file or add instructions or additional information into the file in some way.

Figure 7.17 shows what a simple modification of the `wmplayer.exe.txt` file might achieve. The two modifications made are found in the third and fourth lines of text from the bottom of Figure 7.17. Notice that the URL path has been modified in the fourth line of text from the bottom, and the third line of text from the bottom shows modifications to the "LinkID =" statement. While neither of these modifications by themselves could be harmful, taken together, these modifications could allow the program to be redirected to a website controlled by a hacker and potentially cause the download of modified software onto the end-user system that executes this modified file.

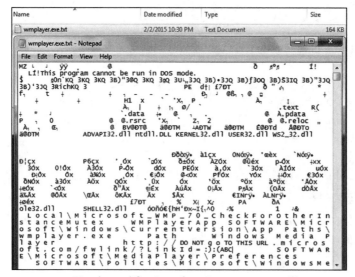

FIGURE 7.17 **Simple modification of** `wmplayer.exe.txt` **file**

Fake Related Extension

Sometimes a fake related extension is what works best for an attack vector. An example of this type of behavior can be seen by examining the Unitrix exploit. Named the Unitrix exploit by Avast after it was used by the Unitrix malware, this method takes advantage of a special character in Unicode to reverse the order of characters in a file name, hiding the dangerous file extension in the middle of the file name and placing a harmless-looking fake file extension near the end of the file name. The Unicode character is U+202E: Right-to-Left Override, and it forces programs to display text in reverse order. Figure 7.18

shows the Unicode Character Map in Windows 8.1, with the U+202E: Right-to-Left Override selected.

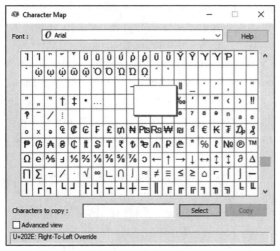

FIGURE 7.18 **U+202E: Right-To-Left Override selection**

The way this would work is that the file's actual name can be something like "Cool song uploaded by [U+202e]3pm.SCR." The special character forces Windows to display the end of the file's name in reverse, so the file's name will appear as "Cool song uploaded by RCS.mp3." However, it's not an MP3 file; it is an SCR file, and it will be executed if you double-click it. Analysis of this exploit showed that the hackers did not directly take over the infected computers. Instead, they had a "pay per installation" network that provided outsourced infection and malware distribution services for other cybergangs, hitting a peak of 25,000 infections daily during the last quarter of 2011.

The security practitioner needs to be focused on what kind of files are being used and made available in end-user systems in order to better understand the potential threats that may exist. Additional file types that could prove to be problematic include the following: .bat, .cmd, .com, .lnk, .pif, .scr, .vb, .vbe, .vbs, .wsh.

Fake Icons

Fake icons are often given to files to make them appear as something safe or trusted, tricking the end user into executing rogue software. Some actors will give file names that appear to be something like a PDF or similar file, and then an icon for PDF files, but they will configure the file so that it runs as an executable.

Password-Protected ZIP Files/RAR

Some malcode attacks can be used to send compressed or encrypted files to potential victims. This helps to bypass some gateway filters that exist to block EXE, COM, SCR, and similar file types known to be of high risk. Such attacks will normally include text or an image to provide the password to a possible victim, instructing them to open the file. Another use for modified .zip files could be to use them to carry out a zip bomb attack. A zip bomb is a malicious archive file designed to crash or render useless the program or system reading it. It is often employed to disable antivirus software in order to create an opening for more traditional viruses. Rather than hijacking the normal operation of the program, a zip bomb allows the program to work as intended, but the archive is carefully crafted so that unpacking it requires inordinate amounts of time, disk space, or memory. One example of a zip bomb is the file 42.zip, which is a zip file consisting of 42 kilobytes of compressed data, containing five layers of nested zip files in sets of 16, each bottom layer archive containing a 4.3 gigabyte file for a total of 4.5 petabytes of uncompressed data.[19]

Hostile Codecs

This family of code spread through multiple vectors, but it always ended up with a user installing a hostile codec of some kind. Various posts are made to forums or users may be directed via e-mail or some other vector to visit a pornography site. Upon visiting the pornography site, or similar content, they are told they cannot view the video without installing a codec first. Installation of the codec gives permission to install Zlob or similar malicious code onto the targeted system, thus opening it up to attack and compromise by the hacker.

E-mail

E-mail is one of the most well-known vectors for spreading malcode. It is heavily used and depended upon by millions daily. Sometimes, e-mail threats can involve a vulnerability related to e-mail clients or even web browsers, such as Internet Explorer, that are used to view HTML-based content. One example of an e-mail attempt to infect end-user systems with malware has been targeted at users of the Google Chrome web browser. Google Chrome users receive an unsolicited e-mail that announces that a new extension for their favorite browser has been developed to facilitate their access to documents from e-mails. A link is provided, and the recipients are advised to follow it in order to download the new extension. Once they click the link, they are redirected to a look-alike of the Google Chrome Extensions page, which, instead of the promised extension, provides them with a fake application that infects their systems with malware. Figure 7.19 shows a sample of the spam e-mail that would be used by the attacker to convince a targeted end user to click the bad URL to force a redirect to the modified web page where the malware would be waiting to be downloaded into the computer once the user attempted to download the extension file.

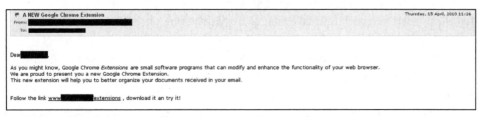

FIGURE 7.19 **Sample spam e-mail**

Another example of e-mail being used as an attack vector against unsuspecting users was targeted at a very narrowly defined silo of users. This attack, launched in the end of October 2013, was targeted at fliers who would be taking Lufthansa Flights on November 4, 2013.

A description of the attack and the image of the e-mail shown in Figure 7.20 is reproduced directly from the Hot for Security blog post, "Fake Lufthansa Ticket Reservation Plants Spyware on Germans' PCs," at `http://www.hotforsecurity.com/blog/fake-lufthansa-ticket-reservation-plants-spyware-on-germans-pcs-7297.html`. These travelers received the e-mail shown in Figure 7.20, which appears to be from Lufthansa customer service.

FIGURE 7.20 **E-mail that appears to be from Lufthansa customer service**

The fake message informs travelers that they have been issued an electronic ticket and that they can use the flight data in the attachment to perform an advance online check-in. The attachment includes a hidden Trojan that deploys spyware on the compromised system. The Trojan spies on users' network activities to steal system data, browser-related credentials, and e-mail login data. The collected data is sent to the attackers' remote servers. These servers tell the malware when and where to download and run files, remove itself from the system, and update its code to avoid detection.

The security practitioner needs to be able to create a culture within their networks that allows users to report unusual events of any kind in order to ensure that attacks such as the ones described do not go unnoticed and, as a result, have the ability to infect multiple systems before they are discovered. While there are many ways for the security practitioner to communicate with users, one of the most effective ways to help users to understand the importance of understanding what an expectation of normalcy may be for a network, and as a result, what a deviation from that baseline is, would be to create security awareness training content that is made available to *all* users of the network, regardless of job role.

Insider Human Threats

The following discussion of insider threats is reproduced directly from the Department of Homeland Security white paper, "Combating the Internal Threat."

> An insider threat is generally defined as a current or former employee, contractor, or other business partner who has or had authorized access to an organization's network, system, or data and intentionally misused that access to negatively affect the confidentiality, integrity, or availability of the organization's information or information systems. Insider threats, to include sabotage, theft, espionage, fraud, and competitive advantage, are often carried out through abusing access rights, theft of materials, and mishandling physical devices. Insiders do not always act alone and may not be aware they are aiding a threat actor (i.e., the unintentional insider threat). It is vital that security practitioners understand normal employee baseline behaviors and also ensure employees understand how they may be used as a conduit for others to obtain information. Some behavioral indicators of malicious threat activity include:
>
> - Remotely accesses the network while on vacation, sick, or at odd times.
> - Works odd hours without authorization.
> - Displays notable enthusiasm for overtime, weekend, or unusual work schedules.
> - Unnecessarily copies material, especially if it is proprietary or classified.
> - Shows an interest in matters outside of the scope of their duties.
> - Signs of vulnerability, such as drug or alcohol abuse, financial difficulties, gambling, illegal activities, poor mental health, or hostile behavior, should

trigger concern. Be on the lookout for warning signs among employees such as the acquisition of unexpected wealth, unusual foreign travel, irregular work hours, or unexpected absences.

Identifying behavioral indicators may be difficult, particularly if they do not occur for a long period of time and therefore do not set a pattern. Therefore, a good understanding of risk characteristics and events that may trigger those characteristics is essential. It's equally important for the security practitioner to create productive and healthy work environments to help reduce the unintentional insider threat. Some countermeasures include:

- Training employees to recognize phishing and other social media threat vectors.
- Training continuously to maintain the proper levels of knowledge, skills, and abilities.
- Conducting training on and improving awareness of risk perception and cognitive biases that affect decision making.
- Improving usability of security tools.
- Improving usability of software to reduce the likelihood of system-induced human error.
- Enhancing awareness of the unintentional insider threat.
- Providing effective security practices (e.g., two factor authentication for access).
- Maintaining staff values and attitudes that align with organizational mission and ethics.

There are several detection, prevention, and deterrence methods to consider:

- Data/file encryption
- Data access monitoring
- SIEM or other log analysis
- Data loss prevention (DLP)
- Data redaction
- Enterprise identity and access management (IAM)
- Data access control
- Intrusion detection/prevention systems (IDS/IPS)
- Digital rights management (DRM)

Finally, continual training is always a recommended option. Below are descriptions of two free of charge courses that organizations may want to consider offering to employees, contractors, and others that meet the description of an "insider."

- The Department of Homeland Security (DHS) offers an online independent study course titled Protecting Critical Infrastructure Against Insider Threats (IS-915). The one-hour course provides guidance to critical infrastructure employees and service providers on how to identify and take action against insider threats.[20]

- The Department of Defense (DoD) also offers an Insider Threat Awareness course free of charge. The course includes a printable certificate after completion and focuses on the insider threat as an essential component of a comprehensive security program.[21]

Insider Hardware and Software Threats

The following list details the most common behaviors that security practitioners should be engaging in on a regular basis to detect insider threats:

- Monitor phone activity logs to detect suspicious behaviors.
- Monitor and control privileged accounts.
- Monitor and control external access and data downloads.
- Protect critical files from modification, deletion, and unauthorized disclosure.
- Disable accounts and connections upon employee termination.
- Prevent unauthorized removable storage mediums.
- Identify all access paths into organizational information systems.

There are many ways that insider threats can be executed inside of a network, many of which can go unnoticed. For example, Knoppix can be loaded onto a thumb drive and then used to boot up a computer and possibly gain unauthorized access to files on the drive or make changes in Linux mode.[22] Another example of this kind of a solution is the Windows To Go feature that is available with the Windows 8 and 8.1 releases. The use of the Windows To Go technology could allow an attacker to use any device that could boot from a USB drive to run a full featured version of Windows 8. The issues that this poses for the security practitioner are as follows. First, this behavior could allow for an unsupported version of a network operating system to be deployed and used within the network. This would violate usage policies and could also have unknown consequences. In addition, and perhaps more importantly, if security has not been set up properly within the network to implement the use of policy based device management and drive encryption, the attacker could potentially gain access to data stored on the local hard drive of the machine being used to run the Windows To Go solution.

Another area of potential compromise involves the use of hardware and software Keyloggers to steal information without the knowledge of the user sitting at the computer.

The German news source Der Spiegel reported that the NSA's elite hacking unit Tailored Access Operations (TAO) conducts sophisticated wiretaps.[23] The NSA, CIA, and FBI routinely and secretly intercept shipments of laptops and computer accessories. The TAO unit diverts shipments to a secret workshops where agents install malware malicious hardware that grants remote access to U.S. intelligence agencies. Since 2009 the NSA has used a USB hardware implant codenamed COTTONMOUTH that secretly provides the NSA with remote access to the compromised machine. COTTONMOUTH-1 provides a wireless bridge into a network and the ability to load exploitative software onto computers.

Another NSA unit named ANT can compromise the security architecture of Cisco, Huawei, Dell, Juniper, and similar companies. The NSA uses malware called FEED-THROUGH to burrow into firewalls and make it possible to smuggle other NSA programs into mainframe computers. These programs can even survive reboots and software upgrades.

Available software and hardware for such purposes runs the full gamut of prices. A rigged monitor cable that shows what is displayed on a targeted monitor is available for $30. An active GSM base station that mimics a mobile phone tower so you can monitor cell phones costs $40,000. Computer bugging devices disguised as USB plugs that can transmit data via radio undetected are sold in packs of 50 for more than $1 million.

The security practitioner faces a large array of potential threats to the confidentiality, integrity, and availability of the systems and information that they are tasked with protecting. Some of these threats are easily identified and mitigated, while others may be impossible to foresee and detect until well after they have done damage to one or more systems. The need for training as well as situational awareness has never been greater. The security practitioner has several responsibilities that are instrumental to the success of creating and maintaining a secure environment within the enterprise. They may need to partner with one or more additional resources, such as a CISSP or senior information systems architect, in order to be able to fully execute on some of the responsibilities discussed here:

1. They must examine the architecture of all systems being used to ensure that any known issues, threats, vulnerabilities, and risks have been identified and plans are drawn up to address them in some way.

2. They must review the documentation for all systems and validate that it is up to date and properly managed through the use of a change management structure.

3. They must ensure that security awareness training is carried out at every level of the enterprise in order to ensure that all team members are aware of their role, the specifics of their role with regards to information and systems security, and also aware of the requirements that any and all policies may put in place with regards to system access and usage.

4. They must analyze all system usage and access policies in order to ensure that they are up to date and accurately represent current technology deployed in the enterprise, as well as current usage patterns of the technology deployed.

SPOOFING, PHISHING, SPAM, AND BOTNETS

Spoofing, phishing, spam, and botnets are all techniques that can compromise security. They sometimes are used in conjunction with each other. This section explores how you can recognize and address each of them.

Spoofing

In the context of network security, a spoofing attack is a situation in which one person or program successfully masquerades as another by falsifying data and thereby gaining an illegitimate advantage. Spoofing is the creation of TCP/IP packets using somebody else's IP address. Routers use the *destination IP* address in order to forward packets through the Internet, but they ignore the *source IP* address. That address is used only by the destination machine when it responds to the source. A common misconception is that "IP spoofing" can be used to hide your IP address while surfing the Internet, chatting online, sending e-mail, and so forth. This is generally not true. Forging the source IP address causes the responses to be misdirected, meaning you cannot create a normal network connection. However, IP spoofing is an integral part of many network attacks that do not need to see responses, such as blind spoofing. Here are some examples of spoofing:

- **Man-in-the-middle**—Packet sniffs on link between the two end points and can therefore pretend to be one end of the connection.

- **Routing redirect**—Redirects routing information from the original host to the hacker's host (this is another form of man-in-the-middle attack).

- **Source routing**—Redirects individual packets by hacker's host.

- **Blind spoofing**—Predicts responses from a host, allowing commands to be sent, but cannot get immediate feedback.

- **Flooding**—The SYN flood fills up receive queue from random source addresses; smurf/fraggle spoofs victim's address, causing everyone to respond to the victim.

Phishing

Phishing is the attempt to acquire sensitive information such as usernames, passwords, and credit card details (and sometimes, indirectly, money) by masquerading as a trust-worthy entity in an electronic communication. Phishing e-mails may contain links to websites that are infected with malware. Phishing is typically carried out by e-mail spoof-ing or instant messaging, and it often directs users to enter details at a fake website whose look and feel are almost identical to the legitimate one. Some of the most common char-acteristics that these forged e-mail messages present are:

- **Use of the Names of Existing Companies**—Instead of creating a company's website from scratch, fraudsters imitate the corporate image and website function-ality of an existing company in order to further confuse recipients of the forged message.

- **Use of the Name of a Real Company Employee as the Sender of the Spoofed Message**—By the fraudsters doing so, if recipients attempt to confirm the authen-ticity of the message by calling the company, they will be assured that the person that acts as spokesperson of the company does actually work for the company.

- **Web Addresses that Seem to be Correct**—Forged e-mails usually take users to websites that imitate the appearance of the company used as bait to harvest the information. In fact, both the contents and the web address (URL) are spoofed and simply imitate legitimate contents. What's more, legal information and other non-critical links could redirect trusting users to the real website.

- **Fear Factor**—The window of opportunity open to fraudsters is very short because once the company is informed that its clients are targets of these techniques, the server that hosts the fake website and harvests the stolen information is shut down within a few days. Therefore, it is essential for fraudsters to obtain an immediate response from users. On most occasions, the best strategy is to threaten them with either financial loss or loss of the account itself if the instructions outlined in the forged e-mail are not followed, which usually refer to new security measures rec-ommended by the company.

In addition to obscuring the fraudulent URL in an apparently legitimate e-mail mes-sage, this kind of malware also uses other more sophisticated techniques:

- In the man-in-the-middle technique, the fraudster is located between the victim and the real website, acting as a proxy server. By doing so, he can listen to all com-munication between them. In order to be successful, fraudsters must be able to redirect victims to their own proxy, instead of to the real server. There are several methods, such as transparent proxies, DNS cache poisoning, and URL obfusca-tion, among others.

- Exploitation of cross-site scripting vulnerabilities in a website, which allow a secure banking webpage to be simulated, without users detecting any anomalies neither in the web address nor in the security certificate displayed in the web browser.

- Vulnerabilities in Internet Explorer, which by means of an exploit allow the web address that appears in the browser address bar to be spoofed. By doing so, while the web browser could be redirected to a fraudulent website, the address bar would display the trustworthy website URL. This technique also allows false pop-up windows to be opened when accessing legitimate websites.

- Some attacks also use exploits hosted in malicious websites, which exploit vulnerabilities in Internet Explorer or the client operating system in order to download keylogger type Trojans, which will steal confidential user information.

- Pharming is a much more sophisticated technique. It consists in modifying the contents of the DNS (domain name server), either via the TCP/IP protocol settings or the lmhost file, which acts as a local cache of server names in order to redirect web browsers to forged websites instead of the legitimate ones, when the user attempts to access them. Furthermore, if the victim uses a proxy in order to remain anonymous while surfing the Web, its DNS name resolution could also become affected so that all the proxy users are redirected to the false server.

How Phishing Works and Is Distributed

The most common attack vector is a forged e-mail message that pretends to come from a specific company, whose clients are the target of the scam. This message will contain links to one or more fraudulent web pages that totally or partially imitate the appearance and functionality of the company, which is expected to have a commercial relation with the recipient. If the recipient actually works with the company and trusts the e-mail to have come from the legitimate source, he is likely to end up entering sensitive information in a malicious form located in one of those websites.

The means of distribution of these e-mails also shares several common characteristics.

Much the same as spam, it is massively and indiscriminately sent via e-mail or instant messaging programs: The message urges users to click a link, which will take them to a website in which they must enter their confidential data in order to confirm it, reactivate their account, etc. It is sent as a financial company alert, warning users of an attack. It includes a link to a website in which they are prompted to enter personal data.

As the message is massively distributed, some of the recipients will actually be clients of the company. The message states that due to some security concerns, users should visit a website and confirm their data: username, password, credit card number, PIN, Social Security number, etc.

Of course, the link does not point to the company page but to a website developed by the fraudsters and that imitates the corporate image of the financial or banking entity. The web address displayed usually includes the name of the legitimate institution so that users do not suspect any deception.

When users enter their confidential data, these are stored in a database, allowing fraudsters to use the harvested information to connect to the accounts and strip all of the funds out.

The main damage caused by phishing is

- Identity and confidential user data theft
- Loss of productivity
- Use of corporate networks resources: bandwidth, mail flooding, etc.

Recognizing a Phishing E-mail

It might be difficult for users who have received a message with these characteristics to tell the difference between a phishing e-mail and a legitimate one, especially for those who are clients of the financial entity from which the e-mail message is supposed to come from.

The From field shows an address belonging to the legitimate company. However, it is very easy for fraudsters to spoof the source e-mail address that is displayed in any mail client.

The message includes logos or images, which have been collected from the legitimate website to which the forged e-mail refers to.

Though the link included seems to point to the original company website, it actually directs the browser to a fraudulent web page, in which user data, passwords, etc., must be entered.

These messages frequently contain grammatical errors or spelling mistakes, or special characters, none of them usual in communication sent from the company that they are pretending to represent.

Spam

Spam is unsolicited e-mail, normally with an advertising content sent out as a mass mailing. Some of the most common characteristics these types of e-mail messages have are:

- The address that appears as that of the message sender is unknown to the user and is quite often spoofed.
- The message does not often have a Reply address.
- An eye-catching subject is presented.

- It has advertising content: website advertisements, ways to make money easily, miracle products, property offers, or simply lists of products on special offer.

- Most spam is written in English and comes from the United States or Asia, although spam in Spanish is also now becoming common.

Although this type of malware is normally spread via e-mail, there are variants, each with their own name according to their distribution channel:

- **Spam**—Sent by e-mail.

- **Spim**—Specific to Instant Messaging applications (MSN Messenger, Yahoo Messenger, etc.).

- **Spit**—Spam over IP telephony. IP telephony consists in using the Internet to make telephone calls.

- **Spam SMS**—Spam designed to be sent to mobile devices using SMS (short message service).

How Spam Works and Is Distributed

Spammers try to obtain as many valid e-mail addresses as possible, i.e., actually used by users. They use different techniques for this, some of which are highly sophisticated:

- **Mail Lists**—The spammer looks in the mail list and notes the addresses of the other members.

- **Purchasing User Databases from Individuals or Companies**—Although this type of activity is illegal, it is actually carried out in practice, and there is a black market.

- **Use of Robots (Automatic Programs)**—These robots scour the Internet looking for addresses in web pages, newsgroups, weblogs, etc.

- **DHA (Directory Harvest Attack) Techniques**—The spammer generates e-mail addresses belonging to a specific domain and sends messages to them. The domain mail server will respond with an error to those addresses that do not actually exist, so the spammer can discover which addresses generated are valid. The addresses can be compiled using a dictionary or through brute force, i.e., by trying all possible character combinations.

Consequently, all e-mail users are at risk from these types of attacks. Any address published on the Internet (used in forums, newsgroups, or on any website) is more likely to be a spam victim.

Protecting Users Against Spam

The mail message filter is a basic measure to prevent spam entering users' mailboxes. There are many applications that can filter e-mails by message, keywords, domains, IP addresses from where the messages come from, etc. The best anti-spam systems should be based on more than just one technology. They should use diverse techniques (heuristic rules, Bayesian filters, white and black lists, digital signatures, sender authentication, etc.) that achieve the basic aim of reducing false positives to a minimum and therefore eliminate the possibility of a user losing a message as a result of a system error, maintaining a high degree of efficiency in the spam detection process. Also, take into account the following guidelines for protecting users against spam and minimizing its effects:

- Do not publish personal e-mail addresses in any public site, such as web pages, for example.
- Never click the "unsubscribe" link in a spam message. All this will do is let the spammer verify that the e-mail address is active.
- Never reply to a spam message.
- Do not resend chain letters, requests, or dubious virus alerts.
- Do not open the spam message.
- Disable the Preview Pane of the e-mail client.
- Do not purchase products offered through unsolicited e-mails.
- Have various e-mail accounts, and use them for separate purposes: personal, work, etc.
- Use an anti-spam filter or an anti-spam solution.
- Install an antivirus solution.
- Install content filter software.

Botnets

A botnet is an army of compromised machines, also known as *zombies*, that are under the command and control of a single *botmaster*. The rise of consumer broadband has greatly increased the power of botnets to launch crippling denial-of-service (DoS) attacks on servers, infect millions of computers with spyware and other malicious code, steal identity data, send out vast quantities of spam, and engage in click fraud, blackmail, and extortion.

How Botnets Are Created

Botnet creation begins with the download of a software program called a *bot* (for example, IRCBot, SGBot, or AgoBot) along with an embedded exploit (or payload) by an unsuspecting user, who might click an infected e-mail attachment or download infected files or freeware from P2P networks or malicious websites. Once the bot and exploit combination is installed, the infected machine contacts a public server that the botmaster has set up as a control plane to issue commands to the botnet. A common technique is to use public Internet relay chat (IRC) servers, but hijacked servers can also issue instructions using HTTPS, SMTP, TCP, and UDP strings. Control planes are not static and are frequently moved to evade detection; they run on machines (and by proxies) that are never owned by the botmaster.

Using the control plane, the botmaster can periodically push out new exploit code to the bots. It can also be used to modify the bot code itself in order to evade signature-based detection or to accommodate new commands and attack vectors. Initially, however, the botmaster's primary purpose is to recruit additional machines into the botnet. Each zombie machine is instructed to scan for other vulnerable hosts. Each new infected machine joins the botnet and then scans for potential recruits. In a matter of hours, the size of a botnet can grow very large, sometimes comprising millions of PCs on diverse networks around the world.

The Impact of Botnets

Botnet-led exploits can take many forms, as detailed here:

Distributed Denial-of-Service (DDoS) Attacks   With thousands of zombies distributed around the world, a botnet may launch a massive, coordinated attack to impair or bring down high-profile sites and services by flooding the connection bandwidth or resources of the targeted system. Multigigabit-per-second attacks are not uncommon. Most common attack vectors deploy UDP, Internet Control Message Protocol (ICMP), and TCP SYN floods; other attacks include password brute forcing and application layer attacks.

Targets of attack may include commercial or government websites, e-mail services, DNS servers, hosting providers, and critical Internet infrastructure, even anti-spam and IT security vendors. Attacks may also be directed toward specific political and religious organizations, as well as gambling, pornography, and online gaming sites. Such attacks are sometimes accompanied by extortion demands.

Spyware and Malware   Zombies monitor and report users' web activity for profit, without the knowledge or consent of the user (and at times for blackmail and extortion). They may also install additional software to gather keystroke data and harvest system vulnerability information for sale to third parties.

Identity Theft   Botnets are often deployed to steal personal identity information, financial data, or passwords from a user's PC and then either sell it or use it directly for profit.

Adware   Zombies may automatically download, install, and display pop-up advertising based on a user's surfing habits or force the user's browser to periodically visit certain websites.

E-mail Spam   Most of today's e-mail spam is sent by botnet zombies.

Click Fraud   The exploit code may imitate a legitimate web browser user to click ads for the sole purpose of generating revenue (or penalizing an advertiser) for a website on pay-per-click advertising networks (such as Google AdWords).

Phishing   Zombies can help scan for and identify vulnerable servers that can be hijacked to host phishing sites, which impersonate legitimate services (e.g., PayPal or banking websites) in order to steal passwords and other identity data.

Botnet Detection and Mitigation

Botnets use multiple attack vectors; no single technology can provide protection against them. For instance, the goal of a DDoS attack is to cripple a server. The goal of a phishing attack is to lure users to a spoofed website and get them to reveal personal data. The goal of malware can range from collecting personal data on an infected PC to showing ads on it or sending spam from it. A defense-in-depth approach is essential to detect and mitigate the effects of botnets.

Traditional packet filtering, port-based, and signature-based techniques do not effectively mitigate botnets that dynamically and rapidly modify the exploit code and control channel, resort to port-hopping (or using standard HTTP/S ports such as 80 and 443), and shuffle the use of zombie hosts. A variety of open source and commercial tools are currently used for botnet detection. Many of them analyze traffic flow data reported by routers, such as Cisco NetFlow. Others use behavioral techniques, for example, building a baseline of a network or system under normal conditions and using it to flag abnormal traffic patterns that might indicate a DDoS attack. DNS log analysis and honeypots are also used to detect botnets, but these technique are not always scalable.

The most common detection and mitigation techniques include:

Flow Data Monitoring   This technique uses flow-based protocols to get summary network and transport layer information from network devices. Cisco NetFlow is often used by service providers and enterprises to identify command-and-control traffic for compromised workstations or servers that have been subverted and are being remotely controlled as members of botnets used to launch DDoS attacks, perform keystroke logging, and perform other forms of illicit activity.

Anomaly Detection   While signature-based approaches try to have a signature for every vulnerability, anomaly detection (or behavioral approaches) try to do the opposite. They characterize what normal traffic is like and then look for deviations. Any burst of scanning activity on the network from zombie machines can be detected and blocked. Anomaly detection can be effectively used on the network as well as on endpoints (such as servers and laptops). On endpoints, suspicious activity and policy violations can be identified and infections prevented.

DNS Log Analysis   Botnets often rely on free DNS hosting services to point a subdomain to IRC servers that have been hijacked by the botmaster and that host the bots and associated exploits. Botnet code often contains hard-coded references to a DNS server, which can be spotted by any DNS log analysis tool. If such services are identified, the entire botnet can be crippled by the DNS server administrator by directing offending subdomains to a dead IP address (a technique known as *null-routing*). While this technique is effective, it is also the hardest to implement since it requires cooperation from third-party hosting providers and name registrars.

Honeypots   A honeypot is a trap that mimics a legitimate network, resource, or service but is in fact a self-contained, secure, and monitored area. Its primary goal is to lure and detect malicious attacks and intrusions. Effective more as a surveillance and early warning system, it can also help security researchers understand emerging threats. Due to the difficulty in setup and the active analysis required, the value of honeypots on large-scale networks is rather limited.

MALICIOUS WEB ACTIVITY

Web-based attacks are one of the most popular ways to spread malcode in the wild. Social network sites can contain vulnerabilities designed to spread malware code through one or more "profiles" that have been crafted by attackers to draw in hundreds and thousands of potential "drive-by" victims. Web-based vectors commonly spread through social engineering and through the exploitation of Internet Explorer as well as Firefox and other browsers. Web attack vectors offer a multitude of possibilities for an attacker to reach thousands of targets in a very short amount of time with little to no effort at all.

Cross-Site Scripting (XSS) Attacks

In general, cross-site scripting refers to that hacking technique that leverages vulnerabilities in the code of a web application to allow an attacker to send malicious content from an end-user and collect some type of data from the victim. According to the CERT Coordination Center:

> "A webpage contains both text and HTML markup that is generated by the server and interpreted by the client browser. Websites that generate only static pages are able to have full control over how the browser interprets these pages. Websites that generate dynamic pages do not have complete control over how their outputs are interpreted by the client. The heart of the issue is that if mistrusted content can be introduced into a dynamic page, neither the website nor the client has enough information to recognize that this has happened and take protective actions."

According to Acunetix:

> "Cross-site scripting allows an attacker to embed malicious JavaScript, VBScript, ActiveX, HTML, or Flash into a vulnerable dynamic page to fool the user, executing the script on his machine in order to gather data. The use of XSS might compromise private information, manipulate or steal cookies, create requests that can be mistaken for those of a valid user, or execute malicious code on the end-user systems. The data is usually formatted as a hyperlink containing malicious content and is distributed over any possible means on the Internet."[24]

To check for cross-site scripting vulnerabilities, use a web vulnerability scanner. A web vulnerability scanner crawls an entire website and automatically checks for cross-site scripting vulnerabilities. It will indicate which URLs/scripts are vulnerable to these attacks. Besides cross-site scripting vulnerabilities, a web application scanner will also check for SQL injection and other web vulnerabilities.

Zero-Day Exploits and Advanced Persistent Threats (APTs)

A zero-day (or zero-hour or day zero) attack or threat is an attack that exploits a previously unknown vulnerability in a computer application or operating system, one that developers have not had time to address and patch. It is called a "zero-day" because the programmer has had zero days to fix the flaw (in other words, a patch is not available). Zero-day attacks occur during the vulnerability window that exists in the time between when vulnerability is first exploited and when software developers start to develop and publish a counter to that threat.

A special type of vulnerability management process focuses on finding and eliminating zero-day weaknesses. This unknown vulnerability management lifecycle is a security and quality assurance process that aims to ensure the security and robustness of both in-house and third-party software products by finding and fixing unknown (zero-day) vulnerabilities. According to Codenomicon, the unknown vulnerabilities management process consists of four phases: analyze, test, report, and mitigate.[25]

- **Analyze**—This phase focuses on attack surface analysis.

- **Test**—This phase focuses on fuzz testing the identified attack vectors.

- **Report**—This phase focuses on reporting of the found issues to developers.

- **Mitigate**—This phase looks at protective measures explained below.

Zero-day exploits can take many forms. One example was announced in early October 2014. In this case, Bugzilla, a system that many developers use to track and discuss bugs in their code, was the target. Patches released for Bugzilla addressed a privilege escalation vulnerability that could have allowed attackers to gain administrative access to software bug trackers based on the open-source application. Bugzilla is developed with support from the Mozilla Foundation, which uses it to track issues for many of its own products. However, the platform is also used by the Apache Software Foundation, the Linux kernel developers, LibreOffice, OpenOffice, OpenSSH, Eclipse, KDE, GNOME, various Linux distributions, and many other projects. The vulnerability was discovered by security researchers from Check Point Software Technologies and was reported to the Bugzilla developers on September 30, 2014. The flaw has been in the software for a long time, and it's unclear whether anyone discovered and exploited it independently in the past.

In July 2014, Google announced a zero-day tracking initiative called Project Zero.[26] Google claims that this project will allow them to document and stop the latest zero-day threats before they can be exploited. Project Zero is a two-pronged attack against zero-days. It creates within Google a team of elite security researchers who have a broad mandate to go bug-hunting. Project Zero also will create a public database of zero-day bugs that will be first reported only to the software vendor, without contacting third parties.[27]

An APT uses multiple phases to break into a network, avoid detection, and harvest valuable information over the long term. This infographic details the attack phases, methods, and motivations that differentiate APTs from other targeted attacks.

The five phases of an APT are detailed here:

- **Reconnaissance**—Attackers leverage information from a variety of areas to understand their target.

- **Incursion**—Attackers break into the target network by using social engineering to deliver targeted malware to vulnerable systems and people.

- **Discovery**—The attacker maps the organization's defenses from the inside out, allowing them to have a complete picture of the strengths and weaknesses of the network. This allows the attacker to pick and choose what vulnerabilities and weaknesses they will attempt to exploit through the deployment of multiple parallel vectors to ensure success.

- **Capture**—Attackers access unprotected systems and capture information over an extended period of time. They will also traditionally install malware to allow for the secret acquisition of data and potential disruption of operations if required.

- **Exfiltration**—Captured information is sent back to the attackers for analysis and potentially further exploitation.

Brute-Force Attacks

A brute-force attack can manifest itself in many different ways, such as an attacker configuring predetermined values, making requests to a server using those values, and then analyzing the response. An attacker may use a dictionary attack, with or without mutations, or a traditional brute-force attack with given classes of characters, e.g., alphanumerical, special, case (in)sensitive. There are several different types of brute-force attacks as listed here:

Dictionary Attack   Dictionary-based attacks consist of automated scripts and tools that will try to guess usernames and passwords from a dictionary file. A dictionary file can be tuned and compiled to cover words potentially used by the owner of the account. The attacker can gather information via many methods such as active/passive reconnaissance, competitive intelligence, dumpster diving, and social engineering to better understand the target.

Search Attacks   Search attacks will try to cover all possible combinations of a given character set and a given password length range. This kind of attack is very slow because the space of possible candidates is quite big.

Rule-Based Search Attacks   The creation of good rules to drive the search can serve to increase the combination space coverage without slowing down the process too much. For example, a password cracking software tool such as John the Ripper can generate password variations from part of the username or modify them through the use of a preconfigured mask word in the input (e.g., 1st round "tool" > 2nd round "t001" > 3rd round "too1t0").[28]

One example of a brute-force attack can be targeting a web application by taking a word list of known pages, for instance from a popular content management system, and simply requesting each known page, and then analyzing the HTTP response code to determine if the page exists on the target server. DirBuster is one tool that can be used to carry out this kind of an attack.[29]

Figure 7.21 shows the main DirBuster tool interface running in Windows 7. Another tool for the SSCP to consider in this area is the OWASP Zed Attack Proxy (ZAP), which can be used to automatically find security vulnerabilities in your web applications while you are developing and testing, as well as once deployment takes place. ZAP is an integrated penetration testing tool that uses automated scanners and a set of tools that can be deployed manually to assess the security of applications and websites. Figure 7.22 shows the ZAP tool.

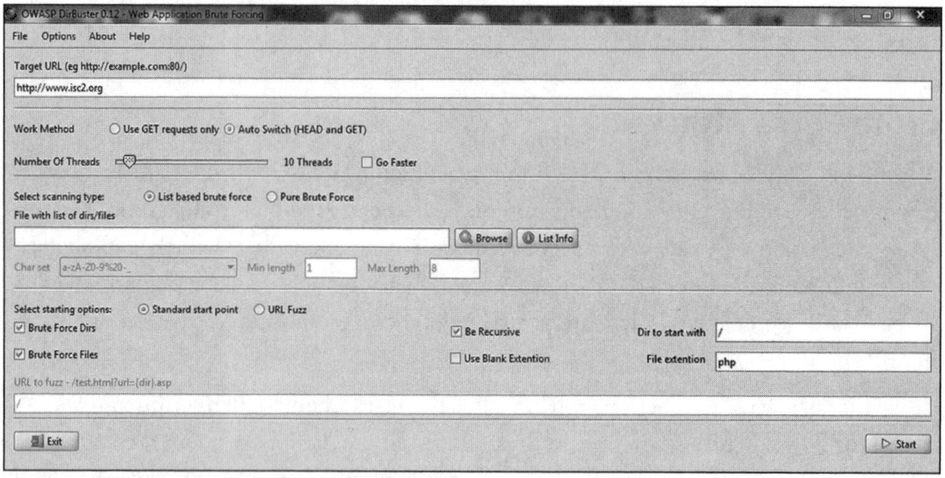

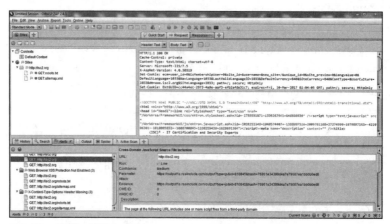

FIGURE 7.21 Main DirBuster tool interface

FIGURE 7.22 The ZAP tool

ZAP uses spiders to discover links through the examination of the HTML code in application responses. There is also a specific spider that can be deployed for AJAX applications that generate JavaScript instead of HTML. ZAP also provides you with the ability to proxy your browser, if you decide that you want to explore the application under review manually instead of using the spiders. ZAP can be used in both active and passive scanning mode, allowing for analysis to be carried out using the content stream provided through spidering, as well as using known attacks against the intended target to probe for additional vulnerabilities.[30]

The security practitioner should become familiar with brute-force attack methodology as well as the tools that are used to execute these attacks in the wild. One of the resources that security practitioners should consider taking advantage of in this regard is the use of defensive tools to help detect brute-force attacks when they are occurring. Php-Brute-Force-Attack Detector is one such tool that could be used for this purpose.[31]

Instant Messaging

Instant messaging (IM) threats may involve exploitation of software to spread code but more frequently rely on social engineering. Kelvir is one such bot, infamous for spreading as a bot through traditional means and also through IM.[32] Historically, IM threats are less likely to be trusted and followed compared to e-mail threats. Most involve a user receiving a message with a link that the user is required to click to visit the hostile site. The remote hostile site may involve social engineering or include an exploit to attack the computer. There was an interesting resurgence of this attack vector in 2010 surrounding the World Cup events being hosted in South Africa. According to Symantec researchers, by the end of 2010, one in 300 IM messages would contain a URL. Also, in 2010, Symantec predicted that overall one in 12 hyperlinks would be linked to a domain known to be used for hosting malware. Thus, one in 12 hyperlinks appearing in IM messages would contain a domain that is considered suspicious or malicious. In mid-2009, that level was one in 78 hyperlinks.

Instant messaging threats are more of a historical issue today for most security practitioners because much of the instant messaging usage taking place across company-owned networks is secured and encrypted traffic, even when it transits across the World Wide Web between federated partners. The advent of instant messaging platforms that use encryption, as well as log user interactions, transcribe conversations, and archive them for storage, subjecting them to retention policies and governance regimes has changed the way this technology is being used by business today, and as a result, the nature of the threats that users may be exposed to. There are still threats that users of instant messaging platforms may face, such as account hijacking and the ability to become a launching pad for the spread of worms through the use of the contact lists maintained by the instant messaging software.

Peer-to-Peer Networks

P2P networks involve hosts sharing files with one another, either directly or through a centralized P2P server.[33] A wide variety of files are shared on P2P networks, including those that are unintentionally shared and pirated, illegal, and warez-type media. Most

P2P downloads are not malicious. However, risk escalates to more than 75% on average once a user starts to search for specific terms like pornography-related words and illegal terms such as "warez" and "crack." Studies analyzing the spread of malware on P2P networks found that 63% of the answered download requests on the Limewire network contained some form of malware, whereas only 3% of the content on OpenFT contained malware. In both cases, the top three most common types of malware accounted for the large majority of cases (99% in Limewire and 65% in OpenFT). Another study analyzing traffic on the Kazaa network found that 15% of the 500,000 file sample examined was infected by one or more of the 365 different computer viruses that were tested for.[34] Most organizations block the use of P2P software for security and liability reasons today. Security practitioners need to be diligent to monitor network traffic for possible rogue P2P installations, as they can lead to unintentional sharing of files. Figure 7.23 shows what typical P2P software looks like on an end-user system.

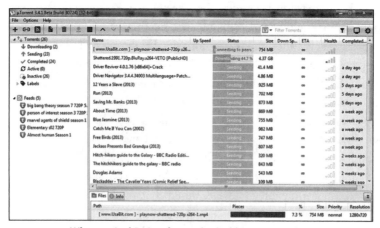

FIGURE 7.23 **What typical P2P software looks like on an end-user system**

Internet Relay Chat

IRC was a big part of how people chatted or communicated near the turn of the century. Today, social networking sites and forums are dominating the scene as IRC falls into the background. IRC is still used by thousands daily and has similar threats to several years ago. It is common to receive spammed messages within IRC chat rooms, private messages from bots by bad actors, and more. Sometimes bad actors attempt to exploit vulnerable software (chat clients) or may send malcode through IRC to the user via links or files directly through a Direct Client to Client Protocol (DCC) connection. [35]

As of December 2014, the largest IRC networks were the following:[36]

- **IRCnet**—Around 50,000 users during peak hours
- **QuakeNet**—Around 40,000 users during peak hours

- **Undernet**—Around 30,000 users during peak hours
- **EFnet**—Around 28,000 users during peak hours
- **Rizon**—Around 25,000 users during peak hours

Rogue Products and Search Engines

There are literally hundreds of rogue security products, such as Antivirus XP 2008/9, Antivirus Pro, and many others. They have legitimate-sounding names and GUIs but are not legitimate programs. They even have successfully hosted advertisements for short periods of time on major websites. Parked domains and manipulated search engine results and abuse can also be used to help spread malcode to computers via social engineering and exploitation. One tip is to scan files before installation with a free multiscanner like Virus-Total (`http://www.virustotal.com`) or Jotti (`http://virusscan.jotti.org/en`) to see if they are detected as malicious.

Infected Factory Builds and Media

Should you scan media for malcode? While it is a rare occurrence, some major cases of media being infected are reported every year. Infected media and computers are a possibility, especially as major changes take place in highly competitive industries with outsourced or overseas operations. Sometimes core builds of various downloads on the Internet are also hacked or compromised by bad actors, leading to malicious installations of software. Again, these cases are rarer than other vectors but do happen and are normally communicated clearly and globally when such incidents take place.

Web Exploitation Frameworks

Web exploitation frameworks are tools that include many exploits and a user interface to launch attacks against computers visiting a website. Exploit kits, also referred to as exploit packs, are a type of malware that allows hackers to exploit vulnerabilities in a given system. The packs might target vulnerabilities in programs such as Adobe Flash Player, which would allow the hacker to gain access to a system remotely by way of a web browser, or they may exploit faulty or non-existent patches in third-party applications or operating systems. Exploit kits can be downloaded for free or purchased.

There are many exploit frameworks available in the wild. A partial listing includes the following: Redkit, Crime Boss, Cool, Sweet Orange, Phoenix, Sakura, Siberia Private, g01Pack, Impact, Popads, and SofosFO. The security practitioner needs to stay up to date on what exploit frameworks are being used in the wild and how to detect their use in order to be able to defend their users and networks from attack.[37]

PAYLOADS

There are a wide range of payloads being used to deliver malcode in the wild today. In the early days, payloads were more related to fame, such as promoting an alias of a virus writing author. Early malcode often asked for permission to spread or simply spread and notified the user. Then destructive payloads followed, resulting in a loss of data. Common payloads are overviewed in this section.

Backdoor Trojans

Backdoor Trojans are malicious software programs that share the primary functionality of enabling a remote attacker to have access to or send commands to a compromised computer. These are the most dangerous, and most widespread, type of Trojan. Backdoor Trojans provide the author or "master" of the Trojan with remote administration capabilities of victim machines. Unlike legitimate remote administration utilities, they install and launch and run invisibly, without the consent or knowledge of the user. Once installed, backdoor Trojans can be instructed to send, receive, execute, and delete files; harvest confidential data from the computer; log activity on the computer; and more.

As the name suggests, these threats are used to provide a covert channel through which a remote attacker can access and control a computer. The Trojans vary in sophistication, ranging from those that only allow for limited functions to be performed to those that allow almost any action to be carried out, thus allowing the remote attacker to almost completely take over control of a computer. A computer with a sophisticated backdoor program installed may also be referred to as a *zombie* or a *bot*. A network of such bots may often be referred to as a *botnet*. Botnets have been well publicized in the news over the years, with different instances being given specific names such as Kraken, Mariposa, Kneber, Virut, ZeroAccess, and Zeus along with claims of hundreds of thousands of nodes belonging to certain networks.

Typical backdoor capabilities may allow a remote attacker to

- Collect information (system and personal) from the computer and any storage device attached to it
- Terminate tasks and processes
- Run tasks and processes
- Download additional files
- Upload files and other content
- Report on status
- Open remote command-line shells
- Perform denial-of-service attacks on other computers

- Change computer settings

- Shut down or restart the computer

Backdoor Trojan horse programs have become increasingly popular amongst malware creators over the years because of the shift in motivation from fame and glory to money and profit. In today's black market economy, a computer with a back door can be put to work performing various criminal activities that earn money for their controllers. Schemes such as pay per install, sending spam e-mails, and harvesting personal information and identities are all ways to generate revenue. The security practitioner needs to be aware of backdoor Trojans and their potential impact they can have on a network.[38]

Man-in-the-Middle Malcode

Man-in-the-middle (MITM) refers generically to any agent that is in between communications or processing and is able to influence it in some regard. It is traditionally used to describe communication flows across the Internet. With regard to malcode, it is more commonly used to describe malcode that infects a host and then plays MITM locally to manipulate traffic and events. A man-in-the-middle attack is a type of attack where a malicious actor inserts him/herself into a conversation between two parties, impersonates both parties, and gains access to information that the two parties were trying to send to each other. A man-in-the-middle attack allows a malicious actor to intercept, send, and receive data meant for someone else, or not meant to be sent at all, without either outside party knowing until it is too late. Man-in-the-middle attacks can be abbreviated in many ways, including MITM, MitM, MiM, or MIM.

Key concepts of a man-in-the-middle attack include the following:

- Man-in-the-middle is a type of eavesdropping attack that occurs when a malicious actor inserts himself as a relay/proxy into a communication session between people or systems.

- A MITM attack exploits the real-time processing of transactions, conversations, or transfer of other data.

- A man-in-the-middle attack allows an attacker to intercept, send, and receive data never meant to be for them without either outside party knowing until it is too late.

There are now phishing attacks that are controlled by malcode that are very sophisticated. In one instance the malcode monitors URLs. If it sees a URL that it targets for phishing, it sends encrypted data over TCP port 80 to a remote C&C. The remote C&C returns customized phishing data to the code in real time to display in the browser instead of the URL accessed by the end user.

Additional examples of MITM attacks have come to light through the activities of Edward Snowden. Some of the documents leaked by him show that the NSA's so-called

STORMBREW program, which involves copying Internet traffic directly off of cables as it is flowing past, is being operated with the help of a "key corporate partner" at about eight strategic locations across the United States where there is access to "international cables, routers, and switches." According to a leaked NSA map, this surveillance appears to be taking place at network junction points in Washington, Florida, Texas, at two places in California, and at three further locations in or around Virginia, New York, and Pennsylvania.

In addition to the STORMBREW program, there is evidence in leaked documents that the NSA and British counterpart/partner, the GCHQ, have directly performed a man-in-the-middle attack to impersonate Google security certificates.[39] One document, apparently taken from an NSA presentation that also contains some GCHQ slides, describes how the attack was carried out to snoop on SSL traffic. The document illustrates with a diagram how one of the agencies appears to have hacked into a target's Internet router and covertly redirected targeted Google traffic using a fake security certificate so it could intercept the information in unencrypted format. Figure 7.24 shows the diagram of the attack vector.

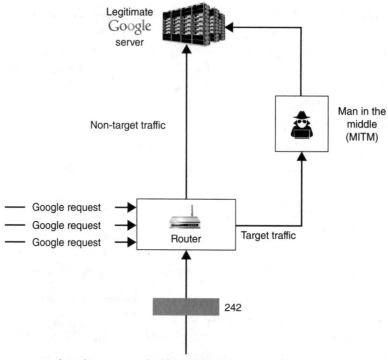

FIGURE 7.24 **Diagram of the Google MITM attack vector**

Documents from GCHQ's network exploitation unit show that it operates a program called "FLYING PIG" that was started up in response to an increasing use of SSL encryption by e-mail providers like Yahoo, Google, and Hotmail. The FLYING PIG system appears to allow it to identify information related to use of the anonymity browser Tor. FLYING PIG has the option to query Tor events and also allows spies to collect information about specific SSL encryption certificates. GCHQ's network exploitation unit boasts in one document that it is able to collect traffic not only from foreign government networks but also from airlines, energy companies, and financial organizations.

IDENTIFYING INFECTIONS

Identification of infections often takes place through network alerts or antivirus scanning results. Unfortunately, these alerts all too often do not include enough details to enable a thorough response by a security practitioner. For example, a network tool may identify a hostile IP address and sample traffic but may not include the domain or original universal resource identifier (URI). As a result the security practitioner may need to perform open source intelligence queries against the IP alone in hopes of identifying possible related malicious activity to know how to follow up on the malcode threat.

In addition, an investigation of cache data and logs from the local host may also be required to investigate a possible infection. Security practitioners need to review policies to ensure that logs are detailed enough and not deleted too quickly to empower malcode mitigation and investigations. For example, a decision to delete detected malicious code removes any samples that could have been quarantined instead and then captured for laboratory analysis.

If antivirus software on a host identifies malcode, it may only be detecting part of the incident. New private code may have been installed following the infection. A second antivirus program and specialty programs like anti-rootkit software may be required to quickly identify other binaries on the system in question. In addition, manual inspection of drive contents or mounting the drive and identifying changes to the system may be required.

There are many tools that the security practitioner may use to evaluate a system's health, as well as to monitor a system in real time. One example of a tool that can be very effective when used to establish a baseline for a system, allowing the security practitioner to understand what system files and processes are present during normal operations, is Process Explorer. The Process Explorer display consists of two subwindows. The top window always shows a list of the currently active processes, including the names of their owning accounts, whereas the information displayed in the bottom window depends on the mode that Process Explorer is in: If it is in handle mode, you'll see the handles that the process selected in the top window has opened; if Process Explorer is in DLL mode, you'll see the DLLs and memory-mapped files that the process has loaded. Process Explorer also has a powerful search capability that will quickly show you which processes have particular handles opened or DLLs loaded. The Process Explorer window lists the processes that are running in the system, along with a variety of additional information. In Figure 7.25, the properties of a specific running process, thun bird.exe, are shown. The security practitioner should take note of the various options and additional information available to them from within the properties area, such as the ability to find and verify the Path, Command Line, Current Directory, and Autostart Location for the process being examined. In addition, the ability to kill the process is also available.

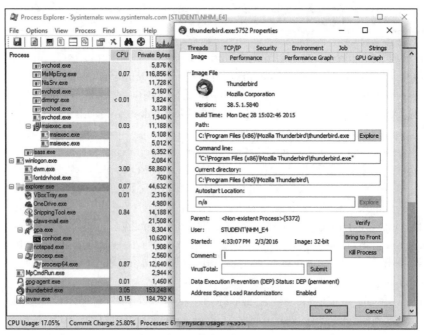

FIGURE 7.25 **Properties of a specified running process are displayed.**

Using a tool such as ProcNetMonitor, the security practitioner will be able to have visibility into what processes are running on a given machine, as well as what ports they are using to communicate. Figure 7.26 shows the information that ProcNetMonitor displays when launched. The javaw.exe process has been selected, and the resulting information displayed in the lower left and right portions of the screen show the Open Network Ports and the Active Network Connections.

Another type of tool that security practitioners should consider using is one that allows for the examination of executable files. This kind of a tool can be used to examine the internal make-up of the executable package, allowing the security practitioner to see if there is potential malware included inside of the .exe file. Figure 7.27 shows PeStudio, a Windows Image Executable Analysis tool that has been used to examine the ca_setup.exe executable (which is the installer for Cain & Able, a password cracking tool). The VirusTotal scores section has been highlighted in the left column, and the resulting information in the right column shows that 21 AV scanning engines have tagged this file as potentially having malware or malware-like components contained within it.

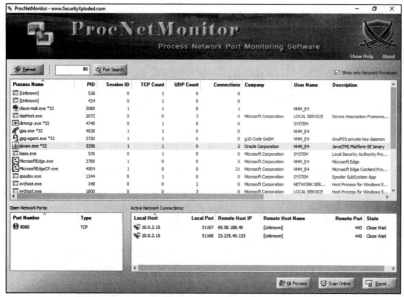

FIGURE 7.26 Information that ProcNetMonitor displays when launched

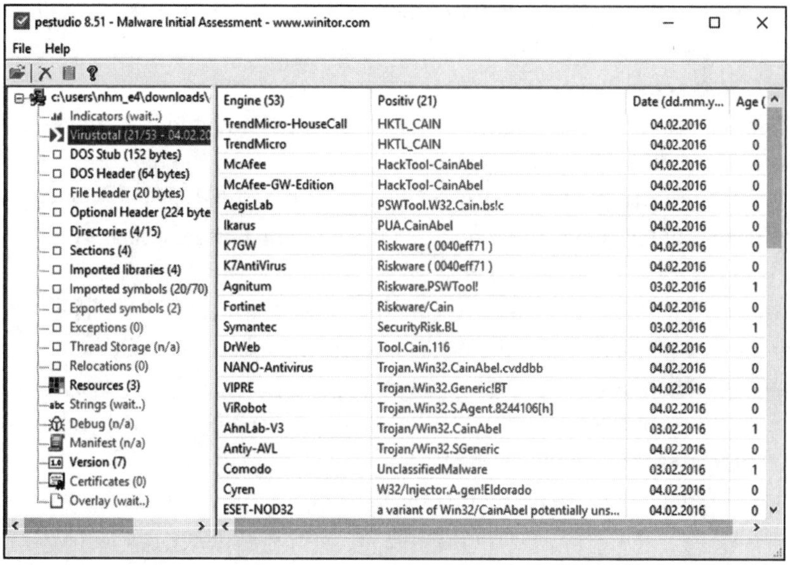

FIGURE 7.27 PeStudio, a Windows Image Executable Analysis tool that has been used to examine the ArpScan executable

An antivirus scanning engine is also a tool that the security practitioner needs to make sure that they are using in order to protect computers, as well as to validate what kind of malware may have been used to infect a specific machine.

Malicious Activity Countermeasures

A wide variety of security solutions exist to help fight malcode on multiple layers. A brief annotation of common areas of concern is outlined in this section. Configuration options of solutions like antivirus software are not covered here since that is specific to each application and policies implemented by individual organizations.

Network Layer

A large number of solutions and managed services exist for working with the network layer of an enterprise. It is very important for a security practitioner to be able to monitor and manage all network traffic across an enterprise. Best practices for managing and securing network traffic include locking down ports that are not used, encouraging the use of nonstandard ports to avoid brute-force attacks against protocols such as FTP and SSH and similar services, as well as using encryption solutions for secure traffic flows. Security practitioners also need to deploy network monitoring to identify questionable egress traffic made by hosts, such as excessive DNS requests, port scanning activities, and worm behavior related to the network. For example, if a backdoor Trojan is discovered on a computer, monitoring for egress traffic can help to identify the C&C server and activity of the code. Monitoring can take place with tools such as Advanced Port Scanner, which maps open ports per host; Open Ports Scanner for mapping processes to ports on a specific host; as well as network solutions like Snort, which can capture network traffic between multiple hosts across a network.

Figure 7.28 shows Advanced Port Scanner being used to scan an IP address range. A security practitioner can use this tool to examine a range of hosts over the network and establish which ports are open per host and, as a result, can understand several things about the hosts being profiled, such as O/S type, services running on the host, as well as unusual traffic patterns based on ports in use.

Figure 7.29 shows TCPView being used to view the network status of a host. The detailed output shows the Process, PID, Protocol, Local Address, Local Port, Remote Address, Remote Port, State, and packet counters for all active processes. A security practitioner can use this tool to examine a single host in depth, gaining detailed understanding of what processes are running on the host, what port they are connecting from, and where they are connecting to. This information can help to uncover if there is malware running on the host, and if so, what ports it may be using to interact with its C&C infrastructure.

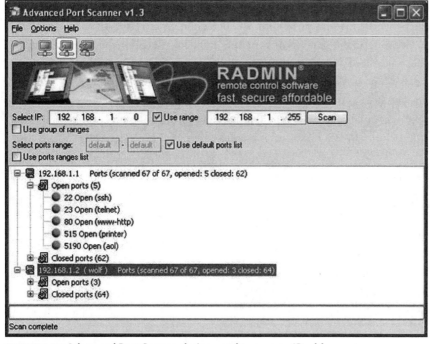

FIGURE 7.28 Advanced Port Scanner being used to scan an IP address range

Process	PID	Protocol	Local Address	Local Port	Remote Address	Remote Port	State	Sent Packe
dasHost.exe	2072	UDP	STUDENT	ws-discovery	*	*		
dasHost.exe	2072	UDP	STUDENT	ws-discovery	*	*		
dasHost.exe	2072	UDP	STUDENT	52996	*	*		
dasHost.exe	2072	UDPV6	student	3702	*	*		
dasHost.exe	2072	UDPV6	student	3702	*	*		
dasHost.exe	2072	UDPV6	student	52997	*	*		
dirmngr.exe	4748	TCP	STUDENT	49739	STUDENT	0	LISTENING	
explorer.exe	2600	TCP	student.globalkno...	54505	195.138.255.27	http	ESTABLISHED	
explorer.exe	2600	TCP	student.globalkno...	54506	195.138.255.27	http	ESTABLISHED	
explorer.exe	2600	TCP	student.globalkno...	54508	a23-60-201-168.d...	http	ESTABLISHED	
explorer.exe	2600	TCP	student.globalkno...	54509	195.138.255.27	http	ESTABLISHED	
gpg-agent.exe	3720	TCP	STUDENT	49753	STUDENT	0	LISTENING	
lsass.exe	536	TCP	STUDENT	49675	STUDENT	0	LISTENING	
lsass.exe	536	TCPV6	student	49675	student	0	LISTENING	
SearchUI.exe	5232	TCP	student.globalkno...	52079	a-0001.a-msedge....	https	CLOSE_WAIT	
services.exe	528	TCP	STUDENT	49668	STUDENT	0	LISTENING	
services.exe	528	TCPV6	student	49668	student	0	LISTENING	
spoolsv.exe	1244	TCP	STUDENT	49667	STUDENT	0	LISTENING	
spoolsv.exe	1244	TCPV6	student	49667	student	0	LISTENING	
svchost.exe	648	TCP	STUDENT	epmap	STUDENT	0	LISTENING	
svchost.exe	856	TCP	STUDENT	49665	STUDENT	0	LISTENING	
svchost.exe	824	TCP	STUDENT	49666	STUDENT	0	LISTENING	
svchost.exe	872	UDP	student.globalkno...	ssdp	*	*		
svchost.exe	872	UDP	STUDENT	ssdp	*	*		
svchost.exe	1000	UDP	STUDENT	ws-discovery	*	*		

Endpoints: 58   Established: 4   Listening: 21   Time Wait: 0   Close Wait: 1

FIGURE 7.29 Open Ports scanner being used to scan a single host

Figure 7.30 shows Snort being initialized and set up to run on a host. Snort is an open source network intrusion prevention and detection system (IDS/IPS) developed by Sourcefire. Combining the benefits of signature, protocol, and anomaly-based inspection, Snort has become a tool that security practitioners are very likely to come across in the enterprise today. The security practitioner should have a working knowledge of Snort and a familiarity with how to install, set up, and configure Snort for basic network monitoring. There is a set of detailed step-by-step guides that walk through the process of configuring a Snort solution for both Windows and Linux-based installations.

```
Administrator: Command Prompt - snort -v -i1                                    –   □

C:\Snort\bin>snort -v -i1
Running in packet dump mode

        --== Initializing Snort ==--
Initializing Output Plugins!
pcap DAQ configured to passive.
The DAQ version does not support reload.
Acquiring network traffic from "\Device\NPF_{396BDAC5-5435-4AF9-A7ED-FBFF36B02813}".
Decoding Ethernet

        --== Initialization Complete ==--

      ,,_         -*> Snort! <*-
     o"  )~       Version 2.9.8.0-WIN32 GRE (Build 229)
      ''''        By Martin Roesch & The Snort Team: http://www.snort.org/contact#team
                  Copyright (C) 2014-2015 Cisco and/or its affiliates. All rights reserved.
                  Copyright (C) 1998-2013 Sourcefire, Inc., et al.
                  Using PCRE version: 8.10 2010-06-25
                  Using ZLIB version: 1.2.3

Commencing packet processing (pid=5252)
█
                                                           Activate Windows
```

FIGURE 7.30 **Snort being initialized and set up to run on a host**

All of the relevant Snort documentation can be found at `https://www.snort.org/documents`. The landing page for setting up a Snort solution in a Windows environment can be found at `http://www.winsnort.com/`.

Deep-analysis capabilities are also required to help identify and mitigate code. For example, if an incident takes place, the security practitioner may benefit greatly from having a PCAP file of how the malcode functions within a laboratory environment. That information can then be used to develop custom Snort signatures or similar solutions across the network. Security practitioners can work with intelligence agencies like iSIGHT Partners to acquire support for malcode incidents of interest and the deep data required to develop Snort signatures or coordinate managed security service provider (MSSP).[40] An MSSP is an Internet service provider (ISP) that provides an organization with some amount of network security management, which may include virus blocking, spam blocking, intrusion detection, firewalls, and virtual private network (VPN) management. An MSSP can also handle system changes, modifications, and upgrades.

Application Layer

The security practitioner will need to ensure that some form of antivirus software is being deployed and used throughout the enterprise. There are two main methods that are used to search for and detect viruses and malcode. The first is signature detection. A signature is a string of bits found in a virus. An effective signature is the string of bits that is commonly found in viruses but not likely to be found in normal programs. Generally, each virus has its own unique signature. All known signatures are organized in a database. A signature-based virus detection tool searches for a known signature in all the files on a system. The second method used is heuristic analysis. Heuristic analysis is useful in detecting new or unknown viruses. Heuristic analysis can be static or dynamic. Static heuristics mainly analyze the file format and the code structure of the virus body. Dynamic heuristics use code emulators to detect unusual behavior while the virus code is running inside the emulator.

Heuristics, if properly employed, can improve detection by 7–10%. There are several different types of heuristic analysis that may be deployed by an antivirus software engine, as noted here:

File Emulation   Also known as sandbox testing or dynamic scanning, file emulation allows the file to run in a controlled virtual system, or sandbox, to see what it does. If the file acts like a virus, it's deemed a virus.

File Analysis   File analysis involves the software taking an in-depth look at the file and trying to determine its intent, destination, and purpose. Perhaps the file has instructions to delete certain files, to format a hard drive, or to replace certain files with altered versions containing the malcode itself, and as a result it should be considered a virus.

Genetic Signature Detection   This technique is particularly designed to locate variations of viruses. Several viruses are re-created and make themselves known by a variety of names, but they essentially come from the same family, or classification. Genetic detection uses previous antivirus definitions to locate these similar "cousins" even if they use a slightly different name or include some unusual characters.[41]

In order to deploy a robust antivirus solution, the security practitioner should use a multilayered approach that is part of a greater enterprise security plan. For example, use one anti-virus engine on the gateway and another on the host. This greatly improves the chances of detecting the malcode since one single antivirus solution is limited to its unique detection capabilities. Two or more layers of antivirus protection help to improve overall detection and mitigation rates.

Third-Party Certifications

To identify what will be an appropriate antivirus solution, the security practitioner will need to do some research. First, identify those solutions that provide the type of centralized management and options required to fulfill the needs of the enterprise. It is then appropriate to consider demonstrations of products as well as reviewing third-party certifi-cations of antivirus software. Several reliable third-party certification sources exist online:

- **AV-Test.org:** `http://www.av-test.org/`
- **Virus Bulletin VB100 Awards:** `http://www.virusbtn.com/vb100/index`

Look for consistency in certifications. Those that regularly obtain certification are generally considered more robust for functionality than those that do not. One of the challenges is how samples are acquired and then used in tests performed by such agen-cies. One of the key components of this historically is what is known as the Wildlist.

The Wildlist

Malcode that actually infects a computer is considered "in the wild," in loose terms. This is different from proof-of-concept (POC) code that may exist only within a laboratory environment or some new code created by an author but not launched against a victim. The technical definition for malcode in the wild is derived from a group known as the Wildlist. The Wildlist maintains a website at `http://www.wildlist.org/`. When two or more Wildlist reporters, experts in the industry, submit the same code, it is considered "in the Wild." A monthly Wild list is published, and samples are shared among WildCore participants for testing and analysis.

Questionable Behavior on a Computer

Questionable behavior may indicate many things, including possible malicious behavior.

Pop-Ups

Pop-ups are one of the most common issues that users will report to a help desk. Take, for example, ad/spyware warnings like the one in Figure 7.31.

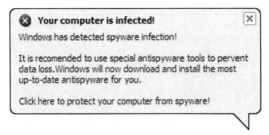

FIGURE 7.31 **Pop-up message**

The pop-up shown in Figure 7.31 is a common message that will appear on a com-puter, and if an unsuspecting user has not been given the proper security awareness train-ing, they may very well choose to follow the instruction to "click here" and infect their machine with spyware. This is where research is required to follow up on such threat reports by end users. The security practitioner would need to be aware of the issue being reported by the end user and then be able to quarantine the computer in order to examine it and uncover whatever malcode may have been installed onto the machine. Figure 7.32 shows two tools that the security practitioner may use to detect malware that has been installed on a targeted computer. Programs such as Malwarebytes and CCleaner can be used to detect malware that is running on a system under investigation. CCleaner is also able to examine and report on what programs have been installed and set to run at startup on the computer.

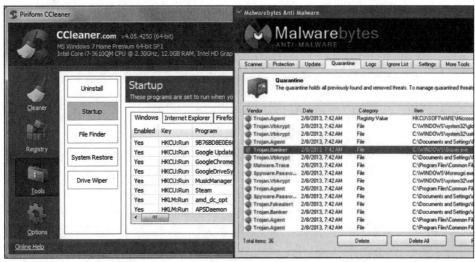

FIGURE 7.32 Two tools that the security practitioner may use to detect malware that has been installed on a targeted computer

Degraded Performance

Degraded performance can happen for many reasons, such as memory-handling issues within the OS, the need to work with large and complex files that are graphic intensive, or incorrect hardware or software settings. If a *noticeable* change in performance takes place, it may be worthwhile for the security practitioner to investigate egress traffic on a computer as well as look at performance and process information on the host. This may lead to an investigation to discover an injected rootkit and malicious process or perhaps just optimization of the computer.

Modified HOSTS File and DNS Changes

Malicious code may modify the HOSTS file to block or redirect traffic on the host. The HOSTS file is located in the Windows\System32\Drivers\ETC directory. It normally has just a few entries, like the sample here showing a printer, Exchange, and a shared drive for VPN access:

```
127.0.0.1         localhost
::1               localhost
HP001635578986    HP001635578986
10.1.100.5        exchange.local
192.168.155.5     SharedDrive
```

However, if it has additional entries that point to questionable content or loopback, it may indicate a malicious code infection. The data here is from an actual HOSTS-related file infected with malcode:

```
0.0.0.0    avp.ch
0.0.0.0    avp.com
0.0.0.0    avp.ru
0.0.0.0    avast.com
```

The previous changes block access to known antivirus domains such as AVP.ch and others. They are redirected to 0.0.0.0, which goes nowhere.

Also, the security practitioner needs to be on guard for changes to the DNS server(s) used by the client. Some malicious codes now change the DNS server to point to a remote rogue server that then acts as an MITM to monitor or manipulate traffic from the infected host.

Inspection of Processes

Inspection of processes on a computer can be very time-consuming and difficult. First, a security practitioner needs to have a baseline of what should be expected on the computer per the enterprise build for that type of host. Then, processes such as Explorer.exe can be looked for in the Windows Task Manager. If a program like Explorer.exe, which renders the Windows GUI for the desktop used by a user, is not visible, it is likely that it is being hidden by a Windows rootkit, as this process should always be visible when viewed via the Windows Task Manager under normal operating conditions.

The more traditional approach to looking for malcode in processes is to look for new processes taking up lots of memory or finding a new or unexpected process in the list of running processes. Programs like Process Explorer help the analyst to dive deep into the code, terminate it, and perform actions not possible from within Windows Task Manager.[42]

Other programs such as EnCase Enterprise include a response component that enables the security practitioner to log in remotely to any host within the network.[43] EnCase then includes MD5 solutions to quickly identify known good (whitelisted) processes, known malicious processes, and those that are in question (unknown). EnCase also includes its own anti-rootkit process that helps subvert such threats. This provides the security practitioner an excellent remote view into what needs to be looked at on a system, possibly captured, and then analyzed for malicious behavior.

Inspection of the Windows Registry

Security practitioners can create Perl scripts to audit a network for possible malicious changes to the Windows registry on hosts of a network. This is a very efficient way to quickly identify any questionable or known malicious entries that may exist in the traditional AutoRun areas of the Windows registry, such as HKLM\SOFTWARE\Microsoft\Windows\CurrentVersion\Run and RunOnce.

Run and RunOnce registry keys cause programs to run each time that a user logs on. The data value for a key is a command line. Register programs to run by adding entries of the form description-string=commandline. You can write multiple entries under a key. If more than one program is registered under any particular key, the order in which those programs run is indeterminate.

The Windows registry includes the following four keys:

- HKEY_LOCAL_MACHINE\Software\Microsoft\Windows\CurrentVersion\Run
- HKEY_CURRENT_USER\Software\Microsoft\Windows\CurrentVersion\Run
- HKEY_LOCAL_MACHINE\Software\Microsoft\Windows\CurrentVersion\RunOnce
- HKEY_CURRENT_USER\Software\Microsoft\Windows\CurrentVersion\RunOnce

By default, the value of a RunOnce key is deleted before the command line is run. You can prefix a RunOnce value name with an exclamation point (!) to defer deletion of the value until after the command runs. Without the exclamation point prefix, if the RunOnce operation fails, the associated program will not be asked to run the next time you start the computer.

By default, these keys are ignored when the computer is started in safe mode. The value name of RunOnce keys can be prefixed with an asterisk (*) to force the program to run even in safe mode. Run and RunOnce keys are run each time a new user logs in.

How to Do It for Yourself: Installing Strawberry Perl in Windows 7 or Windows 8

Perl is a programming language suitable for writing simple scripts as well as complex applications. For more information, see `http://www.perl.org`.

Strawberry Perl is a Perl environment for Microsoft Windows containing everything needed to run and develop Perl applications. It is designed to be as close as possible to the Perl environment on UNIX systems. It includes Perl binaries, compiler (gcc) +

related tools, all the external libraries (crypto, graphics, XML . . .), as well as all the bundled database clients.

Security practitioners should be familiar with scripting languages and how to install and use them in different operating systems.

1. Download the latest version from `http://strawberryperl.com`.

2. Execute the installer by double-clicking the .msi file
   (e.g., `strawberry-perl-5.20.1.1.msi`), and follow the setup wizard.

3. By default, the installer creates the `C:\strawberry` directory and extracts all of its contents there. Installing Perl elsewhere is fine, but the README warns that whatever path you decide to install into needs to have directory names free of spaces (i.e., `C:\isc2 sscp\perl\bin\` is bad).

4. Next, open a command prompt and switch into whatever directory you installed perl into. Type `perl -v`, hit Enter, and you should get the version info.

5. To create an association between the .pl file extension and Strawberry Perl, do the following:

   a. Open Notepad and copy in the following code (line numbers are added simply for reference):

   ```
   1 Windows Registry Editor Version 6.2
   2
   3 [HKEY_LOCAL_MACHINE\SOFTWARE\Classes\.pl\shell\open\Command]
   4 @="\"C:\\strawberry\\perl\\bin\\perl.exe\" \"%1\" %*"
   ```

   b. Save the file to the desktop with a .reg extension.

   c. Double-click it to make it apply the appropriate changes to the Registry.

6. Now, it is time to create a test script. In Notepad, type the following (line numbers are added simply for reference):

   ```
   1 print "Hello, World!\n";
   ```

   When you are done typing, save the file as `script.pl` and in the command prompt `cd` to the directory in which it was saved. Type `perl script.pl` and you should see "Hello, World!" on the screen.

Security practitioners can see the following websites for information and research into Perl:

- `http://www.perl.com/`
- `http://learn.perl.org/`
- `http://www.perlmonks.org/?`

When you are dealing with known questionable or malicious executables, a manual search of the Windows registry can be very useful. Simply type **regedit** into the Start ⇨ Run location on a Windows computer to pull up the Windows registry editor program. Then, use the Edit menu to perform a find for the executable name of interest. Press F3 to move to the next instance, quickly searching the entire Windows registry.

Tools such as Autoruns, cports, and HiJack This! are excellent freeware programs that may also be useful in quickly identifying autostart entries.

Since the functionality of Windows registry keys are often not known or well documented, one must perform queries on the Internet or within various Windows registry guides to identify what the role of a specific entry may be. For example, if one enters a suspect key into an Internet search engine and gets back many replies related to malicious code, a quick review may highly suggest a malicious entry for the host computer being investigated. Once this can be correlated back to a specific code, the security practitioner can then look for files of interest, capture, and qualify the threat in a laboratory environment.

Inspection of Common File Locations

A manual inspection of files is also helpful, but it can be subverted by Windows rootkits that may conceal files. Malicious code changes are typically performed in the Windows and Windows System32 directories.[44] Files are also frequently stored in temporary Internet locations, the user directory, and the root directory of the drive (C:\). It is also common to find files stored within a Windows\System32 subdirectory, such as drivers or a custom directory created by the malcode.

A rootkit is a program that takes fundamental control (in Unix terms "root" access, in Windows terms "Administrator" access) of a computer, often without authorization by the computer's owner. When a rootkit is present on a system, it has the ability to conceal files from the end user. As a result, the end user will typically not be aware of the rootkit's presence in the system. Therefore, it is up to the security practitioner to be able to detect and remove malware such as rootkits. The following discussion is meant to represent a high-level overview of what malware removal from a Windows-based system would be like for the security practitioner. The tools discussed are samples of tools that are available for use, and they are not the only tools available. The circumstances of each infection or outbreak are unique, and as such, the security practitioner will need to assess the situation and choose the most appropriate tools to use based on the circumstances involved.

Some forms of malware will not allow removal utilities and tools to be started while Windows is running normally. As a result, the security practitioner may need to restart Windows in Safe Mode with Networking. It is always a good idea to first attempt to detect and remove malware while the computer is running under normal conditions and only as a secondary option to use safe mode to run detection and removal tools.

To start a computer in Safe Mode with Networking, follow these steps:

1. Remove all floppy disks, CDs, and DVDs and then restart the computer.

2. For Windows XP, Vista, or Windows 7, press and hold the F8 key as the computer restarts. Please keep in mind that you need to press the F8 key before the Windows startup logo appears.

NOTE With some computers, pressing and holding a key as the computer is booting will generate a stuck key message. If this occurs, instead of pressing and holding the F8 key, tap the F8 key continuously until the Advanced Boot Options screen appears. For Windows 8, press the Windows key + C, and then click Settings. Click Power, hold down Shift on the keyboard, and click Restart; then, click Troubleshoot and select Advanced Options.

---

3. In the Advanced Options screen, select Startup Settings, and then click Restart.

4. For Windows XP, Vista, or Windows 7 in the Advanced Boot Options screen, use the arrow keys to highlight Safe Mode with Networking, and then press Enter. For Windows 8, press 5 on the keyboard to Enable Safe Mode with Networking.

Once you have enabled/entered Safe Mode with Networking, then you will need to engage in a process similar to that outlined next, depending on the nature and extent of the problem being addressed.

WARNING The tools discussed here are simply being named and discussed for illustrative purposes to lay out the methodology that the security practitioner would need to follow in general to attempt to clean an infected system. The security practitioner needs to decide which tools would be the best and most effective to use based on the circumstances of the situation that they are addressing in real time.

---

1. **Remove Any Master Boot Record Infections**—As part of their self defense mechanisms, some types of malware will install a rootkit on the infected computer, which will compromise the Windows loading process. In this first step, the security practitioner would run a system scan with Kaspersky TDSSKiller to remove this type of rootkit if present. [45]

2. **Run RKill to Terminate Any Malicious Processes**—RKill is a program that will attempt to terminate all malicious processes that are running on the computer. Because this utility will only stop running processes and does not delete any files,

after running it the security practitioner should not reboot the computer, as any malware processes that are configured to start automatically will just be started up again. In this step, the security practitioner would double-click `iExplore.exe` to start RKill. RKill runs as a working process in the background, and it may take a while to finish, depending on the amount of malware present in a system.[46]

3. **Remove Trojans and Other Malicious Software Using Malwarebytes Anti-Malware**—Malwarebytes Anti-Malware software can detect and remove traces of malware including worms, trojans, rootkits, rogues, dialers, spyware, and more.[47] In this step, the security practitioner would run one of three possible scans on the target computer, or some combination of them, in order to establish what types of malware may be present in the computer. The scans available are shown in Figure 7.33. Once the scans have been successfully run against the computer, then the security practitioner would be presented with a list of the detected malware, as well as mitigation options, as shown in Figure 7.34.

4. **Remove Additional Rootkits with HitmanPro**—HitmanPro is a "second opinion" scanner, designed to disinfect a computer that has been infected with malware despite the security measures that may have been applied prior to running the scanner. In this step, the security practitioner would scan the computer with HitmanPro to establish what malware may still remain resident and active on the computer and then mitigate what is found through whatever actions are appropriate. [48]

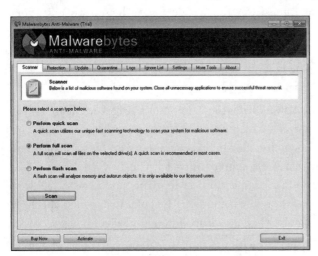

FIGURE 7.33 **Scan types available in tool**

FIGURE 7.34 **A list of the detected malware, as well as mitigation options**

5. **Remove Malicious Registry Keys Added by Malware with RogueKiller**— Malware often modifies the registry of the computer it infects in order to successfully run. Using software such as RogueKiller allows the security practitioner to search for, find, and, if needed, mitigate modified registry keys.[49] In this step, the security practitioner would scan the computer using RogueKiller and then would choose which modified registry keys to delete based on the output of the scan, as shown in Figure 7.35.

6. **Remove Malicious Adware from the Computer Using AdwCleaner**—The Adw-Cleaner utility will scan the computer and browsers for adware files and registry keys that may have been installed on the computer.[50] In this step, the security practitioner would scan the computer using AdwCleaner and then would choose which selected items in the Folders, Files, Shortcuts, and Registry tabs that they would want to remove from the computer. The items that are left checked are removed by the program when the clean button is selected.

7. **Remove Browser Hijackers with the Junkware Removal Tool**—The Junkware Removal Tool is a powerful utility, which will remove malware within Internet Explorer, Firefox, or Google Chrome, on a computer.[51] The Junkware Removal Tool runs from a command prompt and requires the security practitioner to press a key in order to perform the scan of the computer, as Figure 7.36 shows. Once

the security practitioner runs the scan, removal of the malware found during the scan is automated, and a log will be created showing what malicious files and registry keys were removed from the computer.

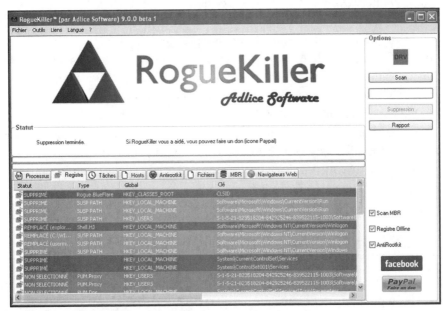

FIGURE 7.35 Modified registry keys shown as output of scan

FIGURE 7.36 Prompt for the security practitioner to press a key to start the scan

Once the security practitioner has completed the previous steps, there will still be a need to monitor the computer to ensure that the malware has been successfully removed and has not returned upon reboot or managed to re-infect the computer due to user interaction. The security practitioner should consider using combinations of tools in an ongoing effort to monitor and maintain the health of the computer proactively once the initial malware infections have been mitigated and removed.

In addition, the security practitioner should also consider the use of a host-based intrusion detection system (HIDS) that will allow for a broad and centralized monitoring and integration with a security incident management/security events management (SIM/SIEM) solution. OSSEC is an open source host-based intrusion detection system that performs log analysis, file integrity checking, policy monitoring, rootkit detection, real-time alerting, and active response. It runs on most operating systems, including Linux, MacOS, Solaris, HP-UX, AIX, and Windows. OSSEC is composed of multiple pieces. It has a central manager monitoring everything and receiving information from agents, syslog, databases, and from agentless devices.[52] There are also managed security services that the security practitioner should consider as a possible solution, depending on the nature and scope of the systems under management. Dell SecureWorks provides an array of managed security services for businesses including a Managed Advanced Malware Protection service.[53] Symantec also provides managed security services, as does Solutionary, among others.[54]

BEHAVIORAL ANALYSIS OF MALCODE

In order for the security practitioner to begin to analyze malcode samples, a test system must be in place to properly analyze malcode behavior. This system should contain a known set of applications, processes, and tools that establish a behavioral baseline. Changes to the system can then be identified manually as well as through various tools useful in the behavioral analysis of malcode. It is important to remind the security practitioner that they must perform their work carefully so as to not bridge networking and spread a threat into the wild. In addition, any laboratory computer used for malcode analysis should be separated from the normal network to avoid any possible contamination or unwanted impact, such as a network worm attempting to exploit or spread to other computers on the network. One tool that the security practitioner can use to analyze suspected malware on a test machine is SysAnalyzer, created by David Zimmer of iDefense Labs.[55] SysAnalyzer is an automated malcode run-time analysis application that monitors various aspects of system and process states. SysAnalyzer was designed to enable analysts to quickly build a comprehensive report as to the actions a binary takes on a system. SysAnalyzer can automatically monitor and compare

- Running processes
- Open ports
- Loaded drivers
- Injected libraries

- Key registry changes
- APIs called by a target process
- File modifications
- HTTP, IRC, and DNS traffic

The main components of SysAnalyzer work off of comparing snapshots of the system over a user specified time interval. The reason a snapshot mechanism was used compared to a live logging implementation is to reduce the amount of data that analysts must wade through when conducting their analysis. When a snapshot system is used, only the persistent changes found on the system since the application was first run are presented to the analyst for examination. When first run, SysAnalyzer will present the user with the configuration wizard, as shown in Figure 7.37; the executable path textbox represents the file under analysis.

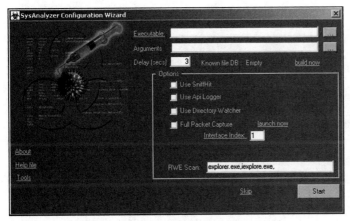

FIGURE 7.37 **Configuration Wizard for SysAnalyzer tool**

The user can specify the following options to be used for the analysis:

- **Delay**—Time in seconds between before and after snapshots
- **Sniff Hit**—Whether to launch a specialized HTTP/IRC sniffer for analysis
- **API Logger**—Whether to inject an API logging DLL into the target
- **Directory Watcher**—Whether to monitor filesystem for all file creation activities

NOTE   SysAnalyzer is not a sandboxing utility. Target executables are run in a fully live test on the system. If you are testing malicious code, you must realize you will be infecting your test system.

SysAnalyzer is designed to take snapshots of the following system attributes:

- Running processes
- Open ports and associated process
- DLLs loaded into `explorer.exe` and Internet Explorer
- System drivers loaded into the kernel
- Snapshots of certain registry keys

Each logged category is stored on its own tab in the main interface. The report link to the bottom right of the main interface will arrange all of this log data and place it into a series of simple text reports for the analyst to view. Figure 7.38 shows one of the associated tools available with SysAnalyzer, called sniff_hit, which scans a selected network interface, capturing and recording traffic across that interface, as well as the associated IP addresses being used and DNS resolution requests being made during the active capture session.

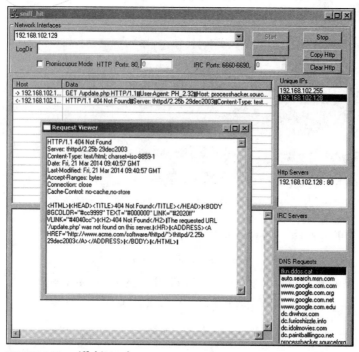

FIGURE 7.38 **sniff_hit tool**

Static File Analysis

Static file analysis is where it all begins for the security practitioner who is looking to analyze malcode. This involves looking at file details and characteristics, as well as using a hexadecimal editor, to properly identify and investigate the suspect code. The security practitioner will need to find an appropriate hex editor for whatever OS platform they are conducting analysis on. The following is a partial list of hex editors for the Windows, Mac, and Linux OS platforms:

- **wxHexEditor** is built specifically for dealing with large files, supporting up to 2^{64} bytes. It is available for all three platforms.[56]
- **DHEX** is built for Linux and Mac OS X.[57]
- **XVI32** is a freeware hex editor running under Windows 9x/NT/2000/XP/Vista/7.[58]
- **Hex Fiend** is an open source hex editor for Mac OS X.[59]
- **Hex Edit** is available for the Microsoft Windows platform.[60]

Figure 7.39 shows the Hex Edit tool being used to examine the `winhex.exe` file. The security practitioner should examine all suspect `.exe` files using a hex editor to establish whether or not the file has been modified, and whether or not there are suspicious items contained within the file that could indicate the presence of malware.

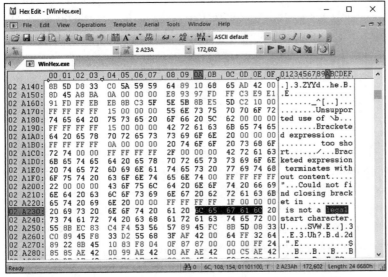

FIGURE 7.39 **Hex Edit tool being used to examine the** `winhex.exe` **file**

File Properties

File properties can be useful in correlating a sample to related samples or data on mal-code of interest. For example, a specific threat may have a static file size or average size related to codes spread by the threat. The security practitioner can correlate the file sizes to identify if it may be related or not. More importantly, exact details about the file may help identify other computers infected with a different filename but similar file size, or modified or created time values. For example, if a worm infected a system on a specific date and time, that information may help correlate network and host logs or manual inspection of targeted computers to look for similar changes around the same date and time on other computers within the network.

Some malcode modify the MAC times (modification, access, and creation times). This can hinder discovery during an incident. For example, when one is looking for changes to a system at a specified time, the modified time is the default value displayed in Windows. If the modified time is changed by the malcode to be something fairly old, it will not show up at the top of the modified time listing when sorted. This is an easy and highly effective way for malcode to subvert code identification by time stamps alone. For this reason, all MAC times should be looked at carefully when attempting to find code that may have infected a system at a specific point in time.

Behavioral tests can also be performed on code, and then a directory dump and difference analysis can be performed to identify what is different pre- and post-installation of the code to identify what is new on the system. Realize, though, that if a Windows rootkit is involved, the post-infection directory dump must be done from a disk mount or boot disk rather than from within the infected operating system itself.

Hash

Hash values, such as MD5 and SHA1, are a cryptographic function used to calculate a unique value for a file. Even a minor change in 1 byte of a file results in a new hash value. Many freeware tools are available to calculate the hash value, such as HashCalc for Windows.[61] In addition, malcode experts are moving toward naming binaries by MD5 values for large malcode archives. If two binaries have the same hash value, they are exactly the same! There are ways to subvert hash systems, but this is not common nor should it be considered a major problem for a security practitioner attempting to identify and correlate malcode binaries of interest.

Portable Executables Header

Portable executables (PE files) for Windows 32- and 64-bit systems have a header that can tell the security practitioner much about the file. Tools such as PEiD help the analyst to identify what type of file and packer is being analyzed.[62] Such tools may also include the EntryPoint, File Offset, EP Section, TimeDateStamp data, and other information useful in initiating reverse engineering of a binary. Figure 7.40 shows PEiD being used to examine the `streams.exe` file.

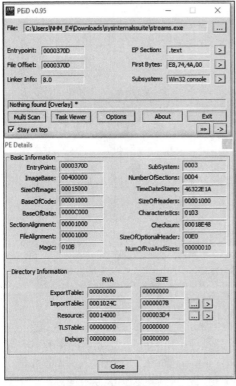

FIGURE 7.40 PEiD being used to examine the `streams.exe` file

String Analysis

A string analysis can be performed on both packed and unpacked files. Strings provide clues to the functionality and various system calls made by code. Comments within the original source code may also be visible in part helping to explain actor attribution or other functionality. Performing a string analysis on packed and unpacked files, including memory captures, may provide many clues, as shown in Figure 7.41.

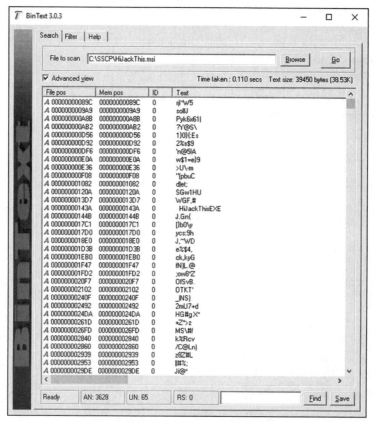

FIGURE 7.41 **A string analysis performed on a packed file**

In Figure 7.41, notice the line numbered 00000000143A lists the string "HiJackThisEXE." This helps to further validate that the binary is indeed an executable. Then, notice that the other listed strings in this file are seemingly random. This string dump does not reveal much because the binary is still packed (i.e., compressed) with UPX. However, if it is unpacked, notice how the strings change, as shown in Figure 7.42.

Strings are very useful to the reverse engineer who understands how to correlate seemingly cryptic data to what one sees while disassembling malcode. The security practitioner can look for common signs of infection, common system calls of interest, URLs, and other data used for initial triage. If detailed string files are captured by the security practitioner, they can then be shared with a reverse engineer to facilitate a deeper analysis of the malcode.

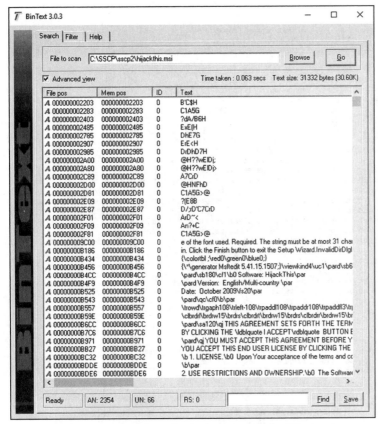

FIGURE 7.42 A string analysis performed on an unpacked file

Hex Editors

There are both freeware and commercial hex editors available that will allow the security practitioner to look at the binary contents of a file. When you are using a hex editor, the information displayed may look confusing at first glance until you know what to look for. The first few characters identify the true file type, irrespective of the extension assigned to the Windows filename. Figure 7.43 shows what should be seen when working with a Windows binary: an MZ header right at the top of the screen. The string of characters 4D 5A on the left is the representation of the MZ header.

Further down towards the bottom of the picture, the file has the string "UPX," indicating that it is likely packed with UPX. This is useful information for the security practitioner that would help them to understand what tools should be used to unpack the file successfully.

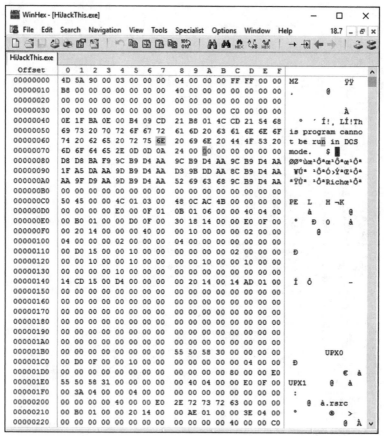

FIGURE 7.43 An MZ header in a Windows binary file

Unpacking Files and Memory Dumps

A simple explanation of software packers, or compression, is that symbols are used to represent repeated patterns in the software code. A packed file can contain malware, and unless your antivirus product knows how to unpack the file, the malware will not be detected. That would seem to be the end of the story, except that we have something called run-time packers. Here is how they work. The packed file is an executable program that is only partially packed. A tiny bit of the program is not packed. The beginning of the program is not packed, so when the packed executable is run, it starts unpacking the rest of the file. The unpacker tool is built right in.

Runtime packers are used by malware authors because it makes it much harder to detect the malware. Antivirus vendors use heuristic technologies that create a virtual computer inside the scanning engine and then run the program inside the virtualized environment. This can force a run-time packed program to unpack itself; there is always a catch, though. The malware programmer can make the program detect that it is running in a virtual environment, and then the program may not unpack itself or may only unpack harmless parts of itself to fool the virus scanning program.

In order to prevent the reverse engineering of a malicious software program and to hinder the analysis of the program's behavior, malware developers may compress or pack their malicious programs using a variety of methods combined with file encryption. Antivirus programs can detect the results of the actions of suspicious packers.

The main features that differentiate behaviors in the suspicious packers subclass are the type and number of packers used in the file compression process. The suspicious packers subclass of malware includes the following behaviors:

- **Suspicious Packer**—Objects that have been compressed, using packers that are designed to protect malicious code against detection by antivirus products
- **MultiPacked**—Files that have been packed several times, using a variety of packers
- **Rare Packer**—Files that have been compressed by packers that are rarely encountered—for example, packers that demonstrate a proof of concept

Unpacking files can be a difficult process involving some patching of the files that have been captured. It may also result in the accidental execution of a binary, so it should always be done within a safe test environment to avoid accidental execution of code on a production machine. Unpacking files first involves trying to identify what program or tool the code was packed with, such as UPX, MEW, or PESpin, which are all free.[63] There are also commercially licensed packer programs available such as EXECryptor, VMProtect, and SoftwarePassport (using the armadillo protection engine). In the case of UPX, the security practitioner would need to run the command `upx -d filename`, where `-d` is for decompress and `filename` is the name of the file. Of course, UPX has a variety of other commands and options that can be used as well. Figure 7.44 shows the UPX interface. At the top of the figure is the usage information. Below this are the core commands that can be used, which deal with compressing, decompressing, and displaying important data. Underneath the commands, you can see a useful array of options to modify these commands further.

WARNING   Locating a packer and unpacker online may result in the security practitioner traveling to high-risk areas of the Internet, such as crack sites and hacker zines. It is important to always run such tools in a test environment, since they may harbor malcode themselves and cannot be trusted. Some packers are very difficult to work with, requiring more creative efforts in unpacking or capturing code from memory.

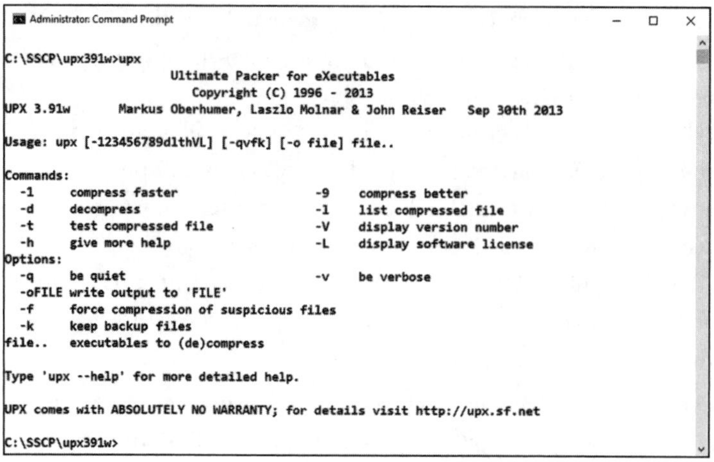

FIGURE 7.44 **UPX tool interface**

Memory dumps can be performed with tools like OllyDbg.[64] Figure 7.45 shows a memory dump performed with OllyDbg's Memory Viewer. Memory dumps are not as good as unpacked binaries and are certainly better than nothing when it comes to analyzing samples. A strong reverse engineer can typically decipher how a program uses or abuses memory using this and a variety of other advanced techniques.

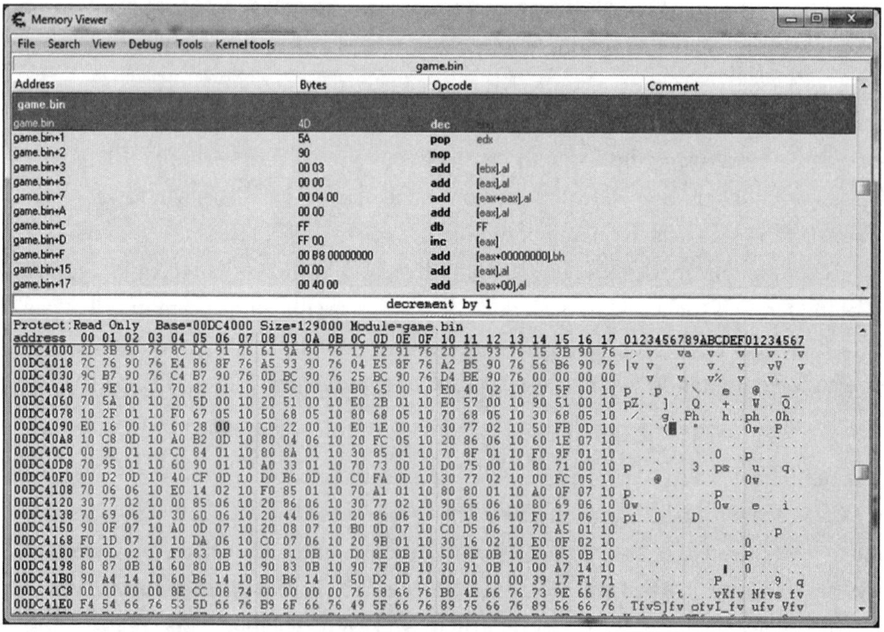

FIGURE 7.45 **A memory dump performed with OllyDbg**

Testing Remote Websites Found in Network Log Files

Log files from firewalls, IDS, IPS, Snort, and others are often configured to only report the basic facts, like the IP address and packet details. Unfortunately, this often leaves out important information like the exact path or domain visited by a victim during an attack. Performing an open source intelligence query is helpful in identifying possible malicious behavior related to the address. Behavioral analysis of the sample may also reveal domains or IPs and related data of interest to a malcode attack. Extensive time-consuming research may be required to best understand an attack and related attack data.

When looking at remote hostile servers, always check into each public directory. For example, `http://badsite.com/images/badfile.exe` may allow a directory list of the image's subdirectory. It is not uncommon in such situations to then locate additional binaries or log files or scripts of interest in an investigation.

Passive DNS Queries [65]

According to the Cisco blog post, "Tracking Malicious Activity with Passive DNS Query Monitoring," (at `https://blogs.cisco.com/security/tracking-malicious-activity-with-passive-dns-query-monitoring`):

> When a client wants to access a service by name, it must resolve that name into a usable IP address. To do this, the client sends a request for the name to a recursive name server and that server will retrieve the information and send it back to the client. From a security perspective, there are two interesting aspects to this activity. The first is the names clients are requesting, and the second is the Internet hosts that are providing the services for any given name. In other words, the security practitioner would want to know who is looking up a service (DNS queries) and would also want to know who is providing a service (DNS answers).

> The DNS answers portion of the problem has been solved by the Internet Systems Consortium's (ISC) Passive DNS Replication Project, and the corresponding ISC DNS Database. ISC's DNSDB is very good at answering questions like "What DNS names have pointed at this IP?" as well as "What IPs have provided services for this name?" The ISC DNSDB project has been transitioned to Farsight Security, a company started by the creators of DNSDB as of 2010. DNSDB is a database that stores and indexes both the passive DNS data available via Farsight Security's Security Information Exchange as well as the authoritative DNS data that various zone operators make available. DNSDB makes it easy to search for individual DNS RRsets and provides additional metadata for search results such as first seen and last seen timestamps as well as the DNS bailiwick

associated with an RRset. DNSDB also has the ability to perform inverse or rdata searches.[66]

To get at the DNS-questions side of the problem would require the security practitioner to ensure that logging has been enabled on all of the organization's recursive resolvers and then searching through those logs. This is an imperfect solution for a number of reasons that include

- Most organizations have a wide variety of nameservers (BIND, Active Directory, etc.) with varying logging abilities and formats deployed.

- Clients and malware can send DNS requests to external services like Google's Public DNS or OpenDNS with little trouble.

- Clients generate a huge volume of DNS queries, and it is difficult and costly to quickly search through such a high volume of logs.

The best open source passive DNS replication database available at the time of this writing is `http://www.bfk.de/bfk_dnslogger.html`. As a service to CERTs and incident response teams, BFK uses passive DNS replication to collect public DNS data. Figure 7.46 shows the results for a query run against the ISC2.ORG namespace.

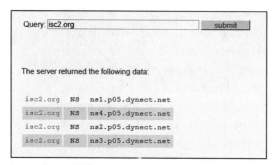

FIGURE 7.46 ISC2.org query results

This website makes it easy for a query to be entered and to then see what information has passively been stored related to that IP or domain. This information must be interpreted carefully by the security practitioner, and it needs to be vetted against additional sources of information to corroborate it thoroughly if it is to be used as part of an investigation.[67]

WHOIS, Reverse IP, Name Servers

There is a wealth of information available on domains, their IPs, reverse IPs, name servers, historical IP addresses, WHOIS registrant name or company affiliations, open source correlation, and more. This can be one of the most time-consuming and difficult components of an investigation to properly understand and follow. Several sites of interest are helpful in collecting such data:[68]

- **Robtex**—Large volumes of information and also what servers are shared with other domains or IPs. Great for looking up related data within various IP ranges or shared resources.

- **DomainCrawler**—Lots of interesting information on domains unique to this server.

- **SpamHaus**—Excellent for identifying if a server is related to known abuse in the past.

- **DNSstuff**—A suite of tools with powerful research options.

- **DomainTools**—A commercial site that offers excellent data including name server spy reports, domain history, domain monitoring, historical IP information, and more.

While all of the sites listed previously are valuable tools that the security practitioner should consider using as needed to establish the authenticity of DNS information during an investigation, Robtex is of special interest due to the graphing function that it provides for the information queried. Figure 7.47 shows the search results from Robtex for isc2.org, specifically the Information section.

Scorecard for isc2.org			
Test⬇	Points⬇	Date⬇	Extra⬇
🗗Domain Name Service	N/A		
🗗Analyzed		Feb 4, 2016 11:06 PM	
Grand total	0-0=0		

Information

DNS Records

Number of IP Records (after resolving CNAME:s and CDN analysis and deduplication):	1
Number of name servers in zone:	4
Number of mail servers:	1
IP Records:	1 68.177.216.201
Name servers in zone:	1 ns1.p05.dynect.net 2 ns2.p05.dynect.net 3 ns3.p05.dynect.net 4 ns4.p05.dynect.net
Mail servers:	1 isc2-org.mail.protection.outlook.com

Checksums

MD5 sum of host name:	621f00bb8c4ba80cce255e8a27a57cbd
SHA1 sum of host name:	6b7ec3f1e1b29cefe423d2d09fabdee8cfc27f26
SHA256 sum of host name:	26714ca7213951bd7bd7afc00bec79fe06b0f19a21f71d1862958895d43cf943

Analysis of the hostname

Split into words:	is c 2, i sc 2

FIGURE 7.47 Robtex search results

The Robtex search produces a significant amount of data; for example, the Records section displays DNS resource records in a table format, as shown in Figure 7.48.

Records

Displays various information related to AS, BGP, Routes and Location.

Base	Record	Preference	Name	IP Number	Reverse	R
isc2.org	A		isc2.org	68.177.216.201		68.176. 68.177. Proxy-re route obj QWEST-
	NS (primary)		ns1.p05.dynect.net	208.78.70.5	ns1.p05.dynect.net	208.78. Dynamic Services DNSINC
			ns2.p05.dynect.net	204.13.250.5	ns2.p05.dynect.net	204.13. Dynamic Services DNSINC
	NS		ns3.p05.dynect.net	208.78.71.5	ns3.p05.dynect.net	208.78. Dynamic Services DNSINC
			ns4.p05.dynect.net	204.13.251.5	ns4.p05.dynect.net	204.13. Dynamic Services DNSINC
	MX		isc2-org.mail.protection.outlook.com	207.46.163.138 207.46.163.170 207.46.163.215 207.46.163.247	mail-bn14138.inbound.protection.outlook.com mail-bn1b4170.inbound.protection.outlook.com mail-bl24215.inbound.protection.outlook.com mail-by24247.inbound.protection.outlook.com	207.46. 207.46. REACH Route) -

FIGURE 7.48 **Output for the domain name search**

Scrolling down further on the Robtex search results reveals the Graph section. The graphical output of the domain name search for isc2.org is produced, as shown in Figure 7.49.

Graph

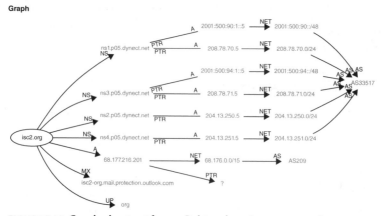

FIGURE 7.49 **Graphed output from a Robtex domain name search**

WARNING Abuse notifications should also be done through an alias instead of from a security practitioner directly because some abuse notifications are sent to the offender.

Scanning a target server with a tool such as Nmap may produce a detailed picture of the services that are running and the open ports available, but the security practitioner needs to exercise caution. Scans are generally considered to be legitimate within the international security community and may be useful in identifying a remote server or the ports it has open related to potential malicious behavior; however, the security practitioner runs the risk of being identified as a potential malicious actor by the target of the scan. Accessing various services, such as opening an FTP connection, may also help to capture banner data of interest in an investigation. Figure 7.50 shows the output of a target scan for the isc2.org domain address using Zenmap, which is a multi-platform graphical Nmap frontend and results viewer, derived from Umit.[69]

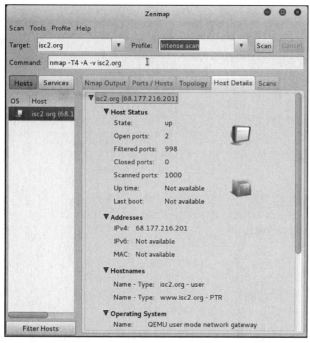

FIGURE 7.50 **Output of a scan using the Zenmap tool**

Deobfuscation of Scripts

Obfuscated JavaScript and similar content may prove to be difficult to decipher for the security practitioner. Fortunately, a few tools exist to help make this easier. One way to capture and examine traffic between machines suspected of harboring malware is to use virtualization technology to "sandbox" the suspect host. Converting the suspect machine into a virtual machine through a physical to virtual (P2V) transformation, and then using the virtual environment to allow the suspect machine to operate within along with a network sniffer being run on the physical host, will allow the security practitioner to identify all of the important network communications performed during an attack against a site or when code is run. Irrespective of any obfuscation that takes place, the links to executables and communications with remote C&Cs cannot be hidden from the sniffer on the host.

Using the Firefox Live HTTP Headers add-on (an extension) is also helpful in sniffing and sorting through traffic related to specific sessions of interest.[70] It is a free and powerful tool that allows the security practitioner to save HTTP headers from a session, replay, and quickly triage data from a session, as shown in Figure 7.51.

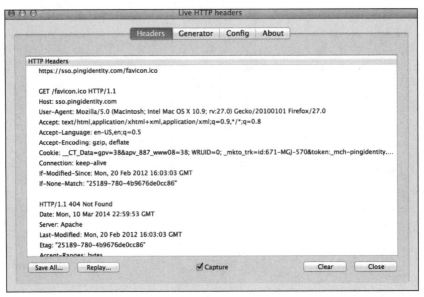

FIGURE 7.51 **Firefox Live HTTP Headers add-on**

Interpreting Data

When working with a remote hostile site, the security practitioner should not make assumptions about the behavior or capabilities of the site under review. Many malcode and exploit sites now check for the IP of the inbound connection and render different behaviors if the IP visits a site a second time. Even 404 errors are sometimes bogus, created as a way to drive security experts away, while C&C activities take place for communications from a bot with a special HTTP header used to identify bot traffic. It is increasingly common for internal self-checks, browser IDs, IP checking, and other anti-security expert scripts to be running on remote hostile servers in the wild.

Anti-VMware capability is another example of being on guard for interpretation of data. If code is anti-VMware, it may detect that it is being executed inside of a virtual environment and then exit. Thus, if nothing happens when the security practitioner attempts to examine a piece of code or unexpected behavior takes place within a virtual environment, the test may need to be performed again on a native "goat" computer used to test malcode on a real physical computer, not one that is virtualized.

Native goat machines must be able to be restored quickly through imaging solutions like Acronis software or Ghost. They ideally mirror the images used in the corporate environment and are put on a separate network for the security practitioner to use in order to run their laboratory tests. It is a good idea for the security practitioner to create multiple goat images based on patched and not patched, to test for exploitation success, and up-to-date builds from the network.

Testing of Samples in Virtualized Environments

VMware is one of the most popular tools used to analyze code in a virtual environment today. Other solutions also exist, like Qemu for Linux and Parallels for Macintosh.[71] Each essentially uses a special drive to write data to a software file instead of to a disk.

Simple behavioral analysis, where one runs the code in a virtual environment, is fairly straightforward but does involve measured and experienced interpretation of data. For example, it is easy to misinterpret data and believe that snapshot changes are caused by malcode when, in fact, they are part of normal computing changes. Security practitioners should have a base system with core tools and techniques that are *proven* and well understood before attempting to run any code with an unknown behavior.

A good way to get started is to simply run various tools on a clean VMware system and interpret the changes when Internet Explorer is opened, files are opened or deleted, etc. Follow this up with testing of malcode captured in quarantine from antivirus that is from a well-documented family that is easy to understand. Run the code and look for documented features to help learn tools and techniques for analyzing malcode. When an unknown sample comes across your desktop, follow the same procedures and also use a third-party sandbox solution to compare results against.

WARNING   Always be very careful when configuring the network settings for a virtual environment being used as a test bed in order to avoid the accidental spread of potential malware through shares or a bridged network connection.

Core tools vary greatly within the industry but should include basic snapshot and real-time monitoring tools for processes, files, and network activity, as well as anti-rootkit programs. Here is a list of helpful tools for the security practitioner to start a toolkit with:

- InstallWatchPro, Regshot, and InCTRL5 for snapshot views of a system that can survive a restart.[72]

- Autoruns, HiJack This!, and cports (CurrPorts) for quick views of open ports and auto-run entries.[73]

- Anti-rootkit programs—as many as possible since no single scanner can detect all rootkits.[74]

- File analysis tools like HashCalc, PEiD, Windows Fila Analyzer, The Sleuth Kit, and WinHex.[75]

- Monitoring tools from Microsoft (formerly SysInternals): Filemon, Regmon, Tdi-Mon, Tcpview, and ProcessExplorer.[76]

- Wireshark, Fport (NT4—Windows XP support only), Advanced Port Scanner, Advanced IP Scanner, Nmap, and NetCat/Ncat for working with networking and remote servers.[77]

Proxy tools or services so that a machine can have different IP addresses for multiple tests against a site that checks for the IP. Tun2socks is a great tool to help make some programs proxy aware if they are not. Tor is also a good freeware solution to meet some needs.[78] There are also web-based anonymous proxy servers that the security practitioner can use if needed. An anonymous web proxy is a type of proxy server that works through a web form, also often called a CGI proxy. Instead of configuring the address of the server in the browser as is done for HTTP or SOCKS proxies, you simply navigate to the home page of the web/CGI proxy, where proxy functionality is then enabled for each browsing session. Some of the most popular web proxies include the following:

- Proxify

- Anonymouse

- Anonymizer

- Ninja Cloak

- Firefox, Adobe Acrobat Reader, and similar programs that may be useful in tests or exploit research.

- OllyDbg with OllyScript, the PaiMai Framework, Immunity Debugger or other debugger or disassembly programs that can be used for reverse engineering.[79]

It is also advisable to create a test image that has certain configurations useful for malcode research, such as changing view settings to show the full extension, show system files, and do not hide known file types or system files. It is also helpful to create shortcut links to common malcode locations such as C:\, Windows, Windows System32, Drivers, Drivers\ETC, and similar directories.

Sometimes, files are difficult to identify or capture from a computer. For example, some files may not allow copying or moving from a virtual machine or may not be visible. Advanced techniques are then required to capture such files.

DiskMount

DiskMount is a free utility provided by VMware that enables a security practitioner to mount a virtual machine that is not currently loaded within VMware. Simply infect a virtual machine and then shut it off (no shut down required). Then, use DiskMount to mount the drive on the HOST machine. It can then be accessed with the full control of the HOST machine. There are a variety of other tools that can be used as well such as DAEMON Tools.[80] The same capability exists in Windows, as Figure 7.52 shows. Using

Windows 7 or Windows 8/8.1, the security practitioner could also mount a VHD/VHDX file as an accessible data drive from within the Computer Management MMC, by using the Disk Management tool. A VHD file can also be mounted using the diskpart tool. In order to do so, create a text file with this content:

```
SELECT VDISK FILE="file path and name of the vhd file"
 ATTACH VDISK
```

To attach the VHD image in a script, use `diskpart -s text file name`.

WARNING   Once a drive is mounted on the HOST, malicious files on the infected guest could be accidentally executed! Handle with extreme caution. Defang any captured files by renaming their extension to something like `badfile.exe_`.

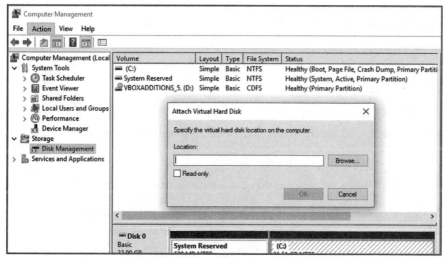

FIGURE 7.52 Attaching a virtual hard disk to a Windows system

A quick way to find files that have been changed on a drive is to use the Windows search function. After mounting the drive, right-click the mounted drive and search. Look for files via a modified date, or created date, for the current day. All the files are loaded and easily captured. However, MAC times can be modified and, therefore, such files potentially missed requiring a manual inspection for any lingering files not yet identified through such methods.

Suspend Memory Captures

VMware supports what is known as a suspend mode. When a running virtual machine is put into suspend mode, the virtual machine's memory state is saved to a `.vmss` file in the virtual machine's working directory. The security practitioner can locate the file type and then analyze it within a hex editor or similar tool to locate files within memory of interest, such as the vmss2core tool created by VMware labs.[81] The same capability exists in the Microsoft Hyper-V solution. The security practitioner would need to use the vm2dmp tool to convert the saved state of a virtual machine into a full memory dump file compatible with debugging tools on Hyper-V Version 1 and Version 2 VMs (basically anything created PRIOR to Windows Server 2012). If you are using Windows Server 2012 or later, then a different approach is required, and the use of either the Livekd tool from Sysinternals or the Debug-VM cmdlet in PowerShell will be required.[82] This is a time-consuming and complicated process that can yield excellent rootkit analysis when necessary.

Linux DD Captures

Linux builds like Knoppix easily boot from a CD or thumb drive. Booting up a system from Linux enables a security practitioner to use a tool called "dd" to capture the MBR or other data from a drive. The tool "dd" can be used to take an image of the disk by using this command:

```
dd if=<media/partition on a media> of=<image_file>
```

Here is an example:

```
dd if=/dev/sdc of=image.dd
```

This can be useful if a machine is suspected of being under the control of a Windows rootkit.

Anti-VMware Code Techniques

Anti-VMware code exists to detect the presence of a virtual machine. In most cases, such code simply exists and does nothing to hinder the analysis of the code. A native goat machine can be used to analyze such code. The security practitioner may also modify default VMware settings to remove common detection vectors used by malcode in the wild. By disabling hardware acceleration and similar components on a virtual machine and then testing code a second time, many malcode fail to detect the virtual environment and then run as expected.

Free Online Sandbox Solutions

There are several free online sandbox solutions available to the public today. When using these scanners, realize that they capture and share or sell the code submitted. Do not use such solutions for sensitive codes. Current online reputable sandbox solutions include the following:

- Anubis
- BitBlaze Malware Analysis Service

- Comodo Automated Analysis System and Valkyrie
- EUREKA Malware Analysis Internet Service
- Joe DD (PDF and MS Office files) and Joe Sandbox (registration required)
- Malwr
- Norman SandBox
- ThreatExpert
- ThreatTrack
- ViCheck
- Xandora
- XecScan (PDF and Microsoft Office files from targeted attacks)

Reports from such sandboxes are invaluable in comparing against laboratory results to confirm or help explain malicious behavior related to a specific binary.

Interactive Behavioral Testing

Interactive behavioral testing is a very time-consuming process and is part of a more advanced reverse engineering process in most cases. Take, for example, a malcode that attempts to connect to a remote IRC server. The security practitioner can create a Linux virtual environment with Snort and an IRC server on the box. The security practitioner can then modify the HOSTS file of the Windows virtual machine to point to the IRC server for the domain requested by the malcode. When the malcode is run, it will be redirected to the internal Linux server and will attempt to log into the IRC server. If it is properly configured, the security practitioner can then interact with the malcode in the IRC server, trying out different commands and watching what it does when various conditions or commands change. The possibilities are almost endless on various virtual networks and solutions that can be implemented to test specific components of code within a laboratory environment.

MALCODE MITIGATION

Malcode mitigation can be a daunting topic of great scope. This overview provides both strategic and tactical direction for the security practitioner to consider.

Strategic

The security practitioner needs to design a defense-in-depth architecture and secure top-down support from senior management for security if they are to be successful at implementing and maintaining a comprehensive security architecture.

An emergency response team and procedures, with the necessary power to act, should be in place before an incident takes place. Ideally, an internal CERT/CSIRT should exist as part of a greater disaster recovery plan. CSIRT stands for Computer Security Incident Response Team. The term CSIRT is used predominantly in Europe for the protected term CERT, which is registered in the United States by the CERT Coordination Center (CERT/CC).[83] There exist various abbreviations used for the same sort of teams:

- CERT or CERT/CC (Computer Emergency Response Team/Coordination Center)
- CSIRT (Computer Security Incident Response Team)
- IRT (Incident Response Team)
- CIRT (Computer Incident Response Team)
- SERT (Security Emergency Response Team)

A CERT/CSIRT is a team of IT security experts whose main business is to respond to computer security incidents. It provides the necessary services to handle incidents and support the team's constituency, enabling them to recover from breaches. In order to mitigate risks and minimize the number of required responses, most CERT/CSIRTs also provide preventative and educational services for their constituency. They issue advisories on vulnerabilities in the software and hardware in use and also inform the users about exploits and viruses taking advantage of these flaws, so the constituents can quickly patch and update their systems.[84]

There are many services that a CERT/CSIRT can choose to offer. Each CERT/CSIRT is different and provides services based on the mission, purpose, and constituency of the team. Providing an incident handling service is the only prerequisite to be considered a CERT/CSIRT. CERT/CSIRT services can be grouped into three categories:

- **Reactive Services**—These services are triggered by an event or request, such as a report of a compromised host, wide-spreading malicious code, software vulnerability, or something that was identified by an intrusion detection or logging system. Reactive services are the core component of CERT/CSIRT work.

- **Proactive Services**—These services provide assistance and information to help prepare, protect, and secure constituent systems in anticipation of attacks, problems, or events. Performance of these services will directly reduce the number of incidents in the future.

- **Security Quality Management Services**—These services augment existing and well-established services that are independent of incident handling and traditionally performed by other areas of an organization such as the IT, audit, or training departments.

The security practitioner may or may not have experience working with a CERT/ CSIRT. They may also not have any knowledge of how to go about setting up a CERT/ CSIRT for their organization if asked to do so. While there are many resources for the security practitioner to turn to if needed, the FIRST website offers several that should be of particular interest. The one that stands out is the `CERT-in-a-box.zip` download. It is from the NCSC-NL, the National Cyber Security Centre of the Netherlands. The project CERT-in-a-Box and Alerting Service-in-a-Box is an initiative of GOVCERT.NL/ NCSC to preserve the lessons learned from setting up GOVCERT.NL and De Waar-schuwingsdienst, the Dutch national alerting service.[85]

Tactical

Hardening systems against attack, including operating system, application, and antivirus updates, and properly backing up and protecting data is core to the tactical approach that the security practitioner should deploy against malcode. The rest of this section will focus on common mistakes that the security practitioner needs to be aware of in order to avoid making them in the field.

- Never remotely log into a potentially infected computer with an account that has administrative rights. If the malware turns out to be a worm, it can very easily spread through the administrative account into the rest of the network.

- The security practitioner always should strive to find the root cause of the problem that is being addressed. For example, if a computer has potentially been compromised by some form of malware, simply reimaging the computer to erase any signs of the malware and nullify its behavior will not allow the security practitioner to search for the root cause of the infection. Rather, this type of activity in the face of a potential infection can actually serve to further the aims of the hacker who may have planted the malware inside the infected system in the first place, as it destroys any possibility for the security practitioner to examine the malware and understand its structure, purpose, functionality, as well as its C&C infrastructure. The security practitioner needs to work hard on developing the skills necessary to allow them to thoroughly investigate a malware incident in order for them to be able to qualify the threat and properly mitigate the risk it poses.

- Do not rely on antivirus solutions to solve all problems. Just because an updated signature now detects code that has infected a host on the network does not mean that the problems are over. Do not forget that other codes that remain undetected may exist on the computers. Use anti-rootkit tools, and take nothing for granted when the integrity of a system has been compromised.

- After a malcode incident, the security practitioner should put special alerts in place within their monitoring infrastructure to watch for egress traffic related to known attack data points such as remote C&C IPs or domains.

- When working with file-infecting viruses that also have worm components, recognize the great challenge that lies ahead. These types of infections within a network environment can be almost impossible to remove unless the security practitioner is highly organized and very diligent in looking at the MD5 values of all targeted files on a drive, such as all `.exe` and `.scr` file types. Without such diligence, legitimate files that are infected with malcode may go undiscovered, reinfecting cleaned boxes as a result.

- Forget about manual disinfection after a malcode outbreak unless it is a short-term fix on a computer that cannot be taken offline immediately. If manual disinfection proves to be necessary, then careful monitoring of the affected computer needs to be put in place to ensure any remaining activity or payloads are captured and alerted on.

- Realize that safe mode can be undermined by some malcode. If an infected computer is started in safe mode, it may still have a malcode running in memory hindering disinfection efforts! Also realize that some malcode now remove all former restore points on a Windows backup solution and then install a new restore point that includes the malcode! Using a clean image from a protected location is important in maintaining the integrity of a system. This works best when user files are not stored on hosts but on a network server, making machine wipes much easier. Additionally, realize that MBR kernel-level threats exist (Mebroot with Torpig) and may require that the MBR of a disk be cleaned before attempting to install a clean image on a computer.

- Just because there is a policy in place that may prevent the use of unauthorized wireless access points (WAPs) within the enterprise does not mean they do not exist on the network. Audit everything to know what is going on inside and in and out of a network at all times!

- Design networks to maximize intelligence load balancing, bandwidth, and upstream host provider anti-DDoS capabilities or throttling and tarpitting techniques to help manage DDoS attacks against one or more network resources.

- Configure routers within internal networks to explicitly limit ingress traffic to only allow IP addresses that are on a whitelist. Also, configure filtering to take place between network address translation (NAT) devices and the ISP to explicitly allow only authorized sources. Deny private, server, and unroutable traffic and direct broadcast packets as appropriate within the network topology.

- Configure routers to block spoofed traffic from within a network.

- Consider using a honeypot to trap bot traffic, analyze it, and ensure countermeasures and auditing is in place over the network to prevent similar attacks on legitimate network resources.

Finally, a complete package of training and technology is required to best mitigate malware. Humans are often the last link and the weakest link, but they can help significantly in mitigating malcode if they are taught to pay attention to the warning signs and are aware of suspicious behavior.

IMPLEMENTING AND OPERATING END-POINT DEVICE SECURITY

When it comes to implementing and operating end-point device security, the SSCP will need to consider several things. Endpoint security implies that technologies such as host-based intrusion detection and firewalls may be used. The skills required to install, configure, and manage these technologies on a specified end-point will require a combination of vendor-specific and operating system–specific knowledge. The SSCP will need to become familiar with the required software interfaces as needed to ensure that these systems are set up and configured correctly. The use of additional technologies and protection measures such as whitelisting, endpoint encryption, and secure browsing are built on top of the host operating system and as a result will be implemented differently based on the version of host operating system being configured. The SSCP will need to take this into account as they seek to operate these systems and manage them securely.

Host-Based Intrusion Detection System

Host-based intrusion detection systems, or HIDS, work by monitoring activity that is occurring internally on a host. HIDS look for unusual activity by examining logs created by the operating system, looking for changes made to key system files, tracking installed software, and sometimes examining the network connections a host makes. They are installed in a particular host, or groups of hosts, and they monitor traffic coming to or from that host only. If there are attacks in any other part of the network, they will not be detected by the host-based IDS. Apart from monitoring incoming and outgoing traffic, a host-based IDS can also analyze the file system of a host, users' logon activities, running processes, data integrity, etc.

According to Internet-Computer-Security.com, there are several types of HIDS:

"Signature Based   Signatures are created by vendors based on potential attacks and attacks that have taken place in the past. These signatures are downloaded by the intrusion detection software/system itself. Any packets arriving into the network are compared to the set of downloaded signatures comparing these for any attacks. Signature based systems are the most common type of IDS. The main issue with these systems is that they cannot detect new attacks because they only compare attacks to the signatures their system currently holds.

"Anomaly Based   In anomaly based, the system would first need to learn the NOR-MAL behavior, traffic, or protocol set of the network/host. When the system has learnt the normal state of a network and the types of packets and throughput it handles on a daily basis, taking into account peak times such as lunch time for web browsing, then it can be put into action. Now, when traffic is detected that is outside of the "normal state" profile created, the anomaly based detection system would take action.

This type of system can detect new attacks as they are happening, unlike a signature based system. The downside to these systems is that the security practitioner has to spend time fine stunning the system and maintaining it in order to produce and update the protection profiles used to discern what the "normal behavior" patterns are. As a result, if this is not done correctly, then the system will usually produce many false positives, stopping normal traffic as a result.

"Rule Based   Rule based systems use a knowledge base programmed with rules paired with an inference engine to examine and assess all traffic flowing through the system. Based on assessment of traffic flows, against the rules in effect, the system makes a deter-mination as to whether or not the traffic flow being measured is legitimate or not."[86]

Host-Based Firewalls

A host-based firewall is made up of software that is installed and configured on an indi-vidual computer. The software acts to monitor the flow of traffic into and out of the host computer. The firewall software uses rulesets to examine all traffic passing through the host, allowing or denying traffic based on the rules and the action specified when a match is found. Traffic may also be examined based on a "whitelist" of either IP addresses or applica-tions. If the traffic is coming from a machine whose IP address is on the whitelist, than that traffic would be allowed. If the traffic is coming from an application on the whitelist, then that traffic would also be allowed. If traffic of any kind, originating from any location, is not found to be "approved" when examined by the firewall, then it is typically discarded. The user may also be prompted by the firewall to allow or deny traffic based on activity being examined that is not on covered by the list of rules already in place.

Application Whitelisting

According to the Systems and Network Analysis (SNAC) Center of the United States National Security Agency, "Application Whitelisting is a proactive security technique where only a limited set of approved programs are allowed to run while all other pro-grams (including most malware) are blocked from running by default. In contrast, the standard policy enforced by most operating systems allows all users to download and run any program they choose. Application Whitelisting enables only the administrators, not the users, to decide which programs are allowed to run. Application Whitelisting is not a replacement for traditional security software, such as antivirus and host firewalls. It should be used as one layer in a defense-in-depth strategy.

"For an application whitelisting solution to be effective:

- "All executable code must be blocked by default so only approved programs can run.

- "Users must not be allowed to modify the files that are allowed to run."[87]

Endpoint Encryption

According to Symantec:

> "When it comes to encrypting data, there are various encryption strategies. Endpoint encryption protects a disk in the event of theft or accidental loss by encrypting the entire disk including swap files, system files, and hibernation files. If an encrypted disk is lost, stolen, or placed into another computer, the encrypted state of the drive remains unchanged, ensuring only an authorized user can access its contents."[88]

Endpoint encryption cannot, however, protect your data when you have logged into the system during startup and leave your computer unattended. In this case, your system has been unlocked, and unauthorized users can access your system just as an authorized user could. This is where file encryption comes in.

According to Symantec, "File encryption encrypts specific files so that when a user successfully authorizes to an operating system, the contents of the file still remain encrypted. File encryption requires user action, whereas drive encryption automatically encrypts everything you or the operating system creates."[89] File encryption can also be paired with an encryption policy server, which allows IT administrators to create and deliver encryption rules across an organization, including automatically encrypting files from various applications and folders.

Trusted Platform Module

The Trusted Computing Group is an international standards body that creates specifications used to define Trusted Platform Modules, and the API's and protocols necessary to operate a trusted environment. According to the Trusted Computing Group:

> "A TPM (trusted platform module) is a computer chip (microcontroller) that can securely store artifacts used to authenticate the platform (your PC or laptop). These artifacts can include passwords, certificates, or encryption keys. A TPM can also be used to store platform measurements that help ensure that the platform remains trustworthy. Authentication (ensuring that the platform can prove that it is what it claims to be) and attestation (a process helping to prove that a platform is trustworthy and

has not been breached) are necessary steps to ensure safer computing in all environments."[90]

Mobile Device Management

Mobile device management (MDM) is the administrative area dealing with deploying, securing, monitoring, integrating, and managing mobile devices, such as smartphones, tablets, and laptops, in the workplace. The intent of MDM is to optimize the functionality and security of mobile devices within the enterprise while simultaneously protecting the corporate network.

Bring your own device, or BYOD, is where employees bring non-company IT into the organization and demand to be connected to everything—without proper accountability or oversight. According to Gartner, BYOD forces the organization and the security practitioner to wrestle with three key operational challenges:[91]

- **Governance and Compliance**—BYOD could cause violation of rules, regulations, trust, intellectual property, and other critical business obligations.

- **Mobile Device Management**—The security practitioner needs to manage growing workforce expectations around mobility. Employees use many devices, and they expect to use any device or application anytime, anywhere.

- **Security**—If left unmanaged, BYOD can lead to loss of control, impact network availability, and cause data loss. Security practitioners need the right network access strategies and policies in place to secure the organization's computing environment.

The security practitioner should consider the following items when crafting the BYOD policy and procedures for the organization:

- How to specify what devices are permitted for use and under what circumstances

- What will the security and service/support policies for allowed devices be and how will they be enforced

- How to differentiate who owns what applications and data, as well as what apps will or will not be allowed to be used

- How to address acceptable usage

- How to "offboard" users that have company data on their devices

According to Scott Kraege of MOBI Wireless Management, COPE (corporate owned, personally enabled) gives both employers and employees the freedom of BYOD while also offering a slew of benefits to each party:

> "The 'corporate owned' portion of the COPE policy helps companies keep their networks and information secure, which has become one of

the biggest backlashes of the traditional BYOD program in the workplace. 'CO' means that the company still owns the line of service and selects its preferred device and usage cost thresholds for employees to consider. "This kind of ownership grants the company the right to wipe or disconnect devices on the corporate network, and ultimately offers the company pre-established security just like the pre-BYOD days. Studies show that up to 77 percent of BYOD employees dislike the use of MDM on their device; the 'personally enabled,' or 'PE,' aspect of COPE changes that as it allows employees to choose the company approved device they prefer while also enabling them to use it both personally and professionally. Employees are allowed to choose the company-approved device they prefer from the predetermined list, which enables them to utilize their device for both personal and professional use—a common perk of BYOD."[92]

Secure Browsing

An up-to-date browser guards you from phishing and malware attacks when you are browsing the Web. It does so by limiting three types of security risk when you are online:

Risk 1: How often You Come into Contact with an Attacker You can be exposed to attackers through a malicious fake website or even through a familiar website that has been hacked. Most modern browsers pre-check each web page you visit and alert you if one is suspected of being malicious. This lets you make an informed judgment about whether you really want to visit that page. For example, Google Chrome uses Safe Browsing technology, which is also used in several other modern browsers. As you browse the Web, each page is checked quickly against a list of suspected phishing and malware websites. This list is stored and maintained locally on your computer to help protect your browsing privacy. If a match against the local list is found, the browser then sends a request to Google for more information. (This request is completely obscured, and the browser does not send it in plaintext.) If Google verifies the match, Chrome shows a red warning page to alert you that the page you are trying to visit may be dangerous.

Risk 2: How Vulnerable Your Browser Is if It's Attacked Old browsers that have not been upgraded are likely to have security vulnerabilities that attackers can exploit. All outdated software, irrespective of whether it's your operating system, browser, or plug-ins, has the same problem. That's why it's important to use the very latest version of your browser and promptly install security patches on your operating system and all plug-ins, so that they're always up-to-date with the latest security fixes.

Risk 3: How Much Damage Is Done if an Attacker Finds Vulnerabilities in Your Browser Some modern browsers like Chrome and Internet Explorer are built with an added layer of protection known as a sandbox. A browser sandbox builds a contained environment to keep malware and other security threats from infecting your computer. If you open a malicious webpage, the browser's sandbox prevents that malicious code from leaving the browser and installing itself to your hard drive. The malicious code therefore cannot read, alter, or further damage the data on your computer.

OPERATING AND CONFIGURING CLOUD SECURITY

Cloud computing environments are complex systems. They are made up of hardware and software, and they use technologies such as virtualization and DLP to provide operating environments and confidentiality protection for data. Cloud systems are deployed using deployment models such as public, private, and hybrid and are consumed using service models such as infrastructure as a service (IaaS), platform as a service (PaaS), and software as a service (SaaS). The protection of data integrity, confidentiality, and availability hinges on the understanding of data as it moves, is used, and is stored across the cloud. The ability to clearly identify what is considered to be part of the data that makes up personally identifiable information (PII), secure that data, and ensure it is managed appropriately, in accordance with the prevailing laws, poses a unique set of challenges for the SSCP. The following sections will discuss these issues and concerns.

The Five Essential Characteristics of Clouds

Although clouds are widespread and diverse, they generally share five essential characteristics:

On-Demand Self-Service   On-demand self-service is the provisioning of cloud resources on demand (i.e., whenever and wherever they are required). From a security perspective, this has introduced challenges to governing the use and provisioning of cloud-based services, which may violate organizational policies.

Broad Network Access   Cloud, by its nature, is an "always on" and "always accessible" offering for users to have widespread access to resources, data, and other assets. Access what you want, when you need it, from any location. In theory, all you should require is Internet access and relevant credentials and tokens, which will give you access to the resources.

Resource Pooling   Resource pooling lies at the heart of all that is good with cloud computing. More often than not, traditional, non-cloud systems may see utilization rates for their resources of 80–90% for a few hours a week and reside at an average of 10–20% for the remainder. What cloud looks to do is to group (pool) resources for use across the user landscape or multiple clients, which can then scale and adjust to the user or client's needs, based on their workload or resource requirements. Cloud providers typically have large numbers of resources available, from hundreds to thousands of servers, network devices, applications, etc., which can accommodate large volumes of customers and can prioritize and facilitate appropriate resourcing for each client.

Rapid Elasticity   Rapid elasticity allows the user to obtain additional resources, storage, compute power, etc., as their need or workload requires. This is often transparent to the user, with more resources added as necessary in a seamless manner. Think of a provider selling 100,000 tickets for a major sporting event or concert. Leading up to the ticket release date, little to no compute resources are needed; however, once the tickets go on sale, they may need to accommodate 100,000 users in the space of 30–40 minutes. This is where rapid elasticity and cloud computing could really be beneficial, compared to traditional IT deployments, which would have to invest heavily up front, using capital expenditures (CapEx) to have the ability to support such demand.

Measured Service   Cloud computing offers a unique and important component that traditional IT deployments have struggled to provide: resource usage that can be measured, controlled, reported, and alerted upon, which results in multiple benefits and overall transparency between the provider and client. Essentially, you pay for what you use and have the ability to get an itemized bill or breakdown of usage.

Deployment Models

According to NIST:

> "*Cloud computing* allows computer users to conveniently rent access to fully featured applications, to software development and deployment environments, and to computing infrastructure assets such as network-accessible data storage and processing."[93]

A cloud computing system may be deployed privately or hosted on the premises of a cloud customer, may be shared among a limited number of trusted partners, may be hosted by a third party, or may be a publically accessible service, i.e., a public cloud. Depending on the kind of cloud deployment, the cloud may have limited private computing resources, or it may have access to large quantities of remotely accessed resources. The different deployment models present a number of trade-offs in how customers can control their resources and the scale, cost, and availability of resources.

Public

According to NIST:

> "The cloud infrastructure is provisioned for open use by the general public. It may be owned, managed, and operated by a business, academic, or government organization, or some combination of them. It exists on the premises of the cloud provider."[94]

Key drivers or benefits of public cloud typically include:

- Easy and inexpensive setup because hardware, application, and bandwidth costs are covered by the provider
- Streamlined and easy use of provisioning resources
- Scalability to meet customer needs
- No wasted resources—pay as you consume

Given the increasing demands for public cloud services, many providers are now offering and re-modeling their services as public cloud offerings. Providers in the public cloud space include Amazon, Microsoft, Salesforce, and Google among others.

Private

According to NIST:

> "The cloud infrastructure is provisioned for exclusive use by a single organization comprising multiple consumers (e.g., business units). It may be owned, managed, and operated by the organization, a third party, or some combination of them, and it may exist on or off premises."[95]

A private cloud is typically managed by the organization it serves; however, outsourcing the general management of this to trusted third parties may also be an option. A private cloud is typically available only to the entity or organization, its employees, contractors, and selected third parties.

The private cloud is also sometimes referred to as the internal or organizational cloud.

Key drivers or benefits of public cloud typically include

- Increased control over data, underlying systems, and applications
- Ownership and retention of governance controls
- Assurance over data location, removal of multiple jurisdiction legal and compliance requirements

Hybrid

According to NIST:

> "The cloud infrastructure is a composition of two or more distinct cloud infrastructures (private, community, or public) that remain unique entities, but are bound together by standardized or proprietary technology that enables data and application portability (e.g., cloud bursting for load balancing between clouds)."[96]

Hybrid cloud computing is gaining in popularity because it provides organizations with the ability to retain control of their IT environments, coupled with the convenience of allowing organizations to use public cloud service to fulfil non-mission-critical workloads and taking advantage of flexibility, scalability, and cost savings.

Key drivers or benefits of hybrid cloud deployments include:

- Retain ownership and oversight of critical tasks and processes related to technology.

- Re-use previous investments in technology within the organization.

- Control over most critical business components and systems.

- Cost-effective means to fulfilling non-critical business functions (utilizing public cloud components).

- "Cloud bursting" and disaster recovery can be enhanced by hybrid cloud deployments. "Cloud bursting" allows for public cloud resources to be utilized when a private cloud workload has reached maximum capacity.

Community

According to NIST:

> "The cloud infrastructure is provisioned for exclusive use by a specific community of consumers from organizations that have shared concerns (e.g., mission, security requirements, policy, and compliance considerations). It may be owned, managed, and operated by one or more of the organizations in the community, a third party, or some combination of them, and it may exist on or off premises."[97]

Community clouds can be on premise or off-site and should give the benefits of a public cloud deployment while providing heightened levels of privacy, security, and regulatory compliance.

Service Models

A cloud can provide access to software applications such as e-mail or office productivity tools (the SaaS service model), can provide an environment for customers to use to build and operate their own software (the PaaS service model), or can provide network access to traditional computing resources such as processing power and storage (the IaaS service model). The different service models have different strengths and are suitable for different customers and business objectives. Generally, interoperability and portability of customer workloads are more achievable in the IaaS service model because the building blocks of IaaS offerings are relatively well-defined, e.g., network protocols, CPU instruction sets, and legacy device interfaces.

SaaS

According to the *NIST Definition of Cloud Computing*, in SaaS,

> "The capability provided to the consumer is to use the provider's applications running on a cloud infrastructure. The applications are accessible from various client devices through either a thin client interface, such as a web browser (e.g., web-based e-mail), or a program interface. The consumer does not manage or control the underlying cloud infrastructure including network, servers, operating systems, storage, or even individual application capabilities, with the possible exception of limited user-specific application configuration settings."[98]

Within SaaS, two delivery models are currently used:

- **Hosted Application Management (hosted AM)**—A provider hosts commercially available software for customers and delivers it over the Web (Internet).
- **Software on Demand**—The cloud provider gives customers network-based access to a single copy of an application created specifically for SaaS distribution (typically within the same network segment).

Software as a service has a number of key benefits for organizations, which include but are not limited to:

- Ease of use and limited/minimal administration.
- Automatic updates and patch management: The user will always be running the latest version and most up-to-date deployment of the software release as well as any relevant security updates (no manual patching required).
- Standardization and compatibility: All users will have the same version of the software release.
- Global accessibility.

Providers in the SaaS space include Microsoft, Google, Salesforce.com, Oracle, and SAP among others.

PaaS

According to the *NIST Definition of Cloud Computing*, in PaaS,

> "the capability provided to the consumer is to deploy onto the cloud infrastructure consumer-created or acquired applications created using programming languages, libraries, services, and tools supported by the provider. The consumer does not manage or control the underlying cloud infrastructure including network, servers, operating systems, or storage, but

has control over the deployed applications and possibly configuration settings for the application-hosting environment." [99]

PaaS and the cloud platform components have revolutionized the manner in which development and software has been delivered to customers and users over the past few years. The barrier for entry in terms of costs, resources, capabilities, and ease of use have dramatically reduced "time to market"—promoting and harvesting the innovative culture within many organizations.

PaaS has a number of key benefits for developers, which include but are not limited to:

■ Operating system can be changed and upgraded frequently, including associated features and system services.

■ Where development teams are scattered globally, the ability to work together on software development projects within the same environment can be extremely beneficial.

■ Services are available and can be obtained from diverse sources that cross international boundaries.

■ Up-front and recurring or ongoing costs can be significantly reduced by utilizing a single vendor rather than maintaining multiple hardware facilities and environments.

Providers in the PaaS space include Microsoft, OpenStack, and Google among others.

IaaS

According to the NIST *Definition of Cloud Computing*, in IaaS,

"the capability provided to the consumer is to provision processing, storage, networks, and other fundamental computing resources where the consumer is able to deploy and run arbitrary software, which can include operating systems and applications. The consumer does not manage or control the underlying cloud infrastructure but has control over operating systems, storage, and deployed applications; and possibly limited control of select networking components (e.g., host firewalls)." [100]

Infrastructure as a service has a number of key benefits for organizations, which include but are not limited to:

■ Usage is metered and priced on the basis of units (or instances) consumed. This can also be billed back to specific departments or functions.

- Ability to scale up and down of infrastructure services based on actual usage. This is particularly useful and beneficial where there are significant spikes and dips within the usage curve for infrastructure.

- Reduced cost of ownership—no need to buy any assets for everyday use, no loss of asset value over time, and reduction of other related costs of maintenance and support.

- Reduced energy and cooling costs, along with "Green IT" environment effect with optimum use of IT resources and systems.

Providers in the IaaS space include Amazon, AT&T, Rackspace, Verizon/Terremark, HP, and OpenStack among others.

Virtualization

Virtualization is the foundation for an agile, scalable cloud—and the first practical step—for building cloud infrastructure. Virtualization abstracts and isolates the underlying hardware as virtual machines (VMs) in their own runtime environment and with multiple VMs for computing, storage, and networking resources in a single hosting environment. These virtualized resources are critical for managing data, moving it into and out of the cloud, and running applications with high utilization and high availability.

Virtualization is managed by a host server running a hypervisor—software, firmware, or hardware that creates and runs VMs. The VMs are referred to as guest machines. The hypervisor serves as a virtual operating platform that executes the guest operating system for an application. Host servers are designed to run multiple VMs sharing multiple instances of guest operating systems.

Virtualization also provides several key capabilities for cloud computing, including resource sharing, VM isolation, and load balancing. In a cloud environment, these capabilities enable scalability, high utilization of pooled resources, rapid provisioning, workload isolation, and increased uptime.

A hypervisor or virtual machine monitor (VMM) is a piece of computer software, firmware, or hardware that creates and runs virtual machines. The hypervisor presents the guest operating systems with a virtual operating platform and manages the execution of the guest operating systems. Multiple instances of a variety of operating systems may share the virtualized hardware resources.

In their 1974 article "Formal Requirements for Virtualizable Third Generation Architectures," Gerald J. Popek and Robert P. Goldberg classified two types of hypervisor:[101]

Type-1: Native or Bare-Metal Hypervisors

These hypervisors run directly on the host's hardware to control the hardware and to manage guest operating systems. For this reason, they are sometimes called *bare-metal hypervisors*. A guest operating system runs as a process on the host. Examples include Citrix XenServer, VMware ESX/ESXi, and Microsoft Hyper-V 2008/2012.

Type-2: Hosted Hypervisors

These hypervisors run on a conventional operating system just as other computer programs do. Type-2 hypervisors abstract guest operating systems from the host operating system. VMware Workstation and VirtualBox are examples of type-2 hypervisors.

There are several different types of virtualization that the security practitioner needs to be familiar with:

Server Virtualization   Using server virtualization, multiple operating systems can run on a single physical server as virtual machines, each with access to the underlying server's computing resources.

Network Virtualization   Network virtualization is the complete reproduction of a physical network in software. Virtual networks offer the same features and guarantees of a physical network, yet they deliver the operational benefits and hardware independence of virtualization—rapid provisioning, non-disruptive deployment, automated maintenance, and support for both legacy and new applications. Network virtualization presents logical networking devices and services—logical ports, switches, routers, firewalls, load balancers, VPNs, and more—to connected workloads. Applications run on the virtual network exactly the same as if on a physical network.

Desktop Virtualization   Deploying desktops as a managed service gives you the opportunity to reduce costs and increase service by quickly delivering the desktop environment needed by the user to any endpoint in the organization.

Application Virtualization   Deploying applications as a managed service gives you the opportunity to reduce costs and increase service by quickly delivering the required application(s) necessary to drive productivity and collaboration to any endpoint in the organization.

Storage Virtualization   Storage virtualization abstracts the disks and flash drives inside your servers, combines them into high-performance storage pools, and delivers these as software. Storage virtualization technology provides a fundamentally better way to manage storage resources, giving the organization the ability to:

- Significantly improve storage resource utilization and flexibility
- Simplify OS patching and driver requirements, regardless of storage topology
- Increase application uptime and simplify day-to-day operations

Legal and Privacy Concerns

Privacy and data protection (P&DP) matters are often cited as a concern for cloud computing scenarios. The P&DP regulations affect not just those whose personal data is processed in the cloud (the data subjects) but also those (the CS customers) using cloud computing to process others' personal data and indeed those providing cloud services used to process that data (the service providers).

Key questions that the security practitioner needs to understand are:

- What information in the cloud is regulated under data protection laws?
- Who is responsible for personal data in the cloud?
- Whose laws apply in a dispute?
- Where is personal data processed?

The following is an overview of some of the ways in which different countries and regions around the world are addressing the varied legal and regulatory issues they face.

The United States has many sector-specific privacy and data security laws, both at the federal and state levels. There is no official national privacy data protection authority; however, the FTC (Federal Trade Commission) has jurisdiction over most commercial entities and has authority to issue and enforce privacy regulations in specific areas (e.g., for telemarketing, spamming, children's privacy, etc.).[102] In addition to the FTC, a wide range of sector-specific regulators, particularly those in the healthcare and financial services sectors, have authority to issue and enforce privacy regulations as well.

Generally, the processing of personal data is subject to *opt out*[103] consent from the data subject, while the *opt in*[104] rule applies in special cases such as the processing of sensitive/health data. However, it is interesting to note that currently no specific geographic personal data transfer restrictions apply.

With regards to the accessibility of data stored within cloud services, it is important to underline that the 4th Amendment to the U.S. Constitution applies: It protects people from unreasonable searches and seizures by the government.[105] The Fourth Amendment, however, is not a guarantee against all searches and seizures but only those that are deemed unreasonable under the law. Whether a particular type of search is considered reasonable in the eyes of the law is determined by balancing two important interests. On one side is the intrusion on an individual's Fourth Amendment rights and on the other side are legitimate government interests, such as public safety.

In 2012 the Obama Administration unveiled a "Consumer Privacy Bill of Rights," as part of a comprehensive blueprint to protect individual privacy rights and give users more control over how their information is handled.[106]

The data protection and privacy laws in the EU members states are constrained by the EU Directives, Regulations, and Decisions enacted by the European Union.

The main piece of legislation is the EU directive 95/46/EC "on the protection of individuals with regard to the processing of personal data and on the free movement of such data."[107] These provisions apply in all the business/social sectors; thus, they cover the processing of personal data in cloud computing services. Furthermore, the EU enacted a privacy directive (e-privacy directive) 2002/58/EC "concerning the processing of personal data and the protection of privacy in the electronic communications sector."[108] This directive contains provisions concerning data breaches and the use of cookies.

On March 12, 2014, the European Parliament formally adopted the text of the proposed EU General Data Protection Regulation for replacing the actual EU privacy directive 95/46/EC and of a new specific directive for privacy in the Police and Criminal Justice sector.[109]

The next steps for both the Regulation and the Directive are for the EU Council of Ministers to formulate a position and for trilateral negotiations between the European Commission, Parliament, and Council to begin. Entry into force is not expected before 2017.

Latin American as well as North Africa and medium-sized Asian countries have privacy and data protection legislation largely influenced by the EU privacy laws.

APEC, the Asia-Pacific Economic Cooperation council, is becoming an essential point of reference for the data protection and privacy regulations of the region.

The APEC Ministers have endorsed the APEC Privacy Framework, recognizing the importance of the development of effective privacy protections that avoid barriers to information flows and ensure continued trade and economic growth in the APEC region. The APEC Privacy Framework promotes a flexible approach to information privacy protection across APEC member economies, while avoiding the creation of unnecessary barriers to information flows.[110]

Understanding Differences Between Jurisdiction and Applicable Law

For P&DP, it is particularly important to distinguish between the concepts of the following:

- **Applicable Law**—Determines the legal regime applicable to a certain matter
- **Jurisdiction**—Usually determines the ability of a national court to decide a case or enforce a judgment or order

The applicable law and the jurisdiction in relation to any given issue may not always be the same. This can be particularly true in the cloud services environment, due to the complex nature of cloud hosting models and the ability to geo-locate data across multiple jurisdictions.

Essential Requirements in P&DP Laws

The ultimate goal of P&DP laws is to provide safeguards to the individuals (data subjects) for the processing of their personal data in the respect of their privacy and will: This is achieved with the definitions of principles/rules to be fulfilled by the operators involved in the data processing. These operators can process the data by playing the role of data controller or data processor.

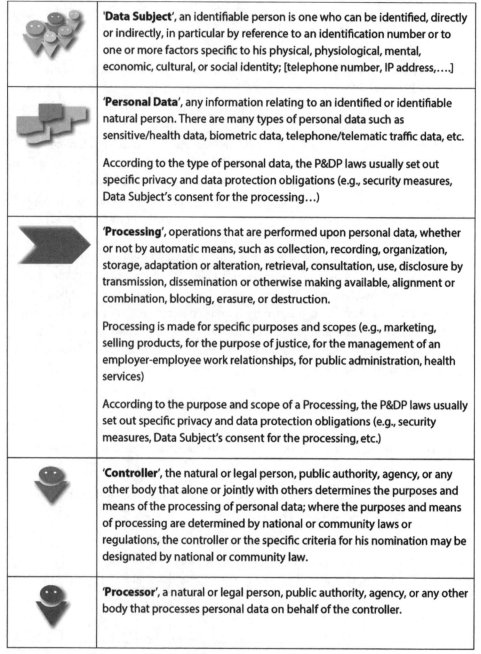

	'Data Subject', an identifiable person is one who can be identified, directly or indirectly, in particular by reference to an identification number or to one or more factors specific to his physical, physiological, mental, economic, cultural, or social identity; [telephone number, IP address,....]
	'Personal Data', any information relating to an identified or identifiable natural person. There are many types of personal data such as sensitive/health data, biometric data, telephone/telematic traffic data, etc. According to the type of personal data, the P&DP laws usually set out specific privacy and data protection obligations (e.g., security measures, Data Subject's consent for the processing...)
	'Processing', operations that are performed upon personal data, whether or not by automatic means, such as collection, recording, organization, storage, adaptation or alteration, retrieval, consultation, use, disclosure by transmission, dissemination or otherwise making available, alignment or combination, blocking, erasure, or destruction. Processing is made for specific purposes and scopes (e.g., marketing, selling products, for the purpose of justice, for the management of an employer-employee work relationships, for public administration, health services) According to the purpose and scope of a Processing, the P&DP laws usually set out specific privacy and data protection obligations (e.g., security measures, Data Subject's consent for the processing, etc.)
	'Controller', the natural or legal person, public authority, agency, or any other body that alone or jointly with others determines the purposes and means of the processing of personal data; where the purposes and means of processing are determined by national or community laws or regulations, the controller or the specific criteria for his nomination may be designated by national or community law.
	'Processor', a natural or legal person, public authority, agency, or any other body that processes personal data on behalf of the controller.

FIGURE 7.53 **Typical meaning for common privacy terms**

The Privacy Roles for Customer and Service Provider

The customer determines the ultimate purpose of the processing and decides on the outsourcing or the delegation of all or part of the concerned activities to external organizations. Therefore, the customer acts as a controller. In this role, they are responsible and subject to all the legal duties that are addressed in the P&DP laws applicable to the controller's role. The customer may task the service provider with choosing the methods and the technical or organizational measures to be used to achieve the purposes of the controller.

When the service provider supplies the means and the platform, acting on behalf of the customer, then he is considered to be a data processor.

As a matter of fact, there may be situations in which a service provider may be considered either as a joint controller or as a controller in his own right depending on concrete circumstances. However, even in complex data processing environments, where different controllers play a role in processing personal data, compliance with data protection rules and responsibilities for possible breaches must be clearly allocated in order to avoid that the protection of personal data is reduced to a negative conflict of competence.

In the current cloud computing scenario, customers may not have room to maneuver when negotiating the contractual terms of use of the cloud services since standardized offers are a feature of many cloud computing services. Nevertheless, it is ultimately the customer who decides on the allocation of part or the totality of processing operations to cloud services for specific purposes.

The imbalance in the contractual power of a small controller/customer with respect to large service providers should not be considered as a justification for the controller to accept clauses and terms of contracts that are not in compliance with P&DP applicable to him.

In a cloud services environment, it is not always easy to properly identify and assign the roles of controller and processor between the customer and the service provider. However, this is a central factor of P&DP, since all liabilities are assigned to the controller role and its country of establishment mainly determines the applicable P&DP law and jurisdiction.

Figure 7.54 shows who is responsible depending on the types of cloud services involved. The following list explores how this applies to customers and service providers in more detail.

- **SaaS**—The customer determines/collects the data to be processed with a cloud service (CS), while the service provider essentially takes the decisions of how to carry out the processing and implement specific security controls. It is not always possible to negotiate the terms of the service between the customer and the service provider.

- **PaaS**—The customer has higher possibility to determine the instruments of processing, although the terms of the services are not usually negotiable.

- **IaaS**—The customer has a high level of control on data, processing functionalities, tools, and related operational management, thus achieving a very high level of responsibility in determining purposes and means of processing.

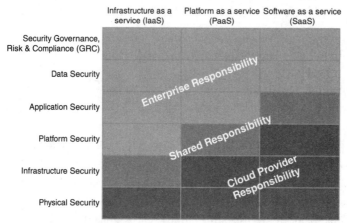

FIGURE 7.54 **Responsibility depending on the type of cloud services**

Therefore, although the main rule for identifying a controller is *to search for who determines the purpose and scope of a processing,* in the SaaS and PaaS types, the service provider could also be considered a controller/joint controller with the customer. The proper identification of controller and processor roles is essential for clarifying the P&DP liabilities of customer and service provider, as well as the applicable law.

A guide that may be helpful to use for a proper identification of controller and processor roles in a cloud services environment in terms of SaaS, PaaS, and IaaS is the NIST document SP800—145, "The NIST Definition of Cloud Computing."[111]

Data Discovery

The implementation of data discovery solutions provides operative foundation for effective application and governance for any of the P&DP fulfillments. Data discovery is focused on the use of tools to discover patterns and trends in large data sets. According to Gartner's IT Glossary, search-based data discovery tools enable users to develop and refine views and analyses of structured and unstructured data using search terms.[112] Data discovery is commonly linked to the concept of big data as well, because it focuses on the three "Vs" that are typically used to describe big data solutions: volume, velocity, and variety. Using data discovery tools, large data sets that are either structured or unstructured from multiple sources can be analyzed quickly, providing the user insights into the data that may otherwise remain hidden.

From the Customer Perspective

The customer in their role of data controller has full responsibility for compliance with the P&DP laws obligations; therefore, the implementation of data discovery solutions together with data classification techniques provide him with sound basis for operatively specifying to the service provider the requirements to be fulfilled and for performing effective periodic audit according to the applicable P&DP laws, as well as for demonstrating, to the competent privacy authorities, his due accountability according to the applicable P&DP laws.

From the Service Provider Perspective

The service provider in their role of data processor has necessity to implement and be able to demonstrate he has implemented in a clear and objective way the rules and the security measures to be applied in the processing of personal data on behalf of the controller; thus, data discovery solutions together with data classification techniques will provide him with an effective enabler factor for his ability to comply with the Controller P&DP instructions.

Implementation of data discovery together with data classification techniques represents the foundation of data leakage/loss prevention (DLP) and of data protection (DP), applied to personal data processing in order to operate in compliance with the P&DP laws.

Classification of Discovered Sensitive Data

Classification of data for the purpose of compliance with the applicable P&DP laws plays an essential role for the operative control of those elements that are the feeds of the P&DP fulfillments. This means that not only the "nature" of the data should be traced with classification but also its relation with the "P&DP law context" in which the data itself shall be processed.

Data classification can be accomplished in different ways, ranging from "tagging" the data by using other external information to extrapolating the classification from the content of the data. The latter one, however, may raise some concerns because, according to the laws of some jurisdictions, this can result in prohibited monitoring actions on the content belonging to data subjects (for example, the laws that restrict or do not allow access to the content of e-mail in employer-employee relationships).

The use of classification methods will be properly ruled in the cloud service agreements between the customer and the service provider in order to achieve efficacy in classification within the limits set out by the laws ruling the access to the data content.

Mapping and Definition of Controls

All the P&DP requirements are important in a cloud service context; however, it is appropriate for the security practitioner to bear in mind the key privacy cloud service factors, depicted in Figure 7.55.

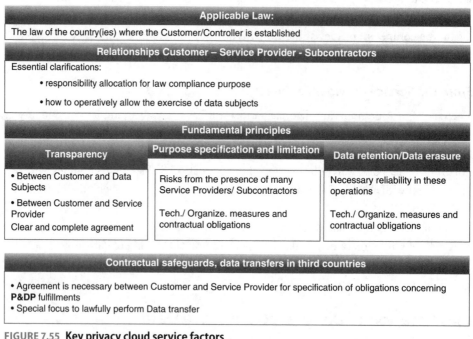

FIGURE 7.55 **Key privacy cloud service factors**
Source: Cloud Security Alliance

These Key Privacy Cloud Service Factors stem from the "Opinion 5/2012 on Cloud Computing" adopted by the WP 29; this working party was set up under Article 29 of Directive 95/46/EC, and it is an independent European advisory body on data protection and privacy, essentially formed by the representatives of all the EU Data Protection Authorities.[113]

These factors show that the primary need is to properly clarify in terms of contractual obligations the privacy and data protection requirements among the customer and cloud service provider.

In this context, the Cloud Security Alliance has defined baselines for compliance with data protection legislation and best practices with the realization of a standard format named the privacy level agreement (PLA). By means of the PLA, the service provider declares the level of personal data protection and security that it sustains for the relevant data processing.

The PLA, as defined by the Cloud Security Alliance:

- Provides a clear and effective way to communicate the level of personal data protection provided by a service provider

- Works as a tool to assess the level of a service provider's compliance with data protection legislative requirements and best practices

- Provides a way to offer contractual protection against possible financial damages due to lack of compliance

All the information concerning the various PLAs is documented by the Cloud Security Alliance on its website.[114]

Application of Defined Controls for Personally Identifiable Information (PII)

Since the application of data protection measures has the ultimate goal to fulfill the P&DP laws applicable to the controller, any constraints arising from specific arrangements of a cloud service operation shall be made clear by the service provider in order to avoid any consequences for unlawful personal data processing. For example, with regards to servers located across several countries, it would be difficult to ensure the proper application of measures such as encryption for sensitive data on all systems.

In this context, the previously mentioned PLAs play an essential role. Furthermore, the service providers could benefit from making explicit reference to standardized frameworks of security controls expressly defined for cloud services.

In this sense, the Cloud Security Alliance Cloud Controls Matrix (CCM) (`https://cloudsecurityalliance.org/research/ccm/`) is an essential and up-to-date security controls framework addressed to the cloud community and stakeholders. A fundamental richness of the CCM is its ability to provide mapping/cross relationships with the main industry-accepted security standards, regulations, and controls frameworks such as the ISO 27001/27002 and ISACA's COBIT and PCI-DSS.

The CCM can be seen as an inventory of cloud service security controls, arranged in the following separate security domains:

- Application and interface security
- Audit assurance and compliance
- Business continuity management and operational resilience
- Change control and configuration management
- Data security and information lifecycle management
- Datacenter security

- Encryption and key management

- Governance and risk management

- Human resources

- Identity and access management

- Infrastructure and virtualization security

- Interoperability and portability

- Mobile security

- Security incident management, e-discovery, and cloud

- Supply chain management, transparency, and accountability

- Threat and vulnerability management

Although all the CCM security controls can be considered as applicable in a specific CS context, from the privacy and data protection perspective, some of them have greater relevance to the P&DP fulfillments.

Therefore, the selection and implementation of controls for a specific cloud service involving processing of personal data shall be performed within the context of an information security managed system:

- This requires at least the identification of law requirements, risk analysis, design and implementation of security policies, and related assessment and reviews.

- The cloud service provider needs to consider the typical set of data protection and privacy measures required by the P&DP laws.

Data Storage and Transmission

At the core of all cloud services, products, and solutions are software tools with three underlying pillars of functionality—tools for processing data and running applications (compute servers), moving data (networking), and preserving or storing data (storage).

Cloud storage is basically defined as data storage that is made available as a service via a network. Products and solutions are the most common cloud storage service building blocks of physical storage systems. Private cloud and public services from SaaS to PaaS and IaaS leverage tiered storage including solid state drives (SSDs) and hard disk drives (HDDs). Similar to traditional enterprise storage environments, cloud services and solution providers exploit a mix of different storage technology tiers that meet different service level objective (SLO) and service level agreement (SLA) requirements. For example, using fast SSDs for dense I/O consolidation—supporting database journals and indices, metadata for fast lookup, and other transactional data—enables more work to be performed with less energy in a denser and more cost-effective footprint.

Using a mixture of ultra-fast SSDs along with high-capacity HDDs provides a balance of performance and capacity to meet other service requirements with different service cost options. With cloud services, instead of specifying what type of physical drive to buy, cloud providers cater for that by providing various availability, cost, capacity, functionality, and performance options to meet different SLA and SLO requirements.

Infrastructure as a Service (IaaS)

Cloud infrastructure services, known as infrastructure as a service (IaaS), are self-service models for accessing, monitoring, and managing remote data center infrastructures, such as compute (virtualized or bare mental), storage, networking, and networking services (e.g., firewalls). Instead of having to purchase hardware outright, users can purchase IaaS based on consumption. Compared to SaaS and PaaS, IaaS users are responsible for managing applications, data, runtime, middleware, and OSs. Providers still manage virtualization, servers, hard drives, storage, and networking. Figure 7.56 shows the differences between object and volume storage types.

IaaS uses the following storage types:

- **Volume storage**—A virtual hard drive that can be attached to a virtual machine instance and be used to host data within a file system. Volumes attached to IaaS instances behave just like a physical drive or an array does. Examples include VMware VMFS, Amazon EBS, RackSpace RAID, and OpenStack Cinder.

- **Object storage**—Object storage is like a file share accessed via APIs or a web interface. Examples include Amazon S3 and RackSpace cloud files.

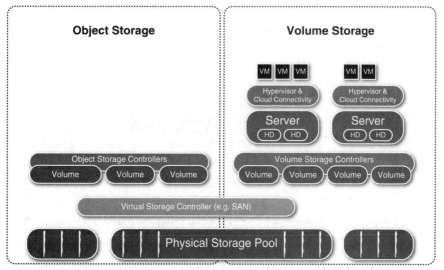

FIGURE 7.56 Differences between object and volume storage types

Platform as a Service (PaaS)

What developers gain with PaaS is a framework they can build upon to develop or customize applications. PaaS makes the development, testing, and deployment of applications quick, simple, and cost-effective. With this technology, enterprise operations, or a third-party provider, can manage OSs, virtualization, servers, storage, networking, and the PaaS software itself. Developers, however, manage the applications.

PaaS utilizes the following data storage types:

- **Structured**—Structured data refers to information with a high degree of organization, such that inclusion in a relational database is seamless and readily searchable by simple, straightforward search engine algorithms or other search operations.

- **Unstructured**—Usually refers to information that does not reside in a traditional row-column database. Unstructured data files often include text and multimedia content. Examples include e-mail messages, word processing documents, videos, photos, audio files, presentations, web pages, and many other kinds of business documents. Note that while these sorts of files may have an internal structure, they are still considered "unstructured" because the data they contain does not fit neatly in a database.

Software as a Service (SaaS)

Cloud application services, or software as a service (SaaS), use the Web to deliver applications that are managed by a third-party vendor and whose interface is accessed on the clients' side. Many SaaS applications can be run directly from a web browser without any downloads or installations required, although some require small plugins. With SaaS, it is easy for enterprises to streamline their maintenance and support because everything can be managed by vendors: applications, runtime, data, middleware, OSs, virtualization, servers, storage, and networking. Popular SaaS offering types include e-mail and collaboration, customer relationship management, and healthcare-related applications.

SaaS utilizes the following data storage types:

- **Information Storage and Management**—Data is entered into the system via the web interface and stored within the SaaS application (usually a back-end database). This data storage utilizes databases, which in turn are installed on object or volume storage.

- **Content/File Storage**—File-based content is stored within the SaaS application (e.g., reports, image files, documents) and made accessible via the web-based user interface. This store also utilizes object and volume storage.

Other types of storage that may be utilized include

- **Ephemeral storage**—This type of storage is relevant for IaaS instances, and it exists only as long as its instance is up. It will typically be used for swap files and other temporary storage needs and will be terminated with its instance.

- **Content delivery network (CDN)**—Content is stored in object storage, which is then distributed to multiple geographically distributed nodes to improve Internet consumption speed.

- **Raw storage**—Raw device mapping (RDM) is an option in the VMware server virtualization environment that enables a storage logical unit number (LUN) to be directly connected to a VM from the storage area network (SAN). In Microsoft's Hyper-V platform, this is accomplished using pass-through disks.[115]

- **Long-term storage**—Some vendors offer a cloud storage service tailored to the needs of data archiving. These include features such as search, guaranteed immutability, and data lifecycle management. The HP Autonomy Digital Safe archiving service uses an on-premises appliance that connects to customers' data stores via APIs and allows search. Digital Safe provides read-only, WORM, legal hold, e-discovery, and all the features associated with enterprise archiving. Its appliance carries out data deduplication prior to transmission to the data repository.[116]

Data Dispersion in Cloud Storage[117]

Data dispersion techniques are used to provide high availability, assurance, and performance when writing data into cloud-based storage systems. By fragmenting the data and writing each bit into different physical storage containers, greater information assurance can be achieved by the data owner. The underlying architecture of this technology involves the use of erasure coding, which takes a data object (think of a file with self-describing metadata) and chunks it into segments. Each segment is encrypted and cut into 16 slices and dispersed across an organization's network to reside on different hard drives and servers. If the organization has access to only 10 of the slices—because of disk failures, for instance—the original data can still be put back together. If the data is generally static with very few rewrites, such as media files and archive logs, creating and distributing the data is a one-time cost. If the data is very dynamic, the erasure codes have to be re-created and the resulting data blocks redistributed.

Threats to Storage Types

Cloud storage is subject to the following key threats:

- Administrators for the cloud provider can technically access your volumes and storage. This can be a challenge for security measures and indeed for compliance (with an emphasis on reporting/auditing).

- Private volume storage can very easily become publically available with a simple configuration change.

- Volumes and their snapshots can be used as an invaluable resource for troubleshooting purposes. Controls and verification should be in place to ensure that the data sent for external company support does not contain sensitive information.

- Object-level storage typically lacks comprehensive security controls (such as access control lists [ACLs], audit, and permissions). All controls for data access should be integrated into the application as well as other supporting mechanisms.

- There can be multi-tenancy issues. When you are using a multi-tenant cloud, your data is placed on the same physical hard drive as other tenants. There is a possibility that any tenant's data can be seized and reviewed as part of an investigation by either the provider or law enforcement. This could mean that your data is seized as part of the investigation, and it may be subject to review and disclosure as well.

Technologies Available to Address Threats

The security practitioner will need to leverage different technologies to address the varied threats that may face the enterprise with regards to the safe storage and use of their data in the cloud. The circumstances of each threat will be different, and as a result, the key to success will be the ability of the security practitioner to understand the nature of the threat they are facing, combined with their ability to implement the appropriate technology to mitigate the threat.

DLP

Data loss prevention, also known as data leakage prevention or data loss protection, are terms used interchangeably by practitioners and indeed businesses alike to describe the controls put in place by an organization to ensure that certain types of data (structured and unstructured) remain under organizational controls, in line with policies, standards, and procedures.

Controls to protect data form the foundation of organizational security, along with enabling the organization to ensure the ability to meet regulatory requirements and relevant legislation (i.e., EU data protection directives, U.S. privacy act, HIPPA, and PCI-DSS). DLP technologies and processes play important roles when building those controls. The appropriate implementation and use of DLP will reduce both security and regulatory risks for the organization.

DLP technology presents a wide and varied set of components that need to be contextually applied by the organization, often requiring changes to the enterprise security architecture. It is for this reason why many organizations do not adopt a "full-blown" DLP strategy across the enterprise. In this module we will not discuss the entire implementation methodology of DLP, or indeed all relevant components, because many of these do not apply to cloud-based services or solutions. For those hybrid cloud users or those utilizing cloud-based services partially within their organizations, it would be beneficial to ensure that DLP is understood and is appropriately structured across both cloud and non-cloud environments. Failure to do so can result in segmented and non-standardized levels of security—leading to increased risks.

DLP consists of three components:

- **Discovery and classification**—This is the first stage of a DLP implementation and also an ongoing and recurring process; the majority of cloud-based DLP technologies are predominantly focused on this component.

- **Monitoring**—Data usage monitoring forms the key function of DLP. Effective DLP strategies monitor the usage of data across locations and platforms while enabling administrators to define one or more usage policies. The ability to monitor data can be executed on gateways, servers, and storage, as well as workstations and endpoint devices. Recently, the increased adoption of external services to assist with DLP "as a service" has increased, along with many cloud-based DLP solutions.

- **Enforcement**—Upon a violation of policy being detected, specified relevant enforcement actions can automatically be performed. Enforcement options can include the ability to alert and log, block data transfers or re-route them for additional confirmation, or encrypt the data prior to leaving the organizational boundaries.

DLP Architecture

DLP tool implementations typically conform to the following topologies:

- **Data in Motion (DIM)**—Sometimes referred to as network-based or gateway DLP. In this topology the monitoring engine is deployed near the organizational gateway to monitor outgoing protocols such as HTTP, HTTPS, SMTP, and FTP. The topology can be a mixture of proxy-based, bridge, network tapping, or

SMTP relays. In order to scan encrypted HTTPS traffic, appropriate mechanisms to enable SSL interception/broker are required to be integrated into the system architecture.

- **Data at Rest (DAR)**—Sometimes referred to as storage based. In this topology the DLP engine is installed where the data is at rest, usually one or more storage subsystems, and file and application servers. This topology is very effective for data discovery and tracking usage but may require integration with network or endpoint-based DLP for policy enforcement.

- **Data in Use (DIU)**—Sometimes referred to as client or endpoint based, the DLP application is installed on a user's workstations and endpoint devices. This topology offers insights into how the data is used by users, with the ability to add additional protection that network DLP may not be able to provide. The challenge with client-based DLP is the complexity, time, and resources to implement across all endpoint devices, often across multiple locations and significant numbers of users.

Cloud-Based DLP Considerations

There are several things you need to take into consideration when implementing DLP:

- Data in the cloud tends to move and replicate, whether it is between locations, data centers, backups, or back and forth into the organizations. The replication and movement can present a challenge to any DLP implementation.

- Administrative access for enterprise data in the cloud could be tricky. Make sure you understand how to perform discovery and classification within cloud-based storage. Sometimes this will require authorization protocols to be involved (like OAUTH) or other processes.[118]

- DLP technology can affect overall performance. Network or gateway DLP, which scans all traffic for pre-defined content, might have an effect on network performance. Client-based DLPs scan all workstation access to data; this can have a performance impact on the workstation's operation. The overall impact must be considered during testing.

DLP Best Practices

There are a number of best practices for working with DLP that can make everything work more smoothly and effectively:

- Start with data discovery and classification process. Those processes are more mature within the cloud deployments and present value for the data security process.

- Cloud DLP policy should address the following:
  - What kind of data is permitted to be stored in the cloud?
  - Where can the data be stored (jurisdictions)?
  - How should it be stored? Encryption and storage access consideration.
  - What kind of data access is permitted? Which devices and what networks? Which applications? Which tunnel?
  - Under what conditions is data is allowed to leave the cloud?
- Encryption methods should be carefully examined based on the format of the data. Format preserving encryption such as information rights management (IRM) is getting more popular in document storage applications; however, other data types may require vendor-agnostic solutions.
- When you are implementing restrictions or controls to block or quarantine data items, it is essential to create procedures that will prevent business process damage due to false positive events.
- DLP can be an effective tool when planning or assessing a potential migration to cloud applications. DLP discovery will analyze the data going to the cloud for protected content, and the DLP detection engine can discover policy violations during data migration.

ENCRYPTION

Encryption is an important technology for the security practitioner to consider and use when implementing systems that will allow for secure data storage and usage from the cloud. While having encryption enabled on all data across the enterprise architecture would reduce the risks associated with unauthorized data access and exposure, there are performance constraints and concerns to be addressed. It is the responsibility of the security practitioner to implement encryption within the enterprise in such a way that it provides maximum security benefits, safeguarding the most mission-critical data, while minimizing system performance issues as a result of the encryption.

Encryption can be implemented within different phases of the data lifecycle:

- **Data in Motion**—Technologies for encrypting data in motion are mature and well defined and include IPSEC or VPN, TLS/SSL, and other "wire-level" protocols.
- **Data at Rest**—When the data is archived or stored, different encryption techniques should be used. The encryption mechanism itself may well vary in the

manner in which it is deployed, dependent on the timeframe or period for which the data will be stored. Examples of this may include extended retention vs. short term storage, data located in a database vs. file system, etc.

- **Data in Use**—Data that is being shared, processed, or viewed. This stage of the data lifecycle is less mature than other data encryption techniques, and it typically focuses on IRM/DRM solutions.

Sample Use Cases for Encryption

The following are some sample use cases for encryption:

- When data moves in and out of the cloud—for processing, archiving, or sharing—you can use encryption for data-in-motion techniques such as SSL/TLS or VPN in order to avoid information exposure or data leakage while in motion.
- Protecting data at rest such as file storage, database information, application components, archiving, and backup applications.
- Files or objects that must be protected when stored, used, or shared in the cloud.
- When complying with regulations such as HIPAA and PCI-DSS, which, in turn, requires relevant protection of data traversing "untrusted networks," along with the protection of certain data types.
- Protection from third party access via subpoena or lawful interception.
- Creating enhanced or increased mechanisms for logical separation between different customers' data in the cloud.
- Logical destruction of data when physical destruction is not feasible or technically possible.

Cloud Encryption Challenges

There are a myriad of factors influencing encryption considerations and associated implementations in the enterprise. The usage of encryption should always be directly related to business considerations, regulatory requirements, and any additional constraints that the organization may have to address. Different techniques will be used based on the location of data, whether at rest, in transit, or in use, while in the cloud. Different options might apply when dealing with specific threats like protecting PII, legally regulated information, or when defending against unauthorized access and viewing from systems and platform administrators.

- The integrity of encryption is heavily dependent on control and management of the relevant encryption keys, including how they are secured. If the keys are held by the cloud provider, not all data threats are mitigated against because unauthorized actors may gain access to the data through acquisition of the keys via a search warrant, legal ruling, or theft and misappropriation. Equally, if the customer is holding the encryption keys, this presents different challenges to ensure they are protected from unauthorized usage as well as compromise.

- Encryption can be challenging to implement effectively when a cloud provider is required to process the encrypted data, even for simple tasks such as indexing, along with the gathering of metadata.

- Data in the cloud is highly portable. It replicates and is copied and backed up extensively, making encryption and key management a complex and sizeable undertaking.

- Multi-tenant cloud environments and the shared use of physical hardware present challenges for the safeguarding of keys in volatile memory such as RAM caches.

- Secure hardware for encrypting keys may not exist in cloud environments, with software-based key storage often being more vulnerable to attack/compromise.

- Storage-level encryption is typically less complex, but it can be most easily exploited/compromised (given sufficient time and resources). The higher you go up towards the application level, the complexity to deploy and implement encryption becomes more challenging. However, encryption implemented at the application level will typically be more effective in protecting the confidentiality of the relevant assets or resources.

- Encryption can impact negatively on performance, especially when dealing with high-performance data processing mechanisms such as data warehouses and data cubes.

- The nature of cloud environments typically requires us to manage more keys than traditional environments (access keys, API keys, encryption keys, shared keys, among others).

- Some cloud encryption implementations require all users and service traffic to go through an encryption engine. This can result in availability and performance issues to both end users and to providers.

- Throughout the data lifecycle, data can change locations, format, encryption, and encryption keys. Using the data security lifecycle can help to document and map all those different aspects.

- Encryption affects data availability. Encryption complicates data availability controls such as backups, DR planning, and co-locations because expanding encryption into these areas increases the likelihood that keys may become compromised.

In addition, if encryption is applied incorrectly within any of these areas, the data may become inaccessible when needed.

■ Encryption does not solve data integrity threats. Data can be encrypted and yet be subject to tampering or file replacement attacks. In this case, supplementary cryptographic controls such as digital signatures need to be applied, along with non-repudiation for transaction-based activities.

Encryption Architecture

Encryption architecture is very much dependent on the goals of the encryption solutions, along with the cloud delivery mechanism. Protecting data at rest from local compromise or unauthorized access differs significantly from protecting data in motion into the cloud. Adding additional controls to protect the integrity and availability of data can further complicate the process.

Typically, the following components are associated with most encryption deployments:

■ **The Data**—The data object or objects that need to be encrypted.

■ **Encryption Engine**—Performs the encryption operation itself.

■ **Encryption Keys**—All encryption is based on keys. Safeguarding the keys is a crucial activity, necessary for ensuring the ongoing integrity of the encryption implementation and its algorithms.

Data Encryption in IaaS

The issues associated with data management and encryption in an IaaS model should be of concern to the SSCP. Due to the nature of the IaaS service model, the cloud service provider is often directly involved in implementing encryption of data on behalf of the customer. As a result, there is a need for the SSCP to understand the issues and concerns associated with this service model as they pertain to data confidentiality, integrity, and availability when storage versus volume-level encryption solutions are deployed. In addition, issues associated with key management and secure data life cycles also need to be considered. The following sections will touch on these issues, as well as solutions for some of the concerns they raise.

Basic Storage-Level Encryption

Where storage-level encryption is utilized, the encryption engine is located on the storage management level, with the keys usually held/stored/retained by the cloud provider. The engine will encrypt data written to the storage and decrypt it when exiting the storage (i.e., for use). This type of encryption is relevant to both object and volume storage, but it will only protect from hardware theft or loss. It will not protect from cloud provider administrator access or any unauthorized access coming from the layers above the storage.

Volume Storage Encryption

Volume storage encryption requires that the encrypted data resides on volume storage. This is typically done through an encrypted container, which is mapped as a folder or volume. Instance-based encryption allows access to data only through the volume operating system and, therefore, provides protection from the following:

- Physical loss or theft
- External administrator(s) accessing the storage
- Snapshots and storage-level backups being taken and removed from the system

Volume storage encryption will not provide protection against any access made through the instance, i.e., an attack that is manipulating or operating within the application running on the instance.

There are two methods that can be used to implement volume storage encryption:

- **Instance Based**—Where instance-based encryption is used, the encryption engine is located on the instance itself. Keys can be guarded locally but should be managed external to the instance.
- **Proxy-Based Encryption**—Where proxy-based encryption is used, the encryption engine is running on a proxy instance or appliance. The proxy instance is a secure machine that will handle all cryptographic actions including key management and storage. The proxy will map the data on the volume storage while providing access to the instances. Keys can be stored on the proxy or via external key storage (recommended) with the proxy providing the key exchanges and required safeguarding of keys in memory.

Object Storage Encryption

The majority of object storage services will offer server-side storage-level encryption as described earlier. This kind of encryption offers limited effectiveness, with the recommendation for external encryption mechanisms to be encrypting the data prior to its arrival within the cloud environments. Potential external mechanisms include:

- **File-Level Encryption**—Such as information rights management (IRM) or digital rights management (DRM) solutions, both of which can be very effective when used in conjunction with file hosting and sharing services that typically rely on object storage. The encryption engine is commonly implemented at the client side and will preserve the format of the original file.

- **Application-Level Encryption**—The encryption engine resides in the application that is utilizing the object storage. It can be integrated into the application component or by a proxy that is responsible for encrypting the data before going to the cloud. The proxy can be implemented on the customer gateway or as a service residing at the external provider.

Database Encryption

For database encryption, the following options should be understood:

- **File-Level Encryption**—Database servers typically reside on volume storage. For this deployment, we are encrypting the volume or folder of the database, with the encryption engine and keys residing on the instances attached to the volume. External file system encryption will protect from media theft, lost backups, and external attack, but it will not protect against attacks with access to the application layer, the instance's OS, or the database itself.

- **Transparent Encryption**—Many database management systems contain the ability to encrypt the entire database or specific portions, such as tables. The encryption engine resides within the DB, and it is transparent to the application. Keys usually reside within the instance, although processing and management of them may also be offload to an external key management system (KMS). This encryption can provide effective protection from media theft, backup system intrusions, and certain database and application-level attacks.

- **Application-Level Encryption**—In application-level encryption, the encryption engine resides at the application that is utilizing the database. Application encryption can act as a robust mechanism to protect against a wide range of threats, such as compromised administrative accounts along with other database and application-level attacks. Since the data is encrypted before reaching the database, it is challenging to perform indexing, searches, and metadata collection. Encrypting at the application layer can be challenging, based on the expertise requirements for cryptographic development and integration.

Key Management

Key management is one of the most challenging components of any encryption implementation. Even though new standards like Key Management Interoperability Protocol (KMIP) are emerging, safe guarding keys and appropriate management of keys are still among the most complicated tasks that the security practitioner will need to engage in when planning cloud data security.[119]

Common challenges with key management include the following:

- **Access to the Keys** — Best practices, coupled with regulatory requirements, may set specific criteria for key access, along with restricting or not permitting access to keys by cloud service provider employees or personnel.

- **Key Storage** — Secure storage for the keys is essential to safeguarding the data. In traditional "in-house" environments, keys were able to be stored in secure dedicated hardware. This may not always be possible in cloud environments.

- **Backup and Replication** — The nature of the cloud results in data backups and replication across a number of different formats. This can have an impact on the ability for long- and short-term key management to be maintained and managed effectively.

Considerations when planning key management include the following:

- Random number generation should be conducted as a trusted process.

- Throughout the lifecycle, cryptographic keys should never be transmitted in the clear and always remain in a "trusted" environment.

- When considering key escrow or key management "as a service," carefully plan to take into account all relevant laws, regulations, and jurisdictional requirements.

- Lack of access to the encryption keys will result in lack of access to the data. This should be considered when discussing confidentiality threats vs. availability threats.

- Where possible, key management functions should be conducted separately from the cloud provider in order to enforce separation of duties and force collusion to occur if unauthorized data access is attempted.

Key storage in the cloud is typically implemented using one or more of the following approaches:

- **Internally Managed** — In this method the keys are stored on the virtual machine or application component that is also acting as the encryption engine. This type of key management is usually used in storage-level encryption, internal database encryption, or backup application encryption. This approach can be helpful to mitigate against the risks associated with lost media.

- **Externally Managed** — In this method keys are maintained separate from the encryption engine and data. They can be on the same cloud platform, internally within the organization, or on a different cloud. The actual storage can be a separate instance (hardened especially for this specific task) or on a HSM. When implementing external key storage, consider how the key management system is integrated with the encryption engine and how the entire lifecycle of key creation through to retirement is managed.

- **Managed by a Third Party**—Key escrow services are provided by a trusted third party. Key management providers use specifically developed secure infrastructure and integration services for key management. The cloud security professional must evaluate any third-party key storage services provider that may be contracted by the organization to ensure that the risks of allowing a third party to hold encryption keys are well understood and documented.

Typically, cloud service providers protect keys using software-based solutions in order to avoid the additional cost and overhead of hardware-based security models.

NOTE Software-based key management solutions do not meet the physical security requirements specified in the NIST Federal Information Processing Standards Publication FIPS 140—2 or 140—3 specifications.[120] The ability for software to provide evidence of tampering is unlikely. The lack of FIPS certification for encryption may be an issue for U.S. federal government agencies and other organizations.

ENCRYPTION ALTERNATIVES AND OTHER DATA PROTECTION TECHNOLOGIES

The solutions discussed so far with regards to data protection have focused on the use of encryption and implementation of a secure data management life cycle. There are other technologies and approaches that can be used to augment the use of encryption or even to replace it, depending on the circumstances and operational requirements of the system being discussed. The SSCP should be able to understand the use of technologies such as data masking, data obfuscation, data anonymization, and tokenization.

Data Masking/Data Obfuscation

Data masking or data obfuscation is the process of hiding, replacing, or omitting sensitive information from a specific data set. Data masking is usually used in order to protect specific data sets, such as PII, and commercially sensitive data in order to comply with certain regulations such as HIPAA or PCI-DSS. Data masking or obfuscation is also widely used for test platforms (where suitable test data is not available). Both techniques are typically applied when migrating test or development environments to the cloud or when protecting production environments from certain threats such as data exposure by insiders or outsiders.

Common approaches for data masking include:

- **Random Substitution**—The value is replaced (or appended) with a random value.
- **Algorithmic Substitution**—The value is replaced (or appended) with an algorithm-generated value (this typically allows for two-way substitution).
- **Shuffle**—Shuffles different values from the dataset, usually from the same column.
- **Masking**—Uses specific characters to hide certain parts of the data. This usually applies for credit card data formats: XXXX XXXX XX65 5432.
- **Deletion**—Simply put a null value or delete the data.

Primary methods of masking data include:

- **Static**—In static masking, a new copy of the data is created with the masked values. Static masking is typically efficient when creating clean nonproduction environments.
- **Dynamic**—Dynamic masking (sometimes referred to as "on-the-fly" masking) adds a layer of masking between the application and the database. The masking layer is responsible for masking the information in the database "on the fly" when it is accessed by the presentation layer. This type of masking is efficient when protecting production environments; i.e., dynamic masking can hide the full credit card number from customer service representatives, but the data remains available for processing.

Data Anonymization

Direct identifiers and indirect identifiers form two primary components for identification of individuals, users, or indeed personal information. Direct identifiers are fields that uniquely identify the subject (usually name, address, etc.) and usually referred to as PII (personal identifiable information). Masking solutions are usually used to protect direct identifiers. Indirect identifiers typically consist of demographic or socioeconomic information, dates, or events. While each standalone indirect identifier cannot identify the individual, the risk is that combining a number of indirect identifiers together with external data can result in exposing the subject of the information. For example, imagine a scenario where users were able to combine search engine data with online streaming recommendations to tie back posts and recommendations to individual users on a website.

Anonymization is the process of removing the indirect identifiers in order to prevent data analysis tools or other intelligent mechanisms from collating or pulling data from multiple sources to identify an individual or sensitive information. The process of anonymization is similar to masking and includes identifying the relevant information to anonymize and the choosing of a relevant method for obscuring the data. The challenge with indirect identifiers is the ability for this type of data to be integrated in free text fields, which tend to be less structured than direct identifiers, thus complicating the process.

Tokenization

Tokenization is the process of substituting a sensitive data element with a non-sensitive equivalent, referred to as a token. The token is usually a collection of random values with the shape and form of the original data placeholder, and it is mapped back to the original data by the tokenization application or solution.

Tokenization is not encryption, and it presents different challenges and different benefits. Encryption is using a key to obfuscate data, while tokenization removes the data entirely from the database, replacing it with a mechanism to identify and access the resources.

Tokenization is used to safe guard the sensitive data in a secure, protected, or regulated environment. Tokenization can be implemented internally where there is a need to secure sensitive data centrally or externally using a tokenization service.

Tokenization can assist with:

- Complying with regulations or laws

- Reducing the cost of compliance

- Mitigating risks of storing sensitive data and reducing attack vectors on that data

The basic tokenization architecture can be seen in Figure 7.57.

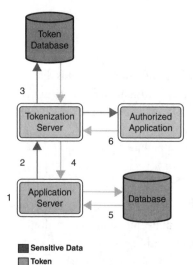

FIGURE 7.57 **Basic tokenization architecture**

There are several considerations when using tokenization with the cloud:

- When you are using tokenization as a service, it is imperative to ensure the provider and solutions have the ability to protect your data.

- When using tokenization as a service, pay special attention to the process of authenticating the application when storing or retrieving the sensitive data. Where external tokenization is used, appropriate encryption of communications should be applied to data in motion.

- As always, evaluate your compliance requirements before considering a cloud-based tokenization solution. The risks of having to interact with different jurisdictions and different compliance requirements will need to be weighed by the security practitioner.

Third-Party/Outsourcing Implications

The need to understand the issues associated with the use of third party/outsourcing solutions is an important area of risk management. The concerns in this area are varied and need to be well understood and documented to be managed successfully within the enterprise. Usage of SLAs and hosting agreements to control cloud-based solutions is a common practice that the SSCP should be comfortable with. The crafting of data retention policies will allow the SSCP to ensure that regardless of whether data is being managed directly within the organization or by a contracted third party, that data is securely maintained for the required period of time to ensure compliance obligations are being met. Data deletion procedures need to be documented and defined so that the SSCP can ensure that all data is being securely destroyed when the time comes to do so, regardless of who will ultimately execute the procedure.

Data Retention Policies

A data retention policy is an organization's established protocol for retaining information for operational or regulatory compliance needs. The objectives of a data retention policy are to keep important information for future use or reference, to organize information so it can be searched and accessed at a later date, and to dispose of information that is no longer needed. The policy balances the legal, regulation, and business data archival requirements against data storage costs, complexity, and other data considerations. A good data retention policy should define retention periods, data formats, data security, and data retrieval procedures for the enterprise.

A data retention policy for cloud services should contain the following key components:

- **Legislation, Regulation, And Standards Requirements**—Data retention considerations are heavily dependent on the data type and the required compliance regimes associated with it. For example, according to the Basel II Accords for Financial Data, the retention period for financial transactions should be between 3 to 7 years, while according to the PCI-DSS version 3.0 Requirement 10, credit card transaction data should be kept available for at least a year with at least 3 months available online.[121]

- **Data Mapping**—The process of mapping all relevant data in order to understand data types (structured, unstructured), data formats (file types), and data location (network drives, databases, object or volume storage).

- **Data Classification**—Classifying the data based on locations, compliance requirements, ownership, or business usage. Classification is also used in order to decide on the proper retention procedures for the enterprise.

- **Data Retention Procedure**—For each data category, the data retention procedures should be followed based on the appropriate data retention policy that governs the data type. How long the data is to be kept, where (physical location, jurisdiction), and how (which technology and format) should all be spelled out in the policy and implemented via the procedure. The procedure should also include backup options, retrieval requirements, and restore procedures as required and necessary for the data types being managed.

- **Monitoring and Maintenance**—Procedures for making sure that the entire process is working, including review of the policy and requirements to make sure that there are no changes and compensating controls such as initiated periodic data access in order to make sure that the process is working.

Data Deletion Procedures and Mechanisms

A key part of data protection procedures is the safe disposal of data once it is no longer needed. Failure to do so may result in data breaches and compliance failures. Safe disposal procedures are designed to ensure that there are no files, pointers, or data remnants left behind within a system that could be used to restore the original data.

A data deletion policy is sometimes required for the following reasons:

- **Regulation or Legislation**—Certain laws and regulation such as HIPAA, GLB Act, and FISMA require specific degrees of safe disposal for certain records.

- **Business and Technical Requirements**—Business policy may require safe disposal of data. Also processes such as encryption might require safe disposal of the clear text data after creating the encrypted copy.

Restoring deleted data in a cloud environment is not an easy task for an attacker because cloud-based data is scattered, typically being stored in different physical locations with unique pointers, and achieving any level of physical access to the media is a challenge. Nevertheless, it is still an existing attack vector that the cloud security professional should consider when evaluating the business requirements for data disposal.

In order to safely dispose of electronic records, the cloud security professional should consider the following options:

- **Physical Destruction**—Physically destroying the media by incineration, shredding, or other means.

- **Degaussing**—Using strong magnets for scrambling data on magnetic media such as hard drives and tapes.

- **Overwriting**—Writing random data over the actual data. The more times the overwriting process occurs, the more thorough the destruction of the data is considered to be.

- **Encryption**—Using an encryption method to re-write the data in an encrypted format to make it unreadable without the encryption key.

Since the first three options are not applicable to cloud computing, the only reasonable method remaining is encrypting the data. The process of encrypting the data in order to dispose of it is called *digital shredding* or *crypto-shredding*.

Crypto-shredding is the process of deliberately destroying the encryption keys that were used to encrypt the data originally. Since the data is encrypted with the keys, the result is the data is rendered unreadable (at least until the encryption protocol used can be broken or is capable of being brute-forced by an attacker).

In order to perform proper crypto-shredding, the security practitioner should consider the following:

- The data should be encrypted completely without leaving any clear text remaining.

- The technique must make sure that the encryption keys are totally unrecoverable. This can be hard to accomplish if the keys are managed by an external cloud provider or other third party.

Data Archiving Procedures and Mechanisms

Data archiving is the process of identifying and moving inactive data out of current production systems and into specialized long-term archival storage systems. Moving inactive data out of production systems optimizes the performance of resources needed there, while specialized archival systems store information more cost-effectively and provide for retrieval when needed.

A data archiving policy for the cloud should contain the following elements:

- **Data Encryption Procedures**—Long-term data archiving with encryption could present a challenge for the organization with regards to key management. Encryption policy should consider which media is used, restoral options, and what the threats are that should be mitigated by the encryption. Bad key management could lead to the destruction of the entire archive and therefore requires the attention of the security practitioner.

- **Data Monitoring Procedures**—Data stored in the cloud tends to be replicated and moved. In order to maintain data governance, it is required that all data access and movements be tracked and logged to make sure that all security controls are being applied properly throughout the data lifecycle.

- **Ability to Perform eDiscovery and Granular Retrieval**—Archive data may be subject to retrieval according to certain parameters such as dates, subject, authors, and so on. The archiving platform should provide the ability to do eDiscovery on the data in order to decide which data should be retrieved.

- **Backup and Disaster Recovery Options**—All requirements for data backup and restore should be specified and clearly documented. It is important for the security practitioner to ensure that the business continuity and disaster recovery plans are updated and aligned with whatever procedures are implemented.

- **Data Format and Media Type**—The format of the data is an important consideration because it may be kept for an extended period of time. Proprietary formats can change, leaving data in a useless state, so choosing the right format is very important. The same consideration must be made for media storage types as well.

- **Data Restoration Procedures**—Data restoral testing should be initiated periodically to make sure that the process is working. The trial data restore should be made into an isolated environment in order to mitigate risks such as restoring an old virus or accidently over-writing existing data.

Event Sources

The relevant event sources that the security practitioner will draw data from will vary according to the cloud services modules that the organization is consuming. The service modules are Saas, IaaS, and PaaS.

SaaS

In SaaS environments, the security practitioner typically will have minimal control of, and access to, event and diagnostic data. Most infrastructure-level logs will not be visible to them, and they will be limited to high-level, application-generated logs that are located on a client endpoint. In order for the security practitioner to maintain reasonable investigation capabilities, auditability, and traceability of data, it is recommended to specify required data access requirements in the cloud SLA or contract with the cloud service provider. The following data sources play an important role in event investigation and documentation:

- Web server logs
- Application server logs
- Database logs
- Guest operating system logs
- Host access logs
- Network infrastructure devices logs
- Application level logs
- Virtualization platform logs and SaaS portal logs
- Network captures
- Billing records
- User access records
- Management application logs

PaaS

In PaaS environments, the security practitioner typically will have control of, and access to, event and diagnostic data. Some infrastructure-level logs will be visible to them, along with detailed application logs. Because the applications that will be monitored are being built and designed by the organization directly, the level of application data that can be extracted and monitored is up to the developers. In order to maintain reasonable investigation capabilities, auditability, and traceability of data, the security practitioner should work with the development team to understand the capabilities of the applications under development and to help design and implement monitoring regimes that will maximize the organization's visibility into the applications and their data streams.

OWASP recommends the following application events to be logged:[122]

- Input validation failures, e.g., protocol violations, unacceptable encodings, invalid parameter names and values
- Output validation failures, e.g., database record set mismatch, invalid data encoding
- Authentication successes and failures
- Authorization (access control) failures

- Session management failures, e.g., cookie session identification value modification

- Application errors and system events, e.g., syntax and runtime errors, connectivity problems, performance issues, third-party service error messages, file system errors, file upload virus detection, configuration changes

- Application and related systems startups and shutdowns, and logging initialization (starting, stopping, or pausing)

- Use of higher-risk functionality, e.g., network connections, addition or deletion of users, changes to privileges, assigning users to tokens, adding or deleting tokens, use of systems administrative privileges, access by application administrators, all actions by users with administrative privileges, access to payment cardholder data, use of data encrypting keys, key changes, creation and deletion of system-level objects, data import and export including screen-based reports, and submission of user-generated content—especially file uploads

- Legal and other opt-ins, e.g., permissions for mobile phone capabilities, terms of use, terms and conditions, personal data usage consent, and permission to receive marketing communications

IaaS

In IaaS environments, the security practitioner typically will have control of, and access to, event and diagnostic data. Almost all infrastructure-level logs will be visible to them, along with detailed application logs. In order for the security practitioner to maintain reasonable investigation capabilities, auditability, and traceability of data, it is recommended to specify required data access requirements in the cloud SLA or contract with the cloud service provider.

The following logs might be important for the security practitioner to examine at some point, but they might not be available by default:

- Cloud or network provider perimeter network logs

- Logs from DNS servers

- VMM logs

- Host operating system and hypervisor logs

- API access logs

- Management portal logs

- Packet captures

- Billing records

Data Event Logging and Event Attributes

In order for the SSCP to be able to perform effective audits and investigations as needed, the event log should contain as much of the relevant data for the processes being examined as possible. OWASP recommends the following data to be integrated into event data:[123]

- When
    - Log date and time (international format)
    - Event date and time—the event time stamp may be different from the time of logging, e.g., server logging where the client application is hosted on remote device that is only periodically or intermittently online
    - Interaction identifier
- Where
    - Application identifier, e.g., name and version
    - Application address, e.g., cluster/host name or server IPv4 or IPv6 address and port number, workstation identity, local device identifier
    - Service, e.g., name and protocol
    - Geolocation
    - Window/form/page, e.g., entry point URL and HTTP method for a web application, dialog box name
    - Code location, e.g., script name, module name
- Who (human or machine user)
    - Source address, e.g., user's device/machine identifier, user's IP address, cell/RF tower ID, mobile telephone number
    - User identity (if authenticated or otherwise known), e.g., user database table primary key value, username, license number
- What
    - Type of event
    - Severity of event, e.g., {0=emergency, 1=alert, . . ., 7=debug}, {fatal, error, warning, info, debug, trace}
    - Security relevant event flag (if the logs contain non-security event data too)
    - Description

Additionally, consider recording:

- Secondary time source (e.g., GPS), event date, and time

- Action—original intended purpose of the request, e.g., log in, refresh session ID, log out, update profile

- Object—the affected component or other object (user account, data resource, file), e.g., URL, session ID, user account, file

- Result status—whether the ACTION aimed at the OBJECT was successful, e.g., success, fail, defer

- Reason—why the status occurred, e.g., user not authenticated in database check, incorrect credentials

- HTTP Status Code (web applications only)—the status code returned to the user (often 200 or 301)

- Request HTTP headers or HTTP User Agent (web applications only)

- User type classification, e.g., public, authenticated user, CMS user, search engine, authorized penetration tester, uptime monitor

- Analytical confidence in the event detection, e.g., low, medium, high, or a numeric value

- Responses seen by the user and taken by the application, e.g., status code, custom text messages, session termination, administrator alerts

- Extended details, e.g., stack trace, system error messages, debug information, HTTP request body, HTTP response headers and body

- Internal classifications, e.g., responsibility, compliance references

- External classifications, e.g., NIST Security Content Automation Protocol (SCAP), Mitre Common Attack Pattern Enumeration and Classification (CAPEC) [124]

Storage and Analysis of Data Events

Event and log data can become very costly to archive and maintain depending on the volume of data being gathered. The security practitioner needs to carefully consider these issues as well as the business/regulatory requirements and responsibilities of the organization when planning for event data preservation.

Preservation is defined by ISO 27037:2012 as the "process to maintain and safeguard the integrity and/or original condition of the potential digital evidence."[125]

Evidence preservation helps assure admissibility in a court of law. However, digital evidence is notoriously fragile and is easily changed or destroyed. Given that the backlog in many forensic laboratories ranges from six months to a year (and that delays in the legal system might create further delays), potential digital evidence may spend a significant period of time in storage before it is analyzed or used in a legal proceeding. Storage requires strict access controls to protect the items from accidental or deliberate modification, as well as appropriate environment controls.

Please also note that certain regulations and standards require that event logging mechanism should be tamper proof in order to avoid the risks of faked event logs.

The gathering, analysis, storage, and archiving of event and log data is not limited to the forensic investigative process, however. In all organizations, the security practitioner will be called on to execute these activities on an ongoing basis for a variety of reasons during the normal flow of enterprise operations. Whether it is to examine a firewall log, to diagnose an application installation error, to validate access controls, to understand network traffic flows, or to manage resource consumption, the use of event data and logs is a standard practice.

What the security practitioner needs to concern themselves with is how they can collect the volumes of logged event data available and manage it from a centralized location. That is where SIEM systems come in.

Security information and event management is a term for software and products services combining security information management (SIM) and security event management (SEM). SIEM technology provides real-time analysis of security alerts generated by network hardware and applications. SIEM is sold as software, appliances, or managed services and are also used to log security data and generate reports for compliance purposes.

The acronyms SEM, SIM, and SIEM have been sometimes used interchangeably. The segment of security management that deals with real-time monitoring, correlation of events, notifications, and console views is commonly known as security event management (SEM). The second area provides long-term storage, analysis, and reporting of log data and is known as security information management (SIM).

SIEM systems will typically provide the following capabilities:

- **Data Aggregation**—Log management aggregates data from many sources, including network, security, servers, databases, and applications, providing the ability to consolidate monitored data to help avoid missing crucial events.

- **Correlation**—Looks for common attributes and links events together into meaningful bundles. This technology provides the ability to perform a variety of correlation techniques to integrate different sources in order to turn data into useful information. Correlation is typically a function of the security event management portion of a full SIEM solution.

- **Alerting**—The automated analysis of correlated events and production of alerts to notify recipients of immediate issues. Alerts can be sent to a dashboard or sent via third-party channels such as e-mail.

- **Dashboards**—Tools can take event data and turn it into informational charts to assist in seeing patterns or identifying activity that is not forming a standard pattern.

- **Compliance**—Applications can be employed to automate the gathering of compliance data, producing reports that adapt to existing security, governance, and auditing processes.

- **Retention**—Employing long-term storage of historical data to facilitate correlation of data over time and to provide the retention necessary for compliance requirements. Long-term log data retention is critical in forensic investigations because it is unlikely that discovery of a network breach will be at the time of the breach occurring.

- **Forensic analysis**—The ability to search across logs on different nodes and time periods based on specific criteria. This mitigates having to aggregate log information in your head or having to search through thousands and thousands of logs.

However, there are challenges with SIEM systems in the cloud that have to be considered when deciding whether or not this technology will make sense for the organization. Turning over internal security data to a cloud provider requires trust, and many users of cloud services will desire more clarity on providers' security precautions before being willing to trust a provider with this kind of information.

Another problem with pushing SIEM into the cloud is that targeted attack detection requires in-depth knowledge of internal systems, the kind found in corporate security teams. Cloud-based SIEM services may have trouble with recognizing the low-and-slow attacks. In targeted attacks, many of the times that organizations are breached, attackers create only a relatively small amount of activity while carrying out their attacks. To see that evidence, you need to know the environment. Cloud services may not be able to do that effectively.

SECURING BIG DATA SYSTEMS

The world's effective capacity to exchange information through telecommunication networks was 281 petabytes in 1986, 471 petabytes in 1993, 2.2 exabytes in 2000, and 65 exabytes in 2007, and it is predicted that the amount of traffic flowing over the Internet will reach 667 exabytes annually by 2014.[126] It is estimated that one-third of the globally stored information is in the form of alphanumeric text and still image data, which is the format most useful for most big data applications.[127]

The term *big data* refers to the massive amounts of digital information companies and governments collect about us and our surroundings. Security and privacy issues are magnified by velocity, volume, and variety of big data, such as large-scale cloud infra-structures, diversity of data sources and formats, streaming nature of data acquisition, and high volume inter-cloud migration.

Though the word "big" implies such, big data is not simply defined by volume; it's about complexity. Many small datasets that are considered big data do not consume much physical space but are particularly complex in nature. At the same time, large data-sets that require significant physical space may not be complex enough to be considered big data. In addition to volume, the big data label also includes data variety and velocity making up the three V's of big data—volume, variety, and velocity. Variety references the different types of structured and unstructured data that organizations can collect, such as transaction-level data, video and audio, or text and log files. Velocity is an indication of how quickly the data can be made available for analysis.[128]

An August 2013 blog post by Mark van Rijmenam titled "Why the 3V's Are Not Suf-ficient to Describe Big Data" added "veracity, variability, visualization, and value" to the definition, broadening the realm even further. Rijmenam stated, "90% of all data ever created was created in the past two years. From now on, the amount of data in the world will double every two years."[129]

Interpretation of big data can bring about insights that might not be immediately vis-ible or that would be impossible to find using traditional methods. This process focuses on finding hidden threads, trends, or patterns, which may be invisible to the naked eye. Sounds easy, right? Well, it requires new technologies and skills to analyze the flow of material and draw conclusions. Apache Hadoop is one such technology, and it is gener-ally the software most commonly associated with big data. Apache calls it "a framework that allows for the distributed processing of large data sets across clusters of computers using simple programming models." Just as big data can be both a noun and a verb, Hadoop involves something that is and something that does—specifically, data storage and data processing. Both of these occur in a distributed fashion to improve efficiency and results. A set of tasks known as MapReduce coordinates the processing of data in different segments of the cluster and then breaks down the results to more manageable chunks that are summarized. Hadoop is open source, and there are variants produced by many different vendors such as Cloudera, Hortonworks, MapR, and Amazon. There are also other products such HPCC and cloud-based services such as Google BigQuery.

From a security perspective, there are two distinct issues: securing the organization and its customers' information in a big data context; and using big data techniques to analyze, and even predict, security incidents.

According to Adrian Lane, CTO at Securosis, the big data phenomenon is driven by the intersection of three trends:[130]

- Mountains of data that contain valuable information

- The abundance of cheap commodity computing resources
- "Free" analytics tools (very low to non-existent barriers to acquire)

When we are talking about the security of big data environments, it is the last item in particular that often raises security concerns. Without knowing where many of these tool sets have come from, how they are architected, and who is behind them, as well as how they are being deployed and utilized within the enterprise, the security practitioner is faced with a significant challenge with regards to data confidentiality and integrity. The addition of distributed computing architectures such as cloud-based systems that allow end point access to data on demand, from anywhere that a network connection can be accessed, adds to the myriad of challenges being faced by security practitioners.

Lane says that these systems use many nodes for distributed data storage and management. They store multiple copies of data across multiple nodes. This provides the benefits of fail-safe operation in the event any single node fails, and it means the data queries move to the data, where processing resources are available. It is this distributed cluster of data nodes cooperating with each other to handle data management and data queries that makes big data so potentially valuable for enterprise architectures, but at the same time it presents such unique challenges to the security of the enterprise.

The security practitioner faces challenges in the areas of trust, privacy, and general security. In the area of trust-related issues, items such as key verification, mitigation of trust-based DoS attacks, and content leakage detection within trusted networks may need to be addressed. Privacy issues may include remote authentication schemes for wireless network access to data, traffic masking to obfuscate data, anonymization of large scale data sets, and decentralized access control solutions for cloud based data access. General security challenges may span a wide range of issues and concerns such as response mechanisms in the face of fast-spreading/fast-acting intrusion vectors, the existence of inconsistent authorization policies and user credentials within distributed databases accessed by cloud-based systems, and the concerns associated with securely, efficiently, and flexibly sharing data using public key cryptosystems.

OPERATING AND SECURING VIRTUAL ENVIRONMENTS

There are many components that go into operating and securing virtual environments. The move to use software definition up and down the virtualization stack in the data center has meant that solutions such as software-defined networking (SDN) are now commonplace, requiring the SSCP to become familiar with them as part of their operational responsibilities. In addition, the use of virtualized security appliances has also become commonplace and requires that the SSCP update their skills with the required vendor-specific knowledge to ensure the successful deployment, configuration, and management of these gateway solutions. Being able to manage and operate environments that are focused on continuity and resiliency of the systems and information that make them up is a daunting challenge, one that the SSCP has to continue to work hard to accomplish.

Software-Defined Network (SDN)

According to Wikipedia, software-defined networking is an approach to computer networking that allows network administrators to manage network services through abstraction of lower-level functionality. This is done by decoupling the system that makes decisions about where traffic is sent (the control plane) from the underlying systems that forward traffic to the selected destination (the data plane).[131]

SDN providers offer a wide selection of competing architectures, but at its simplest, the SDN method centralizes control of the network by separating the control logic to off-device computer resources. All SDN models have some version of an SDN controller, as well as southbound APIs and northbound APIs:

- **Controllers**—The "brains" of the network, SDN controllers offer a centralized view of the overall network, and they enable network administrators to dictate to the underlying systems (like switches and routers) how the forwarding plane should handle network traffic.

- **Southbound APIs**—SDN uses southbound APIs to relay information to the switches and routers "below." OpenFlow, considered the first standard in SDN, was the original southbound API and remains as one of the most common protocols. Despite some considering OpenFlow and SDN to be one in the same, OpenFlow is merely one piece of the bigger SDN landscape.

- **Northbound APIs**—SDN uses northbound APIs to communicate with the applications and business logic "above." These help network administrators to programmatically shape traffic and deploy services.

Virtual Appliances

Virtual appliances are prebuilt software solutions comprising one or more virtual machines that are packaged, updated, maintained, and managed as a unit. Because virtual appliances are preconfigured, they help organizations reduce the time and expense associated with application deployment—including the patching and ongoing management of the software.

A virtual machine has four key virtualized resources (CPU, RAM, storage, and networking). It requires the installation of an OS and runs one or more applications. A virtual appliance functions much like a virtual machine, possessing the four key characteristics of compatibility, isolation, encapsulation, and hardware independence. However, a virtual appliance contains a preinstalled, preconfigured OS and an application stack that is optimized to provide a specific set of services. Because virtual machines contain a general-purpose OS that can run multiple applications, the patches for virtual machines are delivered by both OS vendors and application software vendors. IT administrators, in turn, might need to test these patches for compatibility. In contrast, virtual appliances are a unified offering of Just Enough Operating System (JeOS, pronounced "juice") and a single application. The application-software vendor needs only to provide a single pretested update (containing relevant patches), thereby eliminating the need for testing. JeOS is a stripped-down version of an OS. Several software vendors are creating JeOS variants to support the virtual-appliance paradigm. Examples include Ubuntu 7.04, 7.10 and 8.04, Lime JeOS from Novell, and Appliance Operating System (AOS) from Red Hat.

See the following for more information: `https://www.suse.com/products/susestudio/features/jeos.html`

Continuity and Resilience

A clustered host will be a host that is logically and physically connected to other hosts within a management framework that allows for resources to be centrally managed for the collection of hosts, and for the applications and virtual machines running on a member of the cluster to fail over, or move, between host members as needed to allow for continued operation of those resources, with a focus on minimizing the downtime that host failures can cause. The security practitioner will need to understand the basic concept of host clustering, as well as the specifics of the technology and implementation requirements that are unique to the vendor platforms they support. Within a host cluster, resources are allocated and managed as if they are pooled, or jointly available to all members of the cluster. The use of resource sharing concepts such as reservations, limits, and shares may also be used to further refine and orchestrate the allocation of resources according to certain requirements imposed by the cluster administrator.

Reservations allow for the guaranteeing of a certain *minimum* amount of the clusters pooled resources to be made available to a specified virtual machine.

Limits allow for the guaranteeing of a certain *maximum* amount of the clusters pooled resources to be made available to a specified virtual machine.

Shares allow for the provisioning of the remaining resources left in a cluster when there is resource contention. Specifically, shares allow the cluster's reservations to be allocated and then to address any remaining resources that may be available for use by members of the cluster through a prioritized percentage based allocation mechanism.

Clusters are available for the traditional "compute" resources of the hosts that make up the cluster: RAM and CPU. In addition, there are also storage clusters that can be created and deployed to allow back end storage to be managed in the same way that the traditional "compute" resources are. The management of the cluster will involve the use of a cluster manager or management toolset of some kind. The chosen virtualization platform will determine the clustering capability of the cloud hosts. Many virtualization platforms utilize clustering for high availability and disaster recovery.

For example, according to VMware, a cluster is a collection of ESXi hosts and associated virtual machines with shared resources and a shared management interface.[132]

Microsoft provides the same level of technology to create, manage, and integrate their clustering solutions for virtualized cloud-based resources as well. System Center Operations Manager (SCOM) is used in partnership with the System Center Virtual Machine Manager (SCVMM) and the Performance Resource Optimization (PRO) feature to provide the monitoring component of individual hosts and virtual machines running on them, which would be the equivalent of the DRS functionality in VMware. The HA functionality is provided through the failover clustering technology built into the Windows Server 2012/2102R2 operating systems.[133]

Attacks and Countermeasures

To secure a server, it is essential to first define the threats that must be mitigated. Many threats against data and resources are possible because of mistakes—either bugs in operating system and server software that create exploitable vulnerabilities, or errors made by end users and administrators. Threats may involve intentional actors (e.g., attacker who wants to access information on a server) or unintentional actors (e.g., administrator who forgets to disable user accounts of a former employee). Threats can be local, such as a disgruntled employee, or remote, such as an attacker in another geographical area. Organizations should conduct risk assessments to identify the specific threats against their servers and determine the effectiveness of existing security controls in counteracting the threats; they then should perform risk mitigation to decide what additional measures (if any) should be implemented, as discussed in NIST Special Publication (SP) 800—30 Revision 1, "Risk Assessment Guide for Information Technology Systems."[134] Performing risk assessments and mitigation helps organizations better understand their security posture and decide how their servers should be secured.

The following general guidelines will help the security practitioner to understand the key items that have to be addressed:

- Use of an asset management system that has configuration management capabilities to enable documentation of all system configuration items (CIs) authoritatively.

- Use of system baselines to enforce configuration management throughout the enterprise. In configuration management, a *baseline* is an agreed-upon description of the attributes of a product, at a point in time, which serves as a basis for defining change. A *change* is a movement from this baseline state to a next state. The security practitioner should consider automation technologies that will help with the creation, application, management, updating, tracking, and compliance checking for system baselines.

- Development and use of a robust change management system to authorize the required changes needing to be made to systems over time. In addition, enforcement of a requirement that no changes may be made to production systems unless the change has been properly vetted and approved through the change management system in place. This will force all changes to be clearly articulated, examined, documented, and weighed against the organization's priorities and objectives. Forcing the examination of all changes in the context of the business allows the security practitioner to ensure that risk is minimized whenever possible and that all changes are seen as being acceptable to the business based on the potential risk that they pose.

- The use of an exception reporting system to force the capture and documentation of any activities undertaken that are contrary to the "expected norm" with regards to the lifecycle of a system under management.

- The use of vendor-specified configuration guidance and best practices as appropriate based on the specific platforms under management.

Security Virtualization Best Practices

According to the Infosec Institute, the following are best practices for using virtualized infrastructure securely that the SSCP should consider:[135]

Administrator Access and Separation of Duties   The following are best practices for administrator access and separation of duties:

- Provide administrators with power on/power off rights for their hosts only and no others.

- Give administrators the right to deploy new VMs but not modify existing VMs. Other administrators can then be enabled to modify existing VMs but not create new ones.

- Separate authentication should be in place for each guest OS unless there is a good reason for two or more guest operating systems to share credentials.

Desktop Virtualization and Security   The following are best practices for desktop virtualization and security:

- Update acceptable use policy. Document the exact conditions under which virtualization software can be installed and define what approvals are required. State what software can be run and how it should be protected. Document the repercussions that employees can expect if they don't follow the rules.

- Limit the use of VMs to the users who need them. Limit permissions to a small group of developers and testers for virtual tools and VMs, and help them understand that they still have to conform to corporate security policies.

- Keep virtualization and security software up to date.

- Choose security policies that support virtualization. Make sure that there are not any known security policy conflicts with existing virtualization platforms.

- Create and maintain a library of secure VM builds. Maintain a repository of VM templates containing all of the configuration settings, security software, and patches that users can download, use, and reuse.

Network Security   Following are best practices for network security:

- Disconnect any unused NICs so that there is not an easy way to get onto the network.

- Make sure that the host platform that connects the hypervisor and guests to the physical network is secure by setting file permissions, using access controls for users and groups, and setting up logging and time synchronization.

- Encrypt all traffic between clients and hosts, between management systems and the hypervisor, and between the hypervisor and hosts using SSL/TLS.

- Secure IP communications between two hosts by using authentication and encryption on each IP packet.

- Do not use default self-signed certificates as they are vulnerable to man-in-the-middle attacks.

- Place virtual switches into promiscuous mode for monitoring purposes, and enable MAC address filtering to prevent MAC spoofing attacks.

Storage Networks   The following are best practices for storage networks:

- iSCSI and NFS traffic should be placed on dedicated storage networks or non-routable VLANs.

- Use IPSec to encrypt iSCSI traffic to prevent snooping.

- iSCSI supports Challenge Handshake Authentication Protocol (CHAP), and this should be used to force authentication prior to granting access.

- When using iSCSI or NFS, use physical switches to detect and disallow IP or MAC address spoofing.

- NFS is easy to set up but is the least secure storage choice. Configure the NFS server to restrict access to specific IP addresses related to your hypervisors, or use a firewall to restrict traffic to specific hosts. If the NFS server supports IPSec, use it to secure traffic between the NFS server and the hypervisors.

- All traffic to and from storage repositories needs to be isolated from non-storage traffic.

- Security for Fibre Channel storage networks involves the use of zoning, which is the creation of access control groups at the switch level and is similar to how VLANs operate. Although numerous topologies are available, the simplest secure form is single initiator zoning. This involves a host bus adapter in its own zone with a target device to prevent initiators from trying to communicate with each other.

- Security for Fibre Channel storage networks involves the use of masking, which allows the security practitioner or storage administrator to effectively "hide" one or more LUNs being made available from the storage array, presenting only those LUNs that the endpoint device seeking access is allowed to see.

Auditing and Logging   The following are best practices for auditing and logging:

- Use centralized logging to determine whether guests have gone offline. These guests can get out of sync with regards to patches and updates. Log any VM power events (such as On, Off, Suspended, or Resumed), changes in hardware configurations, or any login events related to those with elevated privileges. VMs that are copied, moved, or deleted should also be logged.

- Audit files should be read only and should be read only by those in an auditing role to ensure forensic integrity. Unauthorized and authorized login attempts to the audit files and other virtual resources should be logged.

- Conduct regular audits of the environment including the virtual network, storage, the hypervisor, the VMs, and the management systems.

- Send log files securely to a remote log server.

Virtual Machine Security   The following are best practices for virtual machine security:

- Turn off any unused VMs.

- Use IPSec or other forms of encryption between the host and VM to secure all traffic.

- Employ VLANs within a single vSwitch to segment traffic.

- When VMs move, active memory and state are sent over the network to the new host in clear text. Isolate this traffic from the production network on an isolated segment that is non-routable and configured with a separate vSwitch or VLAN.

- Policies can be used to make sure that a new VM is not allowed to join a VM group or cluster unless it has a specific configuration and has related updates installed.

- Do not place workloads with different trust levels in the same security domain or on the same physical server. The chance of mixing trust levels is great when users can create and deploy their own VMs.

- Restrict access to archived VMs.

- When two or more VMs are on the same VLAN and vSwitch, the traffic between the VMs is not protected. Consider placing virtual firewalls on these VMs for protection.

- Place a CPU limit on any VMs that can access the Internet. This will ensure that if a VM is compromised, the VM's resources are limited to launch attacks on other hosts.

- If users are allowed to create VMs, consider allowing them to only create VMs from an authorized template.

- Consider deploying a security VM or virtual appliance to eliminate an agent on each VM. This can eliminate antivirus storms and any bottlenecks that would occur when all hosts and VMs start their malware scans simultaneously.

- Disable any copy-paste functionality to protect the confidentiality of the data and the integrity of the hypervisor and VMs.

- A virtual firewall attached to a VM travels with it at all times to ensure that security policy is enforced before, during, and after any moves.

- A security gateway (firewall and IDS/IPS) can be employed to inspect traffic between VMs.

- Make sure that any VMs that process protected information are isolated from other VMs so that the data is not combined with other data or is accessible through other VMs.

Management Systems   The following are best practices for management systems:

- Secure your communications between management systems and the hosts to prevent data loss, eavesdropping, and any chance for man-in-the-middle attacks. Enable one or more of the available SSH, IPSec, and SSL/TLS protocols for this purpose.

- Do not allow a management server to be accessible from all workstations. Compromising this server could affect VMs and data stores. To prevent this, place the management server on a separate VLAN from the user computers' subnet and then place it behind a firewall. These are two completely different security zones. Define access control lists on the network switches, and set appropriate rules on the firewall. Change the default permissions on these servers so that the admin does not have access to the entire environment.

- Separate management servers from database servers.

Hypervisor Security   The following are best practices for hypervisor security:

- Install vendor-supplied patches and updates to the hypervisor as they are released. Support this with a sound patch management process to mitigate the risk of hypervisor vulnerabilities. Place the latest service packs on guests and hosts, and remove any applications with a history of vulnerabilities.

- Disable any unused virtual hardware that connects to the hypervisor.

- Disable unneeded services like clipboard or file sharing.

- Perform constant monitoring of the hypervisor for any potential signs of compromise. Monitor and analyze the hypervisor logs on a consistent basis.

- Disable all local administration of the hypervisor, and require use of a centralized management application.

- Require multi-factor authentication for any admin functions on the hypervisor.

Time Synchronization   The following are best practices for time synchronization:

- Network Time Protocol (NTP) should be enabled and configured to synchronize with a time server close to your network, and NTP should run on a host. Guest VMs should either use the same server as the host or use the host itself as the NTP server. If the VM layer allows a guest OS to sync time directly from the host, then this should be used as this is the simplest to implement.

- Hashing authentication should be used between NTP peers to prevent tampering.

Remote Access   The following are best practices for remote access:

- Remote access management should be limited to a small set of authorized management system IP addresses.

- Any remote access should ask for a username as well as a password backed up with a strong password policy. For strong security environments, use two-factor authentication or one-time-use passwords.

- Remote communication to any management tools should be encrypted and authenticated.

- When using SSH, disable the version 1 protocol, disable the admin or root SSH login, and require users to use role-based access control or their individual user accounts. Use a tool like Sudo because it allows activity to be written to a log that indicates what was done, when it was done, and by whom.

Backups   The following are best practices for backups:

- Encrypt any backup data streams in case a server image is stolen. Data at rest should have access control lists to control copying or mounting of images.

- Network-level protections like VLANs and access control lists should be in place to protect backup data whether at rest or in transit.

- Do not allow root accounts to be used for backup.

- Any backups that are sent to a disaster recovery site over the network should be securely encrypted.

Configuration and Change Management   The following are best practices for configuration and change management:

- Make sure that any physical or virtual servers are hardened before putting them into deployment. Monitor any configuration changes to detect any unauthorized changes or deviations from compliance in regards to updates and patches.

- Harden physical and virtual switches and virtual appliances and gateways before deployment.

- Do not allow changes to the infrastructure without documentation and testing in a lab environment that is as identical to the production environment as possible. Answer these questions before making any changes:
    - What are the implications of the change?
    - Who and what will be affected?
    - How much of a risk does the change represent?
    - Can the change be reversed if necessary?
    - How long will it take to roll back a change?

- Track VM configurations and issue alerts for any changes to a desired configuration.

SUMMARY

Systems and application security is a multidimensional topic made up of many moving parts. The activities and actions of malware, the countermeasures required to mitigate the threats that malware poses, as well as the processes necessary to manage mobile devices all play a part. Adding cloud computing increases the scalability and interactivity of the organization's infrastructure but brings with it its own set of security concerns and issues that the security practitioner needs to understand and manage effectively. The security professional should be able to put all of these issues and concerns into context, understand their main goals, and apply a commonsense approach to typical scenarios. The focus here is to maintain operational resilience and protect valuable operational assets through a combination of people, processes, and technologies. At the same time, security services must be managed effectively and efficiently just like any other set of services in the enterprise.

SAMPLE QUESTIONS

1. "VBS" is used in the beginning of most antivirus vendors to represent what component of the CARO general structure?

   a. Family

   b. Platform

   c. Modifier

   d. Suffix

2. W64.Root.AC is what variant of this malcode?

   a. W64

   b. AC

   c. Root

   d. C

3. W64.Slober.Z@mm spreads through what primary vector, according to Symantec naming conventions?

   a. Mass Mailer

   b. Windows 64-bit

   c. Windows 8/8.1

   d. E-mail

4. A SSCP discovers an antivirus message indicating detection and removal of Backdoor .win64.Agent.igh. What should the SSCP do to monitor to the threat?

a. Use rootkit detection software on the host

b. Update antivirus signature files

c. Run a full host scan

d. Monitor egress traffic from the computer

5. Malcode that infects existing files on a computer to spread are called what?

a. Rootkit

b. Worms

c. Viruses

d. Trojans

6. A Trojan that executes a destructive payload when certain conditions are met is called what?

a. Data diddler

b. Rootkit

c. Logic bomb

d. Keylogger

7. How does a cavity virus infect a file with malcode?

a. Appends code

b. Injects code

c. Removes code

d. Prepends code

8. Mebroot is unique because it modifies what component of a computer to load on system startup?

a. Windows registry keys

b. Kernel

c. Master boot record

d. Startup folder

9. SYS and VXD hostile codes are commonly associated with what type of threat?

   a. Trojans

   b. Userland rootkits

   c. Worms

   d. Kernel rootkits

10. A potentially unwanted program (PUP) refers to software that may include what? (Choose all that apply.)

    a. Monitoring capability

    b. End user license agreement (EULA)

    c. Patch management capability

    d. Ability to capture data

11. "0.0.0.0 avp.ch" is a string found within a Trojan binary, indicating that it likely performs this type of change to a system upon infection:

    a. Downloads code from avp.ch

    b. Modifies the HOSTS file to prevent access to avp.ch

    c. Communicates with a remote C&C at avp.ch

    d. Contains a logic bomb that activates immediately

12. What does it mean when an SSCP does not see `explorer.exe` in the Windows Task Manager on a host machine?

    a. It is normal for `explorer.exe` to not appear in Windows Task Manager.

    b. `explorer.exe` is likely injected and hidden by a Windows rootkit.

    c. `explorer.exe` does not need to be visible if `svchost.exe` is visible.

    d. Internet Explorer is open and running in memory.

13. If an SSCP attempts to analyze suspicious code using a VMware-based test environment and nothing executes, what might be the next steps to take to further analyze the code?

    a. Submit the code to an online sandbox scanner to compare behavioral results.

    b. Modify advanced settings to disable hardware acceleration and similar components and execute the code again.

    c. Call VMware technical support for help in identifying the problem(s) causing the code not to execute.

    d. Run the malcode in a native, non-virtualized test environment to see if it is anti-VMware.

14. What does the "vector of attack" refer to?

    a. Software that can infect multiple hosts

    b. The primary action of a malicious code attack

    c. How the transmission of malcode takes place

    d. The directions used to control the placement of the malcode

15. What is direct kernel object modification an example of?

    a. A technique used by persistent mode rootkits to modify data structures

    b. A technique used by memory based rootkits to modify data structures

    c. A technique used by user mode rootkits to modify data structures

    d. A technique used by kernel mode rootkits to modify data structures

16. What kind of an attack is the following sample code indicative of?

    ../../../

    a. Covert channel

    b. Buffer overflow

    c. Directory traversal

    d. Pointer overflow

17. What does a second generation antivirus scanner use to search for probable malware instances?

    a. Heuristic rules

    b. Malware signatures

    c. Malware signatures

    d. Generic decryption

18. What type of botnet detection and mitigation technique is Netflow used for?

    a. Anomaly detection

    b. DNS log analysis

    c. Data monitoring

    d. Honeypots

19. What kind of tool should be used to check for cross-site scripting (XSS) vulnerabilities?

    a. Rootkit revealer

    b. Web vulnerability scanner

    c. Terminal emulator

    d. Decompiler

20. What are the five phases of an advanced persistent threat (APT)?

    a. Reconnaissance, capture, incursion, discovery, and exfiltration

    b. Reconnaissance, discovery, incursion, capture, and exfiltration

    c. Incursion, reconnaissance, discovery, capture, and exfiltration

    d. Reconnaissance, incursion, discovery, capture, and exfiltration

21. What would a malware author need to do in order to prevent the heuristic technology used by antivirus vendors from detecting the malware code hidden inside of a program file?

    a. Use a runtime packer that is virtual environment aware

    b. Encrypt the malware files

    c. Decompile the malware files

    d. Use a runtime packer that is not virtual environment aware

22. What is a goat machine used for?

    a. Configuration management

    b. Hosting of network monitoring software

    c. Testing of suspicious software

    d. Creation of baseline images

23. Identify whether each of the following activities is strategic or tactical:

    ■ Defense in depth

    ■ Hardening systems

    ■ Senior management support

    ■ Backing up data

    ■ The formation of a CERT/CSIRT team

24. What is the correct description of the relationship between a data controller and a data processor role with regards to privacy and data protection (P&DP) laws?

    a. The processor determines the purposes and means of processing of public data, while the controller processes public data on behalf of the processor.

    b. The controller determines the purposes and means of processing of public data, while the processor processes public data on behalf of the controller.

    c. The controller determines the purposes and means of processing of personal data, while the processor processes personal data on behalf of the controller.

    d. The processor determines the purposes and means of processing of personal data, while the controller processes personal data on behalf of the processor.

25. According to the NIST Definition of Cloud Computing (NIST SP 800–145), what are the three cloud service models?

   a. Software as a service (SaaS), platform as a service (PaaS), and Internet of things as a service (TaaS)

   b. Software as a service (SaaS), platform as a service (PaaS), and infrastructure as a service (IaaS)

   c. Software as a service (SaaS), business process as a service (BPaaS), and infrastructure as a service (IaaS)

   d. Security as a service (SaaS), platform as a service (PaaS), and infrastructure as a service (IaaS)

26. Which of the following are storage types used with an infrastructure as a service solution?

   a. Volume and block

   b. Structured and object

   c. Unstructured and ephemeral

   d. Volume and object

27. What is the Cloud Security Alliance Cloud Controls Matrix?

   a. A set of regulatory requirements for cloud service providers

   b. An inventory of cloud service security controls that are arranged into separate security domains

   c. A set of software development life cycle requirements for cloud service providers

   d. An inventory of cloud service security controls that are arranged into a hierarchy of security domains

28. Which of the following are attributes of cloud computing?

   a. Minimal management effort and shared resources

   b. High cost and unique resources

   c. Rapid provisioning and slow release of resources

   d. Limited access and service provider interaction

29. When using an infrastructure as a service solution, what is the capability provided to the customer?

   a. To provision processing, storage, networks, and other fundamental computing resources where the consumer is not able to deploy and run arbitrary software, which can include operating systems and applications.

   b. To provision processing, storage, networks, and other fundamental computing resources where the provider is able to deploy and run arbitrary software, which can include operating systems and applications.

   c. To provision processing, storage, networks, and other fundamental computing resources where the auditor is able to deploy and run arbitrary software, which can include operating systems and applications.

   d. To provision processing, storage, networks, and other fundamental computing resources where the consumer is able to deploy and run arbitrary software, which can include operating systems and applications.

30. When using a platform as a service solution, what is the capability provided to the customer?

   a. To deploy onto the cloud infrastructure provider-created or acquired applications created using programming languages, libraries, services, and tools supported by the provider. The consumer does not manage or control the underlying cloud infrastructure including network, servers, operating systems, or storage, but has control over the deployed applications and possibly configuration settings for the application-hosting environment.

   b. To deploy onto the cloud infrastructure consumer-created or acquired applications created using programming languages, libraries, services, and tools supported by the provider. The provider does not manage or control the underlying cloud infrastructure including network, servers, operating systems, or storage, but has control over the deployed applications and possibly configuration settings for the application-hosting environment.

   c. To deploy onto the cloud infrastructure consumer-created or acquired applications created using programming languages, libraries, services, and tools supported by the provider. The consumer does not manage or control the underlying cloud infrastructure including network, servers, operating systems, or storage, but has control over the deployed applications and possibly configuration settings for the application-hosting environment.

   d. To deploy onto the cloud infrastructure consumer-created or acquired applications created using programming languages, libraries, services, and tools supported by the consumer. The consumer does not manage or control the underlying cloud infrastructure including network, servers, operating systems, or storage, but has control over the deployed applications and possibly configuration settings for the application-hosting environment.

31. What are the four cloud deployment models?

    a. Public, internal, hybrid, and community

    b. External, private, hybrid, and community

    c. Public, private, joint, and community

    d. Public, private, hybrid, and community

32. When setting up resource sharing within a host cluster, which option would you choose to mediate resource contention?

    a. Reservations

    b. Limits

    c. Clusters

    d. Shares

END NOTES

1. For an overview of CARO's activities, see the following: `http://www.caro.org/`

2. See the following for information on the CARO naming convention: `http://www.caro.org/articles/naming.html`

3. Details on this worm can be found at `https://www.symantec.com/security_response/`

4. The vgrep online search tool can be accessed at `https://www.virusbulletin.com/blog/2012/10/vgrep-rose-revived`

5. The Virus Bulletin website can be found at `https://www.virusbulletin.com/`

6. For a good overall biography of Dr. Cohen, see the following: `http://all.net/resume/bio.html`

   Dr. Cohen is CEO of Fred Cohen & Associates, a firm that does research and advisory services exclusively for the U.S. government, and Management Analytics, a firm specializing in research and advisory services and litigation support for non-Federal customers. Fred Cohen & Associates can be found at `http://fredcohen.net/index.html`

7. The full McAfee white paper on Operation High Roller can be found at `http://www.mcafee.com/sg/resources/reports/rp-operation-high-roller.pdf`

8. For a deep dive on the Zeus/Citadel Botnet, please see the following: "Understanding the Zeus/Citadel Botnet from Blackhat 2012 Europe" presentation by Ken Baylor: `http://www.youtube.com/watch?v=GA7S0JK8o_k`

9. For historical background on macro viruses, and many other interesting areas of computer history, the security practitioner can visit the Computer History Museum: `http://www.computerhistory.org/`

10. For an up-to-date listing of all currently discovered and tracked threats that a security practitioner would need to be aware of, including polymorphic viruses, listings provided by the major antivirus software companies and research institutions are great places to do research in order to stay up to date on new discoveries in the wild that may affect your networks. Some lists to examine are these:

    `http://www.symantec.com/security_response/landing/azlisting.jsp`

    `http://www.mcafee.com/us/threat-center.aspx`

    `http://usa.kaspersky.com/internet-security-center#.UnVBL9rD_IU`

    `http://www.secureworks.com/cyber-threat-intelligence/`

11. See the following for the actual coded exploit from GitHub: `https://gist.github.com/poliva/36b0795ab79ad6f14fd8`

12. "State of Software Security Report: The Intractable Problem of Insecure Software," April 2013. Volume 5. Veracode. `http://www.veracode.com/resources/state-of-software-security`

13. `http://samate.nist.gov/docs/Juliet%201.1%20Oct%202012.pdf`

14. Some examples of phishing attack vectors and explanations about basic phishing techniques may be found here:

    `http://www.microsoft.com/security/online-privacy/phishing-symptoms.aspx`

    `http://www.phishtank.com/what_is_phishing.php?annotated=true`

    `http://www.phishtank.com/what_is_phishing.php?view=website&annotated=true`

    `http://netforbeginners.about.com/od/scamsandidentitytheft/ig/Phishing-Scams-and-E-mail-Cons/`

    `http://www.financialfraudaction.org.uk/consumer-protecting-your-personal-information.asp?pagecontent=2`

    `http://www.it.cornell.edu/security/safety/phishbowl.cfm`

15. For an overview of the kind of issues that end users may face in even the most "innocent" of situations and thus the reasons that security awareness training at all

levels of the organization is critical, see the following: `http://blogs.technet`
`.com/b/fesnouf/archive/2010/09/13/a-great-example-of-a-social-`
`engineering-attack-my-polynesian-friend-marceline-attacked-me-this-`
`morning.aspx`

16. For a summary of the RSA breach, see the following: `http://www.darkreading`
`.com/attacks-and-breaches/rsa-details-securid-attack-`
`mechanics/d/d-id/1096981?`

17. For overviews of each of the attacks, please see the following:

Facebook NATO attack: `http://www.darkreading.com/risk-management/`
`facebook-social-engineering-attack-strikes-nato-/d/d-id/1103308?`

Wal-Mart DefCon attack: `http://money.cnn.com/2012/08/07/technology/`
`walmart-hack-defcon/`

Francophoned attack: `http://www.symantec.com/connect/blogs/`
`francophoned-sophisticated-social-engineering-attack`

18. For a good overview discussion of filename length in various operating systems,
including Windows, see the following: `http://en.wikipedia.org/wiki/Filename`

19. See the following to download a copy of the "42.zip" file: `http://www`
`.unforgettable.dk/`

20. `http://training.fema.gov/EMIWeb/IS/courseOverview.aspx?code=IS-915`

21. `http://cdsetrain.dtic.mil/itawareness/`

22. See the following for more information on Knoppix: `http://knoppix.net/`

23. See the following for the full *Der Spiegel* article: `http://www.spiegel.de/`
`international/world/the-nsa-uses-powerful-toolbox-in-effort-to-spy-`
`on-global-networks-a-940969.html`

24. See the following: `http://www.acunetix.com/websitesecurity/`
`cross-site-scripting/`

25. See the following: `http://www.codenomicon.com/products/defensics/`

26. See the following for the original blog announcement for Project Zero: `https://`
`security.googleblog.com/2014/07/announcing-project-zero.html`

27. See the following for the Google project zero-day bug tracking database: `https://`
`code.google.com/p/google-security-research/issues/list?can=1`

28. See the following to get more information on the John the Ripper tool: `http://`
`www.openwall.com/john/`

29. See the following to get more information on DirBuster and to download the latest build of the tool: `https://www.owasp.org/index.php/Category:`
`OWASP_DirBuster_Project`

30. See the following for more information on the ZAP: `https://www.owasp.org/index.php/ZAP`

31. See the following for more information on the Php-Brute-Force-Attack-Detector tool: `http://yehg.net/lab/pr0js/files.php/php_brute_force_detect.zip`

32. See the following for more information on the W32.Kelvir Worm: `https://www.symantec.com/security_response/writeup.jsp?docid=2005-041414-2221-99&tabid=2`

33. See the following for the original document that lays out the basis for modern computer networks, as well as the concepts of file sharing that underlie the P2P network phenomena: `http://tools.ietf.org/html/rfc1`

34. See the following for information on the studies mentioned above: Goebel, Jan et al (2007). "Measurement and Analysis of Autonomous Spreading Malware in a University Environment." In Hämmerli, Bernhard Markus & Sommer, Robin. Detection of Intrusions and Malware, and Vulnerability Assessment: 4th International Conference, DIMVA 2007 Lucerne, Switzerland, July 12–13, 2007 Proceedings. Springer. p. 112. ISBN 9783540736134.

35. See the following for more information on DCC: `http://en.wikipedia.org/wiki/Direct_Client-to-Client`

36. See the following for daily ranking statistics on IRC channels and usage: `http://irc.netsplit.de/networks/top100.php`

37. See the following for various resources that can help to provide information on trends in the issues that security practitioners may be facing in the wild:

    `http://blog.spiderlabs.com/`

    `https://www.fireeye.com/blog.html`

    `http://www.tripwire.com/state-of-security/`

    `http://www.darkreading.com/`

    `http://www.kaspersky.com/news`

38. See the following for information on BotConf'14, the first conference devoted to fighting botnets: `https://www.botconf.eu/`

39. See the following for the GCHQ homepage: `http://www.gchq.gov.uk/Pages/homepage.aspx`

40. See the following for the iSIGHT Partners website: `http://www.isightpartners.com/`

41. See the following for an interesting article on new research in the area of genetic signature detection: `http://www.v3.co.uk/v3-uk/the-frontline-blog/2244636/researchers-borrow-dna-tricks-to-identify-malwares-genetic-code`

42. See the following for an overview of Process Explorer: `http://technet` `.microsoft.com/en-us/sysinternals/bb896653.aspx`

43. See the following for an overview of EnCase Enterprise: `https://www.guidancesoftware.com/encase-endpoint-investigator`

44. See the following for historical reference works on malware, rootkits, and viruses that every security practitioner should read and be familiar with, as they form the foundational knowledge for this topic:

    Rootkits: Subverting the Windows Kernel by Greg Hoglund and Jamie Butler

    The Art of Computer Virus Research and Defense by Peter Szor

    Malware: Fighting Malicious Code by Ed Skoudis and Lenny Zeltser

45. See the following to download the Kaspersky TDSSKiller software: `http://` `support.kaspersky.com/viruses/utility#TDSSKiller`

46. See the following to download the RKill software: `http://www.bleepingcomputer` `.com/download/rkill/dl/11/`

47. See the following to download the Malwarebytes Anti-Malware software: `http://` `www.malwarebytes.org/mwb-download/`

48. See the following to download the HitmanPro software: `http://www.surfright` `.nl/en/hitmanpro/`

49. See the following to download the RogueKiller software: `http://www.adlice` `.com/softwares/roguekiller/`

50. See the following to download the AdwCleaner software: `https://toolslib` `.net/downloads/viewdownload/1-adwcleaner/`

51. See the following to download the Junkware Removal Tool: `http://thisisudax` `.org/downloads/JRT.exe`

52. See the following for more information on OSSEC: `http://ossec.github.io/`

53. See the following for information on the Dell SecureWorks service offerings: `https://www.secureworks.com/capabilities/security-services`

54. See the following for more information on the Symantec and Solutionary offerings:

    `http://www.solutionary.com/`

    `https://www.symantec.com/services/cyber-security-services/managed-security-services`

55. See the following for more information about iDefense and its services: `http://` `www.verisign.com/en_US/security-services/security-intelligence/index` `.xhtml#home`

56. See the following to download the latest version of wxHexEditor by OS type: `http://sourceforge.net/projects/wxhexeditor/files/wxHexEditor/` `v0.22%20Beta/`

57. See the following to download the latest version of DHEX: `http://www.dettus.net/dhex/`

58. See the following to download the latest version of XVI32: `http://www.chmaas.handshake.de/delphi/freeware/xvi32/xvi32.htm`

59. See the following to download the latest version of Hex Fiend: `http://ridiculousfish.com/hexfiend/`

60. See the following to download the latest version of HexEdit: `http://www.hexedit.com/`

61. See the following to download the latest version of HashCalc: `http://www.slavasoft.com/hashcalc/`

62. See the following to download the latest version of PEiD:

    PEiD: `http://www.softpedia.com/get/Programming/Packers-Crypters-Protectors/PEiD-updated.shtml`

63. See the following to download the latest versions of UPX, MEW, and PESpin:

    UPX: `http://upx.sourceforge.net/`

    MEW: `http://www.softpedia.com/get/Programming/Packers-Crypters-Protectors/MEW-SE.shtml`

    PESpin: `http://pespin.w.interia.pl/`

    For a general overview of executable compression, and a listing of some of the most common tools used to pack files, see the following: `http://en.wikipedia.org/wiki/Executable_compression`

64. See the following to download the latest version of OllyDbg: `http://www.ollydbg.de/version2.html`

65. Passive DNS Queries is a technique invented by Florian Weimer in 2004 to opportunistically reconstruct a partial view of the data available within the global domain name system into a central database where it can be indexed and queried. Passive DNS databases are extremely useful for a variety of purposes. Malware and e-crime rely heavily on the DNS, and so-called "fast flux botnets" abuse the DNS with frequent updates and low TTLs. Passive DNS databases can answer questions that are difficult or impossible to answer with the standard DNS protocol, such as:

    Where did this domain name point to in the past?

    What domain names are hosted by a given nameserver?

What domain names point into a given IP network?

What subdomains exist below a certain domain name?

The original paper published by Weimer is available here: `http://www.enyo.de/fw/software/dnslogger/first2005-paper.pdf`

Florian Weimer also maintains a website with additional resources that may be of interest to the security practitioner: `http://www.enyo.de/fw/software/dnslogger/`

66. See the following for more information on DNSDB and to apply for an account in order to access the DNSDB information: `https://www.dnsdb.info/`

    See the following for a general overview of the Passive DNS solution from FarSight and how it is being used: `https://archive.farsightsecurity.com/Passive_DNS_Sensor_FAQ/`

    `https://www.dns-oarc.net/files/workshop-201010/edmonds_sie.pdf`

    `https://www.defcon.org/html/links/dc-archives/dc-18-archive.html#Vixie`

67. One example of an approach that uses Passive DNS Analysis to find malicious domains can be found here: `https://www.cs.ucsb.edu/~chris/research/doc/tissec14_exposure.pdf`

68. See the following for the websites listed:

    Robtex: `https://www.robtex.com/dns/`

    DomainCrawler: `http://www.domaincrawler.com/`

    SpamHaus: `http://www.spamhaus.org/`

    DNSstuff: `http://www.dnsstuff.com/`

    DomainTools: `http://www.domaintools.com/`

69. See the following to download the latest version of Zenmap: `http://nmap.org/zenmap/`

70. See the following to download the latest version of the Firefox Live HTTP Headers add-on: `https://addons.mozilla.org/en-us/firefox/addon/live-http-headers/`

71. See the following for more information on these software programs:

    Qemu: `http://wiki.qemu.org/Main_Page`

    Parallels: `http://www.parallels.com/`

72. See the following to download the latest versions of these tools:

    InstallWatchPro: http://www.pcworld.com/product/949536/installwatch.html

    Regshot: http://sourceforge.net/projects/regshot/files/latest/download?source=dlp

    InCtrl5: http://www.pcmag.com/article2/0.2817.25126.00.asp

    There are two issues with InCtrl5 that will require a bit of knowledge to use the program effectively. First, InCtrl5 will need to be run in compatibility mode for Windows Vista, 7, or 8/8.1. Secondly, there is an issue with its output results for 64-bit users as it will not display the Software\Wow6432Node registry keys as coming from there, but it will instead show them as coming from simply Software, something to watch out for.

73. See the following to download the latest versions of these tools:

    Autoruns: http://technet.microsoft.com/en-us/sysinternals/bb963902.aspx

    HijackThis: http://download.cnet.com/Trend-Micro-HijackThis/3000-8022_4-10227353.html

    CurrPorts: http://www.nirsoft.net/utils/cports.html

74. See the following for some examples of anti-rootkit tools:

    Sophos: http://www.sophos.com/en-us/products/free-tools/sophos-anti-rootkit.aspx

    Malwarebytes: http://www.malwarebytes.org/antirootkit/

    Kaspersky Labs TDSSKiller: http://support.kaspersky.com/us/viruses/disinfection/5350

    GMER: http://www.gmer.net/

    Bitdefender Labs Rootkit Remover: http://labs.bitdefender.com/rootkit-remover-download-page/

75. See the following to download the latest versions of these tools:

    HashCalc: http://www.slavasoft.com/hashcalc/

    PEiD: http://www.softpedia.com/get/Programming/Packers-Crypters-Protectors/PEiD-updated.shtml

    Windows File Analyzer: http://www.mitec.cz/wfa.html

    The Sleuth Kit: http://www.sleuthkit.org/sleuthkit/desc.php

    WinHex: http://www.x-ways.net/winhex/

76. See the following to download any of the SysInternals tools currently available: http://technet.microsoft.com/en-us/sysinternals/bb545021.aspx

77.　See the following to download the latest versions of these tools:

Wireshark: `http://www.wireshark.org/`

Fport: `http://www.mcafee.com/us/downloads/free-tools/fport.aspx`

Advanced Port Scanner: `http://www.advanced-port-scanner.com/`

Advanced IP Scanner: `http://www.advanced-ip-scanner.com/`

Nmap: `http://nmap.org/`

Netcat/Ncat: `http://nmap.org/ncat/`

Ncat is integrated with Nmap and is available in the standard Nmap download packages (including source code and Linux, Windows, and Mac binaries).

78.　See the following for information on how to set up and use tun2socks and Tor: `https://code.google.com/archive/p/badvpn/wikis/tun2socks.wiki`

79.　See the following to find out more about these tools:

OllyDbg: `http://www.ollydbg.de/`

OllyDbg Plugins (OllyScript): `http://www.openrce.org/downloads/details/106/OllyScript`

The PaiMai Framework: `http://www.openrce.org/downloads/details/208`

Immunity Debugger: `https://www.immunityinc.com/products/debugger/`

80.　See the following for a good overview of how to mount a virtual hard drive for access directly from a host machine: `http://www.reactos.org/wiki/Transfer_files_from_the_host_OS_to_the_virtual_drive`

See the following to download the latest version of DAEMON Tools: `http://www.daemon-tools.cc/downloads`

81.　See the following for an overview of the vmss2core tool: `http://labs.vmware.com/flings/vmss2core`

See the following for a VMware KB article that provides an overview on the various methods available to suspend a virtual machine running on ESX/ESXi to collect diagnostic information (KB article 2005831): `http://kb.vmware.com/selfservice/microsites/search.do?language=en_US&cmd=displayKC&externalId=2005831`

82.　See the following for an overview of the vm2dmp tool: `http://blogs.technet.com/b/virtualworld/archive/2010/02/02/vm2dmp-hyper-v-tm-vm-state-to-memory-dump-converter.aspx`

See the following for the Debug-VM cmdlet documentation: `http://technet.microsoft.com/en-us/library/dn464280.aspx`

See the following for the Livekd Tool: `http://technet.microsoft.com/en-us/sysinternals/bb842062`

83.　See the following for the CERT/CC website: `http://www.cert.org/certcc.html`

84. See the following for RFC 2350, "Expectations for Computer Security Incident Response": `http://www.ietf.org/rfc/rfc2350.txt`

85. See the following to download the CERT-in-a-box project files: `http://www.first.org/resources/guides#bp21`

86. `http://www.internet-computer-security.com/Firewall/IPS.html`

87. See the following: `https://www.nsa.gov/ia/_files/factsheets/Application_Whitelisting_Trifold.pdf`

88. See the following: `http://securityresponse.symantec.com/content/en/us/enterprise/white_papers/how-endpoint-encryption-works_WP_21275920.pdf`

89. See the following: `http://securityresponse.symantec.com/content/en/us/enterprise/white_papers/how-endpoint-encryption-works_WP_21275920.pdf`

90. See the following: `http://www.trustedcomputinggroup.org/resources/trusted_platform_module_tpm_summary`

91. See the following: `http://www.gartner.com/technology/topics/`

92. See the following: `http://www.wired.com/2012/12/cope-the-secure-alternative-to-byod/`

93. NIST Cloud Computing Synopsis and Recommendations `http://nvlpubs.nist.gov/nistpubs/Legacy/SP/nistspecialpublication800-146.pdf`

94. `http://nvlpubs.nist.gov/nistpubs/Legacy/SP/nistspecialpublication800-145.pdf` (page 3)

95. `http://nvlpubs.nist.gov/nistpubs/Legacy/SP/nistspecialpublication800-145.pdf` (page 3)

96. `http://nvlpubs.nist.gov/nistpubs/Legacy/SP/nistspecialpublication800-145.pdf` (page 3)

97. `http://nvlpubs.nist.gov/nistpubs/Legacy/SP/nistspecialpublication800-145.pdf` (page 3)

98. `http://nvlpubs.nist.gov/nistpubs/Legacy/SP/nistspecialpublication800-145.pdf` (page 2)

99. `http://nvlpubs.nist.gov/nistpubs/Legacy/SP/nistspecialpublication800-145.pdf` (page 2)

100. `http://nvlpubs.nist.gov/nistpubs/Legacy/SP/nistspecialpublication800-145.pdf` (page 3)

101. Popek, Gerald J.; Goldberg, Robert P. (1974). "Formal Requirements for Virtualizable Third Generation Architectures." Communications of the ACM 17 (7): 412–421. doi:10.1145/361011.361073.

102. `http://www.ftc.gov/`

103. Consent is by definition already in place, unless the data subject does not express a willingness to withdraw it (thus making opposition to the continuation of processing).

104. The consent of the data subject (with all the features required by the applicable P&DP law, typically free, informed, specific, documented in writing) must be collected in advance to initiate any operation on his/her personal data.

105. http://www.archives.gov/exhibits/charters/bill_of_rights_transcript.html

106. http://www.whitehouse.gov/the-press-office/2012/02/23/fact-sheet-plan-protect-privacy-internet-age-adopting-consumer-privacy-b

107. http://eur-lex.europa.eu/legal-content/EN/TXT/?uri=CELEX:31995L0046

108. http://www.dataprotection.ro/servlet/ViewDocument?id=201

109. See the following for a complete overview of the timeline of activities associated with the process of adoption: http://www.huntonregulationtracker.com/legislativescrutiny/

110. http://www.apec.org/Groups/Committee-on-Trade-and-Investment/~/media/Files/Groups/ECSG/05_ecsg_privacyframewk.ashx

111. See the following for NIST SP800—145: http://nvlpubs.nist.gov/nistpubs/Legacy/SP/nistspecialpublication800-145.pdf

112. http://www.gartner.com/it-glossary/search-based-data-discovery-tools/

113. See the following for the full text of the opinion:http://www.cil.cnrs.fr/CIL/IMG/pdf/wp196_en.pdf

114. https://cloudsecurityalliance.org/group/privacy-level-agreement//

115. The security practitioner will want to be aware of platform specific architectural issues and be able to make the appropriate choices when configuring storage as a result.

    For Microsoft's Hyper-V on Windows Server 2012 R2, see the following with regards to pass-through disks: http://blogs.technet.com/b/askcore/archive/2013/01/24/behavior-change-when-working-with-pass-through-disks-in-windows-server-2012-failover-clusters.aspx

    For VMware's guidance on using RDM's, see the following: http://pubs.vmware.com/vsphere-55/topic/com.vmware.ICbase/PDF/vsphere-esxi-vcenter-server-55-storage-guide.pdf (Chapter 17, pages 155—161.)

116. http://www8.hp.com/us/en/software-solutions/digital-safe-cloud-archiving/

117. One example of a company that is using Data Dispersion technology is Clever-Safe: https://www.cleversafe.com/platform/how-it-works

118. See the following for a general overview of OAUTH: http://oauth.net/2/

    The OUATH v2 RFC is here: http://tools.ietf.org/html/rfc6749

119. See the following for an overview on KMIP: https://www.oasis-open.org/committees/tc_home.php?wg_abbrev=kmip

120. See the following for a complete listing of all NIST FIPS documentation: http://csrc.nist.gov/publications/PubsFIPS.html

121. See the following:

    Basel Accord II: `http://www.bis.org/publ/bcbs128.pdf`

    PCI-DSS version 3.0: `https://www.pcisecuritystandards.org/documents/PCI_DSS_v3.pdf`

122. `https://www.owasp.org/index.php/Logging_Cheat_Sheet`

123. `https://www.owasp.org/index.php/Logging_Cheat_Sheet`

124. See the following for more information on SCAP: `http://scap.nist.gov/`
    See the following for more information on CAPEC: `https://capec.mitre.org/`

125. `https://www.iso.org/obp/ui/#iso:std:iso-iec:27037:ed-1:v1:en`

126. See the following: `http://www.sciencemag.org/content/332/6025/60`

127. See the following: `http://martinhilbert.net/WhatsTheContent_Hilbert.pdf`

128. "The three V's—volume, velocity and variety," concepts originally coined by Doug Laney in 2001 to refer to the challenge of data management in the following blog article: `http://blogs.gartner.com/doug-laney/files/2012/01/ad949-3D-Data-Management-Controlling-Data-Volume-Velocity-and-Variety.pdf`

129. `https://datafloq.com/read/3vs-sufficient-describe-big-data/166`

130. See the following: *Security Implications of Big Data Strategies*, Information Week reports, March 2013.

131. `http://en.wikipedia.org/wiki/Software-defined_networking`

132. For those looking to go deeper with the VMware technologies being discussed, the following landing page for *all* of VMware's documentation by versioned release will be helpful: `https://www.vmware.com/support/pubs/vsphere-esxi-vcenter-server-pubs.html`

133. The following resources may be helpful for those looking to go deeper in the Microsoft technologies discussed:

    `http://technet.microsoft.com/en-us/library/dn282278.aspx`

    `http://technet.microsoft.com/en-us/library/dn743844.aspx`

    `http://technet.microsoft.com/en-us/library/dn440540.aspx`

    `http://technet.microsoft.com/en-us/library/hh831579.aspx`

    `http://technet.microsoft.com/en-us/library/hh205987.aspx`

    `http://technet.microsoft.com/en-us/library/gg610610.aspx`

134. See the following: `http://csrc.nist.gov/publications/nistpubs/800-30-rev1/sp800_30_r1.pdf`

135. See the following: `http://resources.infosecinstitute.com/virtualization-security-2/`

Answers to Sample Questions

DOMAIN 1: ACCESS CONTROLS

1. What type of controls are used in a Rule Set–Based Access Control system?

   a. Discretionary

   b. Mandatory

   c. Role Based

   d. Compensating

   Answer: A

   Rule set–based access controls (RSBAC) are discretionary controls giving data owners the discretion to determine the rules necessary to facilitate access.

2. What framework is the Rule Set–Based Access Controls logic based upon?

   a. Logical Framework for Access Control

   b. Specialized Framework for Access Control

   c. Technical Framework for Access Control

   d. Generalized Framework for Access Control

   Answer: D

   The RSBAC framework logic is based on the work done for the generalized framework for access control (GFAC) by Abrams and LaPadula.

3. View-Based Access Controls are an example of a(n):

   a. Audit control

   b. Constrained User Interface

   c. Temporal constraint

   d. Side Channel

   Answer: B

   View-based access controls (VBACs) are most commonly found in database applications to control access to specific parts of a database. The constrained user interface in VBAC restricts or limits an access control subject's ability to view or perhaps act on "components" of an access control object based on the access control subject's assigned level of authority. Views are dynamically created by the system for each user-authorized access.

   Simply put, VBAC separates a given access control object into subcomponents and then permits or denies access for the access control subject to view or interact with specific subcomponents of the underlying access control object.

4. Which of the following are supported authentication methods for iSCSI? (Choose two.)

   a. Kerberos

   b. Transport Layer Security (TLS)

   c. Secure Remote Password (SRP)

   d. Layer 2 Tunneling Protocol (L2TP)

   Answer: A and C

   There are a number of authentication methods supported with iSCSI:

   - **Kerberos** — Kerberos is a network authentication protocol. It is designed to provide strong authentication for client/server applications by using secret-key cryptography.

   - **SRP (Secure Remote Password)** — SRP is a secure password-based authentication and key-exchange protocol. SRP exchanges a cryptographically strong secret as a byproduct of successful authentication, which enables the two parties to communicate securely.

   - **SPKM1/2 (Simple Public-Key Mechanism)** — SPKM provides authentication, key establishment, data integrity, and data confidentiality in an online distributed application environment using a public-key infrastructure. The use of a public-key infrastructure allows digital signatures supporting non-repudiation to be employed for message exchanges.

   - **CHAP (Challenge Handshake Authentication Protocol)** — CHAP is used to periodically verify the identity of the peer using a three-way handshake. This is done upon initial link establishment and may be repeated any time after the link has been established.

5. According to the following scenario, what would be the most appropriate access control model to deploy?

   Scenario: A medical records database application is used by a health-care worker to access blood test records. If a record contains information about an HIV test, the health-care worker may be denied access to the existence of the HIV test and the results of the HIV test. Only specific hospital staff would have the necessary access control rights to view blood test records that contain any information about HIV tests.

   a. Discretionary Access Control

   b. Context-Based Access Control

   c. Content-Dependent Access Control

   d. Role-Based Access Control

Answer: C

Content-dependent access control is used to protect databases containing sensitive information. Content-dependent access control works by permitting or denying the access control subjects access to access control objects based on the explicit content within the access control object.

Context-based access control is often confused with content-dependent access control, but they are two completely different methodologies. While content-dependent access control makes decisions based on the content within an access control object, context-based access control is not concerned with the content; it is concerned only with the context or the sequence of events leading to the access control object being allowed through the firewall.

In the example of blood test records for content dependent access control, the access control subject would be denied access to the access control object because it contained information about an HIV test. Context-based access control could be used to limit the total number of requests for access to any blood test records over a given period of time. Hence, a health-care worker may be limited to accessing the blood test database more than 100 times in a 24-hour period.

While context-based access control does not require that permissions be configured for individual access control objects, it requires that rules be created in relation to the sequence of events that precede an access attempt.

6. Which of the following is *not* one of the three primary rules in a Biba formal model?

   a. An access control subject cannot request services from an access control object that has a higher integrity level.

   b. An access control subject cannot modify an access control object that has a higher integrity level.

   c. An access control subject cannot access an access control object that has a lower integrity level.

   d. An access control subject cannot access an access control object that has a higher integrity level.

Answer: D

An access control subject cannot access an access control object that has a higher integrity level is not one of the three primary rules in the Biba formal model.

7. Which of the following is an example of a firewall that does not use Context-Based Access Control?

    a. Static packet filter

    b. Circuit gateway

    c. Stateful inspection

    d. Application proxy

    Answer: A

    Context-based access controls also consider the "state" of the connection, and in a static packet filter no consideration is given to the connection state. Each and every packet is compared to the rule base regardless of whether it had previously been allowed or denied.

8. Where would you find a singulation protocol being used?

    a. Where there is a Radio Frequency ID system deployed and tag collisions are a problem

    b. Where there is router that has gone offline in a multi-path storage network

    c. Where there is a Radio Frequency ID system deployed and reader collisions are a problem

    d. Where there is switch that has gone offline in a multi-path storage network

    Answer: C

    Some common problems with RFID are reader collision and tag collision. Reader collision occurs when the signals from two or more readers overlap. The tag is unable to respond to simultaneous queries. Systems must be carefully set up to avoid this problem; many systems use an anti-collision protocol (also called a *singulation protocol*). Anti-collision protocols enable the tags to take turns in transmitting to a reader.

9. Which of the following are not principal components of access control systems? (Choose two.)

    a. Objects

    b. Biometrics

    c. Subjects

    d. Auditing

Answer: A and C

While biometrics devices are used in some access control systems to confirm an individual's identity, they are not considered to be one of the principal components of an access control system.

While auditing is used in many access control systems, it is not a mandatory feature or function of all systems and is not always enabled.

Both objects and subjects are the building blocks of all access control systems.

10. Which of the following are behavioral traits in a biometric device?

    a. Voice pattern and keystroke dynamics

    b. Signature dynamics and iris scan

    c. Retina scan and hand geometry

    d. Fingerprint and facial recognition

Answer: A

Voice pattern, signature dynamics, and keystroke dynamics all are behavioral traits in biometric devices.

11. In the measurement of biometric accuracy, which of the following is commonly referred to as a "type 2 error"?

    a. Cross-over error rate (CER)

    b. Rate of false rejection—False Rejection Rate (FRR)

    c. Input/output per second (IOPS)

    d. Rate of false acceptance—False Acceptance Rate (FAR)

Answer: D

A false reject rate is a type 1 error, false acceptance rate is a type 2 error, and cross-over error rate is the intersection when FRR equals FAR.

12. What is the difference between a synchronous and asynchronous password token?

    a. Asynchronous tokens contain a password that is physically hidden and then transmitted for each authentication, while synchronous tokens do not.

    b. Synchronous tokens are generated with the use of a timer, while asynchronous tokens do not use a clock for generation.

    c. Synchronous tokens contain a password that is physically hidden and then transmitted for each authentication, while asynchronous tokens do not.

    d. Asynchronous tokens are generated with the use of a timer, while synchronous tokens do not use a clock for generation.

Answer: B

Security tokens are used to prove one's identity electronically (as in the case of a customer trying to access their bank account). The token is used in addition to or in place of a password to prove that the customer is who they claim to be. The token acts like an electronic key to access something. All tokens contain some secret information that are used to prove identity. There are four different ways in which this information can be used:

- **Static password token.** The device contains a password that is physically hidden (not visible to the possessor) but that is transmitted for each authentication. This type is vulnerable to replay attacks.

- **Synchronous dynamic password token.** A timer is used to rotate through various combinations produced by a cryptographic algorithm. The token and the authentication server must have synchronized clocks.

- **Asynchronous password token.** A one-time password is generated without the use of a clock, either from a one-time pad or cryptographic algorithm.

- **Challenge response token.** Using public key cryptography, it is possible to prove possession of a private key without revealing that key. The authentication server encrypts a challenge (typically a random number, or at least data with some random parts) with a public key; the device proves it possesses a copy of the matching private key by providing the decrypted challenge.

13. What is an authorization table?

   a. A matrix of access control objects, access control subjects, and their respective rights

   b. A service or program where access control information is stored and where access control decisions are made

   c. A listing of access control objects and their respective rights

   d. A listing of access control subjects and their respective rights

Answer: A

An authorization table is a matrix of access control objects, access control subjects, and their respective rights. The authorization table is used in some DAC systems to provide for a simple and intuitive user interface for the definition of access control rules.

14. What ports are used during Kerberos Authentication?

    a. 53 and 25

    b. 169 and 88

    c. 53 and 88

    d. 443 and 21

    Answer: C

    TABLE A.1 Network Ports Used During Kerberos Authentication

SERVICE NAME	UDP	TCP
DNS	53	53
Kerberos	88	88

15. What are the five areas that make up the identity management lifecycle?

    a. Authorization, proofing, provisioning, maintenance, and establishment

    b. Accounting, proofing, provisioning, maintenance, and entitlement

    c. Authorization, proofing, provisioning, monitoring, and entitlement

    d. Authorization, proofing, provisioning, maintenance, and entitlement

    Answer: D

    In essence, identity management is the process for managing the entire life cycle of digital identities, including the profiles of people, systems, and services, as well as the use of emerging technologies to control access to company resources. A digital identity is the representation of a set of claims made by a digital subject including, but not limited to, computers, resources, or persons about itself or another digital subject. The goal of identity management, therefore, is to improve companywide productivity and security, while lowering the costs associated with managing users and their identities, attributes, and credentials.

    There are five areas that make up the identity management lifecycle:

    - Authorization
    - Proofing
    - Provisioning
    - Maintenance
    - Entitlement

DOMAIN 2: SECURITY OPERATIONS

1. Security awareness training aims to educate users on:

   a. What they can do to maintain the organization's security posture

   b. How to secure their home computer systems

   c. The work performed by the information security organization

   d. How attackers defeat security safeguards

   Answer: A

   The aim of security awareness is to make the organization more resistant to security vulnerabilities and therefore maintain the organization's security posture.

2. Which of the following are operational aspects of configuration management (CM)?

   a. Identification, documentation, control, and auditing

   b. Documentation, control, accounting, and auditing

   c. Control, accounting, auditing, and reporting

   d. Identification, control, accounting, and auditing

   Answer: D

   Configuration management begins with identification of the baseline configuration as one or more configuration items within the configuration management database (CMDB). Once the baseline is established, all changes are controlled throughout the lifecycle of the component. Each change is accounted for by capturing, tracking, and reporting on change requests, configurations, and change history. Finally, auditing ensures integrity by verifying that the actual configuration matches the information captured and tracked in the CMDB and that all changes have been appropriately recorded and tracked.

3. The systems certification process can best be described as a:

   a. Process for obtaining stakeholder signoff on system configuration

   b. Method of validating adherence to security requirements

   c. Means of documenting adherence to security standards

   d. Method of testing a system to assure that vulnerabilities have been addressed

   Answer: B

   Certification reviews the system against the requirements specified in the system security plan to ensure that all required control specifications are met. Answer D is incorrect because while the process may include vulnerability testing, this is only one component of the process and residual risks do not preclude certification against requirements. Answer C is incorrect because the controls specified in the security plan are requirements, not standards. The answer is not A, because the certification process results in a recommendation only; accreditation is the process of obtaining signoff to operate the system.

4. Which of the following is a degausser used to do?

   a. Render media that contain sensitive data unusable.

   b. Overwrite sensitive data with zeros so that it is unreadable.

   c. Eliminate magnetic data remanence on a disk or tape.

   d. Reformat a disk or tape for subsequent reuse.

   Answer: C

   Degaussing eliminates remanence by applying and then removing a strong magnetic field, removing magnetic signals from media. Reformatting does not actually erase data, so D is incorrect. While degaussing may render some media unusable, this is not the aim, so A is also incorrect. Answer B is incorrect because data are not over-written by degaussing; it is removed.

5. A web application software vulnerability that allows an attacker to extract sensitive information from a backend database is known as a:

   a. Cross-site scripting vulnerability

   b. Malicious file execution vulnerability

   c. Injection flaw

   d. Input validation failure

   Answer: C

   An injection flaw occurs when user-supplied data can be sent directly to a command processor or query interpreter; attackers can exploit this flaw by supplying a query string as input to a web application to extract data from a database. Answer A is incorrect; cross-site scripting vulnerabilities allow an attacker to execute scripts, typically in a user's browser. Malicious file execution (B) is a vulnerability in applications that accept file names or object references as input and then execute the files or objects. Answer D is also incorrect, as failures in input validation can have many adverse consequences (not necessarily disclosure of database content).

6. The security practice that restricts user access based on need to know is called:

   a. Mandatory access control

   b. Default deny configuration

   c. Role-based access control

   d. Least privilege

Answer: D

Least privilege grants users and processes only those privileges they require to perform authorized functions, that is, "need to know." Mandatory access control (A) limits access based on the clearance of the subject and the sensitivity of the object and may provide access to objects of lower sensitivity where there is no business purpose for access; therefore, A is incorrect. Answer B is also incorrect; a "default deny" configuration refers to rule-based access control in which only that which is explicitly authorized is allowed; this is implemented in most firewall rule sets and is the premise behind whitelisting. Role-based access control (C) is not correct because while it provides access based on a role a user is associated with, it does not allow for granting individuals access to specific objects based on a need to know and may provide more access than is required to perform a certain function.

7. A security guideline is a:

   a. Set of criteria that must be met to address security requirements

   b. Tool for measuring the effectiveness of security safeguards

   c. Statement of senior management expectations for managing the security program

   d. Recommended security practice

Answer: D

A guideline is a recommended security practice but is not required (as in A or C) or enforced. As a recommended practice, there is no standard of measurement, so B is also incorrect.

8. A security baseline is a:

   a. Measurement of security effectiveness when a control is first implemented

   b. Recommended security practice

   c. Minimum set of security requirements for a system

   d. Measurement used to determine trends in security activity

Answer: C

A baseline is a special type of security standard that specifies the minimum security controls or requirements for a system. Answer A is incorrect because this more accurately describes a configuration baseline established in a CMDB but does not indicate whether requirements have been met. Answer B refers to a guideline and is incorrect. Answer D is incorrect; a benchmark, not a baseline, is a value used in metrics against which to measure variations in performance.

9. An antifraud measure that requires two people to complete a transaction is an example of the principle of:

   a. Separation of duties

   b. Dual control

   c. Role-based access control

   d. Defense in depths

Answer: B

Dual control requires two people to physically or logically complete a process, such that one initiates and the other approves, or completes, the process. Dual control operates under the theory that controls that require more than one person operating together to circumvent are more secure than those under the control of a single individual. Answer A is incorrect; under separation of duties, two individuals may perform two separate, although perhaps similar, processes; that is, they perform separate functions. Answer C is incorrect; this refers to an access control model. Answer D is incorrect because dual control is actually a single control mechanism, not a series of layered controls.

10. The waterfall model is a:

   a. Development method that follows a linear sequence of steps

   b. Iterative process used to develop secure applications

   c. Development method that uses rapid prototyping

   d. Extreme programming model used to develop web application

Answer: A

The waterfall method is a linear sequence of seven steps used in application development. It is not iterative, does not make use of prototypes, and does not use rapid application development (RAD) or extreme programming techniques; thus B, C, and D are incorrect.

11. Code signing is a technique used to:

   a. Ensure that software is appropriately licensed for use

   b. Prevent source code tampering

   c. Identify source code modules in a release package

   d. Support verification of source code authenticity

   Answer: D

   Code signing using hash functions and a digital signature is used in the release process to ensure that the code that is moved to production is the same as that which was approved for production release. Answer A is not correct because the signature is not the same as a license key. Answer B is not correct because signing itself does not prevent tampering, although it can be used to detect tampering. Answer C is not correct; code signing verifies authenticity of the signed code but does not identify discrete components or packages.

12. The role of information owner in the system security plan includes:

   a. Maintaining the system security plan

   b. Determining privileges that will be assigned to users of the system

   c. Assessing the effectiveness of security controls

   d. Authorizing the system for operation

   Answer: B

   The information owner determines who can access the system and the privileges that will be granted to users. The system owner is responsible for A, maintaining the system security plan. The approver or authorizing official is responsible for D, authorizing the system for operation, at the end of the certification and accreditation process. Assessing the effectiveness of security controls (C) is the responsibility of the system security officer.

13. What are the mandatory tenets of the ISC2 Code of Ethics? (Choose all that apply.)

   a. Protect society, the commonwealth, and the infrastructure.

   b. Act honorably, honestly, justly, responsibly, and legally.

   c. Promote and preserve public trust and confidence in information and systems.

   d. Advance and protect the profession.

Answer: A, B, and D

There are four mandatory tenets of the Code of Ethics:

1. Protect society, the commonwealth, and the infrastructure.
2. Act honorably, honestly, justly, responsibly, and legally.
3. Provide diligent and competent service to principals.
4. Advance and protect the profession.

"Promote and preserve public trust and confidence in information and systems" is part of the Code of Ethics canons but it is not one of the four mandatory tenets.

14. What principle does confidentiality support?

   a. Due diligence

   b. Due care

   c. Least privilege

   d. Collusion

Answer: C

Confidentiality supports the principle of *least privilege* by providing that only authorized individuals, processes, or systems should have access to information on a need-to-know basis. The level of access that an authorized individual should have is at the level necessary for them to do their job. In recent years, much press has been dedicated to the privacy of information and the need to protect it from individuals, who may be able to commit crimes by viewing the information. Identity theft is the act of assuming one's identity through knowledge of confidential information obtained from various sources.

15. What two things are used to accomplish non-repudiation?

   a. Proofing and provisioning

   b. Encryption and authorization

   c. Monitoring and private keys

   d. Digital signatures and public key infrastructure

Answer: D

Non-repudiation can be accomplished with digital signatures and PKI. The message is signed using the sender's private key. When the recipient receives the message, they may use the sender's public key to validate the signature. While this proves the integrity of the message, it does not explicitly define the ownership of the private key. A certificate authority must have an association between the private key and the sender (meaning only the sender has the private key) for the non-repudiation to be valid.

16. What are the elements that make up information security risks?

   a. Requirements, threats, and exposures

   b. Threats, vulnerabilities, and impacts

   c. Assessments, vulnerabilities, and expenses

   d. Impacts, probabilities, and known errors

   Answer: B

   Information security risk can be thought of as the likelihood of loss due to threats exploiting vulnerabilities, that is:

   $$RISK = THREAT + VULNERABILITY + IMPACT$$

17. What is an example of a compensating control?

   a. A fence

   b. Termination

   c. Job rotation

   d. Warning banner

   Answer: C

   Compensating controls are introduced when the existing capabilities of a system do not support the requirements of a policy. Compensating controls can be technical, procedural, or managerial. Although an existing system may not support the required controls, there may exist other technology or processes that can supplement the existing environment, closing the gap in controls, meeting policy requirements, and reducing overall risk.

	ADMINISTRATIVE	TECHNICAL	PHYSICAL
Directive	Policy	Configuration Standards	Authorized Personnel Only Signs Traffic Lights
Deterrent	Policy	Warning Banner	Beware of Dog Sign
Preventative	User Registration Procedure	Password-Based Login	Fence

CONTINUES

CONTINUED

	ADMINISTRATIVE	TECHNICAL	PHYSICAL
Detective	Review Violation Reports	Logs	Sentry CCTV
Corrective	Termination	Unplug, Isolate, and Terminate Connection	Fire Extinguisher
Recovery	DR Plan	Backups	Rebuild
Compensating	Supervision Job Rotation Logging	CCTV Keystroke Logging	Layered Defense

18. What is remote attestation?

   a. A form of integrity protection that makes use of a hashed copy of hardware and software configuration to verify that configurations have not been altered

   b. A form of confidentiality protection that makes use of a cached copy of hardware and software configuration to verify that configurations have not been altered

   c. A form of integrity protection that makes use of a cached copy of hardware and software configuration to verify that configurations have not been altered

   d. A form of confidentiality protection that makes use of a hashed copy of hardware and software configuration to verify that configurations have not been altered

   Answer: A

   Trusted Platform Module (TPM) chips provide additional security features such as platform authentication and remote attestation, a form of integrity protection that makes use of a hashed copy of hardware and software configuration to verify that configurations have not been altered.

19. With regards to the Change Control Policy document and Change Management, where should Analysis/Impact Assessment take place?

   a. After the decision making and prioritization activities, but before approval

   b. After the recording of the proposed change(s), but before decision making and prioritization activities

   c. After the approval, but before status tracking activities

   d. After the request submission, but before recording of the proposed change(s)

Answer: B

The change control policy document covers the following aspects of the change process under management control:

1. **Request Submission**—A request for change is submitted to the Change Control Board for review, prioritization, and approval. Included in the request should be a description of the change and rationale or objectives for the request, a change implementation plan, an impact assessment, and a backout plan to be exercised in the event of a change failure or unanticipated outcome.

2. **Recording**—Details of the request are recorded for review, communication, and tracking purposes.

3. **Analysis/Impact Assessment**—Changes are typically subject to peer review for accuracy and completeness and to identify any impacts on other systems or processes that may arise as a result of the change.

4. **Decision Making and Prioritization**—The team reviews the request, implementation, and backout plans, and impacts and determines whether the change should be approved, denied, or put on hold. Changes are scheduled and prioritized, and any communication plans are put in place.

5. **Approval**—Formal approval for the change is granted and recorded.

6. **Status Tracking**—The change is tracked through completion. A post-implementation review may be performed.

DOMAIN 3: RISK, IDENTIFICATION, MONITORING, AND ANALYSIS

1. Which of the following terms refers to a function of the likelihood of a given threat source exercising a potential vulnerability, and the resulting impact of that adverse event on the organization?

   a. Threat

   b. Risk

   c. Vulnerability

   d. Asset

Answer: B

A threat (A) is the potential for a threat source to exercise (accidentally trigger or intentionally exploit) a specific vulnerability. A vulnerability (C) is a flaw or weakness in system security procedures, design, implementation, or internal controls that could be exercised (accidentally triggered or intentionally exploited) and result in a security breach or a violation of the system's security policy. An asset (D) is anything of value that is owned by an organization.

2. The process of an authorized user analyzing system security by attempting to exploit vulnerabilities to gain access to systems and data is referred to as:

   a. Vulnerability assessment

   b. Intrusion detection

   c. Risk management

   d. Penetration testing

   Answer: D

   Vulnerability assessments (A) attempt to determine only if vulnerabilities exist but do not attempt to actively exploit identified vulnerabilities. Intrusion detection (B) is an automated technique for identifying active intrusion attempts. Risk management (C) is the process of assessing and mitigating risk.

3. The process for assigning a dollar value to anticipated losses resulting from a threat source successfully exploiting a vulnerability is known as:

   a. Qualitative risk analysis

   b. Risk mitigation

   c. Quantitative risk analysis

   d. Business impact analysis

   Answer: C

   A qualitative risk analysis (A) assesses impact in relative terms such as high, medium, and low impact without assigning a dollar value. Risk mitigation (B) describes a process of applying risk mitigation strategies to reduce risk exposure to levels that are acceptable to the organization. A business impact analysis (D) assesses financial and nonfinancial impacts to an organization that would result from a business disruption.

4. When initially responding to an incident, it is critical for the SSCP to:

   a. Notify executive management.

   b. Restore affected data from backup.

   c. Follow organizational incident response procedures.

   d. Share information related to the incident with everyone in the organization.

Answer: C

You should always follow the organization's incident response policy when responding to an incident. Information related to the incident should be shared only on a need-to-know basis. Many types of incidents will not require notification to executive management. The incident response policy and procedure should define when notification to executive management is required. Data restoration should not be performed until forensic analyses and evidence gathering is complete.

5. Which of the following are threat sources to information technology systems? (Choose all that apply.)

   a. Natural threats

   b. Human threats

   c. Environmental threats

   d. Software bugs

   Answer: A, B, C, and D

   Natural threats, human threats, environmental threats, and software bugs are all potential threat sources to information technology systems.

6. The expected monetary loss to an organization from a threat to an asset is referred to as:

   a. Single loss expectancy

   b. Asset value

   c. Annualized rate of occurrence

   d. Exposure factor

   Answer: A

   Asset value (B) is the value of a specific asset to the organization. Annualized rate of occurrence (C) represents the expected number of occurrences of a specific threat to an asset in a given year. Exposure factor (D) represents the portion of an asset that would be lost if a risk to the asset was realized.

7. Which risk-mitigation strategy would be appropriate if an organization decided to implement additional controls to decrease organizational risk?

   a. Risk avoidance

   b. Risk reduction

   c. Risk transference

   d. Risk acceptance

Answer: B

Risk avoidance (A) is a strategy that is used to reduce risk by avoiding risky behaviors. Risk transference (C) is a strategy to transfer risk from the organization to a third party by methods such as insurance or outsourcing. Risk acceptance (D) is a strategy in which the organization decides to accept the risk associated with the potential occurrence of a specific event.

8. During which phase of the risk assessment process is technical settings and configuration documented?

    a. Risk determination

    b. Results documentation

    c. System characterization

    d. Control analysis

Answer: C

In the risk determination phase (A), overall risk to an IT system is assessed. During the results documentation phase (B), results of the risk assessment are documented. In the control analysis phase (D), controls are assessed to evaluate their effectiveness.

9. What is the correct order of steps for the NIST risk assessment process?

    a. Communicate, prepare, conduct, and maintain

    b. Prepare, conduct, communicate, and maintain

    c. Conduct, communicate, prepare, and maintain

    d. Maintain, communicate, prepare, and conduct

Answer: B

NIST Special Publication 800-30 R1, "Risk Management Guide for Information Technology Systems," details a four-step risk assessment process. The risk assessment process described by NIST is composed of the following steps (as shown in Figure A-1):

    1. **Prepare** for the assessment

    2. **Conduct** the assessment

    3. **Communicate** the assessment results

    4. **Maintain** the assessment

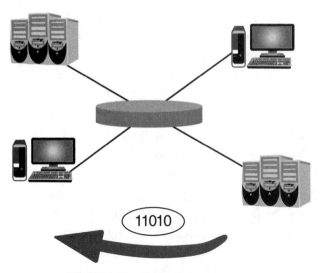

FIGURE A-1 **The NIST risk assessment process**

10. Cross-referencing and stimulus response algorithms are qualities of what associated with what activity?

    a. Vulnerability testing

    b. Penetration testing

    c. Static application security testing

    d. Dynamic application security testing

Answer: A

Vulnerability testing usually employs software specific to the activity and tends to have the following qualities:

- **OS Fingerprinting**—This technique is used to identify the operating system in use on a target. OS fingerprinting is the process where a scanner can determine the operating system of the host by analyzing the TCP/IP stack flag settings. These settings vary on each operating system from vendor to vendor or by TCP/IP stack analysis and banner grabbing. Banner grabbing is reading the response banner presented for several ports such as FTP, HTTP, and Telnet. This function is sometimes built into mapping software and sometimes into vulnerability software.

- **Stimulus and Response Algorithms**—These are techniques to identify application software versions and then referencing these versions with known vulnerabilities. Stimulus involves sending one or more packets at the target.

Depending on the response, the tester can infer information about the target's applications. For example, to determine the version of the HTTP server, the vulnerability testing software might send an HTTP GET request to a web server, just like a browser would (the stimulus), and read the reply information it receives back (the response) for information that details the fact that it is Apache version X, IIS version Y, etc.

- **Privileged Logon Ability**—The ability to automatically log onto a host or group of hosts with user credentials (administrator-level or other level) for a deeper "authorized" look at systems is desirable.

- **Cross-Referencing**—OS and applications/services (discovered during the port-mapping phase) should be cross-referenced to identify possible vulnerabilities. For example, if OS fingerprinting reveals that the host runs Red Hat Linux 8.0 and that portmapper is one of the listening programs, any pre-8.0 portmapper vulnerabilities can likely be ruled out. Keep in mind that old vulnerabilities have resurfaced in later versions of code even though they were patched at one time. While these instances may occur, the filtering based on OS and application fingerprinting will help the security practitioner better target systems and use the security practitioner's time more effectively.

- **Update Capability**—Scanners must be kept up-to-date with the latest vulnerability signatures; otherwise, they will not be able to detect newer problems and vulnerabilities. Commercial tools that do not have quality personnel dedicated to updating the product are of reduced effectiveness. Likewise, open-source scanners should have a qualified following to keep them up-to-date.

- **Reporting Capability**—Without the ability to report, a scanner does not serve much purpose. Good scanners provide the ability to export scan data in a variety of formats, including viewing in HTML or PDF format or to third-party reporting software and are configurable enough to give the ability to filter reports into high-, mid-, and low-level detail depending on the intended audience for the report. Reports are used as basis for determining mitigation activities later. Additionally many scanners are now feeding automated risk management dashboards using application portal interfaces.

11. What is the correct order for the phases of penetration testing?

    a. Information gathering, preparation, information evaluation and risk analysis, active penetration, and analysis and reporting

    b. Preparation, information gathering, active penetration and analysis, information evaluation, and risk analysis and reporting

c. Preparation, active penetration and analysis, information gathering, information evaluation, and risk analysis and reporting

d. Preparation, information gathering, information evaluation and risk analysis, active penetration, and analysis and reporting

Answer: D

Penetration testing consists of five different phases:

- Phase 1—Preparation
- Phase 2—Information gathering
- Phase 3—Information evaluation and risk analysis
- Phase 4—Active penetration
- Phase 5—Analysis and reporting

12. Where do the details as to how the security objectives of a security baseline are to be fulfilled come from?

a. The system security plan

b. A security implementation document

c. The enterprise system architecture

d. Authorization for the system to operate

Answer: B

A security baseline defines a set of basic security objectives that must be met by any given service or system. The objectives are chosen to be pragmatic and complete and do not impose technical means. Therefore, details on how these security objectives are fulfilled by a particular service/system must be documented in a separate security implementation document. These details depend on the operational environment a service/system is deployed into and might, thus, creatively use and apply any relevant security measure. Derogations from the baseline are possible and expected and must be explicitly marked.

13. Shoulder surfing, Usenet searching, and dumpster diving are examples of what kind of activity?

a. Risk analysis

b. Social engineering

c. Penetration testing

d. Vulnerability assessment

Answer: B

Social engineering is an activity that involves the manipulation of persons or physical reconnaissance to get information for use in exploitation or testing activities.

14. What is the most important reason to analyze event logs from multiple sources?

   a. They will help you obtain a more complete picture of what is happening on your network and how you go about addressing the problem.

   b. The log server could have been compromised.

   c. Because you cannot trust automated scripts to capture everything.

   d. To prosecute the attacker once he can be traced.

Answer: A

By analyzing various logs sources, it is possible to piece together a timeline of events and user activity. Answer B is partially correct but not the most fitting answer. This is only a small picture of what the attacker could have done. Answer C may be true but again is not the most important reason. This answer is meant to distract. Answer D may apply in some cases, but this is not the primary goal of correlating event logs.

15. Security testing includes which of the following activities? (Choose all that apply.)

   a. Performing a port scan to check for up-and-running services

   b. Gathering publicly available information

   c. Counterattacking systems determined to be hostile

   d. Posing as technical support to gain unauthorized information

Answer: A, B, and D

Counterattacking systems determined to be hostile is never something an organization wants to do and does not constitute security testing. Answer A is part of security testing. Using a network mapping technique such as nmap can reveal security holes. Answer B can involve Googling an organization to determine information for future attacks. Answer D is an example of social engineering and should be a part of an organization's security testing process.

16. Why is system fingerprinting part of the security testing process?

   a. It is one of the easiest things to determine when performing a security test.

   b. It shows what vulnerabilities the system may be subject to.

   c. It tells an attacker that a system is automatically insecure.

   d. It shows the auditor whether a system has been hardened.

Answer: B

Some versions of an OS or software may be vulnerable, and this information is useful to an attacker. Answer A may or may not be true depending on the system and is not a reason to determine the OS or other system details. Answer C is true, but it does not answer why system fingerprinting is part of the security testing process. Answer D is not true. Just because a machine is running a particular OS, for example, does not mean it has not been updated and patched to prevent certain vulnerabilities.

DOMAIN 4: INCIDENT RESPONSE AND RECOVERY

1. Creating incident response policies for an organization would be an example of:

   a. A technical control

   b. An administrative control

   c. A logical control

   d. A physical control

Answer: B

Administrative controls are "managerial" and are a part of corporate security policy. Technical controls (A) implement specific technologies. A policy would not constitute a specific technological process. Physical controls (D) constitute elements such as Closed Caption Television (CCTV), padlocks, or any other physical barrier or device to bar access. Logical control is a fictitious term.

2. A security audit is best defined as:

   a. A covert series of tests designed to test network authentication, hosts, and perimeter security

   b. A technical assessment that measures how well an organization uses strategic security policies and tactical security controls for protecting its information assets

   c. Employing intrusion detection systems (IDSs) to monitor anomalous traffic on a network segment and logging attempted break-ins

   d. Hardening systems before deploying them on the corporate network

Answer: B

Answers A and C are good examples of a type of security audit but do not answer the question of what a security audit is. Answer D is a security control check used to harden a host against vulnerabilities.

ANSWERS TO SAMPLE QUESTIONS

Domain 4: Incident Response and Recovery   793

3. What is the primary purpose of testing an intrusion detection system?

   a. To observe that the IDS is observing and logging an appropriate response to a suspicious activity

   b. To determine if the IDS is capable of discarding suspect packets

   c. To analyze processor utilization to verify whether hardware upgrades are necessary

   d. To test whether the IDS can log every possible event on the network

Answer: A

The primary purpose of an IDS is to detect known attacks or anomalous activity. Answer B would fall more along the line of an intrusion prevention system or a firewall. Answer C is not correct because CPU utilization is not the primary concern of an IDS, but rather load balancing or bandwidth limiting. Answer D is an unrealistic and storage-consuming goal unrelated to the primary purpose of an IDS.

4. Which of the following is true regarding computer intrusions?

   a. Covert attacks such as a distributed denial-of-service (DDoS) attack harm public opinion of an organization.

   b. Overt attacks are easier to defend against because they can be readily identified.

   c. Network intrusion detection systems (NIDSs) help mitigate computer intrusions by notifying personnel in real time.

   d. Covert attacks are less effective because they take more time to accomplish.

Answer: C

NIDS can monitor data in real-time and notify appropriate personnel. Answer A, a DDOS attack, is an example of an overt attack. Answer B is not true, as overt attacks can be just as complex and hard to defend against as covert attacks. Answer D is certainly not true. A waiter can steal a credit card number just as fast as any overt method.

5. This documents the steps that should be performed to restore IT functions after a business disruption event:

   a. Critical business function

   b. Business continuity plan

   c. Disaster recovery plan

   d. Crisis communications plan

Answer: C

Critical business functions (A) are functions that are integral to the success of an organization, without which the organization is incapable of operating. Business continuity plans (B) focus on the continuity and recovery of critical business functions during and after disaster. A crisis communications plan (D) details how organizations will communicate internally and externally during a disaster situation.

6. During which phase of incident response are the results of incident response activities documented and communicated to the appropriate parties?

    a. Post-incident activity

    b. Detection and analysis

    c. Containment, eradication, and recovery

    d. Preparation

    Answer: A

    During the detection and analysis phase (B), security incidents are initially identified and analyzed to determine if an actual incident has occurred. During the containment, eradication, and recovery phase (C), security incidents are contained, incidents are corrected, and systems are restored to normal operations. During the preparation phase (D), incident response policies and procedures are documented and training is provided to enable the incident response team to be prepared to respond to an incident.

7. What is the first type of disaster recovery testing that should be performed when initially testing a disaster recovery plan?

    a. Simulation

    b. Structured walkthrough

    c. Parallel

    d. Full interruption

    Answer: B

    Simulation testing (A) simulates an actual disaster and is a more in-depth testing approach than structured walkthrough testing. Parallel testing (C) uses testing performed at alternate data processing sites. This test involves significant cost to the organization and should not be performed before structured walkthrough testing. Full interruption testing (D) requires that business operations are actually interrupted at the primary processing facility.

8. This concept refers to the point in time to which data could be restored in the event of a business disruption:

a. Recovery time objective (RTO)

b. Business impact analysis (BIA)

c. Recovery point objective (RPO)

d. Maximum tolerable downtime (MTD)

Answer: C

The recovery time objective (A) indicates the period of time within which a business function or information technology system must be restored after a business disruption. A business impact analysis (B) assesses financial and nonfinancial impacts to an organization that would result from a business disruption. Maximum tolerable downtime (D) is the maximum amount of time that a business function can be unavailable before an organization is harmed to the degree that puts the survivability of the organization at risk.

9. Which RAID level uses block-level striping with parity information distributed across multiple disks?

a. RAID 0

b. RAID 1

c. RAID 4

d. RAID 5

Answer: D

RAID 0 stripes data across multiple disks, but no parity information is included. RAID 1 uses mirroring to store identical copies of data on multiple disks. RAID 4 implements striping at the block level and uses a dedicated parity disk. RAID 4 is not used in practice.

10. The type of data backup that only backs up files that have been changed since the last full backup is called:

a. Full backup

b. Incremental backup

c. Partial backup

d. Differential backup

Answer: D

In a full backup (A), the entire system is copied to backup media. Incremental backups (B) record changes from the previous day or previous incremental backup. A partial backup (C) is not a widely accepted backup type.

11. Selecting this type of alternate processing site would be appropriate when an organization needs a low-cost recovery strategy and does not have immediate system recovery requirements:

   a. Cold site

   b. Warm site

   c. Hot site

   d. Mobile site

   Answer: A

   A cold site is the lowest cost type of alternative processing site. The warm site, hot site, and mobile site are all higher-cost solutions that support quicker recovery requirements.

12. What are the phases of the incident response process? (Choose all that apply.)

   a. Preparation

   b. Detection and analysis

   c. Assessment and recovery

   d. Authorization

   Answer: A and B

   Phases of the incident response process include:

   1. Preparation

   2. Detection and analysis

   3. Containment, eradication, and recovery

   4. Post-incident activity

13. Phases of the incident response process include:

   a. Preparation

   b. Detection and analysis

   c. Containment, eradication, and recovery

   d. Post-incident activity

14. This data backup strategy allows data backup to an offsite location via a WAN or Internet connection:

   a. Remote journaling

   b. Electronic vaulting

   c. RAID

   d. Clustering

Answer: B

RAID (C) refers to a method for writing data across multiple disks to provide redundancy or improve performance. Remote journaling (A) transfers journals and database transaction logs electronically to an offsite location. Clustering (D) uses multiple systems to reduce the risk associated with a single point of failure.

DOMAIN 5: CRYPTOGRAPHY

1. Applied against a given block of data, a hash function creates:

   a. A chunk of the original block used to ensure its confidentiality

   b. A block of new data used to ensure the original block's confidentiality

   c. A chunk of the original block used to ensure its integrity

   d. A block of new data used to ensure the original block's integrity

   Answer: D

   Applied against a block of data, hash functions generate a hash of the original data that verifies the data has not been modified from its original form.

2. In symmetric key cryptography, each party should use:

   a. A publicly available key

   b. A previously exchanged secret key

   c. A randomly generated value unknown to everyone

   d. A secret key exchanged with the message

   Answer: B

   In symmetric key cryptography, each party must exchange a private key in advance of establishing encrypted communications.

3. Nonrepudiation of a message ensures that the message:

   a. Can be attributed to a particular author

   b. Is always sent to the intended recipient

   c. Can be attributed to a particular recipient

   d. Is always received by the intended recipient

Answer: A

The idea of nonrepudiation is to link the actions of an individual to those actions with a great deal of certainty.

4. In Electronic Code Book (ECB) mode, data is encrypted using:

    a. A cipher-based on the previous block of a message

    b. A user-generated variable-length cipher for every block of a message

    c. A different cipher for every block of a message

    d. The same cipher for every block of a message

Answer: D

ECB uses the same cipher for each block resulting in identical ciphertext blocks when encrypting identical plaintext blocks.

5. In Cipher Block Chaining (CBC) mode, the key is constructed by:

    a. Generating new key material completely at random

    b. Cycling through a list of user defined choices

    c. Modifying the previous block of ciphertext

    d. Reusing the previous key in the chain of message blocks

Answer: C

CBC XOR's the previous block of ciphertext with the current block of plaintext to produce the key used to encrypt the block.

6. Stream ciphers are normally selected over block ciphers because of:

    a. The high degree of strength behind the encryption algorithms

    b. The high degree of speed behind the encryption algorithms

    c. Their ability to use large amounts of padding in encryption functions

    d. Their ability to encrypt large chunks of data at a time

Answer: B

Stream ciphers tend to be faster than block ciphers while generally being less robust and operating on single bits of information.

7. A key escrow service is intended to allow for the reliable:

    a. Recovery of inaccessible private keys

    b. Recovery of compromised public keys

c. Transfer of inaccessible private keys between users

d. Transfer of compromised public keys between users

Answer: A

Key escrow services are third-party organizations that can provide a customer organization with archived keys should the recovery of the customer organization's encrypted data be required.

8. The correct choice for encrypting the entire original data packet in a tunneled mode for an IPSec solution is:

a. Generic Routing Encapsulation (GRE)

b. Authentication Header (AH)

c. Encapsulating Security Payload (ESP)

d. Point-to-Point Tunneling Protocol (PPTP)

Answer: C

An IPSec solution that uses ESP will encapsulate the entire original data packet when implemented in a tunnel mode.

9. When implementing an MD5 solution, what randomizing cryptographic function should be used to help avoid collisions?

a. Multistring concatenation

b. Modular addition

c. Message pad

d. Salt

Answer: D

A cryptographic salt is a series of random bits added to a password or passphrase to help avoid a possible hash collision.

10. Key clustering represents the significant failure of an algorithm because:

a. A single key should not generate different ciphertext from the same plaintext, using the same cipher algorithm.

b. Two different keys should not generate the same ciphertext from the same plaintext, using the same cipher algorithm.

c. Two different keys should not generate different ciphertext from the same plaintext, using the same cipher algorithm.

d. A single key should not generate the same ciphertext from the same plaintext, using the same cipher algorithm.

Answer: B

In key clustering, two different keys end up generating the same ciphertext from the same plaintext while using the same cipher algorithm.

11. Asymmetric key cryptography is used for the following:

a. Asymmetric key cryptography is used for the following:

b. Encryption of data, nonrepudiation, access control

c. Nonrepudiation, steganography, encryption of data

d. Encryption of data, access control, steganography

Answer: B

Steganography is the hiding of a message inside of another medium and does not rely on the use of asymmetric key cryptography.

12. Which of the following algorithms supports asymmetric key cryptography?

a. Diffie-Hellman

b. Blowfish

c. SHA-256

d. Rijndael

Answer: A

Diffie-Hellman is an asymmetric algorithm.

13. A certificate authority (CA) provides which benefit to a user?

a. Protection of public keys of all users

b. History of symmetric keys

c. Proof of nonrepudiation of origin

d. Validation that a public key is associated with a particular user

Answer: D

A certificate authority "signs" an entities digital certificate to certify that the certificate content accurately represents the certificate owner. Answer A is not a certificate authority function, because public keys are not meant to be kept secret. Answer B is a function of key management. Answer C is a function of a digital certificate.

14. What is the output length of a RIPEMD-160 hash?

    a. 150 bits

    b. 128 bits

    c. 160 bits

    d. 104 bits

    Answer: C

    Research and Development in Advanced Communications Technologies in Europe (RACE) Integrity Primitives Evaluation Message Digest (RIPEMD) is a hash function that produces 160-bit message digests using a 512-bit block size.

15. ANSI X9.17 is concerned primarily with:

    a. Financial records and retention of encrypted data

    b. The lifespan of master key-encrypting keys (KKM's)

    c. Formalizing a key hierarchy

    d. Protection and secrecy of keys

    Answer: D

    ANSI X9.17 was developed to address the need of financial institutions to transmit securities and funds securely using an electronic medium. Specifically, it describes the means to ensure the secrecy of keys. The ANSI X9.17 approach is based on a hierarchy of keys. At the bottom of the hierarchy are data keys (DKs). Data keys are used to encrypt and decrypt messages. They are given short lifespans, such as one message or one connection. At the top of the hierarchy are master key-encrypting keys (KKMs).

    KKMs, which must be distributed manually, are afforded longer lifespans than data keys. Using the two-tier model, the KKMs are used to encrypt the data keys. The data keys are then distributed electronically to encrypt and decrypt messages. The two-tier model may be enhanced by adding another layer to the hierarchy. In the three-tier model, the KKMs are not used to encrypt data keys directly, but to encrypt other key-encrypting keys (KKs). The KKs, which are exchanged electronically, are used to encrypt the data keys.

16. What is the input that controls the operation of the cryptographic algorithm?

    a. Decoder wheel

    b. Encoder

    c. Cryptovariable

    d. Cryptographic routine

Answer: C

The key or cryptovariable is the input that controls the operation of the cryptographic algorithm. It determines the behavior of the algorithm and permits the reliable encryption and decryption of the message.

17. AES is a block cipher with variable key lengths of?

   a. 128, 192, or 256 bits

   b. 32, 128, or 448 bits

   c. 8, 64, 128 bits

   d. 128, 256, or 448 bits

Answer: A

AES is a block cipher. It has variable key length of 128, 192, or 256 bits; the default is 256 bits. It encrypts data blocks of 128 bits in 10, 12, and 14 round depending on the key size.

18. A Hashed Message Authentication Code (HMAC) works by:

   a. Adding a non-secret key value to the input function along with the source message

   b. Adding a secret key value to the output function along with the source message

   c. Adding a secret key value to the input function along with the source message

   d. Adding a non-secret key value to the output function along with the source message

Answer: C

A MAC based on DES is one of the most common methods of creating a MAC; however, it is slow in operation compared to a hash function. A hash function such as MD5 does not have a secret key, so it cannot be used for a MAC. Therefore, RFC 2104 was issued to provide a hashed MACing system that has become the process used now in IPSec and many other secure Internet protocols, such as SSL/TLS. Hashed MACing implements a freely available hash algorithm as a component (black box) within the HMAC implementation. This allows ease of the replacement of the hashing module if a new hash function becomes necessary. The use of proven cryptographic hash algorithms also provides assurance of the security of HMAC implementations. HMACs work by adding a secret key value to the hash input function along with the source message. The HMAC operation provides cryptographic strength similar to a hashing algorithm, except that it now has the additional protection of a secret key, and still operates nearly as rapidly as a standard hash operation.

19. The main types of implementation attacks which of the following? (Choose all that apply.)

a. Linear

b. Side-channel analysis

c. Fault analysis

d. Probing

Answer: B, C, and D

Implementation attacks are some of the most common and popular attacks against cryptographic systems due to their ease and reliance on system elements outside of the algorithm. The main types of implementation attacks include:

- Side-channel analysis
- Fault analysis
- Probing attacks

Side-channel attacks are passive attacks that rely on a physical attribute of the implementation such as power consumption/emanation. These attributes are studied to determine the secret key and the algorithm function. Some examples of popular side channels include timing analysis and electromagnetic differential analysis.

Fault analysis attempts to force the system into an error state to gain erroneous results. By forcing an error, gaining the results and comparing it with known good results, an attacker may learn about the secret key and the algorithm.

Probing attacks attempt to watch the circuitry surrounding the cryptographic module in hopes that they complementary components will disclose information about the key or the algorithm. Additionally new hardware may be added to the cryptographic module to observe and inject information.

20. What is the process of using a key encrypting key (KEK) to protect session keys called?

a. Key distribution

b. Key escrow

c. Key generation

d. Key wrapping

Answer: D

The process of using a KEK to protect session keys is called *key wrapping*. Key wrapping uses symmetric ciphers to securely encrypt (thus encapsulating) a

---

plaintext key along with any associated integrity information and data. One application for key wrapping is protecting session keys in untrusted storage or when sending over an untrusted transport. Key wrapping or encapsulation using a KEK can be accomplished using either symmetric or asymmetric ciphers. If the cipher is a symmetric KEK, both the sender and the receiver will need a copy of the same key. If using an asymmetric cipher, with public/private key properties, to encapsulate a session key both the sender and the receiver will need the other's public key.

Protocols such as SSL, PGP, and S/MIME use the services of KEKs to provide session key confidentiality, to provide integrity, and sometimes to authenticate the binding of the session key originator and the session key itself to make sure the session key came from the real sender and not an attacker.

DOMAIN 6: NETWORKS AND COMMUNICATIONS SECURITY

1. Which of the following is typically deployed as a screening proxy for web servers?

   a. Intrusion prevention system

   b. Kernel proxies

   c. Packet filters

   d. Reverse proxies

Answer: D

A reverse proxy is a device or service placed between a client and a server in a network infrastructure. Incoming requests are handled by the proxy, which interacts on behalf of the client with the desired server or service residing on the server. The most common use of a reverse proxy is to provide load balancing for web applications and APIs. Reverse proxies can also be deployed to offload services from applications as a way to improve performance through SSL acceleration, intelligent compression, and caching. They can also enable federated security services for multiple applications.

A reverse proxy may either act as a simple forwarding service or actively participate in the exchange between client and server. When the proxy treats the client and server as separate entities by implementing dual network stacks, it is called a *full proxy*. A full reverse proxy is capable of intercepting, inspecting, and interacting with requests and responses. Interacting with requests and responses enables more advanced traffic management services such as application layer security, web acceleration, page routing, and secure remote access.

2. A customer wants to keep cost to a minimum and has ordered only a single static IP address from the ISP. Which of the following must be configured on the router to allow for all the computers to share the same public IP address?

   a. Virtual Private Network (VPN)

   b. Port Address Translation (PAT)

   c. Virtual Local Area Network (VLAN)

   d. Power over Ethernet (PoE)

   Answer: B

   An extension to network address translation (NAT) is to translate all addresses to one routable IP address and translate the source port number in the packet to a unique value. The port translation allows the firewall to keep track of multiple sessions that are using PAT.

3. Sayge installs a new Wireless Access Point (WAP), and users are able to connect to it. However, once connected, users cannot access the Internet. Which of the following is the *most* likely cause of the problem?

   a. An incorrect subnet mask has been entered in the WAP configuration.

   b. Users have specified the wrong encryption type, and packets are being rejected.

   c. The signal strength has been degraded, and latency is increasing hop count.

   d. The signal strength has been degraded, and packets are being lost.

   Answer: A

   The subnet mask is broken into two parts, the network ID and the host ID. The network ID represents the network that the device is connected to. If, for example, the subnet mask in question was supposed to be 255.224.0.0 but instead was entered as 255.240.0.0, then the device would only be able to see other computers in the 255.240.0.0 subnet and the default gateway of the subnet. When the wrong subnet mask is entered for a network configuration, the device will not be able to communicate with any other devices outside of the subnet until the right subnet mask is entered, allowing them to be able to interact with the devices on the network that the subnet mask represents.

4. Which of the following devices should be part of a network's perimeter defense?

   a. Web server, host-based intrusion detection system (HIDS), and a firewall

   b. DNS server, firewall, and a boundary router

   c. Switch, firewall, and a proxy server

   d. Firewall, proxy server, and a host-based intrusion detection system (HIDS)

Answer: D

The security perimeter is the first line of defense between trusted and untrusted networks. In general it will include a firewall and a router to help filter traffic. Security perimeters may also include proxies and devices such as intrusion detection systems to warn of suspicious traffic flows.

5. A Security Incident Event Management (SIEM) service performs which of the following function(s)? (Choose all that apply.)

   a. Coordinates software for security conferences and seminars

   b. Aggregates logs from security devices and application servers looking for suspicious activity

   c. Gathers firewall logs for archiving

   d. Reviews access control logs on servers and physical entry points to match user system authorization with physical access permissions

Answer: B, C, and D

SIEM is a solution that involves harvesting logs and event information from a variety of different sources on individual servers or assets and analyzing it as a consolidated view with sophisticated reporting. Similarly, entire IT infrastructures can have their logs and event information centralized and managed by large-scale SIEM deployments. SIEM will not only aggregate logs but will perform analysis and issue alerts (e-mail, pager, audible, etc.) according to suspicious patterns.

6. A botnet can be characterized as a:

   a. Type of virus

   b. Group of dispersed, compromised machines controlled remotely for illicit reasons

   c. Automatic security alerting tool for corporate networks

   d. Network used solely for internal communications

Answer: B

A bot is a type of malware that an attacker can use to control an infected computer or mobile device. A group or network of machines that have been co-opted this way and are under the control of the same attacker is known a botnet.

7. During a disaster recovery test, several billing representatives need to be temporarily set up to take payments from customers. It has been determined that this will need to occur over a wireless network, with security being enforced where possible. Which of the following configurations should be used in this scenario?

   a. WPA2, SSID disabled, and 802.11a

   b. WEP, SSID disabled, and 802.11g

   c. WEP, SSID enabled, and 802.11b

   d. WPA2, SSID enabled, and 802.11n

   Answer: A

   WPA2 is a security technology commonly used on Wi-Fi wireless networks. WPA2 (Wi-Fi Protected Access 2) replaced the original WPA technology on all certified Wi-Fi hardware since 2006 and is based on the IEEE 802.11i technology standard for data encryption. WPA was used to replace WEP, which is not considered a secure protocol for wireless systems due to numerous issues with its implementation. Disabling the SSID will further enhance the security of the solution, as it requires the user who wants to connect to the WAP to have the exact SSID, as opposed to selecting it from a list.

8. A new installation requires a network in a heavy manufacturing area with substantial amounts of electromagnetic radiation and power fluctuations. Which media is best suited for this environment is little traffic degradation is tolerated?

   a. Shielded twisted pair

   b. Coax

   c. Fiber

   d. Wireless

   Answer: C

   Since fiber-optic cabling relies on light as the transmission mechanism, electromagnetic interference will not affect it.

9. What is the network ID portion of the IP address 191.154.25.66 if the default subnet mask is used?

   a. 191

   b. 191.154.25

   c. 191.154

Answer: C

If the default subnet mask is used, then the network ID portion of the IP address 191.154.25.66 is 191.154. The first octet, 191, indicates that this is a class B address. In a class B address, the first two octets of the address represent the network portion. The default subnet mask for a Class B network address is 255.255.0.0.

10. Given the address 192.168.10.19/28, which of the following are valid host addresses on this subnet? (Choose two.)

   a. 192.168.10.31

   b. 192.168.10.17

   c. 192.168.10.16

   d. 192.168.10.29

Answer: B and D

192.168.10.19/28 belongs to the 192.168.10.16 network with a mask of 255.255.255.240. This offers 14 usable IP address range from 192.168.10.17 – 30.

11. Circuit-switched networks do which of the following tasks?

   a. Divide data into packets and transmit it over a virtual network.

   b. Establish a dedicated circuit between endpoints.

   c. Divide data into packets and transmit it over a shared network.

   d. Establish an on-demand circuit between endpoints.

Answer: B

Circuit-switched networks establish a dedicated circuit between endpoints. These circuits consist of dedicated switch connections. Neither endpoint starts communicating until the circuit is completely established. The endpoints have exclusive use of the circuit and its bandwidth. Carriers base the cost of using a circuit-switched network on the duration of the connection, which makes this type of network only cost-effective for a steady communication stream between the endpoints. Examples of circuit- switched networks are the plain old telephone service (POTS), Integrated Services Digital Network (ISDN), and Point-to-Point Protocol (PPP).

12. What is the biggest security issue associated with the use of a multiprotocol label switching (MPLS) network?

   a. Lack of native encryption services

   b. Lack of native authentication services

A

c. Support for the Wired Equivalent Privacy (WEP) and Data Encryption Standard (DES) algorithms

d. The need to establish peering relationships to cross Tier 1 carrier boundaries

Answer: A

MPLS is often referred to as "IP VPN" because of the ability to couple highly deterministic routing with IP services. In effect, this creates a VPN-type service that makes it logically impossible for data from one network to be mixed or routed over to another network without compromising the MPLS routing device itself. MPLS does not include encryption services; therefore, any MPLS service called "IP VPN" does not in fact contain any cryptographic services. The traffic on these links would be visible to the service providers.

13. The majority of DNS traffic is carried using User Datagram Protocol (UDP); what types of DNS traffic is carried using Transmission Control Protocol (TCP)? (Choose all that apply)

   a. Query traffic

   b. Response traffic

   c. DNNSEC traffic that exceeds single packet size maximum

   d. Secondary zone transfers

Answer: C and D

Most of the attention paid to DNS security focuses on the DNS query and response transaction. This transaction is a UDP transaction; however, DNS utilizes both UDP and TCP transport mechanisms. DNS TCP transactions are used for secondary zone transfers and for DNSSEC traffic that exceeds the maximum single packet size. The original single packet size was 512 bytes, but there is an extension available to DNS that allows the single packet size to be set to 4,096 bytes.

14. What is the command that a client would need to issue to initialize an encrypted FTP session using Secure FTP as outlined in RFC 4217?

   a. "ENABLE SSL"

   b. "ENABLE TLS"

   c. "AUTH TLS"

   d. "AUTH SSL"

Answer: C

Secure FTP with TLS is an extension to the FTP standard that allows clients to request that the FTP session be encrypted. This is done by sending the AUTH TLS command. The server has the option of allowing or denying connections that do not request TLS. This protocol extension is defined in the proposed standard RFC 4217.

15. What is the IEEE designation for Priority-based Flow Control (PFC) as defined in the Data Center Bridging (DCB) Standards?

   a. 802.1Qbz

   b. 802.1Qau

   c. 802.1Qaz

   d. 802.1Qbb

Answer: D

The DCB standards define four new technologies:

- Priority-based flow control (PFC), 802.1Qbb allows the network to pause different traffic classes.

- Enhanced transmission selection (ETS), 802.1Qaz defines the scheduling behavior of multiple traffic classes, including strict priority and minimum guaranteed bandwidth capabilities. This should enable fair sharing of the link, better performance, and metering.

- Quantized congestion notification (QCN), 802.1Qau supports end-to-end flow control in a switched LAN infrastructure and helps eliminate sustained, heavy congestion in an Ethernet fabric. Before the network can use QCN, you must implement QCN in all components in the converged enhanced Ethernet (CEE) data path (converged network adapters (CNAs), switches, and so on). QCN networks must also use PFC to avoid dropping packets and ensure a lossless environment.

- Data Center Bridging Exchange Protocol (DCBX), 802.1Qaz supports discovery and configuration of network devices that support PFC, ETS, and QCN.

16. What is the integrity protection hashing function that the Session Initiation Protocol (SIP) uses?

   a. SHA-160

   b. MD4

   c. MD5

   d. SHA-256

Answer: C

SIP provides integrity protection through MD5 hash functions.

17. Layer 2 Tunneling Protocol (L2TP) is a hybrid of:

   a. Cisco's Layer 2 Forwarding (L2F) and Microsoft's Point to Point Tunneling Protocol (PPTP)

   b. Microsoft's Layer 2 Forwarding (L2F) and Cisco's Point to Point Tunneling Protocol (PPTP)

   c. Cisco's Layer 2 Forwarding (L2F) and Point to Point Protocol (PPP)

   d. Microsoft's Layer 2 Forwarding (L2F) and Point to Point Protocol (PPP)

   Answer: A

   Layer 2 Tunneling Protocol (L2TP) is a hybrid of Cisco's Layer 2 Forwarding (L2F) and Microsoft's Point to Point Tunneling Protocol (PPTP).

18. With regards to LAN-based security, what is the key difference between the control plane and the data plane?

   a. The data plane is where forwarding/routing decisions are made, while the control plane is where commands are implemented.

   b. The control plane is where APIs are used to monitor and oversee, while the data plane is where commands are implemented.

   c. The control plane is where forwarding/routing decisions are made, while the data plane is where commands are implemented.

   d. The data plane is where APIs are used to monitor and oversee, while the control plane is where commands are implemented.

   Answer: C

   The control plane is where forwarding/routing decisions are made. Switches and routers have to figure out where to send frames (L2) and packets (L3). The switches and routers that run the network run as discrete components, but since they are in a network, they have to exchange information such as host reachability and status with neighbors. This is done in the control plane using protocols like spanning tree, OSPF, BGP, QoS enforcement, etc.

   The data plane is where the action takes place. It includes things like the forwarding tables, routing tables, ARP tables, queue's, tagging and re-tagging, etc. *The data plane carries out the commands of the control plane.*

   For example, in the control plane, you set up IP networking and routing (routing protocols, route preferences, static routers, etc…) and connect hosts and switches/routers together. Each switch/router figures out what is directly connected to it and then tells its neighbor what it can reach and how it can reach it. The switches/routers also learn how to reach hosts and networks not attached to it. Once all of the routers/switches have a coherent picture—shared via the control plane—the network is converged.

In the data plane, the routers/switches use what the control plane built to dispose of incoming and outgoing frames and packets. Some get sent to another router, for example. Some may get queued up when congested. Some may get dropped if congestion gets bad enough.

19. There are several record types associated with the use of DNSSEC. What does the DS record type represent?

   a. A private key

   b. A public key

   c. A hash of a key

   d. A signature of an RRSet

   Answer: C

   The DNSSEC trust chain is a sequence of records that identify either a public key or a signature of a set of resource records. The root of this chain of trust is the root key that is maintained and managed by the operators of the DNS root. DNSSEC is defined by the IETF in RFCs 4033, 4034, and 4035.

   There are several important new record types:

   - DNSKEY: A public key, used to sign a set of resource records (RRset)
   - DS: Delegation signer, a hash of a key
   - RRSIG: A signature of a RRset that share name/type/class

20. MACsec (IEEE 802.1AE) is used to provide secure communication for all traffic on Ethernet links. How is MACsec configured?

   a. Through key distribution

   b. Using connectivity groups

   c. Using key generation

   d. Using connectivity associations

   Answer: D

   MACsec is configured in connectivity associations. MACsec is enabled when a connectivity association is assigned to an interface.

   MACsec provides security through the use of secured point-to-point Ethernet links. The point-to-point links are secured after matching security keys—a user-configured pre-shared key when you enable MACsec using static connectivity association

A

ANSWERS TO SAMPLE QUESTIONS

key (CAK) security mode or a user-configured static secure association key when you enable MACsec using static secure association key (SAK) security mode — are exchanged and verified between the interfaces at each end of the point-to-point Ethernet link. Other user-configurable parameters, such as MAC address or port, must also match on the interfaces on each side of the link to enable MACsec.

DOMAIN 7: SYSTEMS AND APPLICATION SECURITY

1. "VBS" is used in the beginning of most antivirus vendors to represent what component of the CARO general structure?

   a. Family

   b. Platform

   c. Modifier

   d. Suffix

   Answer: B

   VBS is short for Visual Basic Script and is a prefix commonly associated with VBS threats. The general structure of CARO as presented in this chapter is `Platform.Type.Family_Name.Variant[:Modifier]@Suffix`.

2. W64.Root.AC is what variant of this malcode?

   a. W64

   b. AC

   c. Root

   d. C

   Answer: B

   The variant is commonly the last element added to a malcode name, AC in this example.

3. W64.Slober.Z@mm spreads through what primary vector, according to Symantec naming conventions?

   a. Mass Mailer

   b. Windows 64-bit

   c. Windows 8/8.1

   d. E-mail

Answer: A

Symantec uses the `@SUFFIX` mailing convention to identify how malcode spreads. In this case the suffix is `@mm`, which stands for mass mailer. Answers B and C are specific to the platform, not to how the malcode spreads. Answer D is also used by Symantec but would be specified as `@m`.

4. A SSCP discovers an antivirus message indicating detection and removal of Backdoor .win64.Agent.igh. What should the SSCP do to monitor to the threat?

   a. Use rootkit detection software on the host

   b. Update antivirus signature files

   c. Run a full host scan

   d. Monitor egress traffic from the computer

Answer: D

The CARO name indicates that this is a backdoor Trojan. Backdoor Trojans provide attackers with remote access to the computer. Monitoring of network communications is critical in identifying egress communications related to the Trojan. Installation or use of various rootkit or antivirus solutions is not helpful in monitoring the threat. Additionally, antivirus has already detected the threat on the system.

5. Malcode that infects existing files on a computer to spread are called what?

   a. Rootkit

   b. Worms

   c. Viruses

   d. Trojans

Answer: C

Viruses require a host file to infect. Trojans do not replicate but masquerade as something legitimate. Worms create copies of themselves as they spread. Rootkits are used for stealth to increase survivability in the wild.

6. A Trojan that executes a destructive payload when certain conditions are met is called what?

   a. Data diddler

   b. Rootkit

   c. Logic bomb

   d. Keylogger

Answer: C

Keyloggers are not destructive but merely steal keystrokes on a system. Data diddler is defined online by Virus Bulletin as a destructive overwriting Trojan, but it does not have a "time" or conditional component to when the payload is executed like that of a logic bomb. A rootkit is a stealthy type of software, typically malicious, designed to hide the existence of certain processes or programs from normal methods of detection and enable continued privileged access to a computer.

7. How does a cavity virus infect a file with malcode?

   a. Appends code

   b. Injects code

   c. Removes code

   d. Prepends code

   Answer: B

   Cavity viruses inject code into various locations of a file. Prepending is to put code before the body of a file. Appending is to put code following the body of a file.

8. Mebroot is unique because it modifies what component of a computer to load on system startup?

   a. Windows registry keys

   b. Kernel

   c. Master boot record

   d. Startup folder

   Answer: C

   Mebroot is a kernel-level rootkit that modifies the master boot record to load before the operating system even runs in memory. Modifications made to the Windows registry keys and startup folder are not unique, as they are used by many programs to load specified settings with the operating system.

9. SYS and VXD hostile codes are commonly associated with what type of threat?

   a. Trojans

   b. Userland rootkits

   c. Worms

   d. Kernel rootkits

Answer: D

Kernel-level rootkits normally have SYS and VXD filenames. Userland rootkits are typically a DLL extension. Trojans and worms are general classifications for malcode that are not as specific as the answer Kernel rootkits.

10. A potentially unwanted program (PUP) refers to software that may include what? (Choose all that apply.)

    a. Monitoring capability

    b. End user license agreement (EULA)

    c. Patch management capability

    d. Ability to capture data

    Answer: A, B, and D

    This is technically legal software that includes an end user license agreement (EULA) but may monitor or capture sensitive data.

11. "0.0.0.0 avp.ch" is a string found within a Trojan binary, indicating that it likely performs this type of change to a system upon infection:

    a. Downloads code from avp.ch

    b. Modifies the HOSTS file to prevent access to avp.ch

    c. Communicates with a remote C&C at avp.ch

    d. Contains a logic bomb that activates immediately

    Answer: B

    The structure of the string is that of a HOSTS file, indicating that it likely modifies the HOSTS file on the computer.

12. What does it mean when an SSCP does not see `explorer.exe` in the Windows Task Manager on a host machine?

    a. It is normal for `explorer.exe` to not appear in Windows Task Manager.

    b. `explorer.exe` is likely injected and hidden by a Windows rootkit.

    c. `explorer.exe` does not need to be visible if `svchost.exe` is visible.

    d. Internet Explorer is open and running in memory.

    Answer: B

    `explorer.exe` provides the Windows desktop graphical user interface (GUI) and should always be visible within the Windows Task Manager. If it is not visible, a Windows rootkit is likely concealing the process after having injected into it.

13. If an SSCP attempts to analyze suspicious code using a VMware-based test environment and nothing executes, what might be the next steps to take to further analyze the code?

   a. Submit the code to an online sandbox scanner to compare behavioral results.

   b. Modify advanced settings to disable hardware acceleration and similar components and execute the code again.

   c. Call VMware technical support for help in identifying the problem(s) causing the code not to execute.

   d. Run the malcode in a native, non-virtualized test environment to see if it is anti-VMware.

   Answer: A, B, and D

   Answer C will not help to identify what the suspicious code may be, to analyze it further, or to learn anything of value about the code, as VMware technical support will not be able to answer any questions regarding the suspicious code itself.

14. What does the "vector of attack" refer to?

   a. Software that can infect multiple hosts

   b. The primary action of a malicious code attack

   c. How the transmission of malcode takes place

   d. The directions used to control the placement of the malcode

   Answer: C

   The vector of attack is how the transmission of malcode takes place, such as e-mail, a link sent to an instant messenger user, or a hostile website attempting to exploit vulnerable software on a remote host. This is one of the most important components of a malcode incident for a security practitioner to understand to properly protect against reinfection or additional attacks on the infrastructure of a corporate network.

15. What is direct kernel object modification an example of?

   a. A technique used by persistent mode rootkits to modify data structures

   b. A technique used by memory based rootkits to modify data structures

   c. A technique used by user mode rootkits to modify data structures

   d. A technique used by kernel mode rootkits to modify data structures

   Answer: D

   Kernel-mode rootkits are considered to be more powerful than other kinds of rootkits since not only can they intercept the native API in kernel-mode, but they can also directly manipulate kernel-mode data structures. A common technique for hiding the presence of a malware process is to remove the process from the kernel's list of active processes. Since process management APIs rely on the contents of the list, the malware process will not display in process management tools like Task Manager or Process Explorer. Another kernel mode rootkit technique is to simply modify the data structures in kernel memory. For example, kernel memory must keep a list of all running processes and a rootkit can simply remove themselves and other malicious processes they wish to hide from this list. This technique is known as direct kernel object modification (DKOM).

16. What kind of an attack is the following sample code indicative of?

    `../../../`

    a. Covert channel

    b. Buffer overflow

    c. Directory traversal

    d. Pointer overflow

    Answer: C

    A directory traversal exploits a lack of security in web applications and allows an attacker to access files. The directory traversal:

    - Uses a common means of representing a parent directory, ../ (dot dot slash) to access files not intended to be accessed.

    - Consists of adding the characters ../ to the right side of a URL, An example is: `../../../../<filename>`.

17. What does a second generation antivirus scanner use to search for probable malware instances?

    a. Heuristic rules

    b. Malware signatures

    c. Malware signatures

    d. Generic decryption

    Answer: A

    A second-generation scanner does not rely on a specific signature. Rather, the scanner uses heuristic rules to search for probable malware instances. One class of such scanners looks for fragments of code that are often associated with malware. An example of this type of scanner would be a scanner that may look for the beginning of an encryption loop used in a polymorphic virus and discover the encryption key. Once the key is discovered, the scanner can decrypt the malware to identify it and then remove the infection and return the program to service. Another second-generation approach is integrity checking. A checksum can be appended to each program. If malware alters or replaces some program without changing the checksum, then an integrity check will catch this change. To counter malware that is sophisticated enough to change the checksum when it alters a program, an encrypted hash function can be used. The encryption key is stored separately from the program so that the malware cannot generate a new hash code and encrypt that. By using a hash function rather than a simpler check-sum, the malware is prevented from adjusting the program to produce the same hash code as before.

18. What type of botnet detection and mitigation technique is Netflow used for?

   a. Anomaly detection

   b. DNS log analysis

   c. Data monitoring

   d. Honeypots

Answer: C

The most common detection and mitigation techniques include:

- **Flow data monitoring**—This technique uses flow-based protocols to get summary network and transport-layer information from network devices. Cisco NetFlow is often used by service providers and enterprises to identify command-and-control traffic for compromised workstations or servers that have been subverted and are being remotely controlled as members of bot-nets used to launch DDoS attacks, perform keystroke logging and perform other forms of illicit activity.

- **Anomaly detection**—While signature-based approaches try to have a signa-ture for every vulnerability, anomaly detection (or behavioral approaches) try to do the opposite. They characterize what normal traffic is like and then look for deviations. Any burst of scanning activity on the network from zombie machines can be detected and blocked. Anomaly detection can be effectively used on the network as well as on endpoints (such as servers and laptops). On endpoints, suspicious activity and policy violations can be identified and infections prevented.

- **DNS log analysis**—Botnets often rely on free DNS hosting services to point a subdomain to IRC servers that have been hijacked by the botmaster and that host the bots and associated exploits. Botnet code often contains hard-coded references to a DNS server, which can be spotted by any DNS log analysis tool. If such services are identified, the entire botnet can be crippled by the DNS server administrator by directing offending subdomains to a dead IP address (a technique known as *null-routing*). While this technique is effective, it is also the hardest to implement since it requires cooperation from third-party hosting providers and name registrars.

- **Honeypots**—A honeypot is a trap that mimics a legitimate network, resource, or service, but is in fact a self-contained, secure, and monitored area. Its primary goal is to lure and detect malicious attacks and intrusions. Effective more as a surveillance and early warning system, it can also help security researchers understand emerging threats. Due to the difficulty in setup and the active analysis required, the value of honeypots on large-scale networks is rather limited.

19. What kind of tool should be used to check for cross-site scripting (XSS) vulnerabilities?

   a. Rootkit revealer

   b. Web vulnerability scanner

   c. Terminal emulator

   d. Decompiler

Answer: B

To check for cross-site scripting vulnerabilities, use a web vulnerability scanner. A web vulnerability scanner crawls an entire website and automatically checks for cross-site scripting vulnerabilities. It will indicate which URLs/scripts are vulnerable to these attacks. Besides cross-site scripting vulnerabilities a web application scanner will also check for SQL injection and other web vulnerabilities.

20. What are the five phases of an advanced persistent threat (APT)?

   a. Reconnaissance, capture, incursion, discovery, and exfiltration

   b. Reconnaissance, discovery, incursion, capture, and exfiltration

   c. Incursion, reconnaissance, discovery, capture, and exfiltration

   d. Reconnaissance, incursion, discovery, capture, and exfiltration

Answer: D

The five phases of an APT are detailed below:

   1. **Reconnaissance**—Attackers leverage information from a variety of areas to understand their target.

   2. **Incursion**—Attackers break into the target network by using social engineering to deliver targeted malware to vulnerable systems and people.

3. **Discovery**—The attacker maps the organization's defenses from the inside out, allowing them to have a complete picture of the strengths and weaknesses of the network. This allows the attacker to pick and choose what vulnerabilities and weaknesses they will attempt to exploit through the deployment of multiple parallel vectors to ensure success.

4. **Capture**—Attackers access unprotected systems and capture information over an extended period of time. They will also traditionally install malware to allow for the secret acquisition of data and potential disruption of operations if required.

5. **Exfiltration**—Captured information is sent back to the attackers for analysis and potentially further exploitation.

21. What would a malware author need to do in order to prevent the heuristic technology used by antivirus vendors from detecting the malware code hidden inside of a program file?

   a. Use a runtime packer that is virtual environment aware

   b. Encrypt the malware files

   c. Decompile the malware files

   d. Use a runtime packer that is not virtual environment aware

Answer: A

A simple explanation of software packers, or compression, is that symbols are used to represent repeated patterns in the software code. A packed file can contain malware and unless your antivirus product knows how to unpack the file the malware will not be detected. That would seem to be the end of the story, except that we have something called run-time packers. Here is how they work. The packed file is an executable program that is only partially packed. A tiny bit of the program is not packed. The beginning of the program is not packed so, when the packed executable is run, it starts unpacking the rest of the file. The un-packer tool is built right in.

Runtime packers are used by malware authors because it makes it much harder to detect the malware. Antivirus vendors use heuristic technologies that create a virtual computer inside the scanning engine and then run the program inside the virtualized environment. This can force a run-time packed program to unpack itself; there is always a catch, though. The malware programmer can make the program detect that it is running in a virtual environment, and then the program may not unpack itself or may only unpack harmless parts of itself to fool the virus scanning program.

22. What is a goat machine used for?

   a. Configuration management

   b. Hosting of network monitoring software

   c. Testing of suspicious software

   d. Creation of baseline images

   Answer: C

   Native goat machines must be able to be restored quickly through imaging solutions like Acronis software or Ghost. They ideally mirror the images used in the corporate environment and are put on a separate network for the security practitioner to use in order to run their laboratory tests. It is a good idea for the security practitioner to create multiple goat images, based on patched and not patched, to test for exploitation success and up-to-date builds from the network.

23. Identify whether each of the following activities is strategic or tactical:

   ■ Defense in depth

   ■ Hardening systems

   ■ Senior management support

   ■ Backing up data

   ■ The formation of a CERT/CSIRT team

   Answer:

   - **Defense in depth:** Strategic

   - **Hardening systems:** Tactical

   - **Senior management support:** Strategic

   - **Backing up data:** Tactical

   - **The formation of a CERT/CSIRT Team:** Strategic

24. What is the correct description of the relationship between a data controller and a data processor role with regards to privacy and data protection (P&DP) laws?

   a. The processor determines the purposes and means of processing of public data, while the controller processes public data on behalf of the processor.

   b. The controller determines the purposes and means of processing of public data, while the processor processes public data on behalf of the controller.

c. The controller determines the purposes and means of processing of personal data, while the processor processes personal data on behalf of the controller.

d. The processor determines the purposes and means of processing of personal data, while the controller processes personal data on behalf of the processor.

Answer: C

The ultimate goal of P&DP laws is to provide safeguards to the individuals (data subjects) for the processing of their personal data in the respect of their privacy. This is achieved with the definitions of principles/rules to be fulfilled by the operators involved in the data processing. These operators can process the data playing the role of data controller or data processor.

Following are typical meanings for common privacy terms:

- **Data Subject**—An identifiable person is one who can be identified, directly or indirectly, in particular by reference to an identification number or to one or more factors specific to his physical, physiological, mental, economic, cultural or social identity; telephone number; IP address; etc.

- **Personal Data**—Any information relating to an identified or identifiable natural person. There are many types of personal data such as, sensitive/health data, biometric data, telephone/telematic traffic data. According to the type of personal data, the P&DP laws usually set out specific privacy and data protection obligations (e.g., security measures, data subject's consent for the processing, etc.)

- **Processing**—Operations performed upon personal data, whether or not by automatic means, such as collection, recording, organization, storage, adaptation or alteration, retrieval, consultation, use, disclosure by transmission, dissemination, or otherwise making available, alignment or combination, blocking, erasure, or destruction. Processing is made for specific purposes and scopes (e.g., marketing, selling products, for the purpose of justice, for the management of an employer-employee work relationship, for public administration, health services). According to the purpose and scope of a processing, the P&DP laws usually set out specific privacy and data protection obligations (e.g., security measures, data subject's consent for the processing) for the controller, the natural or legal person, public authority, agency, or any other body that alone or jointly with others determines the purposes and means of the processing of personal data. Where the purposes and means of processing are determined by national or community laws or regulations, the controller, or the specific criteria for his nomination, may be designated by national or community law.

- **Processor**—A natural or legal person, public authority, agency, or any other body that processes personal data on behalf of the controller.

25. According to the NIST Definition of Cloud Computing (NIST SP 800−145), what are the three cloud service models?

   a. Software as a service (SaaS), platform as a service (PaaS), and Internet of things as a service (TaaS)

   b. Software as a service (SaaS), platform as a service (PaaS), and infrastructure as a service (IaaS)

   c. Software as a service (SaaS), business process as a service (BPaaS), and infrastructure as a service (IaaS)

   d. Security as a service (SaaS), platform as a service (PaaS), and infrastructure as a service (IaaS)

Answer: B

Service Models:

- **Software as a Service (SaaS)**—The capability provided to the consumer is to use the provider's applications running on a cloud infrastructure. The applications are accessible from various client devices through either a thin client interface, such as a web browser (e.g., web-based e-mail), or a program interface. The consumer does not manage or control the underlying cloud infrastructure including network, servers, operating systems, storage, or even individual application capabilities, with the possible exception of limited user-specific application configuration settings.

- **Platform as a Service (PaaS)**—The capability provided to the consumer is to deploy onto the cloud infrastructure consumer-created or acquired applications created using programming languages, libraries, services, and tools supported by the provider. The consumer does not manage or control the underlying cloud infrastructure including network, servers, operating systems, or storage but has control over the deployed applications and possibly configuration settings for the application-hosting environment.

- **Infrastructure as a Service (IaaS)**—The capability provided to the consumer is to provision processing, storage, networks, and other fundamental computing resources where the consumer is able to deploy and run arbitrary software, which can include operating systems and applications. The consumer does not manage or control the underlying cloud infrastructure but has control over operating systems, storage, and deployed applications; and possibly limited control of select networking components (e.g., host firewalls).

26. Which of the following are storage types used with an infrastructure as a service solution?

   a. Volume and block

   b. Structured and object

   c. Unstructured and ephemeral

   d. Volume and object

   Answer: D

   IaaS uses the following storage types:

   - **Volume storage**—A virtual hard drive that can be attached to a virtual machine instance and be used to host data within a file system. Volumes attached to IaaS instances behave just like a physical drive or an array does. Examples include VMware VMFS, Amazon EBS, RackSpace RAID, and OpenStack Cinder.

   - **Object storage**—Object storage is like a file share accessed via APIs or a web interface. Examples include Amazon S3 and Rackspace cloud files.

27. What is the Cloud Security Alliance Cloud Controls Matrix?

   a. A set of regulatory requirements for cloud service providers

   b. An inventory of cloud service security controls that are arranged into separate security domains

   c. A set of software development life cycle requirements for cloud service providers

   d. An inventory of cloud service security controls that are arranged into a hierarchy of security domains

   Answer: B

   The Cloud Security Alliance Cloud Controls Matrix (CCM) is an essential and up-to-date security controls framework that is addressed to the cloud community and stakeholders. A fundamental richness of the CCM is its ability to provide mapping/cross-relationships with the main industry-accepted security standards, regulations, and controls frameworks such as the ISO 27001/27002, ISACAs COBIT, and PCI-DSS. The CCM can be seen as an inventory of cloud service security controls.

28. Which of the following are attributes of cloud computing?

   a. Minimal management effort and shared resources

   b. High cost and unique resources

c. Rapid provisioning and slow release of resources

d. Limited access and service provider interaction

Answer: A

"Cloud computing is a model for enabling ubiquitous, convenient, on-demand network access to a shared pool of configurable computing resources (e.g., networks, servers, storage, applications, and services) that can be rapidly provisioned and released with minimal management effort or service provider interaction."

—N.I.S.T. Definition of Cloud Computing (SP 800-145)

29. When using an infrastructure as a service solution, what is the capability provided to the customer?

   a. To provision processing, storage, networks, and other fundamental computing resources where the consumer is not able to deploy and run arbitrary software, which can include operating systems and applications.

   b. To provision processing, storage, networks, and other fundamental computing resources where the provider is able to deploy and run arbitrary software, which can include operating systems and applications.

   c. To provision processing, storage, networks, and other fundamental computing resources where the auditor is able to deploy and run arbitrary software, which can include operating systems and applications.

   d. To provision processing, storage, networks, and other fundamental computing resources where the consumer is able to deploy and run arbitrary software, which can include operating systems and applications.

Answer: D

According to the *NIST Definition of Cloud Computing*, in IaaS, "the capability provided to the consumer is to provision processing, storage, networks, and other fundamental computing resources where the consumer is able to deploy and run arbitrary software, which can include operating systems and applications. The consumer does not manage or control the underlying cloud infrastructure but has control over operating systems, storage, and deployed applications; and possibly limited control of select networking components (e.g., host firewalls)."

30. When using a platform as a service solution, what is the capability provided to the customer?

   a. To deploy onto the cloud infrastructure provider-created or acquired applications created using programming languages, libraries, services, and tools supported by the provider. The consumer does not manage or control the underlying cloud infrastructure including network, servers, operating systems, or storage, but has control over the deployed applications and possibly configuration settings for the application-hosting environment.

b. To deploy onto the cloud infrastructure consumer-created or acquired applications created using programming languages, libraries, services, and tools supported by the provider. The provider does not manage or control the underlying cloud infrastructure including network, servers, operating systems, or storage, but has control over the deployed applications and possibly configuration settings for the application-hosting environment.

c. To deploy onto the cloud infrastructure consumer-created or acquired applications created using programming languages, libraries, services, and tools supported by the provider. The consumer does not manage or control the underlying cloud infrastructure including network, servers, operating systems, or storage, but has control over the deployed applications and possibly configuration settings for the application-hosting environment.

d. To deploy onto the cloud infrastructure consumer-created or acquired applications created using programming languages, libraries, services, and tools supported by the consumer. The consumer does not manage or control the underlying cloud infrastructure including network, servers, operating systems, or storage, but has control over the deployed applications and possibly configuration settings for the application-hosting environment.

Answer: C

According to the *NIST Definition of Cloud Computing*, in PaaS, "the capability provided to the consumer is to deploy onto the cloud infrastructure consumer-created or acquired applications created using programming languages, libraries, services, and tools supported by the provider. The consumer does not manage or control the underlying cloud infrastructure including network, servers, operating systems, or storage, but has control over the deployed applications and possibly configuration settings for the application-hosting environment."

31. What are the four cloud deployment models?

   a. Public, internal, hybrid, and community

   b. External, private, hybrid, and community

   c. Public, private, joint, and community

   d. Public, private, hybrid, and community

Answer: D

According to the *NIST Definition of Cloud Computing*, the cloud deployment models are

- **Private cloud**—The cloud infrastructure is provisioned for exclusive use by a single organization comprising multiple consumers (e.g., business units). It may be owned, managed, and operated by the organization, a third party, or some combination of them, and it may exist on or off premises.

- **Community cloud**—The cloud infrastructure is provisioned for exclusive use by a specific community of consumers from organizations that have shared concerns (e.g., mission, security requirements, policy, and compliance considerations). It may be owned, managed, and operated by one or more of the organizations in the community, a third party, or some combination of them, and it may exist on or off premises.

- **Public cloud**—The cloud infrastructure is provisioned for open use by the general public. It may be owned, managed, and operated by a business, academic, or government organization, or some combination of them. It exists on the premises of the cloud provider.

- **Hybrid cloud**—The cloud infrastructure is a composition of two or more distinct cloud infrastructures (private, community, or public) that remain unique entities but are bound together by standardized or proprietary technology that enables data and application portability (e.g., cloud bursting for load balancing between clouds).

32. When setting up resource sharing within a host cluster, which option would you choose to mediate resource contention?

    a. Reservations

    b. Limits

    c. Clusters

    d. Shares

Answer: D

Within a host cluster, resources are allocated and managed as if they are pooled or jointly available to all members of the cluster. The use of resource sharing concepts such as reservations, limits, and shares may be used to further refine and orchestrate the allocation of resources according to requirements imposed by the cluster administrator.

- Reservations allow for the guaranteeing of a certain *minimum* amount of the clusters pooled resources to be made available to a specified virtual machine.

- Limits allow for the guaranteeing of a certain *maximum* amount of the clusters pooled resources to be made available to a specified virtual machine.

- Shares allow for the provisioning of the remaining resources left in a cluster when there is resource contention. Specifically, shares allow the cluster's reservations to be allocated and then to address any remaining resources that may be available for use by members of the cluster through a prioritized percentage-based allocation mechanism.

DNSSEC Walkthrough

DNSSEC IS A SET of security extensions to DNS that provide the ability to authenticate DNS records. This walkthrough is designed to illustrate for the SSCP how to implement DNSSEC in a typical enterprise network that is running using Microsoft Windows Server 2012. The ability to move step by step through the implementation of DNSSEC will give the SSCP the ability to fully understand how the technology works and is integrated into the defense-in-depth architecture for the modern enterprise.

HARDWARE AND SOFTWARE REQUIREMENTS

The following are required components of the test lab:

- The product disc or other installation media for Windows Server 2012
- Two computers that meet the minimum hardware requirements for Windows Server 2012

CONFIGURING THE TEST LAB

The following procedures are used to configure computers for the demonstration portion of the test lab:

- DC1 is a domain controller and Active Directory–integrated authoritative DNS server.
- DNS1 is a non-authoritative, caching DNS server.

CONFIGURING DC1

DC1 is a computer running Windows Server 2012, providing the following services:

- A domain controller for the isc2.com Active Directory domain
- An authoritative DNS server for the isc2.com DNS zone
- A DNSSEC key master for the isc2.com DNS zone

To install the operating system and configure TCP/IP on DC1, follow these steps:

1. Start your computer using the Windows Server 2012 product disc or other digital media.
2. When prompted, enter a product key; accept the license terms; configure the clock, language, and regional settings; and provide a password for the local Administrator account.
3. Press Ctrl+Alt+Delete and sign in using the local Administrator account.
4. If you are prompted to enable Windows Error Reporting, click Accept.
5. Click Start, type **ncpa.cpl**, and then press Enter. The Network Connections control panel will open.
6. In Network Connections, right-click Wired Ethernet Connection and then click Properties.

7. Double-click Internet Protocol Version 4 (TCP/IPv4).

8. On the General tab, choose Use The Following IP Address.

9. Next to IP Address, type **10.0.0.1**, and next to Subnet Mask, type **255.255.255.0**. It is not necessary to provide an entry next to Default Gateway.

10. Next to Preferred DNS Server, type 10.0.0.1.

11. Click OK twice, and then close the Network Connections control panel.

To configure DC1 as a domain controller and DNS server, follow these steps:

1. The Server Manager Dashboard is displayed by default. In the navigation pane, click Configure This Local Server.

2. Under Properties, click the name next to Computer Name. The System Properties dialog box will open.

3. On the Computer Name tab, click Change and then type **DC1** under Computer Name.

4. Click OK twice and then click Close.

5. When you are prompted to restart the computer, click Restart Now.

6. After restarting the computer, sign in using the local Administrator account.

7. In Server Manager, under Configure This Local Server, click Add Roles And Features.

8. In the Add Roles And Features Wizard, click Next three times, and then on the Select Server Roles page select the Active Directory Domain Services checkbox.

9. When you are prompted to add required features, click Add Features.

10. Click Next three times, and then click Install.

11. Wait for the installation process to complete, verify on the Installation progress page that "Configuration required. Installation succeeded on DC1" is displayed, and then click Close.

12. Click the Notification flag and then click Promote This Server To A Domain Controller.

13. In the Active Directory Domain Services Configuration Wizard, on the Deployment Configuration page, choose Add A New Forest, and then next to Root domain name, type **isc2.com**.

14. Click Next, and then on the Domain Controller Options page, under Type the Directory Services Restore Mode (DSRM) password, type a password next to Password and Confirm Password. Confirm that Domain Name System (DNS) Server and Global Catalog (GC) are selected and then click Next.

B

DNSSEC WALKTHROUGH

15. Click Next five times and then click Install.

    The computer will restart automatically to complete the installation process.

16. Sign in using the local Administrator account.

Next, a domain administrator account must be created to use when performing procedures in the test lab.

Creating a Domain Administrator Account

To create a domain administrator account, follow these steps:

1. On the Server Manager menu bar, click Tools and then click Active Directory Users And Computers.

2. In the Active Directory Users And Computers console tree, double-click isc2. com, right-click Users, point to New, and then click User.

3. In the New Object – User dialog box, type **user1** under User Logon Name and next to Full Name; then click Next.

4. Next to Password and Confirm Password, type a Password for the user1 account.

5. Clear the checkbox next to User Must Change Password At Next Logon, select the Password Never Expires checkbox, click Next, and then click Finish.

6. Double-click user1 and then click the Member Of tab.

7. Click Add, type **domain admins** under Enter The Object Names To Select, click OK twice, and then close the Active Directory Users And Computers console.

8. Click Start, click Administrator, and then click Sign Out.

9. Sign in to the computer using the user1 credentials by clicking the left arrow next to ISC2\Administrator and then clicking Other User.

Configuring the sec.isc2.com DNS Zone

Next, configure a new DNS zone: `sec.isc2.com`. This zone will be used to demonstrate DNSSEC zone signing.

1. On the Server Manager menu, click Tools, and then click DNS.

2. In the DNS Manager console tree, right-click Forward Lookup Zones and then click New Zone.

3. In the New Zone Wizard, click Next three times and then under Zone Name type `sec.isc2.com`.

4. Click Next twice and then click Finish.

5. Verify that the zone `sec.isc2.com` is displayed under Forward Lookup Zones.

6. Next, add one or more DNS resource records to the `sec.isc2.com` zone.

7. Leave the DNS Manager console open.

To add DNS resource records to the sec.isc2.com zone, follow these steps:

1. Right-click `sec.isc2.com` and then click New Host (A or AAAA).

2. In the New Host dialog box, type **dc1** under Name, type **10.0.0.1** under IP Address, and then click Add Host. The IP address of `dc1.isc2.com` is used here to help demonstrate DNSSEC success and failure scenarios.

3. Confirm that "The host record dc1.sec.isc2.com was successfully added" is displayed and then click OK.

4. Add additional resource records to the zone if desired and then click Done.

Enabling Remote Desktop on DC1

DC1 will be used to demonstrate functionality of a network application in an environment with DNSSEC.

1. In the Server Manager navigation pane, click Local Server.

2. Click Disabled next to Remote Desktop.

3. In the System Properties dialog box, on the Remote tab, click Allow Connections From Computers Running Any Version Of Remote Desktop (Less Secure) and then click OK.

CONFIGURING DNS1

DNS1 is a computer running Windows Server 2012, providing the following services:

- A non-authoritative, recursive DNS server.

- A DNS client computer.

- During the demonstration portion of the test lab, DNS1 will be used to perform recursive DNS queries, host a trust anchor for the `isc2.com` domain, and provide DNSSEC validation for DNS client queries. DNS1 will be used to issue DNS client queries.

Installing the OS and Configuring TCP/IP on DC1

To install the operating system and configure TCP/IP on DC1, follow these steps:

1. Start your computer using the Windows Server 2012 product disc or other digital media.

2. When prompted, enter a product key; accept the license terms; configure the clock, language, and regional settings; and provide a password for the local Administrator account.

3. Press Ctrl+Alt+Delete and sign in using the local Administrator account.

4. If you are prompted to enable Windows Error Reporting, click Accept.

5. Click Start, type **ncpa.cpl**, and then press Enter. The Network Connections control panel will open.

6. In Network Connections, right-click Wired Ethernet Connection, and then click Properties.

7. Double-click Internet Protocol Version 4 (TCP/IPv4).

8. On the General tab, choose Use The Following IP Address.

9. Next to IP Address type **10.0.0.2** and next to Subnet Mask type **255.255.255.0**. It is not necessary to provide an entry next to Default Gateway.

10. Next to Preferred DNS Server, type **10.0.0.2**.

11. Click OK twice and then close the Network Connections control panel.

Installing and Configuring DNS on DNS1

To install and configure DNS on DNS1, follow these steps:

1. In the Server Manager Dashboard navigation pane, click Configure This Local Server.

2. Under Properties, click the name next to Computer Name. The System Properties dialog box will open.

3. On the Computer Name tab, click Change and then type **DNS1** under Computer Name.

4. Under Member Of, select Domain, type **isc2.com**, and then click OK.

5. When you are prompted to provide credentials to join the domain, enter the credentials for the user1 account that was created previously.

6. Confirm that computer name and domain changes were successful, click OK, and then click Close.

7. When you are prompted to restart the computer, click Restart Now.

8. After restarting the computer, sign in using the ISC2\user1 account.

9. In Server Manager, under Configure This Local Server, click Add Roles And Features.

10. In the Add Roles And Features Wizard, click Next three times, and then on the Select Server Roles page select the DNS Server checkbox.

11. When you are prompted to add required features, click Add Features.

12. Click Next three times, and then click Install.

13. Wait for the installation process to complete, verify on the Installation progress page that "Installation succeeded on DNS1.isc2.com" is displayed and then click Close.

14. On the Server Manager menu bar, click Tools and then click DNS.

15. In the DNS Manager console tree, right-click DNS1 and then click Properties.

16. Click the Forwarders tab, click Edit, type **10.0.0.1**, and then click OK twice.

17. Leave the DNS Manager console open.

SIGNING A ZONE ON DC1 AND DISTRIBUTING TRUST ANCHORS

Next, sign in to the `sec.isc2.com` zone and distribute a trust anchor for the zone. Trust anchor distribution is manual for DNS servers that are not running on domain controllers, such as DNS1.

1. In the DNS Manager console tree on DC1, navigate to Forward Lookup Zones ➤ `sec.isc2.com`.

2. Right-click `sec.isc2.com`, point to DNSSEC, and then click Sign The Zone.

3. In the Zone Signing Wizard, click Next and then choose Use Recommended Settings to sign the zone.

4. Click Next twice, confirm that "The zone has been successfully signed" is displayed, and then click Finish.

5. Refresh the DNS Manager console and verify that a new icon is displayed for the `sec.isc2.com` zone, indicating that it is currently signed with DNSSEC.

6. Click the `sec.isc2.com` zone and review the new resource records that are present, including DNSKEY, RRSIG, and NSEC3 records.

7. Leave the DNS Manager console open.

Distributing a Trust Anchor to DNS1

To distribute a trust anchor to DNS1, follow these steps:

1. On DC1, click Windows Explorer on the taskbar.

2. Navigate to C:\Windows\System32, right-click the dns folder, point to Share With, and then click Advanced Sharing.

3. In the dns Properties dialog box, click Advanced Sharing, select the Share This Folder checkbox, verify the Share name is dns, and then click OK.

4. Click Close and then close Windows Explorer.

5. On DNS1, in the DNS Manager console tree, navigate to the Trust Points folder.

6. Right-click Trust Points, point to Import, and then click DNSKEY.

7. In the Import DNSKEY dialog box, type **\\dc1\dns\keyset-sec.isc2.com** and then click OK.

Verifying Trust Anchors

To verify trust anchors, follow these steps:

1. In the console tree, navigate to Trust Points ➤ com ➤ isc2 ➤ sec and verify that import was successful.

2. On any computer, click Windows PowerShell, type the following command, and then press Enter:

   ```
   resolve-dnsname –name sec.isc2.com.trustanchors –type dnskey –server dns1
   ```

3. On DNS1, right-click Windows PowerShell and then click Run as Administrator.

4. Type the following command and then press Enter:

   ```
   get-dnsservertrustanchor sec.isc2.com
   ```

5. Verify that two trust anchors are displayed.

Querying a Signed Zone with DNSSEC Validation Required

The Name Resolution Policy Table (NRPT) is used to require DNSSEC validation. The NRPT can be configured in local Group Policy for a single computer or domain Group Policy for some or all computers in the domain. The following procedure uses domain Group Policy.

1. On DC1, on the Server Manager menu bar, click Tools, and then click Group Policy Management.

2. In the Group Policy Management console tree, under Domains ➤ `isc2.com` ➤ Group Policy Objects, right-click Default Domain Policy, and then click Edit.

3. In the Group Policy Management Editor console tree, navigate to Computer Configuration ➤ Policies ➤ Windows Settings ➤ Name Resolution Policy.

4. In the details pane, under Create Rules and To Which Part Of The Namespace Does This Rule Apply, choose Suffix from the drop-down list, and type `sec.isc2.com` next to Suffix.

5. On the DNSSEC tab, select the Enable DNSSEC In This Rule checkbox and then under Validation select the Require DNS Clients To Check That Name And Address Data Has Been Validated By The DNS server checkbox.

6. In the bottom-right corner, click Create and then verify that a rule for `sec.isc2.com` was added under Name Resolution Policy Table.

7. Click Apply, and then close the Group Policy Management Editor.

8. On DC1, type the following commands at the Windows PowerShell prompt, and then press Enter:

```
gpupdate /force
get-dnsclientnrptpolicy
```

9. Verify that computer and user policy updates were successful and that the value of DnsSecValidationRequired is True for the `.sec.isc2.com` namespace.

Unsigning the Zone

Follow these steps to remove DNSSEC signing from the `sec.isc2.com` zone so that the zone can next be re-signed using custom DNSSEC parameters:

1. On DC1, in the DNS Manager console tree, navigate to Forward Lookup Zones ➤ `sec.isc2.com`.

2. Right-click `sec.isc2.com`, point to DNSSEC, and then click Unsign The Zone.

3. In the Unsign Zone Wizard, click Next.

4. Verify that "The zone has been successfully unsigned" is displayed, and then click Finish.

5. Refresh the view in DNS Manager and verify that the `sec.isc2.com` zone no longer contains DNSSEC signed records and the icon next to the zone indicates it is not currently signed.

Resigning the Zone with Custom Parameters

Follow these steps to re-sign the zone using custom DNSSEC parameters:

1. On DC1, right-click `sec.isc2.com`, point to DNSSEC and then click Sign the Zone.

2. In the Zone Signing Wizard, click Next.

3. Customize Zone Signing Parameters is chosen by default. Click Next.

4. On the Key Master page, The DNS Server DC1 Is The Key Master is chosen by default, because zone signing is being performed on DC1.

5. Ensure that DC1 is chosen as the key master, and then click Next twice.

6. On the Key Signing Key (KSK) page, click the existing KSK (with key length of 2048) and then click Remove.

7. To add a new KSK, click Add.

8. In the New Key Signing Key (KSK) dialog box, under Key Properties, click the drop-down next to Cryptographic algorithm, and select RSA/SHA-512.

9. Under Key Properties, click the drop-down next to Key Length (Bits), select 4096, and then click OK.

10. Click Next until "You have successfully configured the following parameters to sign the zone" is displayed.

11. Review the parameters you have chosen, and then click Next to start the zone signing process.

12. Confirm that "The zone has been successfully signed is displayed," click Finish, and then refresh the view in DNS Manager to verify the zone is signed again.

13. Refresh the view for the Trust Points folder, and verify that new DNSKEY trust points are present that use the RSA/SHA-512 algorithm.

14. At an Administrator Windows PowerShell prompt, type the following commands, and press Enter:

```
Get-dnsservertrustanchor –name sec.isc2.com –computername dns1
Get-dnsservertrustanchor –name sec.isc2.com –computername dc1
```

Glossary of Terms Related to the SSCP

6to4

Transition mechanism for migrating from IPv4 to IPv6. It allows systems to use IPv6 to communicate if their traffic has to transverse an IPv4 network.

Absolute addresses

Hardware addresses used by the CPU.

Abstraction

The capability to suppress unnecessary details so the important, inherent properties can be examined and reviewed.

Accepted ways for handling risk

Accept, transfer, mitigate, avoid.

Access

The flow of information between a subject and an object.

Access control matrix

A table of subjects and objects indicating what actions individual subjects can take upon individual objects.

Access control model

An access control model is a framework that dictates how subjects access objects.

Access controls

Are security features that control how users and systems communicate and interact with other systems and resources.

Accreditation

Formal acceptance of the adequacy of a system's overall security by management.

Active attack

Attack where the attacker does interact with processing or communication activities.

ActiveX

A Microsoft technology composed of a set of OOP technologies and tools based on COM and DCOM. It is a framework for defining reusable software components in a programming language–independent manner.

Address bus

Physical connections between processing components and memory segments used to communicate the physical memory addresses being used during processing procedures.

Address resolution protocol (ARP)

A networking protocol used for resolution of network layer IP addresses into link layer MAC addresses.

Address space layout randomization (ASLR)

Memory protection mechanism used by some operating systems. The addresses used by components of a process are randomized so that it is harder for an attacker to exploit specific memory vulnerabilities.

Algebraic attack

Cryptanalysis attack that exploits vulnerabilities within the intrinsic algebraic structure of mathematical functions.

Algorithm

Set of mathematical and logic rules used in cryptographic functions.

Analog signals

Continuously varying electromagnetic wave that represents and transmits data.

Analytic attack

Cryptanalysis attack that exploits vulnerabilities within the algorithm structure.

Annualized loss expectancy (ALE)
Annual expected loss if a specific vulnerability is exploited and how it affects a single asset. SLE × ARO = ALE.

Application programming interface (API)
Software interface that enables process-to-process interaction. Common way to provide access to standard routines to a set of software programs.

Arithmetic logic unit (ALU)
A component of the computer's processing unit, in which arithmetic and matching operations are performed.

AS/NZS 4360
Australia and New Zealand business risk management assessment approach.

Assemblers
Tools that convert assembly code into the necessary machine-compatible binary language for processing activities to take place.

Assembly language
A low-level programming language that is the mnemonic representation of machine-level instructions.

Assurance evaluation criteria
Check-list and process of examining the security-relevant parts of a system (TCB, reference monitor, security kernel) and assigning the system an assurance rating.

Asymmetric algorithm
Encryption method that uses two different key types, public and private. Also called public key cryptography.

Asymmetric mode multiprocessing
When a computer has two or more CPUs and one CPU is dedicated to a specific program

while the other CPUs carry out general processing procedures.

Asynchronous communication
Transmission sequencing technology that uses start and stop bits or similar encoding mechanism. Used in environments that transmit a variable amount of data in a periodic fashion.

Asynchronous token generating method
Employs a challenge/response scheme to authenticate the user.

Attack surface
Components available to be used by an attacker against the product itself.

Attenuation
Gradual loss in intensity of any kind of flux through a medium. As an electrical signal travels down a cable, the signal can degrade and distort or corrupt the data it is carrying.

Attribute
A column in a two-dimensional database.

Authentication Header (AH) Protocol
Protocol within the IPSec suite used for integrity and authentication.

Authenticode
A type of code signing, which is the process of digitally signing software components and scripts to confirm the software author and guarantee that the code has not been altered or corrupted since it was digitally signed. Authenticode is Microsoft's implementation of code signing.

Availability
Reliable and timely access to data and resources is provided to authorized individuals.

Avalanche effect
Algorithm design requirement so that slight changes to the input result in drastic changes to the output.

Base registers
Beginning of address space assigned to a process. Used to ensure a process does not make a request outside its assigned memory boundaries.

Baseband transmission
Uses the full bandwidth for only one communication channel and has a low data transfer rate compared to broadband.

Bastion host
A highly exposed device that will most likely be targeted for attacks, and thus should be hardened.

Behavior blocking
Allowing the suspicious code to execute within the operating system and watches its interactions with the operating system, looking for suspicious activities.

Birthday attack
Cryptographic attack that exploits the mathematics behind the birthday problem in the probability theory forces collisions within hashing functions.

Block cipher
Symmetric algorithm type that encrypts chunks (blocks) of data at a time.

Blowfish
Block symmetric cipher that uses 64-bit block sizes and variable-length keys.

Border Gateway Protocol (BGP)
The protocol that carries out core routing decisions on the Internet. It maintains a table of IP networks, or *prefixes*, which designate network reachability among autonomous systems.

Bots
Software applications that run automated tasks over the Internet, which perform tasks that are both simple and structurally repetitive. Malicious use of bots is the coordination and operation of an automated attack by a botnet (centrally controlled collection of bots).

Broadband transmission
Divides the bandwidth of a communication channel into many channels, enabling different types of data to be transmitted at one time.

Buffer overflow
Too much data is put into the buffers that make up a stack. Common attack vector used by attackers to run malicious code on a target system.

Bus topology
Systems are connected to a single transmission channel (i.e., network cable), forming a linear construct.

Business continuity management (BCM)
Is the overarching approach to managing all aspects of BCP and DRP.

Business continuity plan (BCP)
A business continuity action plan is a document or set of documents that contains the critical information a business needs to stay running in spite of adverse events. A business continuity plan is also called an emergency plan.

Business impact analysis (BIA)

An exercise that determines the impact of losing the support of any resource to an organization, establishes the escalation of that loss over time, identifies the minimum resources needed to recover, and prioritizes the recovery of processes and supporting systems.

Cable modem

A device that provides bidirectional data communication via radio frequency channels on cable TV infrastructures. Cable modems are primarily used to deliver broadband Internet access to homes.

Cache memory

Fast memory type that is used by a CPU to increase read and write operations.

Caesar cipher

Simple substitution algorithm created by Julius Caesar that shifts alphabetic values three positions during its encryption and decryption processes.

Capability maturity model integration (CMMI)

A process improvement methodology that provides guidance for quality improvement and point of reference for appraising existing processes developed by Carnegie Mellon.

Capability maturity model integration (CMMI) model

A process improvement approach that provides organizations with the essential elements of effective processes, which will improve their performance.

Capability table

A capability table specifies the access rights a certain subject possesses pertaining to specific objects. A capability table is different from an ACL because the subject is bound to the capability table, whereas the object is bound to the ACL.

Carrier sense multiple access with collision avoidance (CSMA/CA)

LANs using carrier sense multiple access with collision avoidance require devices to announce their intention to transmit by broadcasting a jamming signal.

Carrier sense multiple access with collision detection (CSMA/CD)

Devices on a LAN using carrier sense multiple access with collision detection listen for a carrier before transmitting data.

CBC-MAC

Cipher block chaining message authentication code uses encryption for data integrity and data origin authentication.

Cell

An intersection of a row and a column.

Cell suppression

A technique used to hide specific cells that contain sensitive information.

Central processing unit (CPU)

The part of a computer that performs the logic, computation, and decision-making functions. It interprets and executes instructions as it receives them.

Certificate

Digital identity used within a PKI. Generated and maintained by a certificate authority and used for authentication.

Certificate revocation list (CRL)

List that is maintained by the certificate authority of a PKI that contains information on all of the digital certificates that have been revoked.

Certification

Technical evaluation of the security components and their compliance to a predefined security policy for the purpose of accreditation. The technical testing of a system.

Certification authority

Component of a PKI that creates and maintains digital certificates throughout their life cycles.

Change control

The process of controlling the changes that take place during the life cycle of a system and documenting the necessary change control activities.

Channel service unit (CSU)

A line bridging device for use with T-carriers and that is required by PSTN providers at digital interfaces that terminate in a data service unit (DSU) on the customer side. The DSU is a piece of telecommunications circuit terminating equipment that transforms digital data between telephone company lines and local equipment.

Checklist test

Copies of the plan are handed out to each functional area for examination to ensure the plan properly deals with the area's needs and vulnerabilities.

Chosen-ciphertext attack

Cryptanalysis attack where the attacker chooses a ciphertext and obtains its decryption under an unknown key.

Chosen-plaintext attack

Cryptanalysis attack where the attacker can choose arbitrary plaintexts to be encrypted and obtain the corresponding ciphertexts.

Cipher

Another name for algorithm.

Ciphertext-only attack

Cryptanalysis attack where the attacker is assumed to have access only to a set of ciphertexts.

Classless interdomain routing (CIDR)

A method for using the existing 32-bit Internet address space efficiently.

Client-side validation

Input validation is done at the client before it is even sent back to the server to process.

Clipping level

A threshold.

Closed system

Designs are built upon proprietary procedures, which inhibit interoperability capabilities.

Cloud computing

The delivery of computer processing capabilities as a service rather than as a product, whereby shared resources, software, and information are provided to end users as a utility. Offerings are usually bundled as an infrastructure, platform, or software.

CMAC
Cipher message authentication code that is based upon and provides more security compared to CBC-MAC.

CMM
Block cipher mode that combines the CTR encryption mode and CBC-MAC. One encryption key is used for both authentication and encryption purposes.

CobiT
Set of control objectives used as a framework for IT governance developed by Information Systems Audit and Control Association (ISACA) and the IT Governance Institute (ITGI).

Cognitive passwords
Fact- or opinion-based information used to verify an individual's identity.

Cohesion
A measurement that indicates how many different types of tasks a module needs to carry out.

Cold site
Is just a building with power, raised floors, and utilities. No devices are available. This is the cheapest of the three options but can take weeks to get up and operational.

Collision
(1) A condition that is present when two or more terminals are in contention during simultaneous network access attempts. (2) In cryptography, an instance when a hash function generates the same output for different inputs.

Collusion
Two or more people working together to carry out fraudulent activities.

Common criteria
International standard used to assess the effectiveness of the security controls built into a system from functional and assurance perspectives.

Compilers
Tools that convert high-level language statements into the necessary machine-level format (.exe, .dll, etc.) for specific processors to understand.

Compression viruses
Another type of virus that appends itself to executables on the system and compresses them by using the user's permissions.

Concealment cipher
Encryption method that hides a secret message within an open message.

Confidentiality
A security concept that assures the necessary level of secrecy is enforced and unauthorized disclosure is prevented.

Confusion
Substitution processes used in encryption functions to increase randomness.

Content-based access
Bases access decisions on the sensitivity of the data, not solely on subject identity.

Context-based access
Bases access decisions on the state of the situation, not solely on identity or content sensitivity.

Control
Safeguard that is put in place to reduce a risk, also called a countermeasure.

Control functions
Control functions include:

- **Deterrent**—Discourage a potential attacker
- **Preventive**—Stop an incident from occurring
- **Corrective**—Fix items after an incident has occurred
- **Recovery**—Restore necessary components to return to normal operations
- **Detective**—Identify an incident's activities after it took place
- **Compensating**—Alternative control that provides similar protection as the original control

Control types
Administrative, technical (logical), and physical.

Control unit
Part of the CPU that oversees the collection of instructions and data from memory and how they are passed to the processing components of the CPU.

Cookies
Data files used by web browsers and servers to keep browser state information and browsing preferences.

Cooperative multitasking
Multitasking scheduling scheme used by older operating systems to allow for computer resource time slicing.

Copyright
A form of protection granted by law for original works of authorship fixed in a tangible medium of expression.

COSO
Internal control model used for corporate governance to help prevent fraud developed by the Committee of Sponsoring Organizations (COSO) of the Treadway Commission.

Cost/benefit analysis
An estimate of the equivalent monetary value of proposed benefits and the estimated costs associated with a control in order to establish whether the control is feasible.

Coupling
A measurement that indicates how much interaction one module requires for carrying out its tasks.

CRAMM
CCTA (Central Computing and Telecommunications Agency) Risk Analysis and Management Method.

Cross-site scripting (XSS) attack
An attack where a vulnerability is found on a website that allows an attacker to inject malicious code into a web application.

Crosstalk
A signal on one channel of a transmission creates an undesired effect in another channel by interacting with it. The signal from one cable "spills over" into another cable.

Cryptanalysis
Practice of uncovering flaws within cryptosystems.

Cryptography
Science of secret writing that enables an entity to store and transmit data in a form that is available only to the intended individuals.

Cryptology
The study of both cryptography and cryptanalysis.

Cryptosystem
Hardware or software implementation of cryptography that contains all the necessary software, protocols, algorithms, and keys.

Data bus
Physical connections between processing components and memory segments used to transmit data being used during processing procedures.

Data custodian
Individual responsible for implementing and maintaining security controls to meet security requirements outlined by data owner.

Data dictionary
Central repository of data elements and their relationships.

Data diddling
The act of willfully modifying information, programs, or documentation in an effort to commit fraud or disrupt production.

Data execution prevention (DEP)
Memory protection mechanism used by some operating systems. Memory segments may be marked as non-executable so that they cannot be misused by malicious software.

Data hiding
Use of segregation in design decisions to protect software components from negatively interacting with each other. Commonly enforced through strict interfaces.

Data mining
A methodology used by organizations to better understand their customers, products, markets, or any other phase of the business.

Data modeling
Considers data independently of the way the data are processed and of the components that process the data. A process used to define and analyze data requirements needed to support the business processes.

Data owner
Individual responsible for the protection and classification of a specific data set.

Data structure
A representation of the logical relationship between elements of data.

Data warehousing
Combines data from multiple databases or data sources into a large database for the purpose of providing more extensive information retrieval and data analysis.

Database
A cross-referenced collection of data.

Database management system (DBMS)
Manages and controls the database.

Decipher
Act of transforming data into a readable format.

Defense-in-depth
Implementation of multiple controls so that successful penetration and compromise is more difficult to attain.

Delphi method
Data collection method that happens in an anonymous fashion.

Differential cryptanalysis
Cryptanalysis method that uses the study of how differences in an input can affect the resultant difference at the output.

Diffie-Hellman algorithm
First asymmetric algorithm created and is used to exchange symmetric key values. Based upon logarithms in finite fields.

Diffusion
Transposition processes used in encryption functions to increase randomness.

Digital rights management (DRM)
Access control technologies commonly used to protect copyright material.

Digital signals
Binary digits are represented and transmitted as discrete electrical pulses.

Digital signature
Ensuring the authenticity and integrity of a message through the use of hashing algorithms and asymmetric algorithms. The message digest is encrypted with the sender's private key.

Digital subscriber line (DSL)
A set of technologies that provide Internet access by transmitting digital data over the wires of a local telephone network. DSL is used to digitize the "last mile" and provide fast Internet connectivity.

Distance-vector routing protocol
A routing protocol that calculates paths based on the distance (or number of hops) and a vector (a direction).

DNS zone transfer
The process of replicating the databases containing the DNS data across a set of DNS servers.

DNSSEC
A set of extensions to DNS that provide to DNS clients (resolvers) origin authentication of DNS data to reduce the threat of DNS poisoning, spoofing, and similar attack types.

DoDAF
U.S. Department of Defense architecture framework that ensures interoperability of systems to meet military mission goals.

Domain name system (DNS)
A hierarchical distributed naming system for computers, services, or any resource connected to an IP-based network. It associates various pieces of information with domain names assigned to each of the participating entities.

Dual-homed firewall
This device has two interfaces and sits between an untrusted network and trusted network to provide secure access.

Dumpster diving
Refers to going through someone's trash to find confidential or useful information. It is legal, unless it involves trespassing, but in all cases it is considered unethical.

Dynamic host configuration protocol (DHCP)
DHCP is an industry-standard protocol used to dynamically assign IP addresses to network devices.

Dynamic link libraries (DLLs)
A set of subroutines that are shared by different applications and operating system processes.

El Gamal algorithm
Asymmetric algorithm based upon the Diffie-Hellman algorithm used for digital signatures, encryption, and key exchange.

Elliptic curve cryptosystem algorithm
Asymmetric algorithm based upon the algebraic structure of elliptic curves over finite fields. Used for digital signatures, encryption, and key exchange.

E-mail spoofing
Activity in which the sender address and other arts of the e-mail header are altered to appear as though the e-mail originated from a different source. Since SMTP does not provide any authentication, it is easy to impersonate and forge e-mails.

Encapsulating Security Payload Protocol (ESP)
Protocol within the IPSec suite used for integrity, authentication, and encryption.

EncipherK
Act of transforming data into an unreadable format.

End-to-end encryption
The encryption of information at the point of origin within the communications network and postponing of decryption to the final destination point.

Ethernet
Common LAN media access technology standardized by IEEE 802.3. Uses 48-bit MAC addressing, works in contention-based networks, and has extended outside of just LAN environments.

Exposure
Presence of a vulnerability, which exposes the organization to a threat.

Facilitated risk analysis process (FRAP)
A focused, qualitative approach that carries out pre-screening to save time and money.

Failure modes and effect analysis (FMEA)
Approach that dissects a component into its basic functions to identify flaws and those flaw's effects.

Fault tree analysis
Approach to map specific flaws to root causes in complex systems.

Federated identity
A portable identity, and its associated entitlements, that can be used across business boundaries.

Fiber distributed data interface (FDDI)
Ring-based token network protocol that was derived from the IEEE 802.4 token bus timed token protocol. It can work in LAN or MAN environments and provides fault tolerance through dual-ring architecture.

File
A basic unit of data records organized on a storage medium for convenient location, access, and updating.

Foreign key
An attribute of one table that is related to the primary key of another table.

Fraggle attack
A DDoS attack type on a computer that floods the target system with a large amount of UDP echo traffic to IP broadcast addresses.

Frequency analysis
Cryptanalysis process used to identify weaknesses within cryptosystems by locating patterns in resulting ciphertext.

Frequency-division multiplexing (FDM)
An older technique in which the available transmission bandwidth of a circuit is divided by frequency into narrow bands, each used for a separate voice or data transmission channel, which many conversations can be carried on one circuit.

Full-interruption test
One in which regular operations are stopped and processing is moved to the alternate site.

Functionality versus effectiveness of control
Functionality is what a control does, and its effectiveness is how well the control does it.

Fuzzing
A technique used to discover flaws and vulnerabilities in software.

Garbage collector
Tool that marks unused memory segments as usable to ensure that an operating system does not run out of memory.

General registers
Temporary memory location the CPU uses during its processes of executing instructions. The ALU's "scratch pad" it uses while carrying out logic and math functions.

Guideline
Suggestions and best practices.

H.323
A standard that addresses call signaling and control, multimedia transport and control,

and bandwidth control for point-to-point and multipoint conferences.

Hardware segmentation
Physically mapping software to individual memory segments.

Hashed message authentication code (HMAC)
Cryptographic hash function that uses a symmetric key value and is used for data integrity and data origin authentication.

Hierarchical data model
Combines records and fields that are related in a logical tree structure.

High availability
Refers to a system, component, or environment that is continuously operational.

High-level languages
Otherwise known as third-generation programming languages, due to their refined programming structures, using abstract statements.

Honeypots
Systems that entice with the goal of protecting critical production systems. If two or more honeypots are used together, this is considered a honeynet.

Hot site
Fully configured with hardware, software, and environmental needs. It can usually be up and running in a matter of hours. It is the most expensive option, but some companies cannot be out of business longer than a day without very detrimental results.

HTTPS
A combination of HTTP and SSL/TLS that is commonly used for secure Internet connections and e-commerce transactions.

Hybrid cryptography
Combined use of symmetric and asymmetric algorithms where the symmetric key encrypts data and an asymmetric key encrypts the symmetric key.

Hybrid microkernel architecture
Combination of monolithic and microkernel architectures. The microkernel carries out critical operating system functionality, and the remaining functionality is carried out in a client/server model within kernel mode.

Hypervisor
Central program used to manage virtual machines (guests) within a simulated environment (host).

IEEE 802.1AE (MACSec)
Standard that specifies a set of protocols to meet the security requirements for protecting data traversing Ethernet LANs.

IEEE 802.1AR
Standard that specifies unique per-device identifiers (DevID) and the management and cryptographic binding of a device (router, switch, access point) to its identifiers.

Immunizer
Attaches code to the file or application, which would fool a virus into "thinking" it was already infected.

Information gathering
Usually the first step in an attacker's methodology, in which the information gathered may allow an attacker to infer additional information that can be used to compromise systems.

Information technology security evaluation criteria (ITSEC)
European standard used to assess the effectiveness of the security controls built into a system.

Initialization vectors (IVs)
Values that are used with algorithms to increase randomness for cryptographic functions.

Instruction set
Set of operations and commands that can be implemented by a particular processor (CPU).

Integrated services digital network (ISDN)
A circuit-switched telephone network system technology designed to allow digital transmission of voice and data over ordinary telephone copper wires.

Integrity
Accuracy and reliability of the information and systems are provided and any unauthorized modification is prevented.

International Data Encryption Algorithm (IDEA)
Block symmetric cipher that uses a 128-bit key and 64-bit block size.

Internet Control Message Protocol (ICMP)
A core protocol of the IP suite used to send status and error messages.

Internet Group Management Protocol (IGMP)
Used by systems and adjacent routers on IP networks to establish and maintain multicast group memberships.

Internet Message Access Protocol (IMAP)
A method of accessing electronic mail or
bulletin board messages that are kept on a
(possibly shared) mail server. IMAP permits
a client e-mail program to access remote
message stores as if they were local. For
example, e-mail stored on an IMAP server
can be manipulated from a desktop computer
at home, a workstation at the office, and a
notebook computer while traveling, without
the need to transfer messages of files back and
forth between these computers. IMAP can be
regarded as the next-generation POP.

Internet Protocol (IP)
Core protocol of the TCP/IP suite. Provides
packet construction, addressing, and routing
functionality.

**Internet Security Association and Key
Management Protocol (ISAKMP)**
Used to establish security associates and an
authentication framework in Internet connections. Commonly used by IKE for key
exchange.

Interpreters
Tools that convert code written in interpreted
languages to the machine-level format for
processing.

Interrupt
Software or hardware signal that indicates that
system resources (i.e., CPU) are needed for
instruction processing.

Interrupts
Values assigned to computer components
(hardware and software) to allow for efficient
computer resource time slicing.

**Intra-Site Automatic Tunnel Addressing
Protocol (ISATAP)**
An IPv6 transition mechanism meant to transmit IPv6 packets between dual-stack nodes on
top of an IPv4 network.

IPSec
Protocol suite used to protect IP traffic
through encryption and authentication. De
facto standard VPN protocol.

IPv6
IP version 6 is the successor to IP version 4
and provides 128-bit addressing, integrated
IPSec security protocol, simplified header
formats, and some automated configuration.

ISO/IEC 27000 series
Industry-recognized best practices for the
development and management of an information security management system.

ISO/IEC 27005
International standard for the implementation
of a risk management program that integrates
into an information security management
system (ISMS).

ITIL
Best practices for information technology
services management processes developed by
the United Kingdom's Office of Government
Commerce.

Java applets
Small components (applets) that provide various functionalities and are delivered to users
in the form of Java bytecode. Java applets can
run in a web browser using a Java Virtual
Machine (JVM). Java is platform independent; thus, Java applets can be executed by
browsers for many platforms.

Kerckhoffs' principle
Concept that an algorithm should be known and only the keys should be kept secret.

Kernel mode (supervisory state, privilege mode)
Mode that a CPU works within when carrying out more trusted process instructions. The process has access to more computer resources when working in kernel versus user mode.

Key
Sequence of bits that are used as instructions that govern the acts of cryptographic functions within an algorithm.

Key clustering
A weakness that would exist in a cryptosystem if two different keys would generate the same ciphertext from the same plaintext.

Key derivation functions (KDFs)
Generation of secret keys (subkeys) from an initial value (master key).

Keyspace
A range of possible values used to construct keys.

Keystream generator
Component of a stream algorithm that creates random values for encryption purposes.

Known-plaintext attack
Cryptanalysis attack where the attacker is assumed to have access to sets of corresponding plaintext and ciphertext.

Layered operating system architecture
Architecture that separates system functionality into hierarchical layers.

Limit registers
Ending of address space assigned to a process. Used to ensure a process does not make a request outside its assigned memory boundaries.

Linear cryptanalysis
Cryptanalysis method that uses the study of affine transformation approximation in encryption processes.

Link encryption
Technology that encrypts full packets (all headers and data payload) and is carried out without the sender's interaction.

Link-state routing protocol
A routing protocol used in packet-switching networks where each router constructs a map of the connectivity within the network and calculates the best logical paths, which form its routing table.

Logic bomb
Executes a program, or string of code, when a certain event happens or a date and time arrives.

Logical addresses
Indirect addressing used by processes within an operating system. The memory manager carries out logical-to-absolute address mapping.

Machine language
A set of instructions in binary format that the computer's processor can understand and work with directly.

Macro virus
A computer virus that spreads by binding itself to software such as Word or Excel.

Maintenance hooks
Code within software that provides a back door entry capability.

Mandatory vacation
Detective administrative control used to uncover potential fraudulent activities by requiring a person to be away from the organization for a period of time.

Maskable interrupt
Interrupt value assigned to a non-critical operating system activity.

Mean time between failures (MTBF)
The predicted amount of time between inherent failures of a system during operation.

Mean time to repair (MTTR)
A measurement of the maintainability by representing the average time required to repair a failed component or device.

Media access control (MAC)
Data communication protocol sub-layer of the data link layer specified in the OSI model. It provides hardware addressing and channel access control mechanisms that make it possible for several nodes to communicate within a multiple-access network that incorporates a shared medium.

Meet-in-the-middle attack
Cryptanalysis attack that tries to uncover a mathematical problem from two different ends.

Meme viruses
These are not actual computer viruses, but types of e-mail messages that are continually forwarded around the Internet.

Memory card
Holds information but cannot process information.

Mesh topology
Network where each system must not only capture and disseminate its own data, but also serve as a relay for other systems; that is, it must collaborate to propagate the data in the network.

Message authentication code (MAC)
Keyed cryptographic hash function used for data integrity and data origin authentication.

Metro Ethernet
A data link technology that is used as a metropolitan area network to connect customer networks to larger service networks or the Internet.

Metropolitan area network (MAN)
A data network intended to serve an area approximating that of a large city or college campus. Such networks are being implemented by innovative techniques, such as running fiber cables through subway tunnels.

Microarchitecture
Specific design of a microprocessor, which includes physical components (registers, logic gates, ALU, cache, etc.) that support a specific instruction set.

Microkernel architecture
Reduced amount of code running in kernel mode carrying out critical operating system functionality. Only the absolutely necessary code runs in kernel mode, and the remaining operating system code runs in user mode.

Mobile code
Code that can be transmitted across a network, to be executed by a system or device on the other end.

MODAF
Architecture framework used mainly in military support missions developed by the British Ministry of Defence.

Mode transition
When the CPU has to change from processing code in user mode to kernel mode.

Monolithic operating system architecture
All of the code of the operating system working in kernel mode in an ad-hoc and non-modularized manner.

Multilevel security policies
Outlines how a system can simultaneously process information at different classifications for users with different clearance levels.

Multipart virus
Also called a multipartite virus, this has several components to it and can be distributed to different parts of the system. It infects and spreads in multiple ways, which makes it harder to eradicate when identified.

Multiplexing
A method of combining multiple channels of data over a single transmission line.

Multiprogramming
Interleaved execution of more than one program (process) or task by a single operating system.

Multiprotocol label switching (MPLS)
A networking technology that directs data from one network node to the next based on short path labels rather than long network addresses, avoiding complex lookups in a routing table.

Multipurpose Internet mail extension (MIME)
The standard for multimedia mail contents in the Internet suite of protocols.

Multitasking
Simultaneous execution of more than one program (process) or task by a single operating system.

Multithreading
Applications that can carry out multiple activities simultaneously by generating different instruction sets (threads).

Natural languages
Otherwise known as fifth-generation programming languages, which have the goal to create software that can solve problems by themselves. Used in systems that provide artificial intelligence.

Network address translation (NAT)
The process of modifying IP address information in packet headers while in transit across a traffic routing device, with the goal of reducing the demand for public IP addresses.

Network convergence
The combining of server, storage, and network capabilities into a single framework, which decreases the costs and complexity of data centers. Converged infrastructures provide the ability to pool resources, automate resource provisioning, and increase and decrease processing capacity quickly to meet the needs of dynamic computing workloads.

NIST SP 800-30
Risk Management Guide for Information Technology Systems A U.S. federal standard that is focused on IT risks.

NIST SP 800-53
Set of controls that are used to secure U.S. federal systems developed by NIST.

Noise and perturbation
A technique of inserting bogus information in the hopes of misdirecting an attacker or confusing the matter enough that the actual attack will not be fruitful.

Non-maskable interrupt
Interrupt value assigned to a critical operating system activity.

Object
Can be a computer, database, file, computer program, directory, or field contained in a table within a database.

Object-oriented database
Designed to handle a variety of data (images, audio, documents, video), which is more dynamic in nature than a relational database.

Object-relational database (ORD)
Uses object-relational database management system (ORDBMS) and is a relational database with a software front end that is written in an object-oriented programming language.

One-time pad
A system that randomly generates a private key and is used only once to encrypt a message that is then decrypted by the receiver using a matching one-time pad and key. One-time pads have the advantage that there is theoretically no way to break the code by analyzing a succession of messages.

One-way hash
Cryptographic process that takes an arbitrary amount of data and generates a fixed-length value. Used for integrity protection.

Online Certificate Status Protocol (OCSP)
Automated method of maintaining revoked certificates within a PKI.

Open mail relay
An SMTP server configured in such a way that it allows anyone on the Internet to send e-mail through it, not just mail destined to or originating from known users.

Open system
Designs are built upon accepted standards to allow for interoperability.

Open Systems Interconnection (OSI) model
International standardization of system-based network communication through a modular seven-layer architecture.

Operationally critical threat, asset, and vulnerability evaluation (OCTAVE)
Team-oriented approach that assesses organizational and IT risks through facilitated workshops.

Out-of-band method
Sending data through an alternate communication channel.

Packages—EALs
Functional and assurance requirements are bundled into packages for reuse. This component describes what must be met to achieve specific EAL ratings.

Parallel test
One in which some systems are actually run at the alternate site.

Parameter validation
The values that are being received by the application are validated to be within defined limits before the server application processes them within the system.

Passive attack

Attack where the attacker does not interact with processing or communication activities, but only carries out observation and data collection, as in network sniffing.

Patent

Grants ownership and enables that owner to legally enforce his rights to exclude others from using the invention covered by the patent.

Personally identifiable information (PII)

Data that can be used to uniquely identify, contact, or locate a single person or can be used with other sources to uniquely identify a single individual.

Phishing

Phishing is a scam in which the perpetrator sends out legitimate-looking e-mails, in an effort to phish (pronounced fish) for personal and financial information from the recipient.

Ping of death

A DoS attack type on a computer that involves sending malformed or oversized ICMP packets to a target.

Plaintext

A message before it has been encrypted or after it has been decrypted using a specific algorithm and key; also referred to as cleartext. (Contrast with ciphertext.)

Plenum cables

Cable is jacketed with a fire-retardant plastic cover that does not release toxic chemicals when burned.

Policy

High-level document that outlines senior management's security directives.

Polymorphic virus

Produces varied but operational copies of itself. A polymorphic virus may have no parts that remain identical between infections, making it very difficult to detect directly using signatures.

Polymorphism

Two objects can receive the same input and have different outputs.

Ports

Software construct that allows for application- or service-specific communication between systems on a network. Ports are broken down into categories: well known (0–1023), registered (1024–49151), and dynamic (49152–65535).

Post Office Protocol (POP)

An Internet standard protocol used by e-mail clients to retrieve e-mail from a remote server and supports simple download-and-delete requirements for access to remote mailboxes.

Preemptive multitasking

Multitasking scheduling scheme used by operating systems to allow for computer resource time slicing. Used in newer, more stable operating systems.

Pretty good privacy (PGP) cryptosystem

used to integrate public key cryptography with e-mail functionality and data encryption, which was developed by Phil Zimmerman.

Primary key

Columns that make each row unique. (Every row of a table must include a primary key.)

Private branch exchange (PBX)
A small version of the phone company's central switching office. Also known as a private automatic branch exchange. A central telecommunications switching station that an organization uses for its own purposes.

Private key
Value used in public key cryptography that is used for decryption and signature creation and known to only key owner.

Procedures
Step-by-step implementation instructions.

Process
Program loaded in memory within an operating system.

Process isolation
Protection mechanism provided by operating systems that can be implemented as encapsulation, time multiplexing of shared resources, naming distinctions, and virtual memory mapping.

Process states (ready, running, blocked)
Processes can be in various activity levels. Ready = waiting for input. Running = instructions being executed by CPU. Blocked = process is "suspended."

Program counter
Holds the memory address for the following instructions the CPU needs to act upon.

Program status word (PSW)
Condition variable that indicates to the CPU what mode (kernel or user) instructions need to be carried out in.

Protection profile
Description of a needed security solution.

Proxy server
A system that acts as an intermediary for requests from clients seeking resources from other sources. A client connects to the proxy server, requesting some service, and the proxy server evaluates the request according to its filtering rules and makes the connection on behalf of the client. Proxies can be open or carry out forwarding or reverse forwarding capabilities.

Public key
Value used in public key cryptography that is used for encryption and signature validation that can be known by all parties.

Public key cryptography
An asymmetric cryptosystem where the encrypting and decrypting keys are different and it is computationally infeasible to calculate one form the other, given the encrypting algorithm. In public key cryptography, the encrypting key is made public, but the decrypting key is kept secret.

Public-switched telephone network (PSTN)
The public circuit-switched telephone network, which is made up of telephone lines, fiber-optic cables, cellular networks, communications satellites, and undersea telephone cables and allows all phone-to-phone communication. It was a fixed-line analog telephone system, but is now almost entirely digital and includes mobile as well as fixed telephones.

Qualitative risk analysis
Opinion-based method of analyzing risk with the use of scenarios and ratings.

Quantitative risk analysis
Assigning monetary and numeric values to all the data elements of a risk assessment.

Quantum cryptography
Use of quantum mechanical functions to provide strong cryptographic key exchange.

Race condition
Two or more processes attempt to carry out their activity on one resource at the same time. Unexpected behavior can result if the sequence of execution does not take place in the proper order.

RAM
Hardware inside a computer that retains memory on a short-term basis and stores information while the computer is in use.

- It is the working memory of the computer into which the operating system, startup applications, and drivers are loaded when a computer is turned on, or where a program subsequently started up is loaded, and where thereafter, these applications are executed.

- RAM can be read or written in any section with one instruction sequence. It helps to have more of this working space installed when running advanced operating systems and applications. RAM content is erased each time a computer is turned off. RAM is the most common type of memory found in computers and other devices, such as printers. There are two basic types of RAM: dynamic RAM (DRAM) and static RAM (SRAM).

Random number generator
Algorithm used to create values that are used in cryptographic functions to add randomness.

RC4
Stream symmetric cipher that was created by Ron Rivest of RSA. Used in SSL and WEP.

RC5
Block symmetric cipher that uses variable block sizes (32, 64, 128) and variable-length key sizes (0–2040).

RC6
Block symmetric cipher that uses a 128-bit block size and variable length key sizes (128, 192, 256). Built upon the RC5 algorithm.

Real-time Transport Protocol (RTP)
Used to transmit audio and video over IP-based networks. It is used in conjunction with the RTCP. RTP transmits the media data, and RTCP is used to monitor transmission statistics and QoS, and aids synchronization of multiple data streams.

Reciprocal agreement
One in which a company promises another company it can move in and share space if it experiences a disaster, and vice versa. Reciprocal agreements are very tricky to implement and are unenforceable.

Record
A collection of related data items.

Recovery point objective (RPO)
A measurement of the point prior to an outage to which data are to be restored.

Recovery time objective (RTO)
The earliest time period and a service level within which a business process must be restored after a disaster to avoid unacceptable consequences.

Reference monitor
Concept that defines a set of design requirements of a reference validation mechanism (security kernel), which enforces an access control policy over subject's (processes, users) ability to perform operations (read, write, execute) on objects (files, resources) on a system.

Register
Small, temporary memory storage units integrated and used by the CPU during its processing functions.

Registration authority (RA)
The primary purpose of an RA is to verify an end entity's identity and determine whether it is entitled to have a public key certificate issued.

Relational database model
In a relational database, data is organized in two-dimensional tables or relations.

Remote access Trojans (RATs)
Malicious programs that run on systems and allow intruders to access and use a system remotely.

Remote authentication dial-in user service (RADIUS)
A network protocol that provides client/server authentication and authorization, and audits remote users.

Remote journaling
Involves transmitting the journal or transaction log offsite to a backup facility.

Replay attack
This type of attack occurs when an attacker intercepts authentication information through the use of network monitoring utilities. The attacker then "replays" this information to the security system in an effort to gain access to the system.

Residual risk
Risk that remains after implementing a control. Threats × vulnerabilities × assets × (control gap) = residual risk.

Restricted interface
Limits the user's environment within the system, thus limiting access to objects.

Rijndael
Block symmetric cipher that was chosen to fulfil the Advanced Encryption Standard. It uses a 128-bit block size and various key lengths (128, 192, 256).

Ring topology
Each system connects to two other systems, forming a single, unidirectional network pathway for signals, thus forming a ring.

Risk
The probability of a threat agent exploiting a vulnerability and the associated impact.

Rollback
An operation that ends a current transaction and cancels all the recent changes to the database until the previous checkpoint/ commit point.

ROM
Computer memory chips with preprogrammed circuits for storing such software as word processors and spreadsheets. Information in the computer's ROM is permanently maintained even when the computer is turned off.

Rootkit

Set of malicious tools that are loaded on a compromised system through stealthy techniques. The tools are used to carry out more attacks on either the infected systems or surrounding systems.

Rotation of duties

Detective administrative control used to uncover potential fraudulent activities.

Rule-based access

Access is based on a list of rules created or authorized by system owners that specify the privileges granted to users.

Running key cipher

Substitution cipher that creates keystream values, commonly from agreed-upon text passages, to be used for encryption purposes.

SABSA

Framework risk-driven enterprise security architecture that maps to business initiatives, similar to the Zachman framework.

Sandbox

A virtual environment that allows for very fine-grained control over the actions that code within the machine is permitted to take. This is designed to allow safe execution of untrusted code from remote sources.

Schema

Defines the structure of the database.

Screened host

A firewall that communicates directly with a perimeter router and the internal network. The router carries out filtering activities on the traffic before it reaches the firewall.

Screened subnet architecture

When two filtering devices are used to create a DMZ. The external device screens the traffic entering the DMZ network, and the internal filtering device screens the traffic before it enters the internal network.

Scytale cipher

A simple transposition cipher system that employs a rod of a certain thickness around which was wrapped a long, thin strip of parchment.

Secure electronic transaction (SET)

The SET specification has been developed by Visa and MasterCard to allow for secure credit card and offline debit card (check card) transactions over the World Wide Web.

Secure MIME (S/MIME)

Secure/Multipurpose Internet Mail Extensions, which outlines how public key cryptography can be used to secure MIME data types.

Secure Shell (SSH)

Network protocol that allows for a secure connection to a remote system. Developed to replace Telnet and other insecure remote shell methods.

Security assertion markup language (SAML)

An XML standard that allows the exchange of authentication and authorization data to be shared between security domains.

Security assurance requirements

Measures taken during development and evaluation of the product to assure compliance with the claimed security functionality.

Security domain

Resources within this logical structure (domain) are working under the same security policy and managed by the same group.

Security functional requirements

Individual security functions which must be provided by a product.

Security kernel

The central part of a computer system (hardware, software, or firmware) that implements the fundamental security procedures for controlling access to system resources.

Security perimeter

Mechanism used to delineate between the components within and outside of the trusted computing base.

Security policy

Strategic tool used to dictate how sensitive information and resources are to be managed and protected.

Security target

Vendor's written explanation of the security functionality and assurance mechanisms that meet the needed security solution.

Security through obscurity

Relying upon the secrecy or complexity of an item as its security, instead of practicing solid security practices.

Self-garbling virus

Attempts to hide from antivirus software by modifying its own code so that it does not match predefined signatures.

Sender policy framework (SPF)

An e-mail validation system designed to prevent e-mail spam by detecting e-mail spoofing, a common vulnerability, by verifying sender IP addresses.

Separation of duties

Preventive administrative control used to ensure one person cannot carry out a critical task alone.

Server-side includes (SSI)

An interpreted server-side scripting language used almost exclusively for web-based communication. It is commonly used to include the contents of one or more files into a web page on a web server. Allows web developers to reuse content by inserting the same content into multiple web documents.

Service provisioning markup language (SPML)

Allows for the automation of user management (account creation, amendments, revocation) and access entitlement configuration related to electronically published services across multiple provisioning systems.

Session hijacking

An intruder takes over a connection after the original source has been authenticated.

Session Initiation Protocol (SIP)

The signaling protocol widely used for controlling communication, as in voice and video calls over IP based networks.

Session keys

Symmetric keys that have a short lifespan, thus providing more protection than static keys with longer lifespans.

Shielded twisted pair (STP)
Twisted-pair cables are often shielded in an attempt to prevent RFI and EMI. This shielding can be applied to individual pairs or to the collection of pairs.

Shoulder surfing
Viewing information in an unauthorized manner by looking over the shoulder of someone else.

Side-channel attack
Non-intrusive attack that uses information (timing, power consumption) that has been gathered to uncover sensitive data or processing functions. Often tries to figure out how a component works without trying to compromise any type of flaw or weakness.

Simple Mail Transfer Protocol (SMTP)
An Internet standard protocol for electronic mail (e-mail) transmission across IP-based networks.

Simple Network Management Protocol (SNMP)
Provides remote administration of network device; simple because the agent requires minimal software.

Simple Object Access Protocol (SOAP)
A lightweight protocol for exchange of information in a decentralized, distributed environment.

Simulation test
A practice execution of the plan takes place. A specific scenario is established, and the simulation continues up to the point of actual relocation to the alternate site.

Single loss expectancy (SLE)
One instance of an expected loss if a specific vulnerability is exploited and how it affects a single asset. Asset Value × Exposure Factor = SLE.

Six Sigma
Business management strategy developed by Motorola with the goal of improving business processes.

Smart card
Plastic cards, typically with an electronic chip embedded, that contain electronic value tokens. Such value is disposable at both physical retail outlets and online shopping locations.

Smurf attack
A DDoS attack type on a computer that floods the target system with spoofed broadcast ICMP packets.

Social engineering
Gaining unauthorized access by tricking someone into divulging sensitive information.

Social engineering attack
Manipulating individuals so that they will divulge confidential information, rather than by breaking in or using technical cracking techniques.

Software configuration management (SCM)
Identifies the attributes of software at various points in time, and performs a methodical control of changes for the purpose of maintaining software integrity and traceability throughout the software development life cycle.

Software deadlock

Two processes cannot complete their activities because they are both waiting for system resources to be released.

Software escrow

Storing of the source code of software with a third-party escrow agent. The software source code is released to the licensee if the licensor (software vendor) files for bankruptcy or fails to maintain and update the software product as promised in the software license agreement.

Source routing

Allows a sender of a packet to specify the route the packet takes through the network versus routers determining the path.

Spanning Tree Protocol (STP)

A network protocol that ensures a loop-free topology for any bridged Ethernet LAN and allows redundant links to be available in case connection links go down.

Special registers

Temporary memory location that holds critical processing parameters. They hold values as in the program counter, stack pointer, and program status word.

Stack memory

Construct that is made up of individually addressable buffers. Process-to-process communication takes place through the use of stacks.

Standard

Compulsory rules that support the security policies.

Star topology

Network consists of one central device, which acts as a conduit to transmit messages. The central device, to which all other nodes are connected, provides a common connection point for all nodes.

Statement of Work (SOW)

Describes the product and customer requirements. A detailed-oriented SOW will help ensure that these requirements are properly understood and assumptions are not made.

Static analysis

A debugging technique that is carried out by examining the code without executing the program, and therefore is carried out before the program is compiled.

Statistical attack

Cryptanalysis attack that uses identified statistical patterns.

Statistical time-division multiplexing (STDM)

This form of multiplexing uses all available time slots to send significant information and handles inbound data on a first-come, first-served basis.

Stealth virus

A virus that hides the modifications it has made. The virus tries to trick antivirus software by intercepting its requests to the operating system and providing false and bogus information.

Steganography

(1) The method of concealing the existence of a message or data within seemingly innocent covers. (2) A technology used to embed information in for example, audio and graphical material. The audio and graphical materials appear unaltered until a steganography tool is used to reveal the hidden message.

Stream cipher

An encryption method in which a cryptographic key and an algorithm are applied to each bit in a datastream, one bit at a time.

Structured walk-through test

Representatives from each functional area or department get together and walk through the plan from beginning to end.

Subject

An active entity that requests access to an object or the data within an object.

Subnet

Logical subdivision of a network that improves network administration and helps reduce network traffic congestion. Process of segmenting a network into smaller networks through the use of an addressing scheme made up of network and host portions.

Substitution cipher

Encryption method that uses an algorithm that changes out (substitutes) one value for another value.

Symmetric algorithm

Encryption method where the sender and receiver use an instance of the same key for encryption and decryption purposes.

Symmetric mode multiprocessing

When a computer has two or more CPUs and each CPU is being used in a load-balancing method.

SYN flood

DoS attack where an attacker sends a succession of SYN packets with the goal of overwhelming the victim system so that it is unresponsive to legitimate traffic.

Synchronous communication

Transmission sequencing technology that uses a clocking pulse or timing scheme for data transfer synchronization.

Synchronous optical networking (SONET) and synchronous digital hierarchy (SDH)

Standardized multiplexing protocols that transfer multiple digital bit streams over optical fiber and allow for simultaneous transportation of many different circuits of differing origin within a single framing protocol.

Synchronous token device

Synchronizes with the authentication service by using time or a counter as the core piece of the authentication process. If the synchronization is time-based, the token device and the authentication service must hold the same time within their internal clocks.

System development life cycle (SDLC)

The scope of activities associated with a system, encompassing the system's initiation, development and acquisition, implementation, operation and maintenance, and, ultimately, its disposal, which instigates another system initiation.

Target of evaluation (TOE)

Product proposed to provide a needed security solution.

T-carriers

Dedicated lines that can carry voice and data information over trunk lines.

TCP/IP model

Standardization of device-based network communication through a modular four-layer architecture. Specific to the IP suite, created in 1970 by an agency of the U.S. Department of Defense (DoD).

Teredo

Transition mechanism for migrating from IPv4 to IPv6. It allows systems to use IPv6 to communicate if their traffic has to transverse an IPv4 network, but also performs its function behind NAT devices.

Thread

Instruction set generated by a process when it has a specific activity that needs to be carried out by an operating system. When the activity is finished, the thread is destroyed.

Threat

The danger of a threat agent exploiting a vulnerability.

Threat agent

Entity that can exploit a vulnerability.

Threat modeling

A systematic approach used to understand how different threats could be realized and how a successful compromise could take place.

Time multiplexing

Technology that allows processes to use the same resources.

Time-division multiplexing (TDM)

A type of multiplexing in which two or more bit streams or signals are transferred apparently simultaneously as sub-channels in one communication channel, but are physically taking turns on the single channel.

Time-of-check/time-of-use (TOC/TOU) attack

Attacker manipulates the "condition check" step and the "use" step within software to allow for unauthorized activity.

TOGAF

Enterprise architecture framework used to define and understand a business environment developed by The Open Group.

Token ring

LAN medium access technology that controls network communication traffic through the use of token frames. This technology has been mostly replaced by Ethernet.

Total risk

Full risk amount before a control is put into place. Threats × vulnerabilities × assets = total risk.

Trade secrets

Proprietary business or technical information, processes, designs, practices, etc., that are confidential and critical to the business.

Trademark

Protect words, names, product shapes, symbols, colors, or a combination of these used to identify products or a company. These items are used to distinguish products from the competitors' products.

Transmission Control Protocol (TCP)

The major transport protocol in the Internet suite of protocols providing reliable, connection-oriented, full-duplex streams.

Transport mode

Mode that IPSec protocols can work in that provides protection for packet data payload.

Transposition

Encryption method that shifts (permutation) values.

Triple DES (3-DES)
Symmetric cipher that applies DES three times to each block of data during the encryption process.

Trojan horse
A program that is disguised as another program with the goal of carrying out malicious activities in the background without the user knowing.

Trusted Computer System Evaluation Criteria (TCSEC)
U.S. DoD standard used to assess the effectiveness of the security controls built into a system. Replaced by the Common Criteria. Also known as the Orange Book.

Trusted computing base (TCB)
A collection of all the hardware, software, and firmware components within a system that provide security and enforce the system's security policy.

Trusted path
Trustworthy software channel that is used for communication between two processes that cannot be circumvented.

Tunnel mode
Mode that IPSec protocols can work in that provides protection for packet headers and data payload.

Tuple
A row in a two-dimensional database.

Two-phase commit
A mechanism that is another control used in databases to ensure the integrity of the data held within the database.

Type I error
When a biometric system rejects an authorized individual (false rejection rate).

Type II error
When the system accepts impostors who should be rejected (false acceptance rate).

Uncertainty analysis
Assigning confidence level values to data elements.

Unshielded twisted pair (UTP)
Cabling in which copper wires are twisted together for the purposes of canceling out EMI from external sources. UTP cables are found in many Ethernet networks and telephone systems.

User Datagram Protocol (UDP)
Connectionless, unreliable transport layer protocol, which is considered a "best effort" protocol.

User mode (problem state)
Protection mode that a CPU works within when carrying out less trusted process instructions.

User provisioning
The creation, maintenance, and deactivation of user objects and attributes as they exist in one or more systems, directories, or applications, in response to business processes.

Validation
Determines if the product provides the necessary solution for the intended real-world problem.

Verification
Determines if the product accurately represents and meets the specifications.

Very high-level languages

Otherwise known as fourth-generation programming languages and are meant to take natural language-based statements one step ahead.

View

A virtual relation defined by the database administrator in order to keep subjects from viewing certain data.

Virtual local area network (VLAN)

A group of hosts that communicate as if they were attached to the same broadcast domain, regardless of their physical location. VLAN membership can be configured through software instead of physically relocating devices or connections, which allows for easier centralized management.

Virtual memory

Combination of main memory (RAM) and secondary memory within an operating system.

Virtualization

Creation of a simulated environment (hardware platform, operating system, storage, etc.) that allows for central control and scalability.

Virus

A small application, or string of code, that infects host applications. It is a programming code that can replicate itself and spread from one system to another.

Vishing (voice and phishing)

Social engineering activity over the telephone system, most often using features facilitated by VoIP, to gain unauthorized access to sensitive data.

VLAN hopping

An exploit that allows an attacker on a VLAN to gain access to traffic on other VLANs that would normally not be accessible.

Voice over IP (VoIP)

The set of protocols, technologies, methodologies, and transmission techniques involved in the delivery of voice data and multimedia sessions over IP-based networks.

Vulnerability

Weakness or a lack of a countermeasure.

War dialing

When a specialized program is used to automatically scan a list of telephone numbers to search for computers for the purposes of exploitation and hacking.

Warm site

Does not have computers, but it does have some peripheral devices, such as disk drives, controllers, and tape drives. This option is less expensive than a hot site but takes more effort and time to become operational.

Wave-division multiplexing (WDM)

Multiplying the available capacity of optical fibers through use of parallel channels, with each channel on a dedicated wavelength of light. The bandwidth of an optical fiber can be divided into as many as 160 channels.

Web proxy

A piece of software installed on a system that is designed to intercept all traffic between the local web browser and the web server.

Wide area network (WAN)

A telecommunication network that covers a broad area and allows a business to effectively carry out its daily function, regardless of location.

Wiretapping

A passive attack that eavesdrops on communications. It is only legal with prior consent or a warrant.

Work breakdown structure (WBS)

A project management tool used to define and group a project's individual work elements in an organized manner.

Wormhole attack

This takes place when an attacker captures packets at one location in the network and tunnels them to another location in the network for a second attacker to use against a target system.

Worms

These are different from viruses in that they can reproduce on their own without a host application and are self-contained programs.

Zachman framework

Enterprise architecture framework used to define and understand a business environment developed by John Zachman.

Zero knowledge proof

One entity can prove something to be true without providing a secret value.

Index

Numbers

3-DES (triple DES), 869
6to4, 842

A

AAFS (American Academy of Forensic
  Sciences), 310
ABAC (attribute-based access control),
  22–23
absolute addresses, 842
abstraction, 842
acceptable use documentation, 207
accepted ways for handling risk, 842
access, 842
    ABAC (attribute-based access control),
      22–23
    definition, 4
access control matrix, 842
    Bell-LaPadula model, 23
access control model, 842
access controls, 1
    access, 4
    DAC (discretionary access control), 11
        policy implementation, 12
        RSBAC, 12–14
    definition, 842
    logical, 120
    MAC (Mandatory Access Control),
      21–22
    managerial, 121–122
        guidelines, 124–127
        policy documents, 122–123
        policy lifecycle, 123–124

    procedures, 127–130
    standards, 124–127
matrix, 12
NDAC (non-discretionary access
  control), 21
objects, 3–4, 9
operational, 121
public, 120–121
role-based, 14–18
    CBAC, 19–20
    CUI, 18–19
    TRBAC, 20–21
subjects, 3–5
accreditation, 842
ACL (access control list), 12, 13
acoustic sensors, 148
ACPO (Association of Chief Police Offers),
  310
acquisition lifecycle, 95
active attack, 842
ActiveX, 842
address bus, 842
addressing
    absolute addresses, 842
    IP and, 452
    logical addresses, 855
ADDS (Active Directory Directory
  Service), 53
ad-hoc mode, 559
adware, 596–598
    botnets, 637
AES (Advanced Encryption Standard)
    CCMP, 370–371
    Rijndael, 371–374

Agile, 100
AH (authentication header) protocol, 414, 843
air contamination, 174–175
ALE (Annualized Loss Expectancy), 843
algebraic attacks, 386, 842
algorithms
    asymmetric, 843
    definition, 842
    Diffie-Hellman, 850
    El Gamal, 851
    elliptic curve cryptosystem, 851
    encryption, 349, 355–356
    Rijndael, 862
    symmetric, 867
ALU (Arithmetic Logic Unit), 843
analog signals, 842
analytic attack, 842
annual audits, 204
anti-collision protocol (RFID), 32
anti-malware systems, incident response and, 300
anti-spam software, incident response and, 297
anti-virus software, incident response and, 297
API (Application Programming Interface), 843
application layer (OSI)
    protocols, 457–459
    web-based layer, 654–655
Application Whitelisting, 692–693
application-level proxies, 537
applications, 4
    access control and, 9
    virtualization, 703
APTs (advanced persistent threats) attacks, 639–641
architecture. *See also* system architecture
    Bell-LaPadula model, 23–24
    Biba model, 24–26
    Brewer-Nash model, 26
    Chinese Wall model, 26
    Clark-Wilson model, 25–26
    design, 82
        accountability, 88
        authorization, 88
        controls, 89–95
        defense-in-depth, 83–85
        documentation, 89–95
        least privilege, 86–87

        risk-based controls, 85–86
        separation of duties, 88–89
    Graham-Denning model, 26–27
    Harrison-Ruzzo-Ullman model, 27
    trust architecture
        DMZ, 60–61
        extranets, 60
        Internet, 59–60
        intranets, 60
archiving procedures, 731–732
ARP (Address Resolution Protocol), 842
ArpScan, 650–651
ASLR (Address Space Layout Randomization), 842
AS/NZS 4360, 843
assemblers, 843
assembly language, 843
assurance evaluation criteria, 843
asymmetric algorithm, 843
asymmetric cryptography, 376
    algorithms, 377
    confidential messages, 377, 378–379
    Diffie-Hellman, 380
    ECC (Elliptic Curve Cryptography), 380–381
    El Gamal, 380
    open messages, 377–378
    RSA, 380
asymmetric encryption, 348
asymmetric key encryption, 355–356
asymmetric mode multiprocessing, 843
asynchronous communication, 843
asynchronous encryption, 347
asynchronous password tokens, 48
asynchronous token generating method, 843
asynchronous tokens, 31–32
attacks
    active, 842
    algebraic, 842
    analytic, 842
    birthday, 844
    chosen-ciphertext, 846
    chosen-plaintext, 846
    ciphertext-only, 846
    Create or Import a CodeSigning Certificate, 618

confidentiality, 77–78, 847
confusion, 847
contactless card readers, 30–31
containment, incident response and, 306–307
content-based access, 847
context-based access, 847
continuous authentication, 50
continuous monitoring, 248–249
control functions, 848
control types, 848
control units, 848
controls, 848
    design, 89–93
    functionality *versus* effectiveness, 852
    operational, 90
    preventive, 90–91
    recovery, 90–91
    technical, 90
        audit trails, 121
        authentication, 119–120
        identification, 119–120
        logical, 120
        public access, 120–121
    validation, 132
converged communications, 496–497
    FCoE (Fibre Channel over Ethernet), 497–498
    iSCSI (Internet Small Computer System Interface), 498
    MPLS (Multi-Protocol Label Switching), 498–499
cookies, 848
cooperative multitasking, 848
copyright, 848
corrective controls, 90–91
COSO (Committee of Sponsoring Organizations), 848
cost/benefit analysis, 848
COTTONMOUTH, 629
coupling, 848
CPU (central processing unit), 845
CRAMM (CCTA Risk Analysis and Management Method), 848
Create files/write data permission, 6
Create folders/append data permission, 6
Create or Import a CodeSigning Certificate, 618

Credential Harvester Attack Method, 618, 619
CRL (certificate revocation list), 846
cross-referencing malcode names, 585–590
crosstalk, 848
cryptanalysis, 349, 359, 848
    differential, 386, 850
    linear, 386, 855
cryptanalytic attacks
    algebraic, 386
    birthday, 388
    brute force, 385–386
    ciphertext, chosen, 387–388
    ciphertext-only, 387
    dictionary, 388
    differential cryptanalysis, 386
    factoring, 388
    frequency analysis, 387
    implementation attacks, 389
    linear cryptanalysis, 386
    plaintext, 385, 387
    rainbow tables, 386–387
    random number generators, 389
    replay, 388
    reverse engineering, 389
    social engineering, 385
    temporary files, 389
cryptogram, 348
cryptography, 849. *See also* encryption
    asymmetric, 376
        algorithms, 377
        confidential messages, 377, 378–379
        Diffie-Hellman, 380
        ECC, 380–381
        El Gamal, 380
        open messages, 377–378
        RSA, 380
    digital signatures, 383–384
    exercise, 417–439
    hash functions, 357
        attacks, 359–360
        HAVAL, 358
        MD (Message Digest) 2, 4, and 5, 358
        RIPEMD-160, 359
        SHA (Secure Hash Algorithm) 0, 1, and 2, 358
    HMAC, 383

data warehousing, 849
data wiping, 115
databases, 849
    encryption, 108–109, 724
Davis, Michael, 76
DBMS (database management system), 849
DCB (Data Center Bridging) standards, 497
    DCBX (DCB Exchange Protocol), 497
    ETS (Enhanced Transmission Selection), 497
    PFC (Priority-based Flow Control), 497
    QCN (Quantized Congestion Notification), 497
DDoS (Distributed Denial-of-Service), 481, 548–550
    attacks, botnets, 636–637
decipher, 849
decoding, encryption, 349
decryption, 349, 361
defense-in-depth design, 849
degaussing, 115–117
degraded performance, 657
Delete permission, 6
deleting data, 730–731
Delphi method, 850
DEP (Data Execution Prevention), 849
DES (Data Encryption Standard), 355
    3DES, 369–370
    advantages, 367
    block cipher modes, 362–363
    disadvantages, 367
    double DES, 367–368
    meet-in-the-middle, 368–369
    stream modes, 364–367
    symmetric cryptography, 361–370
design
    architecture, 82
        accountability, 88
        authorization, 88
        controls, 89–95
        defense-in-depth, 83–85
        documentation, 89–95
        least privilege, 86–87
        risk-based controls, 85–86
        separation of duties, 88–89
    detailed design, 97

general design document, 97
    release management, 130–132
desktop virtualization, 703
detective controls, 90–91
deterministic routing, 504
deterrent controls, 90–91
development, 95
    Agile, 100
    component development, 101
    component reuse, 101
    extreme programming, 100
    RAD (Rapid Application Development), 100
    spiral model, 100
    waterfall model, 96–99
devices
    endpoint security
        Application Whitelisting, 692–693
        encryption, 693
        HIDS, 691–692
        host-based firewalls, 692
        MDM, 694–695
        secure browsing, 695–696
        trusted platform module, 693–694
    forensics and, 317–318
    peripheral device recognition, 59
    synchronous token devices, 867
DFRWS (Digital Forensic Science Research Workshop), 310
DHCP (Dynamic Host Configuration protocol), 464–465, 850
dictionary attack, 388
differential backups, 334–335
differential cryptanalysis, 386, 850
Diffie-Hellman algorithm, 850
diffusion, 850
digital certificates, 348
digital signals, 850
digital signatures, 348, 383–384, 850
DIM (Data in Motion), 717–718
directive controls, 90–91
disaster recovery, 326–330
disaster/business recovery documentation, 207
disk wiping, 115
distance-vector routing protocol, 850
DIT (Directory Information Tree), 53

ciphertext, 348
cleartext, 348
cloud computing and, 719–729
collisions, 349
confusion, 350
cryptanalysis, 349
cryptogram, 348
cryptology, 349
cryptosystem, 348
cryptovariables, 349
databases, 108–109
decoding, 349
decryption, 349, 361
definition, 348
DES (Data Encryption Standard), 355
diffusion, 350
digital certificates, 348
digital signatures, 348
encoding, 349
endpoint, 693
end-to-end, 851
exercise, 417–439
hash functions, 347–348, 357–360
IV (initialization vector), 349
keys, 110–112, 349, 724–725
    asymmetric, 348
    automated generation, 404
    certificate replacement, 412
    certificate revocation, 412
    clustering, 347
    destruction, 409–411
    distribution, 408–409
    duties, 401–404
    escrow, 413
    financial institutions, 401
    key encrypting keys, 407–408
    length, 406–407
    management, 397–401
    public, 355–356
    randomness, 404–406
    recovery, 412–413
    space, 349
    storage, 409–411
    web of trust, 413
    wrapping, 407–408
    X-KISS, 398
    XKMS, 398
    X-KRSS, 398
KIMP (Key Management Interoperability Protocol), 724–726
link, 855
nonrepuidation, 349, 384–385
permutation, 350
plaintext, 348
public key, 860
RA (registration authority), 348
RC2, 356
RC6, 356
SP-network, 350
stream-based ciphers, 351–352
substitution, 350
synchronous, 347
transposition, 350
vulnerabilities and, 103–104
work fact, 349
work factor, 350–351
endpoint security, 513
    devices, 691–696
    encryption, 693
end-to-end encryption, 851
entrance facility security, 166–167
environment conditions (ABAC), 23
equipment room security, 167
eradication, incident response and, 307
erasing data, 114–115
error handling, vulnerabilities and, 104
escort control, 151–152
ESMTP (Enhanced Simple Mail Transfer Protocol), 486–487
ESP (encapsulating security payload), 414, 851
Ethernet, 475–476, 851, 856
event data analysis, 261–264
event triggered audits, 204
events
    analysis, 736–738
    logging, 735–736
    storage, 736–738
exit interview, security audit, 208
exploitation frameworks, 645
exposure, 851
extranets, 60, 463–464
extreme programming, 100
eye features (biometrics), 40–43

F

facial recognition, 44–45
factoring attacks, 388
fault tree analysis, 851
FC (Function Control module), 13
FCoE (Fibre Channel over Ethernet), 497–498
FCP (Fiber Channel Protocol), 456
FDDI (Fiber Distributed Data Interface), 476, 851
FDM (Frequency-Division Multiplexing), 852
FDMA (Frequency Division Multiple Access), 558
federated identity, 851
FEEDTROUGH, 629
FF (File Flag module), 13
fiber optic cabling, 512–513
Fieldbus protocol, 496
file extensions, malcode and, 619–622
file infectors, 594
file integrity checkers, 248
    incident response and, 297
files definition, 851
FIN scanning, 538
fingerprint verification, 36–38
fire detection, 175–176
fire suppression, 176–177
Firewalk, 466
firewalls, 534–535
    dual-homed, 850
    dynamic packet filtering, 536
    filtering, 535
    host-based, 692
    NAT (Network Address Translation), 535
    PAT (Port Address Translation), 535
    personal, 536
    stateful inspection, 536
    static packet filtering, 536
    tunneling, 517
FIRST (Forum of Incident Response Teams), 318
FMEA (Failure Modes and Effect Analysis), 851
foreign keys, 851
forensics (incident response), 309–311
    AAFS, 310

ACPO, 310
    crime scenes, 311–312
    DFRWS, 310
    embedded device analysis, 317–318
    evidence gathering, 313–315
    evidence identification, 310
    findings, 311
    guidelines, 312–313
    hardware analysis, 317–318
    IOCE, 310
    network analysis, 316
    procedures, 315
    software analysis, 316–317
    SWGDE, 310, 312
FQDN (fully qualified domain name), 478
fraggle attack, 851
fragmentation, IP and, 452
FRAP (Facilitated Risk Analysis Process), 851
frequency analysis, 852
front-end processors, 508
FTP (File Transfer Protocol), 83, 487–488
full backups, 334–335
Full Control permission, 6
full interruption testing, recovery plan, 332–333
full-interruption test, 852
functionality *versus* effectiveness of control, 852
fuzzing, 852
FVC-onGoing (fingerprint recognition), 37–38

G

garbage collectors, 852
gateway testing, 221
general registers, 852
generator power, 172
geometry recognition, 38–39
Graham-Denning model, 26–27
grey box testing, 225
guidelines, 852

H

H.245 (Call Control Protocol for Multimedia Communication), 457
H.323, 852
HAIPE (High Assurance Internet Protocol Encryptor), 416

immunizers, 853
implementation attacks, 389
incident response, 243
    analysis, 301–304
    anti-malware systems and, 300
    communication
        law enforcement, 292–293
        media and, 291–292
        official organizations/agencies, 293
        planning, 291–293
        public relations and, 291–292
    containment, 304, 306–307
    countermeasures implementation,
      308–309
    detection, 296–300
    eradication, 307
    forensics, 304
        crime scenes, 311–312
        embedded device analysis, 317–318
        evidence gathering, 313–315
        evidence identification, 310
        findings, 311
        guidelines, 312–313
        hardware analysis, 317–318
        investigations, 309–318
        media analysis, 315–316
        network analysis, 316
        procedures, 315
        software analysis, 316–317
    IDSes and, 299
    indicators, 297–299
    IPSs and, 299
    NIST guidelines, 288
        team, 294
    NVD (National Vulnerability Database),
      298
    phases, 287–288
    policies, 289–290
    precursors, 297–299
    recovery, 307
        backups, 334–336
        continuity and, 319–326
        disaster recovery, 326–330
        plan testing, 330–333
    SIEM solutions and, 301
    team, 293–296
    user reports, 305

incremental backups, 334–335
infected factory builds, 645
information disclosure spoofing, 554
information gathering, 853
infrared linear beam sensors, 148
infrastructure mode, 559
inheritance, permissions, 10
insider threats, 626–630
instant messaging, 515–516
InstantAtlas, 261
instruction set, 853
integrity, 853
interoperability, 139–140
interpreters, 854
interrupts, 854
    maskable, 856
intranets, 60, 463
IO (Input/Output) server, 493
IOCE (International Organization of
    Computer Evidence), 310
IP (Internet Protocol), 452, 460–461, 854
    fragmentation attacks
        Fraggle, 545
        NFS, 545–546
        NNTP security, 546–547
        NTP, 547
        overlapping fragment attack, 545
        Smurf, 545
        source routing exploitation, 545
        teardrop, 544–545
    networks, classes, 461
    routing tables, 452
IP address spoofing, 551–552
IPSec, 854
IPSs (Intrusion Prevention Systems), 220–221
    incident response and, 299
    wireless networks, 562–563
IPv6, 462, 854
IRC (Internet Relay Chat), 517
    attacks, 644–645
iris scan, 41–43
IRM (Information Rights Management), 112
ISAKMP (Internet Security Association and Key
    Management Protocol), 854
ISATAP (Intra-Site Automatic Tunnel
    Addressing Protocol), 854

iSCSI (Internet Small Computer System Interface), 498
ISDN (Integrated Services Digital Network), 473, 853
iSNS (Internet Storage Name Service), 457
ISO/IEC 27002 series, 854
ISO/IEC 27002:2013, 205
ISO/IEC 27005, 854
ITAM (IT asset management), 104–105
ITIL, 854
ITSEC (Information Technology Security Evaluation Criteria), 853
IV (initialization vector), 349, 853

J

Jabber, 516
Java Applet Attack, 618
Java applets, 854

K

Kali Virtual
    configuration, 271–274
    downloading, 267–268
    scans, launching, 275–277
Kaspersky, 584
KDC (key distribution center), 408–409
KDFs (key derivation functions), 855
KEK (key encrypting keys), 407–408
Kerberos, 55–58
Kerckhoff's principle, 855
kernel mode, 855
kernel-mode rootkits, 595–596
key control, 164–166
keyloggers, 592
keys, 855
    clustering, 855
    encryption, 349, 724–725
        asymmetric, 355–356
        automated generation, 404
        certificate replacement, 412
        certificate revocation, 412
        clustering, 347
        destruction, 409–411
        distribution, 408–409
        duties, 401–404

        escrow, 413
        financial institutions, 401
        key encrypting keys, 407–408
        KMIP, 724–726
        length, 406–407
        management, 397–401
        public, 355–356
        randomness, 404–406
        recovery, 412–413
        space, 349
        storage, 409–411
        web of trust, 413
        wrapping, 407–408
        X-KISS, 398
        XKMS, 398
        X-KRSS, 398
    foreign keys, 851
    primary, 859
    private, 860
keyspace, 855
keystream generator, 855
KMIP (Key Management Interoperability Protocol), 724–726
knowledge (authentication), 29–31
known-plaintext attack, 855

L

LANs (local area networks), 477
    control plane, 522–523
    data plane, 522–523
law enforcement, incident response and, 292–293
layered operating system architecture, 855
LDAP (Lightweight Directory Access Protocol), 53, 483
least privilege, 86–87
lightning protection, 167–168
limit registers, 855
linear cryptanalysis, 386, 855
link encryption, 855
link-state routing protocol, 855
List folder/read data permission, 6
LLC (Logical Link Control), 451
locks
    cipher locks, 159
    electric, 153

RDP (Reliable Datagram Protocol), 456

RPC (Remote Procedure Call), 457, 466–467

RTCP (Real-time Transport Control Protocol), 457

SA (security associations), 415

SCTP (Stream Control Transmission Protocol), 456

S/MIME (Secure/Multipurpose Internet Mail Extensions), 417

SMPP (Short Message Peer-to-Peer), 457

SMTP (Simple Mail Transfer Protocol), 457, 486–487

SNMP (Simple Network Management Protocol), 519–520

SPX (Sequenced Packet Exchange), 456

SSL/TLS (secure socket layer/transport layer security), 416–417

SST (Structured Stream Transport), 456

STP (Spanning Tree Protocol), 866

TCP (Transmission Control Protocol), 456, 462–463

TFTP (Trivial File Transfer Protocol), 488

transport mode, 415

tunnel mode, 415

UDP (User Datagram Protocol), 456, 463

VoIP (Voice over Internet Protocol), 499

XMPP (Extensible Messaging and Presence Protocol), 516

proxies

application-level, 537

circuit-level, 537

proxy server, 860

PSTN (public switched telephone networks), 514, 860

PSW (Program Status Word), 860

public data, sensitivity, 390

public key cryptography, 860

public key encryption, 355–356, 860

public multiscanners, malware naming, 586–588

PVCs (permanent virtual circuits), 473–474

Q

qualitative risk analysis, 860

quantitative risk analysis, 861

quantum cryptography, 861

queries, dynamic, 104

R

RA (registration authority), 348, 862

RACE (Research and Development in Advanced Communications Technologies in Europe), 359

race condition, 861

rack security, 168–169

RAD (Rapid Application Development), 100

RADIUS (Remote Authentication Dial-In User Service), 862

RAID (Redundant Array of Independent Disks), 79, 338–340

rainbow tables, 359–360

RAM (random access memory), 861

random number generator, 861

Rapid Elasticity, 697

RATs (Remote Access Trojans), 862

RC (Role Compatibility module), 13

RC4, 861

RC5, 861

RC6, 861

rcp (remote copy), 520–521

RDN (Relative Distinguished Name), 53

RDP (Reliable Datagram Protocol), 456

Read attributes permission, 6

Read extended attributes permission, 6

Read permissions permission, 6

reader collision (RFID), 32

reciprocal agreement, 861

records, 861

recovery, incident response and, 307

    backups, 334–336

    continuity and, 319–326

    disaster recovery, 326–330

    plan testing, 330–333

recovery controls, 90–91

recursion, DNS, 479

recursive resolver, DNS, 479

reference monitor, 862

reformatting data, 114–115

register, 862

regulated data, sensitivity, 390

regulation compliance audits, 204

voice technologies, 513–514
    PSTN (public switched telephone
        networks), 514
    war dialing, 514
VoIP (Voice over Internet Protocol),
    499–500, 870
volume storage encryption, 723
VPN (Virtual Private Network), 495, 517
VUL (Vulnerability Management), 105
vulnerabilities, 101, 870
    authentication and, 103
    authorization and, 103
    data
        deduplication, 110
        disposal, 113–117
        encryption keys, 110–112
        IRM, 112
        output, 112–113
        retention, 113–117
        scrubbing, 109–110
        storage, 106–109
    dynamic queries and, 104
    encryption and, 103–104
    error handling and, 104
    exposure, 851
    hardware and, 104–106
    incident response and, 298
    input validation and, 104
    out-of-band confirmations and, 104
    session management and, 103
    software and, 104–106
    system information exposure and, 104
vulnerability scanning, 209–218
    false positives, 212
    host scanning, 212–218
    tools, 212

W

WANs (wide area networks), 504, 871
war dialing, 224, 514, 870
war driving, 224
warm sites, 870
water issues, 175
waterfall model, 96–99
WBS (Work Breakdown Structure), 871
WDM (Wave-Division Multiplexing), 870

Web Jacking Attack Method, 618
web proxies, 870
web-based attacks, 638
    APTs (advanced persistent threats),
        639–641
    behavior analysis, 666–668
        interactive, 687
    brute force, 641–643
    countermeasures
        application layer, 654–655
        network layer, 652–654
    degraded performance, 657
    DNS changes and, 657–658
    exploitation frameworks, 645
    file location inspection, 661–666
    HOSTS files and, 657–658
    IM (instant messaging), 643
    infected factory builds, 645
    IRC (Internet Relay Chat), 644–645
    P2P networks, 643–644
    pop-ups, 656–657
    process inspection, 658–659
    remote site testing, 677–682
    rogue products, 645
    sandbox solutions, 686–687
    static file analysis, 669
        file properties, 670
        hash values, 670
        hex editors, 673–674
        memory dumps, 674–676
        PE files, 671
        software packers and, 674–676
        string analysis, 671–673
    Strawberry Perl installation, 659–661
    virtualized environments testing, 683–686
    Windows registry inspection, 659
    XSS (cross-site scripting), 639
    zero-day exploits, 639–641
WEP (Wired Equivalent Privacy Protocol), 559
    vulnerability, 561
white box testing, 225
Whois, 231–232
Wi-Fi, 555
WiMAX, 555–556
Windows Live Photo Gallery, face recognition
    and, 44
Windows rootkit, 595–596

WIPS/WIDS (wireless intrusion protection/ wireless intrusion detection systems), 562–563

wireless MAN, 556

wireless mesh network, 556

wireless networking
    Bluetooth, 555
    cellular networks, 556–557
    FDMA (Frequency Division Multiple Access), 558
    OFDM (Orthogonal Frequency Division Multiplexing), 557
    security issues
        ad-hoc mode, 559
        infrastructure mode, 559
        OSA, 558
        parking lot attack, 560
        shared key authentication, 560–561
        SKA, 559
        SSID flaw, 561
        TKIP attack, 561–562
        WEP, 559
        WEP vulnerability, 561
        WPA/WPA2, 559–560
    spread spectrum, 557
    TDMA (Time Division Multiple Access), 558
    testing, 221–223
    VOFDM (Vectored Orthogonal Frequency Division Multiplexing), 557–558
    Wi-Fi, 555
    WiMAX, 555–556
    wireless MAN, 556
    wireless mesh network, 556
    wireless WAN, 556

WLAN (wireless LAN), 556

WPANs (Wireless personal area networks), 556

wireless WAN, 556

wiretapping, 871

WLAN (wireless LAN), 556

work area security, 169–170

work factor, encryption, 349–351

wormhole attack, 871

worms, 591, 871

WPANs (Wireless personal area networks), 556

WPA/WPA2 (Wi-Fi Protected Access), 559–560

Write attributes permission, 6

Write extended attributes permission, 6

XY

X-KISS (XML Key Information Service Specification), 398

XKMS (XML Key Management specification), 398

X-KRSS (XML Key Registration Service Specification), 398

XMAS scanning, 538

XMPP (Extensible Messaging and Presence Protocol), 516

XOR (exclusive-or), 351

XSS (cross-site scripting) attacks, 639, 848

Z

Zachman framework, 871

zero knowledge proof, 871

zero-day exploits, 639–641

ZingChart, 261

zones, DNS, 480